AMERICAN LITERATURE IN TRANSITION, 1820–1860

The essays in *American Literature in Transition, 1820–1860* offer a new approach to the antebellum era, one that frames the age not merely as the precursor to the Civil War but as indispensable for understanding present crises around such issues as race, imperialism, climate change, and the role of literature in American society. The essays make visible and usable the period's fecund imagined futures, futures that certainly included disunion but not *only* disunion. Tracing the historical contexts, literary forms and formats, global coordinates, and present reverberations of antebellum literature and culture, the essays in this volume build on existing scholarship while indicating exciting new avenues for research and teaching. Taken together, the essays in this volume make this era's literature relevant for a new generation of students and scholars.

JUSTINE S. MURISON is Associate Professor of English at the University of Illinois at Urbana-Champaign. She is the author of *The Politics of Anxiety in Nineteenth-Century American Literature* (Cambridge University Press, 2011). Her work has appeared in *American Literature*, *Early American Literature*, *ESQ*, and *The New Melville Studies*, among other places, and she is a general editor for the new *Broadview Anthology of American Literature*.

NINETEENTH-CENTURY AMERICAN LITERATURE
IN TRANSITION

Editor
Cody Marrs, University of Georgia

Nineteenth-Century American Literature in Transition provides an omnibus
account of American literature and its ever-evolving field of study. Emphasizing
the ways in which American literature has been in transition ever since its
founding, this revisionary series examines four phases of American literary history,
focusing on the movements, forms, and media that developed from the late
eighteenth to the early twentieth century. The mutable nature of American
literature is explored throughout these volumes, which consider a diverse and
dynamic set of authors, texts, and methods. Encompassing the full range of
today's literary scholarship, this series is an essential guide to the study of
nineteenth-century American literature and culture.

Books in the Series

American Literature in Transition, 1770–1828 edited by WILLIAM HUNTTING
HOWELL & GRETA LAFLEUR
American Literature in Transition, 1820–1860 edited by JUSTINE S. MURISON
American Literature in Transition, 1851–1877 edited by CODY MARRS
American Literature in Transition, 1876–1910 edited by LINDSAY RECKSON

AMERICAN LITERATURE IN TRANSITION, 1820–1860

EDITED BY

JUSTINE S. MURISON

University of Illinois at Urbana-Champaign

CAMBRIDGE
UNIVERSITY PRESS

CAMBRIDGE
UNIVERSITY PRESS

University Printing House, Cambridge CB2 8BS, United Kingdom

One Liberty Plaza, 20th Floor, New York, NY 10006, USA

477 Williamstown Road, Port Melbourne, VIC 3207, Australia

314–321, 3rd Floor, Plot 3, Splendor Forum, Jasola District Centre, New Delhi – 110025, India

103 Penang Road, #05-06/07, Visioncrest Commercial, Singapore 238467

Cambridge University Press is part of the University of Cambridge.

It furthers the University's mission by disseminating knowledge in the pursuit of education, learning, and research at the highest international levels of excellence.

www.cambridge.org
Information on this title: www.cambridge.org/9781108475365
DOI: 10.1017/9781108566872

© Cambridge University Press 2022

First published 2022

A catalogue record for this publication is available from the British Library.

Library of Congress Cataloging-in-Publication Data
NAMES: Murison, Justine S., editor.
TITLE: American literature in transition, 1820–1860 / edited by Justine S. Murison.
DESCRIPTION: Cambridge ; New York, NY : Cambridge University Press, 2022. |
SERIES: Nineteenth-century American literature in transition ; volume 2 | Includes bibliographical references and index.
IDENTIFIERS: LCCN 2021060659 (print) | LCCN 2021060660 (ebook) | ISBN 9781108475365 (hardback) | ISBN 9781108466752 (paperback) | ISBN 9781108566872 (epub)
SUBJECTS: LCSH: American literature–19th century–History and criticism. | Literature and society–United States–History–19th century. | BISAC: LITERARY CRITICISM / American / General
CLASSIFICATION: LCC PS208 .A437 2022 (print) | LCC PS208 (ebook) | DDC 810.9/003–dc23/eng/20220216
LC record available at https://lccn.loc.gov/2021060659
LC ebook record available at https://lccn.loc.gov/2021060660

ISBN 978-1-108-47536-5 Hardback

Contents

Figures

Contributors

DAVID ANTHONY is Professor and Chair of the English Department at SIU Carbondale. He is the author of *Paper Money Men: Commerce, Manhood, and the Sensational Public Sphere in Antebellum America* (Ohio State University Press, 2009). His current project, "Sensationalism and the Jew in Antebellum American Literature," is under contract with Oxford University Press.

JOHN LEVI BARNARD is an associate professor of English and Comparative and World Literature at the University of Illinois at Urbana-Champaign. He is the author of *Empire of Ruin: Black Classicism and American Imperial Culture* and has published articles on the relation between empire, economy, and environment in *American Literature* and *American Quarterly*.

DALE M. BAUER, Professor Emerita, University of Illinois at Urbana-Champaign, has written books on feminism and Bakhtin, Edith Wharton, and American women's writing. Her latest book, *Nineteenth-Century American Women's Serial Novels* (Cambridge University Press, 2020), is a study of six commercially successful serial writers, including E. D. E. N. Southworth and Laura Jean Libbey. She has also edited *The Cambridge History of American Women's Literature* (2012).

DORRI BEAM is Associate Professor of English at Syracuse University. She is the author of *Style, Gender, and Fantasy in Nineteenth-Century American Literature* (Cambridge University Press, 2010) and is currently at work on a book entitled *Socialist Form and Literary Experiment in the American "Age of Fourier."*

GINA CAISON is an associate professor of English at Georgia State University where she teaches courses in southern literatures, Native American literatures, and documentary practices. Her first book, *Red*

States: Indigeneity, Settler Colonialism, and Southern Studies (University of Georgia Press, 2018), won the 2019 C. Hugh Holman Award for the best book in southern literary studies. Along with Lisa Hinrichsen and Stephanie Rountree, she is coeditor of *Small-Screen Souths: Region, Identity, and the Cultural Politics of Television* (Louisiana State University Press, 2017) and *Remediating Region: New Media & the U.S. South* (Louisiana State University Press 2021).

CHRISTOPHER CASTIGLIA is Distinguished Professor of English at Pennsylvania State University. He is the cofounder of C19: The Society of Nineteenth-Century Americanists and the author of several monographs, including most recently *The Practices of Hope: Literary Criticism in Disenchanted Times* (NYU Press, 2017).

TESS CHAKKALAKAL is Associate Professor of Africana Studies and English at Bowdoin College where she teaches classes on eighteenth- and nineteenth-century American Literature. She is the author of *Novel Bondage: Slavery, Marriage, and Freedom in Nineteenth-Century America* (University of Illinois, 2013) and co-editor of *Jim Crow, Literature, and the Legacy of Sutton E. Griggs* (University of Georgia Press, 2013) as well as *Imperium in Imperio by Sutton E. Griggs: A Critical Edition* (Greenbook Publication, 2010). Her articles have appeared in *J19*, *South Atlantic Quarterly*, *New England Quarterly*, *American Literary History*, and *American Quarterly*. She is currently at work on coediting a new edition of Charles W. Chesnutt's *Journals* and completing a new biography of the author.

MICHAEL C. COHEN is Associate Professor of English at UCLA. He is the author of *The Social Lives of Poems in Nineteenth-Century America* (University of Pennsylvania Press, 2015), and the co-editor of *The Poetry of Charles Brockden Brown* (Bucknell University Press, 2020).

MARCY J. DINIUS is an associate professor of English at DePaul University and the author of *The Camera and the Press: American Visual and Print Culture in the Age of the Daguerreotype* (University of Pennsylvania Press, 2012) and *The Textual Effects of David Walker's* Appeal: *Print-Based Activism against Slavery, Racism, and Discrimination, 1829–1851* (University of Pennsylvania Press, 2022).

MICHELLE GRANSHAW is Associate Professor and Director of Graduate Studies in the Department of Theatre Arts at the University of Pittsburgh. Her research interests include American and Irish theater and popular entertainment, diaspora and global performance histories, performance and the working class, dramaturgy, and historiography. Her book *Irish on the Move: Performing Mobility in American Variety Theatre* was published in 2019 by the University of Iowa Press. Her essays have appeared in *Theatre Survey, Popular Entertainment Studies, Nineteenth-Century Theatre and Film, Theatre Topics, New England Theatre Journal,* and the *Journal of American Drama and Theatre.*

CHRISTOPHER HANLON is Professor of United States Literature at Arizona State University and the author of *America's England: Atlantic Sectionalism and Antebellum Literature* (Oxford University Press, 2013) and *Emerson's Memory Loss: Originality, Communality, and the Late Style* (Oxford University Press, 2018). He has published widely on nineteenth-century American literature and culture and is currently the editor of the *Oxford Handbook of Ralph Waldo Emerson.*

CHRISTINE HEDLIN is a 2021–2022 Leading Edge Fellow through the American Council of Learned Societies. The program pairs humanities scholars with nonprofits serving public needs; through it, Hedlin is writing on religion for PublicSource, a digital news organization based in Pittsburgh. Previously, Hedlin was a postdoctoral fellow and lecturer at Valparaiso University in Indiana. Her articles have appeared in the *Journal of American Studies* and *Political Theology.* She is currently working on a book project, "Novel Faiths: How Postbellum Fiction Changed American Protestantism."

TONI WALL JAUDON is an associate professor of English at Hendrix College, where she teaches courses in early and nineteenth-century American literatures. Her work has appeared in *American Literature, American Literary History,* and *Atlantic Studies,* among other journals. Her manuscript-in-process examines the liveliness of religious objects in the nineteenth-century Atlantic world.

RODRIGO LAZO is Professor of English at the University of California, Irvine, where he teaches courses in American literature, hemispheric studies, and Latinx literature. His latest book is *Letters from Filadelfia: Early Latino Literature and the Trans-American Elite* (UVA Press, 2020). He has published more than twenty-five articles and book chapters.

JUSTINE S. MURISON is Associate Professor of English and affiliate faculty in Religion at the University of Illinois at Urbana-Champaign. She is the author of *The Politics of Anxiety in Nineteenth-Century American*

Literature (Cambridge University Press, 2011) and is currently finishing a second book, on privacy and secularism in the long nineteenth century. Her work has appeared in *American Literature, ESQ,* and *The New Melville Studies,* among other places, and she is a general editor for the new *Broadview Anthology of American Literature.*

EMILY OGDEN is Associate Professor of English at the University of Virginia and the author of *Credulity: A Cultural History of US Mesmerism* (University of Chicago Press, 2018).

ASHLEY REED is Associate Professor in the Department of English and Affiliate Faculty in the Department of Religion and Culture at Virginia Tech. She is the author of *Heaven's Interpreters: Women Writers and Religious Agency in Nineteenth-Century America* (Cornell University Press, 2020) and has published articles in *J19: The Journal of Nineteenth-Century Americanists, ESQ: A Journal of Nineteenth-Century American Literature and Culture, Religion Compass,* and *Digital Humanities Quarterly.*

KELLY ROSS is an associate professor at Rider University. Her work has appeared in *PMLA,* the *Oxford Handbook of Edgar Allan Poe,* and *Leviathan.*

SUSAN M. RYAN is Professor of English and Associate Dean for Faculty Affairs at the University of Louisville. She is the author of *The Grammar of Good Intentions: Race and the Antebellum Culture of Benevolence* (Cornell University Press, 2003) and *The Moral Economies of American Authorship: Reputation, Scandal, and the Nineteenth-Century Literary Marketplace* (Oxford University Press, 2016). Her current project investigates nineteenth-century Americans' preoccupation with India.

MARTHA SCHOOLMAN is Associate Professor of English at Florida International University, director of the MA program in English, and a scholar of transnational literary abolitionism. She is the author of *Abolitionist Geographies* (University of Minnesota Press, 2014) and coeditor with Jared Hickman of *Abolitionist Places* (Routledge, 2013). Her essays and reviews have appeared in *American Literary History, Arizona Quarterly,* and *ESQ,* among other venues.

KYLA SCHULLER is Associate Professor and Undergraduate Director of Women's, Gender and Sexuality Studies at Rutgers University, New Brunswick. She is the author of *The Biopolitics of Feeling: Race, Sex, and Science in the Nineteenth Century* (Duke University Press, 2018) and

The Trouble with White Women: A Counterhistory of Feminism (Bold Type Books, 2021). With Jules Gill-Peterson, she coedited a special issue of *Social Text* and with Greta LaFleur, coedited the *American Quarterly* volume Origins of Biopolitics in the Americas, which was named Best Special Issue 2020 by the Council of Editors of Learned Journals. Schuller's work has been awarded fellowships from the American Council of Learned Societies and Stanford Humanities Center.

DERRICK R. SPIRES is Associate Professor of Literatures in English and affiliate faculty in American Studies, Visual Studies, and Media Studies at Cornell University. He specializes in early African American and American print culture, citizenship studies, and African American intellectual history. His first book, *The Practice of Citizenship: Black Politics and Print Culture in the Early United States* (University of Pennsylvania Press, 2019), won the Modern Language Association Prize for First Book and the Bibliographical Society/St. Louis Mercantile Library Prize. His work on early African American politics and print culture appears or is forthcoming in *African American Review, American Literary History*, and edited collections on early African American print culture, time and American literature, and the Colored Conventions movement.

JORDAN ALEXANDER STEIN teaches in the English Department and Comparative Literature Program at Fordham University. His publications include *When Novels Were Books* (Harvard University Press, 2020).

CLAUDIA STOKES is Professor of English at Trinity University. She is the author of *The Altar at Home: Sentimental Literature and Nineteenth-Century American Religion* and *Writers in Retrospect: The Rise of American Literary History, 1875–1910*. She is also coeditor, with Elizabeth Duquette, of the new Penguin Classics edition of Elizabeth Stuart Phelps's *The Gates Ajar*. Her new book, *Old Style: Unoriginality and Its Uses in Nineteenth-Century U.S. Literature* (University of Pennsylvania Press, 2021).

NAZERA SADIQ WRIGHT is Associate Professor of English and African American and Africana Studies at the University of Kentucky. She is the author of *Black Girlhood in the Nineteenth Century* (University of Illinois Press, 2016), which won the 2018 Children's Literature Association's Honor Book Award for Outstanding Book of Literary Criticism. Her Digital Humanities project, *DIGITAL GI(RL)S: Mapping Black Girlhood in the Nineteenth Century*, documents the cultural activities of black girls living in Philadelphia in the nineteenth century. In 2019, she was elected to the American Antiquarian Society. Fellowships through the Ford Foundation, the National Endowment for the Humanities, the Andrew W. Mellon Foundation, and the Bibliographical Society of America funded archival research for her second book, *Early African American Women Writers and Their Libraries*.

Series Preface

In the past few decades, as American literary studies has changed and evolved, the long nineteenth century has proven to be a crucial pivot point. *American Literature: The Long Nineteenth Century* captures the dynamism of both this critical moment and the historical period it engages. Emphasizing the ways in which American literature has remained in transition ever since its founding, these four volumes comprise a significant act of literary-historical revisionism. As suggested by the overlapping dates (i.e., 1770–1828, 1820–1860, 1851–1877, 1876–1910), these volumes challenge traditional ways of periodizing literature. This series argues for the contingency and provisionality of literary history in general and of nineteenth-century American literary history in particular. The transitional and mutable nature of American literature is explored throughout these volumes, which address a wide range of topics, methods, and areas of interest, and examine the myriad forms, movements, and media that developed across this era. By drawing together leading and emerging scholars and encompassing the full range of today's American literary scholarship, this series provides an omnibus account of nineteenth-century American literature as well as its ever-evolving field of study.

Acknowledgments

It is with enduring gratitude that I begin by thanking Cody Marrs for his role as our series editor and as a fellow volume editor. Cody and I collaborated on our two volumes from the very beginning of this process, and it has been a joy to work with him. He successfully shepherded these volumes into print, and he provided timely and generous feedback on the introduction to this volume. I would also like to thank Lilya Kaganovsky, Brett Kaplan, and Anke Pinkert, who read an early draft of the introduction. Their advice was instrumental in helping me clarify my thesis and address readers beyond those in the field of nineteenth-century American literature. Thank you to Betsy Duquette for her endless patience and keen editorial eye, and to Leah Becker, for her extraordinary work on the index. Above all, I want to thank the contributors to this volume. Reading and editing their important contributions has changed how I write about and teach this era of American literature, and it was an honor to work with them.

CHAPTER I

Introduction
Literature for Democracy
Justine S. Murison

The chapters in this volume of *American Literature in Transition: The Long Nineteenth Century* were written, for the most part, during the presidency of Donald Trump, an era of social and political crisis that led many scholars of the nineteenth-century United States to identify in the turmoil of the present the unfinished business and ongoing legacies of the past. This was an era, after all, that could be more or less bookended by a white supremacist mob that descended on Charlottesville, Virginia, in August 2017 to rally in the shadow of Thomas Jefferson for the preservation of Confederate monuments, and the January 6, 2021, invasion of the US Capitol by a similar mob, carrying Confederate flags, determined to overthrow the results of a democratic election. Whatever else might be said about these flash points, it would be hard to deny that history was not alive in these moments, and the essays in this volume share this apprehension. This intertwined temporal context – of the essays' composition and of the United States' past – will be apparent to readers of these essays. For while calling attention to the historical moment of composition at the outset may strike some readers as "presentist," that is also part of the goal of the collection: an open and thoughtful embrace of the contingencies of the present as part of the necessary work of interpreting the literary past. The groundbreaking scholarship of the essays in this volume comes out of balancing an orientation to the past with the equally pressing imperative that a deeper knowledge of these decades can help us understand our own current moment of crisis and opportunity.

The overriding thesis of this collection may be said to be twofold: first, all of the essays expand upon the critique in recent decades of the exceptionalist assumptions of the field of US literary studies, a field that continues to center a subset of canonical authors, the novel as the predominant form in literary history, settler-colonial imaginaries, and the organizing principle of the nation-state. Second, the essays reorient the decades under consideration away from the Civil War as an end point.

This is not to say that the essays operate as if the sectional crisis did not happen; rather, they suspend a teleological perspective on the field to widen the scope and scale of such narratives, both literary and historical. The essays in this volume propose ways of approaching the concerns, connections, and trajectories of the period other than as preliminary moments in anticipation of the Big Bang of 1860.[1] After all, no one lives either solely in the present or fully oriented to a future end point, especially one that could be imagined but certainly not predicted in detail. The second intervention, then, is to make visible the various trajectories out of the national past that give this period its fecund imagined futures, futures that certainly included disunion but not *only* disunion.

To follow such varied trajectories in the antebellum years comes up hard against a very fundamental challenge: as a designation, "antebellum" is defined by teleology. The name itself signifies that this is the period that precedes the Civil War. Bookended by two historical events that tie the era together in terms of the coming war – the Missouri Compromise of 1820 and the election of Abraham Lincoln and subsequent secession of South Carolina in 1860 – the scholarly use of the term "antebellum" reinforces the sense that the Civil War is an inevitability. A similar teleology has defined the era's literary history since as early as F. O. Matthiessen's *American Renaissance* (1941): the coming of the five canonical writers (Emerson, Thoreau, Hawthorne, Melville, and Whitman) and their significant texts, which were, with the exception of Emerson's major works, published in the 1850s. Whether we are succumbing to the magnetic pull of the war or Melville's 1851 publication of *Moby-Dick*, scholars of antebellum literature are ever tugged toward predetermined ends.

That "antebellum" announces its own telos is a reminder of a larger truth for those studying nineteenth-century literature: as much as we imagine our brash breaks with exceptionalist narratives about the nation and its literature, the periodization we often deploy continually leads us back to them. But that does not mean we are constrained by them. The essays in this volume embrace the contingency of the present, both the historical present, in which the themes, texts, and writers emerged, and our own present, in which that history feels so vivid and relevant to both our lived experience and our critical practice. They think, in other words, in terms of historical situatedness but never operate with the assumption that historical methods mean the suspension of the present era in favor of fully recovering a past one, a fantasy that, at best, limits the scholarly imagination. Jeffrey Insko puts it well when he notes that, since the historical turn inaugurated by the New Historicism, "historicism in literary studies maintains something of a paradoxical relationship to the old problem of presentism: it is at once that which historicism's contextualizing procedure is designed to avoid and, because of its frequently announced political commitments, its self-consciousness about the representational function of every act of historical (re)creation, and its engagement with the political and critical present, that of which it is sometimes accused."[2] As Insko and others have argued, we can see this fear of anachronism as a result of the way in which literary history has theorized "history" itself. Jordan Alexander Stein locates this problem in how literary historians tend still to conflate "history" with chronology – assuming that to be a good historicist is to tell a story of cause and effect that must organize itself in the order of past, present, and future.[3] The new, vibrant field of queer temporalities forged by scholars such as Elizabeth Freeman and Dana Luciano has theorized this tendency, what Freeman calls "a chronobiological society," in which the "state and other institutions, including representational apparatuses, link properly temporalized bodies to narratives of movement and change."[4] As Freeman indicates here, it is not simply legal or political culture that binds us to modern, capitalist temporalities, but stories and literature more broadly. We can historicize the emergence of modern time scales, as Freeman and Luciano both do, to the nineteenth century, but their insights also allow us to see how the meta-stories we tell about the period – the literary history we organize – also asserts a certain type of chrononormativity. And as Stein suggests, these insights about alternative temporalities have the potential to expand our consideration of historicism itself. The creative and queer anachronisms that reading backward into the past produces, he argues, or the way events and publications web out, circulate, loop, and turn sideways in a culture can turn our focus back on assumptions about what constitutes literary history.

While the essays in this collection do not all make history or historiography their main objects of study, they all challenge us to see the multiple and simultaneous historical trajectories of the antebellum years as well as our scholarly roles in producing and narrating those trajectories. They therefore put pressure on the very chronological organizing principle of the collection itself, which stops at the rupture of the Civil War. While 1860 is a typical point for dividing American literary history, we might do well to consider why ruptures – wars and revolutions especially – guide periodization. As Ted Underwood has shown, the rise of periodization as an organizing principle for literary study preceded modern literature departments; it was a result, he argues, of a Romantic secular embrace of "historical cultivation," which became the central cultural mode for "middle-class self-assertion," one that rejected the continuity of a "collective past" and embraced instead a "periodized, contrastive model of history that emerged toward the end of the eighteenth century" and "can be understood as a tacit attack on the logic of aristocratic distinctions."[5] The end point of a subfield or a syllabus implicitly suggests new eras and dispensations, and traditional literary periodizations, which persist in the organization of survey courses, tend to be organized around the ruptures of war (to 1660, or 1789, or 1865). For American literary study, as Christopher Hager and Cody Marrs have argued, this narrative of rupture has long centered on 1865, and it creates many strange distortions: authors' careers that span the century, like Whitman's or Melville's, find themselves cut off from half of their writing lives in anthologies, arbitrarily designated to one or the other side of the 1865 divide; the common narrative of prewar romance and postwar realism belies the continuities between these two aesthetic and philosophical modes before and after the war and those modes' transatlantic context; and finally the literature of the war itself becomes a strange, haunting absence, rarely read beyond Whitman's and Melville's poetry.

The historical bookends for this volume of the series are, if we follow Hager and Marrs's argument, fairly traditional: 1820–1860. While the volume stops short of 1865, it keeps in place the rupture of the coming war, with Lincoln's election and South Carolina's secession rounding out the year of 1860. And considering how historians often place the 1850s into volumes on the Civil War – perhaps most notably in James M. McPherson's *Battle Cry of Freedom: The Civil War Era* (1988) – the choice of 1860 as an end point reflects not a historical but a literary historical decision, reflective of the continuing influence (however invisible) of the field-defining work of Matthiessen's *American Renaissance*. Yet as Robert Levine has recently pointed out, period distinctions need not become straitjackets, and some demarcations are necessary for an anthology or a syllabus.[6] They do not determine years, texts, or events off limits so much as focus attention, and it is to this looser notion of the period that the essays in this volume push us: concentrating attention on an expansive understanding of the literature published in the period while pointing to a *longue durée* that begins with European settler colonialism and spans to today.

Eighty Years Hence with Matthiessen

Matthiessen's "American Renaissance" is one of the many terms for the literary period spanning 1820–1860 that have declined in use in recent decades. While Matthiessen's title implicitly connects what he calls "our past masterpieces" to the English Renaissance of William Shakespeare, Ben Jonson, and John Donne, Matthiessen dwells more, in the opening paragraph of his book's preface, on the meaning of *renaissance* as an apt characterization of this "extraordinarily concentrated moment of expression."[7] Matthiessen considers how the writers themselves judged their contributions "not as a re-birth of values that had existed previously in America, but as America's way of producing a renaissance, by coming to its first maturity and affirming its rightful heritage in the whole expanse of art and culture."[8] In *American Renaissance*, Matthiessen imagines not the rebirth of the classics in American culture but something more akin to what evangelicals mean by "rebirth," that is, the moment of "first maturity" when American art and culture can hold its own with and make unique contributions to the inherited culture of England.

Crosscut throughout Matthiessen's prefatory "Method and Scope" section is a language for the study of literature that has fallen away in the past three decades: words like "masterpiece," "heritage," and "values." There have been many routes to decentering such terms between Matthiessen's 1941 and today, but all coalesce to tell a story that denies the exceptionalism implied in Matthiessen's elevation of just five authors. One such route was inaugurated in Jane Tompkins's *Sensational Designs* (1985), in which she locates the construction of the American literary canon and some of its most canonical of figures, particularly Nathaniel Hawthorne, as emerging out of a modernist aesthetic that devalued literature that inspired sympathetic feelings and aimed to do cultural work in favor of complexity and defamiliarization. "Cultural work" became a new way to value and evaluate texts that opened the canon to women's fiction, particularly white women's sentimental novels. But just as Ashley Reed argues in her essay for this volume pairing Catharine Maria Sedgwick and William Apess, the projects that recovered and valued white women's novels as "cultural work" also reinforced settler-colonial imaginaries at the center of our teaching and scholarship. Scholarship by Lisa Brooks, Mark Rifkin, and others has challenged both the settler-colonial narratives of Manifest Destiny and the romanticization of native genocide that is so apparent in white liberal texts like Sedgwick's *Hope Leslie* (1827). Their scholarship has also pushed the field to consider the longer historical frames needed to recover Native voices and texts. Lisa Brooks's *The Common Pot: The Recovery of Native Space in the Northeast* (2008) unfolds just such a longer history, a trajectory that runs from the linguistic and cultural formations of Abenaki and Narragansett peoples in and before the seventeenth century to the nineteenth-century writing of William Apess and Jane Johnston Schoolcraft to the present of the author's own composition. But her intervention is more than historical; it is geographic. Brooks writes a place-based history – and the mapping project alongside the book evinces how the past and present overlap in the land itself.[9]

Another crucial critique of the canonical and historical work epitomized by the "American Renaissance" as conceived by Matthiessen came through the work of Black feminist literary critics like Frances Smith Foster, Carla Peterson, and Ann DuCille. These groundbreaking scholars not only recovered scores of African American women writers largely left out of print and understudied – and as such they helped to forge the field of Black print culture before that name was applied to it – but they also made claims for the works on aesthetic, formal, and cultural grounds. Joining these revisions of the canon, "New Americanist" scholars like Donald Pease and Amy Kaplan were instrumental in shifting our focus from the nation-state to American imperialism, hemispheric studies, and other geographic formations that challenged the national narrative so central to early scholarship in the field like Matthiessen's and Perry Miller's. Finally, history of the book and print culture studies shifted scholars' attention away from the author and the form, genre, or aesthetics of their texts and toward the history of these texts' circulation and book histories, as seen in a variety of works in the field from Meredith McGill's deep study of the antebellum culture of reprinting in *The Culture of Reprinting* (2003) to Derrick Spires's argument for new theories of citizenship drawn from a rich archive of Black print culture in the early national and antebellum eras in *The Practice of Citizenship* (2019).

This brief overview of major shifts in the field of American literary study from the 1980s to today testifies to something else for which the "rupture" narrative of literary history and scholarly inquiry often do not have room. All of these scholars' works have profoundly reshaped the field of American literary history, and they influence the writers in this volume. In fact, it is perhaps more accurate to say that the field is not simply deeply indebted to these revisions but still works largely within their frameworks. And that is because the deep ethical commitments of their research continue to be vital to scholars today. While the title of a "Transitions" volume might, at first glance, make a reader conflate that with the rupture narrative of history, the essays here reaffirm what the scholars of the last forty years have shown us: how archives and archival access have shaped the canon in ways that reinforced racial and gendered hierarchies in the field; that our

objects of study must be wider – must include newspapers, book production and marketing, and genres and aesthetics left out of a canon shaped
originally with modernist assumptions in mind – in order to build literary
historical claims; and that the political and cultural work of texts is a
paramount and important focus of any analysis. In many ways, the ethical
coordinates of these projects have been sustained and expanded in much
recent work in the field of American literary history.

With that in mind, what "transition" does this volume then herald?
A good way to explain both the continuities with the recent critical past
and the pivot we might say marks the essays in this collection is found in
Emily Ogden's essay for this collection, "Romance." Romance, Ogden
maintains, "is the narration of a sustaining future out of the fragments of a
failed past," and therefore, she posits, we could say that "criticism is a
romance." Deliberately reorienting critical practice toward such "sorties"
into the past, Ogden explains, "may be necessary at a moment when the
precarity of American Studies and its practitioners – and of the humanities
academy itself – has become obvious." This volume arrives in a world that
feels precarious – economically, environmentally, politically, and profes-
sionally. To synthesize the previous section on temporalities of literary
study with this section on building research on our predecessors' insights,
the real shift this volume offers is a deepened appreciation of the messy,
multidirectional, and overlapping but not necessarily intersecting narratives we can bring forward from the literature in the period between the
Missouri Compromise and Lincoln's election. That the current vanguard
work in the field of American literary studies for the period of 1820–1860
has been built on their predecessor's insights, and that the goal has been to
expand and deepen those studies, is a testament to a desire to *build* a future
rather than to announce ruptures or pivots away from the critical inheritance of the last four decades. As Ogden puts it, the work of criticism is the
work of salvaging.

This provocation to salvage – to rescue and preserve – prompts me to
return with more generous eyes to the project inaugurated in Matthiessen's
American Renaissance. Rereading Matthiessen's groundbreaking mono-
graph not as an interlocutor who needs an urgent reply nor as a member
of a generation looking at the previous one and uncovering its contradictions but as a missive from 1941 to 2021 has helped me to frame further
what the essays in this collection aim to do. Writing a decade into the
Great Depression and on the eve of the United States joining the Allies in
World War II, Matthiessen is exquisitely attuned to the devastating effects
of economic inequality and the rise of fascism, both of which are urgent

and compelling resurgent factors in our lived experiences in the twenty-first century. To be sure, Matthiessen's canon was exceedingly, even excessively restrictive as to race and gender (and, indeed, with only five writers, we can say it barely even scratched the surface of canonical white male authors). Yet what he thought organized Emerson, Thoreau, Hawthorne, Melville, and Whitman together was not simply their aesthetic achievements, though form and aesthetics are central to the book as a whole. Rather, he ends the preface by ruminating that all of these writers "wrote literature for democracy," and they did so "in a double sense." He explains,

> They felt that it was incumbent upon their generation to give fulfillment to the potentialities freed by the Revolution, to provide a culture commensurate with America's political opportunity. Their tones were sometimes optimistic, sometimes blatantly, even dangerously expansive, sometimes disillusioned, even despairing, but what emerges from the total pattern of their achievement – if we will make the effort to repossess it – is literature for our democracy.[10]

The importance of this affirmation of democracy's "political opportunity" is everywhere apparent in the field, even as Matthiessen's focus on the nation-state and these five writers has been decentered. And to be clear, Matthiessen's affirmation is not blind to the wide affective span that the uneven, halting, incomplete project of democracy elicits, not just from writers of the antebellum period but from critics since: optimism that can risk seeming "dangerously expansive" as well as a debilitating disillusionment in response to the gap between ideal and reality. What persists between Matthiessen in 1941 and critics in 2021 is both the recognition of this gap and the affirmation of democracy as a project to bridge it.

What to Expect in the Volume

The essays in this volume move beyond the antebellum period – reaching back to the settler-colonial past and looking forward to the postbellum careers of various authors – and they move beyond the geographic coordinates of the typical story of the Civil War as a coming battle of North and South to consider continental, hemispheric, oceanic, and global frames. They build on their predecessors' insights and they also press on exceptionalisms that still remain endemic to the field. The volume is organized into three parts. The essays in Part I, "Fractures and Continuities," focus on major cultural, political, and economic keywords that have emerged in the last forty years. Collectively, they point to future directions in scholarship on the topics. Part II, "Forms and Formats," collects together essays on an array of genres, forms, and media that have come to dominate the field of antebellum literary study. Each of the essays in Part III, "Authors and Figures," pairs two writers of the period together to move beyond biographical information to introduce the conditions of authorship, the political and cultural preoccupations of the era, and new genealogical coordinates for literary historical work.

While offering a continuity with the important major concepts that have long organized the field, the essays of Part I highlight new directions for research in some of these major keywords. The opening two essays – "Hemisphere" by Rodrigo Lazo and "Empire" by John Levi Barnard – take up the mantle of the New Americanists' unseating of the nation-state in favor of a more accurate meaning for the term "American" in "American literature." Lazo's essay lays out the history of the term "America" as a geographic notation that came to be conflated with the US nation-state, and how, in revealing and exploring that elision, hemispheric studies emerged. But as Lazo explains, "hemispheric American studies" is "an impossibility as a field," and he argues instead for reconfiguring this field as "trans-American studies," which would emphasize movement and transition, as he puts it, "beyond America and across America." In like fashion, John Levi Barnard asks us to revisit a now familiar frame for our studies – empire – to emphasize the ecological devastation wrought by American imperialism. Drawing on indigenous scholars like Jodi Byrd and Kyle Powys Whyte, Barnard emphasizes, first, that empire was always an intrinsic ideological goal of the US nation-state, and, second, that it furthered an extinction-producing economy that we can trace from the earliest local impacts of colonization to the planetary threat of climate change today.

The reorientation of the field to a transnational framework, explained and exemplified in the first two essays of this part, is borne out by the rest, all of which offer fresh approaches and frames of reference to critical keywords in the field. In "Economy," David Anthony points the way to revitalizing studies of literature and the economy – so salient for students and scholars since the 2008 crash – by insisting that any study of the antebellum economy be *global* in its coordinates. Sweeping through a wide array of literature – from the canonical *Walden* and *The Scarlet Letter* to city mysteries published in the wake of the Panic of 1837 – Anthony shows how the concerns of the antebellum economy were international in scale. Likewise, Christine Hedlin and Toni Wall Jaudon introduce readers to new directions that the study of religion and secularism have taken in the last two decades, tracing foundational, field-defining ideas about how the very terms "religion" and "secular" are co-definitive and create the conditions for particular forms of settler colonialism, in which, to cite their essay, "Benevolent Protestants thus made themselves the softening forward edge of the US government's dispossession" of native peoples and took up the mantle of defending the slave system. Secularity, they argue, "binds up forms of religious and racial governance into a normative sociality."

This normative sociality worked to obscure the biopolitical violence of the state, a topic probed in the final three essays of the part. In her essay, Kyla Schuller fully revises what is an evergreen term for the field: "nature." Studies of "nature" in the antebellum world have long been tied to Transcendental writers like Emerson, Thoreau, and Fuller, Romantic visions of the American landscape and the capacities for individual genius to flourish in an "original relation to the universe," as Emerson put it in *Nature* (1836).[11] But as Schuller notes, running parallel to these celebrations of the natural world was an increasingly scientized version of *nature* in the consolidation and promotion of race science and scientific authority. Placing Frederick Douglass at the center of her study, Schuller revolutionizes the approach to a familiar term in the field. While "nature" may have been a *theme* for the Transcendentalist writers, she argues, *naturalizing* was a method used to justify enslavement and removal.

In a similar fashion, the final two essays for the section – Gina Caison's "Removal" and Martha Schoolman's "Abolition" – rewrite into a global frame topics that are often relentlessly nationalized. Caison's essay overviews indigenous studies to critique the overlapping narratives of exceptionalism that quarantine removal from the wider stories of antebellum literature and culture. Moving beyond a narrative of southern exceptionalism – where the South is uniquely cruel in its Removal policies and slave system – and "antebellum exceptionalism" – where Removal happened only in the antebellum period – Caison's essay argues for putting such events as the Indian Removal Act of 1830 and the Cherokee Trail of Tears into a longer transnational and transhistorical trajectory that continues to actively shape the present. In doing so, the essay also models how to center Native voices in the study of antebellum literature. Martha Schoolman's essay, "Abolition," also takes on an exceptionalism in the study of the abolitionist movement: that it was a peculiarly national and *nationally focused* reform movement. On the contrary, as Schoolman asserts, abolition must be understood as a transnational movement with a wider global frame and agenda than the teleology of the Civil War suggests. Indeed, as she shows, Black and white abolitionists saw their struggle as one that was deeply hemispheric and transatlantic, encompassing within it the Haitian Revolution and the contemporaneous emancipation movements in the Caribbean. Drawing on new texts made available through Black bibliographic scholarship and digitizing projects, Schoolman shows how, across the newspapers, books, and tracts published by abolitionists – and particularly by David Walker in his *Appeal* (1829) – we can see an insistence on the transnational coordinates of abolition.

The reframing of the antebellum period away from a variety of exceptionalist stories – including most predominantly the exceptional focus on the nation-state – sets up Part II of the collection, which concentrates on new literary histories that have emerged out of research on genre, form, print culture, and the history of the book in the last twenty years. The rise of recovery projects and print culture studies has thoroughly shifted the ground beneath definitions of "form" and "aesthetics" and what objects of study are central to the field. The first four essays tackle genres and forms that have been the backbone of American literary study: romance, drama, poetry, and the sentimental novel. Yet each essay takes that genre or form in vivid new directions. Emily Ogden's essay, "Romance," opens this section of the collection. Romance, as Ogden traces, was the term under which American exceptionalist literary narratives were pursued, following especially from Richard Chase's *The American Novel and Its Tradition* (1957), which posited the romance as America's foremost contribution to literary history, for it dealt not with history and the real but a mood of "idyl" and "melodrama." Ogden recounts the historiography emerging out of Chase's scholarship, including the significant critiques of his theory of romance by the New Americanists. This genealogy of "romance" allows her to return to the elements of the transatlantic romance – the shared generic modes between British and American literature – to posit a different way for us to think of romance. As she argues, "If romance is the narration of a sustaining future out of the fragments of a failed past, then many, if not all, progressive visions must make some use of it."

While fictional romances from *The Last of the Mohicans* to *The Blithedale Romance* and *Moby-Dick* continue to be central scholarly objects of study, they also testify to the grip of the novel form in our field. Drama and poetry have slid into the margins, a point central to the next two essays. Michelle Granshaw's essay, "Theater," takes readers on a tour of the world of popular theater in antebellum New York City, focusing on (and for many readers introducing them to) the melodramas, burlettas, comedies, and variety sketches popular with white working-class male audiences. The essay, moreover, pitches to scholars of antebellum American literature a method to match this archive by modeling the importance of performance studies for a complete picture of the antebellum theater world. In like fashion, Michael Cohen does not simply offer an archive of popular poetry for the years 1820–1860, poetry that is in large part omitted from college syllabi; rather, he walks us through the methodological questions provoked by the popularity of poetry in the antebellum period. He urges scholars to focus less on authorial innovation and critical reception and more on readers and reading, where we find an absolute saturation of poetic enthusiasm and the traces of a transatlantic and commonplace poetic language that has been obscured by the predominance of prose in scholarship on antebellum literature. The final essay in this cluster on the field's familiar forms, Tess Chakkalakal's essay, "Sentimentality," provides readers with a historiographical overview of criticism on sentimental fiction, with Harriet Beecher Stowe's *Uncle Tom's Cabin* (1852) as the central text, and then turns to a productive new way to rethink antebellum sentimentality. Chakkalakal asks what would happen if scholars placed Black writers at the center of our definition, rather than positioning their works as reactions to or only rejections of sentimentality. Sentimentality, this conceptional shift reveals, still maintains a tacit assumption of being "white," with Black writers as reactive to it rather than shapers of its tradition. By combining the scholarship on Black women's writing starting with Ann DuCille and Carla Peterson with studies of sentimentality by Lauren Berlant, Toni Morrison, and Cindy Weinstein, Chakkalakal ends by sketching the form of sentimentality that might emerge out of this reconfigured field: the embrace of new familiar and kinship connections and the radical politics of love.

The final four essays in Part II shift from the traditional forms of our field to the new forms, methods, and aesthetics scholars are taking up now and will be building on in the coming years. In his essay, "African American Print Culture," Derrick Spires traces the origins of African American print culture studies to the pioneering bibliographic work of Dorothy Porter and through the scholarship of Frances Smith Foster to today's digital projects. In doing so, he maps this dynamic and richly historical field and encourages scholars not just to attend to the canonical texts, but to see how scholars of African American texts are continuing to expand bibliographic and digital methods to enlarge the field's objects of study and methods for studying them. Continuing this focus on the print world of the antebellum United States is "Sexuality in Print," by Jordan Alexander Stein. This essay traces for us the twinned cultural moments of the print explosion and the explosion in print of a discourse of sexuality.

The two, Stein contends, must be thought of together, and his essay seeks to spark further studies by delineating possible archives for the field. The final two essays of this part overview new ways of using these print culture studies for rethinking how we pose formal and aesthetic questions. In "Seriality," Dale Bauer introduces readers to the serial novels of the antebellum period, those big behemoths that started in magazines and newspapers, spoke to audiences about big national debates, but have rarely been anthologized, reprinted, or, indeed, even read by most current scholars. Providing a map to all of the novels you may not have had time to read, Bauer discloses for readers the wild and weird world of serialized novel publishing in the nineteenth century. And finally, in "Unoriginality," Claudia Stokes culminates this part by suggesting that we rethink our literary attachments to *originality*, an aesthetic persistence that has not waned, she argues, despite the ways recovery projects and print culture studies have shown its conceptual and intellectual shortcomings. In a similar vein as in Cohen's essay, Stokes argues that antebellum readers were not particularly invested in – and were even skeptical of – claims to originality, and she demonstrates what we can discover by attending to readers and reading, what is valued and reprinted and inked into commonplace books.

The groundbreaking work of print culture and reception studies has helped decenter the exceptional nature of Matthiessen's five big authors, but the result has not been a full decentering of writers, as such. Indeed, the fundamental challenge of any volume covering the years 1820–1860 is the absolute surfeit of canonical authors in this period. While this is the era of the traditional big names of the nineteenth-century canon – Emerson, Hawthorne, Thoreau, Whitman, Melville, Poe – it is also the era that has seen significant canonization following the feminist and African American recovery projects, such that Douglass, Walker, Stowe, Fuller, Child, Harper, and Sedgwick are also now firmly canonical, as the examples that weave in and out of the essays of the first two parts of the collection attest. Narrowing the final part to a few writers would reinforce a canonical hierarchy, a throwback to Matthiessen's big five; to leave out a section on writers would be to lose the opportunity to highlight the exciting new directions currently being taken in the field. To resolve this dilemma, the essays in Part III pair writers together, some canonical, some emerging into canonicity, some still obscure. This structure allows the contributors to focus not on any single author's life or career but to trace the coordinates of literary marketplaces or to offer new literary genealogies.

The section opens with Ashley Reed's essay on William Apess and Catharine Maria Sedgwick, writers who exemplify the changed trajectories of teaching and writing today. The essay provides for us a double lens on the history and literary history of antebellum America. While Apess and Sedgwick both reworked colonial history to speak to their contemporary moment, Sedgwick's more popular *Hope Leslie* depended on the very settler colonialism Apess excoriated as unchristian in his "Eulogy on King Philip" (1836). And as Reed also shows, the recovery and celebration of white women writers in the 1970s and 1980s positioned such texts as *Hope Leslie* as radical and feminist while obscuring their settler colonialism, a process brought into sharper relief by reading these two authors together. In the next essay, Susan Ryan takes two canonical authors who are rarely if ever written about or taught as a pair – Lydia Maria Child and Henry David Thoreau – to sketch for us their similarities in terms of economic and ethical concerns. Through the course of thinking these two authors together, Ryan reorients both authors past the clichéd figures that they sometimes serve in our scholarship and for the wider culture. Child is more than the sentimentalist she is often positioned as, and Thoreau is far from the crass hypocrite he is often popularly made out to be.

Just as the feminist recovery projects brought Sedgwick and Child into regular circulation in antebellum literature classrooms, the 1970s and 1980s recovery of Black writers made Frederick Douglass and David Walker canonical. In her essay on the two, Marcy Dinius traces the influence of Walker on Douglass's politics and writing, a lineage that decenters Douglass's 1845 *Narrative* in favor of understanding his growing political radicalism through the influence of Walker and other Black activists like Henry Highland Garnet. While Walker and Douglass have become canonical – essential – figures in the field, a fact evinced not just in Dinius's essay but across the entire volume, their writing also helps scholars reframe the work of canonical white male authors, especially in terms of white supremacy. Christopher Hanlon pairs two seeming opposites – Ralph Waldo Emerson and Edgar Allan Poe – to explore how the shifts in scholarship to attend to slavery and race have aligned these two antagonists in the contemporary scholarly imagination. As Hanlon shows, the scrutiny of Emerson and Poe in light of their implicit and explicit white supremacist inclinations align them more closely to writers like Harriet Beecher Stowe, who has been regularly brought to account for her fictional racialism. It is to Stowe, along with Margaret Fuller, that our next essay turns. Returning to Matthiessen's off-handed mention that the book he never wrote was "The Age of Fourier," Dorri Beam recasts two authors who tend to be used as representative presences on syllabi (Stowe the Sentimentalist, Fuller the Feminist) into a new narrative of radicalization via the utopian socialism of Fourier and US Fourierism. "The Age of

Fourier" also, no doubt, included Nathaniel Hawthorne's *The Blithedale Romance* (1852), his probing depiction of utopianism, in which Blithedale "seemed to authorize any individual, of either sex, to fall in love with any other, regardless of what would elsewhere be judged suitable and prudent."[12] As Christopher Castiglia argues in his essay, novels by Hawthorne like *Blithedale* and by his contemporary Theodore Winthrop stand at the beginning of a wider historical sweep, a dawning of an era with a twinned culture of sexuality, one regulatory and the other an informal and contingent world of subcultures, a cultural history that begins in the 1850s and culminates in the 1960s.

Castiglia's positioning of Hawthorne and Winthrop within a much wider historical process is likewise the goal of the final two essays of this part and the volume as a whole. Kelly Ross's "Melville/Whitman" poses perhaps the most traditional of the pairings – two of Matthiessen's five – but offers a truly untraditional interpretation. Focusing on the year 1855, which saw the publication of the first edition of *Leaves of Grass* and *Israel Potter*, Ross produces a new reading of the two authors that deemphasizes their relation to what is coming (the Civil War, and their poetry on it) and instead considers the whole of the period not as an *ante*bellum period but a bellicose period, marked by continual warfare. As Ross puts it, "Melville and Whitman looked back to the American Revolution to discern the roots of this never-ending warfare, seemingly the primary characteristic of the young country." Just as Ross rewrites the antebellum years as bellicose, one that stretches from the American Revolution through the Civil War and beyond, Nazera Sadiq Wright, in the final essay of this part and the volume as a whole, takes on the works of Frances Ellen Watkins Harper and Maria Stewart, positioning them in their newly canonical status but also looking beyond the hard end date of the volume of 1860 and toward the writings of the war and Reconstruction that immediately followed. Wright concentrates on how the two authors wrote about Black girlhood. While Harper's poetry and Stewart's orations may be familiar to readers of this volume, Wright introduces their fictional sketches and autobiographical writing. Wright's essay pushes the boundary of the 1860 end date to the collection, and rightly so for a collection in which the questions of historical periodization, and the rush to the Civil War, have long forestalled a *longue durée* understanding of the century. If the opening essays broke the frame of the nation-state implied in the term *American* literature, Wright's essay brings us back to the inability of literary scholars to draw within the lines of 1820–1860, as writers like Harper continued their impressive literary output long after the war ended.

When Matthiessen organized *American Renaissance* to explore authors who "wrote literature for democracy," he certainly did not include in that lineup Harper or Stewart, Douglass or Child, Walker or Apess, Winthrop or Sedgwick. But that does not mean that his characterization of this era's literature was wildly inaccurate; in fact, what scholars in the last forty years have built is in fact a more democratic canon, one with writers even more explicitly attached to democratic values and ready to call on the United States to live up to them more perfectly. As Emily Ogden writes in her essay for this volume, and as I have expanded upon in this introduction, scholarship is a type of romance, a salvaging, "the narration of a sustaining future out of the fragments of a failed past." We see this ongoing, never fulfilled democratic project of antebellum literature echoed in our present literature as well as in our current scholarship. If in "Crossing Brooklyn Ferry" (1856) Walt Whitman told future readers, "I am with you, you men and women of a generation, or ever so many generations hence," poets today self-consciously acknowledge his invocations. Amanda Gorman's inaugural poem, "The Hill We Climb" (2021), best exemplifies this response, in her Whitmanian catalogs, which sit alongside references to Maya Angelou and Lin-Manuel Miranda's *Hamilton*. But while "The Hill We Climb" is acutely aware of the literary past, it is not backward-looking; rather, Gorman's poem asserts that "democracy and poetry both happen in the future," as Virginia Jackson and Meredith Martin put it.[13] "Being American," Gorman reminded us, "is more than a pride we inherit, / it's the past we step into and how we repair it."[14] Salvaging, repairing, rebuilding the present in light of the past and for a future: we present the essays in this volume as expansions on Gorman's clear-eyed view of the past and equally hopeful investment in the reparative work of the present and future.

Notes

1 See Lloyd Pratt, *Archives of American Time: Literature and Modernity in the Nineteenth Century* (Philadelphia: University of Pennsylvania Press, 2010), 2–3 and in the introduction more generally.

2 Jeffrey Insko, *History, Abolition, and the Ever-Present Now in Antebellum American Writing* (Oxford: Oxford University Press, 2018), 9.

3 Jordan Alexander Stein, "American Literary History and Queer Temporalities," *American Literary History* 25.4 (2013), 863.

4 Elizabeth Freeman, *Time Binds: Queer Temporalities, Queer Histories* (Durham, NC: Duke University Press, 2010), 4.

5 Ted Underwood, *Why Literary Periods Mattered: Historical Contrast and the Prestige of English Studies* (Stanford, CA: Stanford University Press, 2013), 7.

6 Robert S. Levine, "Reimagining 1820–1865," in *Timelines of American Literature*, ed. Cody Marrs and Christopher Hager (Baltimore: Johns Hopkins University Press, 2019), 137–138.

7 F. O. Matthiessen, *American Renaissance: Art and Expression in the Age of Emerson and Whitman* (London: Oxford University Press, 1941), vii.

8 Matthiessen, *American Renaissance*, vii.

9 Visit https://lbrooks.people.amherst.edu/thecommonpot/ for Lisa Brooks's mapping project, *The Common Pot: Recovery of Native Spaces in the Northeast*.

10 Mattihiessen, *American Renaissance*, xv.

11 Ralph Waldo Emerson, *Nature*, in *Ralph Waldo Emerson: Selected Essays,* ed. Larzer Ziff (New York: Penguin, 1982), 35.

12 Nathaniel Hawthorne, *The Blithedale Romance*, ed. Richard H. Millington (New York: W. W. Norton, 2011), 52.

13 Virginia Jackson and Meredith Martin, "The Poetry of the Future," *Avidly*, January 29, 2021. http://avidly.lareviewofbooks.org/2021/01/29/the-poetry-of-the-future/ (accessed January 31, 2021).

14 Amanda Gorman, "The Hill We Climb," transcript in Julia Barajas, "Watch and Read L.A. Native Amanda Gorman's Inauguration Day Poem," January 20, 2021, *LA Times*. www.latimes.com/world-nation/story/2021-01-20/watch-and-read-amanda-gormans-inauguration-day-poem (accessed February 6, 2021).

PART I

Fractures and Continuities

CHAPTER 2

Hemisphere

Rodrigo Lazo

The US Library of Congress tells a story about the naming of America. In accordance with a historical artifact in its vaults, the Library records the naming as a result of a map made in 1507 by the German cartographer Martin Waldseemüller. Trying to capture pictorially the areas reached not long before by Christopher Columbus, Waldseemüller decided to name the lands after the Italian explorer Amerigo Vespucci, who had also made it to the territories. The name *Amerigo* was Latinized and feminized into *America*. But there is a problem with the way the Library of Congress Blog frames the story. On the web page publicizing this treasured map, the implication is that it provides the first naming of the United States – in other words, *America* as a metonym for the United States. "While the colonies may have established it," the page says as a reference to the British colonies, "America was given a name long before."[1] But neither Waldseemüller nor his map ever said anything about North American colonies or a nation that was hundreds of years from being conceptualized. For centuries after the 1490s, *America* referred to all of the territories in the hemisphere. In the nineteenth century, people in the United States increasingly claimed *America* as a national term and it became common usage by the twentieth century – an appropriation of continental proportions considering that the country is named the United States *of* America.

For some scholars, that slippage – America as both a reference to the United States and to the entire hemisphere – provides ample opportunity for debate. Some of us come right out and say it: the term "American literature and culture" is a misnomer if you are talking about US literature and culture. *America* can refer to other parts of the Northern Hemisphere, including Central and South America. Using it as a reference to one nation-state appropriates the term and its associations for a sociopolitical project based in one part of the hemisphere. For scholars, engaging with the literature and culture of the broader Americas calls for different types of analysis than the national frame of US literature and culture. A variety of questions come up when one considers hemispheric American literature: Where is America? Who are the people included in a particular use of America? What are its languages? What types of literary cultures emerge in different parts of the Americas? As implied by the Waldseemüller map, what are the power dynamics involved in the naming and framing of America? How to approach these questions methodologically?

Before elaborating on these considerations, let's back up to recent developments in literary study that brought us to this point of transition toward the methodologies of *trans-American studies*. The term "American literature" for decades most commonly referred to US national texts. In the twentieth century, the field was developed in reference to works of literature (mostly fiction and poetry) written in the English language. In its pre–Civil War manifestation, that included a set of authors (mostly men such as James Fenimore Cooper, Edgar Allan Poe, Nathaniel Hawthorne), certain intellectual and literary movements (romanticism, transcendentalism), and selected historical events that provided a context for the work (the US Revolution, the US Civil War). Revisionist approaches in the late twentieth century began to include more women writers (Harriet Beecher Stowe), African American writers (Frederick Douglass), and the relationship of literature to less-studied historical events (the removal of Native American populations, the US–Mexico War). But another question came up for "American literature" in the 1990s: What if we take *America* seriously as a reference to the hemisphere? How does the terrain of analysis change if we start to think of places, people, and languages beyond the limitations of the United States as a geographic entity and national conception?

In the 1990s, scholars proposed a "literatures of the Americas" approach that was largely comparative and involved lining up writers and texts from the United States alongside and against those of Latin America. For example, James Fenimore Cooper was read alongside Rosario Castellanos or Herman Melville alongside Alejo Carpentier.[2] Doris Sommer and José David Saldívar published influential books taking up new approaches to comparative Americas literary studies.[3] Much of this research and teaching was based on the notions of major writers and major works of literature, and the analysis ranged from studies of influence to the interaction of writers across the Americas. But as we entered the new millennium, the field of American literature moved toward the study of culture; scholars turned from literary texts toward a broader range of texts and historical objects. While today a scholar such as Harris Feinsod deploys poetry across the Americas to study twentieth-century inter-Americanism, the literary text has been decentered as a primary object of study across various literary areas. In nineteenth-century

American, interest in historical research has led to the integration of a variety of textual materials into studies of culture.[4]

A collection of essays that is sensitive to this new array of cultural objects and provides a forceful turn toward the Americas is *Hemispheric American Studies* (2008), edited by Robert S. Levine and Caroline Levander. Inspired by Frederick Douglass, Levine and Levander called for a consideration of the "interconnections among nations, peoples, institutions, and intellectual and political movements in the larger context of the American hemisphere" even as they addressed "the urgent question of how scholars might reframe disciplinary boundaries within the broad area of what is generally called American Studies."[5] For Americanists raised with the largely Anglophone emphasis of US national study, the question of how to interpret materials from different parts of the American hemisphere posed methodological challenges. The collection featured a variety of scholars (myself included) focusing on everything from stage performance to newspaper articles. More often than not, spatial configurations and racial conceptions were the focus, not literary texts. The result was the presentation of numerous routes toward research projects rather than one conclusive answer to the question that inspired the volume: How does one do research across the Americas? We will return to that, but let us consider the difference between the use of "hemispheric studies" and another term: trans-American studies.

While I support the spirit of hemispheric American studies – crossing languages, territories, and textual productions – and have no problem describing myself as someone who studies hemispheric movements, I have argued that hemispheric American studies is an impossibility as a field.[6] By that I mean it is impossible to transfer the terms under which national US literature had been founded as a field toward the broader geographic terrain of the Americas. In other words, the field formation of American literature – the conceptualizing of major texts, major writers, historical events, and methodologies – does not transfer well onto the entire hemisphere because the variety of writers, languages, contexts, histories, and literary traditions across the Americas breaks out of the limitations that structure a field of research. With so much to include, you might as well study the world. My argument against hemispheric studies as a field probably appealed to those with an investment in protecting Anglophone US literary study and Hispanophone Latin American studies in part because I seemed to propose that academic formations call for limitations. But retaining old-school field divisions was not my point, and certainly I did not want to shore up the border between the United States and other Americas. My argument was that scholars need to continue thinking of ways to do research across the Americas rather than turning to a predetermined geographic limitation to structure the way that research is done. Neither pretending to be transnational while continuing to study US authors nor attempting to cover the entire hemisphere was attentive to the new directions of research. (I also suggested that the old model of focusing on canonical literary texts, once venerated, was no longer sustainable.)

I distinguish between hemispheric American studies as invoking a mapping of the hemisphere (itself a cartographic construction) versus trans-American studies as *approaches* that call for a variety of methodologies and offer ample opportunities for new research. Trans-American studies (beyond America and across America) are about conceptualizing research questions that allow for the analysis of new texts and objects, some of which may not be written in the English language. (I retain the hyphen in *trans-American* to emphasize that America as a concept continues to play an important part in this research, whereas the usage *transamerican* offers an adjectival neologism.) Rather than rely on a predetermined set of texts and objectives, trans-American studies seeks new texts, topics, and approaches while keeping in mind that newness is relative and perhaps says more about the field from which a scholar starts than about the object of study. At times, scholars in trans-American studies may bring new lenses to old topics.

Trans-American studies is necessarily interdisciplinary, calling on scholars to draw from a variety of approaches, including but not limited to feminist studies, gender and sexuality studies, various strands of race and ethnic studies, Caribbean studies, and numerous critical schools. This calls for ongoing dialogue and engagement with various types of research that may not be directly in the field. For example, the Recovering the US Hispanic Literary Heritage Project, a strand of Latinx studies, has for years contributed in important ways to US and trans-American studies, bringing us such important texts as the novel *Jicoténcal* (1826) and the novels of María Amparo Ruiz de Burton. All of which is to say that trans-American studies demand consideration of scholarship coming out of various fields and disciplines. Depending on the project, it may be in direct dialogue with African Americas or Latinx studies.

Two important aspects of trans-American studies are language crossing and archival research. The most successful scholars of trans-American studies – among them Raúl Coronado, Anna Brickhouse, Kirsten Silva Gruesz, Jesse Alemán, and Sara E. Johnson – work in at least one language in addition to English, and often they consider the historical and political dimensions of translation. Coronado opens his book *A World Not to Come* with an analysis of a Spanish-language version of the Declaration of the Rights of Man and of the Citizen published in Nueva Granada (later Colombia) in 1793. Part history of print culture, Coronado's book is a reminder of the trans-American connections of US Latinx history.[7] Brickhouse's award-winning *The Unsettlement of America* focuses on translation to track Don Luis Velasco, "an Algonquian-speaking interpreter who traveled from what is now Virginia to Spain, Mexico, Cuba, and the Floridas."[8] Brickhouse puts pressure on the hemispheric version of American literary study to engage with Native American studies and the question of language use. Gruesz also delves into the colonial period in *Cotton Mather's Spanish Lessons*, her book on Mather's connections to the Caribbean, Florida, and other Spanish-speaking parts of the Americas. Alemán interprets intellectual culture in relation to civil wars in Cuba, the United States, and Mexico, at times delving into diaries and letters in the Spanish language to develop his arguments.[9] Johnson brings forward the role of African languages in the Americas in her work on how Kikongo was used by a slaveowner in Saint-Domingue to control laborers of African descent. (Johnson works in French as well as other languages.)[10] This is by no means an exhaustive list of the cross-language work being done, but the point here is that these scholars remind us that trans-American studies encompass a variety of languages, including Spanish, French, and many indigenous and African languages. The question of language crossing is often imbricated in a variety of power dynamics related to colonialism, slavery, and the treatment of indigenous populations, as the work of Brickhouse, Gruesz and Johnson show.

The importance of multilingualism and translation in trans-American studies suggests that we as scholars need new ways to think about the relationship of language study to research. On the one hand, language is not only a medium for unearthing information but the heart of what cultural scholars consider, and thus needs to be taken very seriously. On the other, attempting to gain language mastery before undertaking a research project may limit scholarly possibilities. In a more traditional model of graduate education – one based on disciplinary divisions – scholars specialized in a particular language, often spending years becoming experts in one (usually) European language. Research projects followed the language: for example, someone trained in French would study a francophone literary tradition. This type of dyad connecting language expertise to field of study had the unintended effect of creating Anglophone American literature (practiced by people in *English* departments) even as some scholars sought multilingual dimensions of American literature. But what if we were to invert the way scholars approach language study? What if a particular project invited language understanding rather than a priori language mastery framing a project? A scholar needing to learn a language such as Quechua would try to gain proficiency for research rather than the mastery of a field with a canonical impetus. This is where collaboration may be necessary. (Historians have been more open to this approach, whereas literary scholars have fetishized language study as the terrain of specialists.) Certainly, moving into a new language is not easy, and skeptics will scoff at the idea of graduate students learning new languages in light of decreased funding for graduate education (and a push toward shorter time to degree). But a dissertation on the way to a book might indeed call for years of gaining functional use of a language other than English, and it would be salutary if more indigenous languages were integrated into trans-American studies. Because combining the expertise of scholars could help with the demands of this type of research, trans-American studies could benefit from an increase in collaboration in humanistic inquiry.

Collaboration could further support the archival demands of moving beyond the canonical model of literary study. Many recent trans-American projects, including the ones discussed above, share an embrace of the archival turn in literary studies. Archives, once the purview of historians or historically minded critics, have increasingly become sites of debate as scholars mine them for new objects of analysis. While archives hold materials that can become the focus of research, they also raise questions about ways in which archives themselves structure knowledge. How are archives organized and what types of materials are excluded? Who decides what is included in an archive? What questions are raised by archival holdings that may not be a part of established conversations within disciplines or fields of study? These questions – the effects of theoretical debates that drew Michel Foucault and Jacques Derrida as well as historians and archivists – have significantly affected literary studies, namely, a broadening of the types of texts that scholars locate in an archive and then incorporate into research.[11] All of which is to say, like archives, fields of study are being challenged for the ways in which they institutionalize certain types of knowledge at the expense of others, sometimes in ideological support of social hierarchies. But for trans-American studies and other fields, archives also present ways to reinvigorate research agendas.

Archives make available pamphlets, newspapers, diaries, and other objects that effectively, although possibly inadvertently, deflect the position of canonical literary texts as the central concern of a field of study.

These materials have in some cases been made available across the globe through digitization. Whereas in previous decades, scholars had to travel to archives to read or view the materials held there, today holdings are increasingly made available online (although it is always helpful to see the actual object in that it may present information that is not apparent through the mediation of a screen).

When a researcher is confronted with a new piece from the archive, the types of questions that come up might be very different from those that emerge when someone does research on literary texts. This is a methodological challenge that dovetails with the types of spatial geographic realignments that inform trans-American studies. Just as the Americas can pull scholars in unexpected geographic directions (say, research on Central America), archival materials can push researchers into unsettled terrain. Unsettlement, Brickhouse's keyword to deploy counternarratives to stories of colonization, may indeed be the condition of a trans-American studies that is attentive to archival holdings.

For trans-American studies, it is not enough to go into the archives. One needs to do so while being cognizant of how much larger geopolitical considerations structure perspective, particularly in relation to various forms of colonialism and imperialism. John Patrick Leary, for example, approaches *underdevelopment* in a book that takes as its central concern the way the US empire conceptualizes itself culturally in relation to Latin America. The "contradictory discourses of difference and desire have produced a durable fiction of Latin America as either an incorrigibly backwards other or as an aspirant, but not yet arrived, partner," Leary writes.[12] The concern with perspective and how writers and intellectuals imagine parts of the hemisphere can prompt the type of research that uncovers the myriad ways that historical actors at various periods interpreted power dynamics in the Americas. For example, in the history of US-Latin American relations, the United States shifts from offering revolutionary inspiration (the effects of 1776) to positioning itself as the preeminent power in the hemisphere, most overtly in the US–Mexico War. By the time José Martí offers his critique of a giant "with seven-league boots" in his essay "Our America," the United States has moved from revolutionary inspiration for the world to a hegemonic power attempting to control the Americas economically and geopolitically.[13] Martí presented the oppressed populations of the southern continent against US hegemonic power.

The importance of inter-American geopolitics in the analysis of archival materials can be clarified by considering a concrete example: a pamphlet published in 1818 in Philadelphia titled *The Exposition, Remonstrance and*

Protest of Don Vincente Pazos, Commissioner on Behalf of the Republican Agents Established at Amelia Island, in Florida, under the Authority and on Behalf of the Independent States of South America.[14] When I first read this pamphlet, a variety of questions came up, some quite basic: Who was Vicente Pazos, why was he publishing this in Philadelphia, and what did he need to protest and address the US president in print? If the thirty-two-page pamphlet was a response to a military conflict that took place in Amelia Island off the coast of Florida, what had happened at Amelia and why was Pazos compelled to write about these events? The author, it turned out, was a print-culture warrior born in the highlands of what would become Bolivia, and his full name was Vicente Pazos Kanki (1779–1853). The spelling of his name as "Vincente" was an Anglicization, not a typo. Pazos Kanki had been born among the Aymara and had indigenous background.[15] His pamphlet was translated from the Spanish, and it was a public effort to convince US President James Monroe that the United States had violated international rules of military engagement by sending in troops to take over the island. But several questions remained: What was Pazos doing in the United States? And what were the print-culture conditions that led to the publication of the pamphlet in Philadelphia?

These types of questions call for shifting the frame of research away from the usual contours of US literary culture toward work that crosses the Americas and thus is closer to the type of research traditionally done by historians of Latin America. But whereas some approaches might draw from the pamphlet to develop a historical narrative or even to situate it in a national history (e.g. Pazos Kanki in Bolivia), scholars can also focus on the pamphlet itself as a print-culture object that produces historical discourse. For scholars starting from a US studies vantage point, the challenge is to undertake work that is highly interdisciplinary. For example, in-depth research on Pazos Kanki would call for analysis of his Spanish-language writing in South America. Once additional places are added to a terrain of analysis, the histories, political associations, and literary cultures of countries outside the United States call for additional research.

To situate Pazos Kanki within US print culture and the trans-American public sphere in which he participated, it is important to consider that his work as a journalist and activist opposing colonialism emerged in tandem with the wars of independence that spread throughout the Americas in the late eighteenth and early nineteenth centuries. During the decades following the US Revolution, the Americas changed as a cultural and political landscape. Countries in what became Latin America fought for independence from European colonialism. Mexico, Venezuela, Saint Domingue,

Cuba, and other countries went through social and political transformations as they grappled with colonial rule. Print culture conditions across
the hemisphere were altered with intellectuals making their way to printing
centers such as London and Philadelphia. Some Spanish American cities
received new printing presses and later eliminated restrictions on publication; independence brought with it a rise in the public sphere in places
such as Buenos Aires, where Pazos Kanki made his mark. Newspapers
became an increasingly important part of intellectual culture. As the wars
were progressing in the 1810s, intellectuals such as Pazos Kanki crossed the
Americas and made their way to the United States, where a movement in
support of independence was centered in Philadelphia. That city drew the
poet José María Heredia, the newspaper editor Manuel Torres, and the
Mexican radical priest Fray Servando Teresa de Mier.

Pazos Kanki was among the activist circle of intellectuals who gathered
in Philadelphia to discuss republican government, plan support for the
military fight for independence, and publish materials. He was born into an
indigenous community, learned Quechua, then studied Latin and French as
part of his early education at a seminary in La Paz.[16] Although he studied for
the priesthood, Pazos Kanki instead became a newspaper writer and editor,
which took him to Buenos Aires, London, and Philadelphia. In Buenos
Aires, during years when the region was moving toward independence, he
worked on the *Gazeta de Buenos Ayres* and helped found two additional
papers, *El Censor* and *La Crónica Argentina*, which became a major pro-
independence paper in 1816–1817.[17] As a result of this lively press work,
Pazos Kanki came into conflict with leaders of independence movements in
Buenos Aires, and he was exiled twice, first to London and then later to the
United States, where he quickly became involved in the Amelia Island
action. Throughout his life, he sometimes published under the name
Pazos without using the indigenous Kanki, which suggested a fluidity in
the way he presented himself racially in public.

The military action on Amelia Island was planned by a Philadelphia-
based group supporting independence from Spain and calling themselves
the "The deputies of free America, resident in the United States of the
North." Their plan was to start with Amelia and then continue with a
takeover of eastern Florida. The operation came under the direction of a
Scottish military leader by the name of Gregor MacGregor, who took over
the island with fifty-five men after a hasty Spanish capitulation in June
1817.[18] Pazos Kanki was there for part of the operation.

One of Pazos Kanki's goals in *The Exposition* was to tell the story of this
military effort to counter reports in the press that the operation was a mess

and that the United States needed to step in to restore order. Pazos Kanki defended MacGregor and argued that the Scot not only fought militarily but also did battle against "the machinations and desperate views of a few individuals, who, destitute alike of means and morals . . . soon attempted the subversion of the lawful authorities; and succeeded so far as to subvert military discipline and the public peace."[19] Here Pazos Kanki advocates in public for discipline and lawful behavior in contrast to the riotous troops that had gotten attention in newspapers and led to characterizations of the Amelia Island fighters as unruly. MacGregor eventually departed, and Pazos Kanki portrayed in positive terms the change in leadership: "the Spaniards were repulsed and beaten – the patriots triumphant – and the island pacified" (15).

But while Pazos Kanki and his group framed their action as a strike for republican rule, the James Monroe administration believed a band of adventurers was interfering with its own plans to acquire control of Florida. The different goals clashed here – a group of fighters attempting to declare independence from Spain and form a new government versus US attempts to negotiate acquisition of Florida through diplomatic channels. Although little known today, the Amelia Island conflict was big news in the northeastern United States. At the time, the United States was involved in negotiations with Spain over the future of the Florida territory that would eventually lead to the Adams–Onís Treaty of 1819. That was the geopolitical context for the Pazos Kanki pamphlet. When considered through the historical lens of US imperialist ventures in Latin America, Amelia Island looks like an early version of the numerous times the United States has sent troops into Latin America and the Caribbean to exert its will. While the story of US intervention in Latin America usually gains traction with the war against Mexico, Amelia Island offers an earlier window into attitudes about populations to the south of US borders. It also challenges anachronistic beliefs that US territories are historically fixed; Florida was once part of Spain, and Amelia very briefly part of the "independent states of South America," as the title of Pazos Kanki's pamphlet says.

The Monroe administration decided to respond to the Amelia Island action to prevent it from becoming an issue in negotiations with Spain. After reports surfaced that the Amelia Island group had seized a slave ship and were involved in slave trafficking, the Monroe administration came to see the fighters on Amelia as a nuisance and sent in US troops to dislodge them.[20] At the time, the administration justified the action as expelling an illegitimate force, but this was no less than one in a long line of expansionist and imperialist maneuvers to take over territory.

Pazos Kanki's response was a result of his belief as a newspaper man that print was capable of prompting change in the political arena. When he first saw a printing press in Buenos Aires in 1810, Pazos Kanki described his exhilaration: "Animated with the view of the admirable invention, I fancied I beheld in those mute characters, the types, the fountain of that light, which ere long would burst forth and dissipate the clouds of despotism which darkened the horizon of my beloved country."[21] From his perspective, print had the capacity to change minds – and in the case of colonial rule, the potential to inspire a change toward new government.

Pazos Kanki's faith in print is in full display in *The Exposition, Remonstrance and Protest*. The pamphlet both implicitly and explicitly suggests that the circulation of ideas in a US public sphere might have a more significant effect than private diplomatic correspondence he had already sent to the presidential administration. The *Exposition* was presented as a letter addressed "To James Monroe, president of the United States," on the opening page. The epistolary introduction to what is in effect a political pamphlet helped frame the discussion as an enlightened exchange between elite statesmen sharing letters. The pamphlet's goal was "to protest against the aggression, by force and arms, committed on the authorities . . . and the present occupation of the said island by the troops of the United States: – and to demand reparation; so that the rights of the new republics may not be impaired in the invasion of the said territory" (3). The language is tough, if respectful, accusing the United States of "aggression," "occupation," and "invasion." At the same time, the pamphlet is influenced by the language of diplomatic exchange, and on the title page it presents rhetorical flourishes that are explicit in their admiration for the United States. The title page quotes from the US Declaration of Independence, and Pazos positions himself and his compatriots as following in that tradition as defenders of independent republican government. In the title, Pazos Kanki calls them "republican agents."

Pazos Kanki deployed a rhetoric of friendship and admiration, even as he called out the Monroe administration for unlawful seizure of the territory. This was no less than a contradiction in the position of the Philadelphia Spanish American group: they attempted to draw on a US tradition of anticolonial fighting and printing going back to the US Revolution even as, in this case, the United States had shown itself wanting to take over territory already occupied by other people. Characterizing the US action on Amelia as a misunderstanding comparable "to the quarrels of brethren," Pazos Kanki requested that the United States withdraw from the island and return it to the group that had claimed it first. The

pamphlet simultaneously invokes the importance of anticolonial struggle
as a US tradition and accuses the United States of "violating the rights of
the new republics" (4). Pazos Kanki goes on, "I frankly avail myself of this
occasion, to assure the chief magistrate, that the feelings and attachments
of the patriots of South America, have been always ardent and full of
admiration of this nation, which has prepared the way to the emancipation
and liberty of the New World, and from whose example and precepts they
have been led to break the yoke of their oppressors; and that no man is
more impressed with the same feelings than myself" (4). Here he seems to
appeal to readers in the United States who would have seen independence
movements against Spain as part of hemispheric revolutionary struggles.[22]

Pazos makes a case that because his group of independence fighters had
belligerent status vis-à-vis Spain, they had first dibs on Amelia Island and
Florida in general. The subsequent US seizure, he argues, was the result of
force, not international right. In other words, the *Exposition* frames the
conflict on Amelia as two belligerent powers at war (Spain vs. the independence fighters). The United States steps in as an outside party, taking
an unlawful military action without declaring war before it had completed
negotiations on Florida cession. "The cession or sale of the Floridas having
not yet taken place, the United States have no just right over them," Pazos
wrote (19). In other words, the "independent states of South America" had
full rights to acquire the territory and institute republican government: "As
long as a Spanish possession has not been openly and lawfully detached
from the crown of Ferdinand, it remains liable to all the operations of war,
and to be occupied and dismembered by any power at war with Spain" (18).
Here diplomatic phrases such as "lawfully detached" and "liable to all the
operations of war" are presented in the public sphere as a part of a
reasonable argument.

Rather than follow law, he argues the United States turned to military
strength and mounted an "invasion of the Floridas" (19). Pazos continues,
"The United States have very recently proclaimed their neutrality, and still,
notwithstanding their being at peace with both Spain and the new republics, they have invaded a territory which they now possess, neither by virtue
of any cession from Spain, nor from the states of South America, the only
two powers which have alternately possessed it" (19). This was no less than
an inversion of the accusations that the Amelia group was made up of
filibusters. He challenged US efforts to discredit the men who had originally seized Amelia from Spain. "What would they think of another
nation, which, desirous also of possessing the Floridas, should calumniate

the American nation for having bought them, because they themselves had the same object in view?" (19). From Pazos Kanki's vantage point, it was the United States that took over the territory by force without any rights recognized internationally. Pazos went as far as to accuse US forces of taking "private properties belonging to the citizens of the new republics, captured in the waters of the Floridas, without any other right than that of force" (28).

Angry at having lost both the island and whatever resources his group had while there, Pazos Kanki attempted to sway public opinion in the United States against the US occupation of Amelia Island. The pamphlet was part of a broader diplomatic mission, which included Pazos working with Henry Clay to bring the matter to Congress and a meeting with Secretary of State John Quincy Adams.[23] But Pazos was unsuccessful. The Monroe administration stood by its actions.

Pazos Kanki was a writer and editor who could cross oceans and publish his work. His US publications show that he was eager to address an English-reading audience in the United States after distinguishing himself in Buenos Aires's Spanish-language newspaper culture. His indigenous background is important, in part because Pazos Kanki is an example of an intellectual who could cross racial and economic divisions to write alongside other elites from South America and the Caribbean making their way to the United States in the 1810s and 1820s. At times in print he downplayed his indigenous background, publishing as Vicente (and "Vincente") Pazos without adding his second surname. This fluidity in his self-presentation suggests that at times, participation in a trans-American print culture for Pazos may have called for a downplaying of his indigenous background, a point that needs further research.

Pazos Kanki's pamphlet offers an example of a text that raises the importance of language difference and archival remnants in early nineteenth-century trans-American studies. The *Exposition* is not part of received knowledge, nor is Pazos Kanki a figure particularly well known in either US or Latin American history. His text emerges in the minor crevices of archival holdings and thus requires the development of a research apparatus that is not necessarily beholden to fields of study that have been established with the division between US and Latin American studies. As a trans-American text, the *Exposition* is an example of a work translated for US audiences in order to build an English-language reading public trained on an issue that is of concern across the Americas: power relations between a major power and people trying to gain sovereignty.

Pazos Kanki reminds us of a historical context, the Amelia Island attack, that should be read as a bellwether for US-Latin American relations and depicts what Eduardo Galeano characterized as US actions toward Latin America: "U.S. concerns took over lands, customs houses, treasuries, and governments; Marines landed here, there, and everywhere to 'protect the lives and interests of U.S. citizens.'"[24] But these actions were not always similar, and military operations affected local conditions and populations in various ways. Are there new ways of considering these interactions? Archives contain other pieces of information for future scholars of trans-American studies who are willing to cross languages and field divisions in order to develop new ways to view America.

Notes

1 Erin Allen, "How Did America Get Its Name?" Library of Congress Blog. https://blogs.loc.gov/loc/2016/07/how-did-america-get-its-name/ (accessed February 24, 2020).

2 For examples of these pairings and others, see the collection *Reinventing the Americas: Comparative Studies of Literature of the United States and Spanish America*, ed. Bell Gale Chevigny and Gari Laguardia (Cambridge: Cambridge University Press, 1986).

3 Doris Sommer, *Foundational Fictions: The National Romances of Latin America* (Berkeley: University of California Press, 1991); José David Saldívar, *The Dialectics of Our America: Genealogy, Cultural Critique, and Literary History* (Durham, NC: Duke University Press, 1991).

4 Harris Feinsod, *The Poetry of the Americas: From Good Neighbors to Countercultures* (New York: Oxford University Press, 2017).

5 Robert S. Levine and Caroline Levander, *Hemispheric American Studies* (New Brunswick, NJ: Rutgers University Press, 2008),

6 Rodrigo Lazo, "The Invention of America Again: On the Impossibility of an Archive," *American Literary History* 25.4 (Winter 2013): 751–771.

7 Raúl Coronado, *A World Not to Come: A History of Latino Writing and Print Culture* (Cambridge, MA: Harvard University Press, 2013)

8 Anna Brickhouse, *The Unsettlement of America: Translation, Interpretation, and the Story of Don Luis de Velasco, 1560–1945* (New York: Oxford University Press, 2015), 6.

9 Kirsten Silva Gruesz, *Cotton Mather's Spanish Lessons* (Cambridge, MA: Harvard University Press, forthcoming). For an example of Alemán's work, see "From Union Officers to Cuban Rebels: The Story of the Brothers Cavada and Their American Civil Wars," in *The Latino Nineteenth Century*, ed. Rodrigo Lazo and Jesse Alemán (New York: New York University Press, 2016), 89–109.

10 For an example of the type of work in her forthcoming book, see Sara E. Johnson, "'Your Mother Gave Birth to a Pig': Power, Abuse, and Planter

Linguistics in Baudry des Lozière's Vocabulaire Congo," *Early American Studies* 16.1 (Winter 2018): 7–40.

11 The last three decades have ushered in a variety of theoretical and practical debates about archives and their organization. See, for example, Jacques Derrida, *Archive Fever: A Freudian Impression*, trans. Eric Prenowitz (Chicago: University of Chicago Press, 1995); Michel Foucault, *The Archeology of Knowledge* (New York: Pantheon, 1972); Ann Laura Stoler, *Along the Archival Grain: Epistemic Anxieties and Colonial Common Sense* (Princeton, NJ: Princeton University Press, 2009).

12 John Patrick Leary, *A Cultural History of Underdevelopment* (Charlottesville: University of Virginia Press, 2016), 3.

13 José Martí, "Our America," in *Our America by José Martí*, ed. Philip Foner (New York: Monthly Review Press, 1977).

14 In addition to this pamphlet, Pazos published in the United States a book that offers an interesting mix of history, geography, and politics titled *Letters on the United Provinces of South America, Addressed to the Hon. Henry Clay, Speaker of the House of Representatives of the United States*, trans. Platt H. Crosby (New York: J. Seymour, 1819). These *Letters* are a hybrid text, offering descriptions of recent independence movements in South America, the oppressive treatment of indigenous populations, and religious customs and social classes. In an attempt to promote commercial interaction between the United States and countries to the south, Pazos devotes most of the second half of the book to geographic accounting and detailed information about mines and the availability of minerals. Clay was known as a supporter of independence for Spanish America.

15 The most complete biographical-historical work on Vicente Pazos Kanki was done by Charles H. Bowman in 1975. See his book *Vicente Pazos Kanki: Un Boliviano en la libertad de América* (La Paz, Bolivia: Editorial Los Amigos del Libro, 1975) and "Vicente Pazos and the Amelia Island Affair, 1817," *The Florida Historical Quarterly* 53 (January 1975): 273–295.

16 Bowman, *Vicente Pazos Kanki*, 34–35.

17 *El Censor* published twelve issues between January 7 and March 21, 1812. *La Crónica* published twenty-eight issues between August 30, 1816, and February 8, 1817. Bowman, *Vicente Pazos Kanki*, 49, 57, 90.

18 Bowman, "Amelia Island Affair, 1817," 277.

19 Vicente Pazos, *The Exposition, Remonstrance and Protest of Don Vicente Pazos, Commissioner on Behalf of the Republican Agents Established at Amelia Island, in Florida, under the Authority and in Behalf of the Independent States of South America* (Philadelphia, 1818), 13–14; page numbers hereafter are cited parenthetically.

20 Frank Lawrence Owsley Jr. and Gene A. Smith, *Filibusters and Expansionists: Jeffersonian Manifest Destiny, 1800–1821* (Tuscaloosa: University of Alabama Press, 1997), 140.

21 Pazos, *Letters on the United Provinces of South America*, 18.

22 For a book that considers US attitudes toward Spanish American indepen-
    dence, see Caitlyn Fitz, *Our Sister Republics: The United States in an Age of
    American Revolutions* (New York: Norton, 2016).
23 Charles H. Bowman, "Vicente Pazos, Agent fo the Amelia Island Filibusters,
    1818," *The Florida Historical Quarterly* 53 (April 1975): 435.
24 Eduardo Galeano, *Open Veins of Latin America*, 25th anniversary edition,
    trans. Cedric Belfrage (New York: Monthly Review Press, 1997), 108.

CHAPTER 3

Empire

John Levi Barnard

... then all collapsed, and the great shroud of the sea rolled on as it
rolled five thousand years ago.

—Herman Melville

The Pacific ... churns with its colonial and nuclear legacies.

—Teresia Teaiwa[1]

In the early stages of the Cold War, the United States made the Marshall
Islands a testing ground for its nuclear arsenal, detonating sixty-seven
atomic and hydrogen bombs on the Bikini and Enewetak Atolls between
1946 and 1958. Decades later, the US Department of Defense finally
undertook a project of ecological remediation, ostensibly aimed at removing
residual radioactive material and rendering the islands once again habitable
for the Marshallese, many of whom had been displaced or exposed to the
deadly and damaging effects of the testing. The military consolidated this
hazardous material into the Runit Crater – the blast crater from the "Cactus"
test in 1958 – and capped it with a concrete dome. From the moment of its
conception, this structure was inadequate to the task of containment. Its
unsealed interior has allowed radiation to seep into the groundwater and the
adjacent lagoon, and as global warming accelerates, the dome itself is
threatened by intensifying storms and rising seas.[2]

As both Cold War relic and ongoing hazard, the dome is an example of
what Ann Laura Stoler has called "imperial debris," a category that
encompasses the wide-ranging and enduring evidence of empire as a force
of ruination, one that "lays waste to certain peoples and places, relations,
and things," while at the same time producing an imperial infrastructure
that itself inevitably devolves into ruins.[3] Though the United States
officially transferred sovereignty to the Marshallese in 1979, the Runit
Dome remains as imperial debris, a decaying monument not only to
American nuclear colonialism in the Pacific but also to a longer history
of empire and capital that has been unfolding since the fifteenth century.

While the particular threats of nuclear radiation and the greenhouse effect are generally associated with industrialization and militarization in the twentieth and twenty-first centuries, a longer historical perspective reveals these phenomena as what Kyle Powys Whyte calls an "intensification or intensified episode of colonialism," the planetary manifestations of an imperial project that has been ecologically catastrophic from the outset.[4]

Following Whyte and others who have identified the colonial origins of the crises of the "Anthropocene," in this essay I situate the rise of the United States as an economic and military power in the nineteenth century within a continuous history of what Alfred Crosby called "ecological imperialism," which began with the arrival of Columbus in the Caribbean and now culminates in the present threats of climate change and nuclear disaster.[5] While the displacement of the Marshallese and the deliberate contamination of their islands makes it especially obvious, colonization has always been characterized by what Heather Davis and Zoe Todd describe as a "severing of relations" between Indigenous human societies and the web of life in which they had been embedded. As Davis and Todd argue, settler colonialism was never merely about "dispossession"; it "was always about changing the land, transforming the earth itself, including the creatures, the plants, the soil composition and the atmosphere."[6] These processes of invasion, transformation, and settlement have amounted to a "seismic shockwave" that has "rolled through space and across time" to undermine the viability of the imperial powers that "brought about the rending and disruption of lifeways and life-worlds in the first place."[7]

In the following pages, I survey the ways these transformations and disruptions were central to both US nation-building and the development of an American national literature in the decades prior to the Civil War, while at the same time highlighting the causal relation and essential continuity between the extractive enterprises and imperial expansionism of the early United States and the linked geopolitical and ecological crises of the twenty-first century. If this approach situates early US imperialism in the longer history of colonization and the even deeper temporal frame-work of geological and evolutionary time, my opening in the Pacific emphasizes a widening of the spatial understanding of US empire. Through this attention to the Pacific, I join with other scholars working to dislodge what remains a conventional framing of US empire as conti-nental, to show that the continental was always of a piece with the archipelagic and the oceanic.[8] From the 1790s onward, continental settler colonialism and the projection of imperial power across the Pacific unfolded together, laying the foundations of an empire that has become planetary not only in its geopolitical extent but also in its ecological and even geological ramifications.

Global Market, American Axe

Perhaps no single literary work captures the connection between the continental and Pacific forms of US imperialism, as well as the wide-ranging ecosystemic implications of those imperial activities, more thoroughly than James Fenimore Cooper's 1847 novel *The Crater*. Written in the midst of the Mexican-American War – which would result in the largest US territorial acquisition since the Louisiana Purchase, effectively realizing John L. O'Sullivan's notion that it was the nation's "manifest destiny to overspread the continent" – the novel looks back to the 1790s and the rise of American maritime commerce in the Pacific; but it also features a settler-colonial project that aligns with the literature of continental empire running from Cooper's earlier novels *The Pioneers* (1823) and *The Prairie* (1827) to Francis Parkman's *Oregon Trail*, which appeared serially in the *Knickerbocker* in 1847, coincident with Cooper's writing of *The Crater* and the unfolding of the war itself.[9]

Cooper made the connection to this continental literature quite explicit by drawing on William Cullen Bryant's 1833 poem "The Prairies" for the epigraph to the novel. The publication of Bryant's poem more or less coincided with both the Black Hawk War in Illinois and the regional extinction of the American bison east of the Mississippi, and "The Prairies" offers a condensed vision of empire's reverberations through the entire web of life. Registering both the displacement of Indigenous people and the radical depletions of animal species driven by the fur trade, Bryant's speaker observes that the "beaver builds / No longer by these streams" and the bison "feeds no more" on the prairie, just as the "red man . . . / Has left these beautiful and lonely wilds." What Bryant euphemizes with the language of voluntary departure and inevitable vanishing was in fact the violent transformation of a vital setting of multispecies relations into a landscape, as Jodi Byrd has described it, "emptied and awaiting arrival."[10] Bryant's poem concludes with a vision of that arrival, as white settlers complete the transformation of the prairie ecosystem – home to the bison and the human economies that relied on it – into Euro-American farmland grazed by herds of domestic cattle. In alignment with the prevailing, if not yet explicitly articulated, sentiment of Manifest Destiny, Bryant's poem figures these processes of territorial expropriation and ecological disruption as evidence of both natural order and divine will. "Thus change the forms of being," Bryant concludes: "Thus arise / Races of living things, glorious in strength, / And perish, as the quickening breath of God / Fills them or is withdrawn."

For Cooper, these lines foreshadow his novel's apocalyptic conclusion, in which the utopian colony is destroyed by a geological catastrophe, but the appeal to Bryant's poem about the settler-colonial transformation of the North American biosphere also hints at the similarly radical remaking of the archipelagic ecosystem that is the setting of the novel. *The Crater* is a tale of shipwreck on a Pacific island that proves to be a windfall of natural resources and the site of a flourishing colony. And the colony flourishes on the twin pillars of the economic logic of colonization since Columbus: resource extraction and large-scale agricultural production. The resource extraction proceeds in the rapacious manner that characterized imperial commerce in the Pacific from its beginnings. Cooper's protagonist Mark Woolston – a respectable young sailor from Philadelphia – initially sets out in 1796 as first mate on the merchant ship *Rancocus*, "in quest of a cargo of sandal-wood and beche-le-mer" to be sold on "the Chinese market."[11] And though he is marooned on a deserted island, the shipwreck proves only a minor delay in the rise of Woolston's fortunes. Before long, Mark is rejoined by his shipmate Bob Betts, who brings others: his own wife, Mark's wife Bridget, Bridget's enslaved servants Socrates and Dido, and other friends and relatives who together form the basis of the colony. Dedicating themselves to reengaging the Pacific market, the colonists begin by felling their own forests for shipbuilding, making use of "that glorious implement of civilization, the American axe," to carve out the frame of a schooner large enough not only "to visit any part of the Pacific" but to do so armed with "carronades," which would "effectually give them the command of their own seas, so far as the natives were concerned at least" (I: 231–232). Backed by this threat of force, the colonists venture out to the neighboring islands, where they coerce the Indigenous people to open up their sandalwood groves to exploitation, securing a "contract" for the "cutting and preparing of a considerable quantity of this wood, which was to be ready for delivery in the course of three months, when it was understood that the schooner was to return and take it in."[12]

This naked expropriation of Indigenous resources amounts to primitive accumulation in its plainest form, and Cooper's narrator openly acknowledges that the sandalwood forests are a "mine of wealth," and that "so long as the sandal-wood lasted, so long would it be in the power of the colonists to coin money" (II: 66). Sven Beckert has labeled this kind of forcible extraction and accumulation "war capitalism," and though Beckert applies the term in the context of the Atlantic slave trade and the rise of an "empire of cotton," it is equally applicable – as Michelle Burnham has argued – to American activities in the Pacific from the late eighteenth century onward.[13] And as the rush to accumulate would turn the American hemisphere into a field of imperial contestation among European nations, so too would the various maritime powers compete over territory and resources in the Pacific. Mark Woolston is less concerned with Indigenous resistance to his extractive enterprises than he is with imperial "competitors," who might "rush in, the moment the existence of this mine of wealth should be known" (II: 66). And it is this potential threat to the colony's monopoly on local sandalwood that prompts Cooper's narrator to make explicit the exceptionalist ideology underpinning not only the linked projects of capital accumulation and settler colonialism the novel describes, but also the war against Mexico unfolding as the historical backdrop to the novel's composition:

> It was scarcely possible for man to possess any portion of this earth by a title better than that with which Mark Woolston was invested with his domains. But, what is right compared to might! Of his native country, so abused in our own times for its rapacity, and the desire to extend its dominions by any means, Mark felt no apprehension. Of all the powerful nations of the present day, America, though not absolutely spotless, had probably the least to reproach herself with, on the score of lawless and purely ambitious acquisitions. Even her conquests in open war have been few, and are not yet determined in character. In the end, it will be found that little will be taken that Mexico could keep; and had that nation observed towards this, ordinary justice and faith, in her intercourse and treaties, that which has so suddenly and vigorously been done, would never have even been attempted. (II: 66)

As opposed to the "lawless and ... ambitious acquisitions" of other nations, Mark's claims to his island colony are based on discovery and improvement, and it is critical to the utopian aspect of the project that the islands the colonists actually inhabit – unlike the North American continent prior to colonization or Mexico in 1847 – were indeed previously *uninhabited*. Woolston and his group subsequently transform their "discovered" territory into what Crosby would call a "neo-Europe," with large-scale agricultural and civic development; yet neither discovery nor improvement applies to the neighboring islands, which are inhabited by Indigenous islanders and – despite Cooper's insistence on the liberal language of "contract" – expropriated by force rather than consent.

Beyond the willful disregard for the sovereignty of both Mexico and Indigenous people, Cooper's nationalist rhetoric more or less replicates the enabling logic advanced by the likes of O'Sullivan, who in 1839 – as both the forced migration of the Cherokee and the Second Seminole War were simultaneously unfolding – would argue that it had been the "unparalleled glory" of the United States never to have taken to the battlefield "but in defence of humanity, of the oppressed of all nations, of the rights of conscience, the rights of personal enfranchisement," nor had "the American people ever suffered themselves to be led on by wicked ambition to depopulate the land, to spread desolation far and wide."[14] Both O'Sullivan and Cooper advance the peculiar and historically resilient idea that the United States – a country built on the conquest and colonization of a continent, as well as extraction and expropriation across the Pacific – is somehow incapable of imperialism.

Cattle, Guano, and the Breath of God

Key to this figuration of US history as something other than imperial is the notion embedded in Bryant's poem – and in the settler-colonial literary tradition to which Cooper had contributed across his career – that the course of empire and its impacts on human and nonhuman worlds was *inevitable*, part of a process of national and civilizational development that accorded with both divine providence and the natural order. Just as Bryant's poem figures the depletions of the fur frontier as prerequisite to white agrarian settlement, in Cooper's novel the colonists move from one resource to another as their activities deplete supplies and populations. When the sandalwood becomes scarce, they turn to whaling; and like Bryant's attribution of the regional extinctions of beaver and bison to the "breath of god," Cooper's colonists take the presence of whales off their shores as a sign "that Providence was dealing ... mercifully with them, by turning the people into this new channel of commerce" (II: 127).

Though these extractive enterprises are sanctioned by providence, the larger providential plan is the settlement of the island. In the continental context, extraction and settlement are linked through what Patrick Wolfe has identified as the settler-colonial logic of "elimination" and "replacement."[15] This sequential logic is readily apparent in "The Prairies," where white settlers and their cattle displace Indigenous peoples and native nonhuman species. Listening for the future sounds of the "advancing multitude / Which soon shall fill these deserts," Bryant's speaker hears not only the voices of "children," "maidens," and "Sabbath worshippers" but also the "low of herds." Bryant's poem imagines the fur frontier clearing a path for the agricultural frontier, resulting in a pastoral scene in which human domesticity is tightly correlated with the production and consumption of domesticated animals.

Cooper's imperial fantasy in *The Crater* replicates this transformation, as the capital accumulated through sandalwood and whales is reinvested in the development of the settler colony. This includes the construction of domestic and government buildings – largely by effectively enslaved labor drawn from the neighboring islands – but most importantly the importation and raising of vast herds of cows, pigs, and other livestock, and the development of large-scale agricultural enterprises. Increasing the population of domestic animals is a top priority for Mark Woolston throughout the novel, an interest that reflects what John Ryan Fischer has called "cattle colonialism" extending across the continent and the Pacific, as well as more generally demonstrating the centrality of livestock to the entire project of Euro-American colonization.[16] These animals are what Virginia DeJohn Anderson has called the "creatures of empire," and for white settlers in North America (and eventually in Australia and elsewhere) livestock was not only a critical component of local economies and food systems but was "emblematic of civilized existence" itself. Such settlers regarded raising "crops and animals on well-tended lands" as the expression of an "English agrarian ideal," and the proliferation of these practices would be key to the creation of neo-Europes on expropriated lands across the continent and the Pacific.[17]

Woolston begins his own settler-colonial project with only a handful of pigs and goats that had been shipwrecked with him on the island, but by the end of his reign as the colony's governor Mark presides over a herd of over a hundred head of cattle, "the cows giving milk ... the oxen being used in the yoke," and providing the "islanders" with the occasional treat of "fresh beef" (II: 216). Together with the oxen pulling plows, the pigs rooting in the ground contribute not only to the food economy with their edible flesh but to the "improvement" of the land itself with their labor. Most critically to the colonial enterprise, the pigs were essential in the cultivation of the tract of land Woolston dubs "the prairie." Initially consisting of only a "stratum of mud" coated with a "mass of sea-weed," this area had become "the favourite pasturage of the hogs," and "the work they had done on the Prairie was incredible ... mixing the sea-weed with the mud, and fast converting the whole into soil." Though Cooper's depiction of soil science and composition is dubious, the labor of the hogs results in a grassland that would prove to be "a treasure to the colony," ultimately becoming "a vast range, most of which was green, and all of which was firm enough to bear a hoof" (II: 82).

In many ways, these efforts at livestock raising and agricultural development echo the colonizing project described in Cooper's 1823 novel *The Pioneers*, in which white settlers carve a neo-Europe out of Mohican territory through expropriation, deforestation, depletion of native species, and the introduction of Euro-American practices of farming and animal husbandry. The crucial difference in *The Crater*, of course, is that the land is originally uninhabited, untouched by human hands prior to Woolston's arrival. It is the pure, colonial fantasy of the *terra nullius* that North American settlers would have to create through genocidal violence and imaginative acts of erasure. Unlike Bryant's speaker in "The Prairies," who must at least acknowledge the disappearance of the prior inhabitants, Woolston and his pigs can plausibly claim to be cultivating a virgin soil, unencumbered by the history of violence imperial ideologues like O'Sullivan were intent on denying or assimilating to a Providential plan. Without any human history at all, Woolston's island can truly be what O'Sullivan called the "Great Nation of Futurity," built on neither displacement nor expropriation, but on pure ingenuity and the virtuous application of the tools and technologies of "civilization."

These technologies include not only the "glorious . . . American axe" and the terraforming power of animal labor, but also something more modern and more ominous with respect to the future courses of empire and capital that would follow from the colonial histories Cooper's novels recount. Woolston's first and most important discovery is that his island is covered with rich deposits of "as good guano as was ever found on the coast of Peru" (I: 78). Over the course of the nineteenth century, Europeans and Americans increasingly turned to guano – the excrement of sea birds that collects and ossifies on exposed surfaces of rock – as a fertilizer within an intensifying regime of commodity agriculture.[18] The largest deposits of guano were concentrated in a chain of islands off the coast of Peru, and guano quickly emerged as one of the most valued commodities in the Pacific trade. As the historian Gregory Cushman has observed, in its remarkable capacity to render barren or exhausted soils fertile, guano "captured the fascination of laboratory chemists, experimental farmers, globe-trotting explorers – even an occasional poet."[19] It certainly captured the imagination of Cooper the novelist, and for Mark Woolston and his fellow settlers guano is essential to the success of the colony, for with its application, what had been "for thousands of years" a barren island "in its nakedness," was transformed to a landscape "covered with verdure, and blest with fruitfulness" (I: 104).

If guano was vitalizing to both continental soil and Pacific commerce, at a larger scale its proliferation was pivotal to the transition from what Cushman calls the "ecological old regime" of agricultural production to the modern industrial one. Just as coal, petroleum, and eventually uranium would uncouple human industry from the solar energy cycle, guano initiated a new form of agricultural intensification – based on the application of extracted and later synthetic nitrogen-rich fertilizers – that "allowed ... industrial civilization to escape the limitations imposed by nutrient recycling."[20] This revolutionary fertilizer was "so powerful and profitable," as Cushman explains, "that it inspired a global rush" not only for guano itself but for "other similar resources and substitutes – including the vast nitrate deposits of southern Peru."[21] And this rush would usher in an era of nitrogen extraction and experimentation that would fuel the rise not only of industrial agriculture but also of an explosives industry that would in turn intensify both extractive mining enterprises and the conduct of imperial war.[22]

Guano in *The Crater* is – like the appearance of whales when the sandalwood runs out – just another sign of providence, part of a civilizing process that transforms "a wilderness into a garden" (II: 30). But over the rest of the nineteenth century guano would be a driving concern of an expanding American empire, which would ultimately annex close to a hundred small islands across the Pacific and the Caribbean for the purposes of its extraction. Though most of these islands were, like the ones in Cooper's novel, uninhabited at the time of annexation, their incorporation into imperial networks of extraction and exchange was not without ramifications for the Indigenous peoples of the Pacific. Like Cooper's colonists, who pressed the neighboring islanders – whom Cooper calls "Kannakas" – into extractive labor through coercive contracts, hostage-taking, and other threats of violence, American companies largely drew on Native Hawaiians (Kānaka Maoli in the Hawaiian language) to harvest guano from their Pacific islands.[23] And though Cooper's narrator only speculates about "New Zealand and Tahiti" being "brought under the yoke" along with California and the rest of the Mexican territory soon to be ceded to the United States in the Treaty of Guadalupe Hidalgo, Hawai'i itself would become the primary focus of American imperial ambitions in the Pacific.

At Ahab's Tomb

Critical at first as a node in the network of trans-Pacific trade, from its annexation in 1898 onward Hawai'i would increasingly serve as a stage for the projection of US military power.[24] At the height of the Cold War, this force projection would include a number of nuclear-powered and nuclear-armed vessels. Among these was the USS *Kamehameha*, a ballistic missile submarine named for the Hawaiian monarch who unified the islands around the turn of the nineteenth century, just as the imperial powers of Europe and the United States were escalating their extractive and commercial enterprises across the Pacific.[25] Kamehameha died in 1819, the same year Herman Melville was born and the first American whaling vessel stopped in Hawai'i.[26] Melville himself would arrive in Hawai'i on a whale-ship in 1843, just in time to witness the return of sovereignty to Kamehameha III, a younger son of the original king, after a rogue British naval officer briefly and illegally claimed the islands for the Crown.[27] More broadly, in Hawai'i Melville encountered a colonial scene of missionaries and competing commercial interests and military powers that he would depict in scathing terms in his first novel, *Typee* (1846). Despite the "glowing accounts" disseminated by imperial "philanthropists," Native Hawaiians in Melville's view were hardly the beneficiaries of any supposedly benign civilizing mission, but the "victims" of disruption of local economies and food systems, exposure to "the worst vices and evils of civilized life," expropriation of their land, and exploitation of their labor, having been "civilized into draught-horses; and evangelized into beasts of burden."[28]

Melville eventually joined the US Navy in Honolulu, shipping on the frigate *United States*, the name of which may have lodged the trope of the ship of state in the young sailor's mind. He would rename that ship of state the *Neversink* in his novel *White Jacket* (1850), before reimagining it again as the *Pequod* in *Moby-Dick* (1851). Both the whaleship *Pequod* and the submarine *Kamehameha* demonstrate the settler-colonial determination, as Byrd has described it, to "repeatedly and violently" render internal "what was external," as both vessels enlist Indigenous names in the service of empire: the *Pequod* in the primitive accumulation and rising industrialization of the American economy, the *Kamehameha* in advancing the global war against communism through a policy of mutually assured destruction.[29] And in pursuing these objectives at the expense of all manner of human and nonhuman life, these vessels reveal the willingness Stoler has identified at the heart of the imperial project to lay things to waste and leave them in ruins.[30]

This annihilating tendency was self-evident to Black and Indigenous writers in the nineteenth century, from David Walker's account of white imperial history as an endless chain of atrocities, culminating in the enslavement of innumerable Africans to "dig their mines and work their farms; and thus go on enriching them, from one generation to another," to William Apess's charge that white colonizers "care not whether the Indians live or die" and "would think it no crime to go upon Indian lands and cut and carry off their most valuable timber, or any thing else they chose." The Hawaiian historian Samuel Mānaiakalani Kamakau noted that whites had brought not only imperial violence to the islands but also "fleas and mosquitos," "changes in plant life" and "in the air we breathe," while the Sauk leader Black Hawk would similarly observe that white encroachment constituted a disruption not merely of Indigenous social, economic, and political arrangements but of the entire web of life.[31] "Things were growing worse," Black Hawk lamented in his surrender speech at the end of the war that bears his name: "There were no deer in the forest. The opossum and beaver were fled; the springs were drying up, and our squaws and pappooses without victuals to keep them from starving."[32]

Writing at the same time and about the same prairie landscape, both Black Hawk and Bryant observe the same patterns of disappearance and extinction. But where Black Hawk apprehends what Davis and Todd have described as a "genocide of all manner of kin: animals and plants alike," and a "severing of relations" between human and nonhuman forms of life, Bryant sees the workings of providence, the "forms of being" changing "as the quickening breath of God / Fills them or is withdrawn." Bryant here participates in what Sylvia Wynter calls the "poetics of the *propter nos*," through which the world and all its creatures and resources are understood and represented as being *propter nos homines* (for us humans), while at the same time *nos homines* – the supposedly universal category of the human as a species – comes to refer exclusively to the privileged white Euro-American subject.[33] Through this poetics the elimination of Indigenous peoples, the disruption of ecological relations, and the extinction of non-human species could be plausibly represented as the workings of the "breath of God," just as the atomic bombings of the Marshall Islands could be presented to the Marshallese – as the US military did in justifying their relocation – as being "for the good of mankind."[34]

As Wynter has noted, this providential and universalizing ideology, especially "in the face of the mounting evidence of its costs to the planetary environment . . . as well as to the world-systemic sociohuman one," is not only specious but unsustainable.[35] There is a hint of this unsustainability in Cooper's *The Crater*, as the colony is ultimately destroyed by some "awful catastrophe," leaving only the island's "rocky summit, and its venerable deposit of guano," visible above the surface of the ocean (II: 224). While geological in scope – and thus reflecting a transatlantic romantic literary interest in the ways such geological phenomena conjured up visions of not only the end of human civilization, but the extinction of the human species – there is no suggestion that this catastrophe might be attributed to either ecological disruption or to imperial overreach.[36] If the catastrophe can be read politically, it is as the result of the excesses not of empire but of *democracy*, which had brought about the overthrow of Mark Woolston's benign dictatorship, a political outcome Cooper presents as more or less equivalent to the end of the world. The ascent of an unruly democracy marks the end of what is essentially a utopian fantasy of settler colonialism: the creation of a neo-Europe in a New World that is providentially unencumbered by Indigenous people with prior claims to the land. This desert-island fantasy thus avoids – as Cooper's earlier novels could not – any real acknowledgment of the costs of colonization to Indigenous peoples and the larger ecosystems in which their societies and economies had evolved.

By contrast, the apocalyptic finale of Melville's *Moby-Dick* – a novel that casts a far more critical eye on American extractive and expropriative ambitions in the wake of the Mexican War – registers how the course of empire unfolds through a richly inhabited world, severing relations and laying waste along the way. The impacts of those imperial ambitions are captured in the novel's closing scene, as Tashtego – the Wampanoag harpooneer – continues hammering Ahab's flag into the mast even as the ship sinks beneath the "destroying billows" of the ocean. As Tashtego struggles to finish his task, one of the "sea-hawks" that have been hovering like vultures over the impending catastrophe gets caught between the hammer and the mast. This moment crystallizes what has been the novel's critical perspective on empire and capital, as Tashtego's fidelity to the mission – his dedication to raising Ahab's battle flag no matter what – recapitulates the larger appropriation of Indigenous labor and identity into the imperial enterprise, an appropriation revealed most powerfully in the name of the ship itself. And by ensnaring the sea-hawk as well, the scene emphasizes how both human and nonhuman have been drawn into the project of their own eradication as "captive form[s] folded in the flag of Ahab," going "down with his ship, which, like Satan, would not sink to hell till she had dragged a living part of heaven along with her."[37]

If the sinking of the *Pequod* constitutes a grim prophecy for the future of the American empire, it is worth considering that Melville's depictions of the everyday operations of the whaleship are equally apt as prophetic images for the mechanized industrial future of the world as we know it. If Ahab's determination to "burst his hot heart's shell" on the body of the "all-destroying but unconquerable whale" prefigures the annihilating logic of the nuclear age, ignited first in Hiroshima and Nagasaki, carried on through decades of testing and experimentation across the islands of the Pacific, and embodied in the murderous potential of ships like the *Kamehameha*, then the methodical transformation of whale flesh into market value – which would circulate in turn through an economy of cod fisheries, sugar and cotton plantations, rum distilleries, and textile mills – is of a piece with the more banal operation of coal- and gas-fired power plants, internal combustion engines, and industrial food systems entirely reliant on nitrogen fertilizers and fossil fuels, all of which now contribute to global warming and mass extinction on a planetary scale.[38]

These are the histories – of the fast violence of imperial war and the slow violence of capital accumulation and its externalized ecological costs – that converge at the site of the Runit Dome. Melville recognized the catastrophic potential of both of these historical threads, and described the quotidian operations of the whaleship – encapsulated in the huge boilers that distilled blubber into oil – in terms no less infernal and apocalyptic than those he used for Ahab's fiery hunt. Those boilers, fueled by "fierce flames" in the belly of the ship, smell "like the left wing of the day of judgment" and constitute an "argument for the pit" (470). The fires burn all night, "as if remorselessly commissioned to some vengeful deed," and the ship, "laden with fire, and burning a corpse, and plunging into" the "blackness of darkness" of the ocean at night, seems "the material counterpart of her monomaniac commander's soul" (470–471). Like Ahab's twin forms of mutually assured destruction – the boiling of whales into oil and capital, the drowning of the *Pequod* and its crew – the legacies of US empire will be written equally in the fires of warfare and internal combustion and the waters of a rising sea. That sea, as Ishmael says, will roll on "as it rolled five thousand" and even five million years ago, washing away the imperial ruin of the Runit Dome and rendering coastal cities like New York, New Bedford, and Honolulu – those critical waypoints in Melville's life and writing – a strange new form of watery ruins themselves (634).

Just as Black Hawk surveyed what was already a state of ecological ruin in 1832, the Marshallese poet Kathy Jetnil-Kijiner has borne witness to the ruination of her island home by nuclear colonialism and climate change. Like Black Hawk's ruptured prairie ecosystem, Enewetak was once "whole" – "a whole island," marked by "breadfruit trees heavy with green globes of fruit," where "crabs dusted with white sand scuttled through pandanus roots" and "beneath looming coconut trees beds of watermelon slept." But after the nuclear testing, the island "became tomb ... became concrete shell ... became solidified history." Jetnil-Kijiner has collaborated with filmmaker Dan Lin to create a "video poem" titled "Anointed," in which she walks barefoot across the Runit Dome and recounts a story about Letao, a shape-shifting trickster figure in Marshallese tradition.[39] In her story, Letao transforms a shell into "kindling for the first fire," which he gives to a boy – like Phaethon with the chariot of Helios – who is neither powerful nor wise enough to control it. Against footage of nuclear explosions at Bikini and Enewak, we hear how this boy nearly "burned his entire village to the ground." "This is a story of a people on fire," Jetnil-Kijiner writes, and she concludes by asking, "[W]ho anointed them with the power to burn?" In another poem, she has written of a child "stomping . . . / across the edge of a reef / not yet / under water," and the understated implication of that "not yet" points us toward a corollary question.[40] As the camera retreats at the end of "Anointed," from the dome to the scale of the atoll and then the surrounding ocean, we might also ask – looking back to Ahab's tomb in the Pacific, and forward to the inundations of a warming world – about the equally salient power to drown.

Notes

1 Teresia K. Teaiwa, "bikinis and other s/pacific n/oceans," *The Contemporary Pacific* 6.1 (1994): 88.

2 On Runit Dome, see Michael B. Gerrard, "America's Forgotten Nuclear Waste Dump in the Pacific," *SAIS Review of International Affairs* 35.1 (2015): 87–97; Kyle Swenson, "The U.S. Put Nuclear Waste under a Dome in the Pacific. Now It's Cracking Open," *Washington Post*, May 20, 2019, www.washingtonpost.com/nation/2019/05/20/us-put-nuclear-waste-under-dome-pacific-island-now-its-cracking-open/; and Susanne Rust, "How the U.S. Betrayed the Marshall Islands, Kindling the Next Nuclear Disaster," *Los Angeles Times*, November 10, 2019, www.latimes.com/projects/marshall-islands-nuclear-testing-sea-level-rise/. On US nuclear colonialism in the Marshall Islands, see Darlene Keju-Johnson, "For the Good of Mankind," *Seattle Journal for Social Justice* 2.1 (2003): 309–314; Teaiwa, "bikinis," 87–109; Amanda Kearney, *Violence in Place, Cultural and Environmental Wounding* (Abingdon: Routledge, 2017), 166–171; and Martha Smith-Norris, *Domination and Resistance: The United States and the Marshall Islands during the Cold War* (Honolulu: University of Hawai'i Press, 2016).

3 Ann Laura Stoler, "Imperial Debris: Reflections on Ruins and Ruination," *Cultural Anthropology* 23.2 (2008): 195–196.

4 Kyle Powys Whyte, "Indigenous Climate Change Studies: Indigenizing Futures, Decolonizing the Anthropocene," *English Language Notes* 55.1–2 (2017), 153–154.

5 Alfred Crosby, *Ecological Imperialism: The Biological Expansion of Europe, 900–1900* (Cambridge: Cambridge University Press, 2004). See also Heather

Davis and Zoe Todd, "On the Importance of a Date, or Decolonizing the Anthropocene," *ACME: An International Journal for Critical Geographies* 16.4 (2017): 761–780; Simon L. Lewis and Mark A. Maslin, *The Human Planet: How We Created the Anthropocene* (New Haven, CT: Yale University Press, 2018); and Kathryn Yusoff, *A Billion Black Anthropocenes or None* (Minneapolis: University of Minnesota Press, 2019).

6 Davis and Todd, "On the Importance of a Date," 770.

7 Ibid., 774.

8 See, for example, Arrell Gibson and John S. Whitehead, *Yankees in Paradise: The Pacific Basin Frontier* (Albuquerque: University of New Mexico Press, 1993); Yunte Huang, *Transpacific Imaginations: History, Literature, Counterpoetics* (Cambridge, MA: Harvard University Press, 2008); David Igler, *The Great Ocean: Pacific Worlds from Captain Cook to the Gold Rush* (New York: Oxford University Press, 2013); Gregory T. Cushman, *Guano and the Opening of the Pacific World: A Global Ecological History* (New York: Cambridge University Press, 2013); J. Kehaulani Kauanui, "Imperial Ocean: The Pacific as a Critical Site for American Studies," *American Quarterly* 67.3 (2015): 625–636; and Brian Russell Roberts and Michelle Ann Stephens, "Archipelagic American Studies: Decontextualizing the Study of American Culture," in Roberts and Stephens, eds., *Archipelagic American Studies* (Durham, NC: Duke University Press, 2017).

9 John L. O'Sullivan, "Annexation," *The United States Magazine, and Democratic Review* (July–August 1845): 5.

10 Jodi A. Byrd, *The Transit of Empire: Indigenous Critiques of Colonialism* (Minneapolis: University of Minnesota Press, 2011), xxi.

11 James Fenimore Cooper, *The Crater; or, Vulcan's Peak*, vol. I (New York: Burgess, Stringer & Co., 1847), 29. Hereafter cited in the text.

12 James Fenimore Cooper, *The Crater; or, Vulcan's Peak*, vol. II (New York: Burgess, Stringer & Co., 1847), 53. Hereafter cited in the text.

13 Sven Beckert, *Empire of Cotton: A Global History* (New York: Knopf, 2015); Michelle Burnham, *Transoceanic America: Risk, Writing, and Revolution in the Global Pacific* (New York: Oxford University Press, 2019), 11.

14 John L. O'Sullivan, "The Great Nation of Futurity," *The United States Magazine, and Democratic Review* (November 1839): 427.

15 Patrick Wolfe, "Settler Colonialism and the Elimination of the Native," *Journal of Genocide Research* 8.4 (2006): 387–409.

16 John Ryan Fischer, *Cattle Colonialism: An Environmental History of the Conquest of California and Hawai'i* (Chapel Hill: University of North Carolina Press, 2015).

17 Virginia DeJohn Anderson, *Creatures of Empire: How Domestic Animals Transformed America* (New York: Oxford University Press, 2004), 89.

18 On guano, see Cushman, *Guano and the Opening of the Pacific World*, and Daniel Immerwahr, *How to Hide an Empire: A History of the Greater United States* (New York: Farrar, Straus and Giroux), 46–58.

19 Cushman, *Guano and the Opening of the Pacific World*, 27.

20 Ibid., 40.

21 Ibid., 27.

22 Ibid., 19, 69; Immerwahr, *How to Hide an Empire*, 57.

23 Immerwahr, *How to Hide an Empire*, 53; On Hawaiian guano workers, see Gary Y. Okihiro, *Island World: A History of Hawai'i and the United States* (Berkeley: University of California Press, 2008), 167–168. On the Euro-American application of the term "kanaka" to enslaved or coerced laborers throughout the Pacific Islands, see David A. Chang, *The World and All the Things upon It: Native Hawaiian Geographies of Exploration* (Minneapolis: University of Minnesota Press, 2016), 35.

24 On the militarization of Hawai'i, and Native Hawaiian enlistment in and resistance to it, see Jon Kamakawiwo'ole Osorio, "Memorializing Pu'uloa and Remembering Pearl Harbor," in Setsu Shigematsu and Keith L. Camacho, eds., *Militarized Currents: Toward a Decolonized Future in Asia and the Pacific* (Minneapolis: University of Minnesota Press, 2010), 3–14.

25 On the ship, see the Navy press release on its deactivation: www.globalsecurity .org/military/library/report/2001/kamehameha.htm.

26 Okihiro, *Island World*, 156.

27 Hershel Parker, *Herman Melville: A Biography, vol. 1: 1819–1851* (Baltimore: Johns Hopkins University Press), 257–258. On the loss and restoration of sovereignty, see Noenoe K. Silva, *Aloha Betrayed: Native Hawaiian Resistance to American Colonialism* (Durham, NC: Duke University Press, 2004), 36–37.

28 Herman Melville, *Typee* (New York: Wiley and Putnam, 1846), 251.

29 Byrd, *The Transit of Empire*, 136.

30 Stoler, "Imperial Debris," 196.

31 Silva, *Aloha Betrayed*, 22–23. As Silva notes, when Vancouver arrived not long after Cook, "he left cattle and several kinds of fruit and vegetable plants to improve the landscape," which only further "upset the ecological balance" (24).

32 Samuel G. Drake, *Biography and History of the Indians of North America* (Boston, 1834), 137. On the transcription and publication history of the speech, see Arnold Krupat, *"That the People Might Live": Loss and Renewal in Native American Elegy* (Ithaca, NY: Cornell University Press, 2012), 69–73.

33 Sylvia Wynter, "1492: A New World View," in *Race, Discourse, and the Origin of the Americas*, ed. Vera Lawrence Hyatt and Rex Nettleford (Washington, DC: Smithsonian Institution Press, 1995).

34 Keju-Johnson, "For the Good of Mankind," 309.

35 Wynter, "1492: A New World View," 43–44.

36 On Cooper, geology, and "narratives of extinction," see John Hay, *Postapocalyptic Fantasies in Antebellum American Literature* (Cambridge: Cambridge University Press, 2017), 73–112.

37 Herman Melville, *Moby-Dick; or, The Whale* (New York: Harper & Brothers, 1851), 634.

38 Ibid., 203, 633.

39 Kathy Jetnil-Kijiner and Dan Lin, "Anointed," https://vimeo.com/264867214. On Letao, see Phillip H. McArthur, "Ambivalent Fantasies: Local Prehistories and Global Dramas in the Marshall Islands," *Journal of Folklore Research* 45.3 (2008): 263–298.

40 Kathy Jetnil-Kijiner, *Iep Jaltok: Poems from a Marshallese Daughter* (Tucson: University of Arizona Press, 2017), 79.

CHAPTER 4

Economy

David Anthony

In the first chapter of Henry David Thoreau's *Walden* (1854) – which of course bears the same title as this chapter – Thoreau famously tells us, "The mass of men lead lives of quiet desperation."[1] Here Thoreau doesn't refer simply to the struggling poor. Rather, he's talking about the millions of Americans who, by entering into the marketplace for work or trade, have become alienated, both from their fellow citizens and from themselves. This, he says, is "the curse of trade."[2] Even if financially stable, Americans have exchanged their personal liberty – their individuality – for an eroded and reified form of human presence, one in which people relate to one another less as humans than as objectified commodities. "With consummate skill [man] has set his trap with a hair-spring to catch comfort and independence, and then, as he turned away, got his own leg into it," Thoreau says. "This is the reason he is poor; and for a similar reason we are all poor in respect to a thousand savage comforts, though surrounded by luxuries."[3] Anticipating Marx's discussion in *Capital, Volume I* (1867), of the way in which men have become "mere personifications of economic relations,"[4] Thoreau provides the inverse of the line attributed to Bill Clinton and James Carville during the 1992 presidential campaign: "It's the economy, stupid." For Clinton, it only made sense for Americans to embrace their economic selfhood. This was the centerpiece of his efforts to defeat George H. W. Bush. For Thoreau, this way of thinking was a tragic mistake.

This chapter will examine how the economy – especially the economy as Thoreau described and worried about it – was depicted in American literature from about 1820 to 1860. First, I provide an overview of the way American writers tended to represent the emergence of a new form of economic selfhood in America, one based both on credit and speculation, and on market notions of "success" and "failure." In the second section, I suggest a possible future for economic criticism, one that takes its cue from recent scholarship in Transnational American Studies. Here I'll contend that we can't fully understand how American literature, whether canonical or otherwise, reflects the nineteenth-century economy without framing "economy" in global terms. American historians, especially those working on slavery, have been laying the groundwork in this area for the past ten years or so.[5] Scholars focusing on the economic dimensions of American literature would do well to follow suit.

Money and National Anxiety

There's a moment in Washington Irving's famous short story, "The Legend of Sleepy Hollow" (1819), when we glimpse both Ichabod Crane's true motives in his pursuit of the beautiful Katrina Van Tassel and an emergent form of capitalist selfhood in America. "His heart yearned after the damsel who was to inherit these domains," we're told, "and his imagination expanded with the idea, how they might be readily turned into cash, and the money invested in immense tracts of wild land, and shingle palaces in the wilderness."[6] Ichabod, we realize, is a would-be speculator. Not just willing but actually eager to sell off the Van Tassel estate in order to invest in the sorts of high-risk western real estate ventures that preceded the Panic of 1819, he represents the new type of capitalist personhood described by J. G. A. Pocock in his landmark study, *Virtue, Commerce, and History* (1985). Writing about the shift toward a credit-based paper economy in the eighteenth century, Pocock suggests that since property during this period was "acknowledged as the social basis of personality, the emergence of classes whose property consisted not of lands or goods or even bullion, but of paper promises to repay in an undefined future, was seen as entailing the emergence of new types of personality, unprecedentedly dangerous and unstable."[7] Irving's classic gothic plays out as a sort of morality play about this new class of credit-reliant citizens, with the rural laborer Brom Bones posing as the ghostly Headless Horseman in order to chase the scheming Ichabod out of Sleepy Hollow.[8] Like the banker who is haunted by an apparitional dollar coin in the 1808 political cartoon *The Ghost of a Dollar, or the Bankers [sic] Surprize*, Ichabod is confronted with – and humiliated by – an apparition that embodies the speculative market itself. Indeed, forever conducting a "nightly quest of his head,"[9] the Horseman is in many ways a figure of frustration, failure, and – ultimately – castration. From this perspective, the Horseman is a kind of double for Ichabod.

But he might also be a double for Irving himself, and for most Americans at that time. "Various circumstances have concurred to render me very nervous and subject to fits of depression," Irving wrote to his friend Henry Brevoort in 1819 about the "humiliating alternative" of bankruptcy after the family business that he and his brothers ran collapsed under the weight of overextended credit during the Panic of 1819. "I have not the kind of knowledge or the habits that are necessary for business."[10] Irving was a victim of the Panic of 1819, the first of many economic downturns in the pre–Civil War period. The other two major panics were in 1837 and 1857, but there were numerous smaller upheavals – all of them reminders that capitalism, though heralding new forms of prosperity, was also unsettling the landscape of selfhood in early nineteenth-century America. Historian Scott Sandage suggests that the notion that economic failure equaled personal failure was itself a new concept that began to emerge in the nineteenth century. "Failure troubled, hurried and excited nineteenth-century Americans not only because more of them were going bust," he explains, "but also because their attitudes toward ambition were changing.... An American with no prospects or plans, with nothing to look forward to, almost ceases to exist."[11] Irving, we might say, is exactly the sort of failing capitalist subject Sandage describes. From this perspective, his classic American gothic is a kind of therapy project, one in which he plumbs some of his – and the nation's – deepest anxieties, about both the economy and American selfhood itself.

"The Legend of Sleepy Hollow" isn't alone in staging the kind of market-related nervousness Irving and his contemporaries experienced. Quite the contrary. As scholars of American literature operating from under the general label of the "New Economic Criticism" from about 1990 to the present have shown, the literary and extra-literary material of this period is saturated with these concerns.[12] Gothic tales like "Sleepy Hollow," sentimental novels, plays, minstrel song lyrics, political cartoons, advice manuals, penny press newspapers, even children's literature – over and over, this material reflects the vexed, uneven shift from a mercantilist economy based on property and a gold standard to a more fluid, intangible "paper" economy that revolved around credit, debt, and speculation. It also reflects the "paper money" selfhood accompanying this new form of personhood. This might explain the antebellum preoccupation with stories about found gold and treasure. For example, in stories like Irving's "The Golden Dreams of Wolfert Webber" (1824), Robert Montgomery Bird's *Sheppard Lee: Written by Himself* (1836), and Edgar Allan Poe's "The Gold-Bug" (1843), the narrative revolves around the hunt for Captain Kidd's buried treasure. "[W]e found ourselves possessed of an even vaster wealth than we had at first supposed," we're told at the moment of discovery in Poe's tale. "In coin there was rather more than four hundred and fifty thousand dollars.... All was gold of antique date and of great variety – French, Spanish, and German money.... There was no American money."[13] This is what we might refer to as a nostalgic fantasy of money, one that predates the speculative economy emerging at mid-century – the stage Marx links to the notion of "capital." Moreover, as Frederic Jameson suggests, money-as-treasure is qualitatively different than modern money, precisely in that it precedes modern notions of selfhood based on "success" and "failure." Instead, this money (and the finding of it) is linked to luck and fate, rather than an "invisible hand" guiding the marketplace.[14] This, we can assume, is why there is no "American money" in the version of Captain Kidd's treasure Poe provides.

But even in stories that don't involve the discovery of treasure, money and the economy are ever-present, and central to the action of American narratives. Consider, for example, the dramatic moment in Harriet Beecher Stowe's best-selling *Uncle Tom's Cabin* (1852) when young George Shelby seeks somewhat naively to arrest the commodity status of his good friend, the titular slave Uncle Tom, by giving him his gold dollar. *"I've brought you my dollar!"* George says to Uncle Tom (emphasis in original). Stowe makes it clear that the gift is in direct response to the crisis of debt that has engulfed George's family and forced his father to sell Uncle Tom to the slave trader Haley ("He had speculated largely and quite loosely," we're told of Mr. Shelby).[15] But the repeated sale of Uncle Tom proves that the gold dollar is no match for the vicissitudes of the modern paper economy. Thus, even though sentimentalism is by definition a genre that seeks to heal social wounds, in this famous novel, as in so many others, the forces of market capitalism prevail.

Consider as well the many sensation narratives revolving around financial crisis. Frederick Jackson's *A Week in Wall Street* (1841) and *The Victim of Chancery* (1841), George Lippard's best-selling *The Quaker City* (1845), J. B. Jones's *The City Merchant; or, The Mysterious Failure* (1851) – these and various other pulpy stories offer highly affective, didactic tales about financial crisis and those who suffer from it.[16] Usually, the goal is to convince readers that a return to a gold standard is the only reasonable response to the vicissitudes of the speculative, panic-prose market. Thus in *The City Merchant*, the protagonist Edgar Saxton, sensing trouble on the eve of the 1837 Panic, shifts to a no-credit, specie-only trade policy. His peers are baffled, but he prevails, and becomes "one of the FIRST MERCHANTS IN THE COUNTRY."[17]

Note, however, that in keeping with his surname, Saxon's fiscal wisdom is linked to his racial status. His main market antagonist is a "cunning Jew" named Abraham Ulmar.[18] Living in a section of Philadelphia where "Jews were as thick as blackberries, and almost as dark,"[19] Ulmar buys up notes held against the city's merchants in an effort to gain financial leverage over them. In this and various other sensation novels from this period, the Jew – or the figure whom Jonathan Freedman terms the "capitalist Jew"[20] – acts as the figure onto whom the excessive fiscal desires of the nation are projected. Numerous political cartoons sought to depict this stereotyped character. For example, in a lithograph cartoon entitled *Shylock's Year, or 1840 with No Bankrupt Law* (1840), the Jewish creditor who strangles a Gentile debtor is in many ways like the Headless Horseman of Irving's "Sleepy Hollow": he is the uncanny figure of the fiscal repressed, returned in familiar but unrecognized form to persecute the debtor American capitalist.

Nor is this character limited to stories about the North. Numerous plantation novels from the 1850s deploy the Jew as a foil for fiscal anxiety. In Maria McIntosh's *The Lofty and the Lowly* (1853), Uriah Goldwire acquires the mortgage against the Montrose plantation in Georgia, and threatens the unthinkable: the sale of land and slaves. "Such proceedings as those threatened by Uriah Goldwire had never been known amongst [the neighboring planters]," we're told. "They were lenient creditors to each other – no *gentlemen*, it was their creed, could be otherwise."[21] Here the Jew is viewed by his Georgia neighbors as a northerner who misunderstands the feudal, anticapitalist nature of the plantation economy; in this and other plantation novels, the Jew embodies northern capitalism. But, in fact, Goldwire is a figure for the plantation South's own quite thoroughgoing relationship to capitalism. The character "Jew David" in Catherine Bigelow's lurid Louisiana-based plantation novel, *The Curse Entailed* (1857), does similar work. "We had a sort of plantation there," he says after he is arrested for kidnapping women (both black and white), impregnating them, and selling the children into slavery. As one of his prisoners puts it, Jew David and his partner Moloch (also a Jew) "have become pimps to the lusts of Southern gentlemen, who pay ... well for the vile service."[22] Jew David is cast as a depraved capitalist, but clearly his operation is only in business so long as he can market his goods to a steady stream of southern customers. Here, as in the northern narratives, the "curse of trade" – this time the slave trade and its capitalist underpinnings – has been projected onto the Jew.

There is, however, one author whose work consistently offers story lines and characters that stage effective resistance to the emergence of modern capitalism. This is Herman Melville. Melville is best known for his epic novel *Moby-Dick* (1851), in which the monomaniacal Captain Ahab hunts the white whale Moby Dick. For many critics, the voyage of Ahab's ship, the *Pequod*, provides an allegory of American capitalism.[23] From this perspective, Ahab is an early incarnation of the likes of Amazon's Jeff Bezos, whose goal, it seems, is less wealth per se than limitless economic growth and market domination. But the complicated market critique we see in *Moby-Dick* is also evident in Melville's short story "Bartleby, the Scrivener" (1853). This story shares the urban, white-collar business setting of novels like the above-cited *A Week in Wall Street* and *The City Merchant*. But it turns these narratives on their heads. When Bartleby says, repeatedly, "I would prefer not to" in response to the requests of his boss, the attorney-narrator, to perform various office tasks, he is in effect resisting the machinations of Wall Street itself. Indeed, we might note that the attorney is described as being fully immersed in the new paper money economy. As he puts it, he does a "snug business among rich men's bonds and mortgages and title-deeds," and he has been in the good graces of John Jacob Astor – whose name, the attorney says, "rings like unto bullion."[24]

This is why Bartleby makes the attorney so anxious. "[J]ust in proportion as the forlornness of Bartleby grew and grew to my imagination, did that same melancholy merge into fear, that pity into repulsion," the attorney says toward story's end, when he discovers that Bartleby has actually begun sleeping in his Wall Street office.[25] Like Irving's Headless Horseman or the Jew of the period's sensation novels, Bartleby – described as "the apparition in my room" and a "ghost" who "persists in haunting the building" – represents a return of the repressed for the hapless narrator of Melville's tale.[26] And as Naomi Reed argues, Bartleby is a ghost precisely to the extent that he represents the specter-like nature of the American worker in his alienated, commodity-like form.[27] The fact that Bartleby dies at story's end because he refuses to eat only underscores his posture of renunciation. As Gillian Brown suggests, he is like the modern-day anorectic: seeking to control desire and thus maintain some sort of insulation and self-possession against the intrusions of the marketplace, he expires.[28] At least for Bartleby – and for Herman Melville – "economy" is something that can, and should, be resisted.

The Scarlet Letter and Global Trade

Late in *Walden*, in the chapter entitled "The Pond in Winter," Thoreau muses over the unexpected sight of as many as one hundred laborers cutting blocks of ice from Walden Pond. Their goal: to ship the ice cakes to "the sweltering inhabitants of Charleston and New Orleans, of Madras and Bombay and Calcutta." As he puts it, "the pure Walden water [will be] mingled with the sacred water of the Ganges."[29] But what Thoreau doesn't say is that the ice trade he glimpses represents the fact that the "curse of trade" he rails against early in the text is global in nature. In the second half of this essay, I'd like to provide a reading that suggests how the growing field of "Transnational American Studies" provides a critical lens for scholars of antebellum literature interested in national economic issues. Here, I want to suggest, we can seek with renewed vigor to understand how the national economic issues we encounter in stories like "Bartleby" must be understood in terms of the global markets emerging during this period. Doing so will allow us to understand the logic of capitalism and commodification I describe above as having worldwide, even species-impacting implications. Indeed, we might see how this approach unlocks new readings in texts not often read in terms of the keyword "economy." I'll focus for the rest of this chapter on Nathaniel Hawthorne's classic American novel, *The Scarlet Letter* (1850). This novel has been read from many interpretive angles, but to my knowledge it has yet to be placed in the context of international trade – a trade that, as it happens, is related to the one Thoreau reports on in "The Pond in Winter."

In his preface to the novel "The Custom-House," Hawthorne-as-narrator describes his discovery of Surveyor Pue's long-forgotten manuscript as he staves off the boredom of his workaday existence as a Salem customs agent by "poking and burrowing into the heaped up rubbish" in the second story of the Custom-House.[30] While doing so, he attempts to make the scene more interesting for himself – specifically, by "exerting [his] fancy, sluggish with little use, to raise up from these dry bones an image of the old town's brighter aspect, when India was a new region, and only Salem knew the way thither."[31] In what follows, Hawthorne describes the "rag of scarlet cloth" – the scarlet letter – he finds wrapped around Pue's text.[32] Here, though, I'm interested less in the letter itself than in Hawthorne's reference to India, and to Salem's commerce with India. Indeed, I want to suggest that India and US trade with India provide an important interpretive lens for the novel proper, one that might provide a model for an approach to a range of antebellum texts.

Certainly, critics have addressed the Orientalizing aspects of *The Scarlet Letter* and other works by Hawthorne – what Luther Luedtke calls "the romance of the orient."[33] But I want to push this a bit further, and think about the wealth generated in Salem via trade with India, and, more broadly, India's role in the global textile market. I want to ask what it

might mean to read the novel's obsession with the production and purchase of brightly colored fabrics and textiles in the context of the global
market for such goods – a market that was expanding dramatically during
the three time periods Hawthorne's novel references: the mid-seventeenth
century in which Hester's story is set, the late eighteenth-century moment
in which Surveyor Pue wrote his history of Hester Prynne, and
Hawthorne's own mid-nineteenth-century present. Rather than a novel
of American isolationism and exceptionalism, *The Scarlet Letter* reflects
instead the way America was, in each of these three periods, caught up in
the international flow of goods and money.

Hawthorne's reference in "The Custom-House" to India isn't mere
fancy. Quite the contrary, it would be hard to overstate how central
India was to the economic and cultural life of Salem. For one thing,
Surveyor Pue inhabits the period from the late 1780s to the early 1800s,
when Salem became the wealthiest city per capita in the United States via
the cotton textile trade with India. This financial growth was led by Elias
Hasket Derby, whom Hawthorne refers to in "The Custom-House" as
"old King Derby."[34] A Salem native, Derby made his early fortune in the
American Revolution, during which he worked with his father to fund
privateers commissioned to fight against the British. After the war, Derby
began sending ships to China, and then to Calcutta and other Indian ports
in 1787. By the early 1790s, Derby had become one of America's first
millionaires, primarily via the textile trade. Others followed his lead, and
within less than ten years Salem became the India-linked city Hawthorne
describes in "The Custom-House" – something signaled both by the
popularity of Indian cotton in fabric stores, such as the one owned by
Derby, and by the formation of Salem's East India Marine Society in
1799 by a group of shipmasters and supercargoes who had traveled to the
East. The society built the East India Marine Hall, which was in effect a
museum of eastern curios, featuring samples of Indian textiles, as well as
life-sized clay models of Indian cotton merchants and "coolie" laborers.
Hawthorne's father was a founding member of the Society, and
Hawthorne himself visited the hall at least once, probably numerous times.

The reason for the interest in Indian cotton was its quality. As historian
Sven Beckert explains, cotton textiles from India were lighter and held
bright colors far more effectively than any cotton fabrics found in Europe
or America.[35] This is why Indian cotton was assigned high tariffs in
England, France, and America from the seventeenth to the nineteenth
centuries, and was even banned for long stretches of time in England and
France. It is also why Indian cotton was imitated. Beckert provides

numerous examples of European companies selling knock-off versions of
Indian cotton throughout this period, and of manuals that sought to
educate Europeans and Americans about Indian manufacturing techniques. "All the weaving combs in France should be made according to
the model in Bengal," wrote a French observer in 1807. "Then we will
succeed in equaling the Indians in the manufacture of their muslin."[36]

But as Beckert also explains, the Americans and Europeans weren't the
only consumers of Indian cotton. Indeed, west coast African slave traders
found Indian fabrics highly desirable. As Beckert puts it, "Slaves ... could
only be gotten by exchanging them for the cottons from India."[37] This
requirement that Indian cotton be used as currency in the slave trade
created a complex global dynamic in the years preceding the American
abolition of the international slave trade in 1807 – that is, the period in
which Surveyor Pue is writing. First, English slave traders traveled to India
to purchase large quantities of Indian textiles. Next, they sailed to Africa to
trade these textiles for enslaved men and women. Their ensuing stop was
the Americas – the Caribbean and, until 1807, the US South – to sell the
enslaved. Finally – and this is Beckert's larger point – the cash from these
sales made its way back to the large banks in Liverpool and London. This
money, in turn, was often extended in the form of credit to cotton planters
in the American South, who then increased the size and production of
their plantations by buying more people who could clear land and harvest
ever-larger quantities of American cotton. Thus, to return to Salem, while
a merchant like Elias Hasket Derby wasn't directly involved in the slave
trade, he did benefit from and contribute to it. Moreover, the textiles in his
stores bore the mark of this global network of human exchange.

The question, of course, is how this Indian context relates to the story of
Hester Prynne and her daughter Pearl. As we all know, the novel is
obsessed with the production and sale of brightly colored textiles. In
chapter 5, "Hester at Her Needle," we're told, "By degrees, nor very
slowly, [Hester's] handiwork became what would now be termed the
fashion.... Her needlework was seen on the ruff of the Governor; military
men wore it on their scarves, and the minister on his band."[38] We're also
told here that Hester "had in her nature a rich, voluptuous, Oriental
characteristic, – a taste for the gorgeously beautiful, which, save in the
exquisite productions of her needle, found nothing else, in all the possibilities of her life, to exercise itself upon."[39] In chapter 6, Hawthorne
extends these comparisons to Pearl's attire. "[L]ittle Pearl was not clad in
rustic weeds. Her mother ... had bought the richest tissues that could be
procured, and allowed her imaginative faculty its full play in the

arrangement and decoration of the dresses which the child wore, before the public eye." There are many other such passages, but these suffice to make the point: Hawthorne is interested in both the public taste for exotic fashions and the production of goods that create and feed that taste. And I would suggest that this interest is informed by the market for Indian fabrics I've sketched above. Hawthorne would have seen firsthand the most exotic and beautiful Indian textiles in America at the East India Marine Hall. Accordingly, when Hester seeks the "richest tissues that could be procured" in order to make Pearl's dresses, we should envision textiles that are related to the sort of ornate, brightly colored Indian cottons marketed in both Salem and throughout the world. Similarly, Hester's "handiwork," which bears the mark of her "Oriental characteristic," is unique and valuable in the way that Indian textiles were unique and valuable from the seventeenth to the nineteenth century. That Hester seeks and produces these textiles in the mid-seventeenth century, ahead of the booming Indian textile market, fits Hawthorne's own definition of romance, which invites this collapsing of past and present. As a "Romance," Hester's tale falls "somewhere between the real world and fairy-land, where the Actual and the Imaginary may meet."[40] Simply put, "The Custom House" asks us to read the novel as historically fluid.

The Scarlet Letter isn't the only antebellum novel to reflect this romance of the global cotton market. George Pickering Burnam's *The Belle of the Orient, or, The Hindoo Merchant's Legacy* (1850), Caroline Hentz's *Ernest Linwood* (1856), Mary Jane Holmes's *Dora Dean, or the East India Uncle* (1859) – these and many other narratives provide a context for the reading of *The Scarlet Letter* I'm suggesting.[41] Consider this quote from *Ernest Linwood*, in which the novel's narrator, Gabriella, talks about a gift from the novel's namesake:

> Our dresses were alike. They were of the most exquisite India muslin, simply but elegantly decorated with the finest of lace. I had never before been arrayed for an evening party, and as the gauzy fulness of drapery fell so softly and redundantly over the form I had been accustomed to see[,] . . . I hardly recognized my own lineaments. There was something so light, so ethereal and graceful in the dress, my spirit caught its airiness and seemed borne upwards as on wings of down.[42]

As in many other novels from the period, both American and British, femininity and Indian muslin are here linked; in this case, Gabriella almost literally discovers herself as a desirable woman because of Indian cotton. As Linwood himself puts it, "I am delighted . . . to see you in the only livery youth and innocence should wear."[43] But note too that when the Byronic

Linwood becomes jealous that Gabriella might have another lover, he attempts to murder her and the other man, then departs for India for two years to conduct business. "To India!" Gabriella shouts upon hearing the news. "Then we are indeed parted, – parted for ever!"[44] In this melodramatic novel, India and its products offer both a heightened femininity *and* a national elsewhere that acts as a kind of disposal site for the excessive and wayward emotion of the American male.

The Belle of the Orient offers a related storyline. Here we see the "munificent merchant" Sedd Rajab, who deals in "indigo from Delhi and Bengal" and "silks furnished from Orissa."[45] The problem for Rajab is that his beautiful daughter Katrin – the "Belle of the Orient" – has fallen in love with an English supercargo named Hargreve. Viewing western Christians as "white barbarians,"[46] Rajab interprets his daughter's interest in a westerner as a sign that he has lost his integrity as a businessman. Inevitably, though, Rajab becomes fatally ill and is unable to control his daughter's future. Not long after Rajab's death, Katrin converts to Christianity, marries the English merchant, and moves with him to England. It's another romance of cotton – if not in the strictly Hawthornian sense. Part of the work of that romance is to brush aside Rajab's concerns about Hargreve's shady business practices (he also smuggles opium out of China). Indeed, when at novel's end we're told that Rajab's efforts to disinherit Katrin have failed, and that the fortune he has made trading cotton is turned over to Hargreve, the implication is that this is as it should be: Rajab, it seems, has been a hindrance to global trade. Hargreve's joking line in a letter to his father about his impending marriage to Katrin – he describes it as an "India speculation"[47] – underscores the novel's views on political economy.

While the plotlines of these novels differ from what we see in *The Scarlet Letter*, like Hawthorne's novel they both use India and Indian cotton to organize the depiction of gender. Katrin and Hargreve in *The Belle of the Orient*, for example, help us understand what happens with Pearl at the end of *The Scarlet Letter*. When late in the novel Pearl finally kisses Dimmesdale in public, and becomes what Hawthorne describes as "a woman in" the world, rather than one who "for ever do[es] battle with" it,[48] her conversion from an exotic femininity is similar to Katrin's adoption of Christianity and marriage to Hargreve. This may also be the meaning behind Linwood's gift of muslin to Gabriella in *Ernest Linwood* – which is white, rather than indigo or some other combination of colors. "I abhor the gaudy tinselry which loads the devotees of fashion, indicative of false taste and false principles," he says to her. "But white and pearls remind me of everything pure and holy in nature."[49] Here, it seems, the colors in which Hester dresses Pearl are inappropriate for the sort of femininity Linwood has in mind. But Indian cotton is instrumental just the same. Indeed, Linwood's preference for white muslin is simply the flip side of the coin of brightly colored Indian cotton. At least according to Hentz, American women require economic ties to this far-off region to achieve an ideally white and ethereal form of femininity.

The international slave trade is largely offstage in these novels. But given that enslaved Africans were inextricably linked to the Indian cotton market – remember, Indian fabrics such as those traded by Rajab in *The Belle of the Orient* were a key currency for eighteenth-century slave traders on the west coast of Africa – we can't talk about a taste for Indian muslin without acknowledging the connections between this product and slavery. Thus the white muslin that Linwood buys for Gabriella in Hentz's novel is part of this broader global equation – which is to say that the very idea of a pure, disembodied womanhood presented in *Ernest Linwood* is also linked to the international market for cotton and the global slave trade. (It should come as no surprise that Caroline Hentz is also the author of *The Planter's Northern Bride* [1854], one of the period's most popular anti-abolition novels).[50]

As for *The Scarlet Letter*, if we read the novel through the lens of "The Custom-House" and Hawthorne's nostalgia for Salem's once-booming textile trade with India, we're in a position to see slavery lurking at its edges too – just as it lurked at the edges of other India-interested novels during the period. This doesn't mean that we should read the novel as a full-blown allegory of slavery. But it did leave its traces on the goods and materials in which Hester and her community trade.[51] A "transnational" perspective allows us to see how these traces are more than incidental. Winfried Fluck suggests that transnationalism should be deployed as a "counterprogram to the state of exception that characterizes the American nation-state" – in particular, by identifying and uniting "the outsiders of the world in a new kind of transnational communality."[52] Fluck's example is C. L. R. James's famous reading of *Moby-Dick* in his now-classic *Mariners, Renegades and Castaways* (1953).[53] As Fluck argues, James is exemplary in that his own "dis-interpellation" while detained on Ellis Island helped him read Melville's novel in the context of a transnational community of outlaw subjects.[54]

Hester's sewing operates in a similar way. Viewed through a transnational lens, we can see her work as *itself* an alternative means of production, one that parallels and comments on the production of fabrics thousands of miles away in India. Here the famous quote – "the scarlet letter was her passport into regions where other women dared not tread"[55] – becomes especially suggestive. Hester, we might say, is linked through "the exquisite productions of her needle" to a transnational community of laborers. This community includes the sorts of Indian laborers depicted in the East India Marine Hall, and the enslaved Africans who were traded for the fabrics those workers produced. This link is indirect, and I doubt it's intentional. Hawthorne was no abolitionist. But he did live in a world in which Salem, India, England, Africa, and the plantations of the American South were inextricably bound together in a network of capitalist trade. Hester and her sewing bear the imprint – the "trace" – of this global economic fact. Indeed, this might help explain the dramatic conversation Hester has with Dimmesdale late in the novel. "Is the world then so narrow?" she says to him as they discuss escaping Chillingworth. "There is the broad pathway of the sea!"[56] As we know, Dimmesdale is incapable of acting on this challenge. But Hester is very much up to the task. As such, she embodies the form of "dis-interpellation" Fluck describes. The state of exception she has inhabited on the outskirts of Boston has turned her into a person of exception; for her, it seems, the trade route Thoreau envisions for the water of Walden Pond – "mingled with the sacred water of the Ganges" – has the potential to be transformative, even liberating. This is why she's open to interaction with the sailors who've come ashore to observe Election Day in Boston. "The sailor of that day would go near to be arraigned as a pirate in our own," Hawthorne says of this group.[57] Like these sailor-pirates, Hester is a figure through whom we can see the "traces" of the broad and often ruthless reach of global trade – what Thoreau called its "curse." Simultaneously, and also like these sailors, she's a character through whom to imagine an alternative to it.

This is an important distinction, especially if we understand it in relation to the older and newer critical trends I've described here. Much if not most of the New Economic Criticism to date has shown us that a character like Bartleby represents a return of capitalism's repressed knowledge that, as Thoreau puts it, "we are all poor" precisely to the extent that we have become reified in our relations with one another, and even in relation to ourselves. This is why Bartleby's resistance is so effective. An economic criticism devoted to Transnational American Studies tackles this issue from a different, and broader, perspective. Here, Hester isn't simply isolated on the edges of the modern nation-state and its emerging economy. Instead, we're able to see her in relation to an international community of workers, all of whom are struggling, Bartleby-like, against the dehumanizing forces of capitalism. This doesn't mean we should read

Hester as a figure of unimpeded liberation, or national rejuvenation. Indeed, as Fluck reminds us, we should resist the lure of what he terms "aesthetic transnationalism," in which we celebrate a "happy global mélange" that provides an imagined solution to the nation's problems, economic and otherwise, precisely because it is inherently cosmopolitan.[58] But the broadened view I'm suggesting of this most American of novels, and of antebellum literature more generally, does remind us that we should continue to explore new ways to think about depictions of the economy in early US literature, and new ways to understand resistance to it.

Notes

1 Henry David Thoreau, *Walden* [1854] (New York: Penguin, 1986), 50.
2 Ibid., 113.
3 Ibid., 76.
4 Karl Marx, *Capital, a Critique of Political Economy*, vol. 1 [1867], trans. Ben Fowkes, ed. Ernest Mandel (New York: Vintage Books, 1977), 179.
5 See Edward Baptist, *The Half Has Never Been Told: Slavery and the Making of American Capitalism* (New York: Basic Books, 2014); Sven Beckert, *Empire of Cotton: A Global History* (New York: Vintage, 2014), and Walter Johnson, *River of Dark Dreams: Slavery and Empire in the Cotton Kingdom* (Cambridge, MA: Harvard University Press, 2013).
6 Washington Irving, "The Legend of Sleepy Hollow" [1819], in *The Sketch Book of Geoffrey Crayon, Gent*, ed. Haskell Springer, vol. 8 of *The Complete Works of Washington Irving* (New York: Twayne Publishers, 1978), 280.
7 J. G. A. Pocock, *Virtue, Commerce, and History: Essays on Political Thought and History, Chiefly in the Eighteenth Century* (Cambridge: Cambridge University Press, 1985), 235.
8 Washington Irving, *The Sketch Book of Geoffrey Crayon, Gent*, ed. Haskell Springer, vol. 8 of *The Complete Works of Washington Irving* (Boston: Twayne Publishers, 1978), 273.
9 Ibid., 273.
10 Washington Irving, *Letters, vol. I: 1802–1823*, ed. Ralph M. Alderman, vol. 23 of *The Complete Works of Washington Irving* (Boston: Twayne Publishers, 1978), 549–550, 516.
11 Scott Sandage, *Born Losers: A History of Failure in America* (Cambridge, MA: Harvard University Press, 2005), 13, 20.
12 See, for example, David Anthony, *Paper Money Men: Commerce, Manhood, and the Sensational Public Sphere in Antebellum America* (n.p.: Ohio State University Press, 2009); Jennifer Baker, *Securing the Commonwealth: Debt, Speculation, and Writing in the Making of Early America* (Baltimore: Johns Hopkins University Press, 2005); Gillian Brown, *Domestic Individualism: Imagining Self in Nineteenth-Century America* (Berkeley: University of

California Press, 1990); Joseph Fichtelberg, *Critical Fictions: Sentiment and the American Market: 1780–1870* (Athens: University of Georgia Press, 2003); Lori Merish, *Sentimental Materialism: Gender, Commodity Culture, and Nineteenth-Century American Literature* (Durham, NC: Duke University Press, 2002); and Walter Benn Michaels, *The Gold Standard and the Logic of Naturalism* (Berkeley: University of California Press, 1988).

13 Edgar Allan Poe, "The Gold-Bug" [1843], in *The Fall of the House of Usher and Other Writings*, ed. David Galloway (New York: Penguin Books, 2003), 254.

14 Fredric Jameson, *Ideologies of Theory: Essays 1971–1986* (Minneapolis: University of Minnesota Press, 1988), 52.

15 Harriet Beecher Stowe, *Uncle Tom's Cabin; or, Life among the Lowly* [1852], ed. Ann Douglas (New York: Penguin Books, 1986), 171, 51.

16 Frederick Jackson, *A Week in Wall Street. By One Who Knows* (New York: Booksellers, 1841); *The Victim of Chancery; or, A Debtor's Experience* (New York: University Press, 1841); George Lippard, *The Quaker City; or, The Monks of Monk Hall. A Romance of Philadelphia Life, Mystery, and Crime* [1845], ed. David Reyonolds (Amherst: University of Massachusetts Press, 1995); J. B. (John Beauchamp) Jones, *The City Merchant; or, The Mysterious Failure* (Philadelphia: Lippincott and Grambo, 1851).

17 Jones, *The City Merchant*, 214.

18 Ibid., 66.

19 Ibid., 91.

20 Jonathan Freedman, *The Temple of Culture: Assimilation and Anti-Semitism in Literary Anglo-America* (New York: Oxford University Press, 2000).

21 Maria McIntosh, *The Lofty and the Lowly; or, The Good in All and None All-Good*, 2 vols. (New York: D. Appleton and Co., 1853), II: 119.

22 Harriet Hamline Bigelow, *The Curse Entailed* (Boston: Wentworth and Company, 1857), 414.

23 See, for example, Michael Rogin, *Subversive Genealogy: The Politics and Art of Herman Melville* (Berkeley: University of California Press, 1983); Michael Gilmore, *American Romanticism and the Marketplace* (Chicago: University of Chicago Press, 1985); and John Levi Barnard, "The Cod and the Whale: Melville in the Time of Extinction," *American Literature* 89.4 (December 2017).

24 Herman Melville, "Bartleby, the Scrivener. A Story of Wall-Street" [1853], in *Herman Melville: Selected Tales and Poems*, ed. Richard Chase (New York: Holt, Rinehart and Winston, 1950), 93.

25 Ibid., 111.

26 Ibid., 122, 123, 125.

27 Naomi Reed, "The Specter of Wall Street: 'Bartleby the Scrivener' and the Language of Commodities," *American Literature* 76.2 (June 2004): 247–273.

28 Brown, *Domestic Individualism*, 170–196.

29 Thoreau, *Walden*, 343, 346.

30 Nathaniel Hawthorne, *The Scarlet Letter. A Romance* [1850], ed. Nina Baym (New York: Penguin University Press, 1983), 29–30.

31 Ibid., 30.

32 Ibid., 31.

33 Theodore Ludke, *Nathaniel Hawthorne and the Romance of the Orient* (Bloomington: Indiana University Press, 1989).

34 Hawthorne, *The Scarlet Letter*, 8.

35 Beckert, *Empire of Cotton*, 29–55.

36 Francois-Xavier Legoux de Flaix, *Essai historique, geographique et politique sur l'Indoustan, avec le tableau de son commerce*, vol. 2 (Paris: Pougin, 1807), 331. Quoted in Beckert, *Empire of Cotton*, 50.

37 Beckert, *Empire of Cotton*, 48.

38 Hawthorne, *The Scarlet Letter*, 74–75.

39 Ibid., 75.

40 Ibid., 35.

41 George P. Burnham, *The Belle of the Orient; or, The Hindoo Merchant's Legacy* (New York: Samuel French, 1850s); Caroline Hentz, *Ernest Linwood* (Boston: J. P. Jewett, 1856); Mary Jane Holmes, *Dora Deane, or The East India Uncle* (New York: C. M. Saxon, 1859).

42 Hentz, *Ernest Linwood*, 148.

43 Ibid., 151.

44 Ibid., 410.

45 Burnham, *The Belle of the Orient*, 31.

46 Ibid., 61.

47 Ibid., 68.

48 Hawthorne, *The Scarlet Letter*, 222.

49 Hentz, *Ernest Linwood*, 151.

50 Caroline Lee Hentz, *The Planter's Northern Bride*, 2 vols. (Philadelphia: A. Hart, 1854).

51 On slavery in *The Scarlet Letter*, see, for example, Jonathan Arac, "The Politics of *The Scarlet Letter*," in *Ideology and Classic American Literature*, ed. Sacvan Bercovitch and Myra Jehlen (Cambridge: Cambridge University Press, 1986), 247–266; Jay Grossman, "A Is for Abolition? Race, Authorship, The Scarlet Letter," *Textual Practice* 7.1 (1992): 13–30; and Teresa Goddu, "'Letters Turned to Gold': Hawthorne, Authorship, and Slavery," *Studies in American Fiction* 29.1 (2001): 49–76.

52 Winfried Fluck, "A New Beginning? Transnationalisms," *New Literary History* 42.3 (Summer 2011): 374.

53 C. L. R. James, *Mariners, Renegades and Castaways: The Story of Herman Melville and the World We Live In* [1953]. (Hanover, NH: Dartmouth College: University Press of New England, 2001).

54 Fluck, "A New Beginning?," 374.

55 Hawthorne, *The Scarlet Letter*, 174.

56 Ibid., 171, 172.

57 Ibid., 203.

58 Fluck, "A New Beginning?," 369.

Religion

Christine Hedlin and Toni Wall Jaudon

If there is one concern that is evergreen in American literary study, it is religion – present from the field's early conceptions of nineteenth-century literature as the end point of secularization, the finale in a narrative stretching "Edwards to Emerson,"[1] to its recent concerns with US imperialism, the transnational circuits crossing US peoples and territories. And for good reason. US print culture from 1820 to 1860 was full of religion talk: about who has religion and who doesn't, about what religion is and what it can do, and about what religion definitely should not do, or be, or mean in a modernized nation and a world connected by travel and trade.[2]

So, this chapter asks, What should we do with all the religion talk in literatures of the early to mid-nineteenth century? In taking up that question, we extend a line of inquiry that probes, as a first premise, the conditions under which religion talk became possible, the emergence of "religion" as something distinct from another possible entity. For scholars such as Talal Asad, Tracy Fessenden, Peter Coviello, Michael Warner, and John Modern, any understanding of religion's work in the world – what it enables or disables, how it is experienced or felt – must deal first with the circumstances and ontologies that allowed certain practices to register as "religious" in the first place. The rise of these new conceptual categories in the West comprised the world-altering shift now known in the field of secular studies as *secularization*.[3] The best new work on secularization thus portrays religion as a vexed concept, one society is constantly remaking and re-placing in the world. It also portrays religion as a powerful and fluid concept, one that, in the process of its remaking, reconstitutes the world of which it is supposedly just one isolated part. At stake for American literary study in new theories of secularity, then, are at once insights into the normative – why "normal" feels normal, or how the dominant culture came to be – and insights into its fissures, the persistent cracks in secularism's thrall that dominant historical narratives easily smooth over.

To study these cracks, these fissures, we argue, is, in practice, to attune ourselves to the ways nonwhite and non-Protestant peoples in the mid-nineteenth-century United States experienced the everyday world. What we call "cracks" – disruptions to secularism's "normal" – were, for the people creating them, better known as lives or ways of being, carved out of landscapes rife with racial and religious prejudices and violence. Perceiving these fissures, these alternative ways of being in the mid-century world, requires that we first go back to the beginning: to when religion in nineteenth-century Americans' sense of the word was just emerging.

Becoming Protestant in the Public Sphere

Mid-nineteenth-century US talk about religion had its origins in the Protestant Reformation. Early Protestants separated themselves from the Catholic Church, and from state-sponsored religious institutions generally, on the grounds that to be religious was to affirm a set of principles in words – an individual, voluntary, and verbal response.[4] Catholicism, they felt, was too iconographic, too ritualistic, and too concerned with public participation over internal persuasion. Being religious, in their new for-mulations, required belief – the sincere and free assent of a rational mind to ideas that become persuasive to it.[5] John Locke would give sentinel expression to this notion of religion-as-belief in his *A Letter Concerning Toleration* (1689), and it would hold purchase on Western understandings of religion ever since.[6] As Kirstie M. McClure notes, Locke's theory of religious toleration opens on the premise that religion in its proper form – true religion, the religion that separates the saved from the damned – is irreducibly a product of the individual mind or consciousness.[7] In Locke's formulation, religion is private, it is propositional, and, for those reasons, it is also untouchable by state power or political mandate. Yes, state power can ensure outward compliance with religious practice. However, Locke's idea of religious toleration implied that the state can never produce true religious belief, a turn that can take place only in the individual mind. Bound up with Locke's idea of religion, then, is an understanding that individual interiority is the "chief site of that which might elude political coercion," as Webb Keane suggests.[8] The idea of religion as a set of propositions to which one gives private assent was thus entangled, from the start, with theories of both what it means to be a free individual and the limits of state power.

In a US context, writers like Thomas Jefferson and James Madison took up Locke's argument – that true religion is private and propositional – and used it to suggest states leave religion, by which they largely meant Protestantism, alone.[9] Their insights shaped conversations surrounding the Bill of Rights and lent early energy to arguments for the disestablishment of the new nation's state churches. Madison's 1785 "Memorial and Remonstrance against Religious Assessments," for example, written to oppose a bill that would allocate some tax money to Christian churches, stakes its claim in clearly propositional terms: "Whilst we assert for ourselves a freedom to embrace, to profess and to observe the Religion which we believe to be of divine origin," Madison writes, "we cannot deny an equal freedom to those whose minds have not yet yielded to the evidence which has convinced us."[10] This joint affirmation of freedoms – freedom privately to believe but also privately to accept the propositions that persuade one the most – had consequences for the nascent society as a whole. Thomas Jefferson assessed, for instance, that a polity composed of free individuals freely assenting to religious propositions was one in which religious difference could do no harm. As Jefferson reasoned, "It does me no injury for my neighbour to say there are twenty gods, or no god. It neither picks my pocket nor breaks my leg."[11] In Jefferson's view, states are to be concerned with pickpocketing and leg-breaking, acts they can, and should, use their power to regulate. Privately held religious beliefs, on the other hand, located solely in adherents' minds, can do no harm to social life and thus are not to be regulated by the state. Such a theory especially suited evangelical Protestants, who eyed the era's established churches as competition and saw their own emphasis on individual piety harmonizing nicely with concepts of private religion. By insisting religion was private and propositional, Jefferson and others paved the way for some religious traditions, mainly varieties of white evangelical Protestantism, to enjoy more religious freedom in the United States than others.

One of secular studies' key insights has been that, when the nature of religion changes, so does the nature of the very world people inhabit or experience. And so, with this conceptual shift in the early republic – this new sense of religion as private and propositional – there came, too, a transformation in beliefs about the world itself. This transformation, we might say, was about defining what could be experienced as real, what could be experienced as a world shared in common. The very idea of a "secular" public sphere, such as the arena in which Madison and Jefferson could debate the propriety of established churches, relied on the sense that there is present-tense world, shared by all, that is separate from the supposedly particular, supposedly individual spiritual worlds governing religious adherents' behavior. Talal Asad suggests that "modern secularism" is predicated on precisely this division, this bifurcation of the world into, first, "a world of self-authenticating things in which we *really* live as social beings" and, second, "a religious world that exists only in our imagination."[12] Secularity's privatized, propositional religion clears space for a social world divested of gods and spirits, or at least divested of their legitimate agency or influence.[13] The social world becomes a world of human actors and human interests, no matter how individuals present their own experiences or investments. In the age of modern secularism, the human mind, never the cosmos, is the source of meaning.

In one sense, then, modern secularism alighted in the United States when the social world emerged as a distinct entity. Yet this major conceptual shift, this change in religion talk, did not mean religion actually receded from the public view. Despite the implications of Jefferson's famous "wall of separation between church and state" metaphor, the much-vaunted secularization of the public sphere did more to change how religion entered and influenced public life than to cut off its access entirely.[14] As Tracy Fessenden argues, "secularization" in the United States has mostly marked the process by which Protestant affects and habits of mind came to seem like default modes of participating in public life. To be "moral" – a concept that was not clearly religious – came to mean acting like or having the values of a Protestant. This elision between Protestantism and a set of purportedly secular or democratic values meant early US Protestants could at once support disestablishment – in the name of religious toleration or everyone having rights to their own private beliefs – and also seek the legal enforcement of Christianity's moral ideals, ideals they took to be universals after having used violence and the written word to establish them as such.[15] As historian David Sehat notes, evangelicals who supported the disestablishment of public churches often also argued stridently in favor of "more-stringent moral laws, whose content, they claimed, came directly from the Bible."[16] These evangelicals sought at once "the disestablishment of institutional religion" and "the continued establishment and the strengthened legal enforcement of Christianity's moral ideals" – a paradox that lay at the heart of the so-called secularization of the US public sphere.[17]

In making such claims on the secular, Protestants took advantage of how privatized religion in the United States had always been bound up with concerns about public life – about how, in particular, individuals could be made to appear to be or to behave in the public sphere. Important early writings on disestablishment, including Madison's and Jefferson's, twinned talk of religion's essential privacy with a set of historically specific ideas about self-consistency. These authors inherited from Locke and other Enlightenment thinkers the sense that there is something very, very wrong with forcing someone's interior thoughts to differ from their external behavior. In the mid-nineteenth century, as Justine S. Murison writes, this sense of self-consistency became the justification for those who wanted to see morality, especially Christian or Protestant morality, take a leading role in the public sphere. As Murison describes, "The privatization of religion set in motion the importance of performing publicly one's personal morality," of testifying through one's "public, embodied existence . . . the degree to which one's private life was also a moral life."[18] Privatized religion's insistence on the right to self-consistency became, in this moment, a "mandate," a requirement that "there be no gap between what one believes personally and how one acts publicly."[19] The end result of all this talk of self-consistency was that a supposedly religiously neutral society could square the circle of how to get religion back in the public sphere. Public religiosity could become an apparently necessary consequence of consistently living out one's private morality.

And so it was that mid-nineteenth-century religion talk infused Protestantism into the US public sphere: not as a religion, per se, but as a set of deeply felt social formations, moral norms, and practices of the self. These structures took their priorities directly from the nation's emerging cross-Protestant consensus. Yet they seemed intuitive enough, self-evident enough, to pass for universals. Far from absenting Protestantism from public life, the advent of secularism in the mid-nineteenth century made it all the more present.

Secularity, Normative Sociality, Governmentality

As mid-nineteenth-century religion talk carved out new subterranean places for Protestantism in public life, it also gave nineteenth-century Americans a new means of understanding their everyday worlds as ordinary. As John Lardas Modern describes, nineteenth-century discourses surrounding "true religion," by which most Americans meant private, propositional religion, ushered in an accompanying "normative sociality" that made some ways of inhabiting or experiencing the world feel familiar and others seem improper, unexpected, or impossible.[20] The discourses of secularity, in other words, "generated structures of consciousness through which the world was felt, experienced, and acted upon."[21] In the end, talking about religion was one way nineteenth-century Americans, especially nineteenth-century white Protestant Americans, crafted a world that felt "normal" to them – that "felt right," to borrow Harriet Beecher Stowe's terms. This "felt normal" was all the more influential for its ability to dissociate from all things explicitly religious, to subordinate "religion" to a larger sense of normalcy against which religion could be assessed.

As we might expect, this normative sociality, while making the world feel right for some, created exclusions that made it feel wrong for others – made others feel, in fact, like they were wrong in it. The normative sociality of the secular sought to mark as "illegitimate" all those "ways of knowing the world and living within it" that did not align with its own sense of the real or the familiar.[22] In practice, that meant particularly those forms of social life and knowledge possessed by nonwhite or non-Protestant (or not-properly-Protestant) persons. This marking of illegitimacy is perhaps most evident in the widely circulating reports of the era's Protestant missionaries. Although these missionaries wrote from an explicitly evangelical and Protestant perspective, they sought, in their narratives, to establish how the peoples and cultures they encountered deviated from the secular principles – of self-consistency, sincerity, and rational and natural agency – that rightly ordered the modern world. They framed the everyday worldviews and ontologies of so-called religious and racial others as "failures on the part of individuals and, perhaps, entire communities, to assume their full humanity."[23]

Having failed properly to inhabit modernity, these individuals and communities became targets of various forms of Protestant benevolence that often aligned with forms of US state power. Jennifer Graber offers a prime example in her history of the United States' theft of Kiowa Indian lands. Religion, in the overlapping discourses of US soldiers, missionaries, and government officials, served as both a crucial category for marking difference and a shorthand for their own motivations: they were the Christian "friends of the Indian."[24] These "friends of the Indian" – regardless of their denomination – agreed that the Kiowas and other Native peoples basically needed to renovate their entire ways of life before they could take up their place in the modernizing nation of the United States. Baptist, Quaker, and other Protestant missionaries thus sought to convince the Kiowa and other indigenous peoples to give up their nomadic movements across the broad Plains territory and adopt what they considered the keys to "true freedom": "education, agriculture, and Christian worship."[25] These were, of course, also the pillars of a *settled* life, one requiring much less space than the Kiowas had traditionally occupied. Becoming "civilized," then, meant not just becoming Protestant but adopting the structures of everyday life, the patterns of domesticity, that white Protestants valued: the tidy houses, the regular employment, the "proper" education of Protestant children. In short, in the Kiowas' case and countless others across the nineteenth century and beyond, adopting the "right" religion turned out to be inseparable from adopting the "right" daily habits and social structures – inseparable from participating, in other words, in the normative sociality. Protestants hastened the advancement of the secular through precisely this slippage, this point at which "right religion" and "right living" become impossible to separate.

Of course, in their eagerness to Christianize and civilize, Protestant reformers sometimes found themselves in uneasy alliances with government forces dispatched to remove Native peoples from their lands. Despite expressing concerns over military removal and the violence between white settlers and indigenous peoples, Protestant reformers generally supported settler colonialist attempts to dispossess indigenous nations of their lands and restrict them to smaller reservations. Reformers assessed that the foremost task before mid-century Native peoples was, as Graber describes, to "transform their cultures and rebuild their lives," a task for which reservations provided "adequate space."[26] The missionaries thus committed themselves to what they considered an "ethical expansion" of US territory, one that, in their minds and discourses, liberated Native peoples "to enjoy the blessings of civilization and Christianization."[27] The missionaries' roles, within these narratives, were those of teachers, administrators, and, in a sense, secular messiahs: they would implement the "'grand scheme of deliverance'" to bring the Indian into the modern world.[28]

Benevolent Protestants thus made themselves the softening forward edge of the US government's dispossession of the Kiowa and other indigenous peoples. They lent the normalizing structures of the everyday – the "felt rightness" of particular (Protestant-secular) values and behaviors – to a process that could otherwise have been characterized by its violence and theft. In this way, the same everydayness that secured and authorized white Protestants' experiences of the world also served to normalize imperial expansion. Secularity's everydayness made imperialism feel ordinary, made westward expansion feel like a measured, progressive way to face forward into the world. And, crucially, secularity's normalizing forces did not stop with imperial expansion. What was being "normalized" here was ultimately white Protestantism, as both a way of governing and a way to live one's everyday life. In any instance in which white Protestantism exerted this regulating force, then – among Catholic Irish immigrants, along the Mexican border, in confrontations with indigenous nations, and over enslaved, self-emancipated, and freed Black Americans – we see the normative discourses of secularity at work. Thinking in terms of secularity indeed makes plain that these are not isolated instances of oppression but distinct expressions of the same abuses.

And so the same discourses that allowed for the theft of Kiowa lands, for example, also justified the slave system and its still-reverberating social effects. These are not just parallel but interrelated acts: as Tiffany Lethabo King reminds us, the violences of settler colonialism and genocide are inseparable from those enacted by enslavers and the slave system. These formations, she writes, do not have "edges," even though "each is distinct":

> I do not believe that genocide and slavery can be contained.... Each form of violence has its own way of contaminating, haunting, touching, caressing, and whispering to the other. Their force is particular yet like liquid, as they can spill and seep into the spaces that we carve out as bound off and untouched by the other.[29]

In the same way that King describes, we argue, the secularity that normalized white Protestant efforts to remake Native subjectivity also normalized white Protestant efforts to regulate the habits of enslaved and newly freed Africans and African Americans. Secularity's everydayness made the marking and management of racial and religious "others" feel every day, too. As Vincent W. Lloyd assesses, white Protestants' attempts to govern other people's lives indeed became wrapped up in the felt normalcy of their own, a consequence of secular discourses on religion that sought to manage not just religions but "practices and bodies," the "lives of ordinary people."[30] Talking about religion in the mid-nineteenth century helped make governmentality and its practices part and parcel of everyday life.

In its ability to bind up forms of religious and racial governance into a normative sociality – into a sense of the world that feels right – secularity bears more than a passing resemblance to what Christina Sharpe has called the "weather" of antiblackness in the United States. The weather, in Sharpe's formulation, refers to the ongoing, everyday background conditions through and in which antiblackness organizes American cultural life. It names the system of aggressions – personal and political, structural and individual, micro and otherwise – that "makes domination in/visible and not/visceral."[31] In historical terms, the weather names the transformation of "slave law" into "lynch law, into Jim and Jane Crow," into all the "administrative logics that remember the brutal conditions of enslavement after the event of slavery has supposedly come to an end."[32] The weather is the conditions and logic of the slave system in contemporary form, present as both visceral memory (remembering) and re-creation of bodily experience (re-membering). And in this sense, as Sharpe tells us, "The weather is the totality of our environments; the weather is the total climate; and that climate is antiblack."[33]

Sharpe's weather is good to think with, for our purposes, because it names how antiblackness is operative in US culture as a kind of background condition, a feeling or mood, that organizes the lives of all but threatens the lives and well-being of only some. For if secular studies is correct – if secularism's normative sociality forms a felt backdrop to the lives of people born under its predicates – the fact remains that this normative sociality, the way it feels to live in the secular age of the present, is shot through with antiblack and other racisms. It's not a coincidence, we would argue, that the period in which secularity worked out its normative sociality was also the period in which the slave system took its final official form, or in which debates over the religious rights, freedoms, and capacities of formerly enslaved people were commonplace. The relationship between secularity and antiblackness was causal, we maintain, not correlational.

We want to underscore this point. If secularity names a way the world came to "feel right" in the mid-nineteenth century, antiblackness was a constitutive part of that feeling. So, too, were the period's long strains of thought and practices against indigenous nations, immigrant communities, and many varieties of non-Protestants. What is essential here is that, as secularity sought to adjudicate what was real and not real, as it sought to determine what forms of sociality held what kinds of powers, as it sought to tamp down preferable paths for bodies in the modern world, it also, often silently, aligned those paths with ones routed through racial hatred and violence. As religion talk in the mid-nineteenth century changed, it brought new opportunities for secularist and racist modes of governance to entwine under the umbrella of shared feeling. Quite literally, secularity was a way of making racial domination feel right.

Secularity's Otherwise Possibilities

Yet even as religion talk contributed to a world in which whiteness and "felt rightness" went hand-in-hand – even as it made white Protestants' experiences of the world feel ordinary – it also, in the mouths of those secularism tried to dispossess, opened up alternative ways of being, ways of rendering the secular provisional. Ashon T. Crawley's work on the liberatory possibilities of Black religion, especially Black Pentecostal practice, is apposite here. As Crawley describes, Black Pentecostalism makes evident the "ongoing otherwise possibilities" present within secularity's weather.[34] In a world trying to push secular forms of sociality under the skin, to make them into dominant modes of being, Black Pentecostals use their bodies and live in relation to one another differently. Take, for instance, Crawley's description of how Black Pentecostals cultivate breath in the practices of whooping, prayer, and song:

> [T]he Blackpentecostal tendency for praying and preaching to be inclusive of, and often end with, "whooping" – the speaking of phrases melodically, with excitement, usually breaking into loud exclamations and declarations repetitiously; the disruption of air through intentional, intense breathing [are examples of] what I will index as *black pneuma*, the capacity for the plural movement and displacement of inhalation and exhalation to enunciate life, life that is exorbitant, capacious, and fundamentally, social, though it is also life that is structured through and engulfed by brutal violence. This life, life in blackness, otherwise black life, exceeds the very capacities of seemingly gratuitous violence to be totalizing.[35]

Crawley's account of the breath and embodiment of Black Pentecostal worship calls to mind the songs and dances of the ring shout, a kind of "song performance" that Albert J. Raboteau describes as "crucial" to the communal worship experiences of some enslaved populations and their descendants.[36] The ring shout featured a whole litany of aural patterns and embodied movements woven together: "a strong emphasis on call and response, polyrhythms, syncopation, ornamentation, slides from one note to another, and repetition" as well as "body movement, hand-clapping, foot-tapping, and heterophony."[37] Raboteau suggests that, for its physicality and variability, the African-style ring shout exceeded the chronicling power of white observers' musical notations and, with it, the explanatory power of their secular discourses. Unable to inhabit the reality to which the ring shout belonged, the chroniclers could describe only its disruption to the secular's normative sociality: the song performance was, they said, "'wild,' 'strangely fascinating,' of 'peculiar quality,' and 'barbaric.'"[38]

Crawley's account of Black Pentecostalism resonates in much the same way with Yvonne Chireau's descriptions of Conjure, Hoodoo, and other Black-authored religious-medical traditions of healing and harming. For centuries within these traditions, skilled practitioners opened and closed bodies to supernatural forces as a means of navigating larger communities' concerns. Also for centuries within these traditions, we can witness Black persons whose religious and quasi-religious practices were assessed, critiqued, dismissed, and policed by authorities drawing on secularity's logic. Yet the persistence of these practices amid the attempts to control and regulate them underscores exactly Crawley's point: that "alternative modes, alternative strategies, alternative ways of life *already* exist" within secularity's normative sociality.[39] The embodied practices that enslaved, self-emancipated, and free Black people undertook in the mid-nineteenth century – alongside the Kiowa and all those others living beyond the bounds of white Protestantism – marked the limits of secularity's normative sociality, the discourses and experiences of the world it could not fully reach or overwrite.

To acknowledge these "otherwise possibilities" within secularism's dominant sociality is not to diminish the fact that they arose in a world actively seeking to stamp them out. State powers indeed often established their coherence precisely through such policing efforts, as Crawley points out.[40] Yet to call out such acts of policing without also recognizing the practices that survived them is ironically to reinforce the work of that policing, the attempts of state powers to undercut or deny the realities of non-normative experiences. For this reason, we contend that critiques of secularism's normative sociality best go hand-in-hand with close attention to the everyday ways of being that defy secularity's logics. We might see one such "otherwise possibility" in the story of Betsey Toledano, a free woman of color from New Orleans, whose religious and spiritual practices came under police surveillance in the early 1850s. On July 31, 1850, the New Orleans *Times-Picayune* described Toledano's summons before a local magistrate. Toledano, it seemed, had hosted gatherings of women for the purpose, in the *Times-Picayune*'s terms, of "performing the ceremonies and mysteries of Voudouism."[41] The *Times-Picayune* offered a detailed description of what the officers found when they broke into Toledano's house:

> They found one of the rooms fitted up in some sort as a chapel. The walls were hung round with colored prints of the saints, the apostles, &c. A number of basins or large earthenware bowls, were found, some filled with gravel, others with pebbles, two or three with paving-stones, and one very large one with a single, good-sized, peculiar-looking flint stone. There were several glass vases or goblets found containing some strange kind of liquid.

Toledano explained to the court that "she frequently had meetings of women only, at her house, to go through certain feminine mysteries, sing, &c." The rocks, meanwhile – "scattered about the floor" and gathered in bowls – "were to prevent the house from being struck by lightning," "a custom with the African negroes," as the article explained to readers.[42]

In its detailed attention to the foreign objects and unknown purposes at work in Toledano's gatherings, the *Times-Picayune*'s report resembles others from the period that treated Voudouism and other creole African religious and magical practices. These accounts often played up Voudou's transgressive or seemingly sexualized qualities: they referred to cauldrons, orgies, women in states of undress, and other supposedly "indecent" acts.[43] In practice, though, the gatherings grouped under the heading of "voodoo" forged social bonds among women and provided them with strategies meant to change the circumstances of their everyday lives.[44] The contrast between the salacious news reports and the ordinariness of the lived practices suggests the grounds upon which Voudou was perceived to disrupt secularity's norms. Although the news accounts' most lurid details may well have been hyperbolic or even sheer invention, they make clear that women practitioners of Voudouism generally came under public scrutiny for two charges: both the nature of their gatherings and the understood African roots of their powers. According to the *Times-Picayune*'s report on Toledano's testimony, for example, Toledano sought to introduce the women at her gatherings to a source of power she had accessed through her African ancestors:

> She did not attempt to deny the accusation [that she practiced Voudouism], stating that Voudouism was an African religion with its signs and symbols, that she had been educated in its precepts and mysteries by her grandmother, who came over from Africa, and that she never thought there was any wrong in it.[45]

In this description, Toledano and the *Times-Picayune* underscore the "otherwise possibilities" her gatherings generated. Toledano educated women, both enslaved Black women and occasionally white women, in "the precepts and mysteries" of an "African religion." From the state's perspective, the women's choice to assemble across lines of race, class, and slave status was troubling enough. Toledano would eventually be required to return to the court to answer further charges that she had facilitated "unlawful assemblies of slaves."[46] But that the women sought to engage powers associated with African religions – that must have seemed, to many of the *Times-Picayune*'s white readers, beyond the pale. What the white readers perceived as exotic or disarming, however, was, to those who sought Toledano's aid, foremost a matter of navigating the everyday world. White news sources' exoticizing (and well-preserved) accounts of Voudou can easily obscure that Voudou and other quasi-religious, quasi-magical rites were, for their mid-nineteenth-century practitioners, often mundane, pragmatic affairs. Voudouism offered ways of organizing a life that countered secularism's normative sociality.

Toledano's account of her Voudou gatherings before a court in New Orleans demonstrates Voudouism's capacity to disrupt the everydayness of secularity. Toledano's account is striking, too, for the ways it draws upon the language of propositional religion. As Toledano portrays it, Voudouism fits squarely within the category of "religion." It has its own "signs and symbols," much like the Catholicism practiced by New Orleans' free communities of color.[47] Perhaps more significantly for the history of secularism, it also has "precepts and mysteries" – ideas, propositions – that one must learn. In her argument to the court, Toledano positions Voudou squarely under the umbrella of propositional religion, portrays it, in other words, as possessing the form, if not the content, of Protestant religiosity. Yet her white audiences still meet her claim with derision. The reasons for her failure, we propose, are a signature illustration of secularity's final, ironic logic. Although "the secular" had first arisen from the propositional structures of sincere religion, in the US context at least, it came to signify a more general feeling or mood explicitly tied to racial whiteness. In short, to "feel right" – to align with Protestantism's accepted ways of thinking and believing – was ultimately *less* important, under secularity's measures of normativity, than to be white. In our understanding, secularity is a structure that promises a set of rational, racially neutral terms on which different subjects can live together, even as it always already stacks the deck in whiteness's favor.

Yet if Toledano can be seen here making a bid for respectability under the terms of a nascent secularism, one more attuned to propositional conformity than to diversity within these propositions, there were also limits to her willingness to comply with the imperatives of secular discourse. During the inquiry, Toledano displayed a curious necklace she had inherited from her grandmother, which, she said, "gave her great power over rain, she being able thereby to bring down a shower whenever she pleased."[48] Toledano's description of her powers was met with immediate contempt. As the *Times-Picayune* observed, "One of the by-standers said aloud that he thought the present the proper time to use her power," in order that she might "sprinkle and cool the crowded room."[49] Yet instead of trying to prove her powers to the crowd, Toledano offers something else: she "gave no other answer to this proposition . . . [t]han a scornful toss of the head and curl of the lip."[50] As Lisa Ze Winters has noted, Toledano in this moment refuses to engage on the terms of state power. Instead, she renders both the interior world of Black femininity and the social practices of Black women opaque – to viewers past and present alike.[51] What archives today preserve of that moment is most strikingly Toledano's gesture of refusal: a nonverbal marking-out of an alternative sociality she deliberately chooses to leave off stage.

What does this refusal, this silent preservation of an alternative sociality, mean for us, as we think about the place of religion in the study of mid-nineteenth-century American literature? We might see in it a contour of secularity's edges, of the fault lines and fissures running through a world white Protestantism sought to make "feel right." To comprehend this interplay between the felt ordinary and its disruptions, we might return again to Christina Sharpe's description of the weather of antiblackness. In describing how the weather affects Black persons, Sharpe writes that, although "we are constituted through and by continued vulnerability to that overwhelming force," yet also "we are not only known to ourselves and to each other by [it]."[52] If studying religion helps us see all the ways religion talk solidified dominant cultures – how it shaped the terms upon which people experienced everyday life in a secular age – examples like Toledano's remind us that those terms never told mid-nineteenth-century religion's entire story. What remains for us, then, is to sketch out all the ways the period's nonwhite, non-Protestant others made themselves known to each other and the world – and, too, the terms on which they refused to do so. Such an account lets us see Protestantism's effects far beyond those subjects whose hearts it meant to move or whose behaviors it meant to determine. And it lets us see, too, the forms of life, the otherwise possibilities, that proliferated beyond Protestantism's reach.

Notes

1 For an overview of this history, see Joanna Brooks, "From Edwards to Baldwin: Heterodoxy, Discontinuity, and New Narratives of American Religious-Literary History," *American Literary History* 22.2 (2010): 439–53.
2 On the outpouring of religious (usually Protestant) print culture in the period, see David Paul Nord, *Faith in Reading: Religious Publishing and the Birth of Mass Media in America* (New York: Oxford University Press, 2007), and Candy Gunther Brown, *The Word in the World: Evangelical Writing, Publishing, and Reading in America, 1789–1880* (Chapel Hill: University of North Carolina Press, 2004). A wealth of scholarship exists addressing religion's work in nineteenth-century American literatures. For a helpful introduction, see the special issue "American Literatures/American Religions," ed. Jonathan Ebel and Justine Murison, *American Literary History* 26.1 (2014). Recent interventions include Jonathon S. Kahn and Vincent W. Lloyd, *Race and Secularism in America* (New York: Columbia University Press, 2016); Claudia Stokes, *The Altar at Home: Sentimental Literature and*

Nineteenth-Century American Religion (Philadelphia: University of Pennsylvania Press, 2014); Kevin Pelletier, *Apocalyptic Sentimentalism: Love and Fear in U.S. Antebellum Literature* (Athens: University of Georgia Press, 2015); and others cited below.

3 Scholars have debated extensively what defines secularization. Charles Taylor, for instance, characterizes secularization as a kind of loss, a series of historically specific changes in the Western world that transformed religious belief from virtually a given to just "one human possibility among others." Talal Asad focuses more on the epistemic and ontological categories that make it possible to conceive of a political system in which religious institutions are separated from nonreligious ones and in which religion is relegated to a private sphere distinct from public life. See Charles Taylor, *A Secular Age* (Cambridge, MA: Harvard University Press, 2007), 3, and Talal Asad, *Formations of the Secular: Christianity, Islam, Modernity* (Stanford, CA: Stanford University Press, 2003).

4 Talal Asad, *Genealogies of Religion: Discipline and Reasons of Power in Christianity and Islam* (Baltimore, MD: Johns Hopkins University Press, 1993), 41.

5 For a more thorough version of this history, see also Kirstie M. McClure, "Difference, Diversity, and the Limits of Toleration," *Political Theory* 18.3 (1990): 361–91. In *Genealogies of Religion*, 41, Talal Asad describes more fully the process by which religion became "a set of propositions to which believers gave assent."

6 For more on the law and religious freedom in the US context, see Winifred Fallers Sullivan, *The Impossibility of Religious Freedom* (Princeton, NJ: Princeton University Press, 2005).

7 McClure, "Difference, Diversity, and the Limits of Toleration," 377–78.

8 Webb Keane, *Christian Moderns: Freedom and Fetish in the Mission Encounter* (Berkeley: University of California Press, 2007), 214.

9 Tracy Fessenden speaks to the origins and consequences of these early elisions between "religion" and "Protestantism" in *Culture and Redemption: Religion, the Secular, and American Literature* (Princeton, NJ: Princeton University Press, 2006).

10 James Madison, *A Memorial and Remonstrance, Presented to the General Assembly of the State of Virginia* (1785; repr. Worcester, MA: Isaiah Thomas, 1786), 6.

11 Thomas Jefferson, *Notes on the State of Virginia* (1787; repr. Philadelphia: Mathew Carey, 1794), 231.

12 Asad, *Formations of the Secular*, 194.

13 Compare, for instance, Elizabeth Povinelli's important comments on how Indigenous sacred sites such as Two Women Sitting Down are not granted the same standing as humans or corporations under the law. Elizabeth A. Povinelli, *Geontologies: A Requiem to Late Liberalism* (Durham, NC: Duke University Press, 2016), 34–35.

14 Thomas Jefferson, "Jefferson's Letter to the Danbury Baptists," January 1, 1802, repr. *Library of Congress Information Bulletin* 57.6 (1998), loc.gov/loc/lcib/9806/danpre.html.

15 Fessenden, *Culture and Redemption*, 6.

16 David Sehat, *The Myth of American Religious Freedom* (Oxford: Oxford University Press, 2011), 37.

17 Ibid., 37.

18 Justine S. Murison, "'Nudity and other sensitive states': Counterprivacy in Herman Melville's Fiction," *American Literature* 89.4 (2017): 697–726, 703, 704.

19 Ibid., 704.

20 John Lardas Modern, *Secularism in Antebellum America: With Reference to Ghosts, Protestant Subcultures, Machines, and Their Metaphors* (Chicago: University of Chicago Press, 2011), 11.

21 Ibid., 11.

22 Ibid., 21.

23 Ibid., 21. We might compare Talal Asad's argument that secular societies delineate the very categories "secular" and "religious" in order to set the terms within which "modern living is required to take place" and against which "nonmodern peoples are invited to assess their adequacy." Asad, *Formations of the Secular*, 14.

24 Jennifer Graber, *The Gods of Indian Country: Religion and the Struggle for the American West* (New York: Oxford University Press, 2018), 12, 45.

25 Ibid., 54.

26 Ibid., 65.

27 Ibid., 29, 67.

28 Ibid., 45.

29 Tiffany Lethabo King, *The Black Shoals: Offshore Formations of Black and Native Studies* (Durham, NC: Duke University Press, 2019), x.

30 Vincent W. Lloyd, "Introduction: Managing Race, Managing Religion," in *Race and Secularism in America*, ed. Jonathon S. Kahn and Vincent W. Lloyd (New York: Columbia University Press, 2016), 6.

31 Christina Sharpe, *In the Wake: On Blackness and Being* (Durham, NC: Duke University Press, 2016), 21.

32 Ibid., 106.

33 Ibid., 104.

34 Ashon T. Crawley, *Blackpentecostal Breath: The Aesthetics of Possibility* (New York: Fordham University Press, 2017), 6.

35 Ibid., 38.

36 Albert J. Raboteau, *Slave Religion: The "Invisible Institution" in the Antebellum South* (New York: Oxford University Press, 2004), 69.

37 Ibid., 72.

38 Ibid., 74.

39 Crawley, *Blackpentecostal Breath*, 6

40 Ibid., 6–7.

41 "More of the Voudous," New Orleans *Times-Picayune*, July 31, 1850, *America's Historical Newspapers: Early American Newspapers, Series 3*.

42 Ibid.

43 Examples of these accounts circulated widely both in the 1850s and through-
out the rest of the century. On the circulation of these accounts and their
connection to larger "discourses of white supremacy," see Michelle Y.
Gordon, "'Midnight Scenes and Orgies': Public Narratives of Voodoo in
New Orleans and Nineteenth-Century Discourses of White Supremacy,"
American Quarterly 64.4 (2012): 767–86. On the "indecent" practices
chronicled, see Ina Fandrich, *The Mysterious Voodoo Queen, Marie Laveaux:
A Study of Powerful Female Leadership in Nineteenth-Century New Orleans*
(New York: Taylor and Francis, 2005), 118. See also Carolyn Long,
"Perceptions of New Orleans Voodoo: Sin, Fraud, Entertainment, and
Religion." *Nova Religio* 6.1 (2002): 86–101, and *A New Orleans Voodoo
Priestess: The Legend and Reality of Marie Laveau* (Gainesville: University
Press of Florida, 2006). Scholars are rightly skeptical of the accuracy of these
accounts, which overwhelmingly come from white reporters and informants
who did not participate in the rituals they described. Still, the existence of
records documenting police intervention against Voudou practitioners provides evidence that the gatherings occurred, and of the responses they sum-
moned. For a similar analytic approach to another creole African religion, see
Diana Paton, *The Cultural Politics of Obeah: Religion, Colonialism, and
Modernity in the Caribbean World* (New York: Cambridge University Press,
2015).

44 Fandrich, for instance, describes meetings such as Toledano's as part of a
larger "underground religious organization" that should be considered a
distinct "women's religion" in New Orleans. Fandrich, "Defiant African
Sisterhoods: The Voodoo Arrests of the 1850s and 1860s in New Orleans,"
in *Fragments of Bone: Neo-African Religions in a New World*, ed. Patrick
Bellegarde-Smith (Urbana: University of Illinois Press, 2005), 201, 202.

45 "More of the Voudous."

46 Ibid.

47 On free women of color and Catholicism, see Long, *New Orleans*, 85.

48 "More of the Voudous."

49 Ibid.

50 Ibid.

51 Lisa Ze Winters, *The Mulatta Concubine: Terror, Intimacy, Freedom, and
Desire in the Black Transatlantic* (Athens: University of Georgia Press,
2016), 87.

52 Sharpe, *In the Wake*, 134.

CHAPTER 6

Nature

Kyla Schuller

In the summer of 1854, Frederick Douglass (1818–1895) made a characteristically bold choice. Despite his decade of experience lecturing on the abolitionist circuit, he was preparing a type of public speech that was new to him. Douglass was about to become the first African American to deliver a commencement address at a US college.[1] He wasted no opportunities with this new high-profile platform at Western Reserve College in Hudson, Ohio. Rather than impart benign moral lessons or offer comforting platitudes, Douglass elected to confront head-on a "matter of living importance."[2] Black-white relations in the United States, he instructed the graduating white men, was the single most important topic of the day. Racism was "a moral battle field" that permitted his listeners no middle ground (289). Increasingly, defenders of slavery argued that Black people represented a distinct species from white humanity, and they enlisted scientific authority as support. Interpreting his invitation to Western Reserve to authorize his own truth-telling, Douglass activated race science against itself.[3] He used empirical evidence to undo race science's claims while also side-stepping science's bid for absolute authority. "The Claims of the Negro Ethnologically Considered" finds the uneducated, formerly enslaved Douglass challenging college graduates to take a position in the rise of scientific racism, while also underscoring the impossibility of neutral knowledge and challenging the status of scientific authority itself.

Of all aspects of the then-flourishing institutions of slavery, why might Douglass have chosen to take on race science and scientific authority from this new platform? And why was his speech about the nature of African Americans popular enough that it was published as a pamphlet later that year – reaching an audience far beyond the initial gathering of scholars? The answer, I contend, is that Douglass took on scientific racism and the status of scientific knowledge in recognition that *nature* had become the primary site of the political. This claim may seem contradictory, from the perspective of US literary studies. The natural world, particularly

87

during the decades in which romantic and transcendental writers from Ralph Waldo Emerson to Henry David Thoreau and Margaret Fuller famously extolled its enchanting, incorruptible (if sometimes wild) virtue, seems to be the diametric opposite of the domain of human governance.[4] "Nature," Emerson reflected, "in the common sense, refers to essences unchanged by man; space, the air, the river, the leaf."[5] Emerson underscores the alleged distinctness of the natural, its perceived inability to be affected by the human world. Yet Douglass registered a major sea change of his day. Justifications of slavery, he perceived, were increasingly rooted in scientific ideas of biological difference. The political, the human world of power, representation, and governance, was increasingly grounded in the fleshy aspects of material existence as living beings. In the midst of the transcendental view of nature and humanity as intrinsically divine and altogether distinct from the sphere of the human, another view was simultaneously taking shape: one less *about* nature than it was relentlessly *naturalizing*.

Both literature and science – themselves not yet fully distinct forms of knowledge production – played important roles during the first six decades of the nineteenth century in transforming nature into the key grounds of the political. In this consolidating new perspective, humans were understood to be best governed as part of the natural world – rather than superior to or otherwise distinct from it. Michel Foucault has termed this mode of politics *biopower*. Biopower names a form of power ascendant beginning in the late seventeenth century, and rapidly consolidating in the nineteenth, that understands the natural world to be the key domain of politics.[6] Biopower works through two modes. The first is a disciplinary form of power and it targets the individual body, seeking to mold its flesh and character through institutions such as the school, hospital, factory, the prison – and, as we shall see, the novel and the botanical handbook. Its goal is to produce a docile subject who willingly integrates the economic needs of the state into the subject's daily self-discipline and sense of self. The second mode is termed *biopolitics* and it targets the collective level of the population.[7] Biopolitics approaches its population as "biocapital, a statistical mass of life whose biological economies and embodied interests can, like any other material resource, be mined and administered for maximum productivity," in the words of literary critic Cristin Ellis.[8] Biopolitics ranks groups within a population as relative assets or contagions to the success of the whole. Foucault argues that the modern, biological notion of race difference emerged in the mid-nineteenth century to do precisely this biopolitical work.[9] Biopolitics deems racialized and disabled bodies to be inferior and contaminating material from prehistory whose utility lie in their very disposability. They had utility only in the form of extractable labor, transferable from one body or one region to another; otherwise they could be left or made to die. Meanwhile, biopolitics nurtures and fosters white and/or civilized bodies, treating them as the seeds of a healthy future. Whites' value lies in their inherent impressibility, or the capacity to be affected over time and thus to improve (or, if conditions were poor, to decline).[10] The core of biopolitical governance is cultivating white and able members of the population, and eliminating the racialized and/or disabled, as a method to secure the stability and profitability of the population over time.

Race science is a pernicious example of the rise of biological thinking to naturalize political inequalities, as Douglass noted in the 1850s. In this essay, I turn to a less pronounced but tremendously significant aspect of the rise of biopower. I argue that sentimental culture played a large role in transforming nature into the key site of the political. Sentimentalism is the ideology that dictates that sympathetic feeling for one's fellow man ought to shape ethical and political behavior. Sentimentalism could also be a scientific method. Nature and culture were as yet indistinct in the era, a confluence that gave sentimental ideologies in both science and the arts a strong governing hand in building the new biopolitical world view. I show how sentimentalism helped shape both disciplinary efforts to target the individual and biopolitical measures to regulate the species by focusing on three significant elements of the overlapping realms of the literary arts and sciences. First, I show how sentimental culture had a disciplinary cast, one that sought to transform the mind and body. Second, I show how human life became a species, an organic phenomenon subject to natural law, within a Lamarckian evolutionary paradigm that thoroughly blended what later eras would tease apart into the distinct realms of nature and nurture, biology and culture. And finally, the arts of sentiment and civilization were construed as methods of improving the species over time, as I explore in an extended reading of *Uncle Tom's Cabin*. Together, scientific and literary cultures of sentiment transformed nature from an idyllic – or threatening – alternative to human life into the very substance of human flourishing and productivity. The stakes of nature and the political becoming coterminous, as Douglass highlighted, was that inequality became naturalized.

Sentimental Science

Twenty years before Douglass' ground-breaking commencement speech, the aging English poet Samuel Taylor Coleridge (1772–1834) emerged

from decades-long seclusion with one purpose. He was determined to
confront the researchers at the third meeting of the British Association for
the Advancement of Science and protect his intellectual territory.
Immediately following the opening speech of the 1833 conference,
Coleridge slowly but commandingly rose to his feet. "You must stop calling
yourselves natural philosophers!" he thundered. Poets represented the true
philosopher, he chided, the "real metaphysician." The men gathered there
merely trawled around in the muck searching for clues. Theoreticians like
himself, not tinkerers, alone could claim the mantle of philosophy.[11] Prior to
the 1830s, contemplation of the organic world had largely been the purview
of gentlemen naturalists whose key modes were feeling, observation, and
speculation.[12] Coleridge himself had published on the scientific method.[13]
But a new class of beholder that prioritized transferable, standardizable
empirical tools over individual feeling and abstract reasoning was gathering
momentum.[14] Coleridge's anger backfired. In response to Coleridge's
demand, Trinity College, Cambridge, fellow William Whewell (and conference convener) immediately suggested the new term *scientist*. Whewell's
moniker stuck because it identified an important new phenomenon: the rise
of a professional class of researchers who systematized, and made profitable,
the study of the natural and physical world. Coleridge ironically played a role
in the arts and letters losing their status as the privileged method of truth
telling. By the dawn of the twentieth century, scientists, not philosophers or
metaphysicians, would lay claim to the purest epistemological authority.
This shift in science from an individual act of study and contemplation to a
reproducible, institutionalized set of methods was a key element of the
changing political valence of the natural. The study of nature was not just
a key terrain for individual reflection on the meaning of existence; it was
increasingly becoming a site of knowledge and power, yoked to the development of capitalism.

Yet the professionalization of science progressed slowly and unevenly
over the first half of the nineteenth century. Methods that cultivated the
silent and even emotional observation of the wonders of God's creation
still had many champions, beyond Coleridge. Sentimentalism that cultivated the feeling of spectators, sharpening their observational acumen, was
an accepted approach to early nineteenth-century science on both sides of
the Atlantic.[15] This nonstandardized approach to scientific study was
particularly enabling for white bourgeois women. In the early 1830s,
editor, writer, and botany enthusiast Sarah Josepha Hale defended feeling
as an appropriate approach to the study of the natural world. She looked
forward to a day in which the "blessed days of peace, plenty and

intercourse among all nations shall have arrived, science and sentiment will be found compatible with each other, and refined taste and Christian morality [will have] become synonymous terms."[16] According to Hale, the combination of scientific practice and sentimental feeling would enable the world's path towards civilized refinement, a future that white women would play a key role in bringing to pass. Hale works in this vein, and understands the study of the natural world to refine the observer. "We have an earthly as well as a spiritual nature," Hale advised her readers, "and the last cannot attain its human perfection without a due attention to the former" (273). Hers is not a science of capitalism, but it is a science of disciplinary biopower, enabling white women to cultivate human perfection.

Sentimental science was one of the forms through which biopower took shape in the early nineteenth century for it helped to develop a biologizing view of human problems and solutions. For Hale as for many of her contemporaries, the learned appreciation of the natural world was beneficial for it increased the ability to recognize God's magnificence. This had particular import for white women, who were assigned the racist, imperial task of civilizing white youth and all people of color, but were often denied well-rounded educations that would give them knowledge of the natural world. As editor of *Godey's Ladies Book* from 1837 until 1877, Hale thus filled its pages with treatises on natural history, especially about flowers and plants, widely seen as the only apt scientific topic for feminine study.[17] For Hale, women's limited scientific training threatened their divinely appointed roles as the guardians of the nation's moral development and the shepherds of the world's "backward" peoples.[18] Without instruction in natural history, Hale argued, women's development was stunted, thus limiting their ability to unite science and sentimentalism to civilize their communities and their nation's conquered territories. Hale was deeply committed to promoting white women's role in making settler colonialism work. Beginning in the midst of the US–Mexico War, she fought for thirty-six years to make the national holiday Thanksgiving a reality that would unite newly conquered Western territories with New England tradition.[19] In Hale's work, the links between the appreciation of nature and the imperial goal of civilization are explicit. The sentimental study of nature is also the mastery of civilization. Botanical knowledge is not only about private worship; it is also about political duty. Nature represented a key site of women's civilizing power.

Botanical discourse permeated middle-class daily life. Fern collecting and lavish indoor gardens were a national pastime in both the United

States and United Kingdom. The contemplation of flowers was a wildly popular amusement.[20] Flower poems, floral dictionaries, literary studies of flowers, botanies emphasizing the spiritual aspects of flowers, and texts professing to transcribe the language "spoken" by flowers were wildly popular in the United States, reaching an apex in the 1840s and 1850s.[21] Figures now considered integral to sentimental culture, including Hale, Louisa May Alcott, and Lydia Maria Child, published in these genres, and other writers, such as Catharine Maria Sedgwick, took up the theme of botanical study in their fiction.[22] Other women authors looked to flora for their pseudonyms, including Fanny Fern, Grace Greenwood, Fanny Forrester, and Lily Larkspur. In the 1970s, literary critic Ann Douglas diagnosed these pen names as symptoms of the writers' affliction with sentimentalism: "By such self-baptism, feminine authors become characters in their own sentimental effusions: hothouse products, they are self-announced refugees from history."[23] In Douglas's lively but now generally overturned reading, sentiment and the organic represented a flight from the political.

Far from an escape from the concerns of the human world, the study of nature plunged its observers into the heart of civilizing power. In sentimental culture, flora had a disciplinary function. Botany's promoters, such as prominent author Almira Phelps, encouraged women to study flowers for they provided pious and innocent models to cultivate the grace of white women, thereby reducing their animal nature. Sentimental flower culture "considered flower study the primary means to accomplish both religious and romantic devotion," and Phelps's botanical science promoted the field as a means to learn the function and duties of femininity.[24] Furthermore, nature itself was never neutral ground. In the post-Calvinist United States, nature had a dual meaning. It signified both the innocence and beauty of God's creation and the howling wilderness that had so threatened the Puritans. Nature was the duality of spirit and matter, innocence and depravity, purity and sin. White women were often assigned the duality that Nature itself was seen to embody: part divine grace, part animal matter. White men, on the other hand, were often freed from embodiment altogether, portrayed as able to achieve pure abstract reason and feeling. People of color, denied the distinctions of sex and gender, were often associated with degraded, base, earthly material – nature stripped of romance.[25]

Literary writers followed suit. Susan Warner's novel *The Wide, Wide World* (1850), the nation's first bestseller, charts the process through which an unrefined white orphan girl cultivates herself through her relationship to flowers. The narrator portrays Ellen as akin to "a white camellia . . . the emblem of a sinless pure spirit," yet she also has a wild nature.[26] As she matures, flowers bring out her refinement, quieting her coarser qualities. Warner characterizes flowers as "friends to Ellen ... and [she] seemed to purify herself in the pure companionship. Even Mr. Van Brunt" – the novel's docile and unrefined agrarian farmer – "came to have an indistinct notion that Ellen and flowers were made to be together" (340). In the highly popular sentimental orphan novel genre, the presence or absence of flowers in girls' lives is a recurring indicator of their likelihood to restrain their primitive impulses and attain civilization. Flowers and leisured appreciation of the natural world are key to the formation of middle-class habits and desires. Flowers, in other words, figure as agents of biopower that discipline the individual, targeting the biological aspects of their existence.

Biopower was compatible with, even structurally related to, the ethic of sentimental sympathy.[27] Sentimentalism teaches that the imperative of "right feeling" for one's fellow man, in Stowe's oft-repeated phrase, ought to dictate ethical and political behavior.[28] For literary critic Richard Brodhead, sentimentalism was key to the practice of disciplinary biopower. It taught the subject to bond with power, usually represented by parents and teachers, internalizing it fully. In what he calls "the sentimentalization of discipline," power works through "a strategic relocation of authority relations in the realm of emotion and a conscious intensification of the emotional bond between the authority figure and its charge"[29] Emotional identification becomes the site of disciplinary subjection. Sentimentalism professes an ideal of lateral sympathy and shared tears, but sentimentalism far more often takes the shape of instrumentalizing the suffering of the oppressed to build bourgeois moral virtue, as critics have noted.[30] The suffering of the slave, splayed out on the page, allows for the emotional catharsis and refinement of its true target: the middle-class reader. Yet sentimentalism's connections to biopower reach even deeper. Fundamentally, its ethic of cultivating individual feeling targeted the organic body as much as the eternal soul. Sentimentalism is itself a technology of biopower, at the scale of both disciplinary power targeting the individual and, as we shall see, biopolitical power targeting the population.

Biology as History

We might say that life itself became the great subject of history over the first half of the nineteenth century. Geologists wrested nature from its status as divine creation, called into being a mere 5,000 years ago according to the biblical chronology, and plunged humans into the vastness of deep time. Deep time, the geological notion that the earth has a multimillion-year history, now registered humanity as a relative blip in the planet's lifespan. Other new concepts, including prehistory, extinction, and the ice age – the latter two developed by French naturalist Georges Cuvier – suggested that life did not persist unchanged over time and that existence itself held no guarantees.[31] Nature became embedded in time, featuring a prehistoric past, an ongoing present, and an unpredictable future. A key component of the notion that life not only had a history but *was* history was the idea that animal being itself was a changeable phenomenon. To make nature a temporal phenomenon is to make it a potentially pliable one. Rather than fixed, eternal form, the living world came to represent a site of intervention, agency, and change that could potentially be subjected to human control. Darwin is of course most commonly credited with transforming life itself into a great temporal narrative of change with the publication of *On the Origin of Species* in 1859 and subsequent work. But the Darwinian revolution was slow. Darwin's contemporary readers understood species change to allow for human intervention, and this was generally true until the synthesis of population genetics and theory of natural selection in the 1930s.[32] While we now read natural selection to be completely independent from individual choice, a process of statistically random mutation, chance, and pressure from the environment at the level of the species, scientists and laypeople at the time were alike prone to read *Origin* as a teleological account of evolution in which change meant progress that humans could control. This was partly due to the fact that Darwin's theory entered a popular landscape already somewhat familiar with ideas of species change. Evolutionary theories were important in the antebellum period, decades before Darwin published *Origin*.

Early in the nineteenth century, the French natural philosopher Jean-Baptiste Lamarck stressed that organisms changed over time as a result of interaction with their environments.[33] Adaptation had two central principles: first, the law of use and disuse, which stated that habitual use strengthens and enlarges the relevant parts of the body, while infrequent use atrophies. Second, these modifications are transmitted to the next generation via reproduction. For Lamarck, function determined form. Nature wasn't unchanging, but rather evolved according to its own habitual action. The key feature of life for Lamarck is that organisms absorb the effects pressed upon them by their repeated sensory impressions and transmit these effects down generational time. Experience and history, in other words, were embodied in the flesh. This turn toward understanding the organic body to be a record of its species history was central to nature becoming the key site of the political. The plastic body reflected its circumstance – power writes itself into the flesh. Nature had become a historical force subjected to human experience.

In his short story "The Birth-Mark" (1843), Nathaniel Hawthorne captures the emergent worldview that saw the organic body as both a malleable entity and a historical record of the past. This organic plasticity gave particular power to the scientist himself. To study the natural world not only was to understand its workings; increasingly, it also was to influence its workings. The story satirizes the "faith in man's ultimate control over Nature" on account of extraordinary new discoveries in the world of science, such as electricity.[34] Aylmer, the natural philosopher protagonist of the story, marries a striking young white woman who embodies the duality of nature: grace and damnation. Aylmer is haunted by a birthmark in the shape of a hand on Georgiana's face, "the visible mark of earthly imperfection" that plummets his angel earthward (7). She is so near perfection, and yet this mark – itself seemingly the residue of contact with other bodies and sensations before Aylmer – was "the symbol of his wife's liability to sin, sorrow, decay, and death" (10). The "impress of the crimson hand" radiates from her cheek, unless she blushes – where it disappears under the damning coat of red (17). After marriage, this visible reminder of her earthly nature, both her sexuality and eventual mortality, torments him. He convinces Georgiana to become a specimen of his experimental alchemy and undertakes a highly risky procedure to extract the mark from the "substance" of her cheek (8). The experiment is successful, but it comes at a high price. The cost of Georgiana's bodily perfection is her life itself. Dead, she has become free of flaw, the malleable object of Aylmer's ambition. Was the mark the one limit to her organic worth, or the site of it? Her sensory impressions over her lifetime forged the body itself – thus they could not be removed without killing her organism.

The narrator is explicit that Georgiana's femininity is forged of the duality of nature, both spirit and mortality, while Aylmer and his "under-worker" Aminadab represent purity and sin, respectively, in an absolute sense. Aminidab, with "his shaggy hair, his smoky aspect, and the indescribable earthiness that incrusted him, he seemed to represent man's physical nature; while Aylmer's slender figure, and pale, intellectual face, were no less apt a type of the spiritual element" (20). Aminadab is pure matter, the sin of nature – and accordingly, he loves the birthmark – while Aylmer has all but escaped embodiment altogether. Hawthorne's biting tone suggests that while nature was increasingly malleable in the hands of the scientist, organic plasticity has its own resilience. Hawthorne's tale satirizes the goal of biopower: to use science to cultivate, refine, and perfect; to master earthly nature itself. Biopower is fundamentally about manipulating nature, treating the organic as the site of profitability. Botany could function as a method to elevate and civilize, while the body could serve as a surface for experimentation.

Species-Being

Sentimental writers not only helped shape disciplinary modes of biopower that target the individual body; they also contributed to biopolitical modes that address members of the nation not primarily as individuals bearing or lacking political rights, but as members of an organic species. In the broadly influential Lamarckian view, the body was understood to be porous in the hands of culture. Corporeal form resulted from sensory impressions accumulated over time in the form of species. Evolutionary theories like Lamarck's were key to the emergence of the biopolitical model of biopower: that humans formed the organic phenomenon of the population and were best governed in mass. A population is not merely a grouping of individuals, or the resident inhabitants of a locale or nation. Rather, a population represents biocapital, an organic entity in its own right on the scale of the species. It exists over the time of generations and abides by the laws of evolutionary change. Biopolitics attempts to maximize the profitability of a population through regulating its organic rhythms of species life, such as rates of birth, morbidity, and mortality.

A compelling example of how sentimental fiction helped move politics into the flesh and transform humanity into a species is the now-classic novel of the vexed racial politics of sentiment: Harriet Beecher Stowe's blockbuster 1852 novel *Uncle Tom's Cabin*. The novel is well known for its sympathetic, but ultimately racist, representation of its Black characters; it is also deeply invested in an evolutionary perspective. *Uncle Tom's Cabin* understands not just slavery, but the existence of racial groups in the first place, as the result of habits accumulating over generational time. Stowe's novel seeks to expose how slavery as an institution forges the temperaments and characteristics of the people it involves. Consider the very first line of the novel's preface, where Stowe introduces her Black characters as racial types that have evolved over generations: they are members of "an exotic race, whose ancestors, born beneath a tropic sun, brought with them, and perpetuated to their descendants, a character so essentially unlike the hard and dominant Anglo-Saxon race, as for many years to have won from it only misunderstanding and contempt."[35] Black character is indistinguishable from Black nature in Stowe's rendering. Slavery perpetuates this character that Stowe sees as fit for an exotic clime, but wholly unsuited to the demands of American modernity. Modernity has likewise accumulated over time in the bodies of whites, preparing them for dominance. In later work, she was more explicit about approaching human growth as essentially biological in nature. Stowe stressed that humans and animals were regulated by identical laws of nature and that there was no inherent duality between mind and body, spirit and animal. "The foundation of all moral and intellectual worth must be laid in a good healthy animal," she opined in her conduct manual *Little Foxes* (1866).[36] For Stowe, morals and the mind were essentially organic qualities.

Uncle Tom's Cabin thus stages slavery as primarily an organic problem, rather than a political or economic one. For Stowe, the crux of the dilemma wasn't slavery's status as an institution that maximized profit through unfree labor and helped capitalism consolidate in the transatlantic world. Rather, slavery existed because of the oppositional natures of Blacks and whites. She portrayed enslavement as the result of people of conflicting heritages who had been made to coexist in the same population: "The Saxon, born of ages of cultivation, command, education, physical and moral influence; the Afric, born of ages of oppression, submission, ignorance, toil, and vice!" (268). From her perspective, whites *naturally* assumed dominance over those of African descent. Stowe worked with a Lamarckian evolutionary view that embeds the body in historical time and sees nature to be fully porous with culture.[37] Experience codifies in the body over time as racial type. "Your Kentuckian of the present day is a good illustration of the doctrine of transmitted instincts and peculiarities," her narrator relates (115). A hunter and outdoorsman, the Kentuckian is the "frankest, easiest, and most jovial creature living," genial habits that have accumulated over generations as character (115). By contrast, those involved in the nefarious act of slave-trading bear the effects of their callous disregard of human feeling in the flesh. Speaking of a slave trader, the narrator observes that the "whole air of his physiognomy" bears the impress of his business. "In the head and face every organ and lineament expressive of brutal and unhesitating violence was in a state of the highest possible development" (70–71). Nature here functions as a site of the political, as a canvas for human action and conflict. In Stowe's biopolitical vision, politics is transposed onto flesh.

Stowe's naturalizing perspective underscores the deep racial hierarchies at the core of biopower. In *Uncle Tom's Cabin*, the continued existence of slavery threatens to contaminate vulnerable, impressible whites. This was a relatively common abolitionist argument, though Stowe emphasized the biological nature of this influence. "It takes no spectacles to see that a great class of vicious, improvident, degraded people, among us, are an evil to us, as well as to themselves," warns the slaveowner St. Clare. "They are in our houses; they are the associates of our children, and they form their minds faster than we can; for they are a race that children will always cling to and assimilate with.... We might as well allow the small-pox to run among them" (253). St. Clare figures blackness as a pathogen that threatens the ability of whites to thrive. African Americans are simultaneously a dangerous infection and "degraded" remnants of the past who have never fully matured into the level of development achieved by white adults. They are thus the natural companions of white children. In this view, slavery puts two fundamentally distinct types into close proximity and contaminates the population's greatest biological asset: the malleable bodies and minds of white children.

A biopolitical view thus presents Stowe with her solution to slavery. Since the problem was organic, rather than political or economic in origin, its remedy ought to be organic as well. To solve the problem of two conflicting natures occupying the same soil that for her led to enslavement, the answer was to change both the nature of African Americans and their rights to US residency (citizenship, of course, was still a far-off dream in the 1850s). Her solution, as is typical of biopower in the nineteenth century, deploys disciplinary methods that target the individual body to create biopolitical outcomes affecting the population as a whole. Stowe and other white reformers such as Lydia Maria Child emphasized what they saw as the "childlike" temperament of African Americans (160). In their view, this immaturity implied a degree of capacity to be influenced, and thus to be cultivated, by their white racial superiors. Stowe explicitly portrays Black characters as belonging to "a sensitive and impressible race" – thus trainable if exposed to a different class of sensory impressions (313). The novel relates: "There is all the difference in the world in the servants of southern establishments, according to the character and capacity of the mistresses who brought them up" (224). Stowe portrays enslaved children as vessels, ready to be filled. Or, in terms that much more explicitly invoke her scientific, biopolitical gaze: as "fresh-caught specimen[s]" ready for experimentation (260). The novel stages precisely such an experiment. Slaveowner St. Clare gives his visiting aunt Miss Ophelia an enslaved girl "[f]or [Ophelia] to educate ... and train in the way she should go" (259). The arrangement is a bet between them about the nature of African Americans. St. Clare holds the segregationist perspective that sees natures as fixed and permanently unequal, while northerner Ophelia defends the assimilationist position that characters reflect the environments that made them and thus that Blacks could be improved. As historian Ibram X. Kendi argues, these positions – segregation and assimilation – are the two major forms racism has taken in the United States.[38] Topsy's parents are unknown to her, making her "virgin soil" and thus a perfect specimen (264). "[I] don't think nobody ever made me," she tells Ophelia (263). At first, it is St. Clare's angelic daughter Eva who has the most influence over Topsy, for she extends sympathy and feeling. Cold, unemotional Ophelia eventually follows suit, informing her charge "'*I* can love you,'" a sentiment proven by the "honest tears that fell down her face. From that hour, she acquired an influence over the mind of the destitute child that she never lost" (324). For Stowe and other sentimentalists, sympathy confers the ability to control, change, and mold – or in other words, to discipline. And the discipline of sympathy works both ways: Ophelia, too, is transformed by her work with Topsy. When exposed to a child's allegedly pure love, Ophelia's hard Northern ways give in to tenderness and affection – as if Topsy were a flower, and Ophelia were the true target of her own civilizing project. Yet this disciplinary power was possible to arrange only at the individual level. *Uncle Tom's Cabin* infamously ends with the Black characters all moving to Canada or helping to colonize Liberia. At the populational level, Stowe can envision no future America that accommodates African Americans. Hers is a biopolitics that casts the racialized out of the nation.

Stowe's interest in disciplining and evolving Black workers was not only figural. In Stowe, we see sentimental biopower in full flower. In the years after the Civil War, Harriet Beecher Stowe and her family undertook their own experiment to civilize Black workers. She and her husband bought a cotton and sugarcane plantation on a bend of the St. John's River near Jacksonville, Florida. She boasted that the plantation had once been "the leading one in Florida," over 9,000 acres in size and enslaving more than 500 people.[39] Their twofold goals were to have a comfortable place to escape the Connecticut winters – and to transform laborers "blacker, stranger, and more dismal, than anything we had ever seen" into docile subjects (300). She was convinced that Black people were suited for fieldwork in the harsh southern clime. "[T]he negro is the natural laborer of tropical regions," she explains in her account of her Florida experiment, *Palmetto Leaves* (1873).[40] "[A] boiling spring of animal content is ever welling up within" (281) and they "seemed to make a perfect frolic of this job, which, under such a sun, would have threatened sunstroke to any white man" (282). All might have animal vigor, in Stowe's perspective, but African Americans were more in touch with their animal nature. This ebullience was also a form of disorder. "As the first white ladies upon the ground," Stowe related, "Mrs. F— and myself had the task of organizing this barbaric household, and of bringing it into the forms of civilized life. We commenced with the washing" (306) – as if histories of enslavement could be scrubbed off its survivors, as if cleanliness was the major obstacle to their thriving. Stowe's fictional and domestic work reflect that the possibility of individual transformation was tied to the goal of maximizing the biocapital of the population as a whole. Her sentimental biopolitics endorsed the possibility of transforming African Americans from contagions into assets.

In Stowe's life and work, nature does not appear primarily as an escape from or an alternative to corruptible, market-driven human sociality. She and other sentimental writers were part of an epochal shift in politics: transforming nature into the key site of the political. Biological existence itself became a key new resource for conceptualizing human difference and an administrative target of political power. Human life became naturalized. Today we see race science as a key element of this shift, and Douglass was one of the first to observe this. However, sentimental culture, though most often associated with femininity and the domestic realm, also played a major role. Sentimentalism was a technology of biopower. At the level of discipling the individual, it taught the subject to love how power reached into its soul, through institutions as varied as botany, domesticity, and the novel. At the level of conceiving of humanity as members of a species that ought to be evolving upward, it helped inaugurate this teleological, evolutionary view and to promise that manipulating the impressions of children and workers would engineer the bodies of the future. An ideology that sutured literature and science together in an era in which divisions between them were just beginning to form, sentimentalism helped move politics into the flesh.

Notes

1 Bruce Dain, *A Hideous Monster of the Mind: American Race Theory in the Early Republic* (Cambridge, MA: Harvard University Press, 2003), 249.
2 Frederick Douglass, "The Claims of the Negro Ethnologically Considered," in Philip S. Foner, ed., *The Life and Writings of Frederick Douglass*, vol. 2 (New York: International Publishers, 1976), 289. Hereafter cited parenthetically in the text.

3 Cristin Ellis, *Antebellum Posthuman: Race and Materiality in the Mid-Nineteenth Century* (New York: Fordham University Press, 2018), 41. Ellis emphasizes the material, organic basis of Douglass's critique of slavery.

4 On Thoreau's resistance to the consolidating regime of biopolitics, see Peter Coviello, "The Wild Not Less than the Good: Thoreau, Sex, Biopower," *GLQ: A Journal of Lesbian and Gay Studies* 23, no. 4 (2017): 509–532.

5 Ralph Waldo Emerson, "Nature," in *Nature and Selected Essays*, introduction by Larzer Ziff (New York: Penguin Classics, 2003), 36.

6 Michel Foucault, *"Society Must Be Defended": Lectures at the Collège de France, 1975–1976,* trans. David Macey (New York: Picador, 2003). See also Thomas Lemke, *Biopolitics: An Advanced Introduction* (New York: New York University Press, 2011).

7 Michel Foucault, *Security, Territory, Population: Lectures at the Collège de France, 1977–1978*, trans. Graham Burchell (New York: Picador, 2004).

8 Ellis, *Antebellum Posthuman*, 10.

9 Foucault, *"Society Must Be Defended."*

10 Kyla Schuller, *The Biopolitics of Feeling: Race, Sex, and Science in the Nineteenth Century* (Durham, NC: Duke University Press, 2018).

11 Laura J. Snyder recounts this compelling scene in *The Philosophical Breakfast Club: Four Remarkable Friends Who Transformed Science and Changed the World* (New York: Broadway Books, 2011), 1–4.

12 Laura Dassow Walls, "Textbooks and Texts from the Brooks: Inventing Scientific Authority in America," *American Quarterly* 49, no. 1 (1997): 1–25.

13 Samuel Taylor Coleridge, *A Dissertation on the Science of Method; or, The Laws and Regulative Principles of Education* [1818] (London: Charles Griffin and Co., 1859).

14 Lorraine Daston, "Objectivity and the Escape from Perspective," *Social Studies of Science* 22, no. 4 (1992): 597–618.

15 Jessica Riskin, *Science in the Age of Sensibility: The Sentimental Empiricists of the French Enlightenment* (Chicago: University of Chicago Press, 2002); Schuller, *Biopolitics of Feeling*, 35–67.

16 Sarah J. Hale, "Science and Sentiment," *Ladies' Magazine and Literary Gazette* 6, no. 6 (1833): 276. Hereafter cited parenthetically in the text.

17 Nina Baym, *American Women of Letters and the Nineteenth-Century Sciences: Styles of Affiliation* (New Brunswick, NJ: Rutgers University Press, 2001).

18 For an excellent reading of Hale's union of sentiment and US empire building, see Amy Kaplan's classic essay, "Manifest Domesticity," special issue "No More Separate Spheres!" of *American Literature* 70, no. 3, (1998): 581–606.

19 Ibid., 592.

20 For the role of British and French writers in developing US botanical and flower language discourse, see Vera Norwood, *Made from This Earth: American Women and Nature* (Chapel Hill: University of North Carolina Press, 1993), 1–24.

21 Beverly Seaton, *The Language of Flowers: A History* (Charlottesville: University Press of Virginia, 1995), 87.

22 See, for example, Catharine Maria Sedgwick, "Cacoethes Scribendi" (1830), quoted in Tina Gianquitto, *"Good Observers of Nature": American Women and the Scientific Study of the Natural World, 1820–1885* (Athens: University of Georgia Press, 2007), 18.

23 Ann Douglas, *The Feminization of American Culture* (New York: Knopf, 1977), 186.

24 Gianquitto, *"Good Observers of Nature,"* 25.

25 On racism's efforts to deny gender difference to people of color, see Hortense Spillers, "Mama's Baby, Papa's Maybe: An American Grammar Book," *Diacritics* 17, no. 2 (1987): 64–81. On racism's efforts to deny sex difference to people of color, see Schuller, *The Biopolitics of Feeling*.

26 Susan Warner, *The Wide, Wide World* (New York: Grosset and Dunlap, n.d.), 327. Citations hereafter in text.

27 Lora Romero, *Home Fronts: Domesticity and Its Critics in the Antebellum United States* (Durham, NC: Duke University Press, 1997); Simon Strick, *American Dolorologies: Pain, Sentimentalism, Biopolitics* (Albany: SUNY Press, 2015); Schuller, *The Biopolitics of Feeling*.

28 Cindy Weinstein illuminates the regional and political diversity of sentimental writers, identifying how Southern proslavery and Northern antislavery writers each claimed to articulate the true "right feeling." Cindy Weinstein, *Family, Kinship, and Sympathy in Nineteenth-Century American Literature* (Cambridge: Cambridge University Press, 2004).

29 Richard H. Brodhead, "Sparing the Rod: Discipline and Fiction in Antebellum America," *Representations* 21 (1988): 71.

30 Lauren Berlant, *The Female Complaint: The Unfinished Business of Sentimentality in American Culture* (Durham, NC: Duke University Press, 2008).

31 On the invention of geological time in the period, see Dana Luciano, "Tracking Prehistory," *J19: The Journal of Nineteenth-Century Americanists* 3, no. 1 (2015): 173–181.

32 Peter Bowler, *The Non-Darwinian Revolution: Reinterpreting a Historical Myth* (Baltimore: Johns Hopkins University Press, 1988).

33 Jean-Baptiste Pierre Lamarck, *Philosophie Zoologique*, trans. Hugh Elliot (London: Macmillan, 1914).

34 Nathaniel Hawthorne, *The Birth-Mark* (Boston: Squid Ink Classics, 2016), 6. Hereafter cited parenthetically in the text.

35 Harriet Beecher Stowe, *Uncle Tom's Cabin, or Life among the Lowly* (New York: Signet, 1998), 3. Hereafter cited parenthetically in the text.

36 Qtd. by Jennifer Mason, *Civilized Creatures: Urban Animals, Sentimental Culture, and American Literature, 1850–1900* (Baltimore: Johns Hopkins University Press, 2005), 105. Mason argues that Stowe had deep interest in animal welfare and natural history.

37 Lynn Wardley, "Relic, Fetish, Femmage: The Aesthetics of Sentiment in the Work of Stowe," in *The Culture of Sentiment: Race, Gender, and Sentimentality in Nineteenth-Century America*, ed. Shirley Samuels (New York: Oxford University Press, 1992), 203–220.

38 Ibram X. Kendi, *Stamped from the Beginning: The Definitive History of Racist Ideas in America* (New York: Bold Type Books, 2017).
39 Harriet Beecher Stowe, "Our Florida Plantation," *Atlantic Monthly* 43 (1879): 641–649.
40 Harriet Beecher Stowe, *Palmetto-Leaves* (Gainesville: University of Florida Press, 1968), 283. Citations hereafter in text.

CHAPTER 7

Removal

Gina Caison

Perhaps the most readily recognized moment of Removal in the nineteenth century is the Cherokee Trail of Tears, which forced the vast majority of the Cherokee Nation west to Indian Territory in the late 1830s. This genocidal event, though horrific, is neither singular nor exceptional in the period from 1820 to 1860 in the United States. In fact, the forced removal and relocation of Indigenous peoples defines much of the period, and these events are more than footnotes to the era's other conflicts. They are instead central to the political landscape of the period leading up to the US Civil War, and readers can find these resonances in almost any literary work from the period from virtually every region of the continent.

Many scholars of previous generations often viewed the attempted ethnic cleansing of the Indigenous peoples of the American continent as an anomalous, shameful blip in an otherwise positive uplift narrative of American exceptionalism that imagined the United States as a uniquely just nation founded on universal human freedoms. Rightly, very few contemporary scholars of the period hold onto Cold War–era narratives of American exceptionalism; however, I argue that taking a close look at considerations of Indigenous Removal reveals how scholars can accidentally lapse back into exceptionalist narratives about the United States via southern exceptionalism and an incomplete consideration of Native American literature and history. This insidious creep of American exceptionalism appears today in casual discourse as social media users regularly evoke ideas of "this isn't my country" in response to Trump-ism or suggest that "red state" politics thrive only in southeastern states. In other words, from an Indigenous studies perspective, this has *always* been America, and that America is *everywhere*. Returning to take a close look at Indigenous history and literature in this period illuminates the ways that scholars and students can challenge this logic and appreciate a more complete picture of how Removal continues to affect our present.

For example, examining Removal challenges those interested in the period to see Andrew Jackson not so much as an exceptionally bad (though he was) and thus anomalous individual president but as the product of a long colonial process baked fully within the founding of the United States as a nation. Coverage of various Removal policies and actions was ubiquitous in the era's newspapers, and there can be little doubt that many authors of the period (regardless of race, gender, class, or ethnic background) were highly aware of the cultural debates about the US interaction with Indigenous nations and peoples.[1] In short, there can be little engagement with the cultural landscape of the nineteenth century without a recognition of the ways that the physical land of that landscape was and is Indigenous land.

Perhaps more importantly, studying Removal during this period requires that scholars widen their lenses on the various ways that Removal manifested itself during the period. Removal was and is more than the Indian Removal Act of 1830. Removal was and is more than the forced relocation of entire Indigenous nations. Indeed, Removal encompasses these events, but it also goes well beyond them. It includes the individual intimidation and bullying of Indigenous farmers off their lands on the Atlantic seaboard.[2] It includes the kidnapping of individual Indigenous girls into domestic labor, enslavement, and sexual exploitation.[3] It includes the removal of Native children from their homes by force or coercion into boarding and residential schools.[4] It includes the state-sanctioned murder of California Native peoples during the Gold Rush.[5] It includes the removal of Indigenous peoples from census categories, forcing them into a black and white racial binary.[6] It includes the removal of Indigenous human remains from their graves.[7] It includes all of these actions of individual settlers as well as the supporting policies of state and federal governments. Most importantly, Removal includes the ongoing erasure of Indigenous history and literature in textbooks, literary anthologies, and syllabi focused on the period. Thus, Removal includes the impulse to see Removal as exceptional rather than as foundational to the literature, politics, and history of nineteenth-century America.

While many of us who work in nineteenth-century literary studies no longer profess exceptionalist paradigms or understandings of the period in our scholarship or teaching, American exceptionalism still creeps into our assumptions about the period, and it is buttressed by southern exceptionalism – the belief that the US South represents a distinct region that serves as the exclusive repository of the nation's worst ideologies and simultaneously its down-home authenticity and hospitality. Most students of the period recognize that the idea that the United States is somehow a unique nation founded on the equality of persons is undermined quickly by the fact of the enslavement of Africans and African Americans. Frederick Douglass captures this argument in his 1852 speech "What to the Slave Is Fourth of July?" However, many times the problems of the early nation were and are imaginatively quarantined to the southern states as Jennifer Rae Greeson demonstrates in *Our South: Geographic Fantasy and the Rise of National Literature* (2010). Both within the field of US literary studies and more broadly in US culture, the region of the US South is imagined as holding all of the nation's ills and moral failings, allowing the rest of the nation to float free of its deep material and psychological investments in enslavement economies and white supremacy. Although scholars of the period may no longer structure courses around tenets of progressive fantasies based on American exceptionalism, the idea that the US South and its enslavement system signify an aberration of American ideals unwittingly reinforces exceptionalist narratives. In other words, unexamined southern exceptionalism continually bolsters American exceptionalism even for those who may claim to denounce the latter.

While enslavement is the most well-known example of how southern exceptionalism continues to function in literary histories of the period, Removal is just as often associated with narratives of supposedly unique southern avarice. Without a doubt, the Indian Removal Act focused on the US Southeast is one of the most disgusting examples of US genocidal policies toward Indigenous peoples. The situation was exacerbated by the demands of the region's plantation economy that consistently required more and more land for exploitation. One of the great complexities of the Indian Removal Act is how it affected those southeastern Native individuals who had adopted the plantation economy and the enslavement of Black people as part of their own lives in the region.[8] Many prominent members of southeastern Native nations such as the Cherokee, Creek, Choctaw, and others had begun farming large sections of their tribal lands using enslaved people and consolidating estates that included large houses and multiple industries that were in line with the exploitative practices of their white southern counterparts. Importantly, many of the citizens of southeastern tribal nations were not enslaving African American people, but these threads of life – land theft, enslavement, and Indigenous sovereignty – had become entangled over the previous one hundred years of settler colonialism in the region, and it's very likely the process of Black enslavement affected the lives and worldviews of even those individuals who did not participate in the practice directly. Also complicating matters is the fact that many of the Native families who had adopted the practices of the southern plantation economy also provided educational and economic opportunities for their children, who in many cases became the very people with the most access to the press and the courts to fight the federal Indian Removal Act and the individual states as they attempted to forcibly relocate entire Native nations. Not only were they defending tribal sovereignty, which in many cases remained paramount in their work, but often these men were also defending their own economic interests as plantation owners. Therefore, it remains important to understand how the Indian Removal Act satisfied white southerners who coveted not just mythically "undeveloped" Indigenous land but specific plantation estates and industries, including hotels, taverns, and ferries operated by Indigenous people.

However, scholars should recognize that though the Indian Removal Act was focused largely on the US South, it was by no means unique in policy or practice across the rest of the nation. Writing in 1835, Pequot author William Apess offered strong words about the social reform efforts of white people in Massachusetts who professed themselves as allies of the Cherokee Nation in Georgia but neglected to see the same policies at work against the Indigenous peoples in their home state. He writes:

> As our brethren, the white men of Massachusetts, have recently manifested much sympathy for the red men of the Cherokee nation, who have suffered much from their white brethren; as it is contended in this State, that our red brethren, the Cherokees, should be an independent people, having the privileges of the white men; we, the red men of the Marshpee tribe, consider it a favorable time to speak. We are not free. We wish to be so, as much as the red men of Georgia. How will the white man of Massachusetts ask favor for the red men of the South, while the poor Marshpee red men, his near neighbors, sigh in bondage?[9]

Apess's words in no way excuse the white people of Georgia from their terrible acts (he specifically names Georgia's Governor Lumpkin for his attempt to nullify the Supreme Court ruling in *Worcester v. Georgia*), but he offers a clear example from the period that shows how the ideas of an exceptional South allowed so-called socially progressive white people in Massachusetts to ignore the same issues close to home. Furthermore, he specifically highlights the misplaced belief that Andrew Jackson was an aberration of US leadership, writing, "Other editors speak ill enough of Gen. Jackson's treatment of the Southern Indians. Why do they not also speak ill of all the head men and great chiefs who have evil entreated the people of Marshpee"?[10] The Removal of southeastern Indigenous nations may have served as a focal point for the crises facing Native peoples during the period, but as Apess charges, it was by no means an exceptional occurrence.

In fact, there are so many acts of forced relocation of Indigenous peoples across the continent during this period that it would be difficult to catalogue them all here, and it would be impossible to do justice to the details involved in each specific case. And while federal policy buttressed many of these acts, as Tim Alan Garrison demonstrates in *The Legal Ideology of Removal: The Southern Judiciary and the Sovereignty of Native American Nations* (2002), many of the particular facets of these moments played out in state courts. In fact, the most exceptional occurrence in the history of Removal in this period might very well be those tribal nations and peoples who managed to hold on to traditional homelands despite coercive treaties, intimidation, physical and biological warfare, and economic exploitation. Given the pervasiveness of Removal before the US Civil War, it comes as little surprise that so many of the era's authors at some point explore the meaning of Indigenous land and history in their work.

The non-Native writers of the period who engage questions of Native land dispossession and national memory – usually in troublingly romantic terms – include figures such as Charles Brockden Brown, Washington Irving, James Fennimore Cooper, Catharine Maria Sedgwick, Lydia Sigourney, Lydia Maria Child, Ralph Waldo Emerson, Henry David Thoreau, Nathaniel Hawthorne, Henry Wadsworth Longfellow, Herman Melville, and Walt Whitman, among others. Non-Native writers writing primarily after the US Civil War return to issues of Native American identity, sovereignty, and belonging in the United States; these include but are certainly not limited to Mark Twain, Brett Harte, Henry Adams, Constance Fenimore Woolson, Jack London, and Booker T. Washington. And though he does not name it as such, Charles Chesnutt draws from community and family connections with Indigenous peoples in eastern North Carolina to explore questions of binary racial divides and Black Indigenous identity in the region from the pre–Civil War period through Reconstruction. In other words, the questions that Removal raises for the vast majority of nineteenth-century writers cannot be easily assigned to any one period or to any single group of people.

Therefore, when we focus on Removal we find that we must reexamine our structures of periodization that delineate even the bounded dates of this volume. Even though Removal is most often closely associated with the period leading up to the US Civil War, in many ways Thomas Jefferson was the initial architect for what would become the policy of forced and coerced relocation.[11] As early as 1776, Jefferson advocates for the forced removal of the Cherokee beyond the Mississippi, writing to Edmund Pendelton:

> I hope the Cherokees will now be driven beyond the Mississippi & that this in future will be declared to the Indians that invariable consequence of their beginning a war. Our contest with Britain is too serious and too great to permit any possibility of avocation from the Indians. This then is the season for driving them off, & our Southern colonies are happily rid of every other enemy & may exert their whole force in that quarter.[12]

During his presidency, he also outlined strategies for Removal in his private correspondence, and in the first decade of the nineteenth century, William Henry Harrison worked in Jefferson's administration to negotiate the acquisition of lands and the subsequent relocation of many Indigenous nations in present-day Illinois, Indiana, Michigan, and Wisconsin.[13] Although one could argue that Harrison's work was the result of legally sanctioned treaties, the circumstances of treaty negotiations often involved fraud, false promises, and threats of inevitable violence. Furthermore, Removal continued after the onset of the Civil War, as the cases of the 1864 Long Walk of the Navajo and the 1873 forced relocation of Pacific northwestern Modoc freedom fighters to Indian Territory illustrate.[14] Ultimately, the continued occupation of Indigenous lands by settlers across the continent indicates that Removal policy is ongoing in the twenty-first century as the United States and non-Native individuals continue to reap the benefits of the genocidal past.

In this way, one might say that considerations of Removal also suffer from what could be considered "antebellum exceptionalism," where one imagines that the US Civil War constitutes an event where there is a universal change for the better in the foundational problems of the nation.[15] Certainly, Emancipation and the Thirteenth, Fourteenth, and Fifteenth Amendments constitute an enormous correction of US policy. At the same time, the US Civil War did not change (and in some cases exacerbated) the pressure on Indigenous peoples to give up their lands. President Lincoln oversaw the largest mass execution in US history when in 1862 he ordered the hanging of thirty-eight Santee Dakota fighters from the Dakota War, notably an action he did not pursue against Confederate generals (saving the commander of Andersonville Prison, who was changed with war crimes rather than treason). Although Lincoln commuted the death sentences of 256 fighters, the fact remains that the Dakota War in Minnesota resulted precisely from the US failing to uphold its end of a treaty for land sessions and the relocation of Santee people to reservations.[16] As white settlers moved west during and following the Civil War, Native peoples paid the price.[17] Therefore, Removal cannot be quarantined to the period before the war (or after). And while the conflict between the Union and Confederacy may have worked toward excising the demon of slavery from the nation, scholars and readers of the period should not see the pre–Civil War period as a neat or appropriate divider of Indigenous literature or history.

To participate in any of these exceptionalisms – American, southern, or antebellum – operates to erase Indigenous authors and scholars from conversations about American literature. As a counter to that tendency, it is essential to center Indigenous voices in the study of Removal during the nineteenth century, and in our own era. Frequently, anthologies of American literature cover Removal via the Cherokee Trail of Tears. While there may be one or two Euro-American authors featured on the subject – Ralph Waldo Emerson's letter to Martin Van Buren is a perennial favorite – the Cherokee-authored "Memorials" tend to appear as the central "Indigenous voice" in the matter. Without a doubt these Memorials are immensely important texts that demonstrate rhetorical dexterity and the collective voice of a Nation. They deserve to be included in the discussion. However, anthologies have been slower to include the individual works of other Native voices protesting Removal. Elias Boudinot appears with some frequency because of his editorial leadership of the *Cherokee Phoenix*, but this work is often structured as exceptional. And yet, when one surveys the newspapers of the period, Indigenous thinkers are everywhere. Cherokee authors John Ridge (father of novelist John Rollin Ridge) and David Vann are writing regularly in national newspapers as part of their paid work on behalf of the Muscogee Creek Nation. They produce content both from their own hands and as translators and consultants to Muscogee leadership that opposed Creek entrepreneur/political figure William McIntosh and his work to push through the fraudulent Treaty of Indian Springs.[18] It is important to include these authors in discussions of Removal alongside the collectively authored Memorials – not to fetishize the individual author but to avoid imagining the Indigenous people undergoing extreme abuse as a nameless mass, a structure all too common in the way white America portrays groups of people whom they oppress.

Furthermore, while I – a non-Native scholar – am writing this piece, I want to be unequivocal about a centrally important fact of Removal history: Indigenous peoples are *the only ones* who get to say what the history of Removal means for themselves and for the Indigenous communities of which they are a part. Indigenous scholars with rich interpretations of this period are too numerous to count. Insofar as literary scholarship goes, Cherokee scholar Daniel Heath Justice stands at the forefront of interpretation of the period as he offers a compelling reading of the fraudulent Treaty of New Echota, which resulted in the Trail of Tears, and places it in context both for its time and our own.[19] Similarly, Craig Womack's work in *Red on Red: Native American Literary Separatism* (1999) reckons profoundly with how to read the literature of the Muscogee Creek diaspora while maintaining a sensibility of grounded nationalism. Meanwhile, Jace and Laura Weaver have developed a classroom game for the "Reacting to the Past" series that asks students to grapple with the challenges of the Removal period for the Cherokee Nation.[20] For every type of Removal I outline above and for every instance of Removal that has affected an Indigenous nation or community, there is an Indigenous scholar working on interpreting these historical events for the present in a variety of publications and media. There is no shortage of nuanced sources, and this scholarship should lead the way for those wanting to engage with the topic.

Similarly, the need to see Removal as a phenomenon that stretches beyond the period under examination in this volume extends to how we imagine periodization and the relationship between nineteenth-century literature and contemporary works. Period is far too often taken as ontology ("I am a nineteenth-century Americanist") rather than a useful organizing heuristic for the bureaucratic parts of the academy, including course offerings and tables of contents. As scholars of American literature, we know that the common designations of periods tend to fall in line with certain traumatic moments of disunion and warfare – the Revolutionary War, the Civil War, World War I, and so on. And yet these designations strike me and many others as traumas of *white* America. It ignores the apocalyptic moments of the transatlantic slave trade for enslaved African and later African American people, Removal, the California Gold Rush, Allotment policy, Termination and Relocation under Public Law 280, and many other moments for nonwhite peoples of this continent that do more to explain the content and form of their literary works than white anxieties over the breakup of the United States. Understanding the literature of

Removal means understanding that thinking with only the traditional literary periods just won't do.

As I previously stated, Removal has not ended; it is ongoing. Settlers still occupy lands stolen during the period, and they pay their individual property taxes to the state governments that committed the theft. Therefore, we cannot talk about Removal literature as being of the past or as a discrete moment. Instead, the literature of Removal is as present now as it was in the 1820s. Contemporary authors including LeAnne Howe, Blake Hausman, and Brandon Hobson, among many others, help to illuminate Removal in the twenty-first century.[21] Making this connection is not simply a gesture toward the importance of historical fiction. Instead, I am arguing for a reconsideration of periodization that recognizes that the timeline and designated points we use are a profound example of continued colonialism and that we can engage Indigenous literatures more fully by questioning the assumptions embedded in our temporal construction of periods. So while many American literary scholars have worked to productively complicate many facets of what we might call the American literary canon, I do not think we have quite taken periodization to task as much as we could or as an emphasis on or respect for Indigenous methodologies would require us to do. Our very calendars are colonial impositions and the establishment of an imperial time is yet another act of removing Indigenous knowledges from the world. As scholars such as Lisa Brooks and Mark Rifkin have established, time, and how we mark it, matters immensely for sovereignty.[22] Just as tribal nations have homelands with languages and scientific knowledges specific to that area that we all should make a point of knowing and acknowledging, there are also Indigenous understandings of time and calendar systems rooted to specific geographical places. Or put another way: What year is it where you are?

As demonstrated by the example of temporality, at the heart of examining the literature of Removal is examining the ongoing question of Indigenous sovereignty. Numerous authors, both Native and non-Native, from the 1820s and 1830s articulated this clearly. William Apess stands as a central theorist of Indigenous sovereignty. Similarly, Emerson's letter to Van Buren could take a more central place in our understanding of the relationship between that canonical author's concept of self-reliance and the concept of sovereignty, particularly if we examine Emerson's diary entries in Volumes V and XII of *The Journals and Miscellaneous Notebooks* around the dates of composition of his letter to the President.[23] Issues of sovereignty and territorial control in the early Republic occur across the

1840s memoir *Chainbreaker's War* by the eponymous Seneca leader whom Americans knew as Governor Blacksnake, even though he does not directly address Removal policy.[24] Throughout the history of Indigenous literature, sovereignty has remained paramount, and any discussion of Removal must acknowledge that fact.

Importantly, however, the time between 1820 and 1860 was not marked by easy alliances or allegiances between Indigenous nations or individuals. Removal involved a complex set of events that divided tribal nations as the US government worked in multiple ways to steal Indigenous lands for the ever-expanding nation. These divisions within Indigenous nations can often take center stage as non-Native people (both then and now) subtlely shift the blame onto Native peoples for "not working together" to prevent these crises. This shift in focus and rhetorical construction only works to let the federal and state governments off the hook as the perpetrators of the ultimate crimes.[25] Many treaties that effectuated Removal were made possible by conflicting factions within one Nation. In these cases, it is difficult to determine personal motivations, but it is safe to say that they likely range from personal greed to lofty ideals of "knowing best" how to preserve one's Nation in the face of state and federal officials who would turn their backs on and even openly encourage violence against Indigenous peoples who remained on their homelands.

These interpersonal complexities affected the life of Ojibwe poet Jane Johnston Schoolcraft, whose white Indian-agent husband Henry was a supporter not only of Andrew Jackson but also of Removal policy. As Robert Dale Parker explains: "When [Henry] met Jackson in Washington over the Christmas holiday of 1835, [he] wrote Jane a bubbly, awestruck tale of the meeting. He flattered Jackson and Jackson's secretary's family with gifts from Indian country, including moccasins and cakes of maple sugar from the north, prepared under the direction of Mrs. Schoolcraft."[26] Parker goes on to interpret this event, noting the embedded contradictions of the period writ small onto this one family:

> But these many years later, as we recover the legacy of a barely known Indian writer, it gives one pause to think of Jackson and his entourage savoring her gift of maple sugar, and it underlines how Schoolcraft was integrated into the system that exploited her, just as she and her family's cultural and linguistic knowledge were integrated into her Indian-agent husband's efforts to admire, aid, and at the same time conquer, steal from, and diminish her Indian people.[27]

The Schoolcraft example demonstrates how the political landscape of Removal in the 1830s not only involved politicians in the deep north of the upper Midwest and Indigenous peoples of other Nations, but also set up questions of transitioning gender roles for Native women as they negotiated traditional expectations of their Indigenous communities with those of Euro-American perceptions of women's duties and political allegiances. And while we cannot know directly what Schoolcraft thought about these circumstances, what we do know is that these were the circumstances that she lived and wrote through.

It is no exaggeration to say that Removal touched nearly every facet of life in nearly every part of the continent from 1820 to 1860. Although the US South did not define Removal nor did Removal stop at the borders of southern states, Removal certainly shaped much of the eventual Confederacy and the region today. Particularly in Georgia, Removal policy worked (much like the South Carolina nullification crisis) to test how much the federal government would let individual states ignore federal law or Supreme Court decisions. When students ponder questions such as what made the Confederacy think that it could in fact secede from the Union with little repercussion, as teachers we can turn their attention back to Removal policy and Jackson's willful disregard for the Supreme Court decision in *Worcester v. Georgia*. When examined from this perspective, the better question might be: Why *wouldn't* southeastern states think they could behave however they wanted with regards to policy, property, and human life? As I have argued in my other work, in this schema the Civil War becomes not so much an apocalyptic break but the next item in a predictable set of occurrences where white southerners were emboldened by a series of non-responses to their actions that defied federal and judicial oversight.[28] Put differently, we cannot fully understand the later Civil War without understanding Removal.

Perhaps one of the best examples of this is pro-Removal, pro-Confederacy, proslavery South Carolina writer William Gilmore Simms. Indeed, nearly every last thing about his political and moral stances was abhorrent, but he cannot be dismissed as simply an uneducated outlier among the nation's writers. In fact, Simms was a relatively well-educated writer who considered his own material and philosophical interests as a land-owning white man with some sustained thought, and his deep self-interest in his own material privilege led him to espouse troublingly white supremacist and pro-enslavement viewpoints.[29] Across Simms's work, readers can see the inner machinations of how white southerners made the psychological leap from recognizing themselves as settlers to imagining themselves as embattled patriots defending their "homelands." One especially telling example is Simms's creatively embellished, short nonfiction prose piece "The Broken Arrow" (1844) where he waxes poetic about

William McIntosh, the Creek leader I mentioned earlier who negotiated the fraudulent Treaty of Indian Springs, essentially selling out his fellow Muscogee people so he could retain his own estate.[30] As a result of this negotiation, McIntosh was executed by his own people, as his actions constituted a capital offense. Simms offers a strong depiction of the tragedy he sees as McIntosh's predicament in being both a successful land owner and enslaver who cannot make the masses of his people understand his political position in the plantation economy.[31] Throughout the piece, Simms's sympathy for McIntosh seems on the brink of empathy – a rare moment for the author in his depiction of nonwhite people. However, if read closely, what the story reveals is that Simms is not mourning McIntosh the Creek man; rather, he is positioning him as a martyr of a paternalistic plantation economy that knows best what others with less economic power "need." In this literary example, readers see not just Simms's own narcissistic interest in his material interests as reflected in McIntosh's fate, but something bigger: the relationship that Removal shared with the exponential arrogance of the southern plantation economy. Not only were white southerners able to use stolen lands to extend the abuses of enslavement and destructive agricultural practices; they were then also able to co-opt the trauma of Indigenous Removal stories to explain their own supposed beleaguerment and "victimization" at the hands of the federal government as they approached secession.

Given this history of affective transference and manufactured white pathos, it is all the more important that readers approach Removal stories today aware of the tendency of non-Native audiences to render the history as one that allows personal catharsis, or what Julia Coates calls "the litany of loss."[32] This is as dangerous as it is disturbing. Because while the nineteenth century's many instances of Removal were moments of enormous violence, tragedy, and sadness, they were also moments of great resistance. For an example, one can look to the 1832 armed resistance led by Sauk leader Black Hawk as he led a coalition of Native peoples back to the territory the US government had gained in the disputed Treaty of St. Louis in 1804.[33] Or one could look to the extended military resistance of the Seminole as they worked against their forced removal from the place currently known as Florida.[34] Indigenous peoples also resisted Removal via the press, their literature, and the courts.[35] In other words, non-Native readers should resist the urge to see Removal stories from the nineteenth century as *the end* of the story.

And if non-Native readers acknowledge that Removal is ongoing, then they must too acknowledge that Indigenous resistance to Removal is likewise a story that continues into the present across the continent. As Daniel Heath Justice writes about Cherokee Removal: "the story of the Trail isn't one just of tragedy, although it's unmistakably that, too. It's also a story about defiance, about enduring the unimaginable and still continuing on, living to rebuild and emerge from the ashes sadder but stronger than ever."[36] Although it is important to recognize that Removal stories should not serve as cathartic tragedy narratives for non-Native people, it is also important to resist the urge to romanticize Indigenous resistance in such a way that appropriates it for non-Native causes. Certainly, the Seminole leader Osceola strikes a heroic figure. However, his heroism deserves more consideration than the pathos that Walt Whitman uses to frame his death in the "Second Annex" to the deathbed edition of *Leaves of Grass*.[37] Similarly, and perhaps it should go without saying, honoring Indigenous resistance leaders has no relation to the faux "honor" accorded mascots. Simply put, Removal is not a metaphor. It is a lived event that, in one form or another, has affected the vast majority of Indigenous peoples and that requires more of a response than passing regret from non-Natives. After all, guilt, whether it takes the form of romance or tragedy, is rarely – if ever – a productive emotion.

Therefore, when looking back into the nineteenth century, scholars, students, readers, and thinkers must ask themselves what assumptions and exceptionalisms they bring to the table about stories of Indigenous Removal. Perhaps most importantly, if people are led to ask themselves what they would have done during this period of nineteenth-century transition, then they might also ask themselves what they will do today, for Removal is as ever present now as it was then.

Notes

1 Exemplary primary documents include "Cherokee Indians – Proceedings in Congress," *The Southron*, February 23, 1828; "New York Indians," *Georgia Journal*, January 23, 1830; and Opothle Yoholo et al., "Letter to Col. Thomas L. McKenney," *National Journal*, March 3, 1826. All at the American Antiquarian Society, Worcester, MA.

2 Malinda Maynor Lowery, *Lumbee Indians in the Jim Crow South: Race, Identity, and the Making of a Nation* (Chapel Hill: University of North Carolina Press, 2010).

3 Sarah Deer, *The Beginning and End of Rape: Confronting Sexual Violence in Native America* (Minneapolis: University of Minnesota Press, 2015).

4 K. Tsianina Lomawaima, Brenda J. Child, and Margaret L. Archuleta, eds., *Away from Home: American Indian Boarding School Experiences, 1879–2000* (Phoenix, AZ: Heard Museum, 2000).

5 Jack Norton, *Genocide in Northwestern California: When Our Worlds Cried* (San Francisco, CA: Indian History Press, 1979); Brendan C. Lindsay, *Murder State: California's Native American Genocide, 1846–1873* (Lincoln: University of Nebraska Press, 2015); Benjamin Madley, *An American Genocide: The United States and the California Indian Catastrophe, 1846–1873* (New Haven, CT: Yale University Press, 2016).

6 Douglas J. Smith, "The Campaign for Racial Purity and the Erosion of Paternalism in Virginia, 1922–1930: 'Nominally White, Biologically Mixed, and Legally Negro,'" *Journal of Southern History* 68, no. 1 (2002): 65–106.

7 Devon A. Mihesuah, "American Indians, Anthropologists, Pothunters, and Repatriation," in *Repatriation Reader: Who Owns American Indian Remains?*, ed. Devon A. Mihesuah (Lincoln: University of Nebraska Press, 2000).

8 Tiya Miles, *The House on Diamond Hill: A Cherokee Plantation Story* (Chapel Hill: University of North Carolina Press, 2010).

9 William Apess, "Indian Nullification of the Unconstitutional Laws of Massachusetts, Relative to the Marshpee Tribe: or, The Pretended Riot Explained," in *On Our Own Ground: The Complete Writings of William Apess, a Pequot*, ed. Barry O'Connell (Amherst: University of Massachusetts Press, 1992), 205.

10 Ibid., 238.

11 Anthony Wallace, *Jefferson and the Indians: The Tragic Fate of the First Americans* (Cambridge, MA: Harvard University Press, 1999).

12 Thomas Jefferson, *Writings*, ed. Merrill D. Peterson (New York: Library of America, 1984), 754.

13 Robert M. Owens, *Mr. Jefferson's Hammer: William Henry Harrison and the Origins of American Indian Policy* (Norman: University of Oklahoma Press, 2011).

14 Jennifer Denetdale, *The Long Walk: The Forced Navajo Exile* (Langhorne, PA: Chelsea House Publishers, 2007), and Boyd Cothran, *Remembering the Modoc War: Redemptive Violence and the Making of American Innocence* (Chapel Hill: University of North Carolina Press, 2017).

15 Christopher Hager and Cody Marrs make a similar point. However, they never consider Removal nor Indigenous literature, history, or politics in their argument, which seems like a missed opportunity for showing just how fraught current period delineations are for capturing the nuance of the nineteenth century. Christopher Hager and Cody Marrs "Against 1865: Reperiodizing the Nineteenth Century," *J19: The Journal of Nineteenth-Century Americanists* 1, no. 2 (Fall 2013): 259–284.

16 Scott W. Berg, *38 Nooses: Lincoln, Little Crow, and the Beginning of the Frontier's End* (New York: Vintage Press, 2013), and Gary Clayton Anderson and Alan R. Woolworth, eds., *Through Dakota Eyes: Narrative Accounts of the Minnesota Indian War of 1862* (Minneapolis: Minnesota Historical Society Press, 1988).

17 Dee Brown, *Bury My Heart at Wounded Knee* (New York: Henry Holt & Co., 1970).

18 For example, see John Ridge and David Vann, "Letter," *National Journal,* March 3, 1826, or the above-cited "Letter to Col. Thomas L. McKenney."

19 Daniel Heath Justice, *Our Fire Survives the Storm: A Cherokee Literary History* (Minneapolis: University of Minnesota Press, 2006).

20 Jace Weaver and Laura Weaver, *Red Clay, 1835: Cherokee Removal and the Meaning of Sovereignty* (New York: W. W. Norton, 2017).

21 LeAnne Howe, *Shell Shaker* (San Francisco, CA: Aunt Lute Books, 2001), and *Spiral of Fire,* dir. Carol Cornsilk (Lincoln, NE: Vision Maker, 2005); Blake M. Hausman, *Riding the Trail of Tears* (Lincoln: University of Nebraska Press, 2011); and Brandon Hobson *The Removed* (New York: Ecco/HarperCollins, 2021).

22 Lisa Brooks, "The Primacy of the Present, the Primacy of Place: Navigating the Spiral of History in the Digital World," *PMLA* 127, no. 2 (March 2012): 308–316; Mark Rifkin, *Beyond Settler Time: Temporal Sovereignty and Indigenous Self-Determination* (Durham, NC: Duke University Press, 2019.)

23 Ralph Waldo Emerson. *The Journals and Miscellaneous Notebooks, vol. V: 1835–1838,* ed. Merton M. Sealts (Cambridge, MA: Belknap Press of Harvard University Press, 1965), and *The Journals and Miscellaneous Notebooks, vol. XII: 1835–1862,* ed. Linda Allardt (Cambridge, MA: Belknap Press of Harvard University Press, 1976).

24 Chainbreaker, *Chainbreaker's War: A Seneca Chief Remembers the American Revolution,* ed. Jeanne Winston Adler (Hensonville, NY: Black Dome Press, 2002).

25 Julia Coates, *Trail of Tears* (Santa Barbara, CA: ABC-CLIO, LLC Greenwood, 2014).

26 Jane Johnston Schoolcraft, *The Sound the Stars Make Rushing through the Sky: The Writings of Jane Johnston Schoolcraft,* ed. Robert Dale Parker (Philadelphia: University of Pennsylvania Press, 2007), 45.

27 Ibid., 45.

28 Gina Caison, *Red States: Indigeneity, Settler Colonialism, and Southern Studies* (Athens: University of Georgia Press, 2018).

29 Todd Hagstette, ed., *Reading William Gilmore Simms: Essays of Introduction to the Author's Canon* (Columbia: University of South Carolina Press, 2017).

30 Michael D. Green, *The Politics of Indian Removal: Creek Government and Society in Crisis* (Lincoln: University of Nebraska Press, 1985), and Benjamin W. Griffith, *McIntosh and Weatherford: Creek Indian Leaders* (Tuscaloosa: University of Alabama Press, 1998).

31 William Gilmore Simms, "The Broken Arrow," in *An Early and Strong Sympathy: The Indian Writings of William Gilmore Simms,* ed. John Caldwell Guilds and Charles Hudson (Columbia: University of South Carolina Press, 2003), 81–98.

32 Julia Coates, "None of Us Is Supposed to Be Here: Ethnicity, Nationality, and the Production of Cherokee Histories" (PhD diss., University of New Mexico, 2002).

33 Patrick J. Jung, *The Black Hawk War of 1832.* (Norman: University of Oklahoma Press, 2007).

34 John Missall and Mary Lou Missall, *The Seminole Wars: America's Longest Indian Conflict* (Gainesville: University Press of Florida, 2004).

35 Phillip Round, *Removable Type: Histories of the Book in Indian Country, 1663–1880* (Chapel Hill: University of North Carolina Press, 2010).

36 Justice, *Our Fire Survives the Storm*, 58.

37 Kathryn Walkiewicz, "Portraits and Politics: The Specter of Osceola in Leaves of Grass," *Walt Whitman Quarterly Review*, no. 25 (Winter 2008): 108–115.

CHAPTER 8

Abolition

Martha Schoolman

The US Civil War (1861–1865) was a war to end slavery and preserve the union, but to view it simply as abolitionism's final and most successful phase is to flatten a complex tradition of dissent whose origins and goals were never simply, or even primarily, national. Indeed, one of the more enduring side effects of the US abolitionist movement's apparent victory with Lincoln's issuing of the emancipation proclamation on January 1, 1863, and the confederate surrender on April 9, 1865, is that the movement found itself written into a triumphant state narrative to which it would scarcely have imagined itself subscribing. In their most radical moments, abolitionists offered to stake the very concept of a United States in the cause of emancipation, asserting as Henry David Thoreau did in the context of the Mexican-American War (1846–1848) that "[t]his people must cease to hold slaves, and to make war on Mexico, *though it cost them their existence as a people.*"[1] However, popular histories have taught us to view the US South as the emancipation era's emblematic region of dissent from the nation, with the long racist afterlife of Confederate secession finding voice in contemporary white southern forms of aggrieved commemoration such as KKK rallies and statues of Confederate figures like Robert E. Lee menacing the public square. From this perspective, such "southern nationalism" represents a residually proslavery response to a homogenizing yet also multiracial "northern aggression." The northern winner's version of such a history likewise leaves the normative "Americanness" of antislavery – as an organized protest movement, as a frame for cultural production, as a vague pro-union ethos – unquestioned: if the "lost cause" South is taken to stand for slavery and regionalism, the triumphant North must reciprocally embody both abolition and nationalism.

Recent scholarly trends in the literary histories of slavery and abolitionism have been placing pressure on this settled national-sectional story. Whereas traditional approaches to US literary study tended to read the literature of slavery and abolition as a subset of "Civil War literature," thus implying that its main role was to anticipate, reflect, and then commemorate a crisis in US nation-building successfully overcome, newer research has focused instead on the way this literature engages aspects of slavery and abolition that variously contest, exceed, or elude the simplified national frame. Methodologically speaking, this newer literary history is less preoccupied with discerning literature's role as a mirror or agent of a short menu of already agreed-on ideas of historical causality, and more inclined to dwell on what we might consider to be literature's proprietary hold on history: as a storage site for connections severed or forgotten; as the speculative realm where possibilities are considered, utopias contemplated, and plans fictively realized; as the place where faint anachronistic reverberations are nurtured into life in poetry and prose.

Removing the confining teleological frame of the Civil War opens conceptual space for rethinking the geographic scope of the literary history of slavery and abolition as well. When the US Civil War is placed at the center of inquiry, the United States tends to regard itself as a nation-state uniquely affected by the institution of slavery and the struggle for emancipation. Only one modern nation ended African slavery through a pitched internal war fought principally (although by no means exclusively) among white folk, this mostly tacit chain of reasoning goes, so the struggle over slavery must be a characteristically US struggle, and the literature of slavery and abolition must be nationally distinctive as well. When the frame of analysis expands to acknowledge slavery and abolition in their broad historical sweep and complexity, however, we are able to apprehend the US sectional struggle over slavery as only one in a series of such struggles – local, national, and imperial; armed, discursive, and political – that spanned the Western Hemisphere and continued to shape and then reshape the global resource economy for close to 300 years (depending on how we count). A transnational or postnational approach to the US literatures of slavery and abolition works to access the role of literature in recovering, understanding, promoting, and working through the implications of this much longer history.

To such a comparative, transnational perspective, then, it is little more than an unhelpful cliché to claim, as many still do, that African slavery is "America's original sin."[2] Given its near-ubiquity in the European-colonized Western hemisphere, African slavery is probably better described as "imperialism's original sin," or, more pointedly, as "capitalism's origi*nating* sin." The extractive economics of the plantation were a central feature of the waves of European colonization that took hold in the Caribbean after Columbus and spread outward. African labor was both one of the principal resources extracted by long-distance trade and the principal means used by Europeans to profit from the intensive cultivation of indigo, sugar, coffee, rice, and cotton in the tropical and subtropical regions of the Americas.

From this broadened vantage, the enslaved who found means to resist were the first abolitionists, and the Haitian Revolution (1791–1804) was the first successful large-scale antislavery war. The emancipation process everywhere else was piecemeal by comparison. As the rhetoric of the American and French Revolutions makes particularly clear, the European Age of Revolution harbored certain pervasive, if incompletely acted-on humanistic ideas about what David Brion Davis famously named "the problem of slavery in the age of revolution."[3] Enlightenment conceptions of freedom and equality worked quite successfully as rationales for white bourgeois revolutionary nationalism, a fact whose galling significance as an alibi for continued slaveholding served as a particular spur to furious abolitionist eloquence.[4] But these ideas did likewise provide at least part of the moral context for the abolition of the Atlantic slave trade in 1808 and a patchwork of antislavery policy actions throughout the Americas, including, for example, British West Indian emancipation in 1834, and emancipation in the Danish Caribbean and in the rest of the French West Indies in 1848. The US North initiated a state-by-state emancipation process late in the eighteenth century, and the national revolutions in the former Spanish America were also frequently followed within a few years by emancipation, as was the case in Mexico. The US South was therefore a late entrant into a hemispheric emancipation process that began in Haiti and ended in Brazil in 1888.

Abolitionist activity is thus perhaps best understood as having originated with direct action on the plantation, with what Michel-Rolph Trouillot describes in the case of Haiti as a "[r]evolution ... not preceded or accompanied by an explicit intellectual discourse."[5] But, inspired by the bravery and, in some cases, the threat of black resistance, the movement spread beyond the context of local conditions and into the world of print dissemination as those germinal figures of resistance were subsequently joined by the formerly enslaved, by the occasional former enslaver, and by free whites, diasporic Africans, and Indigenous people in solidarity with their cause. It is with this explosion into print that abolition becomes a literary configuration – built around the morally righteous yet never-far-from-problematic incitement among the free to speak on behalf of the enslaved.

Indeed, it is worth acknowledging here at the outset that the literary production connected to slavery and abolition has experienced a notable precarity in terms of literary favor since the period of its emergence and that the transnational/postnational historicist turn of the 1990s and early 2000s has provided the essential context for its latest return to critical salience. For more than half of the twentieth century, dismissive, inquiry-blocking claims to literary discernment have at various times marginalized whole categories of writing relating to slavery and abolition. The contexts and pretexts for such dismissals were many, but chief among them were two arguments that emerged in the late nineteenth century and crested in the 1950s, but endured into the 1980s: one, that woman-authored senti-mental novels such as *Uncle Tom's Cabin* were of poor aesthetic quality and politically unsophisticated, and thus unworthy of literary attention; and two, that the very abolitionist enthusiasm for publishing the testimony of formerly enslaved intellectuals like Frederick Douglass and William Wells Brown meant that the slave narrative should be regarded as untrust-worthy propaganda rather than either serious literature or a category of historical document worthy of close analysis.[6] Other sites of pervasive marginalization have at various times included the scholarly inattention to writing published in periodical rather than book form, the monumental neglect of African American writing in periodical and almost any other format, and the long-running argument that has arisen from alternately reactionary and critical perspectives that interprets abolitionist radicalism variously as insanity, delusion, and sublimated racism.[7]

Reversing these various forms of critical demotion, recent scholarship on the literatures of slavery and abolition premised on a transnational/post-national historicism has moved along two distinct but often intersecting tracks. The first is studies of the literary circulation and influence of antislavery writing rooted in a recognition of the transnational discursive infrastructure of the abolitionist movement. Such studies proceed from the acknowledgment that abolition depended on transatlantic, inter-American, and circum-Caribbean relations of communication, and finan-cial and tactical support, to bolster what was, within US borders, a minoritarian, censored, and sometimes violently suppressed resistance movement. The second is studies that attend to the literary consequences of black internationalism operating at times alongside and at times apart from the broader interracial antislavery movement. Such work examines the literary implications of the particular trajectories of African diasporic migration and connection, settlement and community-building practices, especially as stepped-up enforcement against fugitives from enslavement along with an intensification of racialized harassment generally after 1850 drove increasing numbers of US-born Black activists to seek temporary exile or permanent expatriation all over the Atlantic world, including in England, Canada, Mexico, Jamaica, Haiti, and Liberia. Viewed together, these intersecting traditions of antislavery literary invention form a diverse and complex discursive field whose implications have begun in recent decades to receive the scholarly attention they deserve.

Atlantic Abolitionism in Circulation

Whereas it is possible to say from our current vantage that the literature of slavery and abolition has always been transnational in scope, this now close-to-consensus academic framing has emerged in recent decades largely as a consequence of a particularly productive merger between two renascent academic modes, Atlantic history and book history. Atlantic history, as Bernard Bailyn, one of its foremost late twentieth-century institution-builders, narrates it, emerged in the middle of the twentieth century as a Cold War articulation of the West as a complex, networked civilization constellated, as one favorite formulation has it, around an Atlantic Ocean conceived of as its "inland sea."[8] This historiographic paradigm, initially reflecting the kind of military-strategic internationalism that gave rise to NATO, nonetheless harbored counterdiscursive implications. Even as the pursuit of an idea of an Atlantic civilization was invested in imperial expansion and unfettered trade, left historians such as Peter Linebaugh and Marcus Rediker, among others, worked to disclose the networked Atlantic as a conduit of dissent, resistance, and proletarian revolution instead.[9]

Scholarship emphasizing the counterdiscursive Atlantic was brought within the compass of US literary scholars with the publication of the British sociologist Paul Gilroy's *The Black Atlantic* (1993), a massively influential study that argued against what Gilroy viewed as the literary nationalism of African American studies in order to posit the black literary internationalism that emerged with abolitionism as "a counterculture of modernity."[10] The popularity of Gilroy's paradigm has given rise to any number of Atlanticist cultural studies projects, including the founding of the journal *Atlantic Studies* (2004), and scholarly work on such topics as "circumatlantic performance," and "the queer Atlantic."[11] But it is worth emphasizing in the present context that the founding insight of Gilroy's study derives from the cosmopolitan mobility and intellectual range of Black abolitionist writers such as Martin Delany and Frederick Douglass. For this reason, one of the scholarly sites where his work has been especially transformative is in the study of literary abolitionism.

The second intellectual trend informing contemporary scholarship on slavery and abolition is the collection of methodologies variously known as book history, print cultural studies, and media studies. Like Atlantic history, book history, as a discipline semi-detached from bibliography and librarianship, began to take shape in its majoritarian guise in the middle of the twentieth century, particularly with the publication of Lucien Febvre and Henri-Jean Martin's *L'Apparation du Livre* in French (1958) and Marshall McLuhan's *The Gutenberg Galaxy* in English (1962). Such work injected a crucial materialism into the historiography of ideas. In its attention to the production, sale, and consumption of print, book history, as Robert Darnton has suggested, holds together the seeming contradiction of "intellectual history ... from below."[12] In US literary studies, print culture studies has assumed increasing salience since the late 1980s, particularly following the enthusiastic reception of the work of two more disciplinary interlopers: the anthropologist Benedict Anderson's *Imagined Communities: Reflections on the Origins and Spread of Nationalism* (1983) and the translation into English by Thomas Burger of a work of 1960s Enlightenment sociology, Jürgen Habermas's *The Structural Transformation of the Public Sphere* (1989).[13] Both scholars emphasize the role of newspapers in forming the bourgeois collectivities that become nations, a focus that proved particularly influential to studies of the print-infused early national United States.[14]

As was the case with Atlantic studies, however, the encounter between print culture studies and the antislavery archive has proved challenging to any easy equation of print-facilitated community and political consensus.[15] Indeed, among the defining characteristics of the literary abolitionist tradition are a deep devotion to the propagation of dissent through print and other media and an active self-archiving practice developed early as a hedge against abolitionism's tendency to draw censorship and repressive violence.[16] As scholars including Trish Loughran and Teresa Goddu have shown, abolitionists used pamphlets, newspapers, books, almanacs, and postal campaigns to publicize their cause, an approach that worked as much to create far-flung networked communities of resistance as to heighten the contradictions that a theoretical print-mediated nationalism would seek to cover over. And precisely as a function of their role as agents of dissent, abolitionists developed their own ways of institutionalizing antislavery reading by establishing lending libraries, reading rooms, and literary societies; hand-selling songsters and slave narratives at antislavery events; and, in the years immediately following the Civil War, publishing memoirs and documentary histories, and making library bequests to secure their fragile legacy.[17]

Indeed, the abolitionist archive might be described as almost self-protectively vast and, thus, either overwhelming or illegible to scholarly approaches not specifically interested in investigating the interplay between race and the social lives of print. Perhaps for that reason, key moments of intensified activity in literary abolitionist scholarship within living memory have followed from shifts not only in ideological priorities and intellectual paradigms but also in the material and institutional conditions of research. One key site of development that continues to drive scholarship on slavery and abolition is the post-1968 concentration of intellectual energy and institutional resources around Black Studies. Black Studies emerged from the Civil Rights and Black Power movements while coinciding with the expansion of US public universities and libraries in the same era.[18] These two developments created a double demand for archival resources and scholarship around slavery and abolition: new libraries needed old titles to fill their empty shelves and scholars drawn to new models of academic inquiry centering race and resistance wanted to read and teach them. Out of these conditions were launched productively heterodox library-oriented reprint series on topics generally related to slavery, abolition, and African American history such as the Greenwood Press/Negro Universities Press and the New York Times/Arno Press series, as well as multiyear, multivolume editing projects such as *The Letters of William Lloyd Garrison* (1971–1981, six volumes) and *The Frederick Douglass Papers* (1973 to present, ten volumes and counting).[19] Martin Delany's *Blake*, the sprawling transnational serialized novel now regarded as central to the literary abolitionist canon, was first published in book format in 1970. As Ashraf Rushdy notes, the years 1968–1972 marked the decisive "restoration of slave testimony as historical evidence," prompting the publication of such compilations as Arna Bontemps's *Great Slave Narratives* (1969), Gilbert Osofsky's *Puttin' on Ole Massa* (1969), and George Rawick's *The American Slave: A Composite Biography* (1972–1976, nineteen volumes), among many others.[20]

As certain subdisciplines of literary studies moved away from archival research in the 1980s, historians and literary historicists continued the work of recovery and interpretation, particularly of Black abolitionist work, including in major projects of collation and interpretation like the *Black Abolitionist Papers* (1985–1992, five volumes, three organized around abolitionist work in United States, one devoted to Canada and one devoted to the British Isles), William Andrews's landmark *To Tell a Free Story* (1986), as well as author-based recovery projects such Frances Smith Foster's editions of Frances Ellen Watkins Harper's early writings (1990 and 1994) and Jean Fagan Yellin's identification of Harriet Jacobs as the author of *Incidents in the Life of a Slave Girl* (1987). Although scholars including Dorothy Porter as well as Foster herself have cautioned against *reducing* early Black expressivity to the abolitionist cause, it is nonetheless remains the case that some of the major scholarly developments around the literary historiography of slavery and abolition in the 1980s and early 1990s did indeed center the Black abolitionism that inspired Gilroy's intervention in that same era.[21]

A second arc of scholarly development in which the present discussion is situated builds on the post–Civil Rights–era groundwork to make possible very specific kinds of print cultural studies approaches facilitated by the explosion in digital archiving and computational humanities from the late 1990s to the present. Bibliography and textual studies are old practices (indeed, older than book history itself), and reprographic technologies like microfilm and microprint likewise, but the explosion in searchable databases of slave narratives and abolitionist newspapers, the availability of digital books, the development of web-based teaching archives, and the advent of new types of collaborative archiving and transcription projects have facilitated a new level of attention to the media cultures of abolition that has brought the transnational archive closer to scholars even as it has driven scholars back to paper-based archival research.[22] Driven by the perhaps conflicting urges to determine what print culture *was* and to use means of searching, sorting, and aggregating information specific to digital culture, the latest iteration of literary abolitionist scholarship has been delving ever deeper into what Goddu calls the "larger media ecology" of abolitionism to yield fundamentally new insights into the geographic reach and intellectual complexity of abolitionist writing.[23]

The Revolutionary 1830s: Boston and Southampton

The fruits of a fully Atlanticist-book historicist framing of US abolitionist literary production are still emerging as of this writing, but the archive around which such scholarship revolves began to take shape around 1830, with a series of closely timed and mutually amplifying textual and material events that the Black abolitionist radical Henry Highland Garnet aptly described in 1848 as constituting "the early part of the Anti-slavery Reformation."[24] They include publication of David Walker's *Appeal to the Colored Citizens of the World* (1829), William Lloyd Garrison's emergence as the principal white spokesman for immediate emancipation with the founding of *The Liberator* (1831), Nat Turner's Rebellion (1831), the publication of Thomas R. Gray's *The Confessions of Nat Turner* (1831), and the rebellion in Jamaica variously known as the Western Liberation

Uprising, the Christmas Rebellion, the Great Jamaican Slave Revolt, and the Baptist War (1831–1832). As was the case with the Protestant Reformation to which Garnet alludes, what was accurately perceived at the time as a rising tide of antislavery militancy was both abetted and publicized by developments in communication technology, particularly the increased ease of long-distance travel and the long-distance circulation of printed matter ushered in by the age of steam. As the book historian Robert Gross notes, "[b]y the early 1830s, the elements were coming into place to make possible, for the first time in American history, the efficient production and distribution of printed goods – *notably, pamphlets and periodicals* – in massive quantities throughout the nation."[25] The antislavery movement proved particularly adept at seizing this new, steam-powered expansiveness in order to spread its message not only across regions of the United States, but on a transatlantic and hemispheric scale as well.

Emerging from this context, Walker's *Appeal* is a remarkable document that engages explicitly and intentionally with the radical potential of printed texts set in motion. Published in three successive editions in Boston, the very audience the *Appeal* names for itself, "the colored citizens of the world, but in particular, and very expressly, . . . those of the United States of America," endeavors to call into being a Black Atlantic readership both rhetorically and materially. A North Carolina–born and Boston-based African American activist and used clothing dealer catering principally to sailors, Walker used his connections to coastal trading networks to get copies of his pamphlet into the hands of the people most likely to be inspired by his outraged catalogue of the "wretchedness" of the lives of enslaved and free African-descended people in the United States, prosecuted at the hands of white folk north and south. Thanks to the crucial work of Peter Hinks, the reach of the *Appeal* as a circulating document, and in particular the panic of interdiction caused by its discovery among African American readers in the US South, has become particularly well known.[26] Robert S. Levine has since shown how Walker's experience as a subscription agent for the early Black newspapers *Freedom's Journal* and *The Rights of All* shaped his material approach to launching his radical ideas into the world.[27] Marcy J. Dinius has demonstrated how Walker's unusual and intentional use of printing technology made the very typography of his work embody the righteous rage of its content.[28] Taken together, such critical attention succeeds in making a case for the *Appeal* as a landmark of abolitionist print culture that functioned as both an index of and a participant in a growing culture of resistance in the 1820s and the early 1830s. The history of its reception furthermore helps us to trace the growing awareness of Black resistance among white people (be they sympathetic, alarmed, or indifferent) across regions.

Walker died in 1830, cutting short his own highly distinctive approach to printing, publishing, and organizing. However, his work was kept alive not only through the secret pathways of print in the North and South, but also through his influence on the northern antislavery movement's own emerging practices of large-scale print publicity. For example, Garrison followed Walker's career closely in the early days of his own, having published a review of *The Appeal* in Benjamin Lundy's *The Genius of Universal Emancipation* in January 1830.[29] As a pacifist himself, Garrison's views on Walker's militancy are famously complicated – he recognized a right of revolution for the enslaved but insisted that northern abolitionists act neither to foment nor to crush Black militancy.[30] And yet, within the first year of *The Liberator*'s operation, Garrison's frequent inclusion of Walker's words nonetheless served to install Walker's writing within the radical interracial abolitionist canon. Indeed, within the robust "culture of reprinting" that the antislavery movement was increasingly constructing for itself, the *Appeal* proved an enduring resource for abolitionist militancy.[31] For example, when Garnet published his own call for the enslaved to overthrow their masters, "An Address to the Slaves of the United States of America," he did so in an 1848 pamphlet that reintroduced Walker to a new generation and reprinted the entirety of Walker's *Appeal* as a companion to his own text.[32]

Beyond such explicit practices of citation and reprinting, Garrison's debt to Walker and the *Liberator*'s debt to the *Appeal* are more profound still. In order to gather the funds needed to begin the *Liberator*'s thirty-five-year run, Garrison courted and received support from Walker's African American community in Boston and repaid their loyalty by publishing editorials advocating for African American civil rights, including a well-received pamphlet of Garrison's own, *An Address to the Free People of Color* (1831).[33] *The Liberator* as a publication moreover shared the *Appeal*'s transnational orientation as well as its incendiary tone. The publication's title evoked "Bolivar and the South American revolutions on the one hand and the Irish defiance of Daniel O'Connell on the other," and its internationalist motto was "Our Country Is the World – Our Countrymen Are Mankind."[34] Echoing Walker's habit of shouting through print, Garrison's famous inaugural editorial responded to calls for him to moderate his rhetoric with a defiant promise to be "as harsh as Truth, and as uncompromising as Justice." Also like Walker, Garrison materialized his promises with printing choices – in this particular case

with the visual militancy of dashes and capital letters: "I am in earnest –
I will not equivocate – I will not excuse – I will not retreat a single inch –
AND I WILL BE HEARD."[35]

The *Appeal* and the *Liberator* were likewise linked by the southern
outrage they elicited and the blame they shared for Nat Turner's
Rebellion, an uprising among the enslaved in Southampton, Virginia, that
killed approximately sixty slaveholders in August 1831. Although evidence
of direct influence will likely always remain elusive, the relative temporal
proximity of the southern circulation of both texts and Nat Turner's
rebellion has tended to align them, most particularly in the minds of the
slaveholders. Virginia Governor John Floyd, for example, insisted that
resistance among the enslaved was possible only as a result of outside
incitement.[36] Indeed, one of the remarkable aspects of this era's archive
from a literary studies perspective is the contrast between the slaveholders'
confidence in the power of texts to directly cause actions among the
enslaved that were (they insisted) previously uncontemplated, and the
abolitionist's and the rebel's rather more subtle combination of devotion
to textual radicalism, and confidence that rebellion need not require or
furnish post-hoc evidence of textual incitement.

Anticipating in a sense Trouillot's position on the Haitian Revolution's
initial independence from discourse, Walker, Garrison, and Turner all
described resistance among the enslaved as both historically inevitable
and divinely foreordained rather than *caused*. Their common approach
to post-Haitian revolutionary political exegesis was to insist that their work
was to *reveal* the revolutionary immanence, not to invent it. Thus Walker,
steeped in the language of African American Methodism, stated that God,
"being a just and holy Being will at one day appear fully in behalf of the
oppressed and arrest the progress of the avaricious oppressors."[37] Thus the
Baptist lay preacher Turner recalled the moment

> on the 12th of May, 1828, [when] I heard a loud noise in the heavens and
> the Spirit instantly appeared to me and said the Serpent was loosened, and
> Christ had laid down the yoke he had borne for the sins of men, and that
> I should take it on and fight against the Serpent, for the time was fast
> approaching when the first should be last and the last should be first.[38]

Thus Garrison, using marginally more secular language, insisted that
immediate abolition was necessary because, without it, uprisings like
Turner's were tragically inevitable: "What we have long predicted, at the
peril of being stigmatized as an alarmist and declaimer – has commenced
its fulfillment.... What was poetry – imagination – in January, is now
bloody reality."[39]

The complex connection among Walker's incitement, Garrison's notoriety, and Turner's actions is in interesting ways refracted by the wide circulation of *The Confessions of Nat Turner*, the account taken down by the white slaveholding attorney Thomas R. Gray on the eve of Turner's execution, and rushed into print. Whereas Walker's was an incendiary work that drew a repressive response, *The Confessions of Nat Turner* is an explicitly repressive and proslavery document that nonetheless caught fire among abolitionists. Gray clearly anticipated a white proslavery readership for his pamphlet, describing his motives in publishing Nat Turner's words as "calculated . . . to demonstrate the policy of our laws in restraint of this class of our population" and assuring his readers that "the insurrection in this county was entirely local, and [Turner's] designs confided to but a few."[40] The text nevertheless became an antislavery classic, used at least as often as Walker's *Appeal* to both commemorate and anticipate resistance on the part of the enslaved. For example, a notably heterogeneous pamphlet circulated by the Black abolitionist Henry Bibb, *Slave Insurrection in Southampton County, Va., Headed by Nat Turner, with an Interesting Letter from a Fugitive Slave to His Old Master: Also a Selection of Songs for the Times* (1850), quotes and paraphrases extensively from the *Confessions*.[41] Harriet Beecher Stowe explored Nat Turner's prophetic example in depth in her second antislavery novel, *Dred: A Tale of the Great Dismal Swamp* (1856), and reproduced large sections of the *Confessions* as an appendix to her own book.[42] The 1859 volume of the *Anglo-African Magazine*, where the first part of Martin Delany's revolutionary novel *Blake; or, The Huts of America* was first serialized, reprinted the *Confessions* in full, this time to provide context to the magazine's coverage of John Brown's Raid on Harpers Ferry (October 1859).[43] In this last case, the *Confessions* is used to illustrate what the editors view, like Garrison, as one option in a fateful choice between race war (Turner) and a racially integrated immediate emancipation (Brown): "These two narratives present a fearful choice to the slaveholders, nay, to this great nation – which of the two modes of emancipation shall take place? The method of Nat Turner or the method of John Brown?".[44]

The Revolutionary 1830s: Jamaica and Britain

Such circuits of communication, resistance, and repression have long been read in interregional rather than international terms, as evidence of a structuring Virginia/Massachusetts dualism rather than as indices of a wider struggle. However, the critical shift toward a hemispheric understanding of slavery and a transatlantic view of abolition has made increasingly clear that these conflicts were part of a larger network of proslavery and antislavery thought and action, neither "entirely local" as Gray insisted nor indeed restrictively national. The importance of this broader frame is particularly well illustrated by the international reverberations of the Jamaican uprising of December 1831–January 1832 widely known as the Baptist War, and the British parliamentary debates leading up to the 1833 Emancipation Act that shortly followed. The uprising itself bore some similarities to Nat Turner's rebellion, particularly in the role Christianity played in creating new social networks and new languages of resistance among the enslaved. But it was the divergent paths and staggered timelines to emancipation that followed each rebellion that proved especially fertile grounds for transnational abolitionist organizing. When US abolitionists found themselves thwarted by a slavery-supporting federal system and apathetic or hostile fellow citizens, the success of their British colleagues provided essential material and ideological support for abolitionist aims as well as ample space for literary exploration. When abolitionism began in the 1850s to lose favor with the British public in the face of post-emancipation economic reversals, the transatlantic literary sensation sparked by Stowe's *Uncle Tom's Cabin* served to reinvigorate the movement.

Because it is less well known in the US context than Nat Turner's Rebellion, I will describe the Jamaican uprising in some detail, emphasizing the extent to which a comparative account of the events there inspired activists then and can serve scholars now. Led by Samuel Sharpe, the Jamaican uprising began as a coordinated work stoppage following the Christmas holidays of 1831, at which time the enslaved had planned to demand wages for their labor. Quickly outstripping Sharpe's pacifist design, however, the strike expanded into an outright rebellion, signaled by a string of fires set on sugar estates over the course of more than a month, and involving tens of thousands of rebels in western Jamaica in oppositional activities ranging from the peaceful to the paramilitary.[45] Like Nat Turner's Rebellion, the Jamaican uprising was led by a Christian rebel: Sharpe was a Baptist deacon in Montego Bay. Both uprisings failed in the sense that they were scuttled by military force, and both were followed by a surge of white retributive vengeance. Indeed, whereas popular history tends to recall the blood shed by whites in Nat Turner's Rebellion, the slaveholders' counterrevolt in the Upper South was sufficiently violent to warrant recasting "the revolt [as] far more a tale of the death of slaves than of masters."[46] In Jamaica, the casualties among whites were minimal – fourteen including three soldiers – but the response was likewise one of disproportionate force: "the plantocracy and the military instituted a reign of terror, with summary trials, savage floggings and hangings."[47] This Jamaican "white insurrection" of 1832 also targeted the dissenting (non-Anglican) Protestant missions and missionaries, particularly Baptists and Methodists, who suffered mob violence, police harassment and imprisonment, religious services disrupted, and church buildings destroyed.

Each revolt/counterrevolt formation was destabilizing enough to its respective slaveholding society to elicit a significant legislative response, although only one led directly to emancipation. As Edward Barlett Rugemer observes, the parallel "the rebellions of 1831" concluded with "Great Britain on the verge of becoming an abolitionist empire, while slaveholders in the United States deepened their power in the governance of the republic."[48] In Britain, the Emancipation Act of 1833 decreed a compensated emancipation process set to begin on August 1, 1834, and initially projected to last as long as a decade. The Virginia legislature debated responses to Nat Turner, including emancipation, in its 1831–1832 session, but chose rather to retain slavery while increasing restrictions on religious assembly among the enslaved. Among the many implications of these divergent outcomes were the relative prestige accorded abolitionist organizing and the differential causality attributed to long-distance communication. Whereas US abolitionists recognized the relevance of Nat Turner's rebellion to their cause while disavowing direct influence on his actions, British antislavery *writing* became implicated with the Jamaican uprising and its aftermath in a way that managed to work to the movement's credit.

Indeed, accounts of Sharpe's revolt almost universally stress the importance of literate "studiation" to his leadership.[49] Nat Turner's *Confessions* acknowledges Turner's alphabetic literacy as a mark of his exceptionality, but, likely as a means to underscore the supposed uniqueness of the revolt itself, famously emphasizes the decisive role of the signs written on the landscape that only he could see and prophetic murmurings only he could hear.[50] By contrast, both contemporary and modern accounts describe Samuel Sharpe and his co-conspirators as remarkably careful readers of the secular news. Edward Kamau Brathwaite recounts the Baptist missionary William Knibb's testimony before Parliament concerning the significance of "those newspapers the slaves had" in sparking the revolt.[51] The white British Methodist missionary Henry Bleby likewise stressed the importance of the news in his memoir of Jamaica in 1832 and 1833, *Death Struggles of Slavery* (1853). Bleby, who narrowly survived a tarring and feathering in the white insurrection, dwells extensively on the importance of print culture in Sharpe's Jamaica, stating, for example, that Sharpe told his co-conspirators "a great deal of what he had read both in the English and colonial newspapers."[52] The rebel Edward Hylton related in one of a series of Thomas Gray–like jailhouse interviews with Bleby that, "on the morning of Christmas-day, 1831, a day or two before the insurrection broke out, he, with several others of the insurgent leaders breakfasted at the house of a black man named Taylor, at the Long Store in Montego Bay. At this meeting an English newspaper was produced from under the bed, from which Taylor read extracts on the subject of slavery."[53]

The summary account that emerges from Bleby and others and that has been widely accepted by historians is that Sharpe's leadership combined the alternative social networks created by the dissenting missions in Jamaica, with a deep understanding of both the shift in British public opinion toward emancipation around 1830 and the Jamaican planters' panicked response to their cratering political fortunes. As Bleby demonstrates, Sharpe was particularly adept at combining news and rumor to spur the enslaved to action. Embroidering on the accurate information that emancipation was gaining traction as part of the British parliamentary reform process of the early 1830s, Sharpe disseminated the false but plausible claim that emancipation had already been decreed in Britain but was being blocked from enactment by Jamaican planters. Drawing moreover on the planters' own well-reported deliberations, Sharpe conveyed the urgency of immediate action by informing the enslaved that the planters were on the verge of withdrawing from the British Empire and seeking annexation to the United States in order to protect their property and status.[54]

This last detail is worth dwelling on. Even though it is more than likely that word of Nat Turner's August rebellion had spread to the news-saturated environment of Montego Bay well before the time of the Christmas uprising, the relative frequency of large-scale rebellions in the British Caribbean would make any claims of decisive north-to-south influence implausible. Rather, the relevant hemispheric insight for Sharpe was that the United States remained supportive of slavery and planters' rights, whereas metropolitan Britain increasingly did not. Although he did not survive to see them, having been executed in May 1832, the legislative developments of 1832–1833 more than bore out Sharpe's assessment, which moreover aligned with the perspective of US abolitionists. Indeed, so discursively salient was the legislative success of metropolitan British antislavery to the US abolitionist work yet to come that, in many quarters, Sharpe's rebellion dropped out of public memory entirely as its proximate cause. To counter that elision, which has served a modern mythos of British Imperial benevolence even as it bolstered some abolitionists' visions of a nonrevolutionary emancipation, many historians today insist, along with Philip Sherlock and Hazel Bennett, that "Sam Sharpe and other freedom fighters reset the timetable for freedom."[55] New research continues to emerge on the importance of regional networks of Black resistance in this period, and much more work remains to be done.[56] Yet despite the density of these multiracial print circuits and hemispheric intellectual and political exchanges, in the era of US abolitionist intensification in the 1830s and 1840s, an enabling fiction of British emancipation as a kind of internal self-correction among white folk prevailed, at least among white abolitionists. As Emerson eloquently but inaccurately described the British emancipation process in 1844, "Other revolutions have been the insurrection of the oppressed; this was the repentance of the tyrant. It was the masters revolting from their mastery. The slave-holder said, I will not hold slaves."[57]

The disproportionate centering of metropolitan abolitionists in the antebellum US version of the British emancipation story retained a productive power, reinforcing US abolitionists' prior understanding of Britain as the hub of Atlantic abolitionism. Indeed, even though the US North was engaged in its own gradual emancipation process in the later decades of the eighteenth century and the early decades of the nineteenth, US abolitionists long had reason to regard Britain as discursive abolitionism's cutting edge. For example, Garrison's doctrine of "immediate emancipation," received in the United States as a radical breakthrough in 1831, was first articulated by the English Quaker abolitionist Elizabeth Heyrick in response to the British parliamentary amelioration measures of 1824.[58] African American abolitionists likewise regarded the greater pre-emancipation British empire as a zone of refuge and support. As Rugemer notes, more than a thousand free African Americans fled legal exclusion and mob violence in Cincinnati, Ohio, in 1829, arrived in western Canada, and were welcomed warmly by the governor of Canada. They established a community named for the British hero of the slave trade abolition movement, William Wilberforce.[59] Indeed, even while acknowledging the persistence of slavery in the British Caribbean at the time of his writing, David Walker likewise anticipated Sharpe's reading of the situation by describing "The English" as "the best friends the coloured people have upon earth ... [T]hey have done one hundred times more for the melioration of our condition, than all the other nations of the earth put together."[60]

In the US-focused abolitionist ferment of the subsequent three decades, the example of British emancipation continued to be a powerful engine of both political thought and literary invention. First and most famously, British free soil became a significant touchstone in abolitionist life and art. Before and especially after the passage of the Fugitive Slave Law in 1850, Canada became the US fugitive's most frequently sought terminus of freedom, and metropolitan Britain continued to be the abolitionists' most reliable source of support. Thanks to the massive popularity of Stowe's *Uncle Tom's Cabin*, the ur-story of literary abolitionism became and arguably remains the flight to Canada. However, it is also the case that the fugitive's life *on* British soil became a significant contribution to Black Atlantic literary modernity. Indeed, Stowe's own popularity in Britain was made possible by the transatlantic connections forged by Black abolitionists in the emancipation era, and moved into a new, expansive phase as the novel (both problematically and productively) further whetted the British appetite for Black writing, oratory, and performance.[61] The Black Abolitionists that traveled to the British Isles in large numbers as part of the antislavery fundraising circuit reaped not just funds in support of the movement, but individual public acclaim and literary patronage.[62] Of the best known of black abolitionist memoirs, some, such as Frederick Douglass's 1845 autobiography and William Wells Brown's of 1847, were published in Boston by William Lloyd Garrison, and were then sold for fundraising purposes on domestic and foreign lecture tours. But other, later ex-slave autobiographies bore London imprints, such as James Pennington's *The Fugitive Blacksmith* (1849), Brown's second memoir, *Three Years in Europe* (1852), Samuel Ringgold Ward's *Autobiography of a Fugitive Negro* (1855), and William and Ellen Craft's *Running a Thousand Miles to Freedom* (1860). Indeed, it is notable that Bleby's own memoir, though very explicitly situated in Jamaica in 1831–1832, was published in London in 1853 and itself bears the stamp of "Uncle Tom Mania." Bleby devotes chapters of the memoir to seemingly *Uncle Tom*–inflected topics such as "Negro Forbearance," "Negro Fortitude," and "Martyred Slaves," and even describes a particularly brutal Jamaican overseer in the terms of *Uncle Tom's Cabin's* chief villain, as "a Scotchman, a broad-shouldered, truculent-looking man, of the Legree school."[63]

But even as Bleby used Stowe's work as an anachronistic point of reference to describe Jamaican slavery, a rather less recognized strain of the US antislavery movement was using the Jamaican emancipation process itself as a site for future-oriented political thought. Indeed, even though in practice the British emancipation process itself was far from utopian or even equitable, abolitionists still found a way to use its vague contours for their own organizational ends. "Emancipation Day" or "The First of August" became a regularly celebrated northern US abolitionist holiday, offered as a pointedly Anglophilic rejoinder to the hopelessly compromised holiday of the Fourth of July. As Benjamin Quarles comments, "August 1 became the Negro's Fourth of July."[64] The First of August yielded its own body of speeches and its own vocabulary of civic rituals and literary touchstones. For example, in 1842 the abolitionists John A. Collins and Samuel Joseph May announced in the *Liberator* their plan to transform the First of August into a widely celebrated day of outdoor festivities. Collins offered banners for sale for the use of local abolition societies, and published a pamphlet titled *The Anti-Slavery Picknick*, which included "speeches, poems, dialogues and songs" to be used at as such events.[65]

In some cases, post-emancipation social transformation in Jamaican society itself became a topic for literary inquiry as abolitionists began producing literary "tours of the West Indies" that included visits to now free-labor plantations and interviews with the formerly enslaved. Such works included James A. Thome and Horace Kimball's *Emancipation in the West Indies* (1838), which became a New England abolitionist touchstone, examined at length in First of August addresses by William Ellery Channing (1840) and Ralph Waldo Emerson (1844). In the 1850s, a movement led by the white Jamaican attorney William Wemyss Anderson sought to attract US labor and investment to a Jamaica increasingly abandoned by the British imperial economic system. This effort produced yet another prominent travelogue, John Bigelow's *Jamaica in 1850*, a text that, in an intriguing inversion of the Jamaican slaveholders' aborted secession hopes, proposed that the US annex Jamaica as the first southern free state instead.[66]

The complex transatlantic and hemispheric networks forged by the abolitionist project proved both a laboratory of literary invention and a conduit for the work of print dissemination. The particularly literary impulses of the transnational antislavery movement produced a remarkably large and diverse body of work, the contours of which are still emerging as literary scholarship delves ever more deeply into nineteenth-century cultures of print. The present moment of scholarly attention toward the literary abolitionist archive should alert us, however, to the extent to which the seeming solidity of the archive changes based on the priorities of the scholars examining it. Transnational abolition has always been there in the folds of time, shouting for justice. But fluctuations in scholarly attention likewise always tease us with the knowledge that Garrison's insistence that he *would be heard* will always be a precarious claim.

Notes

1 Henry David Thoreau, "Civil Disobedience," in *Walden and Civil Disobedience*, ed. Kristen Case (New York: Penguin, 2017), emphasis added.
2 Recent examples include Jim Wallis, *America's Original Sin: Racism, White Privilege, and the Bridge to a New America* (Grand Rapids, MI: Brazos Press, 2016); Ethan J. Kytle and Blain Roberts, *Denmark Vesey's Garden: Slavery and Memory in the Cradle of the Confederacy* (New York: New Press, 2018), the cover of which describes the book as "A 150-Year Reckoning with America's Original Sin"; and Jake Silverstein "Editor's Note," *The 1619 Project*, special issue of the *New York Times Magazine*, August 18, 2019, 4, the opening paragraph of which comments, "This is sometimes referred to as the country's original sin, but it is more than that: It is the country's very origin."
3 David Brion Davis, *The Problem of Slavery in the Age of Revolution, 1770–1823* (New York: Oxford University Press, [1975] 1999).
4 See, for example, Thoreau, "Civil Disobedience"; Frederick Douglass, "What to the Slave is the Fourth of July?," in *The Frederick Douglass Papers, Series One: Speeches, Debates, and Interviews*, vol. 2, ed. John Blassingame (New Haven, CT: Yale University Press, 1982), 359–388; and Garrison's famous burning of the US Constitution as "a covenant of death and an agreement with hell." On the context of this statement, see Daniel Yacovone, "A Covenant with Death and an Agreement with Hell," Massachusetts Historical Society. www.masshist.org/object-of-the-month/objects/a-cove nant-with-death-and-an-agreement-with-hell-2005-07-01 (accessed October 13, 2020).
5 Michel-Rolph Trouillot, *Silencing the Past: Power and the Production of History* (Boston: Beacon Press, 1995), 88.
6 On the reception of *Uncle Tom's Cabin*, see Eric Sundquist, "Introduction," in *New Essays on Uncle Tom's Cabin*, ed. Sundquist (New York: Cambridge University Press, 1986), 1–5. On debates around the veracity of the slave narrative see, for example, Charles T. Davis and Henry Louis Gates, Jr., "Introduction: The Language of Slavery," in *The Slave's Narrative*, ed. Davis and Gates (Oxford: Oxford University Press, 1985); Ashraf Rushdy, *Neo-slave Narratives: Studies in the Social Logic of a Literary Form* (Oxford: Oxford University Press, 1999), 24; and Lara Langer Cohen, *The Fabrication of American Literature: Fraudulence and Print Culture* (Philadelphia: University of Pennsylvania Press, 2011), 101–132.
7 For examples of approaches to US print culture outside of the book form, see, for example, Benjamin Fagan, *The Black Newspaper and the Chosen Nation* (Athens: University of Georgia Press, 2016); Eric Gardner, *Black Print Unbound: The Christian Recorder, African American Literature, and Periodical Culture* (Oxford: Oxford University Press, 2015); Meredith McGill, *American Literature and the Culture of Reprinting, 1834–1853* (Philadelphia: University of Pennsylvania Press, 2003); and Elizabeth McHenry, *Forgotten Readers: Recovering the Lost History of African-American Literary*

Societies (Durham, NC: Duke University Press, 2002); Patricia Okker, *Serial Stories: The Magazine Novel in Nineteenth-Century America* (Charlottesville: University of Virginia Press, 2003); Kenneth M. Price and Susan Belasco Smith, *Periodical Literature in Nineteenth-Century America* (Charlottesville: University of Virginia Press, 1996). Examples of studies that center criticism of the motives and conduct of abolitionists from different perspectives include Stanley Elkins, *Slavery: A Problem in American Institutional and Intellectual Life* (Chicago: University of Chicago Press, 1959); Karen Halttunen, "Humanitarianism and the Pornography of Pain in Anglo-American Culture," *American Historical Review* 100, no. 2 (April 1995): 303–334; Karen Sánchez-Eppler, *Touching Liberty: Abolition, Feminism, and the Politics of the Body* (Berkeley: University of California Press, 1993); and Saidiya V. Hartman, *Scenes of Subjection: Terror, Slavery, and Self-Making in Nineteenth-Century America* (Oxford: Oxford University Press, 1997).

8 Bernard Bailyn, *Atlantic History: Concept and Contours* (Cambridge, MA: Harvard University Press, 2005), 12.

9 Peter Linebaugh and Marcus Rediker, *The Many-Headed Hydra: Slaves, Sailors, Commoners and the Hidden History of the Revolutionary Atlantic* (Boston: Beacon Press, 2000).

10 Paul Gilroy, *The Black Atlantic: Modernity and Double Consciousness* (Cambridge, MA: Harvard University Press, 1993).

11 Joseph Roach, *Cities of the Dead: Circumatlantic Performance* (New York: Columbia University Press, 1996); and Omise'eke Natasha Tinsley, "Black Atlantic, Queer Atlantic: Queer Imaginings of the Middle Passage," *GLQ* 14, nos. 2–3 (June 2008): 191–215.

12 Robert Darnton, "'What Is the History of Books?' Revisited," *Modern Intellectual History* 4, no. 3 (November 2007): 496.

13 Benedict Anderson, *Imagined Communities: Reflections on the Origins and Spread of Nationalism* (London: Verso, 1983); Jürgen Habermas, *The Structural Transformation of the Public Sphere: An Inquiry into a Category of Bourgeois Society*, trans. Thomas Burger (Cambridge, MA: MIT Press, 1989).

14 See, for example, Michael Warner, *The Letters of the Republic: Publication and the Public Sphere in Eighteenth-Century America* (Cambridge, MA: Harvard University Press, 1992).

15 Robert Fanuzzi probes this tension from a Habermasian perspective in *Abolition's Public Sphere* (Minneapolis: University of Minnesota Press, 2003). Trish Loughran uses abolition to test the limits of Anderson's paradigm in *The Republic in Print: Print Culture in the Age of U.S. Nation Building, 1770–1870* (New York: Columbia University Press, 2007).

16 On repressive violence, see Leonard L. Richards, *Gentlemen of Property and Standing: Anti-Abolition Mobs in Jacksonian America* (Oxford: Oxford University Press, 1970); and David Grimsted, *American Mobbing, 1828–1861: Toward Civil War* (Oxford: Oxford University Press, 1998). On censorship, see Richard R. John, *Spreading the News: The American Postal System from Franklin to Morse* (Cambridge, MA: Harvard University Press,

1995), 257–280; Susan Wyly-Jones, "The 1835 Anti-Abolition Meetings in the South: A New Look at the Controversy over the Abolition Postal Campaign," *Civil War History* 47, no. 4 (December 2001): 289–309; and Peter Charles Hoffer, *John Quincy Adams and the Gag Rule, 1835–1850* (Baltimore: Johns Hopkins University Press, 2017).

17 For examples of abolition-era print institutions, see Teresa A. Goddu, *Selling Antislavery: Abolition and Mass Media in Antebellum America* (Philadelphia: University of Pennsylvania Press, 2020). On postwar self-archiving, see Julie Roy Jeffrey, *Abolitionists Remember: Antislavery Autobiographies and the Unfinished Work of Emancipation* (Chapel Hill: University of North Carolina Press, 2008). For an examination of the term "autoarchiving" in a related context, see R. J. Boutelle, "Manifest Diaspora: Black Transamerican Politics and Autoarchiving in Slavery in Cuba," *MELUS* 40, no. 3 (Fall 2015): 110–133.

18 As Carol Nemeyer demonstrates, the combined effect of various Great Society programs including the Library Services and Construction Act of 1964 and Higher Education Act of 1965 was a 90 percent increase in the number of libraries nationally between 1960 and 1970, including the addition of 515 new college and university libraries. Carol A. Nemeyer, *Scholarly Reprint Publishing in the United States* (New York: R. R. Bowker, 1972), 55. On the institutionalization of Black Studies, see Noliwe M. Rooks, *White Money/Black Power: The Surprising History of African American Studies and the Crisis of Race and Higher Education* (Boston: Beacon Press, 2006).

19 It is worth acknowledging here that the Douglass reprint industry emerged along a different timeline befitting his outsize stature through most of the nineteenth and twentieth centuries. For example, the historian Philip S. Foner published his five-volume *Life and Writings of Frederick Douglass* with the Marxist International Publishers between 1950 and 1975, and the first twentieth-century reissue of Douglass's 1845 *Narrative* was published in 1960. For a scrupulously detailed recent analysis of Douglass's publishing and reception history, see Robert S. Levine, *The Lives of Frederick Douglass* (Cambridge, MA: Harvard University Press, 2016).

20 Rushdy, *Neo-Slave Narratives*, 39–40, and Martha Schoolman, "Martin Delany, Blake; or, The Huts of America (1859–1962)," in *Handbook of the American Novel in the Nineteenth Century*, ed. Christine Gerhardt (Berlin: De Gruyter, 2018).

21 Dorothy Porter, "Early American Negro Writings: A Bibliographical Study," *The Papers of the Bibliographical Society of America* 39, no. 3 (Third Quarter, 1945): 192; and Frances Smith Foster, "A Narrative of the Interesting Origins and (Somewhat) Surprising Developments of African-American Print Culture," *American Literary History* 17, no. 4 (Winter 2005): 714–740.

22 Prominent examples of influential digital research collections include *Accessible Archives* (John Nagy, 1990), *Documenting the American South* (University of North Carolina, 1996), *Slavery and Antislavery: A Transnational Archive* (Gale, 2009), and *The Colored Conventions Project*

(P. Gabrielle Forman, 2012). Recent examples of print culture–focused work that draws on the archives of abolitionism beyond those noted elsewhere in this essay include Lara Langer Cohen and Jordan Alexander Stein, eds., *Early African American Print Culture* (Philadelphia: University of Pennsylvania Press, 2012); Marcy J. Dinius, *The Camera and the Press: American Visual and Print Culture in the Age of the Daguerreotype* (Philadelphia: University of Pennsylvania Press, 2012); Jared Hickman, *Black Prometheus: Race and Radicalism in the Age of Atlantic Slavery* (Oxford: Oxford University Press, 2016); Lloyd Pratt, *The Strangers Book: The Human of African American Literature* (Philadelphia: University of Pennsylvania Press, 2016); Jonathan Senchyne, *The Intimacy of Paper in Early and Nineteenth-Century American Literature* (Amherst: University of Massachusetts Press, 2020); Caleb Smith, *The Oracle and the Curse: A Poetics of Justice from the Revolution to the Civil War* (Cambridge, MA: Harvard University Press, 2013); and Derrick R. Spires, *The Practice of Citizenship: Black Politics and Print Culture in the Early United States* (Philadelphia: University of Pennsylvania Press, 2019).

23 Goddu, *Selling Antislavery*, 7.

24 Henry Highland Garnet, *Walker's Appeal, with a Brief Sketch of His Life, by Henry Highland Garnet. And Also Garnet's Address to the Slaves of the United States of America* (J. H. Tobitt, 1848), Project Gutenberg, iii.

25 Robert A. Gross, "Introduction: An Extensive Republic," in *A History of the Book in America, vol. 2: An Extensive Republic: Print, Culture, and Society in the New Nation, 1790–1840*, ed. Gross and Mary Kelley (Chapel Hill: University of North Carolina Press, 2010), 47, emphasis added.

26 Peter P. Hinks, *To Awaken My Afflicted Brethren: David Walker and the Problem of Antebellum Slave Resistance* (University Park: Penn State University Press, 1997). On the *Appeal*'s notoriety in the North, see Lori Leavell, "'Not intended exclusively for the slave states': Antebellum Recirculation of David Walker's Appeal," *Callaloo* 38, no. 3 (Summer 2015): 679–695.

27 Robert S. Levine, *Dislocating Race and Nation: Episodes in Nineteenth-Century American Literary Nationalism* (Chapel Hill: University of North Carolina Press, 2008), 85–110.

28 Marcy J. Dinius, "'Look!! Look!!! At This!!!': The Radical Typography of David Walker's Appeal," *PMLA* 126, no. 1 (January 2011): 55–72.

29 Henry Mayer, *All on Fire: William Lloyd Garrison and the Abolition of Slavery* (New York: Norton, 1998), 84.

30 We get a sense of Garrison's ambivalence in the very first issue of the *Liberator*, which included brief notice of the *Appeal*, noting in part that "In a future number, we propose to examine it ... it being one of the most remarkable productions of the age. We have already publicly deprecated its spirit." "Walker's Pamphlet," *The Liberator*, January 1, 1831. See also Robert H. Abzug, "The Influence of Garrisonian Abolitionists' Fears of Slave Violence on the Antislavery Argument, 1829–40," *The Journal of Negro History* 55, no. 1 (January 1970): 15–26.

31 See McGill, *American Literature and the Culture of Reprinting*.
32 For a detailed textual examination of Garnet's lecture, its publication history, and its connection to Walker, see the exhibit curated by Harrison Graves, Jake Alspaugh, and Derrick Spires in the *Colored Conventions Project*, https://coloredconventions.org/garnet-address-1843/.
33 Mayer, *All on Fire*, 116.
34 Ibid., 107.
35 William Lloyd Garrison, "To the Public," *The Liberator* (January 1, 1831): 1; Mayer, *All on Fire*, 112.
36 See, for example, Floyd's letter to J. C. Harris in Henry Irving Tragle, *The Southampton Slave Revolt of 1831: A Compilation of Source Material* (Amherst: University of Massachusetts Press, 1971), 275–276.
37 Walker, *Appeal to the Colored Citizens of the World*, 5.
38 Kenneth Greenberg, ed. and intro., *The Confessions of Nat Turner and Related Documents* (Boston: Bedford/St. Martins, 1996), 47–48.
39 Tragle, *The Southampton Slave Revolt of 1831*, 31–32.
40 Greenberg, *The Confessions of Nat Turner*, 41–42.
41 Tragle, *The Southampton Slave Revolt of 1831*, 473.
42 Harriet Beecher Stowe, *Dred: A Tale of the Great Dismal Swamp* [1856], ed. and introduction by Robert S. Levine (Chapel Hill: University of North Carolina Press, 2000), 551–561. For an alternative interpretation of this inclusion, see Jeannine Marie DeLombard, *Slavery on Trial: Law, Abolitionism and Print Culture* (Chapel Hill: University of North Carolina Press, 2007), 158–159.
43 *The Anglo-African Magazine* (New York: Arno Press, [1859] 1968), 386–97.
44 Ibid., 386.
45 My account of the uprising draws on Henry Bleby, *Death Struggles of Slavery: Being a Narrative of Facts and Incidents Which Occurred in a British Colony, during the Two Years Immediately Preceding Negro Emancipation* (London: W. Nichols, [1853] 1868); Edward Kamau Brathwaite, "The Slave Rebellion in the Great River Valley of St. James – 1831/2," *Jamaican Historical Review* 13 (January 1982): 11–30; Michael Craton, *Testing the Chains: Resistance to Slavery in the British West Indies* (Ithaca, NY: Cornell University Press, [1982] 2009); Thomas Holt, *The Problem of Freedom: Race, Labor and Politics in Jamaica and Britain, 1832–1938* (Baltimore: Johns Hopkins University Press, 1992); Edward Barlett Rugemer, *The Problem of Emancipation: The Caribbean Roots of the American Civil War* (Baton Rouge: Louisiana State University Press, 2008); and Philip Sherlock and Hazel Bennett, *The Story of the Jamaican People* (Kingston: Ian Randle Publishers, 1998).
46 Greenberg, *The Confessions of Nat Turner*, 19.
47 Sherlock and Bennett, *The Story of the Jamaican People*, 221.
48 Rugemer, *The Problem of Emancipation*, 96.
49 Bleby, *Death Struggles of Slavery*, 123; Brathwaite, "The Slave Rebellion," 17.
50 Greenberg, *The Confessions of Nat Turner*, 46–47.

51 Brathwaite, "The Slave Rebellion," 17.

52 Bleby, *The Death Struggles of Slavery*, 123.

53 Ibid., 124–25.

54 Ibid., 134–38.

55 Sherlock and Bennett, *The Story of the Jamaican People*, 226.

56 See, for example, Christopher Taylor, *Empire of Neglect: The West Indies in the Wake of British Liberalism* (Durham, NC: Duke University Press, 2018); and Ifeoma Kiddoe Nwankwo, *Black Cosmopolitanism: Racial Consciousness and Transnational Identity in the Nineteenth-Century Americas* (Philadelphia: University of Pennsylvania Press, 2005).

57 Ralph Waldo Emerson, "Address ... on ... the Emancipation of the Negroes in the British West Indies," in *Emerson's Antislavery Writings*, ed. Len Gougeon and Joel Myerson (New Haven, CT: Yale University Press, 1995), 26.

58 Mayer, *All on Fire*, 70.

59 Rugemer, *The Problem of Emancipation*, 99–100.

60 Walker, *Appeal*, 43, qtd. in Rugemer, *The Problem of Emancipation*, 107.

61 See, for example, Sara Meer, *Uncle Tom Mania: Slavery, Minstrelsy and Transatlantic Culture in the 1850s* (Athens: University of Georgia Press, 2005), 133–193; and Audrey Fisch, *American Slaves in Victorian Britain: Abolitionist Politics in Popular Literature and Culture* (Cambridge: Cambridge University Press, 2000. The Black abolitionist Samuel Ringgold Ward's contextualized his fundraising trip to England under "the unprecedented influence of Mrs. Stowe's masterpiece" in Ward, *Autobiography of a Fugitive Negro: His Antislavery Labors in the United States, Canada and England* (London: John Snow, 1855), *Documenting the American South*, https://docsouth.unc.edu/neh/wards/ward.html, 227.

62 See Benjamin Quarles, *Black Abolitionists* (Boston: Da Capo Press, [1969] 1991), 116–142, and R. J. M. Blackett, *Building an Antislavery Wall: Black Americans and the Atlantic Abolitionist Movement, 1830–1860* (Baton Rouge: Louisiana State University Press, 1983).

63 Bleby, *Death Struggles of Slavery*, 91.

64 Quarles, *Black Abolitionists*, 124.

65 For a detailed discussion of these events, see Martha Schoolman, *Abolitionist Geographies* (Minneapolis: University of Minnesota Press, 2014), 70–76; and Jeffrey R. Kerr-Ritchie, *The Rites of August First: Emancipation Day in the Black Atlantic World* (Baton Rouge: Louisiana State University Press, 2007).

66 John Bigelow, *Jamaica in 1850; or, The Effects of Sixteen Years of Freedom on a Slave Colony*, introduction by Robert J. Scholnick (Urbana: University of Illinois Press, [1851] 2006), 161; Martha Schoolman, "West Indian Emancipation and the Time of Regionalism in the Hemispheric 1850s," in *Mapping Regions in Early American Writing*, ed. Edward Watts, Keri Holt, and John Funchion (Athens: University of Georgia Press, 2015), 81–96.

PART II

Forms and Formats

CHAPTER 9

Romance

Emily Ogden

Modern romance shuttles back and forth in time between a past in which something failed to happen right, failed to happen all the way, or failed to happen at all, and a future in which failure becomes, somehow, success. The thing that failed before, but will succeed now, might be an image of ethnic purity or national founding, as in the historical romances of Walter Scott and James Fenimore Cooper. It might be a vision of bygone ideal love, as in the modern revivals of medieval chivalric romance that realist Anglophone novelists of the eighteenth and nineteenth centuries set themselves against. "Once and future," as in the title of T. H. White's twentieth-century revival of Arthurian romance, *The Once and Future King* (1958), is the romance's rallying cry. Let me, then, hazard a definition: the modern romance narrates as a sustaining, even a utopian future that which has already failed to come true in the past.

Romance can be reactionary. The genre can long to restore past injustice or to rewrite the past in the name of present injustice. Cooper, in *The Last of the Mohicans* (1826), has to do the complex work of making a white American indigeneity out of a past that actually consisted in settler colonialism. His solution is to have a team of Americans who represent both white settlers and those they exploited and dispossessed conquer the wilderness together. One daughter of enslavers and of the enslaved, two indigenous men, a white couple, a white poet, and a white woodsman cross between the camps of two armies, then by united consent hand off the land and its future to the white couple for re-peopling. To say the very least, such a scene never happened, and it is not only we, the critical readers, who know it. In several ways, *The Last of the Mohicans* registers the failure of the past to conform to the needs of the imagined white supremacist future. It leaves its geopolitical plot open-ended, for example; as love plots conclude, war still rages. And it lavishly imagines a marriage of the black woman and the indigenous man in the afterlife, whereas whether out of shame, decency, or cunning, the white couple's wedding is never depicted. Thus *The Last of the Mohicans* registers the failure of its white supremacist reveries, even as it continues to dream them.

Romance can be reactionary, then, but it does not have to be. If romance is the narration of a sustaining future out of the fragments of a failed past, then many, if not all, progressive visions must make some use of it, and they, too, contain that double register we see in *The Last of the Mohicans*: dreaming the dream, they also register its weaknesses and failures. Audre Lorde writes in "Poetry Is Not a Luxury" (1977) that "there are no new ideas waiting in the wings to save us as women, as human," that "there are only old and forgotten ones, new combinations, extrapolations and recognitions from within ourselves – along with the renewed courage to try them out."[1] To imagine a future that sustains is to loop back to the past that undercut, undermined, and harmed. Sustain: hold up. That which *will*, that which *might* hold up has a history of giving way beneath.

Recent Americanist work by Jennifer Fleissner, Lloyd Pratt, Jared Hickman, Carrie Hyde, and Michelle Sizemore has revealed the romance as a promising means of critique.[2] As Fleissner points out, if our object of scrutiny is not only American empire, but also modernity, secularity, or capitalism's relentless march toward the future as it leaves ruins in its wake, then a future-driving politics may not invariably be what is required. For Fleissner, criticism's purchase "depends on our ability to theorize what is at stake when we find ourselves drawn to look back in time," and romance, as "a child of the Enlightenment that revolts against its parent," might guide this theoretical work.[3] Pratt takes the historical romances of Nathaniel Hawthorne to imagine "a present tense that repeats the past while at the same time differing radically from it."[4] The need for ironic stances such as these, that at once draw on and critique the past, arises (proximately, if not exclusively) from our relation to Enlightenment. Criticism at once rejects and depends on this project of human freedom and of liberation from tyranny that not only failed to come to fruition, but instituted new, ever more totalizing forms of bondage. This cosmic irony is familiar from, to name just one example, Theodor Adorno and Max Horkheimer's *Dialectic of Enlightenment* (1947). And yet somewhere in the failure whose American version, a democratic Constitution that enshrines chattel slavery, Frederick Douglass found he could treat only with a "scorching irony," there may lie, nonetheless, the only possible components with which to build.[5] There is a version of the romantic impulse that, in its shuttling back and forth in time, takes this irony on board, dreaming of freedom even after freedom has been shamefully misused. This version of romance hopes for sustenance from that which has given way, knowing full well the irony of its hope. Such a politics asks, What can be repurposed here? What *has* to be?

Romance Revival

The romance's ironic repurposing of past fragments comes most clearly into view when one dates the modern genre to the romance revival, a scholarly movement of the middle to late eighteenth century. While it has not attracted much attention from Americanist critics, this movement was an inevitable point of reference for antebellum American writers at least indirectly, through the major novelist the movement produced: Walter Scott, who both participated in the scholarship and wrote fiction based on it.[6] Starting in 1765, scholars and enthusiasts collected, edited, and published medieval metrical romances, tales of chivalric love and knightly exploit that had previously been little valued. One key text of the romance revival was Bishop Thomas Percy's *Reliques of Ancient English Poetry* (1765), based on a manuscript compendium Percy had literally snatched from the fire (maids were using it as kindling). Joseph Ritson's *Ancient Engleish Metrical Romanceës* (1802) followed close behind.[7] The term *romance* has a long and varied history.[8] But as Ian Duncan explains, scholars of this period saw romance as preserving "the scattered relics of an ancestral culture that was disintegrating under the pressure of modernization."[9] Antiquarians also recorded contemporary folk practices and tales, with the idea that these had survived from an earlier time and might shed light on the mores of that time. The romance revival, then, took as its premise the idea that forgotten, outmoded, or "primitive" lifeways could be a source of meaning again.

Scott both did this antiquarian work and based a new form of fiction on it.[10] In recovering romances and writing in homage to them, Scott and his followers braved the disdain still preserved in the phrase "incurable romantic." Anti-romance pedagogy of the nineteenth century would have had the products of the romance revival in mind to some degree. Anti-romance pedagogy, often present within the realist novel, takes characters to task when they allow imagination to overwhelm reason, or when they expect life – and especially sex – to conform to chivalric patterns. Incurable romantics, like the character Dorcasina Sheldon in Tabitha Tenney's anti-romance novel *Female Quixotism* (1801), are the people for whom the overwhelming evidence of past failure is not sufficient to kill the hope of future success. Such innocents occasion a gentle pity in people occupying, with respect to them, the realist position.

With an ironic knowingness, historical romancers took seriously these texts of an allegedly pitiable innocence, then raised erotic idealism to a geopolitical scale. They found both source material and formal models in the edited texts of the Romantic scholars.[11] One reason we see faux editorial apparatuses in nineteenth-century romances, from the scholarly footnotes of Cooper to the elaborate fiction of manuscript discovery in the preface to Hawthorne's *The Scarlet Letter* (1850), "The Custom-House Sketch," is that writers are nodding to romance-recovery's fantasy of remaking the past.[12] We find two important texts of the romance revival, Percy's *Reliques* and Scott's *Letters on Demonology and Witchcraft* (1830), a work recording contemporary "superstitions" in Scotland, among the Hawthorne family's borrowings at the Salem Athenaeum's circulating library.[13] As Duncan writes, "for us" – meaning, for us moderns – "romance must always be romance revival."[14] Genres like the romance, as Pratt puts it, "register and compound a pluralization of time – a splitting of time into temporalities – characteristic of modernity."[15] Romance authors had to find sustaining futures in past failures, even if that meant *reinventing* those failures, as Cooper did, in the hopes of recombining their parts into some sort of success.

When Lorde writes in "Poetry Is Not a Luxury" that there are no new ideas, she does not mean there is *nothing* new under the sun, but that what is new is not the ideas. "Right now," she writes, "I could name at least ten ideas I would have found intolerable or incomprehensible and frightening, except as they came after dreams and poems."[16] Lorde defines poetry as "a revelatory distillation of experience" and especially of "feeling."[17] Romance attempts (whether in meter or in prose) this poetic task of creating a ground of dream and feeling on which the intolerable ideas can be differently entertained. The genre loops back under the influence of poetry, which is "not only dream and vision; it is the skeleton architecture of our lives," as though the old faulty engineering could be salvaged and even improved.[18]

The Romance Thesis of American Literature

For some seventy-five years, romance has stood near the heart of American studies, but for most of that time the term has had little to do with the history I have just sketched. To reconnect romance in American studies to the romance revival – and to the Romanticism that followed Enlightenment – is to take stock of romance's ambivalent capacity to construct a future out of the fragments of the past. One can pinpoint the moment when romance's connection to romance revival was accidentally severed: Richard Chase's *The American Novel and Its Tradition*

(1957). Chase argued that where the British literary tradition produced novels, with a rich social texture and fully realized characters, the American tradition instead produced romances, which were characterized by a mood of "idyl" and "melodrama," by intense psychological conflict, and by one-dimensional – indeed, seemingly lame or unsuccessful – efforts at characterization.[19] The argument became known as the romance thesis of American literature. Chase's definition of the romance was peculiar, its sources in intellectual history difficult to parse. It is not clear, as John McWilliams pointed out, that anyone before Chase, romance-writer or scholar, ever wrote with precisely this definition in mind.[20] It is also not clear that Chase cared if they had not; his aim seems less to have been to identify a genre toward which authors wrote than to characterize their productions after the fact.[21] Although Scott's heirs, including Cooper, Hawthorne, and Lydia Maria Child, did write what they understood as romances, there was little historical support, as McWilliams showed, for "Chase's notion of the timeless Romance as a generic term broadly applicable to American fiction."[22]

In spite of its idiosyncrasies, Chase's romance thesis was highly influential in American studies, and it became the point of contention between the liberal Americanists of the 1940s and 1950s and the New Americanists who succeeded them in the 1980s and 1990s. In his introduction to the 1990 special issue of *boundary 2* where the New Americanists called themselves by that name for the first time, a collection republished as the book *Revisionary Interventions into the Americanist Canon* (1994), Donald Pease argued that the romance thesis was an ideological project masquerading as an end to ideology.[23] With its claim that literature in general, and American literature in particular, had to do with timeless archetypes and not with political life, the romance thesis enshrined a separation of the cultural and political realms. It thus permitted Americanists to indulge in the fantasy that their literary pursuits stood over to the side somewhere, separate from and impervious to any emancipatory demands that might disturb the idyl. The romance thesis shored up a white male "whole self," Pease wrote, at the expense of a realistic engagement with slavery, with settler colonialism, with race, class, and gender.[24] For the New Americanists, Chase's romance amounted to a flight inward, a flight to a domain where fantasy could flourish unchallenged by political reality.

As trenchant as the New Americanist critique was, there is one aspect of its characterization of Chase that, as Fleissner has pointed out, does not hold up. "Although Pease argues that Chase valorized romance for its projection of a reassuringly 'whole self,' Chase in fact contrasted the American tradition's production of 'fragments,' ... to ... the movement toward 'harmony' and the 'normative' that he found in the British novel," Fleissner writes.[25] Far from seeing the romance as a domain of wholeness and harmony, Chase characterized it as a genre centrally concerned with the impossibility of these ideals. The flight from political reality in Chase's romance was not a flight to peace but a flight to a place where resolution would be, yet again, impossible. Chase explains in an essay published after *The American Novel and Its Tradition* that romance centrally involves, on his view, a "reduction of personality," a doubt, indeed, of "the very possibility of personality."[26] Romantic characters were not just wooden or inept versions of realist characters; their awkwardness was the author's more or less deliberate staging of personality's dissolution. Chase wrote in this later essay that Walt Whitman's "Out of the Cradle Endlessly Rocking" (1860) could be considered a romance because "after the great aggressive act of creating a superb work of art there follows ... the rather desperate act of neurotic self-exposure," as though the poet had "been led, for whatever reason, to wonder whether the glorious autonomous self has not now become ... 'only a chance bit of wreckage thrown up on the shore of existence.'"[27] The performance of personality itself then becomes a romance: a utopian construction out of the fragments of past failure. As a romance, this performance at once attempts the utopian construction and discloses the failure.

In the Whitman essay, Chase acknowledged the singular nature of his romance definition – perhaps after reading some of the reviews of his book, where critics were widely puzzled about why he would use the term *romance* in the way he did.[28] "I am not entirely happy" with the term, he wrote; "I am sure its meaning will not be immediately clear. After all, 'Out of the Cradle' is not a poem about sexual love and courtship; it is not a medieval allegory; it has no knights in shining armor and no chivalry to speak of."[29] But perhaps these chivalric contents, or at least the eighteenth-century scholarship of their recovery, were not a wholly irrelevant context for Chase's thesis. Intuiting that, as Duncan has written, romance is always romance revival, he sought out a similar armature in the psyche – or in the aesthetic performances of psyche he saw in literature. If romance is always romance revival, self is always self-construction. Affects of wryness, belatedness, and irony brood over both operations. You could say that Chase expanded on the idea that romance narrated a chivalric order that was no longer there to say that it narrated a "whole self" that was no longer there. And in both cases, the absence was part of the narrative.

This problem of the dissolution of personality is one that New Americanists also found themselves having to consider. At the New Americanist turn, the personality of the critic became almost impossible to constitute. Consider a question about Pease's text. Pease wrote in 1990 that romance, beyond indicating a genre, also indexed the field's sustaining fantasies and "the relations between the field's practitioners." Romance "overdetermines the field of American studies."[30] Here's the question: Should I now make, a quarter of a century later, an editorial amendment to the past tense, and write "overdetermine[d]"? Is that over-determination in the past? Notice how, in asking this question, all the definitions of romance that we have visited so far are resonant. I am asking whether Chase's romantic idyl has been, finally, repudiated. I am asking whether Pease's critique of the fantasy that culture is apolitical has effec-tively reformed the field. And my definition of romance as the construc-tion of future possibility out of past failure broods over the question, too. I am asking whether there is *any way* for a field to construct its sustaining future except out of the fragments of its failed past. Indeed, I am asking whether the structure of criticism itself is, in this special sense, romantic.

So: Have Americanists escaped the romance? In that they have repudi-ated Chase's definition and taken Pease's critique on board, the answer is provisionally yes. The notion of an American exception to history called the "romance" is thoroughly discredited. The fantasy of a literature unbe-holden to politics no longer governs the field. The New Americanists' interventions have been institutional as well as intellectual. The teaching canon is transformed, and the research canon and research methods are, too. Americanists still offer readings, but they also do primary work on social and cultural history. Abetting and abetted by this change in orien-tation is a diversification of Americanist faculty and students. These changes are real.

But again: Have Americanists escaped the romance? If what we mean is, "Have Americanists escaped the condition of constructing the future out of the past's failures?," then the answer is no. And such an answer requires revisiting that earlier, provisional yes. Fragments of, relations to, the romance thesis remain. With Fleissner, I'd like to ask here, What if, instead of simply moving ever forward, we chose to circle back past the New Americanists to reconsider the critical past?[31] Were critics to take the stance I want to articulate here, they would wish for the new. But they would realize that the new is to be found only by rummaging around in the old – where one invariably also finds the *old* dreams of the new. The desire to start over is present, again, in the New Americanist turn, as

Fleissner points out. Also present in Pease's introduction to *Revisionist Interventions*, though, is an awareness of the problem that this desire poses. Pease's essay pervasively and, I take it, deliberately raises questions about what the change of regime from the liberal Americanists to the New Americanists could possibly consist in – and thus about how or whether the field can ever be free of romance's overdetermining weight.

Forcefully as Pease articulates his differences with his predecessors, he also understands disciplinary change psychoanalytically.[32] In doing so, he introduces a theoretical framework that presumes the future will always involve recursions to the past. Pease posits that each field has a "disciplinary unconscious" or set of "previously internalized ... norms, working assumptions, and self-understanding[s] of the field."[33] This disciplinary unconscious has a textual location in the critical productions of that field. He calls this textual location the "field-Imaginary."[34] To question the field-Imaginary, Pease said, was virtually to exit the field: "an Americanist cannot describe them as uncritically held assumptions without disaffiliating himself from the field of American Studies."[35] Thus rather than a paradigm shift, what Pease saw the New Americanists as having provoked was a "crisis in the field-Imaginary" of American studies.[36] If a field has an unconscious, then it cannot get over its origins in the same way that a patient gets over a cold. A cure in psychoanalysis is not like a cure for a fever. The contents of the unconscious do not go away; it is only our relationship to them that changes. Practicing analysts have various ways of expressing this idea. The point of analysis, Gary Greenberg proposes, isn't to transform us but "to find ... what it is about ourselves that we have to protect one another from, and then to muster the self-control to do that – and all without ever pretending that we have vanquished the beast within."[37] Analysis is not a transaction, says Adam Phillips: "If you buy a fridge, there are certain things you will be guaranteed. If you buy a psychoanalysis, you won't be."[38] The state of health that psychoanalysis imagines is not one of conversion but of long-term tending. The patient becomes a more able custodian of the unconscious's beast-garden. Such a transformation is not really a transformation at all. It involves not the leaving-behind of the past but the formation of a new relation to it.

By proposing that a discipline has an unconscious located in its texts, Pease has simply taken Fredric Jameson's idea, in *The Political Unconscious* (1981), that *literary* texts can be the point of appearance for the set of principles that are both fundamental to a political order and incontestable within it. He has then extended this idea to *critical* texts. The extension is simple and, when you think about it, almost inescapable. But its consequences are considerable. Once this extension has been made, the questions of what criticism is, what criticism can do, and what it would mean for it to undergo a shift become profoundly vexed and vexing.

Pease's introduction shows an awareness of these problems. Robyn Wiegman, in her reading of what she calls this "founding manifesto of New Americanism," has characterized Pease's handling of his double position as a state of "being situated in the mobility of outside/in": Pease is at once in Americanism and critiquing it, in America and critiquing it.[39] His text performs its attempt to break with the past and with the unconscious, and it also performs the impossibility – indeed, the failure – of this attempt. I mean both that the performance fails and that it is a performance of failure; the text performs what Chase called, when he discerned it in Whitman, "the dissolution of personality." Here, in reading Pease, I am departing decisively from Pease's own technique for handling his predecessors. His introduction to *Revisionary Interventions* was occasioned by a negative review essay written by liberal Americanist Frederick Crews about several of the critics who would become the New Americanists – indeed, Crews was the first to apply that term, which Pease then adopted. Pease treated Crews's writing as a symptom that he, Pease, was in a better position to interpret than Crews was. I do not see Pease's text as a mere symptom or myself as the better interpreter of it. Rather, I see Pease as occupying the position that I myself occupy and that I am tempted to say is the general position of the critic: we generate symptoms, we apprehend those symptoms, and in default of being able to stop the production of symptoms or make them fully transparent to ourselves, we come to deliberately perform them, and also to perform the moment when our analysis breaks down. As with Whitman in Chase's estimation, critical texts can contain a "great aggressive act of creating [what one hopes is] a superb work" – in this case, a work not of art but of criticism. At one and the same time they can harbor, "for aesthetic, moral, or psychological reasons we cannot define" – that is, we cannot tell whether what we are seeing is a symptom or a choice and, if a choice, whether an aesthetic or moral one – "the rather desperate act of neurotic self-exposure."[40] I see self-exposure in Pease, not neurotic or desperate self-exposure, but certainly self-exposure that artfully undermines "the great aggressive act" of founding a field. If, as a critic, I am doing my job right, then others would be able to see both aggression and self-exposure in my writing, too.

To take a characteristic example from Pease's work: in one of the most difficult passages of the essay, he at once articulates the wish for a new critical self and undoes this wish. First, he simply says: "In denying the separation constitutive of the field ... New Americanists have changed the field-Imaginary of American Studies."[41] The unconscious has been replaced, Pease is tempted to say. We are new people; we are a new field. But, Pease knows, he is altogether too skilled a practitioner *not* to know, that such a hope for renewal is precisely what he has been criticizing in the previous generation. He knows, too, that as if this problem were not enough, his psychoanalytic framework has introduced fresh obstacles. He has called the field-Imaginary a "pre-linguistic identification."[42] He has said that to subject it to critique is to exit the field. And so what can he, as a New Americanist, possibly know about the *new* field-Imaginary to which he is committed? What sort of an authority can he be about whatever it is that the field-Imaginary has changed *into*? Hence following the clear statement of a wish, we get the tortured performance of the qualified and impossible nature of that wish: "The political unconscious of the primal scene of [the new Americanists'] New Historicist readings embodies *both* the *repressed relationship between* the literary and the political and the *disenfranchised groups previously unrepresentable in this relationship*."[43] What can the chain of prepositional phrases beginning this sentence possibly mean? What modifies what? Does a reading have a primal scene, which in turn has a political unconscious? If we take only the subject, verb, and predicate here, then the claim is that for the New Americanists, the "political unconscious ... embodies ... disenfranchised groups." Here then is a new fantasy, but the old fantasy is still present, in that the wish here is to atone for the old fantasy's sins. Now those harmed by liberal Americanists, and by America, simply *are* the unconscious material for New Americanists. Indeed, their *bodies* are that unconscious material, so that not even the difference between bodies and texts, let alone the difference between academics and the disenfranchised groups of which they may or may not be a part, is permitted to remain a problem here. The "political unconscious ... embodies ... disenfranchised groups."[44]

It would be a serious misunderstanding of Pease's text to point to such ambivalences as this one with the idea of embarrassing him or convicting him of failure or inconsistency. On the contrary, we see Pease's virtuosity as a critic in this performance of his impossible self-constitution. He is aware of several things: aware that he is no longer a liberal Americanist, aware that it is not for him to say what the New Americanist unconscious consists in, and aware, finally, that it *is* for him to say so, indeed that because he is introducing a collection that debuts this group it is urgently *incumbent upon him* to say so. In the face of this multivalent awareness, he performs contradiction: he manifests for his reader the liquefaction of the arguing self into which these contradictory demands betray him, even as he also continues to occupy the role of the critic who knows how to bring such contradictory demands into rational harmony.

If we take Pease's psychoanalytic framework as seriously as we take his ideology critique – and if we take his performance of the dissolution of the critical self as seriously as we take either of these – then we would have to imagine that field transformations involve not the leaving-behind of a past but instead the *reworking* of that past, the invention of new ways of using those past materials. And we would have to imagine that such reworkings are essentially *performed*, not argued, in the continual activity of salvage, and in the continual exposure of the salvage operation's failure. Criticism is a romance.

Salvage

The "salvage" involved in critical romance can be understood in light of one ordinary meaning of that word: to salvage is to haul in a wreck or, failing that, to cull what is useful from the wreck. But it is also worth taking up Anna Lowenhaupt Tsing's use of "salvage" as a theoretical term in *The Mushroom at the End of the World* (2015). Tsing documents modes of life interlinked by a capitalist supply chain that takes matsutake mushrooms from the post-logging Oregon forests where white Americans and Asian-American immigrants pick them, through a number of intermediate steps, to Japanese markets, where they are a delicacy. In this luxury item that grows in capitalist wastelands, picked by people displaced through imperialist war and the movement of capital, Tsing finds some answers to the question with which she begins: "What do you do when your world starts to fall apart?"[45] Precarity is presupposed by this question, where precarity means "life without the promise of stability." "Salvage accumulation," Tsing writes, "is the process through which lead firms amass capital without controlling the conditions under which commodities are produced." [46] In salvage accumulation, value accrues to these firms in the end – but workers have latitude to shape some aspects of the production process. Tsing's use of the term "salvage" echoes ironically with "salvage anthropology," the late nineteenth- and early twentieth-century study of cultures presupposed to be "vanishing" by anthropologists positioned within the very empire attempting to eradicate them. Tsing's formulation indexes a subsequent form of ruin – empire picking its own bones – that is still haunted by the first. There is no a sunny escape from capitalism here; instead, Tsing is trying to describe in her book how production in "capitalist ruins" may nonetheless throw off creative ways of sustaining life in these ruins.

Romance's sorties into the past, to recover what is usable, might be seen as a similarly compromised, and similarly haunted, mode of picking through ruins. Deliberately reorienting critical practice toward such sorties, which have also always been part of criticism, may be necessary at a moment when the precarity of American Studies and its practitioners – and of the humanities academy itself – has become obvious. Academic departments may, themselves, be a form of salvage accumulation, a means by which (to alter Tsing's formulation), the corporatizing university amasses *cultural* capital without controlling, or not entirely, the means by which production occurs.[47] In these salvage conditions, some Americanists, myself included, still enjoy the promise of stability for ourselves, for now. Even so qualified, this promise is a great privilege. But few if any of us can fail to notice that our friends, colleagues, office neighbors, and the graduates and undergraduates who would like to follow in our footsteps do not enjoy the same promise. Stable, livable jobs exist in small numbers, by sufferance, alongside unstable, unlivable ones. Like many institutions, the university does not automatically and evenly preclude every work condition other than the factory at every stage of production. Its supply chains can incorporate varying conditions: the partial gift economy of teaching; the virtual outwork system by which tenured and tenure-track scholars in the humanities do their research and writing at some research institutions. But these varied conditions may be abrogated at any point, as the threat and reality of new assessment systems and austerity measures continually remind us.

The field-Imaginary of American Studies has tended to presuppose that a field of debate called American Studies can be relied on to exist in perpetuity. Less through criticism than through the bearing down of economic conditions, such a presumption is becoming difficult to maintain. These conditions may bring about a new "crisis in field-Imaginary," not through any masterful critical act, but in response to economic pressure. We might be in a position to say now that the fantasized separation between the cultural and the political perceived by the New Americanists in their liberal predecessors had a distant echo in the institutional form of American studies departments, an institutional structure that continued and indeed redoubled itself through the New Americanist heyday. One cannot now take for granted the prosperity of humanities departments, if one ever could. Pease's anxiety, in *Revisionist Interventions*, to bridge the divide between the academy and what he variously calls the "nonacademic," the "public world," and "outside the academy" belies a trust in the stability of the institutional division, which must be effortfully crossed.[48] The assumption that the academy will persist indefinitely into the future has offered a position from which to criticize, a form of solidarity with emancipatory movements that differs from direct partici- pation in them, and a freedom to reflect on demands before making demands. But as academic lives become more obviously and pervasively precarious, how long can the self-evidence of academic separateness hold?

The absurdity and the advantage of criticizing from a position of tenure even while tenure is vanishing already appear at a founding moment of the American romance: Hawthorne's "The Custom-House Sketch." This cele- brated preface to *The Scarlet Letter* has three main subjects. It theorizes romance. It gives a fictionalized antiquarian provenance for the romance to follow – its nod to the scholarship of the romance revival. And it describes the end of tenure. The real Hawthorne had received, through political patronage, a sinecure as the Surveyor of the quiet Salem Custom-House. Here he draws on that position, imagining a character, Surveyor Hawthorne, who finds in the Custom House attic a manuscript account of the life of Hester Prynne, bound up with a scarlet letter. Having found the letter, Hawthorne receives a ghostly visit from the "local antiquarian" who had penned the life of Hester, a former occupant of Hawthorne's own office. "'Do this,' said the ghost of Mr. Surveyor Pue, emphatically nodding the head that looked so imposing within its memorable wig, 'do this, and the profit shall be all your own! You will shortly need it; for it is not in your days as it was in mine, when a man's office was a life-lease, and oftentimes an heirloom.'"[49] Tenure, in other words, has eroded since Pue's day.

To the bafflement of students everywhere, Hawthorne treats the woes of the tenured at greater length than he treats anything else in "The Custom- House Sketch." But to the tenured themselves, the combination of idle- ness and anxiety that marks official life may well be full of personal interest. Something that looks like idleness but is not – it is thought, it is intellectual life, it is labor, and it is, certainly, privilege – characterizes these late days of the university, too. The condition of impermanence is easy to miss in "The Custom-House Sketch" because Hawthorne treats it with that unlocatable irony that passes, with him, for comedy (our own apprehension of impermanence may sometimes hide behind such an affect, too). But it is there nonetheless. The Surveyor and his fellow officers, all recipients of political favor, tip their chairs back against the wall while fearing the next change of presidential administration. They are safe, but not for long. Hawthorne's own tenure is short before the faction whose patronage he enjoys, the Democratic Party, loses to the Whigs again. He finds himself riding in a tumbril to the "political guillotine," where it's off with his official head.[50]

While employed at the Custom House, Hawthorne says, he could write nothing of *The Scarlet Letter*. A "wretched numbness" afflicted him. Pacing back and forth along the passage between two entrances during the three and a half hours per day when he was stationed at the port, he thought about the *Scarlet Letter* and yet thought about nothing: "On Hester Prynne's story," he writes, "I bestowed much thought" and yet "my imagination was a tarnished mirror."[51] The end of official life brought the return of the capacity to enter, as the "romance-writer" must, that "neutral territory, somewhere between the real world and fairy-land, where the Actual and the Imaginary may meet, and each imbue itself with the nature of the other."[52] But if "official life" is inimical to romance, then why must it be described at such great and such serio-comic length in the preface to a romance?[53] And why are the raw materials of *The Scarlet Letter* – the red A and the manuscript – located in this arid location? The metaphorics of official transition permit a meditation on romance's commitment to revisiting past failures, as the infrastructure and the idleness of official life permit the *Scarlet Letter*'s (fictionalized) raw materials to survive, and then be found. Surveyor Hawthorne is at once a romance-writer here and an antiquarian of the romance revival, a scholar braving disdain for the fragmentary and the insignificant in order to recover their value for the present. When Hawthorne asks why each administration should show such "bloodthirstiness" in sweeping the last one out, he also asks why the relics of the past should be so disdained for their imperfections.[54] Shouldn't that bloodthirstiness be tempered somehow with an acknowledgment that both the officials of the previous administration and the relics of the past are at least inescapable for us their successors – and maybe even serviceable to us?

To salvage is to return to the ruins of the past in order to construct a promising future – the very gesture that romance, at its best, can teach us. If there is any version of critical romance to be lived in the present, it is one tinged, like "The Custom-House Sketch," with irony as well as hope. Like the Surveyor, one kind of critical romancer holds a privileged but precarious tenure, still in possession, but maybe not for long, of a chair in the halls of an academic department. As we know, the academic department is no world elsewhere: it is as squarely located in the capitalist university as the Custom House was in state bureaucracy. And yet this does not mean that our critical habits of careful reading, over long durations of time, are bankrupt. In the unattended spaces of the university's salvage accumulation, members of departments may still elect more or less radical ways of going about their days. A degree of academic separateness makes possible, even as it also contaminates and limits, our critical work. From this vantage point, Fleissner proposes, "we should affirm our distance from knowledge production that *simply* rests on the model of progress, but precisely *not* in favor of endorsing timeless truth or beauty."[55] From this perch of separateness that becomes, as its limits heave into view, both more absurd and more pathos-laden, one could loop back – wryly and without claim to novelty – to the contaminated fragments of the past. Among these fragments are present privileges built on privileges of long standing, texts of reviled and revered critical predecessors, reactionary genres and progressive ones, cultural capital–laden critical editions, and disintegrating archives. Our writing is culled from these ruins.

Notes

1 Audre Lorde, "Poetry Is Not a Luxury," in *Sister Outsider: Essays and Speeches* (Trumansberg, NY: Crossing Press, 1984), 38.
2 Jennifer L. Fleissner, "After the New Americanists: The Progress of Romance and the Romance of Progress in American Literary Studies," in *A Companion to American Literary Studies*, ed. Caroline F. Levander and Robert S. Levine (Malden, MA: Blackwell, 2011), 173–90; Jared Hickman, "Political Theology," in *The Routledge Companion to Literature and Religion*, ed. Mark Knight (Abingdon, UK: Routledge, 2016), 124–34; Carrie Hyde, *Civic Longing: The Speculative Origins of US Citizenship* (Cambridge, MA: Harvard University Press, 2018), 122–28; Lloyd Pratt, *Archives of American Time: Literature and Modernity in the Nineteenth Century* (Philadelphia: University of Pennsylvania Press, 2010); Michelle Sizemore, *American Enchantment: Rituals of the People in the Post-Revolutionary World* (New York: Oxford University Press, 2018).
3 Fleissner, "After the New Americanists," 174, 180.
4 Pratt, *Archives of American Time*, 64.
5 Frederick Douglass, "What to the Slave Is the Fourth of July?," in *My Bondage and My Freedom*, ed. David W. Blight (New Haven, CT: Yale University Press, 2014), 372.
6 Ian Duncan, *Modern Romance and Transformations of the Novel: The Gothic, Scott, Dickens* (Cambridge: Cambridge University Press, 1992), 57.
7 Arthur Johnston, *Enchanted Ground: The Study of Medieval Romance in the Eighteenth Century* (London: Athlone Press, 1964), 75–147.
8 Rita Copeland, "Between Romans and Romantics," *Texas Studies in Literature and Language* 33, no. 2 (Summer 1991): 219; Hans Eichner, introduction to *"Romantic" and Its Cognates: The European History of a Word*, ed. Hans Eichner (Toronto: University of Toronto Press, 1972), 3–16.

9 Duncan, *Modern Romance and Transformations of the Novel*, 4.

10 Ibid., 4–5.

11 Ibid., 20–57; Johnston, *Enchanted Ground*, 4, 46–50.

12 See, on this point, Jerome McGann's discussion of the fictionalization of scholarly apparatus in what he calls the "literary ballad": "The Meaning of the Ancient Mariner," *Critical Inquiry* 8, no. 1 (Fall 1981): 40–41.

13 Marion Louise Kesselring, *Hawthorne's Reading, 1828–1850: A Transcription and Identification of Titles Recorded in the Charge-Book of the Salem Athenaeum* (New York: New York Public Library, 1949), 40, 58.

14 Duncan, *Modern Romance and Transformations of the Novel*, 6–7.

15 Pratt, *Archives of American Time*, 6.

16 Lorde, "Poetry Is Not a Luxury," 37.

17 Ibid., 36–37.

18 Ibid., 38.

19 Richard Chase, *The American Novel and Its Tradition* (Garden City, NY: Doubleday, 1957), 1–5, 12–13.

20 John McWilliams, "The Rationale for 'The American Romance,'" *boundary 2* 17, no. 1 (Spring 1990): 82.

21 Chase, *American Novel and Its Tradition*, 12.

22 McWilliams, "Rationale for 'The American Romance,'" 82.

23 Donald E. Pease, "New Americanists: Revisionist Interventions into the Canon," introduction to *Revisionary Interventions into the Americanist Canon*, ed. Donald E. Pease (Durham, NC: Duke University Press, 1994), 1–37. The special issue is "New Americanists: Revisionist Interventions into the Canon," *boundary 2* 17, no. 1 (spring 1990). See also Amy Kaplan, *The Social Construction of American Realism* (Chicago: University of Chicago Press, 1988), 1–14; McWilliams, "The Rationale for 'The American Romance.'" Nina Baym's historicist critique preceded the New Americanist ideological one: see Baym, "Concepts of the Romance in Hawthorne's America," *Nineteenth-Century Fiction* 38, no. 4 (1984): 426–43.

24 Pease, "New Americanists," 12.

25 Fleissner, "After the New Americanists," 177.

26 Richard Chase, "'Out of the Cradle' as a Romance," in *The Presence of Walt Whitman: Selected Papers from the English Institute*, ed. R. W. B. Lewis (New York: Columbia University Press, 1962), 71.

27 Ibid., 71.

28 See, for example, the following reviews of *The American Novel and Its Tradition*: Roy Fuller, *London Magazine* 5 (August 1957): 58–60; A. C. Kettle, *Review of English Studies* 11, no. 41 (1960): 114–17; Geoffrey Moor, *Listener* 60 (July 24, 1958): 133; Edwin Muir, "Light on Dark," *Observer* (June 1, 1958): 16.

29 Chase, "'Out of the Cradle' as a Romance," 52.

30 Pease, "New Americanists," 30.

31 Jennifer Fleissner has noted a further irony here, in that the New Americanists used "a Freudian vocabulary" even as they energetically distanced themselves

from Chase's concern with the inward and the psychological: Fleissner, "After the New Americanists," 174.

32 Fleissner, "After the New Americanists," 176.
33 Pease, "New Americanists," 3.
34 Ibid., 11.
35 Ibid., 3.
36 Ibid., 9.
37 Gary Greenberg, "America and Its Discontents," *The Baffler*, no. 41 (September 2018).
38 Adam Phillips interviewed by Paul Holdengräber in "The Art of Nonfiction, No. 7," *The Paris Review* (Spring 2014).
39 Robyn Wiegman, "The Ends of New Americanism," *New Literary History* 42, no. 3 (2011): 389–90.
40 Chase, "'Out of the Cradle' as a Romance," 71.
41 Pease, "New Americanists," 31.
42 Ibid., 30.
43 Ibid., 31, emphasis original.
44 Similar examples of a simple wish followed by its complex restatement or retraction can be found in Pease, "New Americanists," 17–19.
45 Anna Lowenhaupt Tsing, *The Mushroom at the End of the World: On the Possibility of Life in Capitalist Ruins* (Princeton, NJ: Princeton University Press, 2015), 1.
46 Ibid., 63.
47 John Guillory, *Cultural Capital: The Problem of Literary Canon Formation* (Chicago: University of Chicago Press, 1993).
48 Pease, "New Americanists," 17, 19, 26.
49 Nathaniel Hawthorne, *The Scarlet Letter*, vol. 1 of *The Centenary Edition of the Works of Nathaniel Hawthorne*, 23 vols., ed. William Charvat, Roy Harvey Pearce, and Claude M. Simpson (Columbus: Ohio State University Press, 1962), 33.
50 Ibid., 41.
51 Ibid., 35.
52 Ibid., 36.
53 Ibid., 40.
54 Ibid., 40.
55 Fleissner, "After the New Americanists," 188.

CHAPTER 10

Theater

Michelle Granshaw

One evening in February 1848, in his red flannel shirt, plug hat, and suspenders, Mose stepped onto the Olympic Theatre stage in Benjamin Baker's *A Glance at New York*. Smoking a cigar, Mose spit and then declared, "I've made up my mind not to run wid der machine anymore."[1] Played by F. S. Chanfrau before a cross-class audience of New Yorkers, Mose the Bowery B'hoy became an overnight sensation, especially with the Bowery b'hoys in the pit. The Bowery b'hoys were white working-class men, often second-generation Irish, who were connected through a "loose confederation of many clubs and semi-fraternal organizations" by the 1830s.[2] Committed Democrats and often firemen, the b'hoys became predominant figures in working-class culture in downtown New York for about two decades.[3] *The Albion* described Mose as "really a character both in the creation by the author and the embodiment by the actor . . . [that was] received with shouts of delight by the thousand originals of the pit."[4] *The Spirit of the Times* similarly praised Chanfrau as Mose and characterized the performance as "the very embodiment of the creature designed to be represented. We cannot speak too highly of the astonishing accuracy with which Mr. Chanfrau plays his part, and we advise our friends to go and see a character often heard of, but owing to his peculiar habits, rarely seen by the larger and better community."[5] First performed on the playwright and prompter Baker's benefit night, the production ran at the Olympic Theatre for seventy-four nights. It held the record for the longest running play until *The Drunkard* in 1850. For the next ten years, Mose plays provided Chanfrau with a series of hits, including *New York as It Is* (1848), *The Mysteries and Miseries of New York* (1848), *Mose in California* (1849), and *Mose in China* (1850), among others.[6]

Mose became an iconic New York stage character, and his influence on the representation of white working-class men lingered in melodramas, burlettas, comedies, and variety sketches for decades. *A Glance at New York* also sparked a fervor for shows illustrating local urban life in the United States, such as *Modern Insanity; or, Fashion and Forgery* (1857) and *The Mysteries and Crimes of New York and Brooklyn* (1858). As a result of its popularity and influence, scholars such as Richard M. Dorson, David Rinear, and Zoe Detsi-Diamanti (among others) have analyzed the production in relation to its political, economic, social, and cultural contexts, especially in terms of working-class culture and the literary genres that inspired the play, such as city mystery novels and the "urban sketches" genre written by moral reformers and journalists.[7] Similar to the majority of nineteenth-century theatrical performances, only fragmented evidence remains for the production, which obstructs how it is studied and understood.

The script for *A Glance at New York* provides critical insight into Mose and the production. However, in many ways, the text alone is an incomplete and unstable window into the show witnessed by audiences on that evening in February 1848. Actors interpreted the texts and often improvised during the performance. Songs and other novelty acts typically filled act breaks or scene changes. Prompter scripts reveal how texts existed as living documents with edits and performance changes that sometimes even went as far as cutting or rearranging acts depending on the night. Spectacular design elements and the composition and behavior of the audience shaped how the performance was understood and interpreted as well as what could be seen or heard. Nineteenth-century performance practices, theater historian Amy Hughes notes, "suggest that the 'literature' of the theater was as provisional and ephemeral as the performances themselves."[8]

It is common for scholars of theater and performance to navigate the tension between what Diana Taylor has characterized as the archive, the "supposedly endurable" physical, often text-based evidence, and the repertoire, the "performances, gestures, orality, movement, dance, singing – in short, all those acts usually thought of as ephemeral, nonreproducible knowledge."[9] According to Matthew Rebhorn, the tenuous relationship between archive and repertoire has led scholars of literary studies to "overlook nineteenth-century American theater and performance," which he claims is "virtually absent" in nineteenth-century literature anthologies.[10] It is critical to investigate the relationship between the unstable text and embodied performance because, as Rebhorn points out, the "cultural work that theatre did remains tied to its repertoire."[11] When reading the reviews of *A Glance at New York*, it is possible see how crucial the repertoire is for our understanding of the play. The reviewers talk about not only how Chanfrau represented Mose and the Bowery b'hoys accurately, but also Chanfrau's excellence at *embodying* the character.

This essay models how scholars of theatrical culture, especially when navigating the textual archive, can use the nineteenth-century repertoire to examine how movement created meaning in the nineteenth-century theater. Drawing on mobility studies as developed by sociologists and cultural geographers, I analyze how movement – conceptualized as a meaning-making, embodied process – helps construct nineteenth-century entertainments. I map *A Glance at New York*'s mobile rhythms and examine how they create what cultural geographer Tim Edensor calls a "mobile sense of place."[12] Through the show's dramaturgical structure and the textual clues about character movement, *A Glance at New York* presents a modern city defined by mobility. At the same time, the urban landscape shapes how people move through space as well as how their movement constructs their class, gender, and racial identities. In the final section, I consider the potential of embodied mobile stage practices to produce affective atmospheres that enable the audience to feel the city that lies beyond the stage.

Traveling through the City

With its comic villains and plot, *A Glance at New York* effectively combined popular city narratives, melodramatic conventions, and comedy to (mostly) celebrate the city. Scholars have analyzed these genres and how they reflected and negotiated political and social anxieties as well as generated meaning through the interactions between text, performance, and audience.[13] Amy Hughes's work on melodramatic spectacle and reform demonstrates the importance of centering the body and affect when examining the cultural resonances of nineteenth-century entertainments. She theorizes how the "spectacular instant" created an affective experience for audience members and held the potential to transform "feeling into one or more recognizable emotions that sustain, challenge, or complicate the values with which [the audience] previously identified."[14] This essay focuses on mobility as one approach to better understanding how embodiment created meaning in the nineteenth-century popular theater as well as how it might be further implicated in the affective experience of the audience.

It is mobility studies' emphasis on the *practice* of mobility that holds potential for theater and performance studies scholars.[15] Cultural geographer Tim Cresswell makes an important distinction between movement and mobility. He defines movement as "an act of displacement that allows people to move between locations" or "mobility abstracted from contexts of power."[16] He explains that mobility is created through power relations and is "socially produced motion."[17] Mobility studies scholars argue that mobility is not simply reflective, but, rather, an active practice through which, in sociologist John Urry's terms, "social life and cultural identity are recursively formed and reformed."[18] Although it is not possible to recover the ephemeral aspects of performance, by analyzing scripts for clues to characters' mobility within a matrix of mobility's meanings generated onstage, scholars can move closer to understanding how embodied practice, the repertoire, may have worked alongside and complicated textual meanings. I map the various ways mobility informs the world of the production, its fundamental dramaturgy, and its development of character in *A Glance at New York*.

The dramaturgical foundation of *A Glance at New York* is rooted in the characters' journey through the city. *A Glance at New York* follows Mose, who along with his old school friend Harry Gordon, gives a tour of New York to Harry's cousin, George Parsells, a naïve tourist from the country. Through their adventures, the main characters visit a range of upscale and impoverished locales, meet local characters, and fight thieves and loafers. The show depicts anxieties about urban life, including its power to corrupt morals and its concerns about urban social problems such as crime and poverty, while championing the resourcefulness of the urban working class. Throughout, thieves repeatedly con George, a plot that represents commonly held fears about how the city took advantage of rural visitors. Their movements and the aspects of city life that facilitate or regulate them, I suggest, create what Tim Edensor conceptualizes as a "mobile sense of place." In Edensor's theorization, "places are always becoming, and a human, whether stationary or travelling, is one rhythmic constituent in a seething space pulsing with intersecting trajectories and temporalities."[19] This notion is contingent not only on representation but also on how the embodied movement through the space of the city, materialized through the live performance, constructs the city and its meanings. The play's structure facilitates this mobile sense of New York through its initial framing of New York as a modern, mobile city and its depictions and embodiment of urban mobility and survival.

A Glance at New York's framing characterizes New York as a modern city always on the move. The show opens at the steamboat pier on Barclay Street, where the city and the water meet. This setting opens the dramatic action at a site of different geographies, temporalities, and mobile rhythms. Newsboys and apple-women sell their goods and sing how "The folks are all waiting to see the fast steamer."[20] As "a profile steamboat approaches," they continue the chorus, exclaiming "Ah! here she is! ... We've been waiting to see her best part of the day!"[21] In 1848, the shipping industry was in the midst of a transition from sailing to steamships, which promised faster and more efficient sea travel. The song characterizes New York as being at the forefront of this change, as modern and technologically advanced and as a critical site of exchange. The chorus points out, "In New York, the fastest boats always land here."[22] As the show progressed, it continued to celebrate the modern city and, as Tice Miller, notes, "the production kept congratulating New Yorkers on how up-to-date they were."[23]

The transitional space of the pier helps introduce the play's mobile dramaturgical foundation. The disembarked passengers move from one form of transport to the next and set up the show's insistence on mobility and speed as fundamental to modern city life. Alongside the pier, a cabman questions the passengers, "Hire a cab to ride through the city, sir?"[24] Even though their destination is not far, Harry tells George, "fashion, my boy, won't allow us to walk there; we must ride."[25] Comments such as Harry's link mobility to social values and class status. At least at this point in the production, walking is considered unsuitable for Harry and George as a result of their class status and, implicitly, their white racial identities. As other passengers walk by into the moving city around them, Harry and George find a cab to begin the play's journey.

For the rest of the play, Harry and Mose walk through the city and show George its high and low life. From the pier, they travel to Broadway, the Ladies Bowling Saloon, Loafer's Paradise, Front Street (several times), and, finally, to Vauxhall Gardens. Although *what* was witnessed at each location provided a view into city life, including the lives of respectable ladies, criminals, drunks, and firefighters, *how* they traveled from location to location also contributed to the construction of the city and its meanings. Early on, Harry comments on how New York's mobile accessibility makes it the "great metropolis of the Western world."[26] He praises the range of amusements available for tourists and then explains how a "five minutes' walk will take you from the extreme of wealth to the extreme of poverty."[27] George's cousin Jane is also touring the city, and, in certain scenes, the plot jumps to her adventures with other respectable middle-class women. In their travels as middle-class white women, mobility and accessibility are linked closely with pleasure and entertainment. While window shopping on Broadway, Jane tells her friend, "[E]verything I see is so much superior to our village that I don't know whether New York belongs to this world or not."[28]

The dramaturgical rhythm of the play and sense of New York develops from these characters' movements. Yet their rhythm is shaped by other characters and the landscape of the city. Characters' identities and mobility are dependent on their interactions with others, as well as the material and often dirty reality of city life. How people walked the city constituted their class, racial, and gender identities. On the Bowery, Bowery b'hoys and g'hals boisterously promenaded down the street in brightly colored clothes. Promenading gave working-class women an opportunity to temporarily claim public space as their own and participate in the republican pride that regularly characterized much of working-class male culture during these decades. This uninhibited claiming of space contrasted with the restrained promenade practices of the middle and upper classes on Broadway or the expectations that Black Americans would walk closest to gutter or step aside for white New Yorkers to pass.[29]

As a result of his participation in this context of practices, how and where Mose walks helps signal his working-class identity and his class aspirations to the play's audience. Harry and George first run into Mose as he crosses Broadway. Surprised, Harry remarks: "[H]ow comes it I find you in this part of the town? I heard that you held Broadway in such contempt, that you could'n be persuaded even to cross it."[30] By crossing Broadway, Mose transgresses class boundaries and social divisions that defined the city. While the Bowery was associated with working-class culture and life, the area around Broadway was considered the purview of the upper classes. Mose implies he intends to move up in the world, responding, "I've got over dat now [his aversion to the non-working-class areas of the city]. The fact is, I'm agoin' to give up runnin' to fires. I aren't been used well, so I'm goin' to locate somewhere in this quarter, if I can find a good boardin'-house."[31] Mose's desire to move up and leave his working-class neighborhood results from his disenchantment with his fire company, which quickly dissipates.

Mose works as a butcher and volunteer firefighter, which the production presents as mobile as opposed to stationary occupations. The audience never sees Mose in the slaughterhouse. Instead, audience members view him as he travels through the city with his cart to sell and deliver meat to his customers.[32] As opposed to being smooth and efficient, his movement is circumscribed by the street sweepers and the dust they kick up along the road. Mose yells after them, "[I]f you kick up such a dust as that when I'm passin', to spile my beef, I'll lam you!"[33] Similarly, the audience never sees Mose and the firefighters putting out a fire, but instead, after the fire bell rings, views "Boys and Men cross[ing] the stage from one side to the other."[34] Mose enters, "pulling on hose ... He runs against George, who falls. Scene closes."[35] This representation is not surprising since "running with the machine" became a colloquial reference to serving as a firefighter, as Mose references on his first entrance. His success in New York is contingent on knowing how to successfully move through city spaces, which Mose demonstrates repeatedly throughout the show.

Unlike Mose, George is frequently frozen in the city, which places him in danger. George is constantly knocked down when standing still on city streets, including by Mose running to put out the fire and by other pedestrians. At one point, George explains, "I've been knocked down in the dirt, had a fire-engine to run along within an inch of my nose; then they told me to get up, as I was in the way. Where shall I go, to get out of the way, I wonder?"[36] He often needs to be told how to move by Harry or Mose. As a rural tourist, he needs to understand how to move in the city to survive, which he begins to learn at the end of the play when he decides to stay and marry a woman he met on his trip.

Middle-class women similarly experience more circumscribed mobility. As feminist critic Janet Wolff highlights in her work, "the consequent suggestion of free and equal mobility is itself a deception, since we don't all have the same access to the road."[37] For example, in New York, in addition to the dangers facing a woman walking alone, a woman walking the streets who did not conform to behavioral codes of the middle- and upper-class women was often considered a criminal or sex worker. Thus in *A Glance at New York*, how a woman moves often depends on her class. The middle-class white women in the play conform to class codes as they stroll down Broadway to shop. They acknowledge the danger men present to them while they bowl in their women-only bowling alley. One woman cheerfully comments, "When once within these walls, we are secure from the intrusion of horrid men."[38] The play mocks these women in their female-only space when Mose, Harry, and George dress as women and sneak into it. As the men try to fit in, at one point, Mose can no longer control himself and he kisses one of the women. Mose exclaims, "Yes, sir-ree, I am a man, and no mistake – and one of de b'hoys at dat."[39] While presented as a comic moment, a mocking of middle-class femininity, this scene also demonstrates the danger presented to women by men in the city. Other than window shopping on Broadway, an acceptable preoccupation, the show does not show middle-class women roaming the city streets, which would have been considered improper.

For working-class white women, the play presents a different version of female mobility and the threat posed by men. Lize is Mose's counterpart, the Bowery g'hal. For Lize, walking is primarily a method of transportation to and from work. Lize is a respectable working-class woman and is comfortable using the street for non-travel purposes only if she is assured no one unintended will see her display.[40] In two instances, she stops in the street to sing, once for Mose and once for her friend Jenny. In both scenes, Mose and Jenny assure her the street is empty. Mose confirms, "[Y]ou're safe."[41] Unlike the middle-class women, Lize can defend herself against men and is supportive of Mose's fighting. When her friend Jenny asks about Sykes "cuttin' round" her, she explains how "Sykesy tried, but I bluffed him off."[42] Similar to Mose, Lize knows how to look after herself and, therefore, at least with what is presented to the audience, successfully navigates the city.

The ending of the play reinforces the sense of a city and people on the move and demonstrates how mobility will continue to inform the world of the play after the curtain goes down. In the show's last scene, Mose, Lize, Harry, and George travel north to Vauxhall Gardens, a pleasure garden with a small theater located on Lafayette Street between 4th and 8th Streets. A waiter alerts Mose that his friend Sykes is calling for his help in a street fight. Mose rushes to fight alongside his friend until Harry stops him and asks him to "not go in that manner."[43] He points to the audience and remarks, "Remember there!"[44] Mose asks the "ladies and gentlemen" of the audience not to "be down on me 'cause I'm goin' to leave you – but Sykesy's got in a muss, and I'm bound to see him righted, 'cause he runs wid our machine, you know."[45] Even with the show's conclusion, Mose remains on the move and leaves the audience with a view of the city and its people as constantly in motion.

Feeling the City

It remains impossible to recover *A Glance at New York*'s repertoire, defined as the embodied aspects of performance. Scripts provide opportunities to glimpse what the repertoire may have signified by exploring the relational meanings and the matrix of mobilities produced on stage that informed and gave shape to the now absent, ephemeral performances. In his exploration of absence and performance, theater historian Odai Johnson tells the story of Giuseppe Fiorelli's plaster. From 1865 to 1875, archeologist

Giuseppe Fiorelli excavated Pompei, which was destroyed by the volcano Vesuvius in 79 CE. During the excavation, he found holes filled with air. As the team uncovered more and more of the holes, Fiorelli decided to fill them with plaster in an attempt to see what they once held. The plaster casts revealed human forms and the final moments of Pompei's residents as the ash overtook them. The residents died and decomposed, but the hardened ash preserved their forms. Johnson uses the metaphor of Fiorelli's plaster to urge theater and performance historians not to reconstruct "the theatre or playbills, or a company's roster, or a provincial circuit, but rather to evoke the potent ghost of performance and the desire for where it left little material trace of itself, to reassert its absent presence back into . . . the narrative of the history of performance in the period."[46] For *A Glance at New York*, the repertoire might remain absent, but a broader consideration of mobilities might help make the absent more present. Since it is impossible to recreate the repertoire of *A Glance at New York*, I want to raise the possibilities presented by considering what the matrix of mobilities may have produced, especially in terms of the affective experience potentially generated through the characters' performances.

When witnessing the world of the city in *A Glance at New York*, the audience had the chance to experience an affective atmosphere created by the production's mobile practice. Anne Jensen discusses the potential of mobile spaces to create affective atmospheres:

> Atmospheres are . . . mobile spaces that we experience. . . . The latent quality and the intensity are immanently related to feeling and to diverse ways of experiencing mobile space. Our becoming subjectivities interweave how we experience mobile spaces as emotional, whilst feelings related to mobility at the same time constitute a basic relation with the atmospheres and senses-capes of mobile spaces . . . in other words, particular mobilities are produced in the interaction between the places and spaces of mobility and the experience and perception of the movement as it happens.[47]

The atmosphere had the potential to interact with the audience's own diverse experiences of city life to invoke feelings about the city and its people. With many in the audience having walked down the streets and locations depicted in the play, the show may have evoked feelings tied to those spaces and their experiences moving through them.

Although it witnesses the mobility onstage only, the audience still contributes to the atmosphere produced by the play. Unlike theater later in the century, US theater audiences had yet to adopt passive behaviors, and audience participation remained an active part of the production. The *New York Herald* described the rowdy atmosphere of the premiere of the second Mose play, *New York as It Is*, which demonstrates the active and involved role of the audience in the Mose shows:

> In the early part of the evening, every available place of accommodation within the theatre was crowded to excess, long before the commencement of the evening's entertainment.... "The Brigand," which preceded the new and attractive piece [*New York as It Is*] was being performed when the crowd became so great that those who were in the front seats in the pit were forced to take refuge, for a time, in that part of the theatre allocated for the orchestra. The shouting and confusion here became almost alarming, and no sooner had those who fled there been seated down, when another rush from behind caused them to start on the stage, over the gas lights, and the play was stopped. Soon wave after wave succeeded ... and some of the young b'hoys were seen to be springing forward on the heads of their different groups of friends from the stage, whom they soon joined in the pit, amid continued laughter.[48]

Through the active auditorium, audiences watching the Mose plays participated in the atmosphere created by the characters' mobility on stage. The reviewer remarks on how the mobile chaos of the auditorium reflected the evening's main attraction. After describing the b'hoys behavior in the pit, the reviewer observes that "perhaps a more graphic illustration of 'New York as It Is,' could not be given with better effect."[49]

For the audience, their previous experiences and understandings of New York and the male working class contributed to their theatrical experience and enjoyment of the play. As Jensen notes, "Intertwining with subjectivities, the atmospheres of particular and situated mobile spaces emerge on the basis of prior understandings and experiences of the subject whilst at the same time stimulating mobile behaviours."[50] Some scholars have suggested that "a hush of wonder greeted [Mose's] entrance, and then a roar of recognition burst from the pit."[51] *A Glance at New York*'s playwright, Benjamin Baker, described a contrasting response to the *New York Clipper* several decades after the premiere. Describing Mose's reception as, at first, "a cool one," Baker claimed that the b'hoys in the audience were first concerned the show might be mocking them. Baker remembered that when Mose saves a baby left behind by his mother, "*That* appealed to the good-heartedness of the fire-laddies, and thenceforward Mose was a triumph."[52] The audience's experience depended not solely on visual recognition of the character but on how he was performed in combination with the show's sentimental scene.

Mose and his plays held the potential to influence audiences beyond the evening's performance. Considering the dialogue of the script alone

provides a limited perspective on a play's cultural impact. Even if mobilities offer only a potential window into the repertoire, they present the
possibility of understanding a more complete picture of the show's performance and its resonances. One example illustrates how the affective
atmosphere and embodied experience of the play may have impacted the
ways the audience moved through New York. Even though Chanfrau
performed Bowery b'hoys' culture, the b'hoys took on the physicality of
Chanfrau's Mose and performed it in the streets of New York, combining
their lived experience with Chanfrau's interpretation. A *New York Herald*
review observed, "The boys in the street have caught [Mose's] sayings, and
yesterday morning, while waiting at one of the North River docks for the
arrival of some friends per steamboat, we were quite amused at seeing a
squal of youngsters enacting 'New York as It Is' on their own account to
the unbounded delight of the bystanders."[53] In the process of performance, the boys collapsed the space between the fictional and lived realities
of the b'hoys through their performance on docks not far from the play's
opening scene. They restaged the embodied performances, complicating
them with their own acting skill (or lack thereof) and imitations. This
example also highlights another potential impact: Chanfrau's popular
Mose may have influenced how to *be* a b'hoy through the ways the
character was brought back into working-class neighborhoods by enthusiastic audience members.

Tracing how the manifestations of Mose traveled and transformed over
time presents another opportunity to assess *A Glance at New York*'s impact.
The idea of Mose on the move is intrinsic to future stage depictions in
other shows, which also took him around the city or sent him traveling to
China and California. Like his character, Chanfrau toured as Mose to cities
across the country, including Philadelphia, Cincinnati, and Chicago, for
years after the character's 1848 debut. Lithographers printed Mose and
Lize's images and sold them in shops and on the street. Artists and writers
continued to define Mose through his mobility with one humorous,
illustrated book, *Mose among the Britishers; or, The B'hoy in London*
(1850)[54] (see Figures 10.1 and 10.2). Investigating the embodied practices
prompted by the ephemera surrounding theater performances thus offers
scholars further insight into shows' cultural impacts and resonances.[55]

To be sure, it is impossible to know what the b'hoys or other audience
members felt embodying or witnessing the characters' journeys. However,
by considering mobile practices as we approach nineteenth-century culture, scholars can better understand nineteenth-century theater and performance and its impacts far beyond the play itself. It is important to study

HE TAKES LEAVE OF LIZE, LITTLE MOSE AND DER MASHEENE.

AND EMBARKS IN THAT NOBLE, FAST-SAIL-ING, AND COPPER-BOTTOMED LINE OF PACKET SHIP, THE CATAWAMPUS ; CAPTAIN JOTHAM GRUFFUMSNORTER COMMANDER.

Figure 10.1 "He Takes Leave of Lize, Little Mose, and 'Der Masheene,'" from *Mose among the Britishers; or, The B'hoy in London*. Image courtesy of the New York Public Library.

theater and performance history, and not simply the scripts and literary remains, because scripts provide an imperfect record of performance and leave fundamental components that shaped meaning – the repertoire and audience – out of the conversation. When limited evidence of the repertoire remains, scholars can utilize scripts and methodologies, such as mobility studies, to question how potential embodiment created meaning and to search for the repertoire's echoes through those leads. Theater history and performance studies are critical fields for learning about the antebellum United States. They provide an opportunity to uncover not only what Americans consumed during their leisure time, but also a living medium that reflected, challenged, and processed identities, ideologies, and cultural conflicts. Theater offers scholars a vital site for examining culture in process, how it impacted its audiences, actively was shaped by dialogue with its consumers, and held the potential to influence physical as well as intellectual practices.

Figure 10.2 "Don Cesar Receiving the Intimation in an Uncourteous Manner," from *Mose among the Britishers; or, The B'hoy in London*. Image courtesy of the New York Public Library.

Notes

1 Benjamin Baker, *A Glance at New York* (New York: Samuel French, n.d.), 10, *Literature Online*, ProQuest Information and Learning, www.proquest.com/lion/docview/2138580721/Z000612330/95BBA41A92DE443CPQ/1?accountid=14657&segment=LitTexts (accessed April 2, 2019).
2 David Rinear, "F. S. Chanfrau's Mose: The Rise and Fall of an Urban Folk-Hero," *Theatre Journal* 33, no. 2 (May 1981): 200.
3 Ibid., 200–201.
4 *The Albion*, February 19, 1848, 96.
5 *The Spirit of the Times*, March 11, 1848, 36.
6 Rinear, "F. S. Chanfrau's Mose," 203–12; Richard M. Dorson, "Mose the Far-Famed and World-Renowned," *American Literature* 15, no. 3 (November 1943): 288–300.
7 Rinear, "F. S. Chanfrau's Mose," 203–12; Dorson, "Mose the Far-Famed and World-Renowned," 288–300; Zoe Detsi-Diamanti, "Staging Working-Class Culture: George A. Baker's 'A Glance at New York' (1848)," *Hungarian Journal of English and American Studies* 15, no. 1 (Spring 2009): 11–26;

Rosemarie Bank, *Theatre Culture in America, 1825–1860* (New York: Cambridge University Press, 1997), 84–92.

8 Amy Hughes, "Theater; or, Looking beyond Plays and Places," *J19: The Journal of Nineteenth-Century Americanists* 6, no. 2 (Fall 2018): 413. See also Matthew Rebhorn, "Introduction: 'Nineteenth-Century' 'American' 'Theater' and 'Performance,'" *J19: The Journal of Nineteenth-Century Americanists* 6, no. 2 (2018): 389–94.

9 Diana Taylor, *The Archive and the Repertoire: Performing Cultural Memory in the Americas* (Durham, NC: Duke University Press, 2003), 19.

10 Rebhorn, "Introduction," 391.

11 Ibid., 391.

12 Tom Edensor, "Walking in Rhythms: Place, Regulation, Style and the Flow of Experience," *Visual Studies* 25, no. 1 (2010): 70.

13 *A Glance at New York*'s narrative adapted the local urban focus of popular burlettas and melodramas that showcased European cities, including the wildly successful *Tom and Jerry; or, Life in London* (first produced in New York in 1823), *The Heart of London; or, The Sharper's Progress* (1830), *London by Night* (1845), and *Les Mystères de Paris* (1844). For more on the French melodramas depicting local urban life and their transatlantic adaptations, see Nicholas Daly, *The Demographic Imagination and the Nineteenth-Century City: Paris, London, New York* (New York: Cambridge University Press, 2015), 46–76. For more on *Tom and Jerry*'s connection to *A Glance at New York*, see Tice Miller, *Entertaining the Nation: American Drama in the Eighteenth and Nineteenth Centuries* (Carbondale: Southern Illinois University Press, 2007), 97–99. For more on confidence men in antebellum cities, see Karen Halttunen, *Confidence Men and Painted Women: A Study of Middle-Class Culture in America, 1830–1870* (New Haven, CT: Yale University Press, 1982). For more on nineteenth-century entertainments, see David Grimsted, *Melodrama Unveiled: American Theater and Culture, 1800–1850* (Berkeley: University of California Press, 1988); Bruce McConachie, *Melodramatic Formations: American Theatre and Society, 1820–1870* (Iowa City: University of Iowa Press, 1992); John W. Frick, "The 'Wicked City' Motif on the American Stage before the Civil War," *New Theatre Quarterly* 20, no. 1 (February 2004): 19–27; Jeffrey D. Mason, *Melodrama and Myth of America* (Bloomington: Indiana University Press, 1993); Bank, *Theatre and Culture in America*; Elizabeth Mullenix, *Wearing the Breeches: Gender on the Antebellum Stage* (New York: Palgrave Macmillan, 2000); Kim Mara, *Strange Duets: Impresarios and Actresses in American Theatre, 1865–1914* (Iowa City: University of Iowa Press, 2009); Lisa Merill, *When Romeo Was a Woman: Charlotte Cushman and Her Circle of Female Spectators* (Ann Arbor: University of Michigan Press, 1999).

14 Amy Hughes, *Spectacles of Reform: Theater and Activism in Nineteenth Century America* (Ann Arbor: University of Michigan Press, 2012), 44.

15 In their studies of theater and performance, Fiona Wilkie, Marlis Schweitzer, and Sabinne Haenni have argued for the critical role of analyzing the

relationship between mobility and performance in relation to contemporary theater and transport, transatlantic Broadway objects and infrastructure, and nineteenth-century immigrant theater and film. See Fiona Wilkie, *Performance, Transport, and Mobility: Making Passage* (New York: Palgrave, 2015); Sabine Haenni, *The Immigrant Scene: Ethnic Amusements in New York, 1880–1920* (Minneapolis: University of Minnesota Press, 2008); and Marlis Schweitzer, *Transatlantic Broadway: The Infrastructural Politics of Global Performance* (Palgrave Macmillan, 2015).

16 Tim Cresswell, *On the Move: Mobility in the Modern Western World* (New York: Routledge, 2006), 3.

17 Ibid. By identifying and analyzing "type, strategies, and social implications," of movement, Cresswell suggests scholars can understand mobility's meanings and how they are generated.

18 John Urry, *Sociology beyond Societies: Mobilities for the Twenty-First Century* (New York: Routledge, 2000), 49. Similar to the literary narratives examined by scholars such as Ann Brigham, nineteenth-century theater "participate[s] in imagining, recreating, and interrogating the term and terms of mobility." Ann Brigham, *American Road Narratives: Reimagining Mobility in Literature and Film* (Charlottesville: University of Virginia Press, 2015), 4. In their efforts to consider how degrees of mobility or immobility function on a spectrum to generate meaning, mobility studies scholars attempt to avoid a mobility/immobility binary. Cresswell, *On the Move*, 14; Hagar Kotef, *Movement and the Ordering of Freedom: On Liberal Governances of Mobility* (Durham, NC: Duke University Press, 2015), 11; Doreen Massey, *For Space* (Thousand Oaks, CA: SAGE Publications, 2005), 86–97; John Urry and Mimi Sheller, "The New Mobilities Paradigm," *Environment and Planning A* 38, no. 2 (February 2006): 210–12.

19 Edensor, "Walking in Rhythms," 70–71.

20 Baker, *A Glance at New York*, 4.

21 Ibid., 4.

22 Ibid.

23 Miller, *Entertaining the Nation*, 98.

24 Baker, *A Glance at New York*, 4.

25 Ibid.

26 Ibid., 5.

27 Ibid.

28 Ibid., 8.

29 Christine Stansell, *City of Women: Sex and Class in New York, 1789–1860* (Urbana: University of Illinois Press, 1986), 90–95; Marvin McAllister, *White People Do Not Know How to Behave at Entertainments Designed for Ladies and Gentlemen of Colour: William Brown's African and American Theater* (Chapel Hill: University of North Carolina Press, 2003), 25. See also David Scobey, "Anatomy of the Promenade: The Politics of Bourgeois Sociability in Nineteenth-Century," *Social History* 17, no. 2 (May 1992): 203–27.

30 Baker, *A Glance at New York*, 11.

31 Ibid., 11.
32 Ibid., 23.
33 Ibid., 22.
34 Ibid., 24.
35 Ibid.
36 Ibid.
37 Janet Wolff, "On the Road Again: Metaphors of Travel in Cultural Criticism," *Cultural Studies* 6 (1992): 253. See also Karen Kaplan, *Questions of Travel: Postmodern Discourses of Displacement* (Durham, NC: Duke University Press, 1996), 65–100; Doreen Massey, *For Space* (Thousand Oaks, CA: SAGE Publications, 2005), 45–47; Beverley Steggs, *Class, Self, Culture* (New York: Routledge, 2004), 45–52.
38 Baker, *A Glance at New York*, 13.
39 Ibid.
40 Ibid., 23, 30.
41 Ibid.
42 Ibid., 30.
43 Ibid., 33.
44 Ibid.
45 Ibid.
46 Odai Johnson, *Absence and Memory in Colonial America Theatre: Fiorelli's Plaster* (New York: Palgrave Macmillan, 2006), 15; for Johnson's discussion of Fiorelli, see 13–14.
47 Anne Jensen, "Power and Representations of Mobility: From the Nexus between Emotional and Sensuous Embodiment and Discursive and Ideational Construction," in *Researching and Representing Mobilities: Transdisciplinary Encounters*, ed. Lesley Murray and Sarah Upstone (New York: Palgrave MacMillan, 2014), 33–34.
48 "Theatrical and Musical," *New York Herald*, April 18, 1848.
49 Ibid.
50 Jensen, "Power and Representations of Mobility," 33.
51 Dorson, "Mose the Far-Famed and World-Renowned," 288. I have yet to find primary evidence to support the audience response described by Dorson.
52 "Mose," *New York Clipper*, April 6, 1878; "Theatrical and Musical," *New York Herald*, April 26, 1848.
53 "Theatrical and Musical," *New York Herald*, April 26, 1848.
54 Thomas Butler Gunn, *Mose among the Britishers; or The B'hoy in London* (Philadelphia: A. Hart, 1850).
55 Robin Bernstein discusses how things script human action. See Robin Bernstein, *Racial Innocence: Performing American Childhood from Slavery to Civil Rights* (New York: New York University Press, 2009).

CHAPTER II

Popular Poetry

Michael C. Cohen

In a long essay on Thomas Campbell's *Specimens of the British Poets* (1819), a writer in the *Edinburgh Review* offered some reflections on the double-edged effect of popular taste on literary history. Although "the fame of a poet is popular, or nothing," and although "present popularity, whatever disappointed writers say, is ... the only safe presage of future glory," popular taste, according to this reviewer, was an effective agent of canon formation only during times of literary scarcity, when few poets competed for readers' attention.[1] "As the materials of enjoyment and instruction accumulate," however, many poems "must thus be daily rejected," such that the "superfluity and abundance of our treasures, therefore, necessarily renders much of them worthless" (471). As more and more poets wrote better and better poetry, a greater and greater number would be forgotten, simply because "there was not room in our memories for all" (471). There is only so much popularity to go around at any one time, and, by 1819, far too many poets were competing for it. Therefore, after reading the seven volumes of Campbell's anthology, the reviewer reached a glum conclusion:

> Next to the impression of the vast fertility, compass, and beauty of our English poetry, the reflection that recurs most frequently and forcibly ... is that of the perishable nature of poetical fame, and the speedy oblivion that has overtaken so many of the promised heirs of immortality. Of near two hundred and fifty authors, whose works are cited in these volumes, by far the greater part of whom were celebrated in their generation, there are not thirty who now enjoy any thing that can be called popularity – whose works are to be found in the hands of ordinary readers – in the shops of ordinary booksellers – or in the press for republication.... It is strange, and somewhat humiliating, to see how great a proportion of those who had once fought their way successfully to distinction ... have again sunk into neglect. (470)

Slyly remarking that no period has ever been "so prolific of popular poetry as that in which we now live," the reviewer "cannot help being dismayed at the prospect which lies before the writers of the present day," noting presciently that in 100 years even the most popular were likely to be unknown to the readers of 1919 (471).

Surveys of "popular" literature, such as this essay you have just begun, often read like excerpts from a forgotten anthology, chock full of names and titles that will never appear on a college syllabus. If the literature syllabus is a synecdoche for the literary canon, as John Guillory suggests, then canonicity and popularity might be understood as related processes of hierarchical organization, constituted by distinct temporalities and criteria.[2] As an evaluative concept, "popularity" is a judgment about a text's contemporary fame, the scale of its distribution, or the size and enthusiasm of its readership, but not its aesthetic quality. *The Song of Hiawatha* was more popular in 1855 than *Leaves of Grass*, by any metric, but that initial preference on the part of prior readers entails no obligation on later students of the 1850s. If anything, a review of once-popular cultural forms, texts, and authors can easily become a catalog of indictments against the bad taste (or worse) of the past. Blackface minstrelsy? City mysteries? Abraham Cowley? Felicia Hemans? Joyce Kilmer? Really?[3]

The literary canon, in this view, is that which endures after the popular has faded into ephemeral oblivion. This Modernist understanding of literature as "news that stays news," which bolstered a masculinist critical tradition against the perceived feminization of the mass market, was paramount to the twentieth-century instantiation of an American literary canon.[4] Works by Van Wyck Brooks, V. L. Parrington, F. O. Matthiessen, and others searched for a "usable past" by rigorously winnowing the popular, in the process discarding nearly all nineteenth-century American poetry besides that of Whitman, Dickinson, and, to lesser extents, Poe, Emerson, and Melville.[5] A poet or a poem's popularity in the nineteenth century was, if anything, a reason for twentieth-century critics not to value it. This intellectual and aesthetic dynamic was so foundational to the field that later efforts to open the borders of the American Renaissance still depended on reading the noncanonical in relation to the canon, with a focus only on prose genres.[6]

As Guillory also argues, however, a literary canon is an abstraction that expresses the cathected values of the institutions that mediate it, particularly the college or university.[7] As such, the concept of the popular can serve the purpose of critiquing canonicity as an elite deployment of cultural power. At any point in time, relatively few people read literature within the mediating authority of a university or a syllabus. "Popular literature," in this view, is what happens outside the classroom, or is what is excluded from the undergraduate survey or the graduate reading list. In this more populist iteration, understanding the preferences, habits, and ideas of so-called ordinary readers enables a better, more comprehensive view into the mentalities of the past.[8]

Such arguments may focus on exclusion, but they also reflect on scholarly methods. How do we know what was popular once? In the most positivist definitions, what was "popular" means something along the lines of what was "cheapest," "best-selling," or "most frequently read," three definitions (easy to conflate) that aim to provide empirical answers to notional questions of taste or canonicity.[9] Scholars seeking these kinds of answers might ask, to borrow the terms of the review with which we began: "Which authors, titles, or genres were found most often in 'the hands of ordinary readers' or the 'shops of ordinary booksellers?'" or "Which appeared the most regularly 'in the press for republication'?" This kind of accounting for literary popularity will often document the discrepancy between a contemporary understanding of the literary past (manifest in a canon or a syllabus), and the literary past itself, and it usually takes a neutral or, in some cases, even a polemical position about the explanatory value of popularity.[10] Thus, for example, Lydia Sigourney's large readership between 1820 and 1860 is not cause for embarrassment, but is instead an opportunity to better understand the culture and values of antebellum America.

In the case of the period in literary history that this volume covers – the United States between 1820 and 1860 – a positivist argument about "popular poetry" will paint an especially weird portrait of the era. In the antebellum decades, most of the poets and poems found most often in the hands of so-called ordinary readers, booksellers, or publishers were neither American nor from the nineteenth century. For instance, no volume of poems by an antebellum American author was reprinted even one-fourth as frequently as Alexander Pope's *Essay on Man* (1734) or Isaac Watts's *Divine Songs for Children* (1713), each of which was published in at least sixty different US editions between 1820 and 1860.[11] And few American poets of the time could compete, in terms of their aesthetic reception or their sales, with Walter Scott, Felicia Hemans, William Wordsworth, and Lord Byron. If literary historians of nineteenth-century America want to know which poems were most likely to have been most familiar to their subjects, they will need to start reading a lot more seventeenth- and eighteenth-century British poetry.

The approaches to the concept of popular literature that I have outlined so far are not necessarily antagonistic. Documenting the size of a print run or tabulating statistics about numbers of reprints may simply provide a different view of a cultural field structured by uneven distributions of power. William St. Clair has claimed that the long endurance in Britain of a canon of ballads and chapbooks – the originating works of "popular literature" – which circulated, in the instance of some titles, for more than 300 years, had little to do with the tastes or opinions of ordinary readers and everything to do with the cartelization of the publishing industry and a legal regime of tight control over copyright under the 1710 Statute of Anne. When perpetual copyright was abolished in 1774, he argues, most of this cheap literature vanished, and was quickly replaced by much more recent and much higher-quality materials.[12] Popular literature, in this view, may be that which has been chosen for readers, rather than that which readers would choose for themselves.

However, focusing too narrowly on which texts were printed, sold, bought, or read the most frequently, or in the greatest numbers, or for the lowest price, is not the most effective way to grasp the popularity of a period's literature. In the settler-colonial, male-dominated, white supremacist state of the antebellum United States, access to every component of literariness, from books, magazines, and newspapers to literacy, schooling, print shops, booksellers, and even paved roads, canals, or railroads, was structurally unequal and dependent on geography, class, gender, language, and race. Only after 1850 did it become feasible for publishers to imagine a nationwide literary market for the books or periodicals they printed, right at the moment when the future of the US state was most uncertain, and a nationwide readership even less likely to be realized.[13] And whenever a text did cross some of these lines – whether geographic, linguistic, or racial – it could change so profoundly along the way that it can be debated whether or not it was still the "same" text it had been.[14] What would it mean for any poem to be "popular" under such conditions?

Rather than staging a conflict between high culture and low, or between the literary canon and popular taste, and rather than seeking to unearth this or that heretofore-unrecognized bestselling, bellwether text, I suggest we consider instead the most common ways that people in the antebellum United States participated in the construction of literariness. Another way to say this is to suggest that instead of asking who or what were the most popular poets or poems, we ask instead about the ways in which most people read poems most of the time. Where did people read poems? How did they read them? And why did they want to?

There are many kinds of sources that can inform an inquiry guided by these kinds of questions. My approach is to follow the lead of nineteenth-century readers and to observe their methods and practices. Our guide will be Lucy Larcom. Larcom is as good a point of entry as any other nineteenth-century reader; although she was hardly "ordinary" – in later life she became a distinguished (and popular) author – she grew up in a working-class family, moved frequently, and had only a primary school education, and her access to literature was mediated in specific ways that are, I argue, characteristic of most readers in the antebellum United States.

Where did Larcom find poems to read? In her 1889 autobiography, *A New England Girlhood*, she gives a detailed answer:

> I began to know that I liked poetry, and to think a good deal about it at my childish work. Outside of the hymn-book, the first rhymes I committed to memory were in the "Old Farmer's Almanac," files of which hung in the chimney corner, and were an inexhaustible source of entertainment to us younger ones. My father kept his newspapers also carefully filed away in the garret, but we made sad havoc among the "Palladiums" and other journals that we ought to have kept as antiquarian treasures. We valued the anecdote column and the poet's corner only; these we clipped unsparingly for our scrap-books. A tattered copy of Johnson's large Dictionary was a great delight to me, on account of the specimens of English versification which I found in the Introduction. I learned them as if they were so many poems. I used to keep this old volume close to my pillow; and I amused myself when I awoke in the morning by reciting its jingling contrasts of iambic and trochaic and dactylic metre, and thinking what a charming occupation it must be to "make up" verses.[15]

Where did she find poems to read, memorize, clip, recite, or make up? In hymnals, almanacs, newspapers, and compendia like the dictionary. The tattered copy of Samuel Johnson's dictionary is perhaps the most idiosyncratic source in Larcom's list, but her phrasing of "specimens of English versification" indicates that she was likely also familiar with anthologies like Campbell's or Samuel Kettell's 1829 *Specimens of American Poetry*, so if we were to generalize from the dictionary, and consider as well other omnibus formats like anthologies, textbooks, and collections of extracts, then we have a good picture of the kinds of sources that brought readers and poems together.

Take the hymnal, the subject of a book by Christopher Phillips. "As objects as well as carriers of text," he writes, "hymnbooks were part of the everyday social practices of hundreds of thousands of English-speakers across two centuries."[16] As Phillips explains, a hymnal published in 1820 would have been difficult to distinguish (at least visually) from other large-format collections of poems: it would have included lineated, metrical text, but no music or tunes, and it would have been the property of an individual or a family, and not a church or congregation. Hymnals were intended for use in church, home, and school, thus situating them intimately within the most common nineteenth-century institutions. Some hymnbooks, such as those by Watts, were already over a century old in 1820, but new collections were constantly being published for different Protestant denominations. If someone in 1820 owned only one book besides the Protestant Bible and the Book of Common Prayer, a collection of hymns would likely be it. Hymns were also a poetic genre that crossed readily, if not easily, over differences of race, caste, region, and literacy, especially when detached from particular material formats. If we think of slave spirituals in relation to other kinds of Protestant hymns, then we likely have identified the poetic genre with the most racially diverse audience in the antebellum period.

An almanac, Larcom's next example, might not seem obvious as an "inexhaustible source of entertainment," but, as she observes, most almanacs of the early nineteenth century published poetry. Adopting the early modern model of the "shepherd's calendar," almanacs usually printed short, stanza-long verses on seasonal topics to accompany each month's table of meteorological, astronomical, and calendric information. Many almanacs also included a selection of longer comic, sentimental, or didactic poems, interspersed with prose dialogues, recipes, and historical anecdotes, in addition to tables of data and government information. For instance, *The Improved New-England Almanack* for 1820 included, as its title page declared, "besides a greater number of Astronomical Calculations than are usual, a great variety of useful, instructive and entertaining matter."[17] As was standard practice, this almanac attached quatrains of seasonal verse to each month's table of data, as in this entry for February:

> Now from the school, the noisy tribe
> Of boys and girls, to skate and slide,
> Betake them to yon icy rill,
> To ply their limbs and show their skill.

The editor of this almanac may have been a more devoted admirer of poetry than others; in addition to writing each of the monthly quatrains himself (they were usually lifted from other sources), he includes a selection of poems at the back of the book: two rebuses, Robert Southey's "Complaints of the Poor," a blackface dialogue on "True African Wit," and a collection of "Agricultural Aphorisms." The poems are short, the rhymes and meter simple, and the texts easy to memorize or imitate, as Larcom did. She notes that her first attempt at writing a poem was a "rainy-day amusement" that resembles the style and content of the almanac's seasonal verse:

One summer day, said little Jane,
We were walking down a shady lane,
When suddenly the wind blew high,
And the red lightning flashed in the sky. (127)

Almanacs belonged to many households that did not otherwise own books, and they were designed to reach places that were remote from urban centers. The purpose of an almanac was not to circulate poetry or enable an encounter with literariness, so the fact that it did so is a striking insight into the popular experience of poetry in the antebellum years.

"The Poets' Corner" of the newspaper was another common site to engage with poetry. Newspapers and magazines were prime publication venues for poems going back to the eighteenth century, and by the antebellum period the Poets' Corner was an established institution. As Ryan Cordell and Abby Mullen argue, "poems [appeared] in nearly every issue of nineteenth-century U.S. papers," typically in the same position within the paper, most often the top half of the left column on the fourth (or final) page, mirroring the masthead on the front page.[18] Most editors devoted around one-third of one column to the Poets' Corner, good for a single poem per issue, though some might devote enough room to print three or more poems at a time. The corner might be demarcated with dark bars or a design flourish at the top, but otherwise the text of the poems blended with the material in the surrounding columns. While the location of a Poets' Corner stayed consistent from issue to issue, the content always varied, in contrast with the middle of the paper, which was typically filled with paid advertisements and notices that stayed the same from issue to issue. The Poets' Corner was therefore one of the features that secured the newspaper as a conventional format and enabled every issue to be simultaneously distinct and familiar.

Newspapers and periodicals anchored a literary culture that was, in Meredith McGill's words, "regional in articulation and transnational in scope."[19] As a result, the Poets' Corner of even the most out-of-the-way local paper tended to be a heterogeneous space that brought readers material from far and wide. Entries might include poems reprinted from British or other US newspapers and periodicals; poems by well-known contemporary British or American authors, who were usually named; and "original" work (i.e., not reprinted from elsewhere) by local authors, who were usually not named. For instance, the September 1, 1820, issue of the Warrenton, Virginia, *Palladium of Liberty* published two poems in its Poets' Corner: "The Grave of Burns," taken "From a Scotch Paper," and "The Wheelbarrow," a short comic dialogue, while the September 1, 1820, issue of the *New England Palladium* published "The Duellists" (by Christopher Smart, though unattributed in this instance) and "Lines on Life," "By John Clare, a British Peasant."

Newspapers dedicated to political causes were similarly eclectic in their choices of poems to print or reprint. The inaugural issue of Frederick Douglass's *North Star* reprinted John Pierpont's famous "The Fugitive Slave's Apostrophe to the North Star," but it also reprinted the Scottish poet James Montgomery's eulogy to Robert Burns:

> What bird in beauty, flight, or song,
> Can with the bird compare,
> Who sang as sweet, and soared as strong,
> As ever child of air?
>
> His plume, his note, his form, could Burns,
> For whim or pleasure change;
> He was not one, but all by turns,
> With transmigration strange.[20]

Douglass's editorial control over the Poets' Corner of his newspapers remained consistent: in most issues of *The North Star*, the lead poem would address topics related to antislavery, while the other poems could be about anything. He would dedicate as much as three columns of an issue to reprinting poems, thereby associating a very broad range of eighteenth- and nineteenth-century verse with antislavery, and associating abolitionist activism with literary culture.

Many nineteenth-century poets got their start in the Poets' Corner of their local paper. John Greenleaf Whittier published several hundred poems in northeastern US newspapers in the 1820s and 1830s before securing his first book publication, and much of his career as an antislavery poet would be fought in the columns of periodicals like *The Liberator* and the *National Anti-Slavery Standard*. For example, among the "Original" entries in the March 14, 1829, issue of the *Haverhill Gazette* was Whittier's poem "The Fire Ship," a kind of mash-up of "Casabianca" (1826) and "The Rime of the Ancient Mariner" (1798), "suggested by a passage in the first volume of 'Salathiel'":

> A ship of flame, with its fierce red sail,
> And its mast of burning fire,
> And a tall form stood on its blazing deck,
> Like a slave at his funeral pyre!
> Nearer and nearer came the ship,
> And the mast of flame rose higher.

> Nearer and nearer came the ship,
> With its fearful tenant there,
> The flame like a robe was round him thrown,
> And his blacken'd arm was bare;
> But his lip was curled, and his brow was bent
> With the sternness of despair.
>
> On – on with the flame of mast and sail
> The spectre ship drew nigh;
> A strange heat burned on every cheek
> As its flaming keel went by!
> And we saw its fiend-like mariner,
> But he uttered forth no cry.[21]

A few weeks later, the *Gazette* reprinted a laudatory article about the twenty-one-year-old Whittier from a Philadelphia paper. "As a poet, Whittier has for the short time he has been before the public attained a distinguished station among American writers. His style, although not so polished and classical as that of some other of our writers, is highly imaginative and nervous, and is replete with many of the best characteristics of poetry."[22] Whittier was a spectacular example of a local poet who used newspaper publication to jump from anonymity to fame, but he was not by any means unique. The Kentucky poet Amelia B. Welby cultivated a large readership, particularly across the southern United States, through the tight relationship she established with her hometown paper, the *Louisville Journal*, which published her poems under the moniker "Amelia," beginning when she was a teenager. "It is now something more than two years, since the sweet and thrilling notes of an anonymous poetess, burst startlingly upon the ear of the literary world, from the wilds of Kentucky," wrote the *Journal* in 1839. "At once and eagerly were those enrapturing strains caught up by melody-lovers throughout the Union, and sung in every peopled valley, and echoed from every sunny hill-side, of our vast domain."[23]

Like Whittier, Welby's close association with a specific region and its paper (her poems were always published with the heading "For the *Louisville Journal*") actually enabled her to circulate widely, a process that was aided by the relative abstraction and anonymity of her work, as in this early instance, "To Mrs. L—":

> Lady, if hope's bright ray
> Deceive thee with its beam,
> If life's joys melt away
> Like love's first witching dream,
> If all earth's tender ties,
> Have from thy heart been riven,
> Look up beyond the skies
> To tenderer ties in heaven.

> If all the buds of earth,
> That promised early bloom,
> Have perished in their birth
> Like beauty in the tomb,
> If love hath seared thy heart,
> A glorious hope is given,
> Which soothes affliction's smart –
> There's purer love in heaven.
>   AMELIA.[24]

In a rhetorical move that is utterly characteristic of antebellum newspaper poetry, this poem teases at disclosing a secret by using a public format to deliver an apparently private and personal message to an addressee, Mrs. L—, whose name is both obscured and revealed. Yet when the "Mrs. L—" of the title becomes the "Lady" of the first line, the poem shifts to address many, if not most, of its readers. Though Welby's stanzas end with didactic tags, many of the most popular poets of the 1840s – Elizabeth Oakes Smith, Frances Sargent Osgood, Edgar Allan Poe – used similar rhetorical strategies to revel in the erotic possibilities of being private in public.[25]

Not all poets enjoyed such happy relationships with the press. Newspapers rarely paid for original contributions, and almost never for reprints, which were by far the largest bulk of all the poetry they published. Poe received $15 for the first publication of "The Raven" (in *The American Review*, under the name "Quarles"), but nothing for any of the dozens of reprints the poem went through over the subsequent year, even though the poem accomplished the unusual feat of being reprinted simultaneously in the *Liberator* and the *Southern Literary Messenger*, to the great admiration of both.[26] In a different vein, Emily Dickinson fumed at the alterations editors imposed on her poems, on the very few occasions during her lifetime when one was published. Poem F 124 appeared in the March 1, 1862, issue of *The Springfield Republican* as "The Sleeping":

> Safe in their alabaster chambers,
> Untouched by morning,
> And untouched by noon,
> Sleep the meek members of the Resurrection,
> Rafter of satin, and roof of stone.
>
> Light laughs the breeze
> In her castle above them,
> Babbles the bee in a stolid ear,
> Pipe the sweet birds in ignorant cadences:
> Ah! what sagacity perished here![27]

Dickinson wrote to the *Republican*'s editor, Samuel Bowles, "If you doubted my Snow – for a moment – you never will – again – I know – Because I could not say it – I fixed it in the Verse – for you to read – when your thought wavers, for such a foot as mine."[28] Interestingly, a few weeks after "The Sleeping" appeared Dickinson sent a copy of "Safe in their alabaster chambers" to Thomas Wentworth Higginson, perhaps hoping for a better reception of the poem as she had written it. As she, Poe, and countless other anonymous authors realized, poets had little control over their work once it entered into the antebellum era's decentralized, recirculatory, loosely controlled mediascape.[29]

Though the local Poets' Corner was sometimes the target of readers' irony (especially the diminished relation it bore to the high monumentality of its namesake in Westminster Abbey), it is clear that most readers engaged interactively with the poems they encountered in the newspaper. As Ellen Gruber Garvey observes, poems are among the items found most commonly in nineteenth-century scrapbooks.[30] Larcom notes that she and her siblings clipped only the anecdotes and poems for their scrapbooks; when she began working as a mill operative a few years later, she explains that she expanded this practice to create her own little library, at a time when she could not afford to buy books:

> I made my window-seat into a small library of poetry, pasting its side all over with newspaper clippings. In those days we had only weekly papers, and they had always a "poet's corner," where standard writers were well represented, with anonymous ones, also. I was not, of course, much of a critic. I chose my verses for their sentiment, and because I wanted to commit them to memory. (175–76)

The newspaper was a site for reading poetry in the moment (even when the poem in question was old), but it also provided readers with resources to create their own kinds of anthologies for future use.

Larcom records in her autobiography that soon after she began writing poetry as a child, "my fame crept out among the neighbors," and she was "invited to write some verses in a young lady's album" (128). Here, again, she is an expert guide to understanding what the experience of poetry was like for most people in the first half of the nineteenth century. The antebellum decades are often cast as an age when steam power industrialized communication, creating a much more expansive and fast-moving system of production and dissemination that has come to be known through the abstraction of "the literary market." Printed matter and professional authorship are the norm for so-called print culture, but this view overestimates the significance of technology and underrecognizes the importance of scribal practices to the experience of reading and writing. The vast majority of antebellum poets were amateur writers who had no serious ambition to become published authors, and the majority of the period's poetry came from the hands of children and young women, in school exercises and poetry albums.

Ralph Waldo Emerson observed in 1840 that a "revolution in literature is now giving importance to the portfolio over the book. . . . The philosophy of the day . . . reckons poetry the right and power of every man . . . and every day witnesses new attempts to throw into verse the experiences of private life."[31] The observations are true, though Emerson's gendered pronouns distort the picture. It is more probable that most amateur poets were young women, like Larcom, who recorded poems in the albums of friends and schoolmates.[32] Anthologies of elegant extracts and "flowers of literature" provided would-be poets with selections of material drawn from a wide expanse of mostly older, mostly British material, which could be adapted for an amateur poet's own inscriptions. For instance, sometime in the mid-1830s, a writer inscribed the following lines in the album of a Philadelphia woman:

> I come with a gift it is a simple flower
> That prehaps may wile a weary hour
> And a spirit within a magic weaves
> That may touch your heart from its simple leaves
> And if those should fail it at least will be
> A tokin of love from me to thee.[33]

This poem, usually titled "The Gift," was a popular inscription text, and it appeared more or less continually during the antebellum years, in annuals and giftbooks such as *The Token and Atlantic Souvenir, The Garland,* and *The Young Ladies' Oasis.* To write a poem such as this in another's book, and claim it as one's own token of love and friendship, was not considered plagiarism; it was simply how poetry fit into an ordinary life.

Like all else about antebellum poetry, the scribal practices of the album were structured by convention, emulation, and recirculation. The practice of inscribing poems into albums was less an innovation of the nineteenth century than it was an expansion, across a much broader swathe of population, of older practices of civility and sensibility that had formerly been the province of elite coteries.[34] The democratization of literariness, in the form of popular participation in the social life of poetry, is perhaps the most important – and invisible – transformation in antebellum American literature.

Notes

1 "Campbell's *British Poetry*," *Edinburgh Review* 31.62 (1819): 466, 470. Hereafter cited parenthetically. Portions of this review were reprinted in US periodicals over the following year. The review was unsigned, but is usually attributed to Francis Jeffrey, the editor of the *Edinburgh Review*.

2 John Guillory, *Cultural Capital: The Problem of Literary Canon Formation* (Chicago: University of Chicago Press, 1993), ix–xiii.

3 Hemans, for one, is enjoying a critical revival: see, for example, Catherine Robson, *Heart Beats: Everyday Life and the Remembered Poem* (Princeton, NJ: Princeton University Press, 2012), 91–121, and Tricia Lootens, *The Political Poetess: Victorian Femininity, Race, and the Legacy of Separate Spheres* (Princeton, NJ: Princeton University Press, 2017), 116–50.

4 Ezra Pound, *ABC of Reading* (London: Routledge, 1934), 29; Ann Douglas, *The Feminization of American Culture* (New York: Knopf, 1977). The fact that Douglas's account of "feminization" discusses no poetry at all can be taken as a sign of just how thoroughly twentieth-century scholarship had erased nineteenth-century American poetry.

5 In my view, the first major work of criticism to adopt this approach was Van Wyck Brooks's 1915 treatise *America's Coming of Age*, though Elizabeth Renker has documented a similar attitude in criticism from the 1880s and 1890s: *Realist Poetics in American Culture, 1866–1900* (Oxford: Oxford University Press, 2018), 16–34.

6 David S. Reynolds, *Beneath the American Renaissance: The Subversive Imagination in the Age of Emerson and Melville* (New York: Knopf, 1988).

7 It is clear that nineteenth-century Americanists have not assimilated this part of Guillory's argument. For instance, in a forum in *J19* on "The End of the End of the Canon?" only one of the eleven contributors considers the institutional setting where scholarly debates about canons achieve most of their effect – the classroom. See *J19: The Journal of Nineteenth-Century Americanists* 4.1 (2016): 125–79.

8 Richard Hoggart, *The Uses of Literacy* (London: Chatto and Windus, 1957); Carlo Ginzburg, *The Cheese and the Worms: The Cosmos of a Sixteenth-Century Miller*, trans. John Tedeschi and Anne C. Tedeschi (Baltimore: Johns Hopkins University Press, 1980); Janice Radway, *Reading the Romance: Women, Patriarchy, and Popular Literature* (Chapel Hill: University of North Carolina Press, 1984); Jonathan Rose, *The Intellectual Life of the British Working Classes* (New Haven, CT: Yale University Press, 2001).

9 Or, in the words of Ryan Cordell and Abby Mullen, a poem "exceedingly popular in its day" would be one that was "anthologized in books of poetry; praised by critics, poets, and readers; and widely reprinted in newspapers and magazines." Note the conflations among the categories in their list – formats (book, newspaper, magazine) overlap with material processes (anthologization, reprinting, reading), which overlap with evaluative processes (criticism, praise), which overlap with types of person (critic, poet, reader). "'Fugitive

Verses': The Circulation of Poems in Nineteenth-Century American Newspapers," *American Periodicals* 27.1 (2017): 30.

10 Jane Tompkins, *Sensational Designs: The Cultural Work of American Fiction, 1790–1860* (New York: Oxford University Press, 1985), 186–201; Matthew Brown, *The Pilgrim and the Bee: Reading Rituals and Book Culture in Early New England* (Philadelphia: University of Pennsylvania Press, 2007), 1–20.

11 My calculation for these imprints is based on the catalog listings in the American Antiquarian Society.

12 William St. Clair, *The Reading Nation in the Romantic Period* (Cambridge: Cambridge University Press, 2004), 339–56. For a different argument about similar materials, see Tessa Watt, *Cheap Print and Popular Piety, 1550–1640* (Cambridge: Cambridge University Press, 1991).

13 Kirsten Silva Gruesz, *Ambassadors of Culture: The Transamerican Origins of Latino Writing* (Princeton, NJ: Princeton University Press, 2002); Elizabeth McHenry, *Forgotten Readers: Recovering the Lost History of African American Literary Societies* (Durham, NC: Duke University Press, 2002); Trish Loughran, *The Republic in Print: Print Culture in the Age of U.S. Nation Building, 1770–1870* (New York: Columbia University Press, 2007); Raúl Coronado, *A World Not to Come: A History of Latino Writing and Print Culture* (Cambridge, MA: Harvard University Press, 2013).

14 Daniel Hack, *Reaping Something New: African American Transformations of Victorian Literature* (Princeton, NJ: Princeton University Press, 2017).

15 Lucy Larcom, *A New England Girlhood, Outlined from Memory* (Boston: Houghton, Mifflin, 1889), 126–27. Hereafter cited parenthetically.

16 Christopher N. Phillips, *The Hymnal: A Reading History* (Baltimore: Johns Hopkins University Press, 2018).

17 Nathan Wild, *The Improved New-England Almanack, and Ephemeris* (Keene, NH: John Prentiss, 1819), title page.

18 Cordell and Mullen, "Fugitive Verses," 30.

19 Meredith L. McGill, *American Literature and the Culture of Reprinting, 1834–1853* (Philadelphia: University of Pennsylvania Press, 2003), 1.

20 [James] Montgomery, "Robert Burns," *The North Star*, December 3, 1847: 4. As Tavia Nyong'o argues, Burns was a favorite poet of Douglass's: *The Amalgamation Waltz: Race, Performance, and the Ruses of Memory* (Minneapolis: University of Minnesota Press, 2009), 124.

21 J. G. Whittier, "The Fire-Ship," *Haverhill Gazette*, March 14, 1829: 1. The novel to which the headnote refers was *Salathiel: A Story of the Past, the Present, and the Future*, by George Croly (1828).

22 "J. G. Whittier," *Haverhill Gazette*, June 6, 1829: 1.

23 "Amelia," *Louisville Journal*, February 2, 1839: 2

24 Amelia, "To Mrs. L——," *Louisville Journal*, March 23, 1837: 2.

25 Eliza Richards, *Gender and the Poetics of Reception in Poe's Circle* (Cambridge: Cambridge University Press, 2004), 60–106.

26 Quarles [Edgar Allan Poe], "The Raven," *American Review* (February 1845): 143–45; Edgar A. Poe, "The Raven," *Liberator*, February 21, 1845: 32; Edgar

A. Poe, "The Raven," *Southern Literary Messenger* (March 1845): 186–88. Kenneth Silverman states that Poe was paid "around fifteen dollars" for the poem: *Edgar A. Poe: Mournful and Never-Ending Remembrance* (New York: HarperCollins, 1991), 530. While other sources sometimes cite different payment amounts, they always do so to the same intent, namely, to underscore how little he received for it.

27 "The Sleeping," *Springfield Republican*, March 1, 1862. The poem was headed "Original Poetry" and given the dateline "Pelham Hill, June, 1861."

28 Dickinson, letter to Samuel Bowles, early 1862; *Emily Dickinson: Selected Letters*, ed. Thomas H. Johnson (Cambridge, MA: Harvard University Press, 1958), 170.

29 Jennifer Putzi, "'Some Queer Freak of Taste': Gender, Authorship, and the 'Rock Me to Sleep' Controversy," *American Literature* 84.4 (2012): 769–95.

30 Ellen Gruber Garvey, *Writing with Scissors: American Scrapbooks from the Civil War to the Harlem Renaissance* (New York: Oxford University Press, 2012). Mike Chasar also discusses the practice of scrapbooking poems, though his focus is on the early twentieth century: *Everyday Reading: Poetry and Popular Culture in Modern America* (New York: Columbia University Press, 2012), 27–79.

31 Emerson, "New Poetry," *The Dial* (October 1840): 220.

32 Karen Sánchez-Eppler, "Copying and Conversion: An 1824 Friendship Album 'from a Chinese Youth,'" *American Quarterly* 59.2 (2007): 301–39; Leon Jackson, *The Business of Letters: Authorial Economies in Antebellum America* (Stanford, CA: Stanford University Press, 2008), 97–109; Laura Zebuhr, "The Work of Friendship in Nineteenth-Century American Friendship Album Verses," *American Literature* 87.3 (2015): 433–54; Michael C. Cohen, "Album Verse and the Poetics of Scribal Circulation," in *A History of Nineteenth-Century American Women's Poetry*, ed. Jennifer Putzi and Alexandra Socarides (Cambridge: Cambridge University Press, 2016), 68–86.

33 EMR, "The Gift," inscribed in the album of Mary Ann Hubbert; Mary Ann Hubbert album, 1834–36, LCP57, Historical Society of Pennsylvania.

34 On the eighteenth-century antecedents, see *Only for the Eye of a Friend: The Poetry of Annis Boudinot Stockton*, ed. Carla Mulford (Charlottesville: University of Virginia Press, 1995), 1–68; David S. Shields, *Civil Tongues and Polite Letters in British America* (Chapel Hill: University of North Carolina Press, 1997); *Milcah Martha Moore's Book: A Commonplace Book from Revolutionary America*, ed. Catherine La Courreye Blecki and Karin A. Wulf (University Park: Pennsylvania State University Press, 1997), 1–106; Joanna Brooks, "Our Phillis, Ourselves," *American Literature* 82.1 (2010): 1–28.

CHAPTER 12

Sentimentality

Tess Chakkalakal

Harriet Beecher Stowe's *Uncle Tom's Cabin* (1852), the most famous sentimental novel in American literary history, is not really about women. Yet as Nina Baym and other readers of women's fiction have rightly noted, it is from this novel, more than any other, that the construct of the sentimental heroine was developed. The construct was based not on a woman character but on a young girl, Little Eva, whose angelic qualities and intimate relationship with the enslaved, namely, Uncle Tom and Topsy, doom her to an early, tear-wrenching death. As Jane Tompkins has shown, her tears and death were not in vain.[1] On the contrary, they moved a nation to sympathy for the enslaved and, more than any other book in American history, prompted hundreds of thousands of readers to become part of one of the largest and most successful social movements in the world: abolitionism. The connection between the sentimental novel and what Andrew Delbanco calls the "abolitionist imagination" distinguishes the nineteenth-century American sentimental literary tradition from its English counterpart.[2] While the tradition of the sentimental novel in the United States formally begins in the eighteenth century, with the publication of William Hill Brown's *The Power of Sympathy; or, The Triumph of Nature* in 1789, it is not until the mid-nineteenth century that the form takes off in the United States.[3] Stowe's sentimental strategy in *Uncle Tom's Cabin* was to tie the power of sympathy inextricably to her critique of slavery, rendering the two virtually synonymous.

At the conclusion of *Uncle Tom's Cabin*, Stowe tells her readers to "*feel right.*" As Cindy Weinstein rightly points out, the injunction is not solely a feature of Stowe's antislavery polemic.[4] "Feeling right" informs almost all sentimental fictions, regardless of their political intentions. And yet, it is the subject of slavery that galvanizes the sentimental novel in America, even long after its abolition, as the later novels of Toni Morrison so eloquently testify.

By the time Morrison published her first novel in 1970, Stowe's sentimentalism had been the object of considerable critique by several

African American writers in the twentieth century. James Baldwin's
"Everybody's Protest Novel" (1949) is perhaps the best-known example.
Though twentieth-century critics regarded sentimentality as "the ostenta-
tious parading of excessive and spurious emotion" to mask what Baldwin
called "the catalogue of violence" found in a novel like *Uncle Tom's Cabin*
or Richard Wright's mid-twentieth-century *Native Son*, readers a century
earlier interpreted sentimental literature as providing a model for sympathy
and moral virtue. The nineteenth-century American project of sentimentality turned on what its critics called "the irrepressible problem of slavery."[5] As
Lauren Berlant argues in her discussion of *Uncle Tom's* Cabin, "when
sentimentality meets politics, it uses personal stories to tell of structural
effect, but in so doing it risks thwarting its very attempt to perform
rhetorically a scene of pain that must be soothed politically."[6] Sentimental
literature could not solve the problem of slavery but it could move a nation
to enter into a war that might. It was this kind of thinking about sentimental
literature that christened Stowe, however apocryphally, as the "little woman
who made this great war."[7] The power of sentimental literature lies in its
ability to move readers through language. Whether we shed tears at the
spectacle of Uncle Tom's excruciating death scene or laugh out loud at
Topsy's antics, readers have a physical and emotional response to the
characters that have the potential to change society for the better.

For all its pitfalls into the language of racial stereotype and paternalism,
sentimental literature did manage to bring about considerable social
change, particularly for African American men and women during the
nineteenth century. Finding common cause with Stowe, Frederick
Douglass described *Uncle Tom's Cabin* as "a work of marvelous depth
and power" and was enthralled by its ability to arouse in so many a hatred
of slavery and sympathy for enslaved people.[8] One might even go so far as
to argue that the allegiance between Stowe and Douglass was the direct
result of the sentimental form found in Stowe's fiction. According to
Robert S. Levine, Douglass championed Stowe because he thought
Uncle Tom's Cabin had the potential to do more good than harm. He
admired Stowe's willingness to "change her mind" on the question of
African colonization, a singular feature of Stowe's sentimental politics.[9]

Stowe's "sentimental power," in Tompkins's evocative phrase, played an
important role in inspiring so many nineteenth-century African Americans
to turn to the pen to try their own hand at writing sentimental fiction
themselves, with the explicit intention of making their case against slavery
on the basis of personal experience or eyewitness accounts.[10] While
nineteenth-century American sentimental novels have most often been

associated with white, relatively well-to-do-women – that "damned mob of scribbling women," as Nathaniel Hawthorne famously referred to them in an 1855 letter to William Ticknor – the role African Americans played in the formation of an American sentimental literary tradition has been relatively underplayed. Expanding the canon of nineteenth-century American sentimental literature to include writers like Douglass, Frank J. Webb, William Wells Brown, Harriet Jacobs, Harriet Wilson, and Hannah Crafts establishes a crucial, though often marginalized, context through which to consider nineteenth-century dispensations of sympathy. Their works, written explicitly from the point of view of someone enslaved, sought to represent the experiences of the two and a half million African American slaves in a nation of roughly 17 million. While events in prominent sentimental novels, such as *The Lamplighter* (1854) and *The Wide, Wide World* (1850), feature the search for family as it is constituted in the structure of a home, the family and home are precisely what is legally prohibited in sentimental works written from the point of view of enslaved men and women. The apparent absence of the conventional family unit – comprised of a mother, father, husband, wife, son, daughter, brother, sister – among enslaved people ostensibly disqualifies works written from the slave's point of view as sentimental literature. Indeed, much criticism on the subject of sentimentalism seems incapable of considering this body of literature for its aesthetic qualities –plot, character, theme, language – focusing instead on its historical value as revealing otherwise unknown truths about the inner workings of slavery in the United States. The subsequent sections of this chapter challenge the view that slaves and free blacks were unable or unwilling to solicit sympathy for themselves as members of families who were bound by love rather than property and blood. The works I examine here question the implication that sympathy could be solicited and conferred only by white writers – usually wives, mothers, sisters – who had no direct experience of slavery. In particular, the nature of sympathy as produced by formerly enslaved or free black nineteenth-century writers offers a view of the family that insists on it as a source of both liberation and love.

I

Nowhere is this tendency more apparent than in the critical conversation concerning William Wells Brown's *Clotel*, first published in London in 1853, just a year after *Uncle Tom's Cabin* had galvanized the English-speaking literary scene. Riffing on the stories of Thomas Jefferson's purported intimate relationship with Sally Hemmings and the children they had together, *Clotel* opens with a powerful assessment of how slavery has affected the constitution of nation. The novel begins with a radical revision of the Victorian paterfamilias:

> With the growing population of slaves in the Southern States of America, there is a fearful increase of half whites, most of whose fathers are slave-owners, and their mothers slaves. Society does not frown upon the man who sits with his mulatto child upon his knee, whilst its mother stands a slave behind his chair. (81)

Like Stowe, Brown's novel focuses on the effects of slavery on the family. But unlike Stowe's fiction, Brown's presents a highly *mixed* family, one in which slaves and their owners are engaged in intimate, though illegitimate, relationships. This feature of Brown's novel comprises a major innovation in American sentimental literature that remains central to its form. Part of *Clotel*'s purpose, then, is to legitimize such relations, which takes its plot and characters well beyond the historical constraints of slavery.

As nearly all of its contemporary reviewers pointed out, *Clotel* was read as an effort to capitalize on the post–*Uncle Tom's Cabin* "mania" for abolitionist fiction in Great Britain, where Brown lived, lectured, and wrote between 1849 and 1854. On December 31, 1853, under the heading "W. W. Brown's New Work," the *National Anti-Slavery Standard* summarizes the content of *Clotel* by informing its readers that "[t]he book before us appears to have been written for the purpose of proving – if any additional proof were needed – that the incidents which the authoress of 'Uncle Tom's Cabin' has related in that admirable work are no mere inventions of fancy, but actual occurrences, the counterparts of which are to be met with in the daily scenes of slave life." But since its publication, *Clotel* has mostly been considered as the first *African American* novel, launching a tradition parallel to the nineteenth-century sentimental novels by white women with which *Clotel* is so obviously engaged. Categorizing *Clotel* by its singularity as the earliest known novel by an African American author potentially thwarts its political purpose. The novel shows the inevitable integration of blacks and whites caused by slavery. That integration, Brown suggests, will bring about slavery's end. However, critical assessments of *Clotel* tend to remark on its distinction from the conventions and discourse of sentimentality. Avoiding the terms of sentimentality altogether, Geoffrey Sanborn reads "the art of *Clotel*" as "the art of the pop-cultural assemblage, the art of making something new out of materials drawn from common pools."[11] For Sanborn, as for a number of the novel's later readers, Brown's borrowings from other works, often word for word, is one of its most striking features.[12]

While there is much value in considering the art and form of *Clotel* as an "assemblage," or "hodgepodge," such readings of its form cannot help but avoid the novel's participation in the sentimental literary conventions of its moment, particularly its representation of "the young slave's feelings" being "very much hurt at hearing the cries of his mother."[13] Brown's personal experience of having been enslaved, as the product of a slave mother and white slave owner himself, permeates almost every page of the novel, even those borrowed from other writers. Unlike the fictions of Stowe and Lydia Maria Child that are so important to the production of *Clotel*, Brown is less interested in the feelings of the white people who sympathize or do not sympathize with the enslaved than the feelings of the enslaved characters themselves. What emerges from a sentimental fiction like *Clotel*, I would argue, is an alternative model of sympathy from that found in northern and southern expressions of sympathy for the slave.

Clotel opens with a long prefatory biography of its author infused by sentimental gestures. Departing from his first autobiography published in 1847, which opens with prefaces by prominent white abolitionists Edmund Quincy and J. C. Hathaway, declaring the book's value to their cause, Brown's novel introduces its author by way of his close and painful relationship with his mother:

> He heard her cry, "Oh, pray! oh, pray! oh, pray!" These are the words which slaves generally utter when imploring mercy at the hands of their oppressors. The son heard it, though he was some way off. He heard the crack of the whip and the groans of his poor mother. The cold chill ran over him, and he wept aloud; but he was a slave like his mother, and could render her no assistance. He was taught by the most bitter experience, that nothing could be more heart-rending than to see a dear and beloved mother or sister tortured by unfeeling men, and to hear her cries, and not be able to render the least aid.[14]

Brown's "bitter" experiences of being deprived of his mother as a slave is decidedly different from "Stowe's Dream of the Mother-Savior" celebrated by critics like Elizabeth Ammons.[15] According to this sentimental formulation of motherhood, the proper role of the mother is to provide children with love and to teach them to internalize the values of hard work and integrity; the avoidance of evil was the sacred, and extremely useful, job of the mother. Slave mothers' inability to perform the proper duties of the mother produces a highly emotional, tear-filled response in the child. Powerlessness characterizes the mother–child bond in *Clotel*, a condition that creates a new series of plot twists, family drama, and identities that become central to the discourse of American sentimentality. The child in this scenario hears the cries of his mother but can do nothing to help her in the face of the "unfeeling men" who surround him.

Though Brown would go on to create over a dozen works of literature – fiction and nonfiction – after the publication of *Clotel*, he would return repeatedly to his first novel, revising, rewriting, and updating its main characters and events so that they spoke directly to the changing circumstances of African Americans living in the United States following the abolition of slavery. By the end of his life, he had published a total of four versions of the novel. Following the 1853 publication of *Clotel; or, The President's Daughter* he rewrote it as *Miralda; or, The Beautiful Quadroon. A Romance of American Slavery, Founded on Fact*, serialized in 1860–61 in the *Weekly Anglo-African*; and then returned to the earlier version in 1864 and 1867 editions, *Clotelle: A Tale of the Southern States* and *Clotelle; or, The Colored Heroine, a Tale of the Southern States.*[16] *Clotel*'s broader impact on the sentimental culture of the late nineteenth century should not be underestimated. Where African Americans were viewed as caricatures in Stowe's novel, either too good, like Uncle Tom, or unable to feel, like Topsy, *Clotel* introduced enslaved characters as lovers and parents, sons and daughters, brothers and sisters, engaged in complex relationships with one another and their owners. This racially integrated family would grant sentimentality a new life, introducing black characters as figures of pathos and striving, which would become a staple of American sentimentality from later nineteenth-century and early twentieth-century novels such as Charles Chesnutt's *The House behind the Cedars* (1900), Pauline Hopkins's *Of One Blood* (1902), and Albion Tourgée's *Toinette* (1874) to recent television shows like *Different Strokes* and *This Is Us*.

II

Brown has retained his status as inaugurating a tradition of African American fiction, despite being deeply invested in the sentimental conventions of family and feeling so central to the discourse of American sentimentality. Writing in the wake of Brown's sentimental novel, the first authored by a former slave, the nonfictional or purely historical status of Harriet Jacobs's *Incidents in the Life of a Slave Girl, Written by Herself* (1861) has likewise distanced it from discussions of sentimentality and family. Though almost all of Jacobs's twentieth-century readers agree that "she skillfully plays on her story's adherence to and departures from sentimental conventions of domestic fiction," few have been willing to call Jacobs a sentimental author.[17] It is instead her historical insights into the world of female slaves that continues to shape critical discussion of Jacobs's life and work. This way of reading is due, in large part, to Jean Fagan Yellin's groundbreaking archival research that uncovered the author's biography. Against the once dominant mode of reading Jacobs's work as "a false slave narrative," Yellin's research enabled later readers to read it "as a historical record." Mark Rifkin insists, for instance, that "Jacobs's narrative should be understood as political theory" – not as a slave narrative and certainly not as sentimental fiction. According to this contemporary critical view it is the novel's investment in history and political theory, rather than familial relationships and sympathy, that makes it important.[18]

But like Brown, Jacobs was a close reader of sentimental fiction, particularly those by Stowe and Child. In her introduction to *Incidents*, Child lauds the "lively and dramatic way" Jacobs tells "her own story."[19] As the book's editor, Child played a crucial role in affirming Jacobs's status as a sentimental author. By doing so, Child includes Jacobs in the growing canon of antislavery sentimental literature. First published in 1861 under the pseudonym Linda Brent, Jacobs tells the singular story of her experiences as a slave in the form of a sentimental novel, reminiscent of early sentimental English novels such as Samuel Richardson's *Pamela, or Virtue Rewarded* (1740) and *Clarissa, or The History of a Young Lady* (1748). Just as in Richardson's sentimental novels written as letters between a young woman and a man who pursues her relentlessly, the letters between Jacobs's heroine and the novel's villain, Dr. Flint, take on a decidedly sinister aspect. Jacobs's status as a "woman reared in Slavery" only enhanced the quality of her particular story to arouse the sympathies of white readers like Child. Considering the aesthetic features of *Incidents*, particularly her creation of a fictional narrator, Linda Brent, who presents her private sexual history as a subject of public concern and sympathy, reveals different meanings of home and family that remain relevant to the representation of black women well beyond its nineteenth-century context.

Carla Peterson usefully reads these features of *Incidents* as "novelizing techniques." By employing characters with fictional names, Jacobs recasts her life story so that she might distance herself from the trauma of her experience in slavery.[20] Peterson's assessment of Jacobs's life story *as* fiction renders the work essentially political. The act of telling a story to an imagined reader allows its author to free herself from the violence she has experienced as a slave.

Jacobs's passage from slavery to freedom is an unconventional one. Unlike her male counterparts, Jacobs describes in some detail falling in love with a free black carpenter, a marriage that was forbidden by her owner because such a marriage would interfere with his own illicit desire for her. What follows are the sordid details of a warped courtship plot in which she introduces another slave owner, Mr. Sands, with whom she has a sexual relationship with the hope that her "freedom could be easily obtained from him." Their relationship leads to Jacobs becoming pregnant and the beginning of her journey to securing her own family and free home. In relating these "incidents" Jacobs accepts the negative judgments that will be made against her. And it is also when she makes her most explicit request for her reader's sympathy: "Pity me, and pardon me, O virtuous reader! You never knew what it is to be a slave" (55). Contrasting her struggle with that of white women portrayed in most sentimental fictions of the moment, she holds them to task for her plight, rejecting their conventional sympathy, where readers are asked to recognize the similarities between slaves and free women, and to replace it with knowledge and action: "Neither do I care to excite sympathy for my own sufferings. But I do earnestly desire to arouse the women of the North to a realizing sense of the condition of two millions of women at the South, still in bondage, suffering what I suffered, and most of them far worse." Directing her "testimony" to women readers of sentimental fiction, Jacobs understands her work as correcting perceptions of slavery "to convince the people of the Free States what Slavery really is." Slavery, in Jacobs's sense, is not *really* (or only) about being deprived of freedom or forced to labor. Slavery also involves coerced sex between slaves and owners, the ramifications of which are huge, far beyond anything Stowe could or was willing to present. Her insistence on the real life of slaves hardly undermines Jacobs's sentimentality; indeed, it intensifies it. "Reader, be assured this narrative is no fiction," Jacobs declares in the opening line of her preface; it is a story carefully crafted to show readers the emotional and physical impact of slavery on America, revealing the divisions between black and white, slave and free, to be a fiction.

III

Harriet E. Wilson locates her discussion of the racial politics found in the North in her powerful novel *Our Nig, or Sketches from the Life of a Free Black*, first published in 1859. Like *Incidents*, it tells Wilson's own story through a renamed character, a precocious six-year-old girl she names

Frado, who is abandoned by her white mother after her "kindly African father" dies. As a mixed-race woman, she becomes an indentured servant in a New England household, administered by a white woman, Mrs. Bellmont, who becomes one of the nastiest villains of nineteenth-century sentimental fiction. Wilson's place within that sentimental tradition remains contested due to the circumstances of its publication and redis-covery by Henry Louis Gates, Jr., in 1983. Situated between "the grim determinism of twentieth-century novels" by Richard Wright, Ann Petry, and Toni Morrison and the writings of Wilson's contemporaries, such as Stowe, Susan Warner, and Maria Cummins, readers struggle with under-standing Wilson's place in American literature. Since its rediscovery, Wilson has followed Brown's fate in being read primarily as the author of "the first African American women's novel." That status, however, has given *Our Nig* a new life and audience among late twentieth- and twenty-first-century readers that has been crucial in broadening our understanding of nineteenth-century sentimentality.

As a young, orphaned child, Frado is the preeminent victim of nineteenth-century white violence and a figure of sentimentality par excellence. From the very first page of this fiction, the reader feels sympa-thy for Frado and wishes for her to be saved from all those who do her harm. But her perpetrators are not the ill-mannered, heavy drinking, sexually depraved slave traders and owners that we find in *Uncle Tom's Cabin* or *Incidents in the Life of a Slave Girl*. Instead, Frado is abused by well-to-do northern white women, those very same readers and writers of antislavery sentimental fiction who shed tears over Uncle Tom's death, opposed slavery, and subscribed to a system of free labor. But it is precisely these women's hypocrisy that Wilson exposes. Wilson's novel throws the black/white, North/South, conventions of American sentimentality into disarray. In *Our Nig*, aggressive, selfish, racist women in the North whip and beat a defenseless child simply because she has been born outside the conventions of white, respectable society. Meanwhile, the novel's male figures – both black and white – are depicted as powerless in the face of the uncontrollable, selfish violence of the strong women who rule the house-hold. Throughout the story of her abuse and development, Frado rejects the white/black racial categories of the time. Wilson produces sympathy for Frado by showing how the maternal figures in her life abuse and abandon her. She must find love and affection elsewhere, perhaps among her unnamed "colored brethren" whom Wilson imagines will read her story and be moved to lend her the support she has, for much of her life, been denied.

Frado's role as a motherless "free black" young woman in the story focuses the fiction on the conventions of family. This is not a story about slavery but a story about racism's effects on both its victims and its perpetrators. As Harryette Mullen points out, "[t]he literary tradition that produces the sentimental novel is concerned with the white woman's assumption of her proper place, upon her internalization of the values of propriety and decorum, while the African American oral tradition represents the exposed black woman."[21] The presence of a black child in this case, Frado, exposes the problems within the conventions of the white American family when she is forced to enter into it. Wilson's novel attempts to correct the false sentiments displayed by the Bellmonts to teach them how "*to feel right*" in the face of so much wrong.

To right Mrs. Bellmont's wrongs, Wilson's novel offers readers a portrait of a New England household where the commitment to separating it into a woman's sphere did great harm to those who lacked the family so essential to its constitution. Frado counters the compartmentalized language of the "two-story white house" in which she is forced to live with the language of true love and marriage, while condemning Mrs. Bellmont's ideals of family that are predicated almost entirely on the acquisition of wealth and white supremacy.[22] The quest for a family of one's own, to have and to hold, without separation, is the driving force of these sentimental fictions that present us with an account of interracial families and intimacies.

Shortly after the rediscovery of Wilson's novel in 1983, Gates went on to find another long-forgotten sentimental fiction written from a female slave's point of view. Hannah Crafts's *The Bondwoman's Narrative* was published in the spring of 2002 but written circa 1855. According to Gates, who coedited the novel to considerable fanfare, the novel was written by a female fugitive slave in the 1850s, though it was never published during the author's lifetime. Like Brown, Crafts borrowed liberally from the sentimental fictions of her day, though her interests, like those of Jacobs, were more in the English tradition of the form. Much of the contemporary criticism concerning *Bondwoman's Narrative* focuses on determining the identity and biography of its author. In his introduction, Gates outlines the process by which the novel was discovered, naming Dorothy Porter as having purchased the original manuscript in 1948 for $85. As one of its first readers, Porter remarks on the manuscript's most distinctive features: first, that it is written in a sentimental and effusive style and, second, that it was strongly influenced by the sentimental fiction of the mid-nineteenth century. The nature of that influence remains an open question.

Unlike Frado in Wilson's story of abandonment and abuse, Hannah forms intimate friendships with white women in her household. Though enslaved on a plantation in North Carolina, Hannah's light skin and literacy afford her certain privileges that lead her to find her mother in the North and marry a man with whom she is in love. The distinguishing feature of Crafts's sentimentality are the bonds formed between women – white and black – that can begin to lay the groundwork for an idea of sentimental kinship, particularly between women, that eschews racial difference.

When Hannah, "though a slave," approaches her mistress to ask her about Mr. Trappe, a crooked lawyer hell-bent on torturing them both, she "forgot [at] that moment the disparity in our conditions" and proceeds to speak "to her as she had been my sister or a very dear friend." The friendship that forms between mistress and slave in *The Bondwoman's Narrative* is without parallel in nineteenth-century sentimental novels. Though friendships between mistresses and enslaved women often develop, we need look no further than *Uncle Tom's Cabin*, in which Mrs. Shelby treats Eliza with "indulgence and liberality" (11). Here it is Hannah who protects and cares for her broken and sorrow-filled mistress when she learns that "her mother was a slave then toiling in the cotton fields of Georgia" (45). Though Crafts and her contemporary slave authors have been left out of the canon of nineteenth-century sentimentality, the consensual and nonconsensual intimate relationships between enslaved women and their owners have come to form a neglected but important cornerstone of the American sentimental tradition.

IV

Published, read, and reviewed in the mid-nineteenth century, Brown's and Jacobs's works altered the very landscape of American sentimentality. The American family was one comprised of blacks and whites, slave and free. The slave family existed inside, not alongside, the free American family. No novel better exemplifies this model of the American family than Frank J. Webb's 1857 novel, *The Garies and Their Friends*. In her preface, Stowe remarks on the identity of its author, who is "a coloured young man, born and reared in the city of Philadelphia" and the novel's importance to answering the most urgent political question of the time: "Are the race at present held as slaves capable of freedom, self-government, and progress?"[23]

This was a question that Stowe herself took up only after the publication of *Uncle Tom's Cabin*. In her second novel, *Dred: A Tale of the Great*

Dismal Swamp (1856), Stowe revises her previous support of colonization – the plan to move emancipated people to Africa – to endorse in her second antislavery novel a far more complex and perhaps radical plan of the formation of interracial settlements in Canada. Following her heroine's death, her betrothed, Edward Clayton, and his sister, Anne, lead their liberated slaves to Canada. Using funds secured from the sale of their plantation to purchase a tract of land in Canada, the Claytons help to establish a black township that, with its integrated schools and thriving farms, becomes a model for a new American society predicated on freedom, self-government, and progress.

Stowe's idyllic scene of interracial prosperity and harmony has its counterpart in Webb's novel, published a year later. In the *Garies*, the fierce opposition to integration results in violence and the destruction of the novel's happy black and interracial families. Though we reach the novel's climax in a scene of gruesome violence by whites against blacks in Philadelphia, the novel begins and ends with scenes of interracial domestic bliss first on a southern plantation and then in a stately mansion in Philadelphia. Its first chapter, "in which the Reader is introduced to a Family of peculiar Construction," constitutes the novel's particular brand of sentimentality. We meet the Garies at their breakfast table, overflowing with "all those delicacies that, in the household of a rich Southern planer, are regarded as almost necessaries of life" (1). The Garies family is made up of Mr. Garie, a gentleman of "a highly refined character"; his wife, Mrs. Garie, "a lady of marked beauty" and of "African extraction"; and their two children, a girl and boy who "showed no trace whatever of African origin." The novel follows this peculiar family, from their southern plantation to their new home on the busy streets of Philadelphia.

Although there are no known American reviews of *The Garies and Their Friends*, there is evidence to suggest that the novel was known at the time. The *New Era* in 1870 describes Webb as "author of the somewhat famous book entitled *The Garies* which had been extensively read in England and in this country." Part of the reason for its apparent popularity was Stowe's preface, which described the book's "truthfully-told story," peopled with characters "faithfully drawn from real life." As a free colored man himself Webb would have been perceived as an authority on the topic. Situating it as a "historical novel of urgent manners," Samuel Otter shows the ways in which Webb reworks Charles Dickens's fiction, particularly *Bleak House*, to tell the stories of three families – the interracial Garies, the black Ellises, and the white Stevens.[24] The fierce opposition to the Garies instigated by the racism of Mr. and Mrs. Stevens leads to a race riot that destroys much of Philadelphia and leads to the death of the Garies. But their legacy lives on in the form of their children, who unwittingly dissolve the racial divide between the Ellis and Stevens families. In the end, there are only interracial families living happily ever after. Woven around these three families, Webb produces a story in which "feeling right" about one's family and friends determines a person's happiness. Though written amid the lively debates over slavery, the novel is less interested in participating in this contemporary debate than in finding a new domestic order *after* slavery through the form of sentimental fiction in which blacks and whites might live together in the United States in peace and prosperity.

Although the cultural work of Webb's sentimental fiction has not received the critical or popular attention of Stowe's, it signals a definitive turn in the form. We need only think of the marriage plots in most sentimental fictions to understand the radical difference of Webb's model of family. From Stowe's perspective, marriages are either between slave owners or between the enslaved. In Webb's fiction, this idea of marriage is exploded by the Garies, who marry legally and, for a time, find happiness in the North among their friends. Introducing such a "peculiar family" offers a conception of the future in which the difference between slaves and citizens, free blacks and whites, might be dissolved by presenting happy interracial families.

In her "Concluding Remarks" to *Uncle Tom's Cabin*, Stowe imagines her readers frustrated by the scenes of slavery presented by her novel, asking in despair, "But, what can any individual do?" Her solution to the problem of slavery was simply "to feel right." Reading the sentimental novels written from the point of view of free blacks like Webb and Wilson and the formerly enslaved like Brown, Jacobs, and Crafts alongside Stowe's extends the injunction to feel right. It is not only about feeling right; sentimentality is about embracing the new families created by slavery. It is these new, no longer peculiar but now conventional American families, that replace the bonds of slavery with those of love.

Notes

1 Jane Tompkins, *Sensational Designs: The Cultural Work of American Fiction, 1790–1860* (New York: Oxford University Press, 1986).
2 Andrew Delbanco, *The Abolitionist Imagination* (Cambridge, MA: Harvard University Press, 2012).
3 For more on the wider market for these early popular novels, see Cathy N. Davidson, *Revolution and the Word: The Rise of the Novel in America* (New York: Oxford University Press, 2004).

4 Cindy Weinstein, *Family, Kinship, and Sympathy in Nineteenth-Century American Literature* (New York: Cambridge University Press, 2009), 66.

5 Shirley Samuels, "Introduction," in *The Culture of Sentiment: Race, Gender, and Sentimentality in Nineteenth-Century America* (New York: Oxford University Press, 1992), 3

6 Lauren Berlant, "Poor Eliza," *American Literature* 70 (1998): 641. Berlant pursues her analysis of sentimental politics into the late twentieth century in *The Queen of America Goes to Washington City: Essays on Sex and Citizenship* (Durham, NC: Duke University Press, 1997), a discussion which is also relevant to reading Harriet Jacobs's *Incidents in the Life of a Slave Girl*. For a related argument about sentimentality that deals with the early nineteenth century, see Bruce Burgett, *Sentimental Bodies: Sex, Gender, and Citizenship in the Early Republic* (Princeton, NJ: Princeton University Press, 1998).

7 For a full account of the story of Abraham Lincoln's meeting with Stowe in which he purportedly greeted Stowe with these words, see David S. Reynolds, *Mightier than the Sword: Uncle Tom's Cabin and the Battle for America* (New York: Norton, 2011).

8 Determining the role sympathy plays in sentimental literature varies among its readers. While Lauren Berlant's reading of sympathy as erasing difference has asserted considerable influence in recent years, Jane Tompkins's 1985 *Sensational Designs* has been pivotal to reclaiming sympathy as a positive force showing the "*value* of a powerful and specifically female novelistic tradition." Tompkins located her readings *for* sentimentality *against* Ann Douglass's now-classic 1977 *The Femininization of American Culture*, which can also be read as a precursor to Berlant. For Douglas, as for Berlant, sentimentality became a way to "obfuscate the visible dynamics of development." Amid the debate over the virtues and vices of sentimentality, Nina Baym in *Woman's Fiction: A Guide to Novels by and about Women in American, 1820–1870* offers a useful catalogue of the novel which comprises the tradition that is indispensable to getting to know the books that comprise sentimentality. More recently, critics like Cindy Weinstein and Marianne Noble have helped to expand Baym's catalogue to understand more thoroughly the variations between the texts and the authors that have contributed to the form.

9 Robert S. Levine, "Introduction," in Harriet Beecher Stowe, *Dred: A Tale of the Great Dismal Swamp* (Chapel Hill: University of North Carolina Press, 1857; rpt. 2006), xvi.

10 Stowe's novel was one of many causes for this turn to fiction writing among African Americans in the mid-nineteenth century. As Carla Peterson points out: "The 1850s constitute a significant moment in the history of African American literary production.... The 1850s were ... such a critical moment for African Americans as they witnessed the dramatic deterioriation of race relations, marked by the passage of the Fugitive Slave Law, the Kansas–Nebraska Act, and the Dred Scott decision, as well as the growing exclusion of blacks from industrialization in the North." See Carla Peterson, "*Doers of*

the Word": *African-American Women Speakers and Writers in the North (1830–1880)* (New Brunswick, NJ: Rutgers University Press, 1998), 146–47.

11 Geoffrey Sanborn, "Introduction," in *Clotel; or, The President's Daughter* by William Wells Brown, ed. Geoffrey Sanborn (Peterborough, ON: Broadview Press, 2016), 11.

12 Aside from Sanborn, see also Robert Levine's "Introduction" to *Clotel*: "Ironically inhabiting and mimicking a hodgepodge of discourses (political, sentimental, reformist, and so on), *Clotel* can be read as a stunning example of literary pastiche – a technique of creating a literary work by borrowing from or imitating other works and styles." William Wells Brown, *Clotel; or, The President's Daughter: A Narrative of Slave Life in the United States* (Boston: Bedford/St. Martin's, 2000), 7. See also Ivy Wilson, "Merely Rhetorical: Virtual Democracy in William Wells Brown's *Clotel*," in *Specters of Democracy: Blackness and the Aesthetics of Politics in the Antebellum US* (New York: Oxford Univ. Press, 2011), 37–59; and Laura Soderberg, "One More Time with Feeling: Repetition, Reparation, and the Sentimental Subject in William Wells Brown's Clotel," *American Literature* 88.2 (2016): 241–67.

13 Brown, *Clotel*, ed. Sanborn, 37–38.

14 Ibid., 49.

15 Elizabeth Ammons, "Stowe's Dream of the Mother-Savior: *Uncle Tom's Cabin* and American Women Writers before the 1920s," in *New Essays on Uncle Tom's Cabin*, ed. Eric J. Sundquist (New York: Cambridge University Press, 1986), 155.

16 To understand the relationship and shifts between these texts, see Christopher Mulvey's electronic edition of *Clotel*, part of the African American Research Library series from the University of Virginia's Electronic Text Center. The site collects the four versions and allows readers to compare them by reading them in either two or three parallel columns. See Christopher Mulvey, ed., *Clotel, by William Wells Brown: An Electronic Scholarly Edition*, Rotunda (University of Virginia Press, 2006). http://rotunda.upress.virginia .edu:8080/clotel.

17 Nell Irvin Painter, "Introduction," in Harriet Jacobs, *Incidents in the Life of a Slave Girl: Written by Herself* (New York: Penguin Books, 2000), 5.

18 For a rich account of the novel's politics and history of publication, see Caleb Smith, *The Oracle and the Curse: A Poetics of Justice from the Revolution to the Civil War* (Cambridge, MA: Harvard University Press, 2013). Relying on Jean Fagan Yellin's biography of Jacobs, Smith argues persuasively that Jacobs's *Incidents* was inspired by John Brown's raid on Harpers Ferry. "But Jacobs," Smith shows, "made the connection explicit when she composed, as her concluding chapter, 'a tribute to Brown'" (184). Departing from Yellin, however, Smith does not consider the creation of Linda Brent as a fictional narrator, reading *Incidents* strictly as autobiography rather than as a sentimental novel. Its sentimentality, Smith suggests, was imposed by Child's editorial "effort to make the narrative conform to sentimental conventions" (185).

19 Harriet A. Jacobs, *Incidents in the Life of a Slave Girl Written by Herself*, ed. Jean Fagan Yellin (Cambridge, MA: Harvard University Press, 2002), 3.

20 Peterson, *"Doers of the Word,"* 148.

21 Harryette Mullen, "Runaway Tongue: Resistant Orality in *Uncle Tom's Cabin, Our Nig, Incidents in the Life of a Slave Girl*, and *Beloved*," in *The Culture of Sentiment*, ed. Shirley Samuels (New York: Oxford University Press, 1992), 246.

22 For a full reading of the ways in which Wilson employs the sentimental conventions of love and marriage, see Ann DuCille, *The Coupling Convention: Sex, Text, and Tradition in Black Women's Fiction* (New York: Oxford University Press, 1993), 5–7.

23 Frank J. Webb, *The Garies and Their Friends* (Baltimore: Johns Hopkins University Press, 1997), xx.

24 Samuel Otter, "Frank Webb's Still Life: Rethinking Literature and Politics through *The Garies and Their Friends*," *American Literary History* 20 (2008): 731.

CHAPTER 13

African American Print Culture

Derrick R. Spires

The prevailing narrative frame for understanding early African American literature has been the movement from enslavement to freedom, and rightly so.[1] By the middle of the nineteenth century, approximately 90 percent of the African descended people in the United States were enslaved; free African Americans were either descended from enslaved people, self-emancipated, or emancipated through state law; and the anti-slavery movement created one of the most robust cultural markets in the antebellum United States, based on images and narratives of Blackness and enslavement. The slave narrative genre in particular, and antislavery culture more broadly, provided fertile ground and a durable framework for the literary imagination, simultaneously following and cultivating public taste for particular kinds of representative Blackness. This cultural movement fed the explosion of African American literature during the 1850s, the period William Andrews and Maurice Lee have described separately as "the first renaissance of Black letters."[2] That decade saw publication of the earliest known novel by an African American (William Wells Brown's *Clotel* [1853]), the "institutionalization of slave narratives" (including Douglass's *My Bondage and My Freedom* [1855]), a number of poetry collections (including Frances E. W. Harper's *Poems on Miscellaneous Subjects* [1854]), short stories (Frederick Douglass's "The Heroic Slave" [*Frederick Douglass' Paper*, 1853], Lucie Stanton Day's "Charles and Clara Hayes" [*Aliened American*, 1854], and Harper's "The Two Offers" [*Anglo-African Magazine*, 1859]), and a ranging cadre of Black periodicals (including *Frederick Douglass' Paper, Mirror of the Times* [1857–1862], *Repository of Religion and Literature* [1858–1863], the *Christian Recorder*, and the *Anglo-African Magazine* [1859–1860]). At the same time, the white taste for representations of enslavement created a marketplace in which, Andrews noted, it seemed a "writer who had not been born a slave" or was not telling a story about enslavement "had no story to tell."[3]

Yet, even before the 1850s, burgeoning African American print cultures made space for precisely the kinds of stories the white cultural market of the 1850s would seem to devalue. Since at least the 1930s, scholars like Dorothy B. Porter, architect of Howard University's Moorland-Spingarn special collections, drew attention to "early Negro writings" from a variety of collectives, including mutual aid societies, religious and fraternal organizations, and literary societies.[4] As Porter observed in her 1945 essay, "Early American Negro Writings: A Bibliographical Study," while many of "the very earliest imprints of Negro writings in this country were declarations or appeals in the cause of freedom," the archive also demonstrates that "before emancipation" African Americans "did by no means confine [themselves] to this subject."[5] Updating this thesis for her 1971 anthology, *Early Negro Writing, 1760–1837*, Porter would argue that early African American print provides "the beginnings of the Afro-American's artistic consciousness ... the first articulations of the appeal of beauty and the moral sense" through poetry, fiction, essays, sermons, and a host of other forms.[6] The choice is not between writings addressing enslavement and some broader archive, but rather about developing methods and language for the breadth and depth of Black thought expressed through print over time.

Studying African American print culture, as Porter and contemporary critics like Frances Smith Foster outline it, means developing thick and textured senses of Black writing that center the content and forms important to early Black writers and reading collectives. As Foster puts it in an update of Porter's thesis:

> Once upon a time long ago in North America, a literate people of African descent lived and promulgated their own print culture. They did this primarily to speak to and for themselves about matters they considered worthy of written words. They did this also in response to their own felt needs to record and to refine their own organizational activities and community developments.[7]

This work means exposing and repairing how the critical tools at hand (bibliography and cataloguing, in Porter's case), assumptions about Black literacy, and literary histories focused narrowly on Black writing for white audiences or on particular forms can render texts by Black writers either invisible or illegible.

Following Porter and Foster, I define the object of study for early African American print culture as the traditions, practices, and infrastructures that include routes and theories of circulation and reading culture; relations to dominant and contemporaneous print models and discourse; shared concerns with reception and racialization; citational, paratextual, and intertextual connections; the interrelatedness and contingencies of print production and identity/racial production; and community formation/identification. While early African American print culture includes the study of literary traditions and canons, it might more accurately be described as the study of the processes, movements, and networks through which African Americans entered, produced, and used print, including books, newspapers, and all manner of ephemera and other objects, as well as the cultures of reading that emerged around print. This understanding of African American print culture does not exclude work on how Blackness circulated in US print through, for instance, fugitive slave ads, but my focus here will be on print generated by Black folk for Black folk in the United States and elsewhere. As a field, early African American print culture exists at the intersections of book history, material and cultural studies, Black studies, Black feminist criticism, bibliography, and African American intellectual history, to name a few key nodal points. The study of African American print culture, then, is also an inquiry into the institutional forces that have kept this archive and Black writing from view and the processes and ethics by which the study of African American print culture might lead to changes in these institutions.

African American print culture revises our received understandings of literary form and reading publics. Carla Peterson, for instance, calls on literary scholars to "[follow] nineteenth-century African-American definitions of what constitutes a literary text." Not doing so risks "[reifying] early African-American texts into a monolithic literary canon or tradition."[8] Centering Black reading culture disrupts narratives that have often prioritized white antislavery organizations, white audience expectations, and the struggle to find Black voices within their framing devices. Studying these spaces and texts, including the classic slave narrative, will remain important. But the work becomes all the richer by attending to a diverse array of Black producers and readers. Elizabeth McHenry's *Forgotten Readers: Recovering the Lost History of African American Literary Societies* (2002) has been crucial on this front in its attention to African American literate practices, as she foregrounds literary societies as key nodes in cultivating African American print culture. Beyond classrooms, McHenry highlights "nonacademic venues like churches, private homes[,] . . . beauty parlors," reading rooms, and other social places where reading was a collective enterprise.[9] These Black readers had diverse interests that included poetry and fiction, but also political treatises, sermons and orations, essays, and sketches. And their engagement with print included not only reading, but also being read to.

Our literary histories of African American print cultures have broadened and deepened dramatically over the last two decades. This work has emphasized periodicals and Afro-Protestantism as principle sites for studying early African American print culture; and new work on gift books, friendship albums, understudied sections of periodicals (such as the women's and children's sections and advertisements), and the colored conventions movement has expanded this core to include less formal networks along with state and national organizations.[10] John Ernest and Stephen G. Hall have outlined a vast genre of African American historiography; Nazera Wright, Anna Mae Duane, and Brigitte Fielder draw attention to early African American thought on Black childhood in general and Black girlhood in particular; Britt Rusert has elucidated African Americans' interventions in science; and Ivy Wilson and Meredith McGill have given us new ways to think about Black poetry and periodical culture. Where much of the foundational work in African American print culture has traditionally drawn from texts produced on the East Coast – New York, Philadelphia, and Boston in particular – Eric Gardner and others are bringing more attention to black print in "unexpected places," those print and geographical sites including periodicals, texts from midwestern and western states and territories, Black writing in languages other than English, and massive collections of periodical poetry that have yet to be fully explored or theorized.[11] Finally, new work in print production by Jonathan Senchyne and Jordan Wingate is recovering how enslaved Black people worked as printers, compositors, and pressmen for early American and antebellum newspapers, north and south.[12] This labor-centered focus expands the purview of African American print culture to include the white papers that existed because of Black labor.

Radiclani Clytus crystallizes what has become a consensus within the field in his study of the neglected genre of pseudonymous sketch writing in *Frederick Douglass' Paper*: "critics shouldn't presume that the cultural imagination that fosters black creativity is not also prioritizing black collective self-regard and artistic innovation over and against the political objectives of anti-racism" (58).[13] The rest of this chapter will expand on these critical trends by focusing on three areas: (1) Black newspapers; (2) pamphlets, with special emphasis on David Walker's *Appeal*; and (3) the colored conventions movement. I conclude with a meditation on new developments in Black Digital Humanities and how they have helped shape conversations around the ethics of recovery.[14] Because of the vastness and rapid growth of this field, the rest of this essay takes the form of a survey and, wherever possible, points readers in the direction of scholarship that takes up these issues and readings in more detail.

Antecedents: Texts, Moments, Movements

Well before the 1820s, a robust Black print culture had developed in lockstep with the revolutionary era and early national print cultures in the United States. This print landscape included well-known books, such as Phillis Wheatley's *Poems on Various Subjects* (1773), narratives such as John Marrant's *A Narrative of the Lord's Wonderful Dealings with John Marrant* (1785), as well as self-published pamphlets, such as Benjamin Banneker's *Copy of a Letter from Benjamin Banneker, to the Secretary of State, with His Answer* (written in 1791, published in 1792), Prince Hall's *Charge Delivered to the Brethren of the African Lodge* (1792), and Absalom Jones and Richard Allen's *Narrative of the Proceedings of the Black People* (1794), the first black text to secure US copyright, a new legal framework in the late eighteenth century. Other important touchstones include Black poetry published in periodicals by Wheatley and others; the many sermons and public addresses published to mark occasions such as the abolition of the transatlantic slave trade in 1808; the constitutions and proceedings of mutual aid societies (e.g., the Free African Society of Philadelphia and the Rhode Island African Society), fraternal organizations (Prince Hall Free Masons), and religious institutions (the Free African Church); the collection of writing Jeannine DeLombard and others describe as gallows literature; and the many petitions enslaved and free Africans submitted to federal, state, and local governments to advocate for themselves.[15]

Black print proliferated well before the 1820s, but exploded afterward with the founding of several newspapers, the growth of structures such as the American Methodist Episcopal Church Book Concern (founded in 1854) and the colored conventions movement (begun in 1830), and the maturation of the second and third post-emancipation generations in states such as New York, Pennsylvania, and Massachusetts. This print culture followed US national trends including new print technologies and the rise of the "industrial book" (the development of stereotype plates and machine-made paper, for instance), innovations in transportation (railroad, canals, and improved roads) and communication (expanding postal service networks and services and the telegraph), and social movements including radical abolitionism and the proliferation of religious tract societies.[16] The development of the Black press and the level of control over print production (editing, printing, publishing, circulation, etc.) it provided Black communities were perhaps the signal factors distinguishing pre- and post-1820s African American print cultures.

Black Periodical Culture: Politics, Literature, Culture

Black writers understood that the republic of letters, while often framed as a meritocratic space of rational critical debate, was functionally a space of racialized and gendered power. "Our warfare lies in the field of thought," proclaimed the Committee on a National Press famously reported at the 1847 National Convention of Colored People.[17] The battleground might be metaphysical – the field of thought – but convention delegates understood that the tools and means of engagement were decidedly material: "In training our soldiers for the field – in marshaling our hosts for the fight – in leading the onset, and throughout the conflict, we need a Printing Press, because a printing press is the vehicle of thought – is a ruler of opinions" (256). Here, "press" was not synonymous with "newspapers," but rather control over the means of print production: a printing press and the infrastructure necessary to keep it viable. The convention was calling not only for the distribution of black writing, but also for black editorial work and proprietorship over newspapers and printing houses and black involvement in the material production of printed matter (including composition, paper making, owning a press, distribution networks, etc.).

Black periodicals were central to this movement, both as venues for Black writing and as a mode for advertising and disseminating material from other sources. They were eclectic, at times multilingual, sites of knowledge production and dissemination, framed with the understanding that Black reading communities needed materials for uplift, education, counters to anti-Black culture, and entertainment.[18] *Freedom's Journal* (New York, 1827–1829), the first Black edited newspaper, made this case in its first editorial on March 16, 1827: "We wish to plead our own cause. Too long have others spoken for us." Ten years later, the editors of *Colored American* (1837–1841) would expand on this premise in their March 4, 1837, opening editorial, "Why We Should Have a Paper": we "must establish and maintain the PRESS and through it, speak out in THUNDER TONES, until the nation repent and render to every man that which is just and equal." The paper must emanate from African Americans themselves, because "no class of men, however pious and benevolent can take our place in the great work of redeeming our character and removing our disabilities." This insistence on the Blackness and autonomy of African American print production would be a consistent refrain for subsequent papers, as largely white publics continually doubted Black print agency, on the one hand, and as established white antislavery organizations consistently attempted to exert authority over them, on the other. Though African American periodicals often pitched themselves as venues for Black speech, they also operated under the assumption that their readerships were interracial and transnational. *Colored American* listed "international agents in Jamaica, Bermuda, and Toronto."[19] *Aliened American* and *Frederick Douglass' Paper* boasted correspondents and readers from England, Cuba, Toronto, Sierra Leone, and elsewhere.[20]

Black women were central yet often underacknowledged movers of African American print – in contemporary scholarship and in their day. While some official spaces made Black women's labor and participation in the print culture invisible, newspapers reveal a host of ways that Black women generated, supported, and participated in the broader print culture. Julia Williams Garnet, for instance, led a group of Black women that included Martha M. Wright, J. W. Loguen, and Mary A. Jeffrey in organizing an 1849 bazaar to support Samuel Ringgold Ward's *Impartial Citizen*.[21] Black women also appear on subscriber lists and as contributors, both pseudonymously and under their own names, and Mary Ann Shadd Cary would found the *Provincial Freeman* in 1854. But limiting this research to fundraising or to women's presence on mastheads misses the more invisible labor undertaken by someone like Harriet Myers, who, we learn from her obituary, "was also endowed with more than the ordinary share of literary ability, and was a faithful student." "It is a fact worthy of special notice," the obituary reveals, "that she did perform most of the editorial labors upon the *Northern Light*, published some years since by Mr. Myers, and was entrusted by him with the reading of the proof-sheets for its columns."[22] The obituary leaves unclear whether or not "editorial" applies to "reading of the proof-sheets" only or if it means that she was more involved in the newspaper's running and writing the editorial content, but Stephen Myers's active travel schedule suggests the latter.

As Harriet Myers's example suggests, Black periodicals offer a complex terrain for interrogating the meaning of terms like "editor," "publisher," and "Black press," as well as how papers shape their identities.[23] Is a periodical "Black" if the editors are African Americans, but the printers are not, or if the editors are white, but the owner is Black? As Fagan outlines, the *Colored American* began as the *Weekly Advocate* (New York) with Phillip A. Bell as editor and proprietor and Robert Sears, a white man, as its printer. The paper underwent a name change after a few months, when Samuel Cornish became its editor, but by the end of the paper's run, "the *Colored American*'s masthead listed [Charles B.] Ray as its sole editor and proprietor."[24] In 1854, *Frederick Douglass' Paper* listed Douglass as "publisher" and William Oliver, a white man, as printer. Julia Griffiths, a white British woman, was Douglass's business manager and fulfilled many of the paper's day-to-day editorial duties in its early years.[25] These lines of production point to how the Blackness of Black print does not depend entirely on the blackness of those involved. As John Ernest argues in relation to the *Anglo-African Magazine*, these periodicals' Blackness inheres as much to their approach and style as to the makeup of their offices.

These periodicals also reflected larger tendencies in Black activism where sacred and secular institutions did not conform to binary oppositions and where religious institutions, especially Afro-Protestantism, were often hubs for activist and intellectual culture.[26] Both *Freedom's Journal* (founded by Boston Crummel, Cornish, and John B. Russworm) and *Colored American* (founded by Bell and Charles B. Ray) explicitly frame their missions in jeremiadic terms: to prick the nation's heart, to advocate on behalf of their enslaved brothers and sisters, and to guide Black communities toward moral and economic uplift. They saw their activism as part of their ministry, and, as David Walker outlines so forcefully, they saw enslavement and racism as sins for which the United States would suffer. At the same time, their orientation toward moral uplift could lead to tensions with readers who rejected calls to be respectable in public or for women to adhere to contemporaneous cultures of true womanhood, which called for piety, submission to male leadership, and other protocols relegating women to domestic space away from public and print politics. Other papers framed themselves as explicitly secular. William Howard Day, for instance, proclaimed in the April 9, 1853, inaugural issue of the *Aliened American* (Cleveland, Ohio) that the paper would "favor Literature, Science, and Art" and would be "independent: independent in religion – independent in politics – independent in everything; – the organ of no Party, and yet a Political paper; and the humble supporter of all good men." In these cases, "secular" meant that these papers would cover a range of topics and eschew religious or political affiliation or dedication to a single issue. For Thomas Hamilton, editor of the *Anglo-African Magazine* (1859–1860) and *Weekly Anglo-African* (1859–1861), "secular" meant attending explicitly to Black intellectual culture rather than "the general news or the mere gossip of the hour."[27]

Where Ray and Cornish foregrounded moral reformism, Day and Hamilton foregrounded intellectual culture, but the difference was a matter of emphasis rather than exclusion. All of these papers were hubs for Black literature that arrived "freighted with information for all," including poetry, short fiction, convention minutes, essays, and sketches. *Freedom's Journal*, for instance, published "Theresa: A Haytien Tale," by "S.," perhaps the first short story published by an African American; *Frederick Douglass' Paper* published Frederick Douglass's "The Heroic Slave" (1852) before it appeared in the *Autographs for Freedom* (1853) collection; Martin R. Delany's *Blake* was serialized across several periodicals; and *Weekly Anglo-African* (1859–1861) serialized William Wells Brown *Miralda*, his first reworking of *Clotel* (1853). Poetry was even more plentiful. Many of Frances E. W. Harper's poems, for instance, appeared first in *Frederick Douglass' Paper*, the *Aliened American*, and (later) the *Christian Recorder* and *Anglo-African Magazine* before they were collected and printed in pamphlet and book form. As Ivy G. Wilson notes, "returning to the periodical offers one way of reconstructing the historical context in which a poem was published, a way often obfuscated by the assumed thematic continuity of the self-contained volume per se."[28] Examining the periodical contexts for this literature, especially poetry, opens up new avenues for interpretation and for thinking about audience and textual interpretation.

In addition to original content, Black periodicals participated in a robust antebellum reprint culture: readers of *Douglass' Paper*, for instance, might find serialized installments of Charles Dickens's *Bleak House*, Harriet Martineau's novels, references to Sir Walter Scott's Waverly novels, and a host of poetry, children's literature, and fiction from contemporaneous newspapers and literary journals.[29] Readers of Black newspapers would also find inaugural addresses from the US President, convention minutes from colored conventions and antislavery conventions, congressional proceedings, scientific essays, and other items the editors thought their readers would find edifying, useful, or entertaining.

While short stories, serial novels, and poetry have long been the focus of our literary histories, periodicals also draw attention to other genres and forms central to nineteenth-century Black literary culture but understudied today, including the sketch and pseudonymous writing. The 1840s and 1850s saw the development of a robust culture of pseudonymous writing, with a cadre of correspondents for *Colored American, Douglass' Paper, Provincial Freedman*, and other papers writing under names such as Observer, Cosmopolite, Fanny Homewood, and Home Maria. Their names were less about maintaining anonymity (many were known to each other and to at least some of their readers) and more about style, tone, and history. James McCune Smith published ten installments of "Heads of the

Colored People" under the pseudonym "Communipaw," over several years in *Frederick Douglass's Paper*.[30] William J. Wilson often sparred with Smith through city sketches under his pseudonym, Ethiop, and reveled in describing African American cultures, including dress, dance, visual arts, and business. This writing participated in an urban sketch genre that included contemporaneous white writers like Charles Dickens, whose *American Notes* featured a section on New York, and George Foster, whose *New York by Gas-light* series appeared in the *New York Tribune* and traded in racist caricatures of Black life.

Like other elements of African American print, however, Black sketch writers used the form to challenge negative representations of Blackness and to forward their own aesthetic agendas. As Peterson notes, "the pen names revealed each man's [or woman's] particular perspective on what it meant to be black in America." They "functioned as signposts, informing readers of the personae's orientation toward the world and their representation of it in their writings."[31] "Veritas," for instance, signals an engagement with truth, a call back to revolutionary-era writing, and Roman mythology, while Ethiop invokes African origins (Ethiopia) and Phillis Wheatley, whose speaker in "To the University of Cambridge" referred to themselves as "an Ethiop." This tradition would continue into the twentieth century, with Ida B. Wells writing under Iola and Pauline Hopkins and George Schuyler publishing under various pseudonyms; yet each era brought with it a different inflection and purpose to this practice.

Black Pamphlets: Spreading the Word

In conjunction with newspapers, pamphlets and self-published books were key elements of African American print culture. Touchstone pamphlets and treatises printed between 1820 and 1860 include David Walker's *Appeal, in Four Articles; Together with a Preamble, to the Coloured Citizens of the World, but in Particular, and Very Expressly, to Those of the United States of America* (1829, 1830), Maria Stewart's *Productions* (1835), Richard Allen's *The Life, Experience, and Gospel Labours of the Rt. Rev. Richard Allen* (1833), Jarena Lee's *Religious Experience and Journal of Mrs. Jarena Lee* (1836), Hosea Easton's *A Treatise on the Intellectual Character, and Civil and Political Condition of the Colored People of the U. States* (1837), and Martin R. Delany's *The Condition, Elevation, Emigration, and Destiny of the Colored People of the United States* (1852). The pamphlet gave writers the potential to spread their words widely, and, for those on the lecture circuit – whether antislavery, lyceum, or evangelical – the form allowed them to travel with their work and print new copies on demand. Advances in stereotyping enabled Lee, for instance, to commission new printings of her *Religious Experience* as needed, as she traveled preaching across the country, and, as McGill demonstrates, Harper published the antebellum editions of *Poems on Miscellaneous Subjects* (1854, 1857) as pamphlets that could be reprinted and distributed easily on the lecture circuit.[32] The decade also saw works of literary criticism, including William G. Allen's *Wheatley, Banneker, and Horton* (1849); works of history, including William C. Nell's *The Colored Patriots of the American Revolution* (1855); and, as I will discuss in more detail in the next section, a host of documents emerging from colored conventions. And yet, no text attests to the effects of Black print, and Black bound pamphlets and books, as much as Walker's *Appeal*, published in three editions between 1829 and 1830.

One of the most important works of the nineteenth century, Walker's *Appeal* called on enslaved people to assert their right to freedom and wages as citizens, to organize collectively, and to meet enslavers' violence with counterviolence. Walker drew on the jeremiad tradition to condemn white Americans for perpetuating the most inhumane system of enslavement ever conceived, for not adhering to the principles they themselves articulated in the Declaration of Independence and federal Constitution, and for the hypocrisy of claiming to be Christians while oppressing their fellow citizens.[33] On a very basic level, the *Appeal* is a book about the cultivation of black reading culture and a call to generate more Black discourse, in print and otherwise. "It is expected," Walker's posits in his Preface, "that all coloured men, women and children, of every nation, language and tongue under heaven, will try to procure a copy of this *Appeal* and read it, or get someone to read it to them, for it is designed more particularly for them." Walker also expected this reading public (which includes readers, those being read to, and those hearing of the *Appeal*) to interrogate other texts: the Declaration, the Christian Bible, grammar books, histories, and, most prominently, Thomas Jefferson's *Notes on the State of Virginia* (1785). "[B]uy a copy of Mr. Jefferson's 'Notes on Virginia,' and put it in the hand of [your] son," Walker tells Black men, because "we, and the world wish to see the charges of Mr. Jefferson refuted by the blacks themselves."[34] Walker calls back to *Freedom's Journal* and demonstrates the close relationship between Black print modes. Walker's earlier writings appeared in *Freedom's Journal* and he served as one of the paper's Boston subscription agents, a role that likely helped him establish circulation routes for his *Appeal*.[35]

In recent years, the *Appeal* has gained attention for Walker's unique use of typography as much as for its radical message. As Marcy Dinius notes in her article on the *Appeal*'s typography,

> The striking typography of Walker's *Appeal* is the sign, site, and agent of this violence: with each stab of an exclamation point, each pointing manicule (or punch of a printer's "fist"), every letter that rises up to become a capital or that rushes forward as an italic, the text graphically acts out its resistance. In the visually and rhetorically radical text that results, the master's house is dismantled with one of his most historically significant tools – movable type.[36]

Indeed, the *Appeal is* visually stunning, with manicules (a symbol of a pointing hand, ☞), CAPS, SMALL CAPS, *italics*, and copious exclamation points. Walker uses this strategy to full effect in one of the *Appeal*'s most famous references to the Declaration: "Do you understand your own language? Hear your language, proclaimed to the world, July 4th, 1776 –☞ "We hold these truths to be self-evident – that ALL men are created EQUAL!! that they *are endowed by their Creator with certain unalienable rights*; that among these are life, *liberty*, and the pursuit of happiness!!"[37] Even as Walker's argument calls on white readers to "compare your own language" to the practice of enslaving African descended people, his typography communicates his rage and incredulity at having to "point" them to this language.[38] The overall effect is a document that functions as a script for oral performance, an aid to memorization, and a visual marker of righteous anger.

The *Appeal* demonstrates simultaneously the importance of printedness – the book-ness of Walker's *Appeal* as a material object in circulation across the United States – the fluidity between oral and print cultures, and how following print reveals vast networks in African American reading cultures that include bar owners, book sellers, ministers, sailors, and others. Walker had the *Appeal* printed in Boston and editions began surfacing as far afield as Georgia and Louisiana in a matter of weeks. Walker's circulation network included white sympathizers like E. H. Burritt (publisher of the *Milledgeville Statesman & Patriot*) and an interracial group of sailors and ship's stewards.[39] Peter Hinks reports that by 1830 Thomas Lewis, a free Black Virginian, had at least thirty copies; Jacob Cowan, an enslaved tavern-runner in North Carolina had 200 copies, and white mariner Edward Smith had several copies in South Carolina.[40] Walker's circulation network also included the state legislators who denounced him and any newspapers that reprinted passages from the *Appeal*. Whether in condemnation or approbation, Walker's words spread.

Southern enslavers and their supporters responded to the *Appeal's* circulation with immediate legal action. They amplified or promoted quarantine laws restricting black sailors' movements. Georgia, for instance, passed a quarantine law requiring that "Vessels carrying negro sailors that entered Georgia ports must go into quarantine for forty days and Negro sailors of such vessels who stepped on shore were subject to imprisonment." Georgia, Louisiana, and North Carolina also enacted anti-literacy and censorship laws punishing "any one found guilty of introducing into the state or circulating any publication for the purpose of exciting a revolt among the slaves." This generated increasing tensions between states around the limits of federal citizenship, free speech, and state's rights. Massachusetts and other states responded in the 1830s–1840s with legislation and legal action to protect their "citizens" sailing to and from the south.[41] The legal battle between states reverberated as Georgia disseminated its resolutions to other states, including the claim that black Americans had never been citizens and were not included in the term at the time of the revolution, a prelude to Chief Justice Roger B. Taney's *Dred Scott v. Sandford* (1857) opinion. At the same time, while William Lloyd Garrison and other white organizers disavowed the most radical aspects of Walker's *Appeal*, it is clear that Walker's words, in conjunction with the work and funding from other Black activists, including Richard Allen, James Forten, and Maria Stewart, demonstrated the need for more radical action on their part.

We may never know how many enslaved people encountered Walker's text, but what we do know is that the specter of active reading in slave society frightened enslavers and their supporters. The *Appeal* likely circulated much more than we can account for, especially when we include reprinted excerpts in newspapers and recited passages. Whether in support or opposition, in practice newspapers had the effect of providing Walker yet another vector for reaching his stated audience of enslaved African Americans. This vector becomes especially important when we take seriously narratives from formerly enslaved people like Frederick Douglass and Harriet Jacobs, who describe newspapers – even proslavery newspapers – as key sources for literacy and information. Dinius's work, including her essay in this volume, covers this circulation and effects of the *Appeal* in more detail, including places that we have not traditionally associated with Walker. I'll just note here that these multiple vectors offer a case study for examining how African Americans, free and enslaved, accessed print, especially in the South and especially in spaces like Baltimore, Maryland, and Savannah, Georgia, where enslaved and non-enslaved Black people

lived in fairly close proximity. We can clearly see Walker's influence on the
rhetoric of the colored conventions, especially on Henry Highland Garnet,
who reprinted the second edition of the *Appeal* in 1848 with his own
"Address to the Slaves of the United States"; and, as Emory University's
recent acquisition of W. E. B. Du Bois's copy of the first edition of the
Appeal reveals, the *Appeal*'s reach extends well past the Civil War.[42]

Colored Conventions: Activism, Print, Circulation

The colored conventions movement has become a third key venue for
studying black print culture. While a number of antebellum state and
national conventions have been available for study thanks to the efforts of
Bernard Bell, Eric Foner, and George E. Walker, the Colored Conventions
Project's community-sourcing efforts have increased the number and
availability of convention proceedings exponentially.[43] The conventions
participated in a form of collective self-authoring and collective narration,
offering "a paradigm of Black being and belonging centered not in individual rights and singular authorship but in collective writing and organizing."[44] Colored Conventions developed initially as a response to the threat
of fugitive slave legislation and the rise of the American Colonization
Society, a white-founded organization that supported Black emigration to
Africa based on the premise that African descended people were inferior and
incompatible with US democracy. According to Jim Casey, some "2,000
delegates attended at least forty-eight conventions between 1830 and 1864."
As Casey, Foreman, and Paterson note, "the inaugural Colored Conventions
meeting predates the establishment of the American Anti-Slavery Society by
a full three years and ... the Massachusetts Anti-Slavery Society (1831), the
New England Anti-Slavery Society (1832), and the American Anti-Slavery
Society (1833) were all founded after the convention movement's first
convening."[45] This chronology, along with the publications of *Freedom's
Journal* and Walker's *Appeal*, reveals the degree to which African American
print culture led to the development of the antebellum white antislavery
print culture explosion, not the other way around. Black activism laid the
moral and intellectual groundwork for radical abolitionism.

Colored Conventions were more than single events; they involved
printed calls to local meetings with agendas often published in newspapers,
pre-conference debates, post-conference media coverage, and the circulation of printed minutes and proceedings. As Douglas Jones has demonstrated, convention minutes and other documents surrounding the event
mirrored David Walker's *Appeal* in their status as performative texts,

documents generated with the understanding that they would be read and rehearsed collectively. Convention planning often began in the pages of newspapers, and the infrastructure around the conventions – advertisements, boarding houses, meals, travel, and the like – offers key insights into early African American political and travel culture. Official convention proceedings were documents made of many different kinds of texts and discourses. In addition to resolutions, addresses, petitions, and other documents meant for further circulation, convention proceedings also included debates over tactics and, importantly, Black science writing, including what Patterson has called "Black demography," the collection of black population data including employment and education statistics, census data, and health numbers.

Studying the colored conventions has been one tool for making visible the infrastructure Black women provided – from housing to printing minutes to fundraising – despite silence on this front in official convention documents. As Jewon Woo's work reveals, Black women in Ohio threatened to boycott the 1849 convention if they were not recognized. Two years later, the minutes name the women – "Miss L. A. Stanton, Miss M. J. Hopkins, Mrs. L. M. Jenkins, Mrs. C. Hacley, Mrs. S. Mason, Mrs. S. P. Scurry, Miss L. Harper" – who "[pledged] themselves to furnish means to publish the proceedings of this Convention."[46] First among these is Lucie A. Stanton (Day Sessions), who would go on to help finance William Howard Day's *Aliened American* and provide the paper with one of its first pieces, her short story "Charles and Clara Hayes." This brief moment offers one nodal point connecting colored conventions, black periodicals, black fiction, and black feminism. As Gardner and Denise Burgher have demonstrated separately, tracking public speaking engagements by Frances Harper, Mary Ann Shadd Cary, and others advertised or reported in newspapers close to convention dates provides another clue to which women might have attended and participated in a given colored convention. Harper, whose consistent presence at conventions in the 1850s and 1860s does not appear in convention minutes, would make this connection even more explicitly in her fiction for the *Anglo-African Magazine*, when Jane Rustic dreams of an "Anti-Sun Shine" (ASS) Convention that banned women from speaking but welcomed their fundraising. These Black feminist critiques show us that we must read Black print – and print culture more broadly – with an eye for the ethics of who has voice in the room – and who has a hand in constructing and financing the room and the building, for that matter. Otherwise, we miss the point of a good deal about Black print cultural production.

Antebellum Black Print Now: Ethics, Black Digital Humanities, and Access Beyond Recovery

The increasing availability of black texts in digital spaces combined with the flourishing of Black Digital Humanities projects, from recent efforts such as the Colored Conventions Project, Black Self-Publishing, and Umbra Search to long-standing work such as the North American Slave Narrative Archive and the Project in the History of Black Writing, has made it clear that Black print was no outlier and that our focus on the slave narrative or "traditional" literary forms (the novel, the short story, or the single book) needs revision. These calls move well beyond adding to the canon; they speak to the need to develop new methodologies and interpretive frameworks for assigning value in the canon we already have. They also call us to patiently unravel and revise our origin narratives as new texts come into view and as digital methods provide new ways of engaging already-canonical texts.

Indeed, there is more going on here than recovery. Black print culture studies also changes and challenges how we do this work, with scholars and projects focusing simultaneously on the ethics of studying Black print and life at the same time as they engage in an ongoing reconsideration of archives, power, and our relation to them.[47] "Recovery," Laura Helton, Justin Leroy, Max A. Mishler, Samantha Seeley, and Shauna Sweeney argue, "must have a political purpose beyond documenting black presence, or it is merely a plea for inclusion within the foundational premises of liberal modernity – a critique of its boundaries but not of its essence."[48] As Brigitte Fielder and Jonathan Senchyne note in their introduction to *Against a Sharp White Background* (2019), "while it is exciting and necessary to do recovery work on early black writing and print, it is equally necessary to study the historical library bibliographical standards and contemporary digital architectures that kept such works 'hidden' and in need of recovery today."[49] Rather than a panacea for inclusion and equality, these editors invite us to think of recovery as a "site of contestation" over "what forms of historical inquiry are best suited to addressing the contradictions of the political present" (11).[50]

The field of early African American print culture continues in these efforts even as it enters a new phase in lieu of new interrogations of the archive, its ability to give us access to a Black past, and its political power. Black Digital Humanities projects have been at the forefront of this work.[51] The Project in the History of Black Writing (PHBW) and the Colored Conventions Project (CCP) have been among the most explicit projects in thinking about the ethics of the archive and scholarship and in linking these principles not only to Black studies and Black feminist practices but also to the ideas about Black print itself. The CCP, for instance, "affirms Black women's centrality to nineteenth-century Black organizing even as official records erase and anonymize the very contributions, labor and infrastructure that made the Colored Conventions movement possible" and pledges "to account for Black women's labor and leadership in our own historical work and in our own project practices."[52] The project's model – its insistence on "community sourced" rather than "crowd sourced" terminology, for instance – reinforces community, horizontal organization, and collaboration as key principles in a mirror of the Color Conventions the project archives. Similarly, the PHBW and Black Book Interactive Project (both led by Maryemma Graham at the University of Kansas) take their ethics directly from the principles of accessibility and institutional transformation found in Black studies and continues Dorothy Porter's work of developing metadata schemas that make Black writing – Black novels, in this case – visible for further study.[53] At the same time, these projects remind us that understanding and learning from the wisdom and tactics articulated in and through early Black print culture is a matter of life and death for democracy in the United States. As Kim Gallon argues in a recent essay titled "What the Mainstream News Media Can Learn from the History of the Black Press," "The history of the Black Press reveals that speaking truth to power requires a more complex approach that depends on a commitment to not only routing out lies but also combatting injustice."[54] While Gallon's essay centers the Black press of the early twentieth century, we might apply her argument to antebellum Black print culture, as well: antebellum Black print reveals the power and necessity of *parrhesia* – fearless speech. For people studying this work in the twenty-first century it demands that our methods and analyses meet that challenge.

Notes

1 As Houston A. Baker, Jr., put it, "The locus classicus of African American literary discourse is the slave narrative." See Baker, "Archaeology, Ideology, and African American Discourse," in *Redefining American Literary History*, ed. A. LaVonne Brown Ruoff and Jerry W. Ward, Jr. (New York: Modern Language Association of America, 1990), 169.

2 William Andrews, "The 1850s: The First Afro-American Literary Renaissance," in *Literary Romanticism in America*, ed. William Andrews

(Baton Rouge: Louisiana State University Press, 1981), 441; and Maurice S. Lee, "The 1850s: The First Renaissance of Black Letters," in *A Companion to African American Literature*, ed. Gene Andrew Jarrett (Chichester: Wiley-Blackwell, 2010), 105.

3 Andrews, "The 1850s," 441.
4 For more on Porter, see Laura Helton, "On Decimals, Catalogs, and Racial Imaginaries of Reading," *PMLA* 134, no. 1 (2019): 99–120; Zita Nunes, "Cataloging Black Knowledge," *Perspectives on History*, November 20, 2018, www.historians.org/publications-and-directories/perspectives-on-history/december-2018/cataloging-black-knowledge-how-dorothy-porter-assembled-and-organized-a-premier-africana-research-collection; and Janet Sims-Wood, *Dorothy Porter Wesley at Howard University: Building a Legacy of Black History* (Charleston, SC: History Press, 2014).
5 Porter, "Early Negro American Writing: A Bibliographical Study," *The Papers of the Bibliographical Society of America* 39 no. 3 (Third Quarter, 1945): 192.
6 See Porter, introduction to *Early Negro Writing, 1760–1837* (Baltimore: Black Classic Press, 1995), 3. Robert Stepto usefully outlines "the quest for freedom *and* literacy" as the "Afro-American pregeneric myth" (18, emphasis original). Robert Stepto, "Teaching Afro-American Literature: Survey or Tradition, the Reconstruction of Instruction," in *Afro-American Literature: The Reconstruction of Instructions*, ed. Dexter Fisher and Robert Stepto (New York: Modern Language Association of America, 1978), 8–24.
7 Frances Smith Foster, "A Narrative of the Interesting Origins and Somewhat Surprising Developments of African-American Print Culture," *American Literary History* 17, no. 4 (Winter 2005): 715.
8 Carla L. Peterson, *"Doers of the Word": African American Women Speakers and Writers in the North (1830–1880)* (New Brunswick, NJ: Rutgers University Press), 5.
9 Elizabeth McHenry, *Forgotten Readers: Recovering the Lost History of African-American Literary Societies* (Durham, NC: Duke University Press, 2002), 10.
10 See, for instance, Katharine Capshaw and Anna Mae Duane, eds., *Who Writes for Black Children?: African American Children's Literature before 1900* (Minneapolis: University of Minnesota Press, 2017); Benjamin Fagan, *The Black Newspaper and the Chosen Nation* (Athens: University of Georgia Press, 2016); P. Gabrielle Foreman, Jim Casey, and Sarah Lynn Patterson, eds., *The Colored Conventions Movement: Black Organizing in the Nineteenth Century* (Chapel Hill: University of North Carolina Press, 2021); and Jasmine Nichole Cobb, "'Forget Me Not': Free Black Women and Sentimentality," *MELUS: Multi-Ethnic Literature of the U.S.* 40, no. 3 (2015): 28–46.
11 In addition to the work previously cited, foundational work includes Dickson D. Bruce, *Origins of African American Literature* (Charlottesville: University of Virginia Press, 2001); Henry Louis Gates, Jr., *Figures in Black: Words, Signs, and the "Racial" Self* (New York: Oxford University Press, 1987); Frances Smith Foster, *Written by Herself: Literary Production by African American Women, 1746–1892* (Bloomington: Indiana University Press, 1993); John

Ernest, *Liberation Historiography: African American Writers and the Challenge of History, 1794–1861* (Chapel Hill: University of North Carolina Press, 2004); P. Gabrielle Foreman, "A Riff, a Call, and a Response: Reframing the Problem That Led to Our Being Tokens in Ethnic and Gender Studies; or, Where Are We Going Anyway and with Whom Will We Travel?," *Legacy* 30, no. 2 (2013): 306–322; Katy Chiles, "Within and without the Raced Nations: Intratextuality, Martin Delany, and *Blake; or, The Huts of America,*" *American Literature* 80, no. 2 (2008): 323–352; Jeannine Marie DeLombard, "African American Cultures of Print," in *A History of the Book in America, vol. 3: The Industrial Book, 1840–1880,* ed. Scott E. Casper, Jeffrey D. Groves, Stephen W. Nissenbaum, Michael Winship, and David D. Hall (Chapel Hill: University of North Carolina Press, 2007), 360–373; Leon Jackson, "The Talking Book and the Talking Book Historian: African American Cultures of Print – The State of the Discipline," *Book History* 13 (2010): 251–308; Joycelyn Moody, *Sentimental Confessions: Spiritual Narrative of Nineteenth-Century African American Women* (Athens: University of Georgia Press, 2001); Ivy Wilson, *Specters of Democracy: Blackness and the Aesthetics of Politics in the Antebellum U.S.* (New York: Oxford University Press, 2011). Key edited volumes and journal issues include James Philip Danky and Wayne A. Wiegand, eds., *Print Culture in a Diverse America* (Urbana: University of Illinois Press, 1998); Brigitte Fielder and Jonathan Senchyne, eds., *Against a Sharp White Background: Infrastructures of African American Print* (Madison: University of Wisconsin Press, 2019); George Hutchinson and John K. Young, eds., *Publishing Blackness: Textual Constructions of Race since 1850* (Ann Arbor: University of Michigan Press, 2013); Jordan Alexander Stein and Lara Cohen, eds., *Early African American Literature in Theory and Practice* (Philadelphia: University Pennsylvania Press, 2012); and "African American Print Culture," ed. Joycelyn Moody and Howard Rambsy II, special issue of *MELUS: Multi-Ethnic Literature of the U.S.* 40, no. 3 (Fall 2015). For an account of African American print culture that decenters the East Coast, see Eric Gardner, *Unexpected Places: Relocating Nineteenth-Century African American Literature* (Jackson: University Press of Mississippi, 2009), and *Black Print Unbound: The Christian Recorder, African American Literature, and Periodical Culture* (New York: Oxford University Press, 2015).

12 Senchyne, "Under Pressure: Reading Material Textuality in the Recovery of Early African American Print Work," *Arizona Quarterly: A Journal of American Literature, Culture, and Theory* 75, no. 3 (2019): 109–132.

13 For more on Ethiop, see Radiclani Clytus, "Visualizing in Black Print: The Brooklyn Correspondence of William J. Wilson aka 'Ethiop,'" *J19: The Journal of Nineteenth-Century Americanists* 6, no. 1 (2018): 29–66; Spires, *The Practice of Citizenship: Black Politics and Print Culture in the United States* (Philadelphia: University of Pennsylvania Press, 2019), chapters 3 and 4; and Wilson, *Specters,* chapter 7.

14 I do not include slave narratives or the novels of the 1850s in detail, because those subjects have been taken up ably elsewhere and because I want to focus

on African American print produced with African Americans as the stated primary audience. For the slave narrative in particular, see Nicole Aljoe and Ian Finseth, eds., *Journeys of the Slave Narrative in the Early Americas* (Charlottesville: University of Virginia Press, 2014); Teresa A. Goddu, "The Slave Narrative as Material Text," in *The Oxford Handbook of the African American Slave Narrative*, ed. John Ernest (Oxford: Oxford University Press, 2014), 149–164; Teresa A. Goddu, *Selling Antislavery: Abolition and Mass Media in Antebellum America* (Philadelphia: University of Pennsylvania Press, 2020), 55–82; and Robert B. Stepto, *From behind the Veil: A Study of Afro-American Narrative*, 2nd ed. (Urbana: University of Illinois Press, 1991).

15 See Joanna Brooks, "The Early American Public Sphere and the Emergence of a Black Print Counterpublic," *William and Mary Quarterly* 62, no. 1 (2005): 67–92; Tara Bynum, "Phillis Wheatley on Friendship," *Legacy: A Journal of American Women Writers* 31, no. 1 (2014): 42–51; Jeannine Marie Delombard, *In the Shadow of the Gallows: Race, Crime, and American Civic Identity* (Philadelphia: University of Pennsylvania Press, 2012); Joseph Rezek, "The Orations on the Abolition of the Slave Trade and the Uses of Print in the Early Black Atlantic," *Early American Literature* 45, no. 3 (2010): 655–682; and Xiomara Santamarina, "Thinkable Alternatives in African American Studies," *American Quarterly* 58, no. 1 (March 2006): 245–253.

16 See Michael Winship, "Manufacturing and Book Production," in Casper et al., eds., *A History of the Book in America*, 40–70, for a discussion of developing print technologies during the first half of the nineteenth century.

17 "Proceedings of the National Convention of Colored People and Their Friends; held in Troy, NY; on the 6th, 7th, 8th, and 9th of October, 1847," Colored Conventions Project Digital Records, accessed March 30, 2020, https://omeka.coloredconventions.org/items/show/279.

18 This account of Black periodicals draws on Jacqueline Bacon, *Freedom's Journal: The First African-American Newspaper* (Lanham, MD: Lexington Books, 2007); Ernest, *Liberation*; Fagan, *Black Newspaper*; Frankie Hutton, *The Early Black Press in America, 1827 to 1860* (Westport, CT: Greenwood Press, 1993); Todd Vogel, ed., *The Black Press: New Literary and Historical Essays* (New Brunswick, NJ: Rutgers University Press, 2001); Wilson, "Periodicals, Print Culture, and African American Poetry," in *A Companion to African American Literature*, ed. Gene Andrew Jarrett (Malden: Wiley-Blackwell, 2010), 133–148. For examples of multilingual Black newspapers, see *The Literary Album, Journal of Young People* (*L'Album Litteraire, Journal des Jeunes Gens*) (1843) and *The Union* (*L'Union*) (1862–1854), both out of New Orleans.

19 Fagan, *Black Newspaper*, 44.

20 See letter from Mahalia McGuyre, *Aliened American*, April 9, 1853

21 Julia W. Garnet, "Circular by the Provisional Committee of the Impartial Citizen August 1849," *Impartial Citizen*, September 5, 1849, in Ripley, *Black Abolitionist Papers*, 4: 38–41.

22 "Harriet Myers," *Anglo-African*, August 26, 1865.

23 For a sample of the exciting work coming out of editorship studies, see the 2020 forum on Editorship Studies in *American Periodicals*, edited by Jim Casey and Sarah H. Salter. For Black print, see especially Casey and Salter's introduction, "Challenges and Opportunities in Editorship Studies," *American Periodicals: A Journal of History & Criticism* 30, no. 2 (2020): 101–104; and Jewon Woo, "The *Colored Citizen*: Collaborative Editorship in Progress," *American Periodicals: A Journal of History & Criticism* 30, no. 2 (2020): 110–113.

24 Fagan, *Black Newspaper*, 44.

25 See ibid., 43.

26 See Frances Smith Foster, "African Americans, Literature, and the Nineteenth-Century Afro-Protestant Press," in *Reciprocal Influences: Literary Production, Distribution and Consumption in America*, ed. Steven Fink and Susan S. Williams (Columbus: Ohio State University Press, 1999), 24–35; Frances Smith Foster and Kim D. Green, "Ports of Call, Pulpits of Consultation: Rethinking the Origins of African American Literature," in Jarrett, ed., *A Companion to African American Literature*, 45–58.

27 Hamilton, "Our Paper," *The Weekly Anglo-African*, July 23, 1859.

28 Wilson, "Periodicals," 147.

29 See Daniel Hack, *Reaping Something New: African American Transformations of Victorian Literature* (Princeton, NJ: Princeton University Press, 2017). On reprinting more generally, see Meredith McGill, *American Literature and the Culture of Reprinting, 1834–1853* (Philadelphia: University of Pennsylvania Press, 2007).

30 See Clytus, "Visualizing Black Print"; Peterson, "Mapping Taste: Urban Modernities from the Tatler and Spectator to Frederick Douglass' Paper," *American Literary History* 32, no. 4 (2020): 691–722; Spires, *Practice*, 121–160; and John Stauffer, Introduction, in *The Works of James McCune Smith*, ed. John Stauffer (New York: Oxford University Press, 2006), xiii–xl.

31 Peterson, "Mapping Taste," 702.

32 For Lee, see Moody, *Sentimental*, 56; Katherine Clay Bassard, *Spiritual Interrogations: Culture, Gender, and Community in Early African American Women's Writing* (Princeton, NJ: Princeton University Press, 1999); and Lee, *Religious Experience and Journal of Mrs. Jarena Lee* (1836) in *Sisters of the Spirit: Three Black Women's Autobiographies of the Nineteenth Century*, ed. William L. Andrews (Bloomington: Indiana University Press, 1986), 6. For Harper, see McGill, "Frances Ellen Watkins Harper and the Circuits of Abolitionist Poetry," in *Early African American Print Culture*, ed. Lara Langer Cohen and Jordan Alexander Stein (University of Pennsylvania Press, 2012), 53–74.

33 On the jeremiad in American and African American literature, see Sacvan Bercovitch, *The American Jeremiad* (Madison: University of Wisconsin Press, 1978); and David Howard-Pitney, *The African American Jeremiad: Appeals for Justice in America*, revised and expanded ed. (Philadelphia: Temple University Press, 2005).

34 David Walker, *Walker's Appeal, in Four Articles; Together with a Preamble, to the Coloured Citizens of the World* (1830), ed. Paul Royster, Zea E-Books in American Studies, 17. http://digitalcommons.unl.edu/zeaamericanstudies/15.

35 McHenry *Forgotten*, 27. See also Gene Andrew Jarrett, "'To Refute Mr. Jefferson's Arguments Respecting Us': Thomas Jefferson, David Walker, and the Politics of Early African American Literature," *Early American Literature* 46, no. 2 (2011): 291–318; and Melvin Rodgers, "David Walker and the Political Power of the Appeal," *Political Theory* 43, no. 2 (2015): 208–233.

36 Marcy J. Dinius, "'Look!! Look!!! at This!!!!': The Radical Typography of David Walker's Appeal," *Publications of the Modern Language Association of America* 126, no. 1 (2011): 68.

37 Walker, *Walker's Appeal, in Four Articles*, 85.

38 On Walker and anger, see Bynum, "Why I Heart David Walker," *J19: The Journal of Nineteenth-Century Americanists* 4, no. 1 (2016): 13. See also Jacqueline Bacon, "'Do You Understand Your Own Language?' Revolutionary 'Topoi' in the Rhetoric of African-American Abolitionists," *Rhetoric Society Quarterly* 28, no. 2 (1998): 55–75; and Mia Bay, "'See Your Declaration Americans!!!': Abolitionism, Americanism, and the Revolutionary Tradition in Free Black Politics," in *Americanism: New Perspectives on the History of an Ideal*, ed. Michael Kazin and Joseph A. McCartin (Chapel Hill: University of North Carolina Press, 2006), 25–52.

39 On the sailors as a "deep-sea proletariat," see Peter Linebaugh and Marcus Rediker, *The Many-Headed Hydra: Sailors, Slaves, Commoners, and the Hidden History of the Revolutionary Atlantic* (Boston: Beacon Press, 2000), 214. For a detailed account of the *Appeal*'s circulation in newspapers, see Lori Leavell, "'Not intended exclusively for the slave states': Antebellum Recirculation of David Walker's Appeal," *Callaloo* 38, no. 3 (Summer 2015): 679–695.

40 See Peter Hinks, *To Awaken My Afflicted Brethren: David Walker and the Problem of Antebellum Slave Resistance* (University Park: Pennsylvania State University Press, 1997), 118–145.

41 See Clement Eaton, "A Dangerous Pamphlet in the Old South," *The Journal of Southern History* 2, no. 3 (1936): 323–334; and Michael A. Schoeppner, *Moral Contagion: Black Atlantic Sailors, Citizenship, and Diplomacy in Antebellum America.* (Cambridge: Cambridge University Press, 2019), 146.

42 For a general overview of Garnet's "Address to the Slaves" and his use of Walker's *Appeal*, see Leavell, "Recirculating Black Militancy in Word and Image: Henry Highland Garnet's 'Volume of Fire,'" *Book History* 20 (2017): 150–187; and Spires, "'Flights of Fancy': Black Print, Collaboration, and Performance in 'An Address to the Slaves of the United States of America (Rejected by the National Convention, 1843),'" in Casey et al., eds., *Colored Conventions in the Nineteenth Century and the Digital Age*, 125–153. On Du Bois's copy of the *Appeal*, see Emory Libraries, "W. E. B. Du Bois's Copy of Rare Anti-Slavery Book now Held by Rose Library," *Emory News Center*,

March 7, 2016. https://news.emory.edu/stories/2016/03/lib_walkers_appeal/campus.html.

43 See Howard Holman Bell, *Minutes of the Proceedings of the National Negro Conventions, 1830–1864* (New York: Arno Press and the *New York Times*, 1969); Bell, *A Survey of the Negro Convention Movement, 1830–1861* (New York: Arno Press and the New York Times, 1969); Philip S. Foner and George E. Walker, eds., *Proceedings of the Black State Conventions, 1840–1865, vol. 1: New York, Pennsylvania, Indiana, Michigan, Ohio* (Philadelphia: Temple University Press, 1979); and Jim Casey, P. Gabrielle Foreman, and Sarah Lynn Patterson, eds., *Colored Conventions in the Nineteenth Century and the Digital Age* (Chapel Hill: University of North Carolina Press, 2021).

44 See Spires, "Imagining a Nation of Fellow Citizens: Early African American Politics of Publicity," in Cohen and Stein, eds., *Early African American Print Culture*, 274–289.

45 Jim Casey, P. Gabrielle Foreman, and Sarah Lynn Patterson, "How to Use This Book and Its Digital Companions: Approaches to and Afterlives of the Colored Conventions," in Casey et al., eds., *Colored Conventions in the Nineteenth Century and the Digital Age.*

46 Jewon Woo, "Deleted Name but Indelible Body: Black Women at the Colored Conventions in Antebellum Ohio," in Casey et al., eds., *Colored Conventions in the Nineteenth Century and the Digital Age*, 179–192; State Convention of the Colored Citizens of Ohio (Columbus, 1851), "Minutes of the State Convention of the Colored Citizens of Ohio, Convened at Columbus, Jan. 15th, 16th, 17th and 18, 1851," *Colored Conventions Project Digital Records*, https://omeka.coloredconventions.org/items/show/249.

47 See, for instance, Nellie Y. McKay, "Guest Column: Naming the Problem That Led to the Question 'Who Shall Teach African American Literature?'; or, Are We Ready to Disband the Wheatley Court?," *PMLA* 113, no. 3 (1998): 359–369; Foreman, "A Riff"; and the subsequent forum in *Legacy* 31, no. 1 (2014).

48 Laura Helton, Justin Leroy, Max A. Mishler, Samantha Seeley, and Shauna Sweeney, "The Question of Recovery: An Introduction," *Social Text* 33, no. 4 (December 2015): 11.

49 Fielder and Senchyne, *Against a Sharp White Background*, 9.

50 Nicole N. Aljoe, Eric Gardner, and Molly O'Hagan Hardy, "The Just Teach One: Early African American Print Project," in *Teaching with Digital Humanities: Tools and Methods for Nineteenth-Century American Literature*, ed. Travis Jennifer and DeSpain Jessica (Urbana: University of Illinois Press, 2018), 117–132; Brigitte Fielder, "Recovery," *American Periodicals* 30, no. 1 (Spring 2020): 18–21; and Barbara McCaskill, "Beyond Recovery: A Process Approach to Research on Women in Early African American Print Cultures," *Legacy: A Journal of American Women Writers* 33, no. 1 (2016): 12–18.

51 I emphasize the "Black" in Black Digital Humanities because of Black DHers'
    centering the ethics of the work at their projects' inception and their attention
    to how digital methodologies risk reinforcing silences and the institutional
    structures that have historically disappeared minoritized people's work – past
    and present. See, for instance, "Black Code," the 2017 issue of *The Black
    Scholar* edited by Jessica Marie Johnson and Mark Anthony Neal,
    "Introduction: Wild Seed in the Machine," *The Black Scholar* 47, no. 3
    (2017): 1–2; Jim Casey, "Parsing the Special Characters of African
    American Print Culture: Mary Ann Shadd and the * Limits of Search," in
    Fielder and Senchyne, *Against a Sharp White Background*, 109–128; and Kim
    Gallon, "Making a Case for the Black Digital Humanities," in *Debates in the
    Digital Humanities 2016*, ed. Matthew K. Gold and Lauren F. Klein
    (Minneapolis: University of Minnesota Press, 2016), 42–49.

52 "Colored Convention Project Principles," Coloredconventions.org. https://
    coloredconventions.org/about/principles/ (accessed July 10, 2020).

53 See Fagan, "Chronicling White America," *American Periodicals: A Journal of
    History & Criticism* 26, no. 1 (2016): 10–13; and Ashley Farmer, "Archiving
    While Black," *The Chronicle of Higher Education*, July 22, 2019, www
    .chronicle.com/article/archiving-while-black/.

54 Kim Gallon, "What the Mainstream News Media Can Learn from the
    History of the Black Press," The Black Press Research Collective. http://
    blackpressresearchcollective.org/2020/05/21/what-the-mainstream-news-
    media-can-learn-from-the-history-of-the-black-press-in-the-age-of-a-pan
    demic/ (accessed May 21, 2020).

CHAPTER 14

Sexuality in Print

Jordan Alexander Stein

The decades between 1830 and 1850 in the Northeastern United States gave rise to what historians have called the antebellum print explosion.[1] In 1830, printing was a largely artisanal and preindustrial activity; by 1850 it had transformed in nearly every aspect, as steam-powered presses overtook hand presses, stereotype plates came into wide use, type foundries multiplied, and paper-making technologies modernized, while many of the different specializations associated with printing (including not only typesetting and papermaking, but also book binding, shipping, and sales) consolidated under incorporated printing houses.[2] Together, these changes generated a massive increase in the volume of domestic print production that simultaneously lowered costs and expanded circulation, making printed objects – books, pamphlets, newspapers, broadsheets, documents, ledgers, cards, and much besides – an increasingly ordinary feature of everyday life, especially in the also expanding urban centers of the United States. The multiple cultural and political implications for the antebellum Americans now living in what historians and literary scholars have come to shorthand as a "print culture" prove at once undeniably large and yet difficult to pinpoint. Evidence of change over time abounds, yet that change happened in ways that were gradual and uneven, often without discernible tipping points.

Print amplified the views of those who could access it, often producing more contestation than consensus, and one of the most significant areas of human experience to be developed, challenged, and debated in the antebellum print explosion was sexuality. In print, antebellum Americans debated what sexuality was, how it should be valued, and who had authority over its regulation. The theories of sexuality that emerged in this period challenge and at moments contradict one another, but we should also see that part of the coexistence of these different theories has to do with the fact that they circulated in printed texts aimed at different audiences. For example, vernacular theories registered in pamphlets and books aimed at young men, "bachelors," and other gender-specific, work-ing-class audiences, typically in urban areas, whereas evangelical organiza-tions often maintained separate printing presses and distribution mechanisms by which to circulate their materials. An emerging educated class of doctors, scientists, and other specialists exchanged books suited to their professional needs; and domestic novels, concentrating love, mar-riage, and family into concentric circles, marketed themselves to middle-class women.[3] As sexuality finds its way into print, in other words, it is represented and debated simultaneously by and for different people, with different meanings, and under different auspices. The work of the present essay is to survey some of these different examples of sexuality in antebel-lum print. A single essay cannot resolve the methodological challenges attendant upon the historical study of print, or of sexuality. But this essay aims to contribute to an understanding of how those challenges themselves stand to nuance our historical understanding of sexuality and its relation-ship to print in the antebellum period.

Definitions

Let's start with definitions. The "print" in "print culture" refers to at least three non-identical things.[4] First, print is a material activity, *printing*, and so when we speak of a print culture we can refer to the social, economic, political, and technological relationship among the producers and con-sumers of print: authors, publishers, typesetters, bookbinders, and readers, among others. This material and technological sense of "print culture" has been favored by book historians such as Jean-Henri Martin, Lucien Febvre, Robert Darnton, and Elizabeth Eisenstein.[5] Second, print is a means of communication, and so when we speak of a print culture we can also refer to the phenomena of mass production and impersonal circula-tion, by which printed texts move into the hands of readers, consumers, collectors, and other audiences often beyond their creators' imagining. This sense of print culture interprets material processes in terms of their more abstract implications, and it is the sense of the term favored by cultural historians such as Benedict Anderson, Ronald J. Zboray, and Trish Loughran.[6] Third, print refers to a noetic activity, usually affecting subjectivity, so when we speak of a print culture we can furthermore refer to print's capacity to encourage new ways of being or of imagining one's self, as in historical accounts where print has been tied to the rise of a public sphere, to middle-class individualism, or to celebrity culture. This sense of the term is the most abstract, pushing toward the psychological and epistemological implications of technology. It is generally the sense favored by scholars of the antebellum period, including those influenced by Jürgen Habermas, such as Glenn Hendler, Michael Warner, and Lauren Berlant.[7]

These three senses of print (the material, the communicative, and the noetic) obviously interact, and all three were certainly part of the antebellum print explosion. Yet the overlap among these three senses bespeaks the problem of scale with which this essay began. The material activities associated with printing are fairly concrete and indeed can be tracked empirically, for example, with methods commonly employed by bibliographers such as collation or description.[8] By contrast, the communicative aspect of print is far more challenging to reconstruct, as it leaves fewer traces in the historical record and so requires substantial evidence in support of generalizations about who actually received and read what.[9] Moreover, conclusions about the noetic aspect of print often demand even wilder speculations and, far from belonging to the purview of most historians, are consigned to the interdisciplinary work of "theory."

Consider, for example, the frontispiece from a printed antebellum pamphlet called *Prostitution Exposed* (1839) (Figure 14.1). This frontispiece is a woodcut engraving, not an especially technically sophisticated one, printed on cheap rag paper, in a pamphlet with a stitch binding. The image depicts a naked woman, presumably, given the pamphlet's title, a sex worker, though her bejeweled accessories and her modestly draping hair make her look as much like an allegorical figure – Botticelli's Venus, for instance – as a person. In describing these material aspects of this image, it is easy enough to say that the representational content of the image is sexual and, depending on your orientation to such things, possibly erotic – it is representing a naked woman in the context of a guide to New York's sex workers – and it is not difficult to imagine that the material form of the pamphlet (lightweight, inexpensive, with illustrations and other attention-grabbing visual interests) is designed for circulation and, in that sense, the communicative aspect of print. The printed image, in other words, in its material and communicative aspects, represents something sexual. But if we can say that the representational content of the printed image is sexual, does it represent *sexuality*? Is a representation of sex also a representation of sexuality?

The answer to these questions depends on what we mean by "sexuality." To be sure, "sexuality" is not a word that carried significant meaning in the nineteenth century. The *Oxford English Dictionary* dates the word to the final years of the eighteenth century, but only in its biological sense: "The

Figure 14.1   Woodcut by "A Butt Ender," frontispiece to *Prostitution Exposed; or, A Moral Reform Directory* (1839).
Courtesy of the American Antiquarian Society.

quality of being sexual or possessing sex. Opposed to asexuality." The more modern sense, having to do with sexual orientation or identity, dates to Havelock Ellis and John Addington Symonds's *Sexual Inversion* (1897), but here its use was technical and largely idiosyncratic, and their sense of the word did not filter into common usage until the middle of the twentieth century.[10] Indeed, as late as 1964, an earlier version of the

OED defined "sexuality" as, effectively, sex: "The biological properties associated with male and female, respectively." We might reasonably ask, with respect to what?

Though the movement through print circulation of Ellis and Symonds's definition of "sexuality" could provide us with a case study in itself, it was ultimately a different book that generated consensus (at least in academic conversations) about the meaning of the term. For Michel Foucault in the first volume of his *History of Sexuality* (1976; translated to English in 1978), "sexuality" names a form of discourse whose deployment of knowledge about an individual's interior or private life works in the service of juridical, medical, and governmental power.[11] Sexuality, in short, names a truth of the self, and the work of Foucault's book was to challenge this means of telling the truth by pointing to the ways that sexuality discursively concentrates the authority for sexual knowledge into narrow and self-reinforcing circuits of power. (If you don't believe me, consider how differently you might answer the identical question, "Are you sexually active?" depending on whether it was posed to you by your doctor or by a stranger on the bus.) Foucault was far less interested in a positive account of sexuality than in a critique of its deployment; possibly for this reason, his book spares little attention for actual sex acts and instead focuses on the moments when such acts become the subject of abstract discourses – as he puts it in his analysis of one of the volume's only examples, sex becomes discourse by becoming "a judicial action, a medical intervention, a careful clinical examination, and an entire theoretical elaboration."[12]

Yet because sexuality in Foucault's sense is at once extracted from the private and interior reaches of an individual person, and also circulated through the inexorably public pathways of juridical, medical, and political power, it can be surprisingly difficult to pinpoint. As a concept, sexuality, we might say, has a problem of scale cognate to that of print. Just as print can name, narrowly, a specific material activity and, far more broadly, a noetic aspect of modern subjectivity, so sexuality at once is a smallest unit of what makes a person themselves at the same time as it saturates nearly every modern social institution at its most abstract level.[13]

To return, then, to the frontispiece image from *Prostitution Exposed*, its ability to represent sexuality depends not (or not specifically) on the undeniably sexual content of the image – the naked woman represented – as it depends on the context and authority that surrounds the image in the pamphlet as a whole. It follows that the same point would be true even in cases of sexual representation that more explicitly depict or represent sexual activities (what we now designate as "pornographic"). So, in other words, the claim here is that it is the content of the representation and/or the techniques of representation that allow us to see *sex* in print, but it is the perceptual, epistemological, and knowledge-making aspects of print that allow us to see *sexuality* in this media form. If we want to understand something about the relationship between sexuality and print, it is the noetic sense of the term – print's bearing on subjectivity – that serves us best.

Genres

With these definitions of "print" and "sexuality" in place, let's turn now to a partial taxonomy of some antebellum US print genres, to think about how they might be useful to the study of sexuality and sexual cultures in the time before understanding such as those of Ellis and Symonds obtained – before the modernizing imperatives of the late nineteenth century left Americans, as Peter Coviello has written, "too bleakly stranded" in the modern binary of homosexual and heterosexual identities.[14] These genres span a number of antebellum audiences, and they include moral reform directories, Flash Press weeklies, "fancy books," city mysteries, sentimental novels, slave narratives, medical literature, phrenological writing, and poetry.

Moral Reform Directories

One of the earliest antebellum print genres with overtly sexual content was, ironically, the moral exposé. Sometimes these works were produced by zealous missionaries identifying brothels, houses of assignation, or other locations of urban vice. They alerted their readers of places to avoid, while also seeking to expose amoral and possibly criminal activity to the light of day. Yet the problem with moral reform directories is that they engage in what is effectively an indexical form of representation – they point to their subject, and in the same way that smoke is an index of fire, a guide to avoiding the locations of vice is also a way to find them. Quickly, and unsurprisingly, they generated parodies, like *Prostitution Exposed*, which, in the guise of hand-wringing moralism, provided the reader with a tongue-in-cheek guide *to* brothels and similar kinds of businesses. The imagined reader of the book, moreover, is conjured by the pseudonym of the author of *Prostitution Exposed*, "A Butt Ender." In addition to signaling an obviously bawdy pun, this pseudonym also refers to a faction of egalitarian, prolabor Democrats (Butt Enders, more commonly known as Locofocos).

The name, in other words, suggests masculine and heterosexual prerogatives that, by twenty-first-century standards at least, rather significantly
qualify the democratic commitment to equality that such a book might
have represented to its initial audience.[15]

Flash Press Weeklies

Also emergent in the 1840s, and with similar audiences in mind, was the
"flash" press, a series of inexpensive broadsheets and papers, including the
Flash, the *Whip*, the *Rake*, and the *Libertine*, printed and predominantly
circulated in New York City, usually on a weekly basis.[16] These papers too
were marketed toward young white men, often of a democratic persuasion,
with sexual interests in women; yet most historians agree that the aim of
the flash press fell more on the side of entertainment than politics. The
papers are numerous and their contents various, but it is clear that
challenges to propriety and respectability were understood to be the kinds
of things that sold papers to their imagined audiences.

In the flash pages, sex was discussed frequently and openly, in hetero-
and homoerotic registers, as were a range of attendant sexual practices like
prostitution, adultery, infidelity, and "amalgamation," or interracial sex
acts. The flash press also made recourse to fairly explicit discussions of
homoerotic sexual possibility, though often expressed in a homophobic
attitude. One such account from the *Flash* in 1842, for example, decries
"the hoary headed old villain" described as a sodomite, a "rascal" who
"attempted to fool with me as if I were of the sex feminine," and yet also
"intimated to him the propriety of his visiting the Five Points [i.e., lower
Manhattan's vice district], where possibly he would not be repulsed."[17] As
with prostitution in the moral reform directories, the effort to avoid
homoerotic encounters in the flash press also indexes locations where they
can occur.

Fancy Books

Finally, a third, explicitly pornographic genre of the antebellum period
were what were advertised in the period as "fancy books."[18] These tended
to be reprints of existing, often well-known, erotic titles, such as John
Cleland's *Fanny Hill* (1748), though printed and bound in relatively lavish
ways, such as with illustrations, cloth binding, generous margins, or larger
page size. The "fancy" of fancy books, then, refers almost exclusively to the
material conditions of their printing and to the price point (advertisements

put these books at $2, a significant economic bracket ahead of newspapers that sold for pennies). Fancy books were the same kinds of pornography that circulated to men in cheaper forms, now repackaged for middle-class readers in possession of disposable income for luxury items. While the contents and male audiences of fancy books were congruent with those of the flash press, the economic bar to access and, presumably, the class sensibilities of their audience were importantly distinct.

City Mysteries

Another print genre that relies on the depiction of sexual activity and nudity was the genre of city mysteries. Tracing its origin to European fictions like Eugène Sue's *Mysteries of Paris* (1843) and George W. M. Reynolds's *Mysteries of London* (1844), the genre was aggressively transplanted to the United States almost immediately, with works like Ned Buntline's *Mysteries of New York* (1844), but also more geographically unlikely instances such as the anonymous *The Mysteries of Nashua* (1844), Osgood Bradbury's *The Mysteries of Lowell* (1844), and Frank Hazelton's *The Mysteries of Troy* (1847).[19] As a genre, such works traffic in the revelation of dark rites, secret religious sects and brotherhoods, hidden passageways, trap doors, and heaving, undraped bosoms. What these various objects and props have in common, ultimately, is that they are all hidden things whose narrative interest is that they can be revealed, and the city mystery genre plays extensively with the relationships between secrecy and disclosure, between what stays secret and what gets known. Though significantly different in narrative shape than the moral exposé genre, city mysteries work in similar epistemological terrain. As Donna Dennis has observed, city mysteries were often sold in larger print markets like New York City alongside more explicitly pornographic works – and were protested by moral authorities alongside them as well.[20]

Like moral reform directories, flash press weeklies, and fancy books, city mysteries would have likely reached different audiences along class and social lines. All these kinds of printed materials largely imagined their audiences to be men whose primary sexual interests were in women. Antebellum erotic publications were thus an early instantiation of a more or less explicitly gendered market for print, though not at a mass or other culturally momentous scale. Instead, it was print for women that, in Lauren Berlant's words, contributed to the "first mass-marketed intimate public in the United States of significant scale."[21] While print numbered among other media that made up the substance of nineteenth-century women's commodity culture, one of its key genres, the sentimental novel, was undeniably central to the story of antebellum print.

Sentimental Novels

Sentimental novels written in English had existed in some form since the mid-eighteenth century and were among the relatively few fictional prose narratives printed in the United States between the Federalist period of the 1790s and the advent of mechanized printing in the 1830s.[22] Several, like William Hill Brown's *The Power of Sympathy* (1789) or Susanna Rowson's *Charlotte: A Tale of Truth* (1791; printed in the United States in 1794 as *Charlotte Temple*), organize plots around incest, rape, or illicit pregnancy, providing readers with cautionary tales that are both salacious and sad. As the nineteenth century moved on, sentimental novels gradually developed in a domestic direction, and popular examples from the 1850s, such as Susan Warner's *The Wide, Wide World* (1850) or Maria Cummin's *The Lamplighter* (1854), concern themselves with the education of young women as they graduate from the complexities of childhood to the emergent conventions of heterosexuality. Though sentimental novels were read by men as well as women, they offered an influential vision of heterosexual gender among the emerging middle-class readers of the period.[23] The readership of sentimental novels may not have restricted itself by race, but the novels themselves tend overwhelmingly to focus on white people's lives and conventions. And so, at a more subtle and insidious level, sentimental novels can be seen to shore up whiteness as a terrain for sexuality.[24]

These concerns about race, gender, and sexuality come together with concerns about print in the case of the best-selling antebellum sentimental novel, *Uncle Tom's Cabin*. Harriet Beecher Stowe's antislavery melodrama, following its year-long serial publication by installment, sold 300,000 copies in 1852, shattering the record of the previously biggest selling US novel (George Lippard's *The Quaker City* [1845]) by five times.[25] Part of the measure of Stowe's text is that it not only proliferated in print (with responses, sequels, illustrated editions, and other extensions of its cultural footprint) but also left print behind, migrating to other media forms including theatricals, games, dolls, and eventually, film.[26] The many responses and adaptations to *Uncle Tom's Cabin* suggest that the text generated cultural types, whose adaptations were also, significantly, adoptions or imitations. Though it participated in the material and circulatory senses of print, *Uncle Tom's Cabin* also participated in the noetic form of print – that is, instantiating forms of subjectivity to be imitated and adapted, but also to be refused and derided, for example, when we might disapprove of someone's complacency by calling them an Uncle Tom.

What may seem less than obvious is whether this noetic sense that emerges from the characters in *Uncle Tom's Cabin* is precisely sexual, as it is certainly not the case that *Uncle Tom's Cabin* represents sex in the same way that the moral exposé or the flash press do. Yet no less an authority on human sexuality than Sigmund Freud wrote of *Uncle Tom's Cabin* in his 1919 essay "A Child Is Being Beaten."[27] There Freud shared the experiences of children he encountered in a clinical setting who were incited to erotic sadistic and masochistic fantasies as a result of reading *Uncle Tom's Cabin*.[28] If we were to class this sentimental novel as sexual, then, we would be regarding it not in terms of representations of sex acts, which are noticeably absent, but in terms of the text's engagement with bodies, power, and the complexities of pleasure (including the aspects of pleasure that are voyeuristic, phantasmatic, sadistic). We have come comparatively far from the world of moral reform directories and their basically indexical accounts of sex to a world where reading is and is not, but always could be, a sexual activity in its own right.

Slave Narratives

But even in such a noetic account of sexuality in print, the indexical is never far off. As Stowe insisted in her *Key to Uncle Tom's Cabin* (1853), her earlier novel's scenes of whipping were drawn from life, and certainly resonantly violent accounts appear in narratives written by formerly enslaved people.[29] Frederick Douglass's *Narrative* (1845), for example, includes a gruesome scene where his Aunt Hester is sadistically whipped by a sexually jealous Master Anthony while Douglass, a child, watches in horror and identification.[30] Antebellum slave narratives offer some of the only existing self-authored evidence of the range and complexity of sexual experiences – including, as Douglass shows, voyeurism – of enslaved people. Sometimes that documentation extends also to analysis, as in the case of Harriet Jacobs's remarkable *Incidents in the Life of a Slave Girl* (1861). Jacobs writes of her own sexual harassment and attempted assault by a white master, but she also skillfully connects her personal experience to a larger structural pattern:

> No pen can give an adequate description of the all-pervading corruption
> produced by slavery. The slave girl is reared in an atmosphere of

licentiousness and fear. The lash and the foul talk of her master and his sons are her teachers. When she is fourteen or fifteen, her owner, or his sons, or the overseer, or perhaps all of them, begin to bribe her with presents. If these fail to accomplish their purpose, she is whipped or starved into submission to their will. She may have had religious principles inculcated by some pious mother or grandmother, or some good mistress; she may have a lover, whose good opinion and peace of mind are dear to her heart; or the profligate men who have power over her may be exceedingly odious to her. But resistance is hopeless.[31]

Antebellum slave narratives, including the few written by formerly enslaved women like Jacobs, are important documents of the sexual economy of slavery in the United States, and these arguably depict and describe sexual culture on plantations in a way roughly analogous to the moral reform directories depicting and describing vice culture in the city, leading a number of contemporary scholars to detect in slave narratives elements of pornography.[32]

Medical Literature

Another nonfictional genre that at times strayed into elements of the pornographic was antebellum medical literature. Medical authority in the United States was just beginning to consolidate under credentialing bodies like medical schools and professional associations (the American Medical Association, for example, was founded in 1847), and so the period's medical literature betrays a perhaps surprising range of authors and audiences. Helen Lefkowitz Horowitz observes four theories of sexuality in circulation during these decades. One was a vernacular sexual culture, based in humoral theory, which emphasized bawdy humor and male sexual pleasures. A second stemmed from evangelical Christianity, which preached a distrust of the flesh and a regulation of bodily and sexual appetites. A third, emergent theory based itself in research on human sensation and especially on the new science of nerves. Finally, a more distinctly modern framework placed sexual life at the center of human experience, consciousness, and society.[33]

Useful as this four-part taxonomy is, some texts traversed these categories. Sylvester Graham's *Lectures to Young Men on Chastity* (1834), for example, arguably cut across all four. Though Graham was not precisely an evangelical and did not write explicitly bawdy books, nonetheless his writings are animated by a vernacular conception of human body, which could be optimized through regulation by diet and the avoidance of masturbation, in pursuit of optimizing sensational experience and sexual gratification in marriage.[34] Speaking across audiences encouraged Graham's many pamphlets to sell briskly, as did the associated lifestyle products he sold, including flour for his famous graham cracker.[35] Other medical writers achieved success with more niche audiences. For example, Augustus Kinsley Gardner, a New York physician, wrote a number of pamphlets on reproduction, sterility, and birth control, aimed at more specialist audiences. His chief contribution to the period's medical literature is the notion of a "spermatic economy," according to which semen is imagined to be finite, and so its nonreproductive expenditure through activities like masturbation would diminish a man's chances to produce an heir – a theory now totally discredited.[36] Yet both specialist writings like Gardner's and more popular medical treatises like Graham's interacted with and influenced printed works beyond the medical sphere. Herman Melville was arguably responding to both in the famous sperm-squeezing chapter late in *Moby-Dick* (1851).[37]

Phrenological Writing

Another antebellum print genre that plays extensively on mystery and knowledge is phrenological writing. Now recognized as a pseudoscience, phrenology primarily focused on measurements of the human skull, based on the theory that the brain is the organ of the mind and that certain brain areas have localized, specific functions or modules. Phrenological literature included both theoretical treatises and how-to guides, and all of these encouraged readers to imagine, much as city mysteries did, that visible surfaces contain mysterious depths that only an informed reader can plumb. Phrenology, as Christopher Castiglia has suggested, offered a version of sexuality in very much the sense that Foucault critiques – a truth of the self, legible to an authorized interpreter credentialed by a medical regime.[38] Put more in alignment with the present terms, phrenological works, as printed books, are noetic in the sense that they bring into being a set of unknowns in order then to begin to think about how we can know ourselves through them.

That is not to say, however, that phrenology and sexuality in the sexier sense of term were always so far apart. One of the most enduring and prolific phrenological publishers of the antebellum period was a firm called Fowler and Wells, operating out of a nineteenth-century printing backwater on Long Island called Brooklyn.[39] Their catalog extended beyond strictly phrenological publishing to include scientific literature, and in

1855 an aspiring poet convinced them to print his otherwise self-published volume of poetry under the title *Leaves of Grass*. The homoerotic aspects of Walt Whitman's poems are well known. Yet the adjacency of these poems, in their initial printing, to phrenology's concerns with bodily secrets, perhaps makes sense of one of the kinkiest moments in *Leaves of Grass*: the scene in what later became section XXIV:

I believe in the flesh and the appetites,
Seeing hearing and feeling are miracles, and each part and tag of me is a miracle.

Divine am I inside and out, and I make holy whatever I touch or am touched
    from;
The scent of these arm-pits is aroma finer than prayer,
This head is more than churches or bibles or creeds.[40]

The play of inside and out, the idea that the smells the body exudes reveal the divinity within – this verse engages one of the major tropes we have seen running though these different antebellum print genres. It is also for the period a highly idiosyncratic representation of the elevations of bodily and sensual pleasure.

Historiography

This chapter has argued that there are three senses of print operative when we talk about "print culture" (the material, the communicative, and the noetic). Thinking about these multiple senses of print against a taxonomy of print genres has allowed us to see sexuality as something that emerges in antebellum print in moments other than those that represent sex acts as such. Glancing across a range of antebellum print genres (the moral expose directory, the flash press, fancy books, city mysteries, sentimental novels, slave narratives, medical literature, and phrenological writings), this essay has pointed to some possibilities for thinking about how extensively sexuality is located in the archives of antebellum print, if you know where to look. The reason to emphasize these possibilities for a broadened interpretation of sexuality in antebellum print is to challenge some of the predominant understandings, which can be curiously narrow.

One of the most enduring such understandings is offered by David S. Reynolds in his landmark 1988 study, *Beneath the American Renaissance*.[41] There, Reynolds argues that sexual expression in the ante-bellum period is characterized by an indirectness, or as he puts it, in the 1840s "public expressions of erotic impulses always had a perverse, bizarre aspect" characterized by techniques like euphemism and voyeurism, "which permitted indirect glimpses rather than the warm exposure of human physicality."[42] This characterization of "indirectness" depends entirely on what one imagines "direct" sexual expression to be, and implicit through Reynolds's study, it would seem that the representational norms of post-1970s sexual liberation offer him a benchmark.[43] While this is not a terrible standard by any means, it also makes little sense of, for example, the armpit-sniffing scene in *Leaves of Grass*. In a poem variously celebrated and derogated for its undisguised homoeroticism, this deeply kinky moment, which corresponds perhaps to a sexual practice but not exactly an identity, gets readily lost in an analysis that privileges directness, meaning sexual explicitness, over whatever Whitman is doing. The analytical direction in which this essay is instead pointing aims to hold open the space to try and understand that *whatever* a little better.

Moreover, what also gets lost in Reynolds's analysis but comes back with considerations of the relationship between sexuality and print in texts like *Leaves of Grass, Uncle Tom's Cabin*, or *Narrative of the Life of Frederick Douglass* is the possibility that sexuality in the antebellum period is often nongenital; indeed, that representations of sexuality in the noetic sense are, we might say, intuitively nongenital. This point may be true of what antebellum texts represent, and at the same time it may be true of what it was like for antebellum Americans to read them in real time. Though this last point is considerably more difficult to prove, Michael Millner's suggestive study of "reading badly" has argued that reading "obscene" materials in the antebellum period represents not a retreat from rational-critical thinking but a more complex form of engaging them, in terms of bodily sensation, affect, and pleasure, in addition to ideation.[44] By this line of argument, what Whitman was using armpit sniffing to represent, as well as what his readers might have found it to mean, are open questions in the study of sexuality and print in the antebellum period. The answers to these questions do not necessarily fit into received understandings of what sex or sexuality is, how it works, or where it is most likely to be found on the body or the page.

The act of holding open such questions gets lost not only in analyses like Reynolds's, which take the often unequivocally genital terms of post-1970s sexual liberation as their benchmark, but also in the long nineteenth-century history of vice raids and obscenity trials, whose legal definitions and criminal prosecutions of what comes to be called "obscene" or "sexually explicit materials" likewise hold to an oddly, narrowly genital standard.[45] Such a standard, however, is precisely what the foregoing essay has argued against, because that standard implies that representations and circulations of sex are the same as sexuality. It leads our thinking to a place where sexual possibility is defined by its regulation, whereas in the antebellum period we have seen that sexuality can be tracked instead by its robust circulations. A deeper examination of the relationship of sexuality and print might allow us to undo the accumulated historical work of regulation a little and to restore to the history of sexuality not only some of its material underpinnings but also some of its, to our eyes, weirder and more creative expressions.

Notes

1 John William Tebbel, *A History of Book Publishing in the United States*, vol. 1 (New York: R. R. Bowker, 1972); William Charvat, *The Profession of Authorship in America, 1800–1870* (New York: Columbia University Press, 1992); Lara Langer Cohen, *The Fabrication of American Literature: Fraudulence and Antebellum Print Culture* (Philadelphia: University of Pennsylvania Press, 2012).

2 For a useful overview, see Michael Winship, "Manufacturing and Book Production," in *A History of the Book in America, vol. 3: The Industrial Book, 1840–1880*, ed. Scott E. Casper, Jeffrey D. Groves, Stephen W. Nissenbaum, and Michael Winship (Chapel Hill: University of North Carolina Press, 2007), 40–69.

3 On audiences, see David Paul Nord, *Faith in Reading: Religious Publishing and the Birth of Mass Media in America* (New York: Oxford University Press, 2004); Ronald J. Zboray, *A Fictive People: Antebellum Economic Development and the American Reading Public* (New York: Oxford University Press, 1993); Lauren Berlant, *The Female Complaint: The Unfinished Business of Sentimentality in American Culture* (Durham, NC: Duke University Press, 2008). Cathy N. Davidson makes an influential argument about gendered access to reading in the pre-antebellum period in *The Revolution and the Word: The Rise of the Novel in America* (New York: Oxford University Press, 1986), while I have traced the emerging distinctions between religious and secular publishing in the last quarter of the eighteenth century in Jordan Alexander Stein, *When Novels Were Books* (Cambridge, MA: Harvard University Press, 2020).

4 I am adapting here from Harold Love's indispensable essay "Early Modern Print Culture: Assessing the Models," *Parergon* 20.1 (2003): 45–65.

5 Lucien Febvre and Henri-Jean Martin, *The Coming of the Book: The Impact of Printing, 1450–1800* [1958], trans. David Gerard (London: Verso, 2010); Elizabeth L. Eisenstein, *The Printing Press as an Agent of Change: Communications and Cultural Transformations in Early Modern Europe*, 2 vols. (Cambridge: Cambridge University Press, 1979); Robert Darnton, "What Is the History of Books?," *Daedalus* (Summer 1982): 65–83.

6 Benedict Anderson, *Imagined Communities: Reflections on the Origin and Spread of Nationalism*, rev. ed. (New York: Verso, 1991); Zboray, *A Fictive People*; Trish Loughran *The Republic in Print: Print Culture in the Age of U.S. Nation Building, 1770–1870* (New York: Columbia University Press, 2007).

7 Glenn Hendler, *Public Sentiments: Structures of Feeling in Nineteenth-Century American Literature* (Chapel Hill: University of North Carolina Press, 2001); Michael Warner, "Publics and Counterpublics," *Public Culture* 14.1 (2002): 49–90; Berlant, *The Female Complaint*. See also Jürgen Habermas, *The Structural Transformation of the Public Sphere: An Inquiry into a Category of Bourgeois Society* [1962], trans. Thomas Burger, with the assistance of Frederick Lawrence (Cambridge, MA: MIT Press, 1989).

8 As described, for example, in Fredson Bowers, *Principles of Bibliographic Description* (Princeton, NJ: Princeton University Press, 1949).

9 For example, see Joan W. Scott, "The Evidence of Experience," *Critical Inquiry* 17.4 (Summer 1991): 773–797.

10 Havelock Ellis and John Addington Symonds, *Sexual Inversion* (London: Wilson and Macmillan, 1897).

11 Michel Foucault, *The History of Sexuality, vol. 1: An Introduction*, trans. Robert Hurley (New York: Vintage, 1990).

12 Ibid., 31.

13 See, for example, Elizabeth A. Povinelli, "Notes on Gridlock: Genealogy, Intimacy, Sexuality," *Public Culture* 14.1 (2002): 215–238.

14 Peter Coviello, *Tomorrow's Parties: Sex and the Untimely in Nineteenth-Century America* (New York: NYU Press, 2013), 1–5.

15 On "Butt Enders," see Donna Dennis, *Licentious Gotham: Erotic Publishing and Its Prosecution in Nineteenth-Century New York* (Cambridge, MA: Harvard University Press, 2009), 22; Patricia Cline Cohen *The Murder of Helen Jewett* (New York: Vintage, 1999), 424, n. 28.

16 See *The Flash Press: Sporting Male Weeklies in 1840s New York*, ed. Patricia Cline Cohen, Timothy J. Gilfoyle, and Helen Lefkowitz Horowitz (Chicago: University of Chicago Press, 2008).

17 Ibid., 195.

18 For the best discussion of fancy books, see Dennis, *Licentious Gotham*, 93–126.

19 See Paul Erickson, "Welcome to Sodom: The Cultural Work of City-Mysteries Fiction in Antebellum America" (PhD diss., University of Texas at Austin, 2005); Lara Langer Cohen, "The Depths of Astonishment: City Mysteries and the Antebellum Underground," *American Literary History* 29.1 (2017), 1–25.

20 Dennis, *Licentious Gotham*, 93.

21 Berlant, *The Female Complaint*, 5.

22 See Charles Evans, *American Bibliography: A Chronological Dictionary of All Books, Pamphlets, and Periodical Publications Printed in the United States of America from the Genesis of Printing in 1639 Down to and Including the Year 1820*, 10 vols. (Chicago: For the author by the Blakely Press, 1903–1914).

23 See Mary Chapman and Glenn Hendler, eds., *Sentimental Men: Masculinity and the Politics of Affect in American Culture* (Berkeley: University of California Press, 1999).

24 For elaborations of the ideological and biopolitical work of reading these novels, see Dana Luciano, *Arranging Grief: Sacred Time and the Body in Nineteenth-Century America* (New York: NYU Press, 2007); Kyla Schuller, *The Biopolitics of Feeling: Race, Sex, and Science in the Nineteenth Century* (Durham, NC: Duke University Press, 2018); Elizabeth Freeman, *Beside You in Time: Sense Methods and Queer Sociabilities in the American Nineteenth Century* (Durham, NC: Duke University Press, 2019).

25 The publication history of *Uncle Tom's Cabin* is a well-studied subject. Among the best analyses, see Michael Winship, "'The Greatest Book of Its Kind': A Publishing History of 'Uncle Tom's Cabin,'" *Proceedings of the American Antiquarian Society* 109.2 (1999): 309–332; Claire Parfit, *The Publishing History of Uncle Tom's Cabin, 1852–2002* (Burlington, VT: Ashgate, 2007); Barbara Hochman, *"Uncle Tom's Cabin" and the Reading Revolution: Race, Literacy, Childhood and Fiction, 1851–1911* (Amherst: University of Massachusetts Press, 2011). On the pitfalls of the term "best seller" for pre-twentieth century books, see Loughran, *The Republic in Print*, 40–42, 57–58.

26 See Thomas F. Gossett, *Uncle Tom's Cabin and American Culture* (Dallas, TX: Southern Methodist University Press, 1985); Lauren Berlant, "Poor Eliza," *American Literature* 70.3 (September 1998): 635–668.

27 "A Child Is Being Beaten" is reprinted most accessibly in Sigmund Freud, *Sexuality and the Psychology of Love*, with an introduction by Philip Rieff (1963; reprint New York: Touchstone Books, 1997), 97–122. See also Marianne Noble, *The Masochistic Pleasures of Sentimental Literature* (Princeton, NJ: Princeton University Press, 2000).

28 Freud, *Sexuality and the Psychology of Love*, 98.

29 Harriet Beecher Stowe, *A Key to Uncle Tom's Cabin* (Cleveland, OH: John P. Jewett, 1853).

30 Frederick Douglass, *Narrative of the Life of Frederick Douglass* [1845], introduction by David W. Blight (Boston: Bedford, 1993), 42–43.

31 Harriet Jacobs, *Incidents in the Life of a Slave Girl* [1861], ed. Jean Fagan Yellin (Cambridge, MA: Harvard University Press, 2009), 65.

32 Saidiya V. Hartman, *Scenes of Subjection: Terror, Slavery, and Self-Making in Nineteenth-Century America* (New York: Oxford University Press, 1997); Dwight A. McBride, *Impossible Witness: Truth, Abolitionism, and Slave Testimony* (New York: NYU Press, 2001); Vincent Woodard, *The Delectable Negro: Human Consumption and Homoeroticism within US Slave Culture*, ed. Justin A Joyce and Dwight McBride (New York: NYU Press, 2014).

33 Helen Lefkowitz Horowitz, *Rereading Sex: Battles over Sexual Knowledge and Suppression in Nineteenth-Century America* (New York: Vintage, 2002), 3–15.

34 Kyla Wazana Tompkins, *Racial Indigestion: Eating Bodies in the Nineteenth Century* (New York: NYU Press, 2012), 53–88.

35 On Graham's circulation of pamphlets, see Stephen Nissenbaum, *Sex, Diet, and Debility in Jacksonian America: Sylvester Graham and Health Reform* (Westport, CT: Greenwood, 1980).
36 G. J. Barker-Benfield, *The Horrors of the Half-Known Life: Male Attitudes toward Women and Sexuality in Nineteenth-Century America* [1976], 2nd ed. (New York: Routledge, 2000).
37 Herman Melville, *Moby-Dick; or, The Whale* [1851], ed. Andrew Delbanco (New York: Penguin, 1992).
38 Christopher Castiglia, *Interior States: Institutional Consciousness and the Inner Life of Democracy in the Antebellum United States* (Durham, NC: Duke University Press, 2008), 172–173.
39 Hugh Ryan, *When Brooklyn Was Queer: A History* (New York: St. Martin's Press, 2019).
40 Walt Whitman, *Leaves of Grass*, ed. Scully Bradley and Harold W. Blodgett (New York: Norton, 1973), 53.
41 David S. Reynolds, *Beneath the American Renaissance: The Subversive Imagination in the Age of Emerson and Melville* (New York: Oxford University Press, 1988).
42 Ibid., 222.
43 For a particularly clear-eyed historicization of these norms, see Damon R. Young, *Making Sex Public and Other Cinematic Fantasies* (Durham, NC: Duke University Press, 2018).
44 Michael Millner, *Fever Reading: Affect and Reading Badly in the Early American Public Sphere* (Durham: University of New Hampshire Press, 2012).
45 See again Dennis, *Licentious Gotham*.

CHAPTER 15

Seriality

Dale M. Bauer

Starting before the 1820s and flourishing beyond 1860 and well into the twentieth century, serial fiction became a familiar, even customary way of reading novels. Famous publishers of the time – particularly Robert Bonner and T. B. Peterson – invested in the best-selling capacity of producing fiction in this way. And writers such as Fanny Fern, E. D. E. N. Southworth, Ann Stephens, Harriett Beecher Stowe, George Lippard, Sylvanus Cobb Jr. (who wrote approximately 130 serials for the *New York Ledger*), Bertha M. Clay, and T. S. Arthur made huge fortunes from writing regularly for such magazines as *National Era, Peterson's, Godey's Ladies Book, Ladies Companion*, and, by the mid-1850s, Bonner's *Ledger*.

Serial novels appeared in installments – approximately over a year's time – and attracted audiences through incredible or sensational yet also sympathetic stories. According to Frank Kelleter, these serials depended on both repetition and variety to intrigue readers.[1] Along with monthly serials, publishers also brought forward story papers and "pamphlet novels," as they were called, creating a vogue for the 1860s dime novel.[2] Such literary weeklies depended on high circulation to survive, and they flourished through the appeal of their serial fiction. Serial fiction of all kinds invoked the power of mass publication in newspapers and magazines. They generally did so to propose new narratives about changing US citizenship, which means highlighting particular American anxieties and potential traumas. These serials then offered temporary resolutions for these dilemmas.

Whether called pamphlet or "magazine novels," as Patricia Okker names them, or as a "brand" of fiction, as Rachel Ihara suggests that Southworth wrote, one of the key claims about seriality is that these novels are not like individual printed books.[3] The question of what was a "novel" was indeed up for grabs.[4] Serial authors' novels are marked by the rhetorical mode of repetition, and what recurs most are the issues central to the development of US identity and culture. Along with the standard cast of heroes, heroines, and villains, the novels also defined and described new modern personality types for men and women. This recurrence to similar plots and character types serves a particular function: to highlight certain American traumas, resulting from family pride, family dysfunction, violence, and what was known as "moral insanity." These writers came back to similar issues, not because of the drive for originality – as Lara Langer Cohen argues about Fanny Fern – but because of the desire to forgo innovation in order to attract repeat customers.[5] Habituated readers meant greater remuneration and prestige. Increasingly, editors like Bonner fought other publishers for control of careers like Fern's (the first author that he recruited for the *Ledger*) and Southworth's, even as he invested money in up-and-coming writers like Laura Jean Libbey.

This essay charts the flourishing of serial fiction – with its famous "mechanic accents," as Michael Denning outlines – and the deliberate staking-out of national reputations.[6] Cheap magazines appeared in the 1830s, with story papers appearing in the 1840s and 1850s. Emerging in the 1830s and 1840s, and selling for a penny and as much as six cents, newspapers began to introduce serial fictions. Later, readers paid from 12 to 25 cents for their reading; the price dropped to a dime when Beadle first published dime novels (and then a "nickel" series).

There are two different, if complementary, readerly sources of appeal for these serials: the first is the collective reading process; the other is author-based. There were also several kinds of serials, including "city mysteries," "sensational" accounts, romance and family novels, "domestic" fiction, travel fictions (in Europe, the American West, Cuba, or elsewhere in the Caribbean), crime stories, adoption fiction, and reform fiction (antislavery and temperance fiction), among many subgenres. The national appetite for so much narrative variety often derived from a sense of readers' relation to the author, as well as from the authors' desires to keep in close contact with readers. Such interactions often led to increasing magazine popularity, along with greater salaries for the serial authors themselves.

Publishers and Readers

By the early nineteenth century, novels were beginning to be marketed in magazines rather than as stand-alone books, and then, as widely circulated journals and periodicals.[7] Okker cites Jeremy Belknap's *The Foresters* as the first American novel about the US colonies to be serialized. It appeared in 1787 as a promise of a serialized novel in Philadelphia's *Columbian Magazine*, yet it was never fully published as a complete serial.[8]

Charles Brockden Brown, with *Stephen Calvert* (June 1799–June 1800) and Susanna Rowson, with *Sincerity* (1803–1804), also published serials. Yet such efforts were often limited by the circulation of magazines, which did not proliferate until the 1830s when Charles Dickens's serialized novels in England profoundly influenced such publications in the United States. At the same time, paper production was cheaper because of cylinder machine–produced paper and due to the move from rag paper and wood pulp paper to cotton pulp paper, resulting in amazingly low printing costs.

Although women writers were some of the most popular of serial authors, their popularity had also kept them from serious literary consideration. Women writers sustained their careers as paid writers. Mary Kelley has assessed how much various women authors earned in the nineteenth century, for example, in the increasing rates of pay for Southworth's fiction in Bonner's gifts of money and her investment in bonds.[9] Melissa Homestead and Pamela Washington claim that Libbey was "an astute self-promoter," making the industrious and lucrative Southworth look "pale in comparison."[10] Fanny Fern, Stephens, and Southworth all benefited from the great publicity such that their names were worth gold to their publishers. Women were assumed to be the main segment of the magazine audience, with over a hundred magazines designed for women published during 1820 to 1860.[11] Chief among these were the popular *Godey's Lady's Book*, edited for over forty years by Sarah Josepha Hale. Barbara Sicherman has also studied the readings of women – and one group of family women in particular – and their devotion to sentimental fiction, with Southworth a favorite.[12] Class likewise was hailed by different magazines, which accentuated an opposition between working-class (see Denning) and middle-class (see Streeby, Pawley, and Homestead) readerships.

In addition to authors' popularity and publishers' preferences, scholars of seriality address the cultural forces that led readers to pick up a Southworth or a Buntline story. A significant aspect of this attraction was in the interactive nature of the relation to the author: readers could affect the writers' plots and decisions about characters' fates – through letters to editors and writers alike. Southworth even writes to Bonner that she wants to know what her readers think: "I like you to tell me how the numbers strike the reader. Please do not hesitate to do so. It does help one, I think."[13] This dependency on readers' loyalty suggests that the prospect of interaction among the audience, editors, and writers galvanized the interest over serials. For one of the great enticements of reading serial fiction was a sense of the relation to the author, who felt in need to keep in close contact with readers.

For readers, the choice of which serial publication to read is a question about how to spend one's leisure, how to decide which reading is appropriate, and what remained as amusing reading. Both instruction and engagement were crucial for serial readers. Christine Pawley analyzed the circulation records of the Osage, Iowa, public library for the number and kind of books people checked out between 1870 and 1900.[14] Southworth proved to be one of the most significant of these "sensational" choices. Since adult literacy had grown by 1840, magazine editors wanted to profit from an increase in the numbers of readers. Serial novels paid in terms of immediate readerships and future profits.

Serials, Decade by Decade

The subjects on which US serials focused changed from decade to decade, in large part because of transformations in what was considered "American" and what challenges US citizens faced. In the early part of the century, we see an abiding interest in mental and moral illness, as well as national belonging. By the height of serial novels in the 1840s and 1850s, writers emphasized women's personalities and men's economic security, especially after the Panics of 1837 (one of the most pivotal in the nation's history) and 1857 when writers turned to economic anxiety in their "panic fictions." Perhaps unsurprisingly, by the end of the 1850s and throughout the 1860s, the Civil War and abolition, slave revolution, and African American resistance found voice in serial novels. In what follows, I trace the normative cultural values of serial fiction through the Civil War.

The early national period – roughly through the 1820s and 1830s – was marked by the rise of periodicals and grand ideas about mass marketing news and print, appealing to all kinds of different interests (from law, history, and culture to family life). Once the second Great Awakening subsided, readers perhaps felt free to move away from religious tracts and toward the realms of personal and family leisure. Machine-made paper made publishing cheaper, and readers increasingly turned to newspapers for knowledge and entertainment. Magazine publishing greatly expanded in the 1830s, especially after the introduction of the penny papers in the *New York Sun* in 1833.[15] *The Knickerbocker* was perhaps the best-known; the *Southern Literary Messenger* appeared in 1834, enabling those outside the Northeast to claim some literary status. The *Southern Literary Messenger* published parts of Edgar Allan Poe's *The Narrative of Arthur Gordon Pym*, and it appeared as a novel in 1838.

The incredible popularity of Eugéne Sue's *Mysteries of Paris* (serialized from 1842 to 1843) cannot be underestimated. Its impact proved so wide that US authors similarly began to exploit the appetite for crime, poverty, abuse, and violence, amid some retribution for these social ills. Ned Buntline wrote such "mysteries" about New York City, while others took on Philadelphia, New Orleans, and Lowell, Massachusetts, among many other places. The secrets behind such "mysteries" involve paternity, secret marriages, dead babies, serial adoptions, and eventually abolition. Serials also addressed social reform, whether in terms of temperance, abolition, or violence against women.

Consider the cases of four different authors whose novels illustrate the major types of serials published in the 1840s. George Lippard's *The Quaker City: Monks from Monk Hall* (1844–45) depends on cultural fears of a society immured in corruption and sexual violence. Following the "city mystery" novels devoted to Paris and London, this novel orchestrates the dangers of urban Philadelphia life, including rampant sexual desire and expression, sham marriages and forgeries, frauds and swindles, violence, and revenge.[16] As Paul Erickson explains, "this body of literature helps reveal the ways that popular writers, as well as elite thinkers, were coming to terms with the sudden increase in the size, density, and diversity of urban areas in antebellum America," challenging the past norms of moral and religious life (2).[17] These "adventures" in a corrupt urban life add sensation to trauma, as well as the pleasure of experiencing the effects of such transgressions.

In *The Quaker City*, the danger of seduction is arguably the major secret that the city has to tell. Disreputable men attend bawdy houses in a subterranean lair and are determined to do mischief – "cutting up shines" (294) – perhaps even embarking on an evil "spree." They set their eyes on Mary, a merchant's innocent daughter, whom one of them marries in a sham ceremony, and then rapes. She dies, despite her brother's desperate attempt to save her. Alcohol, sexual intrigue, cuckoldry, orgies at Monk Hall, "bewitching" women, and what Lippard calls "slewers" (299) and roguish men – all are "desolators of the beautiful" (325). At Monk Hall, these rich men devote themselves to spectacular debaucheries. The novel's plot provides a temporary resolution, enough to end the novel but not to banish the fears of such social deterioration. Such resolutions mark how serial novels offered new and innovative, albeit fleeting and incomplete, modes of solutions to American trauma and pain.

To the end of addressing American citizens' pain, Southworth published her first novel, *Retribution* (1849), as a serial in the *National Era*, with a narrative dedicated to the heroine's desire for abolition versus her friend's jealousy of her wealth. Southworth later returns to the idea of abolition in *India/Mark Sutherland* (1853). As Paul Jones contends, Southworth owned one particular slave – Mandy – whom she manumitted, maintaining (ambivalently) the moral righteousness of abolition.[18] She continued promoting this moral stance in novels of the 1850s like *The Mother-in-Law* (1850–51) and *The Curse of Clifton* (1852–53).

Southworth's early novels – from *The Mother-in-Law* to *Hickory Hall* (1861) – illustrate the conflicts between mothers and daughters, especially in terms of the daughter's much-desired independence. Often in these plots, mothers lose control over their children, as the heroine discovers in *The Discarded Daughter* (1852), when she finds that her father has buried her mother alive; she immediately rescues her from an imminent death. Sons, too, clash with their parents' desires, especially when a wife is chosen for a son and he rejects the match, as in *The Fatal Marriage* (1863). In this serial, the antihero is connected to a young wife in a "baby marriage," and he ends up committing bigamy when he marries the wild Lionne and then finds that his first wife was not dead. At his trial, he takes prussic acid to poison himself, and Lionne dies also as a result of her vengeance against him.

A nativist who was anti-immigrant, a supporter of the Know-Nothing Party, and a defender of poor white workers and hater of the wealthy (according to Reynolds and Gladman), George Thompson, whose pseudonym was "Greenhorn," wrote sensational "pulp" fiction, with *Venus in Boston; A Romance of City Life* (1849) and *City Crimes of Life in New York and Boston* (1849), both appearing in the same year.[19] Like Lippard's *Quaker City*, these novels follow the "city mystery" tradition, detailing the erotic violence of urban life. Thompson subsequently wrote about sixty serialized novels, many appearing in the 1850s, some published in *The Broadway Belle*, which he edited.[20]

Condemned for its representation of vulgar and brutal happenings in the city, *Venus in Boston* is nevertheless a serious narrative about the male hero who saves from treachery a virtuous woman, in this case, an innocent fourteen-year-old girl. The young "Sow Nance" is the opposite of the heroine, an ugly sex worker, given over to thieving and trickery, who traps the heroine and imprisons her in a brothel. Yet the revolting acts of the villain are entirely more engaging in enacting what Reynolds and Gladman call the "subversion of domesticity," where families are destroyed by a member's willingness to enter the net of crime – as a procuress, rake, or blackmailer.[21]

Thompson's work served as a kind of nineteenth-century pornography, attracting readers in the fine details of sexual revelry and power, insofar as the characters engage in sexual pleasure without any repercussions.[22] Thompson is determined to reveal "the secret history of things hidden from the public gaze" (3), including in *Venus* the abducting and procuring of young girls, forcing them into underground prisons (20), their rape, desperation of poverty and isolation (20), and the dangers posed by "loafers," Jews, and "mixed" race people in the street (22–23). Also in *Venus*, readers confront branding people, adultery, drinking blood-infused wine, incubus dreams with a "gigantic reptile" as the incubus (81), libertinism, and finally the voluptuous Venus herself (who "sucks in" an old gentlemen for his money [70]). Old, rich people are shown for what Thompson believes they are: stupid fools, easily blackmailed. The novel ends with this address to the reader: "Dear reader, thanking thee for the patience with which thou hast accompanied us in our devious wanderings, and hoping that thou hast not always found us to be a dull companion, we bid thee farewell" (104). This deviousness opposes the presumably "dull," conventional readings in weekly papers.

Ann Stephens's career, begun in the 1840s, might be considered the opposite of Thompson's: Stephens became a major figure in moral serial fiction, with roughly twenty-six novels. We might name *Fashion and Famine* (1854) as her most significant novel, but *The Gold Brick* (1868), *The Reigning Belle* (1855), and *The Noble Woman* (1871) all detail the plight of women's criminality and innocence. *The Gold Brick* starts with the Santo Domingo Revolution and ends with a Christianized couple renewing their moral vows after some eight years in the Newgate underground prison. Katharine Allen is imprisoned after the death of her baby, which she had crushed during her bout of brain fever. In the Newgate Prison, Katharine meets her secret husband, who has been sent to this prison for bigamy (marrying Mrs. Mason after secretly marrying Katharine). Katharine becomes the "prison angel" and turns into a "noble woman" – Stephens's term for the women who preserve culture and American morals. In a great number of Stephens's novels, such as *Bertha's Engagement* (1875), "bad men" are set against the "noble woman" or, on occasion, a noble man.

The 1850s introduced a major change in the function of magazines – from editors' work to a greater emphasis on authors, readers, and their interactions.[23] These magazines also showed a much greater range of topics, intended to pique readers' new interests. By the 1850s, magazines like *Godey's Lady's Book* had huge, national subscriptions, while other magazines begun in the Midwest and West were geared toward specific regional audiences. As Belasco states, there were about 100 magazines in production in the 1850s, with the three most significant ones being *Harper's New Monthly*, *Putnam's Monthly*, and the *Atlantic Monthly*.[24] By 1859, the *Anglo-African Monthly* was the first black-run press magazine in the United States (see below on Delany). By 1859–1861, Street and Smith Publishers also began publishing their *New York Weekly*, which included authors such as Metta Victor and Horatio Alger, among many others.

Perhaps one of the most powerful and lasting serial novels of this decade has to be Harriet Beecher Stowe's *Uncle Tom's Cabin*, serialized for nearly a year in 1851–1852 in the *National Era*. For Stowe, the installment formula led her to end various chapters with cliffhangers – as a result of readers' responses to her installments and the editor Gamaliel Bailey's desire to increase readership. At the end of the first installment, for example, George Harris's future as a slave is foretold – in Stowe's word and font – as "WORSE" than hanging, and the reader is compelled to read more. For this effort, Stowe earned a remarkable amount of money and wrote a number of serial novels after this first one, such as *My Wife and I* in the *Christian Union* (1870–71), though better-known books like *Dred* and *Oldtown Folks* were not serials, largely because of their length.[25]

Ann Stephens's *Fashion and Famine* (1854) is perhaps her most serious indictment of the prison system. The heroine – Julia – and her grandfather are both imprisoned: she as the witness to her grandfather's likely killing of the villain Leicester, who actually has committed suicide. In prison, Julia becomes the "pet" of an African American prisoner, and she, in turn, makes one of the children in the prison become her "pet." By the end of the novel, the grandfather dies in prison, and Julia is released, becoming a happy bride. *The Old Homestead* (1855) also shows the trauma women faced at the public asylum at Bellevue, where the heroine must confront her mother who is a prisoner and is forced to nurse women patients in the poor hospital.

Perhaps the most violent of Stephens's novels, *Mary Derwent* (1858) turns on a mother's insane violence against her daughter. Dorri Beam analyzes the "wrought prose" of Stephens's short story "Mary Derwent" to argue for the aesthetic, stylistic, and political connections, so that reading becomes a "manifold space for possibility."[26] Yet this original version of the plot published in the *Ladies' Companion* in 1838 does not include the maternal violence of the 1858 novel. There, Derwent's mother falls in love with another man despite being already married. During her brain fever, she throws her daughter out the window, thus maiming her with the hunchback from which she then suffers. As a result, Mary is beyond what

Stephens calls "human love," so the girl devotes herself instead to her extended family in the Derwents, bringing them to the estate she inherits as she herself becomes the Lady of Ashton.

Beginning with *Tempest and Sunshine* (1854), Mary Jane Holmes published thirty-nine novels, the most famous of which, *'Lena Rivers* (1856), details the "white trash" fear of family dysgenics and marital failure. Holmes is crucial to the history of US seriality because her corpus attends to the hierarchies of social class that solidified in mid-nineteenth-century culture. In *Tempest and Sunshine*, two sisters vie for family pride, with one sister betraying the other for the rights to the sister's fiancé. Only at the wedding scene does the tempestuous sister reveal her plots and "bleed" from her mouth onto her wedding dress. After her confession, she disappears, and everyone thinks her dead because a young female maniac is found drowned. Eventually, the estranged sister returns, filled with remorse for her sins against her tranquil sister, who eventually marries the fiancé whom Tempest almost stole. Such family disaster leads to Holmes's resolution about the need for people to commit to the value of work, of labor of any kind.

In *'Lena Rivers*, the following questions fuel the novel's plot: Did the heroine's mother really marry her father, or was this a secret marriage that the husband himself never acknowledged? After her mother dies, poor 'Lena Rivers is left in a dangerous circumstance, without any paternity to support her. This tenuous situation hinders her own potential marriage to a very rich man, who doubts her sexual innocence. Eventually, the father acknowledges his daughter, even as 'Lena questions him about how long it took to recognize and admit to his fatherhood. The novel raises the question of paternity – and family pride in it – which is one concern that Holmes's novels repeat. For Holmes, honest labor replaces the dreaded family pride. Along these lines, Holmes published a number of novels in the 1850s – including *The English Orphans* (1855), *Homestead on the Hillside* (1856), *Meadow Brook* (1857), *Dora Deane; or, The East India Uncle* (1859), and *Cousin Maude* (1860). These fictions establish the author's engagement with dilemmas about the health of the family – whether in terms of orphanage, insanity, or white trash. She writes almost exclusively about the detriment of "family pride" to heredity and community.

Southworth's *The Hidden Hand* (first serialized in 1859, then again in 1868–69, and then again in 1883) is certainly her best-known novel, and arguably her best because of its heroine, Capitola Black, whose cross-dressing distinguishes her from the more timid and sentimental heroines

of other popular serial novels. As critics have suggested, the novel is filled
with much more, including the consequences of the Mexican War as
determining national – as well as sexual and gender – boundaries.[27]
Southworth's critique of insane asylums, especially for women, presents a
bitter rendering of women's vulnerability, and her indictment of capital
punishment is equally framed against "injustice, immorality, and ineffi-
ciency."[28] By the end, Capitola has established her own status as Old
Hurricane's heiress, saves Black Donald's life, and lives with – in the last
words of the novel – "a fair amount of human felicity."

By 1859, African American writers turned to seriality to advance their
causes, particularly in the first black literary magazine. One major example
is Martin Delany's *Blake, or, The Huts of America*, an unfinished serial in
the *Anglo-African Magazine*. Part I came out in this magazine; part II
appeared in the *Weekly Anglo-African*. As Robert Levine argues, the novel
was designed to show a "successful hemispheric black revolution," but it
was unfinished and so that success is suspended for readers of the novel.[29]
Blake leads this revolt, the novel following his plans for resisting oppression, to which he offers a "religious" conviction "never to serve a white
man living!" (299). The novel describes both vocal and physical resistance
to submission, including – as the "secret" of the novel – the planned
"successful overthrow of slavery!" Although the reader never sees the
insurrection happen, Delany outlines the plot for such violence. Henry
Blake plans the uprising to avenge his wife, whose "disgrace" had been
averted but whose master still sells her. Without a victory, the novel maps
Blake's moves around the United States, connecting with various peoples
to take part in his insurrection. From the Native Americans of the "United
Nation of Chickasaw and Choctaw Indians" (chapter 21) and the enslaved
people of different states, all commit to back his plan "for the redemption
of his race in the South" (chapter 26). This travel through the United
States and Cuba and in the "middle passage" enables Blake to report on the
tragedies and torture of enslaved African Americans. Such violence and
brutality inflame Blake's desire for revenge and to wrest power.

Blake sees what is meant by white superiority in the United States. In
the serial, a southern judge, acting in the North, explains his racism in this
way: "I hold as a just construction of the law, that not only has a
slaveholder a right to reclaim his slave when and wherever found, but by
its provision every free black in the country, North and South, are liable to
enslavement by any white person. They are freemen by sufferance or
slaves-at-large, whom any white person may claim at discretion. It was a
just decision of the Supreme Court – though I was in advance of it by

action – that persons of African descent have no rights that white men are bound to respect!" (chapter 15). In Cuba, this judge must acknowledge a black man's rights, but he does so only with disgust.

Blake and his wife escape to Havana, where they find some refuge from slavery. The wife recounts her story of being sold and resold and sold again because she refuses to consent to sex with a master. Blake decides to avenge her wrongs, promising the destruction of the enslavers. He enlists his cousin Placido, a well-known poet, for help in destroying American slavery. While in Cuba, a daughter is brutally accosted on the street, and when she sadly returns home, her family is shocked at the aggression she experienced. This, the last scene of the novel, highlights what the chapter title calls "American Tyranny" in the "oppression" of African slaves. Even unfinished, Delany's serial is a call to rebellion against this oppression.

Readers in the 1860s – especially during and after the Civil War – engaged a tremendous appetite for narratives exploring the consequences of this national war and the changes to the United States that such race violence established. By the time of the first Beadle and Adams novel (a publisher of cheap items and the first "dime novel" printer) in 1860, Ann Stephens circulated *Malaeska, or, The Indian Wife of a White Hunter* and later *Myra* (1860) and *The Indian Queen* (1864) as three dime novels to advance her reputation as one of the most accessible and committed serial writers. The first of these Beadle novels was *Malaeska*, based on her original story published as "The Jockey Cap" in 1836 in *Portland Magazine*. Malaeska "marries" the white hunter, and after he dies during a fight with a Native American, she follows his deathbed wish and takes their son to his parents in Manhattan. The grandfather is horrified by his grandson's mixed-race heritage, and he makes the mother become the maid in his house, which is her only way to oversee her son. The novel ends with Malaeska's death after her son commits suicide when he learns of his biracial status. As he exclaims to his mother, "I – an Indian – was about to give my stained hand to a lovely being of untainted blood."[30] Soon after, he throws himself into a river, drowning in front of his mother, who dies of shock. The son's fiancée remains alive – grieving – and laments her own loneliness.

A number of serial novels about US violence and the Civil War appeared after the war, like Southworth's *Fair Play* (1868) and *How He Won Her* (1869), along with Holmes's *Rose Mather* (1868), *Purified by Suffering* (1867) and *Hugh Worthington* (1865). These serials tried to bring some immediate perspective to the violence of the war, often focusing on a cultural impasse between northern pride and southern poverty. One of Southworth's most incisive novels, *The Prince of Darkness* (1869), shows the tragedy of a mixed-race son, Wolfgang Wallraven, who marries a white woman. This wife kills Wallraven when she finds out that his mother was a quadroon, a maid to his grandmother. Slave Nell announces the tragedy of the mother, whose children include the melancholy Wolfgang and a set of fraternal twins. After Wolfgang dies, his wife is kept in their home instead of an asylum or prison, with her insanity a result of race hatred.[31]

In 1868 both *Fair Play* and *Rose Mather* were published and contended for equality of some sort. *Fair Play*, one of the most dramatic and protofeminist of Southworth's works, focuses on the lives of four women who have just finished their careers at Bellemont College. The heroine, Britomarte, is a "man-hater," a woman who refuses to marry because of her sister's demise as a wife to a brute. Instead, she sets off to India as a Christian messenger, but the boat capsizes and she is left stranded on an island along with the man who loves her (the brother of one of her college friends) and an Irish servant. After two years, they are rescued, and in the sequel, *How He Won Her*, she cross-dresses during the Civil War and is imprisoned in Libby Prison. Freed only when her lover, Justin, who is aware of her cross-dressing, manages her escape, she confesses her sister's secret to him, and they marry as a proof of the novel's moral: "MARRIAGE IS MUTUAL CONSENT" (228, Southworth's emphasis), an argument that undergirds the novel's vision of newly discovered equality and women's consent. Similarly, Holmes's *Rose Mather* shows how northern and southern gentlemen/soldiers – though fighting on opposite sides – are equally valuable. The soldiers are horrid whether they come from the North or South. Two women prove themselves worthy during the war itself: the North's Rose Mather and the South's Maude De Vere. Thus, Holmes justifies a necessary peace between North and South equals.

Southworth's favorite novel by her own pen was *Ishmael* (1884), the story of a reputable orphan who becomes a well-known lawyer. The novel's sequel, *Self-Raised, or, From the Depths*, continues with Ishmael's eventual marriage to Bee and also includes the tale of the wicked Mrs. Faustina Dugald. She ends up imprisoned for her crimes, and turns from a reckless woman to one who is "settled" by prison discipline. The novel's ending illustrates Southworth's investment in a lawyer attuned to women's property rights: "Ishmael loved, prayed, and worked – worked more than ever, for he knew that though it was hard to win, it was harder to secure fame. He went on from success to success. He became illustrious. The end" (411). Such heroes are part of the key element of her fictions. These later novels arguably deliver a more powerful moral in their revolt against the violence of the Civil War (see below), and especially women's concerns in this war.

Ultimately, serial novels moved beyond themes centered on the Civil War and testified to the emergence of a new modernity that shaped the concerns of fiction, with characters worrying about how to face major changes in modern culture. Later in the century, other writers, like Horatio Alger, advanced the serial novel and its new emphasis on class transition for many struggling boy-laborers: *Marie Bertrand: The Felon's Daughter*, serialized in Street and Smith's *New York Weekly* in 1864, as well as the various writers of the Frank Reade ("boy inventor") series of detective novels. The serialized fiction of Henry James (who thought serialization was not a serious way to read), William Dean Howells, Mark Twain, Sarah Orne Jewett, and Edith Wharton all suggested how serious serial reading became for middle- and leisure-class readers. In the meantime, Libbey's seventy-plus popular novels were read by working women to advance their sense of class possibilities and mobility. By the end of the century, Pauline Hopkins continued the serial novel in *Colored American Magazine* with three different novels and with the unfinished "Topsy Templeton" in the 1916 *New Era*. Serials at the end of the century provided transitional stories of characters devoted mostly to individual rather than communal challenges to identity and belonging.

Theory and Pedagogy of Serials

One way to teach serial fiction is to offer serials in installments. In doing so, one can make long novels more manageable as self-contained sections. Such a method leads to discussions about rates of pay (by the word vs. a predetermined contract, as many of the serial writers received, rates based on the author's desirability); some payment depended on how long each installment was meant to be; some on the details and organization of each installment. Another way is to provide context of the entire magazine's content and to highlight the function of detail- or "slow reading." Then the next phase might be to trace the movement from serial to book – such as in the process of turning the short fiction "Mary Derwent" (1838) to a much more violent novel (1858). Such reading requires analyzing the magazine itself, including its other articles, along with its illustrations, advertising, opinions, and format of the serial's publication (its publisher, potential readers, social perspective) in relation to the stand-alone novel (to the reviews and revenues it received). Scholars can question the accessibility of serials based on social class and one's access to leisure time. By the end of the nineteenth century, as Nan Enstad argues, working girls turned to fiction and fashion specific to their desires.[32] Thus, reading of serials was part of a "developing class structure" into the twentieth century.

Most recently, Frank Kelleter has perhaps provided the most influential theory of serials, especially his attention to repetition in his consideration of 1850 serials, including such contemporary versions as HBO's *The Wire* (2002–2008) and popular seriality in general. How do serials influence a reader's sense of reality, in terms of rhythm and habit? Kelleter also examines the uncertainty about endings and a sense of a renewed resolution that temporarily – until the next installment – solves a social problem. Conclusions are just temporary and call for more serials to provide a variety of possible endings. Kelleter argues that

> series can be defined as self-observing systems. And self-observing systems always produce theories about their own motions – they do so in order to keep moving. Likewise, series usually experiment with formal identities and they "think" about their own possibilities of continuation. However, when I say that series are "doing" these things, I don't mean that they are intentional entities. Of course series do not act like human beings – or instead of human beings. But they *involve* people and intentions.[33]

Kelleter's key terms – "self-observing systems," "thinking" and "doing" by authors and readers alike – indicate how temporary serial resolutions work for readers' intentions.

The temporary resolutions of mid-nineteenth-century serials, like their counterparts today, may be sufficient to finish the plot dilemmas within the novel, but they resist closing off painful or anxious topics. For another serial can return to the same trauma or social problem. There is always another villain, another reform, and even another brain surgery. These resolutions, then, model how citizens should behave – morally and ethically, sanely and sincerely – as the United States changed between the Panics of 1837 and 1857, and then between antebellum and postbellum culture. Serials depicted various new personalities and moved beyond temperance, abolition, slavery to other issues like vulnerability, disability, and social alienation, which became the larger social and political questions of the era. That is, serials' recursive format needs to keep open the very plots that keep readers reading.

Notes

1 Frank Kelleter, "All about Seriality: An Interview with Frank Kelleter (Part One)." Henry Jenkins blog. May 4, 2017. Henryjenkins.org.
2 Colin T. Ramsey and Kathyrn Zabelle Derounian-Stodola, "Dime Novels," in *A Companion to American Fiction, 1780–1865*, ed. Shirley Samuels (Malden, MA: Blackwell, 2004), 264.
3 Patricia Okker, *Social Stories: The Magazine Novel in Nineteenth-Century America* (Charlottesville: University Press of Virginia, 2003), 11; Rachel

Ihara, "'Like beads strung together': E. D. E. N. Southworth and the Aesthetics of Popular Serial Fiction," in *Must Read: Rediscovering American Bestsellers*, ed. Sarah Churchwell and Thomas Ruys Smith (New York: Continuum, 2012), 84.

4 Barbara Hochman, "Novels," in *US Popular Print Culture to 1860*, ed. Ronald J. Zboray and Mary Saracino Zboray (New York: Oxford University Press, 2019), 421.

5 Lara Langer Cohen, "Mediums of Exchange: Fanny Fern's Unoriginality," *ESQ: A Journal of the American Renaissance* 55.1 (January 2009): 62–65.

6 Michael Denning, *Mechanic Accents: Dime Novels and Working-Class Culture* (New York: Verso, 1997), 2–5.

7 Jared Gardner, "Serial Fiction and the Novel," in *The American Novel, 1870–1940*, ed. Priscilla Wald and Michael A. Elliott (New York: Oxford University Press, 2014), 291.

8 Okker, *Social Stories*, 29.

9 Mary Kelley, *Private Woman, Public Stage: Literary Domesticity in Nineteenth-Century America* (New York: Oxford University Press, 1984), 162–63.

10 Melissa J. Homestead and Pamela T. Washington, eds., *E.D.E.N. Southworth: Recovering a Nineteenth-Century Popular Novelist* (Knoxville: University of Tennessee Press, 2012), xxvi, n. 12.

11 Susan Belasco, "Magazines from 1820 to 1860," in *US Popular Print Culture to 1860*, ed. Ronald J. Zboray and Mary Saracino Zboray (New York: Oxford University Press, 2019), 378.

12 Barbara Sicherman, *Well-Read Lives: How Books Inspired A Generation of American Women* (Chapel Hill: University of North Carolina Press, 2010), 31, 39.

13 E. D. E. N. Southworth, letter to Robert Bonner, April 7, 1887, Library of Congress.

14 Christine Pawley, *Reading on the Middle Border: The Culture of Print in Late Nineteenth-Century Osage, Iowa* (Amherst: University of Massachusetts Press, 2001), 78–79.

15 Paul Joseph Erickson, "Welcome to Sodom: The Cultural Work of City-Mysteries Fiction in Antebellum America" (PhD diss., University of Texas–Austin, 2005).

16 Hochman, "Novels," 422.

17 Erickson, "Welcome to Sodom," 2.

18 Paul Christian Jones, "'Her Little Maid Mandy': The Abolitionist Slave Owner and the Rhetoric of Affection in the Life and Early Fiction of E.D.E.N. Southworth," *J19* 1.2 (Spring 2014): 54.

19 David S. Reynolds and Kimberly R. Gladman, "Introduction," in *Venus in Boston and Other Tales of Nineteenth-Century City Life*, by George Thompson (Amherst: University of Massachusetts Press, 2002), xxi.

20 Ibid., xv.

21 Ibid., xxxiii.

22 Ibid., xxxvi.

23 Belasco, "Magazines from 1820 to 1860," 371.

24 Ibid., 381–82.

25 Michael Winship, "'The Greatest Book of Its Kind': A Publishing History of 'Uncle Tom's Cabin,'" *American Antiquarian Society Proceedings* (2002): 309–32.

26 Dorri Beam, *Style, Gender, and Fantasy in Nineteenth-Century American Women's Writing* (Cambridge: Cambridge University Press, 2010), 173.

27 Shelley Streeby, *American Sensations: Class, Empire, and the Production of Popular Culture* (Berkeley: University of California Press, 2002), 33–34.

28 Jones, "'Her Little Maid Mandy,'" 134.

29 Robert Levine, ed., *Martin R. Delany: A Documentary Reader* (Chapel Hill: North Carolina University Press, 2003), 297.

30 Ann Stephens, *Malaeska: The Indian Wife of a White Hunter* (1860), in *Reading the West: An Anthology of Dime Westerns*, ed. Bill Brown (Boston: St. Martins, 1997), 57–164 (159).

31 Dale M. Bauer, *Nineteenth-Century American Women's Serial Novels* (Cambridge: Cambridge University Press, 2019).

32 Nan Enstad, *Ladies of Labor, Girls of Adventure: Working Women, Popular Culture, and Labor Politics at the Turn of the Twentieth Century* (New York: Columbia University Press, 1999), 50.

33 Kelleter, "All about Seriality."

CHAPTER 16

Unoriginality

Claudia Stokes

It has long been an axiom of literary study that innovation and the pursuit of originality are the hallmarks of artistic achievement. This truism found its most succinct expression in Ezra Pound's famed dictum "make it new," which appointed creative invention the fundamental task of the artist. For generations, scholars and critics have used originality as an evaluative standard to determine which texts and writers merit study and which, by extension, merit erasure from literary memory. Harold Bloom, for instance, deemed novelty a precondition for a text's inclusion in the canon, and he defined this attribute as a "strangeness, a mode of originality that either cannot be assimilated, or that so assimilates us that we cease to see it as strange."[1] Originality – whether in content, form, or style – has become so central to our discipline that we have forgotten that this standard emerged only relatively recently, amid modernism and the professionalization of the literary academy following World War I. We have also forgotten that writers and readers of the nineteenth century did not share our modern esteem for originality, and yet for the last century we have used this twentieth-century measure to appraise texts and writers who did not especially aspire to "make it new."

On the contrary, nineteenth-century American literary history indicates that readers regarded originality with considerable skepticism. In the second quarter of the nineteenth century, improvements in printing technology and distribution caused significant changes in print culture, and readers found themselves inundated with cheap new print material – like newspapers and novels – that could be discarded after a single reading. As a result, the new abundance of print dissolved the practices of preservation and rereading that had governed reading for generations.[2] Readers suddenly faced a dizzying array of new choices, and critics advised Americans to resist the allure of novelty and select only familiar, time-tested books of reliable quality. For these critics, literary originality signified not creativity or artistic ambition but, at best, the unpredictability and variable quality of the new literary market and, at worst, the sensationalism required to attract attention in a crowded marketplace. Though twentieth-century critics regarded originality as evidence of artistic achievement and canonicity, readers a century earlier interpreted this quality as confirmation of a text's irregularity, unwholesomeness, and disposability. The bewildered critical response to Herman Melville's *Moby-Dick* (1851), dubbed by one critic "a primitive formation of profanity and indecency," confirms that nineteenth-century readers and critics neither sought nor esteemed originality as an intrinsic literary virtue but often regarded it with suspicion and distaste.[3] It is for this reason that Melville would have to wait until the twentieth century to find a receptive critical response.[4]

Amid this new literary abundance, critics in the first half of the century urged readers to favor the reliable, familiar texts enshrined in literary tradition: Milton, Shakespeare, the essays of Addison and Steele, sturdy histories of antiquity, and the like. Inscriptions in commonplace books of the second quarter of the nineteenth century confirm that readers often adhered to this advice, diligently copying passages taken from these respectable older sources (though these inscriptions should not be taken as evidence that these readers had not also read splashy new books).[5] In her 1831 child-rearing manual, *The Mother's Book*, Lydia Maria Child explained why older books were preferable over newer material: "Amid the multiplicity of modern books, the old standard works are too much neglected. Young people had better read Plutarch's Lives, and Anacharsis' Travels in Greece.... To read every new thing fosters a love of novelty and a craving for excitement; and it fritters away time and intellect to little purpose."[6] Literary originality, Child warns, might cause young readers to become capricious and overstimulated, and a taste for novelty could undermine a mother's efforts to cultivate good habits and constancy in her children. Children should opt instead for the old and familiar over the new and unusual; such books could be relied on to cultivate good taste and judgment, and, because they required more attention than cheap new publications, they trained young readers in the rewards of diligence and exertion.

Popular poet Lydia Sigourney made this point explicit in directing young readers to avoid the "the flood of desultory literature" in favor of the careful study of familiar books:

> The time must soon come, should your days be prolonged, when you will be young no more. Life will then be like a "twice-told tale." The present will be disrobed of novelty, and the future of its charm, and the mind will

turn for solace to the gatherings of the past. Furnish now your intellectual store-house for that day of need. Be willing to labour for knowledge, to learn long lessons, and to encounter difficult studies.[7]

Sigourney here compares the changes wrought by maturity to the differences between reading an ephemeral work of novelty and a more demanding, familiar book. She explains that life to a young person may feel like an exciting new tale, but adulthood, with its burdens and repetitions, is more akin to the familiar, challenging works in the canon, and so she urges young people to prepare for adult life by reading such books. Because these works have been favored for generations, they may also impart a reverence for custom and tradition as well as a fidelity to the inheritances of the past. True maturity, Sigourney intones, "will turn for solace to the gatherings of the past," and with this statement Sigourney articulated the era's continuing reverence for literary familiarity and tradition, despite the growing enticements of novelty and change.

Twentieth-century critics characterized early nineteenth-century opposition to originality as evidence of its hidebound, stagnant character, and they often identified Ralph Waldo Emerson as the crucial lever that would finally dislodge American literature from its backward-looking resistance and cause it to embrace newness and change.[8] Indeed, it was in response to this literary climate that Emerson in 1837 famously deplored the continuing influence of the literary past – which, even more troubling, was often of English origin – and called for Americans to produce a homegrown national literature anchored in the present.[9] However, nineteenth-century advocates perceived literary familiarity and tradition not as obstacles to progress, as did their twentieth-century counterparts, but as reliable markers of respectability, taste, and education. In an era in which periodicals seemed to spring up practically overnight and novels were frequently published without authorial attribution, familiarity and traditionalism served as the era's primary literary lodestar and provided a stable measure of quality: though readers might not know for certain the identity of a new book's author or the source of a periodical's reprinted contents, a text's visible dependence on respectable source material provided reassuring credentials and attested to its author's taste and propriety.[10] Andrew Piper has described this deliberate invocation of familiar sources as indicative of the era's "bibliographic imagination," which assigned literary value not according to a text's originality but according to its "fundamental . . . reproducibility."[11] Critics have characterized this predilection for familiarity as a regrettable detour on the nation's route to literary independence and innovation, but it bears stressing that, in the first half of the nineteenth century, unoriginality was a legitimate and recognized literary style that conferred prestige and created advantageous networks of influence and citation, in which writers emulated predecessors who had themselves imitated familiar figures and texts. This deliberate unoriginality did not undermine writers' reputation, as we might expect, but allowed them to present themselves as the scions and protectors of a grand literary tradition. In this way, unoriginality affirmed their pedigree and literary bona fides.

Perhaps no writer better demonstrates the benefits of unoriginality than Washington Irving, whose career was built on his faithful reproduction and preservation of the past, whether through his famed *History of New York* (1809) or his biographies of George Washington and Christopher Columbus. From the very outset of his career, Irving adopted the style, forms, and persona of an earlier literary era, and he thus presented himself as the continuation of literary tradition: wholesome, durable, and familiar. This self-presentation began from the very outset of Irving's career, with the publication of a series of letters in which he adopted the persona of an elderly man. Though Irving was only twenty-one years old, he assumed the public affect not of youth, with its anticipatory and generative energies, but of venerable, retrospective age. This demeanor continued throughout Irving's career: as the nation's first international literary celebrity, Irving might have presented himself as the literary avatar of the nation's youth and promise, but he instead built his reputation by styling himself a faithful steward of literary and historical memory, often that of the European Old World. Irving's career reminds us that, in the literary history of the early national period, novelty and newness were discomfiting reminders of the nation's own youthful uncertainty, whereas a solid grounding in history and tradition offered reassurances of stability, continuity, and heritage. Irving's career was thus built on his skillful use of the affordances of literary unoriginality.

Washington Irving adopted pseudonyms throughout his career – the Dutch historian Dietrich Knickerbocker, the sketch author Geoffrey Crayon – but his first pseudonym announced his fidelity to literary tradition. Between 1802 and 1803, Irving adopted the pen name "Jonathan Oldstyle" to publish a series of narrative letters in the *Morning Chronicle*. This moniker openly broadcast Irving's particular attachment to the "old style" of literature as well as his plan to continue this antiquated mode in his own work.[12] In keeping with his pen name, Irving's letters were visibly modeled after the serialized essays of the English eighteenth century and imitated the arch social commentary favored in such periodicals as *The Spectator, The Tatler,* and *The Guardian.*[13] Though Irving's series was short-lived, it adopted the wry conversational style of Joseph Addison, and it similarly commented on changes in courtship, manners, and other social institutions.[14] (This transatlantic imitation was also aided by the fact that the *Morning Chronicle,* edited by Irving's brother Peter, was itself named after an English newspaper of the same title.) Irving supported this imitation of an earlier literary era by fashioning Jonathan Oldstyle as an elderly man who disdained modern life and expressed yearnings for the ways of the past. For instance, in his second letter, published on November 20, 1802, Jonathan Oldstyle described his difficulty adjusting to change and his partiality for the customs of an earlier era: "Nothing is more intolerable to an old person than innovation on old habits. The customs that prevailed in our youth become dear to us as we advance in years; and we can no more bear to see them abolished, than we can to behold the trees cut down under which we have sported in the happy days on infancy."[15] Presaging Sigourney's similar discussion of childhood, Irving here offered a poignant explanation for the period's resistance to disruptive changes in print culture: innovation ushers in not improvement but loss, for it permits the erosion of long-standing custom and memory. These comments offer a salient rejoinder to the twentieth-century insistence on originality, but they also convey that Irving, from the very beginning, sought to present himself as a steadfast literary counterweight to these disruptions. Where other American writers of his generation might have sought to imitate Lord Byron or other sensational contemporaries, Irving launched his career by asserting his commitment to tradition and its viability in the present. That Irving soon became an international celebrity confirms both the continuing appeal of these literary modes among early nineteenth-century readers as well as Irving's canniness in fashioning himself a traditionalist in an age of change.

Irving consolidated this reputation with the publication of *A History of New York,* in which he explicitly announced his intention of protecting historical memory from erasure. New York's early Dutch dwellers, Irving laments, are aging, their memories and lore dying with them, but their children have been so "engrossed by the empty pleasures or insignificant transactions of the present age" that they have failed to preserve their parents' wisdom. "[P]osterity shall search in vain, for memorials of the days of the Patriarchs. The origin of our city will be buried in eternal oblivion."[16] Amid the "empty pleasures ... of the present age," historical memory teeters on the brink of disappearance, and, in the guise of the

Dutch historian Dietrich Knickerbocker, Irving presents his garrulous regional history as a bulwark against this loss. In this undertaking he likened himself to Herodotus, but nineteenth-century readers noted that Irving's *History* seemed visibly patterned after more recent sources. According to Charles Dudley Warner, Walter Scott discerned a marked resemblance to Jonathan Swift, commenting, "'I have never ... read anything so closely resembling the style of Dean Swift as the annals of Dietrich Knickerbocker.'"[17] William Cullen Bryant detected other influences: "I find in this work more manifest traces than in his other writings of what Irving owed to the earlier authors in our language. The quaint poetic coloring and often the phraseology betray the discipline of Chaucer and Spenser. We are conscious of a flavor of the olden time, as of a racy wine of some rich vintage."[18] Irving's biographer Stanley Williams described it as "[u]nquestionably the most allusive of American literary compositions written before 1825," and he identified a wealth of sources: Tobias Smollett, Ben Jonson, John Dryden, Henry Fielding, Jonathan Swift, Richard Sheridan, Lawrence Sterne, and many others.[19] Though these readers differed in their assessments of Irving's models, they all recognized that *A History of New York* seemed allusive and familiar, evoking a range of recognizable styles and voices. Critics in the twentieth century, such as Stanley Williams, would condemn this quality as "servile" and proof of Irving's lesser creative ability, but in the context of the book's own stated ambitions, it conveys Irving's conviction that the task of historical preservation entails not only content – accounts of important episodes, portraits of notable figures – but also literary style. In his evocation of innumerable earlier sources, Irving reproduced the literary qualities, forms, and writers that had been popular during the period he examines.[20] For Irving, literary style and technique are no less deserving of conservation than historical memory.

Readers similarly recognized familiar sources in Irving's *The Sketch Book of Geoffrey Crayon, Gent.* (1819–20), the serial that secured Irving's international renown. Readers detected so many similarities to Walter Scott's work that a rumor circulated that Scott himself was the book's author.[21] William Hazlitt observed, "Not only Mr. Irving's language is with great taste and felicity modelled on that of Addison, Goldsmith, Sterne, or Mackenzie: but the thoughts and sentiments are taken at the rebound."[22] Perhaps because Irving had encountered similar comments about *A History of New York*, he incorporated the topic of unoriginality within the contents of *The Sketch Book*. The short story "The Art of Book Making" begins by marveling at the "extreme fecundity of the press," which "teem[s] with voluminous productions" despite the evident "barrenness" of "so many heads."²³ The story thus begins by acknowledging the era's new literary abundance and by questioning the origins of the countless new publications that suddenly inundated the market. Where do all of these new books come from? he wondered. The story answers this question by depicting an unnamed speaker's visit to a secluded room in the British Museum, populated by "pale, studious personages" who summon ancient tomes upon which they then "fall, tooth and nail, with famished voracity." The visitor soon realizes that these researchers are in fact authors, who eagerly mine these ancient tomes to find material for their own books. One author picks "a morsel out of one [book], a morsel out of another, line upon line, precept upon precept" in order to assemble the contents of his own book. This practice, Irving asserts, is the origin of all literature: all texts originate in the extraction and repurposing of prior writers' work. In defense of this undertaking, the narrator concludes that this "pilfering" lies at the foundation of nature itself, for even birds steal seeds and deposit them elsewhere, enabling plants to grow in distant locations. These literary extractions similarly ensure that the "seeds of knowledge and wisdom shall be preserved from age to age," and he notes that these appropriations may result in new growth of an altogether different kind:

> What was formerly a ponderous history, revives in the shape of a romance – an old legend changes into a modern play, and a sober philosophical treatise, furnishes the body for a whole series of bouncing and sparkling essays. Thus it is in the clearing of our American woodlands; where we burn down a forest of stately pines, a progeny of dwarf oaks start up in their place; and we never see the prostrate trunk of a tree, mouldering into soil, but it gives birth to a whole tribe of fungi. (811)

Irving here provides a hearty defense of literary unoriginality: the reuse of prior literary material not only preserves the wisdom of the past but also proves fruitful, with old content generating new forms and styles. Thanks to the labors of thrifty, resourceful writers, old trunks may sprout new branches and leaves. Unoriginality, he contends, allows the past to flourish and thrive in the present.

Irving would dramatize the continuing appeal of the past in "Rip Van Winkle," the collection's most famous story. It recounts the return of a town idler after a potent beverage, offered by mysterious Dutchmen, causes him to sleep for twenty years. When Rip awakes and returns home, he finds the town strangely changed: in his absence, his long-suffering wife has died and his home fallen into decay, but the drowsy community now bustles with energy and the inn's portrait of King George has been replaced by that of George Washington. Rip's slumber has proved generative, for in his absence the nation has achieved independence and grown toward maturity. However, despite the town's advancement and the community's evident desire to make a clean break with its monarchical past, Rip's reappearance illustrates the continuing influence and circulation of the past in the present. For instance, though it might seem that time has passed Rip by, leaving him obsolete in a modern era, he returns to find two seeming copies of himself, both a grandson named in his honor and his namesake son, "a precise counterpart of himself" who is just as feckless as his father.[24] Throughout Rip's absence, a familiar duplicate stood in his place all along, just as Irving's Jonathan Oldstyle letters adapted Addison's *Spectator* to the modern American literary scene. In keeping with Irving's assertion in "The Art of Book Making" that the practices of unoriginality are quite literally natural, "Rip Van Winkle" suggests that genetic inheritance likewise confirms the inevitability and biological naturalness of unoriginality: we are all copies of our parents, who were themselves copies of their forebears.

Rip's return also demonstrates the adaptability and endurance of the putatively vanished past, which does not conveniently disappear but finds ways to adapt and flourish in the present. A remnant of a presumably vanished era, Rip returns to resume many of his prior habits, taking up his usual seat near the inn's door but befriending some new companions. Though his wife had often chastised him for his indolence, Rip has reached the age where he may legitimately idle, and so he now has license to resume his typical habits. That is, Rip takes advantage of recent changes in order to justify reviving the practices of the past in the present. The adaptability of the past is also evident in the inn's portrait of George Washington: the painting is not actually new but is in fact a repurposed portrait of George III, which has been updated with a few changes of color and accessories. The familiar vestiges of the past have elastic and recombinant value, and what might seem new and original, Irving suggests, is visibly derived from a prior model.

Irving explained his own tendency toward unoriginality in *Bracebridge Hall* (1822), a collection of sketches about an English manor. He wrote, "I am aware that I often travel over beaten ground, and treat of subjects that have already been discussed by abler pens. Indeed, various authors have been mentioned as my models, to whom I should feel flattered if I thought I bore the slightest resemblance."[25] Irving disavowed any deliberate attempt to imitate and attributed this tendency to his "hope that some new interest may be given to such topic" as well as his upbringing in a new country with little history: "To a mind thus peculiarly prepared," he explained, "the most ordinary objects and scenes, on arriving in Europe, are full of strange matter and interesting novelty." Though the sights of Europe might be "stale" to English readers, to "a man from a young country all old things are in a manner new" (10, 11). In this way, Irving offered an explanation for his attraction to familiar subjects and styles: old things seem fresh and new in the eyes of an American, and, for the denizen of a young country, an antiquity is a veritable novelty. For Americans, he insisted, anything that smacks of history or venerable tradition is a rare treat, and so his unoriginality, he suggested, was nothing of the sort for American readers, who delighted in literary scenes familiar to English readers.

Irving's unoriginality would lead later critics to dismiss him as a literary underachiever content to write insipid, nostalgic portraits of country life. According to this assessment, Irving was merely a tentative early step toward the full development of American literature, and his Anglophilic nostalgia had to be outgrown for the nation to reach full literary maturity. However, Irving's career was more influential than this literary historical narrative suggests. Irving's *Sketch Book* continued to circulate widely long after its initial publication, and pieces taken from this collection were omnipresent for decades, for, like the returning Rip Van Winkle, they reappeared virtually everywhere – in gift books, periodicals, and anthologies. Furthermore, Irving's *Sketch Book* found a home in the American classroom, and generations of students learned to write by studying and imitating Irving's example; as a result, Irving displaced Addison's essays, which had long served as an exemplar of rhetorical style and which Irving himself had imitated.[26] Americans for decades were taught to copy Irving, and it is perhaps for this reason that Irving stood at the center of a lively and productive literary network of writers who sought to reproduce his success by adopting his style, affect, and literary forms. Though Irving famously remained a bachelor and lacked direct biological offspring, his many imitators provided Irving with an alternate mode of reproduction. Like the birds sowing seeds in "The Art of Book Making," Irving's literary descendants kept his style and forms in wide circulation, and in this respect Irving's unoriginality proved generative and productive.[27]

The most famous of these imitators was doubtless Henry Wadsworth Longfellow, who in his youth planned to model his literary career after Irving and commenced writing after receiving encouragement from his idol in 1827.[28] Longfellow's first book, *Outre-Mer* (1835), is a patent imitation of *The Sketch Book*: a travel memoir composed of sketches of

European locales and personages, *Outre-Mer* employs a similarly meandering structure, and it likewise adopts a conversational, genial narrative voice.[29] Longfellow openly admitted his intention of imitating Irving: in a letter he confessed that throughout his travels his mind was "'full of Hendrick Hudson and his crew at nine-pins – the Doolittle Inn – and Rip Van Winkle," and in another letter he described *Outre-Mer* as a "kind of Sketch-Book of scenes in France, Spain, and Italy."[30] *Outre-Mer* was even designed to resemble *The Sketch Book*: it was similarly issued in an octavo size, with a taupe cover, an identical font, and marbleized endpapers. In *Outre-Mer*, Longfellow presented himself as Irving's literary heir and suggested that he would continue Irving's mission and similarly preserve the literary past from loss. Longfellow wrote, "But now I will stay the too busy hand of time, and call back the shadowy past," and he fulfilled this ambition by recounting tales of the Old World and including numerous oral ballads he recorded in the European countryside, just as Irving had included the lore of rural England in *Bracebridge Hall*.[31]

Longfellow would eventually find his own literary style and abandon his plan to imitate Irving, but Irving nonetheless had a wide coterie of imitators who built entire literary careers on emulating Irving and extending his legacy. For instance, John Pendleton Kennedy's *Swallow Barn* (1832), a portrait of a southern plantation, was widely recognized as a southern adaptation of Irving's *Bracebridge Hall*. Just as Irving's book described the sojourn of an American to an English major house, so Kennedy's version depicted a northerner's visit to a cousin's Virginia plantation. Like its prototype, *Swallow Barn* uses the sketch form to offer a full portrait of a large household, and it likewise uses a courtship plot to create a narrative through-line. As if to showcase its literary lineage, *Swallow Barn* contains numerous allusions to Irving, such as the bachelorhood of the novel's narrator, Mark Littleton, whose marital status evoked that of Irving himself, the era's most famed bachelor. The novel also included the character Rip Meriwether, who, like his namesake, is similarly unkempt and recalcitrant, as well as the indefatigable governess Barbara Winkle, who resembles Dame Van Winkle.

Theodore S. Fay, editor of the New York *Mirror*, was another known imitator whose *Dreams and Reveries of a Quiet Man* (1832) and *Crayon Sketches by an Amateur* (1833) included sketches that revisited topics made famous by Irving, such as English city streets, Christmas revelries (a subject that figured prominently in *Bracebridge Hall*), rural schoolmasters, and the Alhambra (the subject of Irving's 1832 book). Fay broadcast Irving's influence by dedicating *Crayon Sketches* to his famed forebear, his dedication acknowledging his influence on Fay's youth: "In early boyhood the charms of literature first broke upon me through the productions of your pen; gratitude, therefore, as well as respect and admiration, induces me to dedicate to you the following compositions of one who also warmly appreciates the treasures which you have added to the English language."[32] In describing Irving's work as "treasures," Fay suggested that Irving had achieved the status of a prized literary inheritance, passed from generation to generation, like the canonical writers Irving himself had imitated.

Donald Grant Mitchell, however, was the most successful imitator of both Irving and these predecessors, often following the example of the acolytes who came before him. For instance, like James Pendleton Kennedy, Mitchell devised his pseudonymous literary persona, Ik Marvel, as a bachelor and thereby presented himself as Irving's literary descendant. And like Longfellow's *Outre-Mer*, Mitchell's *Fresh Gleanings* (1847) was a travel memoir composed of sketches and folktales modeled on *The Sketch Book*, and its subtitle, *A New Sheaf from the Old Fields of Continental Europe*, presented Mitchell's book as the latest outgrowth of a venerable literary tradition. In emulation of both Longfellow and Irving, Mitchell began his memoir by asserting his fidelity to the traditions of the past: "For my own part, I like to see now and then such residuary customs of the Past . . . it freshens memories, and makes an agreeable coincidence, and puts the quickest possible edge upon a man's appetite for seeing and living over again the times that are gone."[33] Like Theodore Fay, Mitchell dedicated his book *Dream-Life* (1851) to Irving, whom he described as his "teacher," to whom he is "indebted" for his "facility in the use of language" as well as his "truthfulness of feeling."[34] In this way, Mitchell admitted that, in accord with the common educational uses of Irving's *Sketch Book*, his own style had been shaped by careful imitation of this literary antecedent. *Dream-Life* corroborates this assertion, for it contains innumerable allusions and homages to Irving: in one sketch, a boy's romantic daydream about matrimony constitutes a visible allusion to Irving's "The Wife," which describes a similar scenario. Mitchell's "The Country Church" likewise offers a revision of Irving's sketch of the same name. In another sketch, Mitchell describes the presence of *The Sketch Book* in a Harvard chamber, as if to remind his reader of the centrality of Irving's work in his own education. Irving responded warmly to Mitchell's homage, writing, "Could you witness the effect of the perusal of [*Dream-Life*] upon us all, you would feel satisfied of your success in touching the true chords. Be assured your little work will remain one of the household favorites of our literature, making its ways into every American home and securing a niche for its author in every American heart."[35] In this way, Irving suggested that Mitchell too had achieved canonical status, his imitation of Irving affording him entrance to American literary tradition. Following this exchange, the two men became close personal friends, and Irving, in his late life, effectively gave Mitchell his blessing and appointed him his literary successor.[36]

As Irving's letter suggests, Mitchell staked his own literary reputation on that of Irving's, and the declining literary fortunes of his idol precipitated Mitchell's own waning status. As a result, Mitchell emerged as one of Irving's chief defenders following Irving's death. At the 1883 celebration in honor of the centenary of Irving's birth, Mitchell acknowledged that Irving's unoriginality had elicited public criticism: he wrote, "I know there is a disposition to speak of [Irving's writing] rather patronizingly and apologetically – as if it were reminiscent . . . [and] conventional – as if he would have done better if he had possessed our modern critical bias."[37] This comment confirms that by 1883 unoriginality had already lost its status as a respectable literary mode and that realism had made significant inroads in shaping public literary taste. Mitchell conceded that "[f]ashions of books may change – do change: a studious realism may put in disorder the quaint dressing of his thought; an elegant philosophy of indifference may pluck out the bowels from his books" (47). However, Mitchell insisted that "the fashion of his heart and of his abiding good will toward men will last – will last while the hills last" (47). The sincere fidelity and affection that underlay this unoriginality, Mitchell avers, will enable Irving's works to endure, despite the passage of time.

Irving has retained his status as the bachelor father of American literature, though his followers have largely disappeared from literary memory. In 1881, Charles Dudley Warner reflected on Irving's waning status and concluded that the changes in print culture that initially framed Irving's literary conservationism would end up overtaking him: despite his efforts to protect and revitalize literary tradition, Irving could not outrun the "flood of new books" and the mounting taste for novelty and originality. As a result, "the standard works of approved literature remain for the most part unread upon the shelves," Irving's among them.[38] Abandoned by the reading public, the traditional canon would soon find a new home in the university, which would entirely invert the customary standards of literary appraisal. Where traditionalism had once conferred respectability and refinement, it now came to seem staid and devoid of creativity. Furthermore, the qualities that a century before had branded a text as sensationalist and cheap – such as unconventionality and novelty – would now become markers of artistic ambition and creative ability. Irving had gained entrance to the canon by imitating and invoking its works, but later writers would have to deviate from tradition and produce something new in order to achieve admission: only by diverging from tradition could writers hope to gain inclusion within it. Despite Irving's best efforts, a contested aesthetics of novelty has achieved absolute supremacy in American literary studies.

Notes

1 Harold Bloom, *The Western Canon: The Books and School of the Ages* (New York: Harcourt Brace, 1994), 3.
2 David D. Hall, *Cultures of Print: Essays in the History of the Book* (Amherst: University of Massachusetts Press, 1996), 87-88; William J. Gilmore, *Reading Becomes a Necessity of Life: Material and Cultural Life in Rural New England, 1780–1835* (Knoxville: University of Tennessee Press, 1989), 39–40.
3 Review published in New York *Independent*, November 20, 1851.
4 For a recent reappraisal of Melville's reception history, see Jordan Alexander Stein, "'Copyright, 1892, by Elizabeth S. Melville': Rethinking the Field Formation of Melville Studies," *Leviathan* 21 (March 2019): 97–119.
5 The commonplace book of Susan Storey Tappan, for instance, included the following suggestive passage from Milton's *Aeropagitica*, which confirms her belief in the importance of selecting quality reading material: "Books are not absolutely dead things, but do contain a progeny of life in them, to be as active as that soul was whose progeny they are; nay, they do preserve as in a vial, the purest efficacy and extraction of that living intellect that bred them. I know they are as lively and as vigorously productive as those fabulous dragon's teeth; and being sown up and down, may chance to spring up armed men." Susan Storey Tappan, Commonplace-book, 1841–1935, Massachusetts Historical Society, Ms. N-2337.
6 Lydia Maria Child, *The Mother's Book* (1831; reprint, New York: Arno, 1972), 95.
7 Mrs. L. H. Sigourney, *Letters to Mothers* (Hartford: Hudson and Skinner, 1838), 145, 43.
8 In 1920 George Santayana described New England letters in the first half of the century as the barren "harvest of leaves" that awaited the fructifying influence of more original writers such as Walt Whitman. George Santayana, "The Moral Background," in *The Genteel Tradition*, ed. Douglas L. Wilson (Cambridge, MA: Harvard University Press, 1967), 78.
9 For a fuller discussion of Emerson's interest in the present, see Jeffrey Insko, *History, Abolition, and the Ever-Present Now in Antebellum American Writing* (Oxford: Oxford University Press, 2019), 93–126.
10 John Mullan, *Anonymity: A Secret History of English Literature* (Princeton, NJ: Princeton University Press, 2007), 4–5.

11 Andrew Piper, *Dreaming in Books: The Making of the Bibliographic Imagination in the Romantic Age* (Chicago: University of Chicago Press, 2009), 54.

12 Andrew Burstein, *The Original Knickerbocker: The Life of Washington Irving* (New York: Perseus, 2007), 21.

13 Martin Roth, "Irving and the Old Style," *Early American Literature* 12 (Winter 1977/1978): 256.

14 Leonard Tennenhouse has commented on the importance of English models in the development of early American literature. See Leonard Tennenhouse, *The Importance of Feeling English: American Literature and the British Diaspora, 1750–1850* (Princeton, NJ: Princeton University Press, 2007).

15 Washington Irving, "Letters of Jonathan Oldstyle, Gent.," in *History, Tales and Sketches* (New York: Library of America, 1983), 7.

16 Irving, "A History of New York," in *History, Tales and Sketches*, 377.

17 Charles Dudley Warner, *Washington Irving* (Boston: Houghton, Mifflin, 1881), 74.

18 William Cullen Bryant, "Washington Irving," in *Prose Writings of William Cullen Bryant*, vol. 1 of 2, ed. Parke Godwin (New York: Russell & Russell, 1964), 343–44.

19 Stanley T. Williams, *The Life of Washington Irving*, vol. 1 of 2 (New York: Oxford University Press, 1935), 114–15.

20 Ibid., vol. 1, 115.

21 Burstein, *Original Knickerbocker*, 156.

22 William Hazlitt, *The Spirit of the Age; or, Contemporary Portraits* (London: Oxford University Press, 1960), 300.

23 Washington Irving, "The Sketch Book," in *History, Tales and Sketches*, 808.

24 Washington Irving, "Rip Van Winkle," in *History, Tales and Sketches*, 781. Michael Warner has examined the rhetoric of obsolescence that animates much of Irving's work. See Michael Warner, "Irving's Posterity," *ELH* 67 (2000): 773–99.

25 Washington Irving, *Bracebridge Hall, Tales of a Traveller, The Alhambra* (New York: Library of America, 1991), 7.

26 Van Wyck Brooks, *The World of Washington Irving* (n.p.: E. P. Dutton, 1944), 159; Williams, *Life of Washington Irving*, vol. 1, 191.

27 This argument revises Michael Warner's assertion that Irving's life and work illustrated the failures of paternity. See Michael Warner, "Irving's Posterity," *ELH* 67 (2000): 773–99.

28 Williams, *Life of Washington Irving*, vol. 1, 176–77; Burstein, *Original Knickerbocker*, 195–96.

29 Kent P. Ljungquist, "The 'Little War' and Longfellow's Dilemma: New Documents in the Plagiarism Controversy of 1845," *Resources for American Literary Study* 23.1 (1997): 45; Sidney P. Moss, *Poe's Literary Battles: The Critic in the Context of His Literary Milieu* (Durham, NC: Duke University Press, 1963), 27;

30 Quoted in Williams, *Life of Washington Irving*, vol. 2, 277; Samuel Longfellow, ed., *Life of Henry Wadsworth Longfellow with Extracts from His Journals and Correspondence*, vol. 1 of 2 (Boston: Ticknor, 1886), 171. This letter is dated May 15, 1828.

31 Henry Wadsworth Longfellow, "Outre-Mer," in *The Complete Prose Works of Henry Wadsworth Longfellow with His Later Poems* (Boston: Houghton, Mifflin, 1883), 1025.

32 Theodore S. Faye, *Crayon Sketches by an Amateur*, vol. 1 of 3 (New York: Conner and Cooke, 1833), iii.

33 Ik Marvel, *Fresh Gleanings; or, A New Sheaf from the Old Fields of Continental Europe* (New York: Harper & Brothers, 1847), 11.

34 Ik Marvel, *Dream-Life: A Fable of the Seasons* (Philadelphia: Henry Altemus, 1894), iii.

35 Quoted in Williams, *Washington Irving*, vol. 2, 207.

36 Burstein, *Original Knickerbocker*, 317.

37 Donald Grant Mitchell, "Address," in *Washington Irving: Commemoration of the One Hundredth Anniversary of His Birth by the Washington Irving Society* (New York: G. P. Putnam's Sons, 1884), 42.

38 C. D. Warner, *Washington Irving*, 8.

PART III

Authors and Figures

CHAPTER 17

Apess/Sedgwick

Ashley Reed

When the literary works of Catharine Maria Sedgwick were recovered in the 1970s and 1980s, she was heralded by feminist critics as a worthy but neglected contemporary of James Fenimore Cooper. Like Cooper, Sedgwick had taken inspiration from the historical romance genre for which Sir Walter Scott had become famous, shaping it to fit the unique materials that could be mined from the American past. Also, like Cooper, she had published prolifically during her lifetime and gained both critical accolades and international fame. Unlike Cooper, who emerged from the nineteenth century as a canonical figure (despite the ridicule heaped upon him by Mark Twain), Sedgwick had been relegated to the footnotes of literary history by early twentieth-century critics for whom the fact of her gender rendered her definitionally inferior to her male contemporaries.[1]

Among the literary historians and critics who recovered Sedgwick's work, attention quickly coalesced around her 1827 novel *Hope Leslie, or Early Times in the Massachusetts*. A sweeping tale set in the Massachusetts Bay Colony in the decades after the Pequot War, *Hope Leslie* wove insightful commentary about religious difference, social class, and national formation into a story rife with romance, intrigue, violence, and suspense. Perhaps *Hope Leslie*'s most striking contribution to the historical novel genre was the character of Magawisca, a brave, self-sacrificing, and rhetorically gifted member of the Pequot tribe, the original inhabitants of the land that would become New England. By placing a true narrative of the Pequot War in Magawisca's mouth – one in which white colonists were the aggressors, rather than the innocent victims, in a cowardly, one-sided attack – Sedgwick had countered some of the more demonizing and historically inaccurate portrayals of native peoples that circulated in the early nineteenth century.[2] And in contrast to Cooper's "inherently malevolent" Native American characters, such as Magua in *The Last of the Mohicans*, Sedgwick had portrayed the Pequots as canny historical actors for whom violence was a rational response to threats against their families and their sovereignty.[3]

What *Hope Leslie* did have in common with other historical novels of its time, however, was its fidelity to the myth of the vanishing Indian. At the close of the story, after Magawisca has been imprisoned by Puritan authorities and freed by her white friends, those friends beg her to stay in the colony. "'It cannot be – it cannot be,'" she mourns, "'the Indian and the white man can no more mingle, and become one, than day and night.'" Magawisca and the last of her people, including her father, the Pequot chief Mononotto, make "their pilgrimage to the far western forests" and disappear into "the deep, voiceless obscurity of those unknown regions."[4] For most of Sedgwick's contemporary readers, Magawisca's declaration was axiomatic: the Indian and the white man were irrevocably separated by time, distance, and history, and the native tribes that had once flourished in New England – the Wampanoags, Narragansetts, Mohegans, and Pequots, among others – were little more than a memory.[5]

And yet in 1829, two years after *Hope Leslie* depicted Magawisca and the last of the Pequots disappearing forever from colonial New England, the Pequot author and minister William Apess began insistently publishing records of his own and other New England native peoples' lives. In the 1830s, when Apess pursued his public career, the Pequot tribe had not only not disappeared from New England but maintained an official claim to two reservations in the state of Connecticut. One was in North Stonington and the other in Ledyard, but small communities of Pequots also lived in proximity to the reservations and throughout New England.[6] Apess himself was born in Colrain, Massachusetts, and after growing up in poverty, first with his Pequot grandparents and then as a foster child or indentured servant to white families, he converted to Methodism, became an exhorter and then a licensed preacher, and entered on a career as a writer. He produced the first published autobiography by a native American, spiritual narratives by his fellow converts, a sermon, and political and historical writings that exposed white narratives of native "disappearance" as the dangerous fallacies they were.

Unlike his white contemporaries, who relegated native peoples to the past or regarded them as remnants of dying cultures, Apess gave the story of native North Americans "a contemporary resonance, connecting the past treatment of Indians to present policy and calling for change."[7] He engaged in a written and spoken form of what the Anishinaabe scholar and artist Gerald Vizenor has termed "survivance." Rather than mourning or preemptively memorializing an ostensibly lost or dying culture, narratives of survivance entail "an active sense of presence, the continuance of native stories, not a mere reaction. Native survivance stories are renunciations of dominance, tragedy and victimry."[8] Arnold Krupat has called Apess a "storier of survivance" because his writings highlight "the ongoing agency and activity of the native[,] ... insist on Indian presence rather than absence; and ... rewrite tragic narratives in the ironic mode."[9] Apess's writing consistently recognized, embraced, and proclaimed not only his own worth as a native man but the persistence and sovereignty of native New England communities both past and present.

Reading Catharine Maria Sedgwick and William Apess together reorients our understanding not only of literary production in the early nineteenth century but of American history itself. Expanding the canon of early national historical fiction to include Sedgwick (as well as her contemporaries Lydia Maria Child, Harriet Vaughan Cheney, Lydia Sigourney, Eliza Buckminster Lee, and others) offered a female perspective on colonial and revolutionary events.[10] But that perspective was still dominated by a settler-colonial ideology that required that the violent displacement of native peoples be imaginatively repackaged as an unfortunate but inevitable byproduct of Euro-American progress.[11] Reading Apess alongside Sedgwick highlights the rhetorical violence embedded in white historical fiction – even in those texts most sympathetic to the native's plight. Apess's refusal to capitulate to narratives of "disappearance" or "degradation" exposes how white-authored historical fiction by both men and women conspired in the processes of displacement and erasure that threatened the indigenous peoples of North America.

Sedgwick and Apess as New England Authors

Speaking strictly in geographical terms, Catharine Maria Sedgwick and William Apess grew up on the edges of civilized society, at least by the standards of late eighteenth-century New England. Stockbridge, Massachusetts, where Sedgwick was born in the winter of 1789, was located in the far western reaches of the newly formed state, and while it boasted its own set of rigid social hierarchies, it remained, at least in the minds of urbane coastal dwellers, a barely tamed frontier.[12] Apess was born nine years later in Colrain, in northwest Massachusetts, a farming community founded in the eighteenth century by Scots-Irish emigrants but with a significant population of Native and African Americans.[13] Beyond geography, however, their situations could not have been more different.

Catharine's father Theodore Sedgwick had settled in Stockbridge to pursue a career as a lawyer and had improved his social status when he married Pamela Dwight, whose family could be traced to the earliest English settlers. By the time Catharine, the sixth of seven children, was born in the winter of 1789, Theodore had held positions in the Massachusetts legislature and as a representative to the Continental Congress; during her childhood and adolescence he served in the US House of Representatives (including two years as Speaker), in the US Senate, and on the Supreme Judicial Court of Massachusetts. While Catharine would remember her Stockbridge childhood as often idyllic – largely because of her loving relationship with her siblings and with Elizabeth Freeman, an African American servant and "second mother" to the Sedgwick children – she would later revolt against the rigid and, she believed, hypocritical religion of its Congregationalist inhabitants. Sedgwick's first novel, A New-England Tale, was published in 1822, and it alienated her Stockbridge neighbors with its attack on Calvinist theology. But it also established her reputation as a new literary voice at a time when the young nation was striving to distinguish itself, both culturally and politically, from the mother country. Sedgwick's second novel, Redwood, published in 1824, told the story of two southern travelers, the religious skeptic Mr. Redwood and his self-absorbed daughter Caroline, who are thrown on the mercies of an earthy Vermont family after a carriage accident. The domestic plot sutured sectional divisions by uniting the southern Redwood and northern Lenox families, while also recommending a pluralistic approach to religious concerns.

Though A New-England Tale and Redwood had brought Sedgwick into the public eye, it was her third novel, Hope Leslie, or Early Times in the Massachusetts, that elevated her to the first rank of American authors, and she produced two more novels in the decade after its publication. Clarence (1830) was a contemporary novel of manners detailing the ups and downs of the titular family. Set among the fashionable circles of New York, the novel offered a critique of that city's nouveau riche: their social machinations, their aspirations to aristocracy, and their sudden reversals of fortune. Five years later she published The Linwoods, or Sixty Years since in America (1835), another homage to Scott (the "sixty years since" of the title is a direct nod to Waverley), this one set during the Revolutionary War. Like Hope Leslie – and unlike Cooper's historical novels – The Linwoods made (white) women's self-determination a central concern of the American story.[14] After it appeared, Sedgwick did not publish another novel for two decades, when she produced Married or Single? (1857). The titular question had been a personal one to her: she never married or established an independent household, choosing instead to divide her time between her brothers' homes in Lenox, Massachusetts, and New York City while pursuing her career and devoting her attention to a bevy of beloved nieces and nephews. In addition to her novels, she produced over ninety short stories, sketches, travel narratives, and "didactic novellas," and she continued publishing well into the final years of her life.[15]

From the beginning to the end of her career, Sedgwick consistently drew on her experiences of New England life to bring texture and specificity to her writing. But her own family origins included a history of native displacement that her published works only obliquely addressed. Sedgwick's hometown of Stockbridge had been founded in the 1730s as a missionary outpost explicitly tasked with Christianizing and civilizing the Housatonic Indians. While a mission school was established there by white donors and populated by both Mahicans and members of the Six Nations tribes, the white families who settled Stockbridge to serve as exemplars to the natives grew increasingly greedy. Led by the Williams family, who were among Catharine Sedgwick's relatives on her mother's side, they eventually appropriated all of the land intended for the natives. The "Stockbridge Indians," unable to secure redress or an end to white encroachment, finally relocated to New York to live among the Oneida. The last of the town's native population left in 1788, a year before Catharine was born. The home she grew up in was built on land that Theodore Sedgwick had purchased during "the final land grab" that definitively dispossessed the Stockbridge Indians.[16]

William Apess's life as a New England Native American was marked by patterns – pity and disdain, patronage and abuse – that repeated in microcosm the treatment of the Stockbridge Indians. Born to impoverished parents, including a mother who claimed to be descended from King Philip and a father of mixed white and native ancestry who had joined himself to the Pequot tribe, Apess was first raised by his maternal grandparents, then taken from them when they proved abusive. His first foster family, the Furmans, regarded him with suspicion because of his race; when a white servant girl falsely accused Apess of threatening her with a knife, Mr. Furman called him an "Indian dog" and beat him.[17] When Furman decided to sell William's indenture, he selected Judge William Hillhouse, who had served in the Continental Congress with Theodore Sedgwick in 1786 and 1788; Hillhouse would later transfer his indenture to another well-heeled white family, the Williamses. Apess received some schooling during these years, but in later accounts of his early life he remembered most vividly his encounters with traveling missionaries – particularly those from the newly ascendant Methodist sect – and the ridicule heaped upon them by his white masters.

After a decade of being shuffled from place to place without his consent or consultation, Apess fled from servitude and found himself in New York, where he enlisted (illegally, since he was underage) in the War of 1812. After being discharged without the salary, land, or bounty promised to those who had fought, he spent a few years performing odd jobs before rejoining his Pequot relatives in Groton, Connecticut, where he attended Methodist services led by his aunt Sally George. He soon began speaking in public as a traveling exhorter, then sought a preaching license from the Methodist Episcopal Church. When it became clear that anti-native prejudice, rather than lack of talent or fervor, was preventing him from obtaining his license, Apess joined the Methodist Society, a less hierarchical and more racially diverse denomination, and received his preaching license in 1829, the same year he issued his autobiography, *A Son of the Forest*.

Like Sedgwick, then, Apess entered on his writing career with religious motives. But whereas Sedgwick used fiction to espouse genteel religious sentiments built on the intellectualized model of Boston Unitarianism, Apess wrote nonfiction that combined a fiery evangelicalism with explicitly political aims. In 1831 he reissued *A Son of the Forest* and published his only extant sermon, *The Increase of the Kingdom of Christ*. Two years later he offered to the public *The Experiences of Five Christian Indians of the Pequot Tribe*, a collection of conversion narratives written or dictated by his family members and acquaintances, including his wife Mary and his aunt Sally George. Between 1833 and 1835, Apess embraced the cause of the Mashpee Indians, descendants of the Wampanoag tribe who sought to defend their small reservation from white dispossession; after being libeled in the white press as a rabble-rouser and even a revolutionary, Apess published a true and thorough account of the Mashpees' situation titled *Indian Nullification of the Unconstitutional Laws of Massachusetts Relative to the Marshpee Tribe; or, The Pretended Riot Explained* (1835). In 1836 Apess issued the printed text of a lecture he had delivered at least twice, his *Eulogy on King Philip*, which extolled the Wampanoag chief Metacomet as a hero who like "the immortal Washington lives endeared and engraven on the hearts" of his "grateful descendants," the native peoples of North America.[18] It was his final published work; Apess died in 1839 in a boarding-house in New York.

Contesting the "Vanishing Indian"

As New England authors of the early nineteenth century, Apess and Sedgwick participated in the flurry of national mythologization that characterized their era, but their racial and political investments were diametrically opposed. Sedgwick, born into a privileged political, social, and religious elite, frequently mined the history of colonial North America for tales of heroism and struggle that could be incorporated into the nation's new self-image. While these stories often depicted New England's original inhabitants as noble or self-sacrificing, they also located native existence firmly in the past. Apess, the living example of native survivance in the New England of the nineteenth century, built his short but significant career on a persistent refusal to accede to white ideologies that positioned his people as perpetually vanishing. His vocation as a native speaker and writer (and as a Christian minister) consisted in the physical and textual embodiment of native presence, the exposure of white crimes, and the representation of native peoples as moral and spiritual agents with ongoing and active investments in the political and social life of North America.

Though much of Sedgwick's published writing included Native American characters or drew on native legends, it skirted the material details of displacement and dispossession – processes her own family had perpetuated – and invoked instead the prevailing ideologies of the early nineteenth century. Most famously, *Hope Leslie*, by introducing Magawisca as a possible romantic pairing for the white protagonist Everell Fletcher before ushering her offstage at novel's end, offered a supersessionist history in which the dawning of Anglo-American civilization followed, inevitably, the setting of the native sun.[19] But many of Sedgwick's shorter historical works likewise reified the ideology of the vanishing Indian by depicting once-thriving native communities that were in the process of succumbing to ostensibly inevitable decline. Her tale "The Catholic Iroquois" (1826) tells the story of an eighteenth-century Jesuit priest, Pere Mesnard, and his adopted native daughters, then traces the destruction of this created family as one sister becomes a nun while the other is martyred in an Iroquois attack. "Amy Cranstoun" (1836) features a Puritan maiden of Providence, Rhode Island, who is captured during King Philip's War by the Pokanoket warrior Annawan and his nephew Mantunno. Mantunno falls in love with Amy and sacrifices his life to save her from an attack by his jealous cousin; her rescue by her white lover precipitates the capture of Annawan by Captain Benjamin Church and the English victory in the war.

Despite the fact that native communities persisted in New England throughout Sedgwick's lifetime – a fact to which William Apess's career attests – her works with contemporary settings portrayed native characters only as remnants: solitary, degraded figures whose stubborn presence served to reinforce white ideas about native inferiority. *Redwood* features a lone native man, Sooduck, who is corrupted by drink and conspires in the kidnapping and captivity of a white woman. Though Sooduck maintains native knowledge and practice as a skilled medicine man, Sedgwick's narrator characterizes him as one of those "individuals of the aboriginal race who ... remain among us [as] monuments of past ages."[20] The 1832 story "Berkeley Jail" tells of a "full-blooded Indian," a Seneca man named Sam Whistler, who embodies all of the contradictions of white ideology surrounding Native Americans. He wears a "half savage costume" and lives in a hut that attracts "all those outlaws and vagrants that hang on the skirts of a civilized society." And yet he retains characteristics of the noble savage, including "a feeling of innate and indestructible superiority" and "revelations of a noble origin and high destiny."[21] When Sam vanishes at the end of "Berkeley Jail," he seems to fulfill the "high destiny" of his people by removing himself from the white settlements of Berkeley County. Perhaps Sedgwick's most ideologically revealing depiction of indigenous Americans occurs in a short section of *The Travellers* (1825) in which the white Sackville family spends a few hours on the Oneida reservation in New York. Though *The Travellers* takes place in 1818, Mr. Sackville, upon viewing the spectacle of native families happily weaving baskets, tending their gardens, and playing at jack-straws, opines, "'One might almost fancy here ... that the march of time had been stayed, and the land spell-bound, by some mighty magician.'"[22] Steeped in the "well-worn trope that the race of Native Americans, if they belonged anywhere, belonged to the past,"[23] Sedgwick's Mr. Sackville can only respond to clear evidence of native communal persistence by imaginatively relocating native peoples outside or beyond time.

Across the length of his short career, William Apess's writing defied all of these ideological tropes that sought to render native New Englanders and other indigenous Americans invisible, inferior, and disposable. In narrating his own spiritual development and that of his fellow Pequots, Apess presented native North Americans as active moral agents rather than silent objects of white charity. In publishing the true narrative of the Mashpee tribe's complaints against the Massachusetts government, he championed native sovereignty and the right to occupy ancestral lands. In extolling King Philip as the equal – or the superior – of America's white Founding Fathers, he reinserted native New Englanders into a history from which they were being both physically and rhetorically erased. Neither the Pequots nor the other remaining northeastern tribes, Apess's work vehemently and repeatedly insisted, either had or would disappear.

The first published autobiography by a Native American, Apess's *A Son of the Forest* follows the conventions of the early American spiritual autobiography²⁴ while simultaneously linking all of the occurrences of his life to his identity as a "Native."²⁵ Apess begins his self-narration in *A Son of the Forest* with an account of white injustice against the Pequots – a theme to which the autobiography returns again and again. Apess blames his abusive grandparents' alcoholism on whites who "introduced among my countrymen that bane of comfort and happiness, ardent spirits" and who "committed violence of the most revolting kind" – that is, sexual violence – "upon the persons of the female portion of the tribe."²⁶ He notes the lack of consent involved in his many indentures and finds it particularly galling "to be sold to and treated unkindly by those who had got our fathers' lands for nothing."²⁷ He describes the racist bullying practiced on him by his fellow soldiers, who threatened to "stick my skin full of pine splinters, and after having an Indian powwow over me, burn me to death."²⁸ As Drew Lopenzina has noted in his discussion of *A Son of the Forest*, Apess offered his story of "childhood indentures, warfare, and spiritual and economic struggle" because it was "also the story of thousands of other Natives being written out of the historical and geographical landscapes of nineteenth-century New England."²⁹ In *A Son of the Forest* and the texts that followed, Apess sought to write native North Americans – including himself – into history as vibrant participants rather than silenced victims.

Each of Apess's published works evidenced his complex identification as Pequot, as American, and as Christian – identities that were not "closed, fixed, distinct or even perpetually in competition with one another but instead [were] mutually sustaining, interactive, and dialectic."³⁰ Apess's 1831 publication *The Increase of the Kingdom of Christ* offered theological assertions about the trinity and substitutionary atonement – subjects common to white preachers' sermons as well – but also condemned white Christians for persecuting their native brethren who, Apess believed, were descendants of the lost tribes of Israel.³¹ Similarly, each of the conversion narratives in *The Experiences of Five Christian Indians* both follows the established patterns of that genre and reflects on the hypocrisy of whites who falsely claim to love all Christian brethren equally. Mary Apess, William's wife, relates how she was ridiculed by her white employers for heeding the call of a traveling missionary. Hannah Caleb confesses that she felt an early conviction of sin but resisted conversion because of white Christians' racism: "They openly professed to love one another," and yet "the poor Indians . . . were set at nought by those noble professors of grace, merely because we were Indians."[32] And Anne Wampy, whose testimony Apess transcribed in broken English, relates that she had been overcome with God's grace even though "Me no like Christians, me hate 'em, hate everybody."[33] For each of these native converts, conviction of grace required not only the full acceptance of Christ's sacrifice on the cross but the rejection of white Christian example.

The Experiences was accompanied in print by a short essay, "An Indian's Looking-Glass for the White Man," which, as its title suggests, held up a mirror to white missionary efforts among native peoples. The "Looking-Glass" drove home the *Experiences'* point that native converts were not only the equals but the superiors of white Christians and that white Christian racism was hindering Christian evangelism to people of color (and thus delaying the coming millennium). Addressing corruption, sexism, and prejudice among white missionaries, the "Looking-Glass" also exposed and decried white brutality. Apess imagined a convention of all of earth's "skins" where "each skin had its national crimes written upon it" and asked, "[W]hich skin do you think would have the greatest?"[34] Exhibit A in this cavalcade of crimes, Apess went on to assert, was the enslavement of Africans.[35]

Given Apess's repeated condemnation of white Christian crimes against native peoples, contemporary scholars have debated the significance of his career as a Methodist preacher – his choice, as a native person, to adopt the religion of the colonizer. While some critics have read Apess's conversion to Christianity as a rejection of his Pequot identity,[36] Mark Rifkin has argued that the Methodist religion practiced by Apess and led by his aunt Sally George was inextricable from his identity as Pequot and from his attachment to the Mashantucket Pequot reservation.[37] In the context of the Second Great Awakening, Apess's particular attachment to the growing Methodist sect – and his scorn for more settled denominations like the Presbyterians – represented a repudiation of class and race hierarchies among white Christians, since the Methodists were known (and denigrated by upper-class whites) for welcoming women, the poor, and people of color. And as Rochelle Rainieri Zuck and Shelby Johnson have discussed, Apess's embrace of the "Ten Lost Tribes" theory "allow[ed] Apess to present a vision of a unified Indian 'past' so as to combat Anglo-American attempts to divide Indian peoples from one another."[38] Though the destructive role played by Christianity in European colonization is undeniable, Apess's identification as Methodist cannot be disentangled from his personal development, his professional vocation, and his complex identity as a member of the Pequot tribe.[39]

Apess's writing was always simultaneously pious and political, but his work took an even more radical turn when he published *Indian Nullification of the Unconstitutional Laws of Massachusetts Relative to the Marshpee Tribe; or, The Pretended Riot Explained*. The "pretended riot" of the title was an incident in which Apess had asked the Mashpees' white neighbors to stop stealing timber from their reservation; for this offense they had him bound over to the Court of Common Pleas. While it is sometimes difficult to determine in the collaboratively authored *Indian Nullification* which voice belongs to Apess, the themes that had come to animate all of his writing – native persistence and dignity, native Christians' claim to equal treatment by their white brethren, and the honest elaboration of white crimes – remain clearly visible throughout the text. The *Eulogy on King Philip* offers a similarly radical reading of native interaction with whites, this time in the context of King Philip's War. Though dedicated to Philip, the *Eulogy* begins with a detailed account of early relations between native North Americans and white colonizers in colonial New England; as he presents each vignette, Apess carefully shows how white settlers robbed, attacked, and provoked the natives they encountered, so that every story of native "vengeance" or "savagery" – including the war itself – can be traced to white abuses. As always in his writing, Apess decries the hypocrisy of white Christians: these "pretended pious," he asserts, have been "the foundation of all the slavery and degradation in the colonies toward colored people."[40] Though the *Eulogy* ends with a plea for reciprocity and equal rights, the text's thundering condemnation of white crimes – from the earliest years of contact to the present – leaves little hope for reconciliation.[41]

The last of Apess's published works, the *Eulogy* explicitly addresses the pernicious and persistent myth of the vanishing Indian that had begun with the Puritan settlers and that undergirded so much of Sedgwick's writing and that of her white contemporaries. In the *Eulogy* Apess asserts that "there is a deep-rooted popular opinion in the hearts of many that Indians were made, etc., on purpose for destruction, to be driven out by white Christians, and they to take their places; and that God had decreed it from all eternity."[42] Apess's entire career, from *A Son of the Forest* to the

Eulogy, undermined this ideology and embodied Pequot survivance. He was the living, speaking, and writing representative of a people that, though abused, scattered, and despised, had persisted in the face of white social, economic, ideological, and military efforts to erase their existence.

The recovery of Sedgwick and other women writers of historical fiction marked a crucial step in the reformation of American literary studies at the end of the twentieth century. Expanding the early national canon beyond the works of James Fenimore Cooper, Washington Irving, and William Cullen Bryant brought into view female perspectives on religion, history, national expansion, and a host of other subjects. But those perspectives remained stubbornly Eurocentric. If women writers often presented more even-handed portrayals of Indian–white relations than did their male contemporaries, their writing nevertheless perpetuated ideologies of vanishing and decline that consigned Native Americans to a mythical past. Those ideologies were not merely inaccurate but dangerous, facilitating the removal of Native American tribes from the American South and excusing crimes against the remaining native communities in New England and the Northeast.

Such abuses continue: as recently as September 2018, statements by the US Department of the Interior brought into question the tribal status of the Mashpee Wampanoags – the same tribe Apess defended in his *Indian Nullification*. These statements threatened (and continue to threaten) the sovereignty and survival of the tribe.[43] Studying William Apess's writing alongside that of his white contemporaries rather than as a footnote to them throws into sharp relief the cultural strategies of settler colonialism as they operated in the early nineteenth century and as they continue to operate today. But it also offers evidence of native resistance and survival that can illuminate and guide our scholarship, our teaching, and our action in the world.

Notes

1 See Patricia Larson Kalayjian, "Cooper and Sedgwick: Rivalry or Respect," *James Fenimore Cooper Society Miscellaney* 4 (1993): 9–19.

2 For a history of the Pequot Massacre, see Alfred A. Cave, *The Pequot War* (Amherst: University of Massachusetts Press, 1996). For a discussion of the Massacre as Sedgwick employs it in *Hope Leslie*, see Philip Gould, "Catharine Sedgwick's 'Recital' of the Pequot War," *American Literature* 66, no. 4 (1994): 641–62. For an enumeration of the historical sources Sedgwick drew from in writing *Hope Leslie*, see R. D. Madison, "Sedgwick's Memorials: *Hope Leslie*

and Colonial Historiography," *Literature in the Early American Republic* 4 (2012): 1–9.

3 Sandra Zagarell, "Expanding 'America': Lydia Sigourney's *Sketch of Connecticut*, Catharine Sedgwick's *Hope Leslie*," *Tulsa Studies in Women's Literature* 6, no. 2 (1987): 234.

4 Catharine Maria Sedgwick, *Hope Leslie; or Early Times in the Massachusetts* (London: Penguin Books, 1998), 349, 359.

5 On the myth of the vanishing Indian, see Philip J. Deloria, *Playing Indian* (New Haven, CT: Yale University Press, 1998); Brian Dippie, *The Vanishing American: White Attitudes and U.S. Indian Policy* (Middletown, CT: Wesleyan University Press, 1972); Richard Slotkin, *Regeneration through Violence: The Mythology of the American Frontier, 1600–1860* (Midletown, CT: Wesleyan University Press, 1973); and, more recently, Roxanne Dunbar-Ortiz and Dina Gilio-Whitaker, *"All the Real Indians Died Off" and 20 Other Myths about Native Americans* (Boston: Beacon Press, 2016).

6 Native peoples can be difficult to trace in the documentary record of New England because many lived in poverty and official records often list them as "colored" or even "negro." For information on the Pequot tribe, see Laurence M. Hauptman and James D. Wherry, eds., *The Pequots in Southern New England: The Fall and Rise of an American Indian Nation* (Norman: University of Oklahoma Press, 1990), and Daniel R. Mandell, *Tribe, Race, History: Native Americans in Southern New England, 1780–1880* (Baltimore: Johns Hopkins University Press, 2010).

7 Barry O'Connell, ed., *On Our Own Ground: The Complete Writings of William Apess, a Pequot* (Amherst: University of Massachusetts Press, 1992), 276.

8 Gerald Vizenor, *Manifest Manners: Narratives on Postindian Survivance* (Lincoln: University of Nebraska Press, 1999), vii.

9 Arnold Krupat, "William Apess: Storier of Survivance," in *Survivance: Narratives of Native Presence*, ed. Gerald Vizenor (Lincoln: University of Nebraska Press, 2008), 103.

10 For discussion of Sedgwick among other women writers of history (fictional and factual), see Nina Baym, *American Women Writers and the Work of History, 1790–1860* (New Brunswick, NJ: Rutgers University Press, 1995).

11 See Anna Johnston and Alan Lawson, "Settler Colonies," in *A Companion to Postcolonial Studies*, ed. Henry Schwarz and Sangeeta Ray (Malden, MA: Blackwell Publishing, 2005), 360–67.

12 Biographical information about Sedgwick and her family can be found in Edward Halsey Foster, *Catharine Maria Sedgwick* (New York: Twayne Publishers, 1974); Jane Giles, "Catharine Maria Sedgwick: An American Literary Biography" (PhD diss., City University of New York, 1995); and Timothy Kenslea, *The Sedgwicks in Love: Courtship, Engagement and Marriage in the Early Republic* (Boston: University Press of New England, 2005). See also *The Power of Her Sympathy: The Autobiography and Journal of Catharine*

Maria Sedgwick, ed. Mary Kelley (Boston: Massachusetts Historical Society, 1993).

13 For biographical information on Apess, see Philip F. Gura, *The Life of William Apess, Pequot* (Chapel Hill: University of North Carolina Press, 2015); Drew Lopenzina, *Through an Indian's Looking-Glass: A Cultural Biography of William Apess, Pequot* (Amherst: University of Massachusetts Press, 2017); and O'Connell, *On Our Own Ground*.

14 See Nina Baym, "The Women of Cooper's Leatherstocking Tales," *American Quarterly* 23, no. 5 (1971): 696–709.

15 For a detailed list of Sedgwick's publications, see "Chronological Bibliography of the Works of Catharine Maria Sedgwick," in *Catharine Maria Sedgwick: Critical Perspectives*, ed. Victoria Clements and Lucinda L. Damon-Bach (Boston: Northeastern University Press, 2003), 295–314, or the bibliography on the website of the Catharine Maria Sedgwick Society, https://cmsedgwicksociety.org/sedgwick-bibliography/. For a discussion of the full range of Sedgwick's cultural production over the course of her lifetime, see Melissa Homestead, "The Shape of Catharine Sedgwick's Career," in *The Cambridge History of American Women's Literature*, edited by Dale M. Bauer (Cambridge: Cambridge University Press, 2012), 185–203.

16 Karen Woods Weierman, "Reading and Writing *Hope Leslie*: Catharine Maria Sedgwick's Indian 'Connections,'" *The New England Quarterly* 75, no. 3 (2002): 415–43. For further discussion of the Stockbridge Indian mission, see Patrick Frazier *The Mohicans of Stockbridge* (Lincoln: University of Nebraska Press 1992); and James Axtell, "The Rise and Fall of the Stockbridge Indian Schools," *Massachusetts Review* (Summer 1986): 367–78.

17 William Apess, *A Son of the Forest*, in O'Connell, *On Our Own Ground*, 12.

18 William Apess, *Eulogy on King Philip*, in O'Connell, *On Our Own Ground*, 277. In the *Eulogy* Apess refers to Philip as "king of the Pequot tribe of Indians," and critics are unsure whether this misidentification of Philip, who was leader of the Wampanoags, was erroneous or strategic. See Roumania Velikova, "'Philip, King of the Pequots': The History of an Error," *Early American Literature* 37, no. 2 (2002): 311–35.

19 On native "vanishing" in *Hope Leslie*, see Judith Fetterley, "'My Sister! My Sister!': The Rhetoric of Catharine Sedgwick's *Hope Leslie*," *American Literature* 70, no. 3 (1998): 491–516; Dana Luciano, "Voicing Removal: Mourning (as) History in *Hope Leslie*," *Western Humanities Review* 58, no. 2 (2004): 48–67; and Maureen Tuthill, "Land and the Narrative Site in Sedgwick's *Hope Leslie*," *ATQ: 19th Century American Literature and Culture* 19, no. 2 (2005): 95–114.

20 Catharine Maria Sedgwick, *Redwood: A Tale*, vol. 2 (New York: Garrett Press, 1969), 74.

21 Catharine Maria Sedgwick, "Berkeley Jail," in *Atlantic Souvenir* (Philadelphia, 1832), 25, 26.

22 Catharine Maria Sedgwick, *The Travellers: A Tale, Designed for Young People* (New York: E. Bliss and E. White, 1825), 32.

23 Lopenzina, *Through an Indian's Looking-Glass*, 3.

24 On the conventions of the spiritual autobiography in early America, see Patricia Caldwell, *The Puritan Conversion Narrative: The Beginnings of American Expression* (New York: Cambridge University Press, 1983); Susan Juster, "'In a Different Voice': Male and Female Narratives of Religious Conversion in Post-Revolutionary America," *American Quarterly* 41 (1989): 34–62; and Virginia Lieson Brereton, *From Sin to Salvation: Stories of Women's Conversions, 1800 to the Present* (Bloomington: Indiana University Press, 1991), 3–13.

25 Apess preferred this term to "Indian." See Apess, *A Son of the Forest*, in O'Connell, *On Our Own Ground*, 10. On the differences between the first and second editions of *A Son*, see O'Connell, *On Our Own Ground*, 314–24, and Gura, *Life of William Apess*, 44–51.

26 Apess, *A Son*, 7.

27 Ibid., 16.

28 Ibid., 27.

29 Lopenzina, *Through an Indian's Looking-Glass*, 2.

30 Carolyn Haynes, "'A Mark for Them All to ... Hiss At': The Formation of Methodist and Pequot Identity in the Conversion Narrative of William Apess," *Early American Literature* 31, no. 1 (1996): 25–60.

31 This theory was widespread in the early nineteenth century; Sedgwick mentions it, without endorsement, in "Amy Cranstoun." Apess discussed the Lost Tribes theory in both an essay he published with *The Increase* and an appendix that accompanied *A Son of the Forest*. The latter account, though largely borrowed from Elias Boudinot's *A Star in the West* (1816), contains some of Apess's most scathing critique of white bigotry and dishonesty.

32 William Apess, *The Experiences of Five Christian Indians of the Pequot Tribe*, in O'Connell, *On Our Own Ground*, 145.

33 Ibid., 152.

34 Ibid., 157.

35 Philip Gura describes Apess's time in Boston's Beacon Hill neighborhood, the mixed-race community that fostered the activist work of David Walker, Maria Stewart, and others. See Gura, *Life of William Apess*, 54–71.

36 See, for instance, Arnold Krupat, who finds in *A Son of the Forest* evidence of Apess's desire "to be the licensed speaker of a dominant voice that desires no supplementation by other voices" – to be the "mouthpiece of the Lord." Krupat, *The Voice in the Margin: Native American Literature and the Canon* (Berkeley: University of California Press, 1989), 148.

37 Mark Rifkin, "Shadows of Mashantucket: William Apess and the Representation of Pequot Place," *American Literature* 84, no. 4 (2012): 691–714.

38 Rochelle Raineri Zuck, "William Apess, the 'Lost Tribes,' and Indigenous Survivance," *Studies in American Indian Literatures* 25, no. 1 (2013): 3; Shelby Johnson, "Histories Made Flesh: William Apess's Juridical Theologies," *MELUS: Multi-Ethnic Literatures of the U.S.* 42, no. 3 (2017): 6–25.

39 For more scholarly discussion of Apess's Methodism, see Joshua David Bellin, *The Demon of the Continent: Indians and the Shaping of American Literature* (Philadelphia: University of Pennsylvania Press, 2012), 88–97; Laura E. Donaldson, "Making a Joyful Noise: William Apess and the Search for Postcolonial Method(ism)," *Interventions: International Journal of Postcolonial Studies* 7, no. 2 (2005): 180–98; Haynes, "'A Mark'"; and Harry Brown, "Tribal Christianity: The Second Great Awakening and William Apess's Backwoods Methodism," in *Mapping Region in Early American Writing*, ed. Edward Watts, Keri Holy, and John Funchion (Athens: University of Georgia Press, 2015), 181–98.

40 William Apess, *Eulogy on King Philip*, in O'Connell, *On Our Own Ground*, 304.

41 See Patricia Bizzell, "(Native) American Jeremiad: The 'Mixedblood' Rhetoric of William Apess," in *American Indian Rhetorics of Survivance: Word Medicine, Word Magic*, edited by Ernest Stromberg (Pittsburgh: University of Pittsburgh Press, 2006), 34–49.

42 Apess, *Eulogy on King Philip*, 287.

43 See https://mashpeewampanoagtribe-nsn.gov/standwithmashpee.

CHAPTER 18

Child/Thoreau

Susan M. Ryan

Though they were near-contemporaries (Child was some fifteen years older) and coresidents of Massachusetts for most of their lives, with a number of friends and acquaintances in common, Lydia Maria Child and Henry David Thoreau rarely appear in the same scholarly and pedagogical conversations. We tend to frame Child as a sentimentalist and Thoreau as a Transcendentalist; Child as a long-neglected, now-"recovered" writer, as opposed to Thoreau's longer presence in the canon as, among other accolades, one of F. O. Matthiessen's "big five" (i.e., the figures he treated in depth in his landmark 1941 study *American Renaissance*).[1] The distinctions persist in how we characterize their writerly modes – Child is most often analyzed as a writer of fiction, though her editorial, polemical, and didactic work garners attention as well. Thoreau, meanwhile, is known as an essayist and memoirist whose work combines meticulous observation and sardonic humor. We analyze Child alongside other novelists (e.g., James Fenimore Cooper, Catharine Maria Sedgwick, and Harriet Beecher Stowe), abolitionists (e.g., Theodore Weld, David Walker, Stowe again), and domestic writers (e.g., Catharine Beecher), while Thoreau is typically paired with Emerson and his circle and, more recently, with authors of various eras interested in natural science and ecology.

The differences between the two figures extend beyond literary-historical categorization, of course. Thoreau's work evidences far more engagement with the natural world than does Child's, while she is more intrigued by urban spaces than he is – and especially by the hierarchies and injustices that their configurations foreground.[2] Child's work is considerably more invested than Thoreau's in the lives of women and children, and in the complex roles that affect plays in both narrative and activism. She also worked in a wider range of genres, wrote more overall – in part because she lived much longer – and sold more books than did Thoreau (within their lifetimes, that is). While Thoreau is by far the more famous figure in the early twenty-first century, Child was almost certainly better known in the mid-nineteenth century.

I want to suggest, however, that Child and Thoreau had more in common than these distinctions admit of. In terms of their personal lives, neither enjoyed much in the way of economic security, much less wealth. Both taught school early in their careers. Both were childless and approached romantic partnership in unconventional ways – that is, Thoreau avoided it altogether, while Child remained married to her difficult, improvident husband, but lived apart from him much of the time and took steps to keep her earnings out of his control, despite the persistence of legal structures that presumed his authority in that arena.[3] Both took issue with their era's social reform organizations – Thoreau generally eschewed membership in formal groups, whether by temperament or on principle, while Child participated in the American Anti-Slavery Society for years and edited its newspaper, *The National Anti-Slavery Standard*, in the early 1840s, but grew frustrated over time with the movement's fractiousness. In their writing, both were advice-givers, with a shared interest in the merits of thrift; more broadly, they engaged in forms of social protest, advocating especially forcefully for the abolition of slavery in ways that risked backlash – Child, by publishing an early and quite graphic antislavery polemic (*An Appeal in Favor of That Class of Americans Called Africans* [1833]), and Thoreau, by endorsing John Brown's raid on Harpers Ferry in 1859.

In this essay, I invite readers to look past these authors' divergent styles and paths to literary canonization in order to consider the degree to which two key preoccupations animated their respective work: first, what constitutes a good life and how might people of limited or moderate means achieve it within a volatile and unforgiving US economy; and second, how might individuals conceive of and act upon their responsibilities to suffering others, especially enslaved Americans, and what should one's disposition be toward injustice more generally? These are in some sense interlocking concerns, insofar as both address the matter of debt (what do we owe to others, whether creditors, friends, or strangers, and under what circumstances should we incur or throw off such obligations?) and both require individuals to examine and (re)calibrate their interpersonal commitments. Thinking through Child's and Thoreau's ways of navigating such questions allows us to discern a number of intriguing alignments between these apparently dissimilar authors – and to plumb some of their more illuminating points of departure.

Frugal Homes

Lydia Maria Child's domestic advice book *The Frugal Housewife* (retitled *The American Frugal Housewife* from 1832 onward, to distinguish it from an English work of the same name) first appeared in the fall of 1829, just over a year into her marriage and accompanying launch into the titular role. The book, which went through thirty-five editions by 1870 (according to Child's biographer Carolyn Karcher), brought the author at least $2,000 in its first two years. *The Frugal Housewife* offers recipes, cleaning tips, and food-storage methods, all the while advising wives and mothers on how to run their households and feed their families as cheaply as possible. Recommended strategies include buying in bulk, guarding against waste of all kinds, and cooking and sewing at home rather than purchasing ready-made items from merchants. Housewives, Child writes, should purchase vinegar by the barrel rather than the gallon, as it's cheaper in large quantities; cheese, meanwhile, can be kept "free from insects for years" if wrapped "carefully with paper, fastened on with flour paste," and stored "in a dry, cool place."[4] Further, items that appear to be spoiled or without purpose can be restored to utility: "pulverized alum," she notes, can be used to purify water; used "vials and bottles" should be saved and sold to "apothecaries and grocers"; and sour beer "may be used to advantage for pancakes and fritters" (14, 16). While some of the advice seems downright bizarre ("ear-wax," Child insists, makes for an effective and ever-available analgesic ointment and lip balm [116]), elsewhere the text offers entirely creditable tips – silk does wash better in "almost cold" water, as Child tells us, and shouldn't be subjected to the use of a hot iron (14). Among the book's most detailed segments are those that deal with the preparation of meats. In addition to charts identifying the various cuts of mutton, pork, veal, and beef, Child offers specific instruction with regard to salting and smoking meats, selecting the most economical segments (in which regard "a fore-quarter of mutton" is a better option "than a hind-quarter" [46]), and making soup or shortening from the bones.

As these passages make clear, Child's imagined housewife is neither physically delicate nor squeamish. She is tasked with roasting whole pigs, cutting and packaging portions of meat and hauling them down into cool cellars, and cleaning and boiling the heads of livestock, all with an eye to expedient methods: when boiling a calf's head, Child helpfully notes, "It is better to leave the wind-pipe on, for if it hangs out of the pot while the head is cooking, all the froth will escape through it" (47–48).

This perspective was not universally applauded. As Karcher has shown, some reviewers criticized the book's downscale diction and candor with regard to the indelicate aspects of domestic labor, not to mention its sustained – one might say relentless – attention to money. Nathaniel Parker Willis, whom Child knew personally, was especially harsh, remarking on the book's "thorough-going, unhesitating, cordial freedom from taste."[5] These complaints notwithstanding, the fact that *The American Frugal Housewife* sold so many copies and went through so many editions suggests that a wide swath of the reading public appreciated its offerings. Surely, these buyers were not engaging with the book primarily in order to snicker – as Willis apparently did – at its infelicities. Further, Child's preoccupation with thrift mirrors the fact that she desperately needed the earnings that the book's robust sales brought her. In that sense, *Housewife* evinces a satisfying alignment between the circumstances and goals of the author and those of her implied audience, with the result that its tone, though occasionally judgmental and often demanding, generally avoids condescension. Instead, its advice registers most often as a communication among peers.

While we don't typically think of Thoreau's *Walden* as an advice manual (or, in a more contemporary lexicon, as "self-help"), many of its passages recall and enact that very mode. Much as Child dedicates her book to "those who are not ashamed of economy," Thoreau writes that he does "not speak to those who are well employed . . . but mainly to the mass of men who are discontented, and idly complaining of the hardness of their lot or of the times, when they might improve them."[6] The last part of that sentence is crucial – Thoreau premises his book on the notion that "improvement" is within reach; as he puts the matter early on, he asks readers "about your condition, especially your outward condition or circumstances in this world, in this town, what it is, whether it is necessary that it be as bad as it is, whether it cannot be improved as well as not" (4). What would it mean, in other words, to cease "doing penance in a thousand remarkable ways" (4)? While these extracts sound considerably more spiritual than Child's directions on brining pork, Thoreau interleaves among his first-person narration and abstractions a good deal of practical advice on saving money. *Walden*'s opening chapter is titled, fittingly enough, "Economy," which at the time meant both frugality and the general management of resources. In it, Thoreau writes that "strict business habits . . . are indispensable to every man" (20). In keeping with that maxim, he relates (at a level of detail comparable to that of Child's spot-removal directions) how, precisely, he built his cabin: "I hewed the main timbers six inches square, most of the studs on two sides only, and the rafters and floor timbers on one side, leaving the rest of the bark on" (42). He goes so far as to enumerate his own "pecuniary outgoes" and his income from "day-labor" and the sale of produce, in part to satisfy the curiosity of his neighbors, a project that the book's second paragraph asserts as its reason for being, but also to provide a model of thrift and careful accounting. It is clear, meanwhile, that this is not simply one man's experiment: in one of the book's many slippages from personal narrative to direct address, he enjoins his readers to "consider first how slight a shelter is absolutely necessary" (28), thus implying that most people build homes that are larger, more expensive, and more difficult to maintain than what they truly need.

Here *Walden* aligns with *The American Frugal Housewife*'s admonitions against buying expensive furnishings and housewares, when other, more pressing needs might then go unmet. Indeed, commonalities between the two texts abound. Thoreau writes at length on the merits of old, worn, and homemade clothing, noting that "a winter cap" can be purchased "for sixty-two and a half cents, or a better be made at home at a nominal cost" (24) and advising readers to "beware of all enterprises that require new clothes, and not a new wearer of clothes" (23). Child, meanwhile, instructs readers on how to extend the life of clothing through proper modes of cleaning, storage, and repair, and warns that, through frivolous travel, clothes "are worn out and defaced twenty times as quick as they would have been at home" (100). As these excerpts suggest, Thoreau and Child share a settled disdain for extravagance of all kinds. Child, for example, notes that "no prudent housekeeper will make [French coffee], unless she has boarders, who are willing to pay for expensive cooking" (though she goes on to explain how to make an excellent pot of it) and remarks that "those who love to be invalids" should "drink strong green tea, eat pickles, preserves, and rich pastry," as those foods, in her view, bring on ill health (83, 88). Coffee figures among Thoreau's targets as well: in his conversation with the "honest, hard-working, but shiftless" Irishman John Field (204), Thoreau points out that he himself "did not use tea, nor coffee, nor butter, nor milk, nor fresh meat, and so did not have to work to get them ... but as [Field] began with tea, and coffee, and butter, and milk, and beef, he had to work hard to pay for them, and when he had worked hard he had to eat hard again to repair the waste of his system" (205). On some level both authors recur to the matter of health in grounding their disapproval, though for Child it's the rich food itself that makes "invalids," whereas for Thoreau, the trouble inheres in the physical labor required to procure such fare.

My point in offering these comparisons is not that *Walden*, long
venerated as a kind of countercultural scripture, is instead utterly conventional – a domestic advice manual merely leavened by its author's affinity
for the outdoors. Thoreau's book certainly comprises some mainstream
passages, reminiscent not just of Child's more popular guide but also of
Benjamin Franklin's paeans to thrift and no doubt scores of other advisory
texts.[7] But in drawing attention to these features, I wish to suggest that
frugality itself, despite its prosaic reputation, admitted of some markedly
unconventional elements. Child's text, for example, popular at a juncture
when female delicacy was emerging as a much-touted, if class-bound,
cultural value, reminds readers that women are – or should be – physically
strong, unfazed by blood and guts (of livestock or of afflicted family
members), and fully cognizant of household finances. The developing
capitalist economy – both brutal and unpredictable, in her rendering –
does not allow for wilting flowers, at least among the non-elite. What is
unusual about *Walden*, meanwhile, is its assertion that frugality matters
insofar as it liberates time – time to do things other than worry over money
or work to accumulate more of it.

Child and Thoreau agree, then, that frugality is a great virtue, but they
define its value in strikingly different ways. Child represents thrift (and its
partner, industriousness) as an abstract good, in keeping with the long-
standing New England tradition in which she was raised, but she also
frames it as a bulwark against future hardship – her book is replete with
admonitions to "lay up" butter, to put aside a portion of one's earnings
even when all seems secure, and to make at home even those items that can
be purchased cheaply (like stockings). *The American Frugal Housewife*, that
is, posits a domestic economy ever on the brink of ruin, warning that
whatever hardships or constraints the current moment might present, the
future will almost certainly be worse. While the book's advice presumes
that its addressees have stable housing – including abundant storage space
for those bulk purchases – potential losses (of income, of property, of
security) are ever lurking at the margins, as this young author (just twenty-
seven when the book was published) writes in the voice of a time-worn,
seen-and-survived-it-all matriarch. Her youth notwithstanding, Child's
sense of financial gloom is entirely warranted. The economic struggles that
the book identifies and foretells have already presented themselves in
Child's personal circumstances, as her husband, David Lee Child, was
deeply in debt (and would spend six months of the following year incar-
cerated for a libel conviction). More broadly, the "hard times" that the text
references would grow far worse in the years after its initial publication in

1829, culminating in the Panic of 1837 and the long economic downturn that ensued.[8]

Thoreau, who completed his studies at Harvard in 1837, was almost twenty-eight in 1845 when he moved into his cabin at Walden Pond – approximately the same age as Child when she penned *The Frugal Housewife*. But instead of warning readers to "lay up" against some possible or impending crisis, *Walden* suggests that we are all living in the aftermath of economic disaster. The neighbors to whom the narrator so often refers are egregiously in debt, not only through their mortgaged farms (their inheritance of which Thoreau calls a "misfortune" [5]) but through their failure to imagine a life other than the one they are living ("they honestly think," he writes, that "there is no choice left" [8]). "The mass of men," Thoreau declares in a line that has become famous, "lead lives of quiet desperation" (8) – "mean and sneaking" lives (6) that leave the "finer fruits" out of reach (6). The crisis isn't looming, as Child would have it; instead, it's ambient, pervasive – and probably permanent. How, then, do we devise a life we might find worth living under these circumstances? And what would such a life look like?

Thoreau's response, though today trivialized by its use in myriad graduation cards and motivational posters, remains resonant for many: he urges readers to consume less in order to work less; to use that liberated or reclaimed time in order to think, read, write, observe, and converse; and to take on only those responsibilities that are consonant with a sustainable balance between labor and (productive) leisure. In one of his most often-cited sentences – "I went to the woods because I wished to live deliberately" (90) – we see the starkness of this program. Individuals must choose between life and not-life, rejecting as they do so the received wisdom, social expectations, competition, and comparisons that lock them into ultimately unsatisfying patterns. Child would agree wholeheartedly with much of that program – especially with Thoreau's admonitions against allowing "a love of novelty" or "a regard for the opinions of men" to override considerations of "utility" (21) – but she conceives of time very differently. Child opens her "Introductory Chapter" with the assertion that "the true economy of housekeeping is simply the art of gathering up all the fragments, so that nothing is lost. I mean fragments of time, as well as materials" (3). In the following paragraph she repeats the aphorism "Time is money" and asserts throughout the book that the two are inextricably linked to household management (3). That is, she urges her readers to spend time in order to save money, not, as Thoreau would have it, to figure out how to need less money in order to free up time. And yet, Child herself carved out time for writing (sometimes producing work that was likely to sell, but often not), for activism, and for interpersonal engagement. In other words, despite her book's insistence that all activity recur to a prudent industriousness, the author herself was no domestic automaton.

Another crucial difference between the two texts is the gendering of their implied audiences. Child is quite explicitly writing to women – wives and mothers living in crowded households, where they occupy productive, managerial, and caretaking roles. Accordingly, the book pays attention not just to the particulars of cooking, sewing, and cleaning but also to the care and feeding of husbands and children and to their appropriate management. While Child works to accommodate both urban and rural households (with a lean toward the latter), her emphasis is on families, each with a prodigiously hard-working woman at its center, who is tasked with raising the next generation of daughters to do their frugal best.[9] Thoreau, meanwhile, is writing to men – discontented men, men who feel cheated or left behind by economic forces beyond their control, young men, "poor students" (4). And he foregrounds a household of one that, while not entirely solitary – the text recounts any number of visitors and walks into town – is certainly not communal. In Thoreau's version of what is now often termed "nesting," a minimalist masculinity prevails, entailing a simultaneous investment in and disavowal of home comforts. He takes pride, for example, in his "tight light and clean house," where he lives "so sturdily and Spartan-like," yet appreciates the coziness of being confined indoors during "long rain storms," when, well sheltered, he is "soothed by their ceaseless roar and pelting" (205, 91, 132).

For all Thoreau's attention to his domicile in *Walden*, though, it's fair to say that Child took up the question of home across a broader range of texts. Her early novel *Hobomok* (1824), for example, moves among a range of domestic settings: the protagonist, Mary Conant, leaves her overbearing father's repressive home for a domestic life in the woods with the Indigenous hero after whom the book is named, but then she re-Anglicizes at the end, returning to the English settlement, mixed-race son in tow, in order to marry and form a household with her first love, Charles Brown (who has not, as she had believed, died at sea). Throughout, Mary defines and locates her homes in light of her affective relationships with men – an orientation on which *The American Frugal Housewife* premises its domestic arrangements but then largely ignores. Nearly twenty years later, in the short story "Slavery's Pleasant Homes" (1843), Child combined sentimental and lurid tropes in order to anatomize American slavery's destruction of domestic values. When George

Dalcho, an enslaved man of mixed racial ancestry, kills his half-brother/ master in order to avenge the rape and murder of his pregnant wife, it's clear that slavery has corrupted siblinghood, marriage (the dead man has betrayed his white wife as well), and reproduction, such that the titular "pleasant homes" are unmasked as nightmarish reversals of proper domesticity. Child's enslaved characters, meanwhile, lack access to the home spaces assumed in her advice book, the ever-improvable sites of industry and restraint that won her so many readers.

Social Justice

Thoreau's 1849 essay "Resistance to Civil Government," in which he recounts and meditates on a brief sojourn in the town jail for refusing to pay his "poll-tax," is widely regarded as one of the most influential American texts on social responsibility, with such distinguished admirers as Mohandas K. Gandhi and Martin Luther King, Jr.[10] And yet the essay still engenders unease some 170 years after its initial publication. The crux of Thoreau's argument is his assertion that "It is not a man's duty, as a matter of course, to devote himself to the eradication of any, even the most enormous, wrong; he may still properly have other concerns to engage him; but it is his duty, at least, to wash his hands of it, and, if he gives it no thought longer, not to give it practically his support."[11] The notion that we are not obligated to intervene in even the "most enormous" injustice seems underwhelming, even wrong-headed – and yet when we consider what it would actually mean to withdraw our practical support from all forms of injustice (including via our purchases, tax remittances, and institutional affiliations), the charge seems impossibly daunting. Thoreau, in other words, asks too little and too much of us at once.

In *Letters from New-York* (1843), Child addresses a rather different set of contradictions. After describing at length a "ragged, emaciated woman" – a recent immigrant, Child surmises, who is experiencing wretched poverty and whose circumstances contrast with the luxury items on display in a shop window behind her – Child imagines addressing her directly: "Pence I will give thee, though political economy reprove the deed. They can but appease the hunger of the body; they cannot soothe the hunger of thy heart; that I obey the kindly impulse may make the world none the better – perchance some iota the worse; yet I must needs follow it – I cannot otherwise."[12] Child interrogates her own responses along two axes: first, what good will a few pennies do when this woman's despair runs so deep, encompassing spiritual and emotional as well as material deprivations? And second, in light of the era's abundant warnings against giving alms to apparently suffering strangers lest they turn out to be frauds or advantage-takers, might her donation make matters worse by encouraging or reward-ing idleness? But these questions ultimately yield to compulsion – Child's textual avatar "must ... follow" her "kindly impulse." In this piece Child emphasizes a moment of connection with a specific individual (though the two can communicate only nonverbally due to a language barrier) and expresses a keen interest in how the encounter will affect the other woman and the broader society – will a small donation ease her suffering at all? Will it make "the world ... some iota the worse"? Thoreau, meanwhile, trains his attention in "Resistance" on a kind of principled withdrawal, a process of disembedding oneself from a nexus of moral outrages – in this case, by withholding tax money from a government that was then pursuing an expansionist war with Mexico that many saw as a ploy to extend US slavery westward. He thus offers a version of social activism that requires self-sacrifice but not the vexed engagement that Child dramatizes (and second-guesses).

Thoreau's and Child's divergent modes are intriguingly on display in their expressions of support for the militant abolitionist John Brown, whose raid on the arsenal at Harpers Ferry in October 1859 resulted in his capture and eventual execution. Thoreau's "A Plea for Captain John Brown," first delivered as a speech in Concord, Massachusetts, on October 30, 1859 (three days before Brown was hanged), offers a curious mix of admiration for the prisoner and affective distance from his impending death – an ambivalence foreshadowed in his opening address to his auditors, in which he says, "I trust that you will pardon me for being here. I do not wish to force my thoughts upon you, but I feel forced myself."[13] The speech goes on to recount details of Brown's history and mode of living (with attention, unsurprisingly, to his "Spartan habits"), to rail against northern media coverage of Brown's raid ("as if an ordinary malefactor ... had been caught"), and to compare Brown to divine beings, including Christ ("Some eighteen hundred years ago Christ was crucified; this morning perchance, Captain Brown was hung") and "an Angel of Light." But Thoreau also insists on the necessity – even the desirability – of Brown's death: "I *almost fear*," he writes, "that I may yet hear of his deliverance, doubting if a prolonged life, if any life, can do as much good as his death." Thoreau's speech is angry and triumphal by turns, lambast-ing the nation's failure to recognize Brown's righteousness and foretelling a time when his heroism will be lauded – but his tone is decidedly *not* sorrowful.

If Thoreau resisted the impulse to lament or identify with or attempt to ameliorate Brown's suffering, Child took the opposite tack. On October 26, just four days before Thoreau delivered his speech, she wrote to Governor Wise of Virginia, articulating her desire to visit the wounded Brown in prison: "He needs a mother or sister to dress his wounds and speak soothingly to him," she averred. "Will you allow me to perform that mission of humanity?" Enclosed was a letter to Brown himself, in which Child wrote: "In brief, I love you and bless you" and "I long to nurse you – to speak to you sisterly words of sympathy and consolation."[14] These two letters initiated a multiparty correspondence that fascinated Child's contemporaries across the political spectrum. Most immediately relevant was the response from Brown himself, who asked Child not to visit him: "I cannot see how your coming here can do me the least good," he wrote, "and I am quite certain you can do immense good where you are"; instead of traveling to Virginia, Brown asked Child to raise funds on behalf of his (soon-to-be) widow and other family and friends in New York.[15] Child's initial letter expresses a wish to remake the jail cell as a domestic space, a move that recalls her long-standing preoccupation with homes, and to install herself as Brown's loving family member – though she is careful throughout to express her support for the man and his cause without endorsing his specific methods.

In responding to Brown's circumstances, then, Child emphasizes connection (interpersonal, familial, emotional, tactile), albeit without complete ideological alignment, while Thoreau offers a fuller endorsement of Brown's actions, but does so through distanced contemplation and abstraction. But the starkness of this divergence misleads as much as it illuminates, at least with regard to Child. That is, Child's strategies varied over time and from text to text (Thoreau's reformist rhetoric, meanwhile, hewed to a narrower tonal range), such that the moments I've explored here should not be taken to represent her entire approach to social justice and persuasion.[16] Her 1833 *Appeal* – a watershed not only in her developing boldness as a reformer but in terms of abolitionist print culture generally – provides an apt counterweight to her more personalistic and atomized interventions. Though she begins her preface in a deferential mode, "beseech[ing]" readers "not to throw down this volume as soon as you have glanced at the title," the book's overall tone is more assertive than supplicating.[17] Child's historical overview, for example, of the transatlantic slave trade and of American slaveholding emphasizes violence over sentimental attachment, relating specific means by which enslaved people were controlled, tortured, and killed. Further, her account of slavery's effects on the master class attends to hypocrisy, corruption, and sexual exploitation of enslaved women; and her comparative discussion of slavery over time and across geographical distance foregrounds the laws operating in various states and territories. Throughout, Child bombards the reader with evidence, including drawings that depict shackles and torture devices; quotations from noted authorities; transcriptions of various statutes; demographic data; and illustrative anecdotes. Her own persona reemerges at the end, when she writes that "the expectation of displeasing all classes has not been unaccompanied with pain. But it has been strongly impressed upon my mind that it was a duty to fulfil this task [i.e., of writing the book]."[18] But elsewhere in the *Appeal* that identifiable authorial self is largely submerged, as Child offers instead a forceful but rather impersonal style of argumentation, with any number of passages that sound more like Thoreau in "A Plea" or "Slavery in Massachusetts" (1854) than like the struggling alms-giver depicted in *Letters from New-York*. For instance, in calling out North Carolina's "law subjecting any vessel with *free* colored persons on board to thirty days' quarantine," Child ridicules state law-makers for implying that "freedom were as bad as the cholera" (68–69) – a move that anticipates not just Thoreau's mordant tone but also Frederick Douglass's 1849 piece "Colorphobia in New York," whose titular conceit likens racial prejudice to a communicable disease.

Recent scholarly work on Child reinforces this more capacious take on her reformist modes, strategies, and topics. A 2017 *Legacy* forum devoted to Child, for example, addresses such disparate matters as her treatment of the environment; the complications of citizenship, gender, and labor; and the implications of her work for such contemporary American crises as mass incarceration and anti-immigrant sentiment.[19] Thoreau's social justice writings, for their part, continue to draw astute analyses, including a recent recuperation of the political utility of disobedience within democracy (via *Walden* and "Resistance to Civil Government"), and any number of studies that address Thoreau's antislavery rhetoric or that use his principles of observation and restraint to analyze the twenty-first-century's environmental catastrophes.[20] Both figures are now classed among American literature's most important voices in matters of justice, inequality, and sustainability.

In looking at a few specific moments in these authors' bodies of work, I have suggested that easy distinctions between the two do not hold up well under scrutiny. Admittedly, some texts – or at least some passages within particular texts – allow us to associate Child with sentiment and Thoreau with sarcasm; Child with commercial savvy and Thoreau with a willful (or principled) disregard for what might sell; Child with accessibility and Thoreau with difficult wordplay. And yet a closer examination reveals intriguing complications: Child's *Appeal* deploys irony and an avalanche of historical detail to bring attention to slavery's daily cruelties, while paying scant attention to matters of sentiment. And though she used her understanding of the book market to profitable effect in many instances – discerning and producing texts that would sell – she also wrote out of principle on many occasions, with a clear understanding that doing so would hurt her bottom line. Thoreau, meanwhile, avoids sentimental strategies as the field has come to define them, but at a number of junctures he evinces a keen interest in affect more broadly conceived: *Walden*'s meditations on the self-inflicted miseries of conventional economic life, for example, form a master class in understated desperation, while the anger that animates his antislavery writings erupts palpably amid his more reserved rhetorical moves. Both Child and Thoreau, in other words, produced multivalent bodies of work that require sustained critical attention. Reading them together allows us to consider their recurring tropes and strategies against the grain of the usual taxonomies.

The usefulness of pairing Child and Thoreau extends beyond these insights into their individual bodies of work, however. Their writings, especially when considered in tandem, seem remarkably and perhaps newly salient in the wake of the Great Recession of 2008 (our 1837, it seems) and within a cultural and political present rife with environmental disasters and a renewed fractiousness over such matters as immigration, citizenship, and social responsibility. The resurgent debate over reparations for the descendants of enslaved Americans, for example, could only be enriched by a return to Child's and Thoreau's writings on abolition. A generation coming of age in a time of increasing economic inequality and insecurity, meanwhile, could do worse than to consider these authors' insights into debt and financial anxiety more generally. While their specific domestic advice is dated at best, their broader dispositions toward earning and owing seem eerily prescient. Child and Thoreau wrote within and about their own (shared) historical moment, to be sure, but many of their assertions and meditations speak to our own times with an eloquence and urgency that invite close attention.

Notes

1 Although Child knew several of the figures central to American Transcendentalism (including Margaret Fuller and Ralph Waldo Emerson), her work is only occasionally analyzed within a Transcendentalist frame. See, for example, Jane Duran, "Lydia Maria Child: Abolitionism and the New England Spirit," *The Pluralist* 10.3 (2015): 261–73, and Jeffrey Steele,

"Sentimental Transcendentalism and Political Affect: Child and Fuller in New York," in *Toward a Female Genealogy of Transcendentalism*, ed. Jana L. Argersinger and Phyllis Cole (Athens: University of Georgia Press, 2014), 207–26.

2 Child's *Letters from New-York* (First Series, 1843; Second Series, 1845) are illuminating in this regard.

3 On Child's financial arrangements vis-à-vis David Lee Child, see Carolyn Karcher, *The First Woman in the Republic: A Cultural Biography of Lydia Maria Child* (Durham, NC: Duke University Press, 1994), 293–94.

4 Lydia Maria Child, *The American Frugal Housewife, Dedicated to Those Who Are Not Ashamed of Economy*, 16th ed. (Boston: Carter, Hendee, 1835), 14. Subsequent citations are from this edition, with page numbers noted parenthetically in the text.

5 Qtd. in Karcher, *First Woman*, 134. On the book's overall reception, see 133–36. As Gillian Brown has shown, American domestic advice would take an upmarket turn in Catharine Beecher's popular *Treatise on Domestic Economy*, first published in 1841. Instead of Child's "frugal" home, Beecher urges women to "sustain a prosperous domestic state"; as Brown notes, Beecher's (and her acolytes') "encomiums to the virtues of womanhood and home simultaneously sublimated and denied anxieties about unfamiliar and precarious socioeconomic conditions" (*Domestic Individualism: Imagining Self in Nineteenth-Century America* [Berkeley: University of California Press, 1990], 3).

6 Henry David Thoreau, *Walden*, ed. J. Lyndon Shanley (Princeton, NJ: Princeton University Press, 1971), 16. Subsequent citations are from this edition, with page numbers noted parenthetically in the text.

7 Child's title page includes an epigraph from Benjamin Franklin: "A fat kitchen maketh a lean will."

8 Child writes (before the Panic of 1837): "Perhaps there never was a time when the depressing effects of stagnation in business were so universally felt, all the world over, as they are now" (*American Frugal Housewife*, 108); she goes on to deplore the sartorial extravagance she sees around her, which persists in spite of economic risks. Are those well-dressed women, she wonders, oblivious to the fact that "the stunning effect of crash after crash, may eventually be felt by those on whom they depend for support?" (108).

9 On raising industrious daughters, see Child's "Hints to Persons of Moderate Fortune," which was first published in the *Massachusetts Journal* and then incorporated into editions of *The Frugal Housewife* from 1830 onward.

10 The essay first appeared in *Aesthetic Papers*, ed. Elizabeth Peabody (Boston: The Editor, 1849), 189–211.

11 Henry David Thoreau, "Resistance to Civil Government," in *The Norton Anthology of American Literature*, 9th ed., vol. B, ed. Robert S. Levine (New York: Norton, 2017), 957.

12 Lydia Maria Child, *Letters from New-York*, ed. Bruce Mills (Athens: University of Georgia Press, 1998), 61.

13 Henry David Thoreau, *A Plea for Captain John Brown*, Project Gutenberg digital edition (www.gutenberg.org/files/2567/2567-h/2567-h.htm), accessed June 10, 2019, unpaginated.

14 *Correspondence between Lydia Maria Child and Gov. Wise and Mrs. Mason, of Virginia* (Boston: American Anti-Slavery Society, 1860), 3, 4.

15 Ibid., 16. These letters and Child's spirited counter-responses appeared in a range of newspapers and were eventually released as a freestanding publication, priced at 5 cents, which reportedly sold some 300,000 copies. Though that figure is difficult to verify, if accurate, it far exceeds the sales of Child's other writings during her lifetime. The tract was still being advertised in the *Liberator* in late March of 1861, some fifteen months after the original letters were sent.

16 On Child's use of sympathy and sentiment, see Laura L. Mielke, "Sentiment and Space in Lydia Maria Child's Native American Writings, 1824–1870," *Legacy* 21.2 (2004): 172–92, and Travis M. Foster, "Grotesque Sympathy: Lydia Maria Child, White Reform, and the Embodiment of Urban Space," *ESQ: A Journal of the American Renaissance* 56.1 (2010): 1–32.

17 Lydia Maria Child, *An Appeal in Favor of That Class of Americans Called Africans* (Boston: Allen and Ticknor, 1833), n.p.

18 Ibid., 232.

19 *Legacy* 34.1 (2017): 4–32. Forum contributors include Sarah Olivier, Carolyn Karcher, Karen Kilcup, Hildegard Hoeller, Bruce Mills, Robert Fanuzzi, and Dana D. Nelson.

20 Sandra Laugier and Daniela Ginsburg, "Disobedience as Resistance to Intellectual Conformity," *Critical Inquiry* 45.2 (2019): 420–33; on Thoreau and slavery, see Deak Nabers, "Thoreau's Natural Constitution," *American Literary History* 19.4 (2007): 824–48, and Sandra Harbert Petrulionis, "Slavery and Abolition," in *Henry David Thoreau in Context*, ed. James S. Finley (Cambridge: Cambridge University Press, 2017), 185–95; on Thoreau and the environment, see Sarah Dimick, "Disordered Environmental Time: Phenology, Climate Change, and Seasonal Form in the Work of Henry David Thoreau and Aldo Leopold," *ISLE: Interdisciplinary Studies in Literature and Environment* 25.4 (2018): 700–721; Wai Chee Dimock, "The Global Turn: Thoreau and the Sixth Extinction," in *The Cambridge Companion to Literature and Science*, ed. Steven Meyer (Cambridge: Cambridge University Press, 2018), 195–206; and Jason Gladstone, "Low-Tech Thoreau; or, Remediations of the Human in *The Dispersion of Seeds*," *Criticism* 57.3 (2015): 349–76.

CHAPTER 19

Douglass/Walker

Marcy J. Dinius

Slavery, politics, and time have conspired to estrange David Walker and Frederick Douglass. Consequently, it has gone unnoticed – even in David W. Blight's magisterial 2018 biography of Douglass – that Walker's *Appeal to the Coloured Citizens of the World* most likely occasioned Douglass's early lessons in literacy being cut short by his master Hugh Auld in Baltimore in 1830.[1] Douglass probably didn't recognize this himself, either at the time or subsequently when writing his life story, in that he heard only the reasons that Auld gave his wife for halting her religiously minded instruction and, from them, inferred the larger lessons about literacy, subjectivity, and power that he acted on and wrote about subsequently. In Douglass's recollections of the episode in his autobiographies, Auld makes no reference to Walker's *Appeal* having reached Baltimore and occasioned the very alarm about enslaved people reading, becoming discontent, and resisting their masters that he voices to his wife. Only in time did Douglass come to recognize the broad political and historical significance of Walker's *Appeal*, as we begin to see in his reprinting of a biographical sketch of Walker in the July 14, 1848, *North Star* and ultimately in his describing the *Appeal* in 1883 as "startl[ing] the land like a trump of coming judgment" and Walker as "before either Mr. [William Lloyd Garrison] or Mr. [Benjamin] Lundy."[2]

That scholars have not made this important connection between Walker and Douglass in his early life either – as part of the significant attention that Douglass's 1845 and 1855 autobiographies have received since the expansion of the American literary canon, or in recently renewed attention to the complexities of antislavery, Douglass's biography, and African American print – suggests that many gaps in knowledge and understanding remain in these vibrant fields, even in its most thoroughly analyzed texts. Attending to the influence of Walker's *Appeal* on Douglass's life and political activism offers an important opportunity to bring some of the

318

most insightful new scholarship in African American history, literature, and print cultural studies to bear on both Douglass's and Walker's works. Particularly relevant are arguments that decenter the so-called slave narrative in African American literary histories that seek to broaden and deepen our understanding of black print in the nineteenth century, that find in this expanded archive examples of engaged citizenship in theory and practice, and that theorize the inevitabilities of loss and recovery in African American archives and other forms of cultural memory and lived experience.[3]

Specifically, to recognize that Walker's *Appeal* played a significant role in Douglass's relationship to literacy is to recover an important case study of the dual effects of Walker's pamphlet and its radical messages on the lives of enslaved people. We have long known that discoveries of the *Appeal* circulating in the South prompted some of the most restrictive legislation on black mobility and literacy, with many states legally punishing whites for teaching enslaved people to read and write and prohibiting both free and enslaved black people from moving in places and ways that could access, circulate, and activate so-called incendiary print.[4] And scholars frequently have speculated that Nat Turner may have read Walker's *Appeal* and been inspired by Walker's message to lead fellow enslaved people in violently resisting their masters in 1831 in an area where Walker is known to have circulated his pamphlet.[5] Yet actual records of how individual enslaved people's lives were directly affected by either Walker's message or the restrictions and violence that the *Appeal* and responses to it occasioned are quite rare. Douglass's autobiographies offer just such a record, hiding in plain sight in some of the best-known and most frequently taught texts in all of nineteenth-century American literature.

More broadly, revisiting Walker in the decade of Douglass's rise to prominence as an activist and author will add to our increasingly nuanced histories of the politics and print of antislavery activism – especially black antislavery – by focusing on how the politicization of print was a major issue in the movement at the time. While Walker recognized and exploited print as a powerful weapon against racism and slavery and did his utmost to activate it in the hands of enslaved people in 1829 and 1830, black activists in the 1840s – including Douglass – were more conflicted about the relationship between print and violence. Freedom of the press and questions about who would run it, what it would print, and its potential effects divided leaders and delegates at the National Colored Conventions of the 1840s. I focus on this debate because it became personal for Douglass and Henry Highland Garnet – Walker's most direct successor as a vehement defender of enslaved people's right to violent resistance – as they were vying for leadership of both the black antislavery movement and its press, examining how it culminated in Garnet's 1848 republication of Walker's *Appeal* along with his controversial "Address to the Slaves." By bringing Walker's *Appeal* back into print with his "Address" in a year of worldwide revolution, Garnet renewed Walker's message of violent resistance not just for a new generation, but also in dramatically different national and international political circumstances that had significantly changed conversations about slavery, freedom, and revolution since Walker's time.

With respect to Douglass, I consider how Garnet's vehement and persuasive arguments at the conventions for enslaved people's resistance by any means necessary and his edition of Walker's *Appeal* contributed significantly to Douglass's move away from moral suasion and his break with Garrison and his adherents. In what follows, I revisit Douglass's 1840s speeches on Madison Washington and his 1853 fictionalization of Washington's revolt in *The Heroic Slave* specifically for how they come to terms with Walker, Garnet, and violent resistance. These readings will help strengthen important ties between Douglass and his works and other influential black activists and their writings, deepening our understanding of the crucial role that black political theorizations of freedom and citizenship played in Douglass's evolution from advocating nonviolent resistance to justifying it as an equal right and a sign of black Americans' capacity for self-government.[6] Ultimately, examining the connections between Walker and Douglass reveals more of, and more about, the dense and complex network of literary activists and political activism in which they were embedded, furthering efforts to rethink Douglass's singularity and isolation that we now recognize as effects of his hypercanonicity and of years of situating his works primarily in relation to white authors and activists.[7]

Walker published and widely circulated three editions of his *Appeal* between September 1829 and the spring of 1830.[8] In its most impassioned and argumentatively extreme moments, Walker presents white people as black people's "natural enemies"; claims that modern white Christian Americans are "ten times more cruel, avaricious, and unmerciful" than the worst heathen Greeks, Romans, and Europeans in history; and instructs the enslaved, "[I]f there is an *attempt* made by us" to resist, then "kill or be killed," reasoning "that it is no more harm for you to kill a man who is trying to kill you, than it is to take a drink of water when thirsty."[9] "Walker only made the words of his pamphlet more terrifying to whites," historian Peter P. Hinks explains, "when he set about circulating it as widely as possible among the slaves in the South."[10] "By early 1830, the coastal South was in an uproar over the circulation of the *Appeal*, ever anxious about the scope of its penetration and the degree of its own subject population's excitement for it."[11]

Southern newspapers played a crucial role in fanning the flames by steadily publishing articles that branded the *Appeal* as "incendiary" and a "firebrand" hurled from Boston into the South. They also regularly reported on new laws that most southern state legislatures proposed and passed to thwart Walker's pamphlet and any future "insurrectionary" publications from reaching enslaved people.[12] In January 1830 in Baltimore, the long-running antislavery newspaper *The Genius of Universal Emancipation* carried its first notice of Walker's *Appeal* in an article headlined "Singular Panic."[13] Following excerpts from southern newspaper articles responding to the pamphlet, William Lloyd Garrison – who was at the paper's helm while founding editor Benjamin Lundy was away fundraising – editorializes: "We have had this pamphlet on our table for some time past, and are not surprised at its effects upon our sensitive southern brethren. It is written by a colored Bostonian, and breathes the most impassioned and determined spirit. We deprecate its circulation, though we cannot but wonder at the bravery and intelligence of its author." For slavery's defenders as well as for Garrison, who was committed to a nonviolent end to slavery, Walker's *Appeal* circulating freely meant that violent resistance was likely wherever it appeared.

Garrison's remarks indicate that the pamphlet had reached Baltimore shortly after Walker published his first edition in late September 1829. According to Blight, Douglass "was about eleven years old" when "Hugh Auld suddenly forbade with stern anger any further instruction in reading for the young slave" (39). If this estimate is correct, the year of Auld's interdiction would have been 1829 or 1830.[14] Blight keeps close to Douglass's accounts of this turning point by noting only the suddenness of Auld's action without suggesting its potential cause. But when we look beyond Douglass's autobiographies to the *Genius of Universal Emancipation* and other contemporary newspapers for what might have motivated Auld, the "singular panic" occasioned by the arrival of Walker's *Appeal* in Baltimore and in port cities farther south in late 1829 becomes apparent as the cause.

The reasons that Hugh gives Sophia Auld, and that Douglass hears and remembers, further cement cause and effect:

> Mr. Auld found out what was going on, and at once forbade Mrs. Auld to instruct me further, telling her, among other things, that it was unlawful, as well as unsafe, to teach a slave to read. To use his own words, further, he said, "If you give a nigger an inch, he will take an ell. A nigger should know nothing but to obey his master – to do as he is told to do. Learning would *spoil* the best nigger in the world. Now," said he, "if you teach that nigger (speaking of myself) how to read, there would be no keeping him. It would forever unfit him to be a slave. He would at once become unmanageable, and of no value to his master. As to himself, it could do him no good, but a great deal of harm. It would make him discontented and unhappy."[15]

This is the first version of Auld's words and reasoning that Douglass offers in 1845 and they remain largely consistent across the four versions of Douglass's autobiography. What is more, Auld's language and logic are also consistent with responses to Walker's *Appeal* that frequently appeared in the popular press beginning in late 1829 and continuing through 1831. The following editorial remark from the *Tarborough* [North Carolina] *Free Press* – published in the wake of Nat Turner's rebellion in 1831 and reprinted in *The Liberator* – especially resonates with what Douglass represents his master explaining to his wife:

> The excitement produced a few months since in the Southern country, by the discovery of several copies of the notorious "Walker Pamphlet," is doubtless still fresh in the recollection of most of our readers.... [I]t appears that some misguided and deluded fanatics are still bent on exciting our coloured population to scenes at which the heart sickens on the bare recital, and which instead of improving their moral or physical condition, cannot fail to overwhelm the actors in ruin, and curtail the privileges of all the others. Let them view the first fruits of their diabolical projects in the Southampton massacre, and pause – an awful retribution await[s] them.[16]

In Douglass's 1855, 1881, and 1892 reflections on this turning point, he describes Auld's "exposition" of the dynamics of slavery to his wife as "oracular."[17] But as the *Tarborough Free Press*'s editorial suggests, Auld was more parrot than oracle; his language and arguments effectively repeat at home what was being said about Walker's *Appeal* in newspapers throughout the South between 1829 and 1831.

With Garrison launching *The Liberator* on New Year's Day in Boston in 1831 and the founding of the American Anti-Slavery Society in

1833, white abolitionists quickly came to dominate antislavery print.[18] The AASS seized on advances in printing technology by buying power presses, thereby issuing an unprecedented volume of print and forcing a national debate on slavery. In response to the Great Postal Campaign of 1835, in which nearly 200,000 pieces of antislavery print were mailed south, bounties were put on the heads of Arthur and Lewis Tappan – two of the AASS's most prominent founders and funders – and a mob stole and burned bags of the Society's tracts from the Charleston, South Carolina, post office in late July 1835. By the 1840s, black abolitionists clearly had abundant evidence of the power of the press to shape the national conversations about slavery and race – as well as ample reason to want to reharness that power to plead their own causes, as both the black-published and short-lived newspaper *Freedom's Journal* (1827–29) and Walker's *Appeal* had done and urged others to do.[19] At the 1843 National Convention of Colored Citizens in Buffalo, New York, convention leaders named a committee "to take measures to establish a press, to be the organ of the colored people of this country."[20]

Convention delegate and newspaper editor Henry Highland Garnet specifically and ardently agitated to maintain and use print's "mysterious" power to intimidate slaveholders, urging the convention to adopt and publish his controversial address to enslaved people that he had delivered at the meeting as a stand-alone pamphlet. On the convention floor, he insisted that his address be adopted and endorsed as written, not edited by a committee that would be sensitive to "some points in it that might in print appear objectionable" – specifically his point that the enslaved have both a right and a duty to use all available means to resist their masters. With this argument, Garnet distinctly renewed Walker's *Appeal* for a new generation of black activists before putting it back into circulation five years later. At the Convention, though, he had to convince delegates that his address was worth publishing, given the aggressive suppression of Walker's pamphlet just over a decade earlier. He spoke for an hour and a half, both defending his address and effectively redelivering it so that its most salient points would be included in the convention's official published minutes. In making his case for resistance, he invoked Denmark Vesey, Nat Turner, and, significantly, Madison Washington. The *Minutes* note, "It was a masterly effort, and the whole Convention, full as it was, was literally infused with tears," with Garnet concluding "amidst great applause."[21]

If Frederick Douglass was among those moved, the *Minutes* seem to suggest that he quickly suppressed his emotions as he immediately followed Garnet's defense with objections representing the Garrisonian position at the convention:

> Mr. Douglass remarked, that there was too much physical force, both in the address and the remarks of the speaker last up. He was for trying the moral means a little longer: that the address, could it reach the slaves, and the advice, either of the address or the gentleman, be followed, while it might not lead the slaves to rise in insurrection for liberty, would, never the less, and necessarily be the occasion of an insurrection; and that was what he wished in no way to have any agency in bringing about, and what we were called upon to avoid.[22]

With these objections, Douglass not only voices Garrison's policy of nonviolent resistance, but also sounds an alarm that echoes Hugh Auld's to Sophia for why she must not abet the literacy of an enslaved child: the likelihood of it leading to insurrection. Garnet's Walker-like, step-by-step program for enslaved people's resistance in his "Address" – reading his printed address, learning from it their duty to confront their masters, then refusing to work and demanding for their freedom, followed by defensive counterviolence against their resistant masters – likely spurred for Douglass some memory of the specter of violence in Auld's prohibition of reading that, consciously or not in the moment, informed his warning to convention delegates about insurrection being a likely consequence of their printing Garnet's address. His concerns proved effective as delegates twice voted against adopting and publishing Garnet's address. In doing so, they were heeding Douglass's significant, if implied, modification of his master's claim about whose lives would be endangered by reading insurrectionary print: enslaved people's organized resistance of their masters, Douglass reasoned, ultimately would do both them and free black Americans more harm than good because it inevitably would provoke an overwhelmingly violent response from slaveholders and their defenders. Garnet remained committed to the possibility of violent resistance and to publishing his "Address to the Slaves" despite Douglass's reasoning and his losing the vote for publication at the Buffalo Convention. Five years later, he published it himself along with a reprinting of Walker's *Appeal* in one fearsome pamphlet that made his ideological alignment with, and debt to, Walker materially explicit.[23]

A series of speeches that Douglass gave through the rest of the decade indicate that Garnet's and, through him, Walker's provocative arguments and actions both moved Douglass and stayed with him.[24] Douglass continued to debate violent resistance with himself for several years, specifically doing so through the example of an actual – and successful – rebellion by enslaved people led by Madison Washington aboard the ship *Creole* in 1841. As Robert S. Levine, John Stauffer, and John R. McKivigan note in their 2015 scholarly edition of Douglass's fictionalization of Washington and his actions, *The Heroic Slave*,

> Douglass did not speak or write about the *Creole* rebellion in the early 1840s, or if he did, those comments are no longer extant. But beginning in the fall of 1845, when he commenced a nearly two-year antislavery lecture tour in Great Britain and Ireland, Douglass regularly referred to Madison Washington and the *Creole* rebellion in his speeches, praising both the bravery of the *Creole* rebels and the courage of the British in refusing to return the former slaves to their U.S. owners.[25]

Being in the United Kingdom instead of the United States and, thus, away from both Garrison and Garnet gave Douglass space to think and speak for himself about violent resistance. With that space, he began to move away from Garrison and closer to Garnet's and Walker's position, as we see especially in a speech that he gave on October 27, 1845, in Cork, Ireland – the first known instance in which Douglass addresses Washington and the *Creole* rebellion. As part of narrating this "glorious illustration of affection in the heart of a black man" who "has made some noise in the world by that act of his," Douglass makes a point of noting that Washington had met with Garnet in Troy, New York, on his way back to Virginia from Canada to liberate his wife. In Douglass's account, Garnet specifically discourages Washington from returning South, arguing that "it would be perfectly fruitless." Despite this warning from "a highly intellectual black man," as Douglass describes Garnet, Washington continues his return to Virginia, where he is reenslaved, and ultimately leads the revolt aboard the *Creole*. Douglass narrates how Washington "came to the resolution," then "seized a handspike, felled the Captain – and found himself with his companions masters of the ship."[26] While Washington initially seems to be at odds with Garnet in Douglass's telling of the story, Washington's actions aboard the *Creole* make clear that he is making good on the duty to resist that Garnet insists on in his "Address to the Slaves" and that Walker first insisted on in his *Appeal*. As Garnet told his enslaved audience, "Your condition does not absolve you from your moral obligation. The diabolical injustice by which your liberties are cloven down, neither God, nor angels, nor just men, command you to suffer for a single moment. Therefore it is your solemn and imperative duty to use every means, both moral, intellectual, and physical, that promise success."[27] In concluding his telling of

Washington's successful rebellion, Douglass specifically counters claims
that "none but those persons who have a mixture of European blood ...
distinguish themselves" as revolutionary heroes who insist on their natural
rights by offering the example of Garnet, whom he again praises, this time
as "the most intellectual and moral colored man that is now in our
country" and "a man in whose veins no European blood courses."[28]
With this and the rest of Washington's story Douglass clearly signals that
he and Garnet are no longer as opposed, personally or politically, as the
print record of their debate at the 1843 convention suggests. And in
Douglass's specific invocation of the idea that race and revolution were
matters of biological inheritance, I want to suggest, we also glimpse an
early moment in his coming to recognize himself as no less a descendant
than Garnet of his black intellectual and moral fathers, most prominently
Walker, who defended black Americans' right to revolution.

From this point through the rest of the decade in speeches that he gives
in both the United Kingdom and back in the States, Douglass regularly
calls up Madison Washington as the exemplary black revolutionary, building toward his 1853 novella *The Heroic Slave*.[29] To understand this major
reversal in Douglass's philosophy of resistance, scholars have focused
almost exclusively on Garrison's influence, reading Douglass's explicit
embrace of the possibility of violence as a rejection of both the father
figure–like man and his message.[30] Yet a more positive understanding of
Douglass's political evolution is not just possible, but necessary. When we
shift our focus from Garrison to Garnet and see Douglass's repeated
invocations of Madison Washington as an extended engagement with
Garnet and, through him, Walker, we understand that his turn away from
Garrisonianism was also a critically developed turn toward his black
intellectual and political peers in the movement. This positive turn is
especially visible in a speech that Douglass gave in Walker's and
Garrison's Boston at a New England Anti-Slavery Society Meeting, in
which he links Washington and Nat Turner as representative of the
"many" in the South "who would assert their right to liberty." As the
June 9, 1848, issue of *The Liberator* captured the speech, Douglass
concludes by sounding – and, in print, looking – very much like David
Walker: "[Y]ou will say that I, and such as I, are not *men*.... But,
nevertheless, we are MEN! (Cheers.) ... WE ARE MEN. (Immense
cheering)."[31] Memorably, in Article I of his *Appeal*, Walker both asks
and insists – with emphatic small and all caps, and exclamation points
instead of question marks – "Are we MEN! ! – I ask you, O my brethren!
are we MEN?"[32]

Given the date of Douglass's speech – May 30, 1848 – he may well have been borrowing directly from Walker's text, and not simply alluding to it, as Garnet reissued the *Appeal* in print that same month. Douglass was well aware of the new edition as Garnet had placed an advertisement for it in the *North Star* on May 5, announcing that it would be "ready in a few days."[33] In the same advertisement, Garnet pointedly notes that the new edition also will contain his "Address to the Slaves" that "was rejected by the National Convention at Buffalo in 1843" – notably omitting that the editor of the paper that readers had in hand had led the move to reject his address at the convention. The ad does not note that the edition also features "A Brief Sketch of the Life and Character of David Walker" that Garnet had written as a preface to the *Appeal*. Douglass reprinted the sketch – without attribution to Garnet as its author – in the July 14, 1848, *North Star*. Such a recognition of Walker's significance as a writer and radical, even at the expense of Garnet's, stands as another important index of Douglass's gradual shift away from Garrisonianism toward the rightful resistance first voiced by Walker and powerfully seconded by Garnet.[34]

For Garnet to bring his "Address to the Slaves" into print for the first time bound with Walker's *Appeal* – back in print for the first time since 1830 – and to issue and circulate both together in 1848 – a year of worldwide revolutions from below – was to convert personal frustration into the perfect political opportunity, connecting both his arguments with Walker's and uprisings of enslaved people in the United States with democratic revolutions occurring throughout the world. Newspaper coverage of these revolutions was frequently positive, drawing comparisons to the American Revolution and praising the global realization of its ideals.[35] Garnet recognized and seized on the opportunity by binding together Walker's and his addresses to enslaved people. By doing so, he effectively added to Walker's arguments and their urgency in this new global political moment without changing a word of Walker's original text. "Brethren, the time has come when you must act for yourselves," Garnet declares in his address to the enslaved, essentially activating Walker's instructions to them to act decisively when the time for liberation comes.[36] In turn, for Garnet, binding together his "Address" with Walker's *Appeal* in one pamphlet provided both argumentative and material support for his previously thwarted address, in a time when Garrison's position of abolition by moral suasion alone still dominated and in a way that gave his relatively brief address more physical heft.

The resulting pamphlet – especially the preface that Garnet wrote for Walker's *Appeal* and his biography of Walker – reads as a genealogy that shows all black revolutionary thought – including his own and Douglass's – as necessarily evolving from Walker's original arguments about enslaved people's right and duty to resist. As Garnet declares in the preface, Walker's *Appeal* "is valuable, because it was among the first, and was actually the boldest and most direct appeal in behalf of freedom, which was made in the early part of the Anti-Slavery Reformation." Thus he concludes, "When the history of the emancipation of the bondmen of America shall be written, whatever name shall be placed on the list of heroes, that of the author of the Appeal will not be second" – to Garrison's name, to Douglass's, or to his own.[37]

In Douglass's extended fictionalization of the *Creole* rebellion, he, too, begins by addressing the historical record and his hero's place in it. While "History has not been sparing in recording" the names or deeds of Virginia's statesmen and heroes, "some strange neglect" has caused "*one* of the manliest, and bravest of her children*" to hold "no higher place in the records of that grand old Commonwealth than is held by a horse or an ox," the narrative voice of *The Heroic Slave* sardonically observes.[38] Just as this introduction allows Douglass to suggest the real-life Madison Washington's equally heroic standing with his Founding Father name-sakes, Douglass's and Garnet's shared concern with history also follows the model of their black revolutionary forefather Walker, who begins his *Appeal* by surveying and correcting the historical record, particularly with respect to white Americans' unprecedented cruelty in their practice of racial slavery. Furthermore, in explicitly grounding Washington's heroic deeds in the ideals and language of the American Revolution, Douglass also shares common ground with Walker, who concludes his *Appeal* with an emphatic reprinting of the Declaration of Independence's declarations about equality, rights, and the duty to revolt against despotism. In his final argument about these rights and duties applying equally to white and black Americans, Walker demands, "Now Americans! I ask you candidly, was your sufferings under Great Britain, one hundredth part as cruel and tyrannical as you have rendered ours under you?" At the same time, he acknowledges and ridicules how some whites "believe that we will never throw off your murderous government and 'provide new guards for our future security,'" as the Declaration demands.[39] Douglass may have been responding to this charge as Walker articulates it by embedding the story of Washington's revolt in a barroom debate between two white sailors, one of whom was aboard the *Creole* at the time as its first mate and the other who is incredulous, from his barstool, that black people could want either to resist their bondage or to successfully execute a revolution. In the mate Grant's eyewitness account, Washington pointedly uses rhetoric and logic from the American Revolution, much as Walker does at the end of his *Appeal*, declaring, "God is my witness that Liberty, not malice, is the motive for this night's work."[40] Numerous scholars have examined both Walker's and Douglass's debt to what the mate Grant calls "the principles of 1776."[41] But as Garnet's "Address to the Slaves" compels us to see, Walker and Douglass are not simply extending American democratic discourse and revolutionary potential to African Americans in their ultimate justifications of violent resistance, but also importantly reestablishing these rights as universal and God-given. Or, as Garnet specifically puts it in his address, these rights and duties are God-authored, thereby implying, like Walker, that they are not Jefferson-authored: "You should therefore now use the same manner of resistance, as would have been just in our ancestors, when the bloody foot prints of the first remorseless soul thief was placed upon the shores of our fatherland.... Liberty is a spirit sent out from God, and like its great Author, is no respecter of persons."[42]

With respect to the question of authorship, scholars also have read *The Heroic Slave* as a black-authored fictional response to – and, thus, implicit critique of – Harriet Beecher Stowe's fictional representation of slavery and Christian nonviolent resistance in *Uncle Tom's Cabin*.[43] But as I hope this essay begins to show, we have many good reasons to give equal attention to the novella as a significant aspect of the extended, dynamic conversation between Frederick Douglass and Henry Highland Garnet, and through Garnet and Madison Washington, with David Walker. Douglass not only thought but wrote his way to embracing Walker's original appeal for a violent end to slavery, and by doing so, he strengthened his bonds with Walker, Washington, Garnet, and all other members of the complex network of free and enslaved black theorists and activists who were working for freedom using all available means – especially language and print. Walker's and Garnet's tenaciousness and Douglass's commitment to rethinking his positions offer a productive tension that we should strive to maintain as scholars, as we continue to think and write our way to understanding this network, its intricacy, and the many forms of activism, agency, and experience that its members both embody and model.

Notes

1 David W. Blight, *Frederick Douglass: Prophet of Freedom* (New York: Simon & Schuster, 2018).
2 [Henry Highland Garnet,] "Sketch of the Life and Character of David Walker," *North Star* 1.29 (July 14, 1848): 4; Frederick Douglass, "Our Destiny Is Largely in Our Own Hands: An Address Delivered in

Washington, D.C., on 16 April 1883," in *The Frederick Douglass Papers*, vol. 5, ed. John W. Blassingame and John R. McKivigan (New Haven, CT: Yale University Press, 1992), 68-69.

3 For recent considerations of the diversity within the slave narrative as a genre as a material text and challenges to its coherence as a literary genre, see Teresa A. Goddu, "The Slave Narrative as Material Text," in *The Oxford Handbook of the African American Slave Narrative*, ed. John Ernest (New York: Oxford University Press, 2014), 149–64, and Michaël Roy, "Cheap Editions, Little Books, and Handsome Duodecimos: A Book History Approach to Antebellum Slave Narratives," *MELUS* 40.3 (Fall 2015): 69–93. On the breadth and diversity of antebellum African American literature beyond the slave narrative, see Eric Gardner, *Literature in Unexpected Places: Relocating Nineteenth-Century African American Literature* (Jackson: University of Mississippi Press, 2009), and Cheryl A. Wall, *On Freedom and the Will to Adorn: The Art of the African American Essay* (Chapel Hill: University of North Carolina Press, 2018). On black citizenship in theory and practice, Derrick R. Spires, *The Practice of Citizenship: Black Politics and Print Culture in the Early United States* (Philadelphia: University of Pennsylvania Press, 2019). For theorizations and studies of gaps, loss, and distortion in archives, memory, and lived experience, see Saidiya Hartman, "Venus in Two Acts," *Small Axe* 12.2 (June 2008): 1–14, and, most recently, *Wayward Lives, Beautiful Experiments: Intimate Histories of Social Upheaval* (New York: W. W. Norton, 2019); and Marisa J. Fuentes, *Dispossessed Lives: Enslaved Women, Violence, and the Archive* (Philadelphia: University of Pennsylvania Press, 2016).

4 Maryland was among the southern states that did not pass antiliteracy laws, but as E. Jennifer Monaghan notes, "whether or not their state legislated against literacy, slaves in any state had so few legal protections that if their masters objected to any kind of instruction, that decision had the force of law" ("Reading for the Enslaved, Writing for the Free: Reflections on Liberty and Literacy," *Proceedings of the American Antiquarian Society* 108.2 [October 1998]: 338).

5 Peter P. Hinks notes that the "impulse to create a direct connection between Nat Turner and David Walker has been so strong that commentators, even at the time of the Southampton revolt, could not resist it" and surveys twentieth-century historians' temptation to do the same, but ultimately concludes, "At this point we can only speculate whether Turner actually saw or was aware of David Walker's *Appeal*" (*To Awaken My Afflicted Brethren: David Walker and the Problem of Antebellum Slave Resistance* [University Park: Pennsylvania State University Press, 1997], 167, 169).

6 Robert S. Levine has examined the formation of Douglass's political thought in relation to other black political theorists in *Martin Delany, Frederick Douglass, and the Politics of Representative Identity* (Chapel Hill: University of North Carolina Press, 1997); *Dislocating Race and Nation: Episodes in Nineteenth-Century American Literary Nationalism* (Chapel Hill: University

of North Carolina Press, 2008), chapter 4; and *The Lives of Frederick Douglass* (Cambridge, MA: Harvard University Press, 2016). Alex Zamalian has specifically considered Douglass in relation to Walker in chapter 1 of *Struggle on Their Minds: Political Thought of African American Resistance* (New York: Columbia University Press, 2017). On Douglass and citizenship, see Spires, *The Practice of Citizenship.*

7 For an early critique of Douglass's exceptionalism in the literary canon, see Deborah E. McDowell, "In the First Place: Making Frederick Douglass and the Afro-American Narrative Tradition," in *African American Autobiography: A Collection of Critical Essays*, ed. William L. Andrews (Englewood Cliffs, NJ: Prentice Hall, 1993), 36–58.

8 To date, Peter P. Hinks offers the most thorough documentation published of Walker's pamphlets' publication and circulation in *To Awaken My Afflicted Brethren*, and in his Introduction and Editor's Note to *David Walker's Appeal to the Coloured Citizens of the World* (University Park: Pennsylvania State University Press, 2000). Leon Jackson has undertaken significant archival research that promises new understandings of how Walker's *Appeal* was circulated and received for his in-progress book *David Walker's World: Communication and Emancipation in Antebellum America.* He presented some of this ongoing work in the paper "David Walker in the Archive" at the American Literature Association Annual Conference, Boston, May 25, 2019 (unpublished conference paper). My thanks to Leon for sharing this work in progress.

9 David Walker, *Walker's Appeal to the Coloured Citizens of the World*, 3rd ed., (Boston: s.p., 1830), 30, 20, 30.

10 Hinks, Editor's Note, xxxviii.

11 Ibid., xxxix.

12 The headline "The 'Incendiary Pamphlet'" of a March 4, 1830, *Boston Courier* article reprinted from the *Richmond Enquirer* captures how the phrase had become strategic and widely recognized shorthand among whites in the South and North for Walker's *Appeal* and its notoriety. A letter from Boston Mayor Harrison Gray Otis responding to Savannah, Georgia's mayor's request for an investigation into Walker and his pamphlet parrots back southern authorities' and newspapers' language for describing Walker's pamphlet and intentions: "You may be assured, sir, that a disposition would not be wanting on the part of the city authorities here, to avail themselves of any lawful means, for preventing this attempt to throw fire-brands into your country" ("Excitement in the South," *Niles' Weekly Register* 38:967 [March 27, 1830]: 87). Lori Leavell has examined how northern newspapers eagerly reprinted these sensational articles, thereby extending the pamphlet's notoriety, and spreading Walker's words by adding excerpts from the pamphlet to illustrate the South's cause for alarm. See "'Not intended exclusively for the slave states': Antebellum Recirculation of David Walker's *Appeal*," *Callaloo* 38.3 (Summer 2015): 679–95.

13 [William Lloyd] G.[arrison], "Singular Panic," *Genius of Universal Emancipation* 4.19 (January 15, 1830): 147.

14 Of Douglass's uncertain birth date, Blight explains, "Douglass lived most of his life believing that he had been born in 1817, but a handwritten inventory of slaves, kept by his owner at birth, Aaron Anthony, recorded 'Frederick Augustus, son of Harriet, Feby. 1818" (9).

15 Frederick Douglass, *Narrative of the Life of Frederick Douglass, an American Slave* (Boston: Anti-Slavery Office, 1845), 33.

16 Reprinted in *Liberator* 1.41 (October 8, 1831): 1.

17 Douglass, *My Bondage and My Freedom* (New York: Miller, Orton and Mulligan, 1855), 146.

18 David Paul Nord has examined the significance of print to the AASS and other reform movements of the time, noting that the society's founders specifically emphasized "the press as one of the most powerful engines of reform" and accordingly "devoted to it as much effort as the state of the treasury would allow" ("Benevolent Books: Printing, Religion, and Reform," in *A History of the Book in America*, vol. 2, ed. Robert A. Gross and Mary Kelley [Chapel Hill: American Antiquarian Society and University of North Carolina Press, 2010], 242).

19 In the debut issue of *Freedom's Journal*, editors Samuel Cornish and John Russwurm declared in their introductory "Note to Our Patrons," "We wish to plead our own cause. Too long have others spoken for us" (*Freedom's Journal* 1.1 [March 16, 1827]: 1). After refuting Thomas Jefferson's racist claims in *Notes on the State of Virginia*, Walker declares, "We, and the world wish to see the charges of Mr. Jefferson refuted by the blacks *themselves*" (*Walker's Appeal*, 3rd ed., 17–18). After *Freedom's Journal* – for which Walker was a subscription agent – ended publication, black readers throughout the North turned to Garrison's paper as it filled the void, providing crucial financial support as subscribers to *The Liberator* in its vulnerable early years. For another consideration of the significance of a national newspaper to black activists in the 1840s, see the introduction of Benjamin Fagan's *The Black Newspaper and the Chosen Nation* (Athens: University of Georgia Press, 2016) and, in this volume, Derrick R. Spires's essay "African American Print Culture."

20 *Minutes of the National Convention of Colored Citizens* (New York: Piercy & Reed, 1843), 25. The *Minutes* is also the official report of the Convention's Committee on the Press that attempted to wrest back from the South the dominant narrative about print's power to inspire black Americans to action. It reads in part, "Your committee ... are of the opinion that, if the press, with its almost mysterious influence, is so productive of mischief to us, as they [slavery's defenders and racists] really believe it has been, ... the same power, in proper hands, especially in our own, would be exerted, or at least might be, not only merely to counteract the influences against us, but be made an instrumentality to promote positive good, the tendency of which would be to elevate the people; in other words, a press in our own hands would be wielded to disabuse the public mind in respect to us, and correct the false views and sentiments entertained of us, and of questions necessary to our general welfare, and would be the means of promoting [these] correct views and

sentiments" (*Minutes*, 28). For a more detailed consideration of the Colored Conventions' focus on print as key to their activism, see Spires's essay in this volume.

21 *Minutes*, 13.

22 Ibid., 13.

23 Henry Highland Garnet, *Walker's Appeal, with a Brief Sketch of His Life, and also Garnet's Address to the Slaves of the United States of America* (New York: J. H. Tobitt, 1848).

24 Levine also considers the influence of Garnet's address to the slaves at the 1843 Buffalo Convention on Douglass in *The Lives of Frederick Douglass*, 133–35. Levine's extended consideration of the impact of Washington's story on Douglass and of *The Heroic Slave* focuses primarily on the autobiographical resonance of Washington's story for Douglass.

25 Robert S. Levine, John Stauffer, and John R. McKivigan, "Douglass on the *Creole* and Black Revolution," in Frederick Douglass, *The Heroic Slave: A Cultural and Critical Edition*, ed. Levine, Stauffer, and McKivigan (New Haven, CT: Yale University Press, 2015), 111.

26 Douglass, "American Prejudice against Color," October 23, 1845, in Levine et al., "Douglass on the *Creole* and Black Revolution," 114.

27 Garnet, "Address to the Slaves of the United States of America," in *Walker's Appeal*, 93.

28 Levine et al., "Douglass on the *Creole* and Black Revolution," 115.

29 Levine, Stauffer, and McKivigan have collected the known speeches in which Douglass discusses Madison Washington in part 3 of their scholarly edition of *The Heroic Slave*.

30 Levine offers an important exception to this narrow focus on Douglass's split with Garrison by considering at length Douglass's engagement with the story of Madison Washington in chapter 3 of *The Lives of Frederick Douglass*. Most recently, Blight highlights Douglass's "hypersensitivity to criticism" and how "rivalry had long been part of the personality" that fellow black activists "tolerated" as a way of setting up Douglass's final break with Garrison, which he casts as Douglass rejecting a father figure (222–26). While I do not mean to suppress this side of Douglass, I do want to foreground his more internal, and less public – even though print-mediated – coming to terms with other powerful black activists who thought differently than he did.

31 Levine et al., "Douglass on the *Creole* and Black Revolution," 122. Levine also notes the echo of Walker in Douglass's speech in *The Lives of Frederick Douglass*, 140.

32 Walker, *Appeal*, 19.

33 Garnet, "New Publications" advertisement, *North Star* 1.19 (May 5, 1848): 3.

34 [Henry Highland Garnet], "Brief Sketch of the Life and Character of David Walker," *North Star* 1.29 (July 14, 1848): 4.

35 Timothy Robert's *Distant Revolutions: 1848 and the Challenge to American Exceptionalism* (Charlottesville: University of Virginia Press, 2009) offers a nuanced study of the full range of responses to the 1848 revolutions in US

popular and political culture. Fagan focuses on coverage of the revolutions in the *North Star* in his essay "*The North Star* and the Atlantic 1848," *African American Review* 47.1 (Spring 2014): 51–67.

36 Garnet, "Address," 93.

37 Garnet, Preface to Walker's *Appeal*, unnumbered page iv.

38 Douglass, *The Heroic Slave*, in Levine et al., 3.

39 Walker, *Appeal*, 86.

40 Douglass, *Heroic Slave*, 48.

41 Douglass, *Heroic Slave*, 51. On Douglass's application of American Revolution theory and discourse in *The Heroic Slave*, see Krista Walker, "Trappings of Nationalism in *The Heroic Slave*," *African American Review* 34.2 (Summer 2000), and Kelvin C. Black, "Bound by 'the Principles of 1776': Dilemmas in Anglo-American Romanticism and Douglass's *The Heroic Slave*," *Studies in Romanticism*, 56.1 (Spring 2017): 93–112. Hinks asserts Walker's admiration of the American Revolution and reformist insistence on the full realization of the Founding's principles in *To Awaken My Afflicted Brethren* (247–48), and Elizabeth Beaumont focuses on Walker's formal and ideological debt to the Constitution in *The Civic Constitution: Civic Visions and Struggles in the Path toward Constitutional Democracy* (New York: Oxford University Press, 2014).

42 Garnet, "Address," 93.

43 On *The Heroic Slave* as a response to *Uncle Tom's Cabin*, see Robert B. Stepto, "Sharing the Thunder: The Literary Exchanges of Harriet Beecher Stowe, Henry Bibb, and Frederick Douglass," in *New Essays on Uncle Tom's Cabin*, ed. Eric J. Sundquist (Cambridge: Cambridge University Press, 1986), 135–53. Robert S. Levine offers an analysis of Douglass's extended and multidimensional engagement with Stowe and her novel in "*Uncle Tom's Cabin* in *Frederick Douglass' Paper*: An Analysis of Reception," *American Literature* 64.1 (March 1992): 71–93.

CHAPTER 20

Emerson/Poe

Christopher Hanlon

In some ways Ralph Waldo Emerson (1803–1882) and Edgar Allan Poe (1809–1849) make for such an antithetical pair out of nineteenth-century US literary history. Consider the only surviving remark Emerson made of Poe, which Emerson never bothered to write down. It comes to us through William Dean Howells, who included the anecdote in a 1900 reminiscence:

> He asked me if I knew the poems of Mr. William Ellery Channing. . . .
> I answered then truly that I knew them only from Poe's criticisms: cruel
> and spiteful things which I should be ashamed of enjoying as I once did.
> "Whose criticism?" asked Emerson.
> "Poe's," I said again.
> "Oh," he cried out, after a moment, as if he had returned from a far search
> for my meaning, "you mean the jingle-man!"[1]

That is a story that continues to circulate in undergraduate seminars in American literature because it seems to say so much about the disconnection between the two writers. Emerson, philosopher of ever-expanding circles, optimism, and light; and Poe, whose *Eureka* describes a universe in the process of collapse, who is constantly drawn to pathology and darkness. In a way the story gives Emerson the last word on someone who had trolled him and other transcendentalists as pretentious "frogpondians," someone of whom Emerson had been reminded at the moment Howells reports for his detractions of the son of a close friend. (In his 1843 review of Channing, son of the famous minister of the same name, Poe snarked: "His book contains about sixty-three things, which he calls poems, and which he no doubt seriously supposes so to be. They are full of all kinds of mistakes, of which the most important is that of their having been printed at all. They are not precisely English – not will we insult a great nation by calling them Kickapoo; perhaps they are Channingese."[2]) In yet another way the anecdote encapsulates Poe's reputation as a perpetual outsider and *l'enfant terrible* as well as Emerson's own as a clubby blueblood. Certainly, it captures the cliquishness of the northeastern literary establishment that

335

had so irked Poe: possibly, Emerson was posturing as he claimed barely to recall the name of the author of "The Raven" – though possibly not, given his own increasing dementia during the 1860s. Either way, Howells's implication is that Poe was hardly worth entering the consciousness, to say nothing of the essays, the journals, or the lectures, of Emerson.

And yet thinking about the ways scholars have treated Emerson and Poe over the past few decades can provide a useful chart of concerns that have animated the larger field of American literary scholarship. Though the guiding terms of scholarship on Emerson and Poe refract through multiple biographical, historical, and ideological lenses, the two writers connect in at least one way concerning their critical reception since about 1990. That is, the most recent outpourings of scholarship for both figures have explored questions concerning their engagements with the subjects of race and slavery. In this focus there is, again, such obvious divergence between the two. Emerson is on record for having embraced immediatist abolition, sharing stages with William Lloyd Garrison, Frederick Douglass, and Wendell Phillips, among others; while Poe wrote stories and a novel with barely submerged white supremacist subtexts and may have also authored – but even if he did not, he nevertheless published in the *Southern Literary Messenger* while serving as its editor – at least one proslavery screed arguing that African Americans are congenitally servile. And yet questions relating to Emerson's and Poe's responses to slavery link the two writers in that the airing of those matters cleared space for the most energetic exchange of critical perspective either writer has occasioned over the past thirty years. This is not to gainsay other examples of influential writing on Emerson or Poe to emerge over the same period but that focused on other issues (for instance, one of Emerson's most influential readers, Stanley Cavell, had virtually nothing to say about Emerson's abolitionism) but, rather, to suggest that the positioning of both writers in relation to the racial politics of the antebellum period has provided Americanist scholars with a series of challenges complex enough to sustain ongoing and layered critical exchange. And in both cases, the nature of that exchange altered in significant ways Emerson's and Poe's canonical standing and reputation even as it registered Americanist scholars' increasing investments in charting the ways race and slavery shaped nineteenth-century literary history.

Emerson's Transcendental Abolition

The most recent cascade of Emerson scholarship occurred near the end of the millennium as several scholars raised a series of questions surrounding the history of Emerson's antislavery oratory. John Carlos Rowe, writing in *At Emerson's Tomb: The Politics of Classic American Literature* (1996), argued that Emerson's shift to the abolitionist platform after the 1850 passage of the Fugitive Slave Law marked by necessity the abandonment of his prior transcendentalism, which was too mystical, abstruse, and ultimately solipsistic to support anything like a socially minded consciousness. Rowe notes, for example, Emerson's great hesitancy as he embraced the cause, writing even as late as 1855 to his brother William, "I am trying hard in these days to see some light in the dark slavery question to which I am to speak next week in Boston. But to me as to many tis like Hamlet's task imposed upon so unfit an agent as Hamlet."[3] Though Rowe does not mention it, Emerson's various addresses before abolitionist audiences during the 1850s often began with some such apologia. Speaking in Concord on May 3, 1851, he began with the words, "Fellow citizens, I accepted your invitation to speak to you on the great question of these days, with very little consideration of what I might have to offer. For there seems to be no option. The last year has forced us all into politics, and made it a paramount duty to seek what it is often a duty to shun."[4] Over the course of two trenchant chapters, Rowe asks, essentially: Why does Emerson imagine it "a paramount duty to shun" "politics"? Repeatedly, Emerson speaks as if he owes his audiences some explanation, as if by inveighing against what was then called the Slave Power he compromises some core commitment to an avoidance of the public sphere. And so his March 7, 1854, speech in New York begins with Emerson venting his inner turmoil over the implications of speaking at all. "I do not often speak to public questions," he begins, once again opening with apologia: "they are odious and hurtful, and it seems like meddling or leaving your work." After gesturing toward his (he implies "our") "own spirits" that suffer neglect when the self turns outward, away from the infinitude of the private man, Emerson seems to deride many of those with whom he shared the platform that day in New York:

> And then I see what havoc it makes with any good mind – this dissipated philanthropy. The one thing not to be forgiven to intellectual persons is not to know their own task, or to take their ideas from others and believe in the ideas of others. From this want of manly rest in their own, and foolish acceptance of other people's watchwords, comes the imbecility and fatigue of their conversation. For, they cannot affirm these from any natural experience, and, of course, not with the natural movement and whole power of their nature and talent, but only from their memory, only from the cramp position of standing for their teacher. – They say, what they would have you believe, but which they do not quite know. (*LL* 1: 334)

One can hear in this monologue echoes of "Self-Reliance" (1841), especially the passages where conformity becomes the very worst thing that we
do. What dissipates the kind of philanthropy Emerson derides here is a
discourse defined by its "foolish acceptance of other people's watchwords,"
by an acquiescence that generates the "imbecility and fatigue of their
conversation." Not marking properly that place where one's own thinking
ends and the thinking of other people begins, Emerson's dissipated philanthropists are like the "timid and apologetic" conformists of "Self-
Reliance" who dare "not say 'I think,' 'I am,' but quotes some saint or sage"
(*CW* 2: 38). Repeatedly, after all, the title virtue of "Self-Reliance" comes
down to the way we speak: "We are like children who repeat by rote the
sentences of granddames and tutors," he writes there, "and, as they grow
older, of the men of talents and character they chance to see, – painfully
recollecting the exact words they spoke."[5] Those recited words constitute for
Emerson a cacophony calling us forth – "a conspiracy to importune you
with emphatic trifles." "[A]ll knock at once at thy closet door and say, –
'Come out unto us.' But keep thy state; come not into their confusion" (*CW*
2: 41). So at least as early as that essay of 1841, Emerson was articulating a
rationale for disengagement and nonparticipation.

By the moment of his January 25, 1855, speech at Tremont Temple in
Boston, he had walked back somewhat his reticent tone. "I approach the
grave and bitter subject of American slavery with diffidence and pain," he
said. "It has many men of ability and devotion who have consecrated their
lives to do it. I have not found in myself the right qualifications to serve
this any more than other political questions by my speech, and have
therefore usually left it in their honored hands" (*LL* 2: 1). But even there,
Rowe would point out that Emerson's embrace of abolition skewed from
those earlier notions out of "Self-Reliance" that seem to prioritize solitude over society. Thus Rowe insists that "When Emerson in the mid-
1840s did turn seriously to the political issues of his day – women's rights
and the abolition of slavery, he was faced with the problem of adapting
his transcendentalism to the pragmatics of political activism."[6] This,
Rowe argues, he could not actually pull off, and so Emerson found
himself in pendulum swing from action to abstraction and back:
"When he endorses a liberal political position," Rowe writes, "he must
abandon transcendentalist principles; when he embraces transcendentalism, his politics are patronizing and impractical as the formula for
'reform' in *Nature* and his other early writings. In short, Emersonian
transcendentalism and political activism in mid-nineteenth-century
America were inherently incompatible."[7]

Rowe conveys his account of Emerson's abolitionist commitments to demonstrate the political uselessness of his transcendentalism. But *At Emerson's Tomb* was only part of a pitched exchange conducted by Emerson scholars attending to the archive of Emerson's abolitionist oratory. Other participants in this conversation sought to illustrate what they saw as an implicit radicalism inherent in works like *Nature* (1836) or *Essays*, first and second series (1841, 1844), an unsettling force of which Emerson's eventual activism was the expression and fruition, not the abandonment. In his 1990 *Virtue's Hero: Emerson, Antislavery, and Reform*, Len Gougeon examines Emerson's engagement with abolition to argue that while "the problem of slavery would remain a moral and philosophical abstraction for Emerson until August 1844" (when Emerson would deliver the abolitionist and yet moderate "Emancipation in the British West Indies"), eventually it was not, but that development was not experienced by Emerson himself as some break with his prior idealism. In fact, Gougeon points out that an association of transcendentalism with political quietism would have been familiar to Emerson as it was also well circulated in his day, especially during the 1830s. Emerson acknowledged the accusation in an 1837 address wherein he stated, "The young man relying on his instincts who has only a good intention is apt to feel ashamed of his inaction and the slightness of his virtue when in the presence of the active and zealous leaders of the philanthropic enterprizes, of Universal Temperance, Peace, and Freedom."[8] But as the 1840s witnessed so many prominent self-identified transcendentalists embracing abolition, the apparent connection between passivism and transcendentalism loosened. "Ultimately," Gougeon contends, "any discussion of the relationship of transcendentalism to abolitionism necessarily requires a careful consideration of which transcendentalist and time period one is discussing."[9]

In Gougeon's account, Emerson's 1837 statement on slavery at Concord's Second Church revealed his reluctance to commit himself to any cause along with his disgust at slavery's influence over American culture. "The concept of external social reform brought on by the agitation of groups ran counter to his commitment to individuality and self-redemption," Gougeon writes: "many of the abolitionists themselves ... he perceived to be shallow and self-aggrandizing."[10] And yet Emerson was moved to give the address out of his revulsion at the murder of abolitionist publisher Elijah Lovejoy by a proslavery mob in Alton, Illinois (though as Gougeon suggests, Emerson equivocated on this occasion by weighting the speech away from abolition and toward matters concerning freedom of expression). In Gougeon's account of what came after this moment, Emerson entered a silent period of seven years during which he further percolated his intellectual convictions as a Unitarian, according to which "social improvement would be 'a by-product of the salvation of individuals.'"[11] Antislavery advocacy, according to Gougeon, became for Emerson a task not of abandoning self-reliance but of instilling moral self-reliance among Americans who had heretofore adapted their principles to economic, political, or racist prerogatives.

Gougeon's study did not simply provide a view of Emerson that might have dissuaded Rowe. It swept aside an account of an apolitical Emerson that had extended at least as far back as Stephen Whicher's 1953 *Freedom and Fate: An Inner Life of Ralph Waldo Emerson*, which had insisted that Emerson's life's task was to resist the call of social engagement and thus more sublimely to sound the inner ocean. Whicher argued that Emerson's greatest achievement was in satisfying "his wish for independence," which "clashed also with his sense of obligation to be useful to the society he repudiated."[12] And well after Whicher, other readers, including not only Rowe but George Kateb, Sacvan Bercovitch, and Cornel West, wrote of Emerson during this period of the 1990s in ways that tended to understand Emerson's activism as a deviation from his more typical commitment to inwardness.[13] But other scholars, like Gougeon, noted that antebellum Americans experienced Emersonian transcendentalism as a politically disruptive force that was at least implicitly abolitionist in its core principles.

Indeed, such interests shaped the research agendas of Emerson scholars in all sorts of ways. One intriguing article-length study in this sense was Matthew Guinn's 1999 "Emerson's Southern Critics, 1838–1862," which noted that the critique of Emerson as a "reckless iconoclast [and] an enemy to tradition" "was nowhere more pronounced than in the South," where "[t]he southern press tended to perceive Transcendentalism as a dangerous, alien force with Emerson as its figurehead – the preacher of an egalitarian philosophy that threatened the foundations of the South's hierarchical slaveholding society."[14] Others whose work on Emerson would bridge the gap Rowe had insisted separates transcendental abstraction from political serviceability included Martha Schoolman, whose "Emerson's Doctrine of Hatred" re-reads "Self-Reliance" – particularly, the passage Schoolman positions as "Emerson's best-known statement on social reform":

> If malice and vanity wear the coat of philanthropy, shall that pass? If an
> angry bigot assumes this bountiful cause of Abolition, and comes to me
> with his last news from Barbadoes, why should I not say to him, "Go love
> thy infant; love thy wood-chopper: be good-natured and modest: have that

grace; and never tarnish your hard, uncharitable ambition with this incredible tenderness for black folk a thousand miles off. Your goodness must have some edge to it, – else it is none. The doctrine of hatred must be preached as the counteraction of the doctrine of love when that pules and whines. (*CW* 2: 30)

Schoolman notes that the passage has often been cited as evidence of Emerson's hostility to organized abolition. Indeed, even Gougeon had treated the essay as an artifact of Emerson's thinking prior to his conversion to abolitionism, evident in his 1844 address on emancipation in the British West Indies, which was nearly simultaneous with the publication of the second series of *Essays*. But Schoolman rejects that reading and in so doing discards the conversion narrative implicit in Rowe, insisting instead that the passage reveals the essence of Emerson's abolitionism, which was Garrisonian in its copping of a combative, trenchant political bearing intended to disrupt and upend.[15] (Though if that is so, it is a Garrisonian disposition Emerson also seems to have suspended for the 1844 address on British abolition, where Emerson urges moderation and gradualism: "Let us withhold every reproachful, and, if we can, every indignant remark. In this cause, we must renounce our temper, and the risings of pride" [*CW* 11: 100].) So for Schoolman, Emerson's transcendentalism was always headed in the direction of emancipation.

Reading Poe's White Supremacy

Even as this surge of scholarship drew on the nature of Emerson's commitment to abolition – producing a variegated exchange concerning whether, as Maurice Lee has since put it, Emerson's transcendentalism could "get along" with his activism[16] – the terms that have most recently energized exchange over Poe concern his relationship with antebellum white supremacist thought. It should be noted here that, unlike Emerson, Poe was never fully included within the US literary tradition established by twentieth-century formalists such as F. O. Matthiessen (who excluded Poe along with other writers now considered "major," like Dickinson and Douglass, from his 1941 pantheon of writers in *American Renaissance*). During his own lifetime, Poe sometimes seemed to work at excluding himself, writing withering reviews of Nathaniel Hawthorne and William Ellery Channing, among many others, and making allegedly humorous remarks about Margaret Fuller's nonbinary gender. Nevertheless, during the postwar period of the twentieth century a subfield of Poe Studies emerged – eventually spawning a society, two academic journals, and sustained scholarly attention, even if amounting to nothing like the fuller focus that developed around Emerson.

During the two decades prior to this more recent upwelling of interest in Poe's attitudes toward African Americans, the major strains in Poe criticism had focused on (1) his detective fiction and its influences and (2) psychoanalytic approaches to Poe's work – energized especially by Jacques Lacan's and Jacques Derrida's debate, influential among postmodernists, over the intersubjective and libidinal structures of Poe's "The Purloined Letter" (1844).[17] But by the end of the 1990s the exploration of Poe's apparent obsessions with whiteness, insurrection, and enslavement offered Poe scholars a different center of gravity. Two key treatments in this regard were Teresa Goddu's *Gothic America: Narrative, History, and Nation* (1997), which traced the engagement of American gothic narrative with slavery, and Terrence Whalen's *Edgar Allan Poe and the Masses: The Political Economy of Literature in Antebellum America* (1999), which situated Poe in relation to the burgeoning publishing world of antebellum America. Following Toni Morrison's suggestion that Poe is America's most important practitioner of African Americanism (what Morrison described as an aesthetic that "rose out of collective needs to allay internal fears and to rationalize external exploitation," a "fabricated brew of darkness, otherness, alarm, and desire that is uniquely American"[18]), Goddu outlined Poe's unique position in southern literature as the architect of a linkage between race and gothic romance.[19] Whalen's fundamental purpose two years later was to indicate the extent to which Poe's outsider status – his poverty, certainly, but also his externality to the northeastern publishing coteries that sustained writers like Emerson, who in turn shaped them back – makes him a uniquely sensitive barometer of the exigencies of capitalist literary markets of the nineteenth century, but his argument too carried implications for understanding Poe's attitudes concerning race.

Goddu's argument described Poe's fixations on an ethereal whiteness and sinister blackness as part of emergent fantasy-structures that had everything to do with the development of the literary marketplace of the United States between the Revolution and the Civil War. Similarly, Whalen would focus on Poe's situation within the literary economies of the antebellum United States. But central to the latter argument is Whalen's treatment of Poe's racial attitudes as indicated in publications such as *The Narrative of Arthur Gordon Pym of Nantucket* (1838) and (possibly) the so-called Paulding-Drayton Review, a proslavery manifesto published under Poe's editorship in *The Southern Literary Messenger* in

1836 under the title "Slavery." As early as 1974 Poe scholar Bernard Rosenthal had hypothesized that Poe had actually authored the review, which included for example the following racist arguments:[20]

> [W]e shall take leave to speak, as of things *in esse*, of a degree of loyal devotion on the part of the slave to which the white man's heart is a stranger, and the master's reciprocal feeling of parental attachment to his humble dependent, equally incomprehensible to him who drives a bargain with the cook who prepares his food, the servant who waits at his table, and the nurse who doses over his sick bed. That these sentiments in the breast of the negro and his master, are stronger in the breast of the negro and his master, are stronger than they would be under like circumstances between individuals of the white race, we believe.[21]

In a review published in the *Poe Studies Association Newsletter* in 1992, Joseph V. Ridgely attempted to unsettle Rosenthal's argument, citing correspondence between Poe and Beverly Tucker, a prominent apologist for slavery whom Ridgely contended was the more likely author of the review.[22] For his part Whalen would take up and bolster Ridgely's exculpatory account in *Edgar Allan Poe and the Masses*. Indeed, Whalen's approach to such questions concerning Poe's connections with the racist ideologies of his day was largely absolving, as if to settle that Poe was not the author of the Paulding-Drayton Review, or to demonstrate that the violent end of *The Narrative of Arthur Gordon Pym* – concerning more of which presently – may also be read as an allegory of the figurative violence of the publishing industry, vindicates texts that seem to revel in racist fantasy.

In an essay published in *American Literature* three years prior to Whalen's book, Joan Dayan outlined the habit of "decorous forgetting" by which, she insisted, the Poe Society policed scholarship dealing with Poe's attitudes toward slavery. (After delivering a lecture connecting Poe's love poetry to the Paulding-Drayton Review, Dayan received an invitation from the Society to publish the lecture in its annual proceedings volume, but with the advice that she drop the material dealing with the review.[23]) And yet Poe's fiction and poetry repeatedly beg the questions scholars such as Dayan and Goddu raise. Another moment from *Pym* Whalen declines to treat, for instance, seems to offer up a trope of racial separatism based on an anxiety over amalgamation. Pym, exploring the island of the Tsalalis (indigenous people so black, we are told, that even their teeth are black, and also "among the most barbarous, subtle, and bloodthirsty wretches that ever contaminated the face of the globe" [*WEAP* 5: 208]), at one instance discovers a strange brook with practically supernatural characteristics:

> It was not colourless, nor was it of any one uniform colour – presenting to the eye, as it flowed, every possible shade of purple; like the hues of a changeable silk. This variation in shade was produced in a manner which excited as profound astonishment in the minds of our party as the mirror had done in the case of Too-wit. Upon collecting a basinful, and allowing it to settle thoroughly, we perceived that the whole mass of liquid was made up of a number of distinct veins, each of a distinct hue; that these veins did not commingle; and that their cohesion was perfect in regard to their own particles among themselves, and imperfect in regard to neighbouring veins. Upon passing the blade of a knife athwart the veins, the water closed over it immediately, as with us, and also, in withdrawing it, all traces of the passage of the knife were instantly obliterated. If, however, the blade was passed down accurately between the two veins, a perfect separation was effected, which the power of cohesion did not immediately rectify. The phenomena of this water formed the first definite link in that vast chain of apparent miracles with which I was destined to be at length encircled. (*WEAP* 5: 195)

Composed of "distinct veins" of water, "each of a different hue," veins "that did not commingle," this is water that becomes like the blood that flows within other veins, its resistance to admixture and tendency to separate an apt representation of popular notions of biological racial separations circulating within antebellum America. But even that vehicle for a fantasy of racial purity is nothing compared with the end of *Pym*. Having escaped the treacherous natives of Tsalal, Pym proceeds to a South Pole of blinding, supernatural white (his prisoner, the Tsalali Nu-Nu, simply dies on the spot as they reach the epicenter of this region of nearly metaphysical whiteness occupied by a giant figure "the perfect whiteness of the snow"). Such aspects of Poe's fiction, and also from his poetry (like the vertiginous blackness of the Raven, who spends most of the 109 lines of that poem threateningly atop the milky-white bust of Pallas Athena), have caused readers such as Morrison, Goddu, and Dayan to link Poe's work with the fixations that underpinned the plantation society Poe knew: anxieties over miscegenation, over the alleged illegibility of black affect such as over which Jefferson expressed such dread in *Notes on the State of Virginia*, over the threat of insurrection.[24] All three of these sources of white dread circulate through Poe's final short story, "Hop-Frog" (1849). There the title character, a captive from some foreign land now enslaved within the court of a tyrannical king, achieves his liberation first by manipulating the king and his court into allowing him to disguise them as "Eight Chained Ourang-Outangs," a ruse he promises will provide them gratification by inciting "fright" "among the women." In Poe's denouement, Hop-Frog (whom Poe at one point explains "more resembled ... a small monkey, than a frog") not only subverts the racial tropes of the plantation system in transforming masters to apes; he lynches his masters, immolating them before the horrified subjects of the king (*WEAP* 1: 332, 342).

Is "Hop-Frog" a text that channels the same white anxieties that had, at least since Nat Turner's rebellion of 1835, fomented mass dread over insurrection that in turn tightened the police state of plantation society? Or does it, rather, channel Poe's sympathy with Hop-Frog, and perhaps his sense that enslaved black people had been severely provoked by white victimizers? Or is the story, as Whalen suggested in *Poe and the Masses*, another example of the revenge narratives through which Poe imagined exacting pounds of flesh from publishers, editors, readers?[25] Poe, Whalen argues, allows us to comprehend the existence of a sort of "average racism" extant within antebellum America: according to this view Poe harbored notions about slavery and about black people that reflected the bigotry of his society, but that was still a far cry from a more vitriolic racism to be found, for example, in the Paulding-Drayton Review. Though Whalen's conception of average racism helped to contextualize Poe within a literary marketplace that not only tolerated but rewarded the circulation of particular white supremacist notions, other scholars interested in Poe and race, in addition to those I have mentioned, have written about the subject in ways that were less exonerating. For example, Whalen also appeared in an important collection of essays on Poe's attitudes toward slavery and black people edited by J. Gerald Kennedy and Liliane Weissberg, *Romancing the Shadow: Poe and Race* (2001). These nine essays charted Poe's writerly engagement with slave law, amalgamation, insurrection, and other aspects of racial politics in antebellum America, sometimes taking up Whalen's work as a provocation. John Carlos Rowe's contribution, for example, charged Poe for developing "an 'American' rhetoric of imperial power that reinstates ... racial hierarchies."[26] Betsy Erkkila offered her argument that Poe's "To Helen" is "a perfect emblem of the Western ideal of white beauty, white value, and white art" that led to "The Raven" and its fixations on dark otherness.[27] Lindon Barrett, examining Poe's "The Murder of the Rue Morgue," argued that the tale enacted a contrast between the logical Dupin and his adversary (again, apparently a fixation for Poe, a homicidal orangutan) that reinstated antebellum racial hierarchies. The only other entry in the collection to treat "Murders," Elsie

Lemire's "'The Murders in the Rue Morgue': Amalgamation Discourses and the Race Riots of 1838 in Poe's Philadelphia" argued that Poe's use of a homicidal orangutan registered northern dread over a northern black population gaining in sociopolitical power. So, by the first years of the twenty-first century, a full-throated exchange was underway concerning Poe's racism, whether average or not.

Evil and Sin

Such scholars, along with others who enjoined disagreements over the sufficiency of Emerson's abolition, represented a larger field of nineteenth-century Americanists who were in the process of shifting from paradigms that had dominated the field's formation decades earlier, and according to which Puritanical belief systems provided the core fixations of US literary history. Readers such as Rowe, Gougeon, Goddu, and Whalen, engaged though they were in disagreements over Emerson and Poe, all helped pivot the study of these writers toward a new interest in slavery and white supremacy as defining circumstances for US literary production as well as a burgeoning sense that contemporary interests in social and racial justice had a place in defining research programs within American literary studies. A prior generation of mid-century formalists had read northeastern writers as if they were constantly refining the Puritan project of the seventeenth century, even if in post-Revolutionary, post-Enlightenment, Romantic, or transcendentalist guise. Matthiessen's *American Renaissance* (1941) cleared space for Henry Nash Smith's *Virgin Land* (1950) and Perry Miller's *The New England Mind* (1954) and *The Errand into the Wilderness* (1956) as well as R. W. B. Lewis's *The American Adam* (1955), which in turn informed deeply Leo Marx's *The Machine in the Garden* (1964) and Sacvan Bercovitch's *The Puritan Origins of the American Self* (1970) and *The American Jeremiad* (1978). In varying and fascinating ways, these monographs configured the writings of nineteenth-century authors alongside the fixations that had defined the mindset of a first generation of English settlers 200 years before, but those configurations provided a foil for the work of the scholars already described in this chapter.

In a way, in referring the struggles of nineteenth-century writers to those of Puritan forebears – people consumed with problems of evil far more theological and abstract than those that preoccupied Americans who lived through the 1840s and 1850s – those mid-century formalists took their cues from the generation or readers to hold forth just after Emerson's, some of whom inaugurated the Emerson industry that fixed the terms of his canonization around questions that might have been more meaningful for Puritans than for antebellum Americans. Reviewing James Eliot Cabot's 1887 biography of Emerson, Henry James remarked on Emerson's failure to appreciate either Austen or Dickens even as he recalled Emerson's similarly deadened response to works of art in the Louvre and – most gallingly to James – Hawthorne's fiction. "I was struck with the anomaly of a man so refined and intelligent being so little spoken to by works of art," he wrote. "It would be more exact to say that certain chords were wholly absent." Turning to the novelists Emerson would or could not value, James continued,

> Mr. Cabot makes use of a singular phrase when he says, in speaking of Hawthorne, for several years our author's neighbor at Concord and a little – a very little we gather – his companion, that Emerson was unable to read his novels – he thought them "not worthy of him." This is a judgment odd almost to fascination – we circle round it and turn it over and over; it contains so elusive an ambiguity.... Hawthorne's vision was all for the evil and sin of the world; a side of life as to which Emerson's eyes were thickly bandaged. There were points as to which the latter's conception of right could be violated, but he had no great sense of wrong – a strangely limited one, indeed, for a moralist – no sense of the dark, the foul, the base. There were certain complications in life which he never suspected.[28]

James's assessment of Emerson's immunity to Hawthorne's purportedly more unafraid willingness to probe "evil and sin" reads so differently in light of the divergent ways in which the two authors contended with slavery – not only in their varying willingness to speak frankly of the lives it devoured, but in their sense for the obligations of those who claimed personally to object. Does James seriously contend that of the two "neighbor[s] at Concord," *Emerson* was the one who "had no great sense of wrong"? Hawthorne is on record for excusing repeatedly the northern Democratic Party's accommodation of their southern wing's proslavery platform, just as he is on record for having benefited materially in his role as a Party loyalist whose college friend, Franklin Pierce, would serve as the nation's chief enforcement officer of the Fugitive Slave Law. Whatever "complications of life" James thought Emerson "barely suspected," those complications surely did not include that law or the complications it introduced for asylum-seeking black people and for northeastern conscientious objectors to whom Emerson offered encouragement in 1855: "The crying facts are these, that, in a Republic professing to base its laws on liberty, and on the doctrines of Christianity, slavery is suffered to subsist:

and, when poor people who are the victims of this crime ... run away into states where this practice is not permitted, – a law has been passed requiring those of us who sit here to seize these poor people, tell them they have not been plundered enough, and must go back to be stripped and peeled again, as long as they live" (*LL* 2: 2). Emerson's eyes were bandaged? It's a judgment odd almost to fascination.

Of course, like Emerson, Poe also hated novels, just as he hated long poems for destroying the unity of effect he extolled in "The Philosophy of Composition." And if James had a point that the subjects of evil, perversity, and pathology bored Emerson, how much more so than Hawthorne's would Poe's fiction and poetry have struck Emerson as beneath interest? Their political distance notwithstanding, Emerson's private writings about Hawthorne almost always show him struggling against his sense that some invisible, common ligature connected them. But as Howell's anecdote about Emerson and the jingle-man relays, he struggled in no such way over his disregard for Poe. Maybe the sticking point had to do with their divergent poetic aesthetics: Emerson, of course, issued in his 1841 essay "The Poet" his famous call for "metre-making argument," while Poe described his own composition of "The Raven" in order to emphasize a workmanlike process that couldn't be further from Emerson's notion of the poet as a passive conduit for a form of expression that "was all written before time was" (*CW* 2: 6). (And contrast that sentiment against Poe's un-Emersonian remark in "The Philosophy of Composition," according to which "originality ... is by no means a matter, as some suppose, of impulse or intuition.")[29] So maybe Emerson was sneering at the onomatopoeia and repetition of "The Bells" when he called Poe a jingle-man. On the other hand, maybe the fluctuating reputation of either writer tells us much more about what it is we readers need from the literary history of the United States as we read the past through the aperture of our own national present.

Notes

1 William Dean Howells, *Literary Friends and Acquaintance: A Personal Retrospect of American Authorship* (New York: Harper & Bros, 1900), 63.
2 See Edgar Allan Poe, *The Works of Edgar Allan Poe*, 10 vols., ed. Edmund Clarence Stedman and George Edward Woodberry (Chicago: Stone and Kimball, 1895), 8: 207. Further references to this edition are made parenthetically within the text as *WEAP* and include volume and page number.
3 Qtd. in John Carlos Rowe, *At Emerson's Tomb: The Politics of Classic American Literature* (New York: Columbia University Press, 1996), 18.

4 Ralph Waldo Emerson, *The Later Lectures of Ralph Waldo Emerson*, 2 vols., ed. Ronald A. Bosco and Joel Myerson (Athens: University of Georgia, 2001), 1: 259–60. Further reference to *Later Lectures* will be cited parenthetically as *LL* and include volume and page number.

5 Ralph Waldo Emerson, *The Collected Works of Ralph Waldo Emerson*, 10 vols., ed. Joseph Slater et al. (Cambridge, MA: Harvard University Press, 1971–2013, 2: 39. Further references to this edition will be cited parenthetically as *CW* and include volume and page number.

6 Rowe, *At Emerson's Tomb*, 21.

7 Ibid., 21.

8 Qtd. in Len Gougeon, *Virtue's Hero: Emerson, Antislavery, and Reform* (Athens: University of Georgia Press, 1990), 51.

9 Ibid., 50–51.

10 Ibid., 38.

11 Ibid., 41.

12 Stephen Whicher, *Freedom and Fate: An Inner Life of Ralph Waldo Emerson* (Philadelphia: University of Pennsylvania Press, 1953), 64.

13 See George Kateb, *Emerson and Self-Reliance* (Lanham, MD: Rowman & Littlefield, 1995), 25: "I believe that Emerson gives us indications throughout his work that self-reliant existence or action and endeavor can only be marginal or eruptive; it is dependent on the chances the world gives to make a difference. If the idea of self-reliance is to be realized more self-sufficiently, less contingently – difficult as its realization must always be – it must find its location elsewhere than in worldly appearance or activity. Self-reliance must then refer primarily to the work of the inner life, to the life of the mind." Also see Sacvan Bercovitch, who in *The Rites of Ascent: Transformations in the Symbolic Construction of America* (New York: Routledge, 1993) suggests that Emerson "never really gave serious thought to social reform" (325); and Cornel West, *The American Evasion of Philosophy: A Genealogy of Pragmatism* (Madison: University of Wisconsin Press, 1989). West maintains that though Emerson was in some ways disposed to imagine various possibilities for social reorganization, he was "simply by temperament contemplative and solitary. Institutions, organizations, movement, parties repulsed him" and even that he "wanted the best of two worlds – the world of bourgeois prestige, status, and influence and the world of solitude and contemplation" (23).

14 Matthew Guinn, "Emerson's Southern Critics, 1838–1862," *Resources for American Literary Study* 25.2 (1999): 174. Guinn points out that while other scholars had noted Emerson's difficulties with southern critics throughout his career (certainly, Emerson's disastrous lecture at the University of Virginia after the war, which UVA students disrupted, was connected with this hostility), these prior scholars had tended to ascribe the trend to the notion (as put by Jay B. Hubbell) that Emerson "held particular difficulties for Southern readers" since "it was difficult for any Southerner to understand the Unitarian-Transcendentalist background out of which Emerson's writings had grown" (qtd. in ibid., 174). Whether some sectional perplexity shaped the

southern response to Emerson, as Hubbell suggests, Guinn demonstrates that Emerson also emerged as "a nemesis in southern thought" among southern readers who perceived in his lectures and essays a hostility to the plantation system itself.

15 Schoolman writes that "[b]y presenting abolitionism in terms of an intersubjective dialectic in which 'grace' is answererd with 'gracelessness' and 'love' with 'hatred,' ... Emerson performs rather than criticizes key terms of garrisonianism's famously disruptive publicity." See Martha Schoolman, "Emerson's Doctrine of Hatred," *Arizona Quarterly* 63.2 (Summer 2007): 2.

16 Maurice Lee, *Slavery, Philosophy, and American Literature, 1830–1860* (Cambridge: Cambridge University Press, 2005), 182.

17 Lacan's and Derrida's dispute over "The Purloined Letter" was published, along with several commentaries, in *The Purloined Poe: Lacan, Derrida, and Psychoanalytic Reading*, ed. John P. Muller and William J. Richardson (Baltimore: Johns Hopkins University Press). It would be difficult to overstate the extent to which postmodernist obsession with the Lacan/Derrida dispute – the labyrinthine terms of which would require another essay to outline – guided Poe's circulation in scholarship and probably university curricula during the 1990s.

18 Toni Morrison, *Playing in the Dark: Whiteness and the Literary Imagination* (New York: Random House, 1992), 38.

19 Teresa Goddu, *Gothic America: Narrative, History, and Nation* (New York: Columbia University Press, 1997), 75.

20 See Bernard Rosenthal, "Poe, Slavery, and *The Southern Literary Messenger*: A Reexamination," *Poe Studies* 7.2 (December 1974): 29–38. In her 1992 *The Word in Black and White: Reading "Race" in American Literature* (New York: Oxford University Press, 1992), Dana Nelson describes a "recent trend to sweep Poe's politics under the rug" while drawing attention back to Rosenthal's 1974 essay (91).

21 "Slavery," *The Southern Literary Messenger* 2.5 (April 1836): 338.

22 See Joseph V. Ridgely, "The Authorship of the Paulding-Drayton Review," *PSA Newsletter* 20.2 (Fall 1992): 1–3, 6.

23 Joan Dayan, "Amorous Bondage: Poe, Ladies, and Slaves," *American Literature* 66.2 (June 1994): 239–40.

24 Thomas Jefferson, *The Writings of Thomas Jefferson*, 12 vols., ed. Paul Leicester Ford (New York: G. P. Putnam's Sons, 1904), 4: 50.

25 For Whalen the protagonists of such righteous vengeance narratives include Dupin, who has a personal debt to repay the Minister of "The Purloined Letter"; Legrand of "The Gold-Bug," who has lost his wealth due to "a series of misfortunes [that] had reduced him to want"; and indeed Hop-Frog, who "having been more thoroughly degraded, exacts a more terrifying retribution" See Terrence Whalen, *Edgar Allan Poe and the Masses: The Political Economy of Literature in Antebellum America* (Princeton, NJ: Princeton University Press, 1999), 37–38.

26 J. Gerald Kennedy and Liliane Weissberg, eds., *Romancing the Shadow: Poe and Race* (Oxford: Oxford University Press, 2001), 77.

27 Ibid., 52.

28 Henry James, *The American Essays*, ed. Leon Edel (Princeton, NJ: Princeton University Press, 1956), 74–75.

29 Edgar Allan Poe, "The Philosophy of Composition," *Graham's American Monthly Magazine of Literature, Art, and Fashion* 28.4 (April 1846): 166.

CHAPTER 21

Fuller/Stowe

Dorri Beam

In the preface to his field-defining *American Renaissance: Art and Expression in the Age of Emerson and Whitman*, F. O. Matthiessen confides, "The Age of Fourier" is one of "the important books I have not written."[1] With this, Matthiessen nods to and, though with a tinge of regret, parts with the great political and social ferment of the period. Yet the invitation to consider another American Renaissance under the banner of a French philosopher and inaugurator of European socialism is certainly provocative. Could a body of literature credited with the founding of democratic individualism really have any traffic with European socialism – a European socialism premised on a critique of the family, no less? Might the social experiment and the aesthetic experiment of the "age" in fact be thought together?

Fourier's socialism was distinct from the later, now more familiar, version of Karl Marx in that it connected the relations of labor with the relations of family. For Fourier, the "isolated household" was the chief bane of "Civilisation," the term he used for the darkest, most chaotic stage of human development.[2] It was the organization of labor and affection into the enclosed economic and social unit of the household that wasted resources of time, material, and, most of all, passion. Movement was a key component of Fourier's cosmos, and the crucial, generative resource of passion must keep moving from object to object, whereas the isolated household locked up passion by making domestic labor drudgery and binding men, women, and children to each other for a lifetime through so arbitrary a pretense as genealogy. The passions could be expressed only within a collectivity, and marriage was particularly incarcerating for women's passion (Fourier has been credited with coining the term *feminism*). As historian Gareth Stedman Jones puts it, "the basic unit in Fourier's theory was not the individual, but the group, his minimum number was three."[3] Fourier's great "science," as he called it, of putting the world together anew was also an art.[4] Passion flowed most freely, he held, through ongoing series of novel and various combinations of

352

anything from pastries to jobs to lovers. As Roland Barthes put it, Fourier's theory of serial relation was a "cutting up," rather than a cutting down, of the world, "an exalting, integrating, restorative reading, extended to the plethora of universal forms."[5] The composition and movement through such series Fourier related to the composition and enjoyment of musical scales, and deemed it the highest of pleasures (*seriism*).[6] For Marx and Engels, there was "poetry" in Fourier's system that his practical followers could not always capture. Margaret Fuller herself remarked that in his "arrangement of groups and series," Fourier was "a seer of the divine order, in its musical expression."[7] As these thinkers attest, Fourier's socialism proposed there was an art to assembling and organizing collectivities, one that would yield the poetry of a collective way of being.

Fourier lived long enough to see his ideas take practical root in the United States in a way they did not in France. In 1845 when Margaret Fuller published *Woman in the Nineteenth Century*, the country was in the midst of a decade-long surge in communal utopian experiments, most of them Fourierist. As Larry Reynolds has documented, the European revolutions of 1848, many galvanized by socialism, had a profound effect on American social thought and on the literary authors of the period, especially Fuller, who, until her untimely death in 1850, covered the Italian Revolution from Rome as European correspondent for the New York *Tribune*, a position Marx would also later assume.[8] By the early to mid-1850s, when Harriet Beecher Stowe published her trio of major abolitionist works, *Uncle Tom's Cabin*, *A Key to Uncle Tom's Cabin*, and *Dred: A Tale of the Great Dismal Swamp*, the tide of social agitation was urgently concentrated on the task of abolition, as the defense of slavery and its expansion into new territories accelerated with unprecedented boldness and at a staggering rate. Historians such as Manisha Sinha have recently moved abolition to the center of radical, transnational social movements, including "utopian socialism, feminism, and pacifism," thereby rejecting its traditional casting as a bourgeois movement "burdened by racial paternalism and economic conservatism."[9] Abolition's "steady radicalization on women's rights, organized religion, politics, and direct action" and its embrace of a Black radical perspective can be traced over the course of Stowe's pages as well, as Robert Levine and Martha Schoolman have shown.[10] While abolition's condemnation of slavery's perversion of the family is well known, as is Stowe's role in that narrative, the sequencing of Fuller and Stowe invites us to think about the ways in which late radical abolition took up a radical critique of the family from the utopian socialist and feminist fronts with which it came to align.

Reframing both authors in an American Age of Fourier makes clearer their contributions as social theorists and brings into view both the critique of the family and consequent concern with reassembling social order at the center of both feminism and abolitionism in their work. While critics frequently place Fuller's radicalization at the moment of her later exposure to and participation in the European revolutions of 1848, her explicit engagement with Fourier began in the pages of *Woman in the Nineteenth Century* in ways that align her gender politics with his radical critique of the "isolated household" and with the many intentional communities that sought alternative organizations of labor, economics, and sex. Stowe's later abolitionist texts develop a penetrating analysis of slavery as an institution, indeed as a system, that co-opts the family to capitalism while disavowing the family's relation to either capitalism or slavery. Nested within this attack is a more radical critique of the family as complicit with the aims of racial capitalism than Stowe is generally credited with.

Putting Fuller's and Stowe's work in dialogue allows for a new approach to form in their work as well, particularly the way they put the elements of their texts together. Rather than the unidirectional didacticism with which both Stowe and Fuller are frequently charged, their texts are compositional, networked texts, responding to others, open to the reader and thinking through large-scale systems of relation. Robert Levine points to Stowe's willingness to "situate her ideas in a dialogical context."[11] Her dialogism can be extended to her works, where she fleshes out points of view to put them in play with others, an arrangement which subtly comments without commenting. Fuller is well known for preferring spoken "conversation" to written narrative or monologue. *Woman in the Nineteenth Century* in fact develops out of the formal "Conversations" she held for women in Boston, encouraging them to weigh, synthesize, and order multiple perspectives in response to her verbal prompts.[12] In both authors' texts, these dialogues also turn out to the reader, who bears responsibility for weighing perspectives and composing the organizational logic of the text through the act of reading. Less concerned with authoring or originating discourse, their texts seek to limn the social and textual in ways that activate dialogue, coordinating new conversations and new combinations of participants.

Stowe's and Fuller's works are formally characterized by distinctive organizational modes attempting to enact their goals for political organization. Fuller's *Woman* and Stowe's *A Key to Uncle Tom's Cabin*, Stowe's second and overlooked abolitionist text, are particularly striking feats of assembly, actively composing myriad documents, dialogues, instances, and figures. Stowe's novels likewise gather wide swaths of characters and place them in novel combinations with each other and with scenes and events. Notably, both writers fashion themselves as divinators, gleaning "signs of the times" – often literally piecing together items from the newspaper (and not missing the import in their mastheads – *The Times, The Herald*) to divine the underlying source of trouble.[13] Summoning this vast array of material, they discern patterns, obscured logics, and operations of power, seeking to bring into view large-scale phenomena of social organization that can be seen only in the aggregate – the naturalized system of gender and the vast, authoritarian machinery of slavery – but, in doing so, they also partake of the visionary insistence of the Age of Fourier – that the social world can be put together differently. Orchestrating and arranging their vast archives of figures, data, and voices, Fuller and Stowe summon the editorial arts of compilation and arrangement to "make up" their texts and activate new social logics toward collective life and transformative change.

As Fuller wrote of Rome on January 6, 1850, the "seeds for a vast harvest of hatreds and contempts are sown" by authoritarian rule and await "a fire that will burn down all, root and branch, and prepare the earth for an entirely new culture. The next revolution, here and elsewhere, will be radical."[14] With her research into the American slave system for her 1853 *A Key to Uncle Tom's Cabin*, and her subsequent 1856 novel *Dred: A Tale of the Dismal Swamp*, the titular hero of which was based on Nat Turner, Stowe moved into and promulgated an understanding that slavery was a domestic authoritarian system that needed to be fully and finally eradicated. For both Fuller and Stowe, violence was a legitimate and increasingly necessary response, but the longer and more difficult revolution would be in the building of a radical, "entirely new culture."[15]

Composing Woman

Woman in the Nineteenth Century itself is arguably the trail of Fuller's visionary instantiation of repeated series of women, from contemporary instances to historical to mythological. In each of these series, she seeks to divine the full "scale" of the phenomenon "Woman." The goal is not to present static role models but to place exemplary women in combinations that become more than the sum of their parts and project extensional forms that would allow passions to flourish and yield the human variety that society had yet to endorse, a variety visible in the arrayed series of the text. Thus, for Fuller, the "Woman" of *Woman in the Nineteenth Century* is not a single idea; rather, it is an assemblage of many possibilities. This is what Fuller means by her notoriously confusing title of the earlier, shorter version of *Woman*, "The Great Lawsuit. Man versus Men: Woman versus Women," published in the Transcendentalist small press journal *The Dial*, while she was at the editorial helm. The parts (individual women) cannot be confused for the whole (Woman). The whole (Woman) is never fully contained in a particular woman, and in fact Woman, as a gender principle, exists in tension with Man in every person. The title demanded that readers think about Woman relationally. That is, while the text sought to understand the relation of women to the entire phenomenon of Woman, it also sought to know the relation of the phenomenon of Woman to that of Man. Fuller understood gender to be dialectical. Hers is not simply a call for female self-realization or rights; Fuller's attempt to restructure the relation between masculinity and femininity, and between women and men, strikes at the heart of social organization, finding that society is not organized to give Woman (or Man for that matter) its full breadth, sweep, and force.

Through its repeated catalogs of women, *Woman* sets out gender as a series of possibilities rather than a rigid binary. Like Fourier's phalanxes – the grouped and serialized structures he imagined would facilitate people's movement through varied occupations or into attractive combinations of interests – Fuller builds out the structure of Woman as a category, giving it breadth and dynamism and making it habitable, allowing the range of movement and variety necessary. She summons women from the past to come before us in newly meaningful combination: "a Semiramis, an Elizabeth of England, a Catherine of Russia," with "the lonely Aspasia," and the exclamatory "Sappho! Elosia!" ring out the martial aspects of Woman.[16] "The Diana, Minerva, and Vesta," the celibate series, flanked by "Sita in the Ramayana," "the Egyptian Isis," and the Sphinx, are gathered to indicate both their singularity (and singleness) but also their typicality, the way they mark out a significant aspect of Woman, with the definite article before their names.[17] These were not to be static cookie-cutter types: Fuller is interested in the dynamic relation between the units in each array, the way each warrior plays off the others, refining the intricacy of female heroism with some new aspect of how she unfolded the martial face of Woman within the particular set of relations in which she found herself. The connective tissues of Fuller's series are the narratives Fuller gives each woman, where the finer grain of the women in Woman can be seen. The project is ever to see the individual in her historical and transhistorical placement within the greater sweep of a social world, a social world so arranged by Fuller to bring Woman in to view.

In her challenges to sex and gender complementarity, Fuller's efforts rest on a serialized span of possible combinations indebted to Fourier's model, as she posits series of sex and gender positionalities in which gender "has not been given pure to either [man or woman], but only in preponderance."[18] "A zodiac of the busts of gods and goddesses, arranged in pairs" as well as "whole calendars of female saints" serve Fuller as formal models.[19] Gazing on the zodiac, she observes, "The circle breathes the music of a heavenly order. Male and female heads are distinct in expression, but equal in beauty, strength, and calmness.... Could the thought, thus expressed, be lived out, there would be nothing more to be desired. There would be unison in variety, congeniality in difference."[20] Fuller stretches the dualism of masculine and feminine over a series of positions, each with a male and a female version that are not, she states, oppositional "complement[s]" but mutual "companion[s]."[21] The consequence of Fuller's division of gender types according to the proportion of a quality, rather than its definitive absence or presence, is that she understands gender to be a matter of degree rather than of positive category. In another example, Fuller attempts to define the poles of masculinity and femininity, breaking out of the prose style of *Woman* and using the structure of verse to order them visually on the page:

> The growth of man is two-fold, masculine and feminine.
> As far as these two methods can be distinguished they are so as
> Energy and Harmony.
> Power and Beauty.
> Intellect and Love.[22]

Even as Fuller repeats a dualistic gender structure within each line, the lines also create a set, and as a set work to proliferate the terms of the dualism. That is, she begins to serialize, if we think of this list form as neither a linear progression nor a random catalog but instead a series of related but varied repetitions on a form, visually ordered on the page. When she goes on to suggest that "if these two developments were in perfect harmony, they would correspond to and fulfill one another, like hemispheres, or the tenor and bass in music," she uses a term that became widely associated with Fourierism: harmony.[23] Fuller's interest is not in a bland unification of diverse elements but in music. Harkening to Fourier as "a seer of the divine order, in its musical expression," Fuller riffs on his use of musical harmony as a template for social organization, one that combines a number of elements in a dynamic composition, by positioning gender duality on a musical scale that ascends and descends through a variety of notes that play off each other, music that we are perhaps to hear in her verse-like list as well.[24]

Like Fourier, Fuller understood marriage as fundamental to the problem of female restriction to an isolated domestic sphere, because it was at the center of a sex/gender system that produced woman and man as binary complements, that required sexual difference and the division of labor. Fuller devotes a significant section of *Woman* to classifying and describing four types of marital partnership, which she places on a spectrum from the most practical of matches to a union infused with religious dedication to a higher cause. Marriage is a problem not only for women as individuals, restricted to certain roles; it is a problem for the social order, because the couple, in which the woman is absorbed, becomes the smallest viable unit of the polity. Fuller's interest in marriage is thus two-pronged: in the abstract, marriage should reflect the dynamic relation of "Woman" to "Man," rather than the confining complementarity or, worse, the gender hierarchy, that the institution actually imposed on women and men. Until the marriage relation was transformed, or dispensed with, it both distorts the dynamism of gender, in its narrow depiction of the relation of masculinity to femininity, and suppresses women's participation in the social order by absorbing them instead into the isolated household. Moreover, unequal marriage and the underdevelopment of women for and by marriage creates a heritable condition of female underdevelopment and dependency. Marriage produces wives, not women, and daughters who become wives.

Fuller seems to realize that even an ideal and equitable marriage cannot escape the complementarity of the couple form, and she restlessly turns to consider the "old maid." The unmarried aunt or uncle, she proclaims, can "rove about," as she puts it, "like mental and moral Ishmaelites, pitching their tents amid the fixed and ornamented homes of men."[25] Here these ancillary figures, linked to no single relationship, pose a challenge to the enclosure of the family. They "suppl[y] defects" in the "busy" household, like co-op parents. They "gain a wider, if not so deep existence" because they "are not intimately and permanently linked with others," and here she registers the socialist value of Fourier's breakdown of the isolated household, where roving aunts and uncles can distribute "truth and love," as well as their talents, "for the use of all men, instead of a chosen few, and interpret through it all the forms of life."[26] The aunt and uncle's non-exclusive relation to children and to companion adults opens them out to more capacious and varied (roving!) relations.

Fuller famously concludes that "we must have units before we can have union."[27] Fuller's units can certainly tend toward a romantic individualism, as her exemplars are sometimes seen retreating to caves or mountaintops to discover an inmost being. But Fuller is displaying her mediation of Goethe's romantic individualism and Fourier's socialistic new order. She wishes women to be the "companion" not "complement" to men. Her concern is as much with the way Goethean "self-culture" might allow women to distribute their social relation as it is with the growth of women as individuals: "A being of infinite scope must not be treated with an exclusive view toward any one relation."[28] Thus, Fuller's units are also her building blocks for a new social organization, and those units must have the ability to form a much larger structure. Her panoply of virgins and single/singular women, while each intensely focused inward, is not unlike Walt Whitman's later "comrades" in refusing the familial unit, or the closed-off couple, as a basis for a social democracy. Fuller insists that this breaking-off of relations is preliminary to the founding of a new social order. Fuller's concern with gender is not simply a plea for inclusion in an existing structure – the structure will need to change. Indeed, the structure will change by virtue of putting its parts together differently.

Just as Fuller builds an expansional structure of Woman for women to inhabit and increase, she also builds an extensional structure between women through time. As Wai Chee Dimock argues of *Woman in the Nineteenth Century*, "a large-scale paradigm makes for a different kind of kinship."[29] Fuller's exemplary women are not isolated exceptions when they are connected through time, so that, for instance, De Stael's "*statistical* offspring" can be identified in the schoolgirl who recites her; as Fuller says of Sappho and Eloisa, "with time enough, space enough, their kindred appear on the scene."[30] In what Dimock calls a kind of "reproduc[ing] through the archives" in Fuller's *Woman*, De Stael's very existence guarantees the likelihood there will be descendants.[31]

Dimock's thinking points to a different kind of history writing and a different kind of relationship to the future. A woman from the past – a de Stael, a Boadicea, or even a Fuller – does not simply represent a flat "type" of woman, a complete ideal to which one must live up or within which subsequent women are trapped. That is, Fuller makes Woman an ongoing relational structure, a "kinship" that engenders both indebtedness to and inheritance of the ongoing task of Woman. Rather than positing complete ideals, Fuller insists that one must add to the never-to-be-finished ideal. Each of Fuller's significant women is only a part of an ongoing effort that must be carried forth through time. We might say that self-culture is not about cultivating an interior private essence or "finishing" a socially performative self; it is about cultivating and tending Woman, tapping into and contributing to a much larger, more extensive collective project.

Fuller ends *Woman* with a trail of appendixes, each offering a new or revisited cameo appearance of some type of Woman, many lushly presented in ornate dress or dramatic tableaux. But the types are not ordered and arrayed as they were within the body of the text. Nor do we have Fuller's studied editorial and critical mediation – these are leaves left on the cutting-room floor unassembled after the arrangement of *Woman* is done, giving a peek at the materials and the labor of the composition: one number is simply "an extract from a letter addressed to me from one of the monks of the nineteenth century," another is a "quote from memory" of an extract "I have mislaid," a long poem is not translated from the Italian, and another excerpt is "borrowed from the papers" of an even younger "Miranda" than we had already heard from in *Woman*, indulgently allowed to appear as is ("I trust the girlish tone of apostrophizing rapture may be excused").[32] Miranda collapses temporal and spatial divides to come face to face with Woman, announcing, "As I look up I meet the eyes of Beatrice Cenci," and apostrophizing, "Beautiful one" and "Beatrice!"[33] The girlish apostrophizing of the "memoranda" of Miranda, a character generally taken to be pseudonymous for Margaret, seems to provide a kind of primal scene for the origins of *Woman*. The vagaries of passionate attraction, rather than the methods of critique or classification, seem the glue of this virtual gallery of spectacular, lovingly described women that Fuller gathers into felicitous association. The arrangement, here no more than a loose gathering, reveals that Woman is most visible, most attractive, in the company of other women. A new erotics, not simply generational kinship, shimmers in the passionate labor of searching for and bringing forth Woman, of reproduction from the archives. Fuller flips the cards out to the reader in disarray, seemingly unvetted, challenging the reader to passionately take up, adore, and increase Woman.

Assembling Dre(a)d

Stowe's work is part of a larger abolitionist organizational project, one that has perhaps been muted by an intensive critical focus on questions of the extension of sympathy, white advocacy, or representational politics. These are frequently aspects of abolitionist texts and of *Uncle Tom's Cabin*, but studies of Black print culture and the broader coalitional abolitionist press of which Stowe's work is part have begun to emphasize the shared and networked quality of abolitionist expression, "modes of textual production that exceed origination to encompass reading, maneuvering, and rearrangement" in which editing, citation, and composing become creative acts that accede to prominence over the authorial function.[34] Susan Gillman has argued that *Uncle Tom's Cabin* must be seen within the web of its entire phenomenon, as itself a networked text – reread, rewritten, and redistributed at every node.[35] Indeed, as Robert Levine has shown, Stowe's subsequent texts are part of that phenomenon as she carries on the process of creative revisionism in dialogue with Frederick Douglass, Frances Harper, and Martin Delaney in particular, and African American writing and testimony more generally.[36] As Cindy Weinstein and Susan Ryan have argued, Stowe's response to slavery was equally honed, and radicalized, by her deepening exposure to the southern defense of slavery (itself galvanized and intensified by *Uncle Tom's Cabin*).[37] These critical contexts remind us that abolitionist texts are products of a social movement, arising out of highly networked conversations and coordinated speech and action, as well as emerging from and for different fronts, rather than springing *sui generis* from an individual imagination.

The elaborate character systems of Stowe's novels work something like her networked writing process and the circuits of reception, response, and agitation her novels enter. Though criticism has focused on the representation of character and the mode of sentiment in *Uncle Tom's Cabin* (and the novel is indeed character-driven), its form also seeks to put characters in relation and to modify them by that relation. The novel is built around an intricate network of characters who meet and change. Her form investigates these exterior relations and their effect, rather than diving into interiority or psychological motivation. When a Tom, or an Eva, or a George is viewed in isolation, they are diminished and often distorted by the loss of these relations. Because this character system is so tightly woven, the events of *Uncle Tom's Cabin* tend to take place because of character agency, which networked and modified as it is by others, nonetheless appears the primary causal agent of events. Failure to act on the part of Shelby or St. Clare sends Tom deeper into the South, while Legree's excessive agency condemns Tom to death, placing the weight of slavery on individual failures of will and moral conscience. The too-eager martyrdom of Tom, on the one hand, and the too-decisive flight of George, on the other, diminish the power of slavery. Too often Tom's plight appears to be his choice; too easily George is able to choose and successfully negotiate his escape, moved along his path by those other whole-cloth dissenters, the Quakers.

The prominence of character seen in *Uncle Tom's Cabin* recedes into the scale and power of the slave system in Stowe's next two works, a process that is patent in the form of *A Key*. Stowe's characters, defended as relevant lenses on slavery in the first section of *A Key*, are soon eclipsed by the forces of public sentiment, organized religion, and law unflinchingly documented in the three dense, double-columned succeeding sections. While sentiment, religion, law, and personal character all offered grounds for hope and resistance in *Uncle Tom's Cabin*, *A Key*'s careful documentary reconstruction reveals instead that in the slave South, as in the complicit North, none of these features of social and civic life is any contest for US slavery; each is conditioned by "the absolute despotism of the slave law."[38] The problem of slavery is no longer a matter of individuals feeling wrong or right, exercising power over others, or seeking to change them, as readers of *Uncle Tom's Cabin* might expect. The problem, as *A Key* comes to see it, is rather that slavery is a total system closed to individual agential action.

Before the first section is over, *A Key* has left its defense of her characters (and their author) and is focused on dismantling, piece by piece, the South's fictional portrait of slavery, the "dream [of] the oft-fabled poetic legend of a patriarchal institution, and all that" as Stowe called it, with irony that has been underestimated, on the first pages of *Uncle Tom's Cabin*.[39] Rhetorically styled less on the nuclear, isolated family than on the patriarchal tribes of distant biblical eras or pastoral feudalism, the proslavery portrait promoted a "bright" picture of the plantation as itself a communal experiment. This was a flagrant distortion of property, labor, and familial relations in slavery, and yet it is one that has continued to mask the ways in which capitalism emerged out of slavery, particularly the form developed in the United States in the last thirty years before the Civil War, with the rise of cotton and the cessation of the international slave trade.[40]

Stowe harvests information from myriad sources – legal cases, ecumenical conferences, revival sermons, book reviews and magazine essays, news reports, classified ads, letters from her friends and readers, Black and white, North and South, fugitive slave accounts, and abolitionist pamphlets. Citation, compilation, and documentation are recurring forms across abolitionist genres, but *A Key* performs critique through composition, rather than decomposition or fragmentation, by gathering, arranging, and piecing together fragments from the newspaper, slave codes, and sermons.

Against popular assumptions and southern assertions that the slave trade had ended, *A Key* tallies auction advertisements from eleven southern papers for two weeks to yield an astonishing estimate of "sixty or eighty thousand human beings being raised yearly and sold in the market" from the "slave-raising states" in the Upper South to the "slave-consuming" states.[41] *A Key* reads the robust continuance of a slave trade and the forced migration of children, teens, and young adults in the description of the traders' lots. It exposes the extraction of labor by torture and the disposability of laborers in a running list of citations from enslaved people, tourists, and southern expatriates, documenting the failure of most slave owners to provide habitable shelter, more than one garment, or enough food. In an entire, visually arresting compilation of slave auction inventories and fugitive slave advertisements from the classified ads from 200 southern newspapers, *A Key* reads the torture of those enslaved in the scars described in almost every ad, the rape of women in the color of the escapees, and a trade in children and teens in the young ages of the auction lists. These methods of compilation demonstrate, in their collation and sheer repetition, the frequency of torture, the extent and distribution of abuse, and the vast scale and machinery of the enterprise of slavery. Through this compiling of evidence, a picture develops of a total system. Over the course of *A Key*, then, Stowe comes to understand her task as a question of the true political economy of slavery. In *Dred* she will continue to interrogate slavery, and resistance, through the lens of political and social organization, rather than characterological representation and individuated agency.

Dramatizing a number of the legal cases, vigilante scenes, and slave testimonies she had compiled in *A Key*, *Dred* is distinguished from *Uncle Tom's Cabin* in that it concerns itself less with the wrongs of slavery as experienced by individual victims and witnesses than with the vast coordination of slavery's systematized exploitation of Black lives. Stowe turns also in *Dred* to the question that headed the final chapter of *A Key*: "What is to be done?" This is a markedly different orientation from the protest novel's focus on exposing present ills, involving speculation toward a future. The question, however, was not an easy one in 1856, after the Kansas–Nebraska Act seemed to cede new territory to slavery, the caning of Charles Sumner on the Senate floor heralded the end of civility, and the looming Dred Scott decision would soon declare the Black man had no rights that white men were bound to respect. These events only reinforced the perspective in *A Key* that reforms to, compromises with, or the containment of slavery will not be effective because, as *A Key* had shown, the authority of slavery is absolute, and must be so to sustain it.

Such dark, uncertain times also sparked new urgency and activism: as Derrick Spires argues, the "spirit of '56" echoed but also recast that of '76 among abolitionists.[42] In the absence of state, political, legal, or religious institutions driving the abolition of slavery, Stowe looks to revolutionary, nonstate change. Most obviously, she turns to slave revolt, styling her titular hero after Nat Turner and, in an instance of creative kinship through the archives, makes him a son of Denmark Vesey. *Dred*'s revolutionism presses beyond the emphasis on a parricidal battle between men that Eric Sundquist reads in Turner's *Confessions*.[43] In the figure of Cora Gordon, Stowe adds the maternal revolutionism of Margaret Garner to the pantheon of Black revolutionaries. Garner killed her child in early 1856 rather than have her retaken into slavery after the family's daring flight across the Ohio River, and came to embody the Spirit of '56 for Black radical abolitionists such as Frances Harper and Frederick Douglass.[44] Stowe seems to twin the revolutionary violence of Garner with that of Turner when Cora Gordon's clear-eyed, unflinching testimony of her act echoes Turner's tone in the *Confession*, reprinted by Stowe in the appendix. Cora/Garner's terrifying violence, both intimate and symbolic at once – the killing of her child to put an end to the heritable condition and social reproduction of slavery – is the reverse edge of Turner's killing of the entire white slave-owning family, wives, daughters, and infants included. Turner and Garner's revolutionary acts strike at the familial foundations – both genetic and patriarchal – of slavery. In the character of the homonymic "Livy Ray," Stowe's Gordon is also flanked by the suggestion of radical women's rights and abolitionist activist Lucy Stone, who visited Garner in prison and speaks at her trial. Entwining arguments against marriage with those against slavery, Stowe's novel seems to make the case less for their analogy than for the interdependence of the two institutions.

Dred has been criticized for failing to stage the revolt it plots. In fact, Dred, the revolutionary hero, is cut down before the time is right for the anticipated contest. A second major protagonist, Nina Gordon (the white half-sister of Cora), who is involved in what appears to be a Plantation Novel marriage plot, is also cut down, by a cholera plague that rains down indiscriminately on the area plantations, as if in extension of Dred's Turner-like prophecies of divine retribution. But *Dred*, like other antislavery experiments with genre, is "retell[ing]" received narratives "through formal failure"; in this case, the romantic narratives of heroic agency, and of female *Bildung* and marriage, must be undone, de-formed, to open up other possibilities.[45] In cutting down her protagonists, Stowe acknowledges the serious limit on agency in an authoritarian system. But in its working desire to effect a breach with the patriarchal proslavery narrative and disrupt the genealogical and hierarchical structure of the plantation, the novel actively submerges the heroine and hero into the making of new collectives, moving from character to collectivity, from patriarchy to communitarianism, and from heroic agency to collective movement.

Stowe's narrative in fact tests associationist ideas throughout and uses the ending to reorganize her characters into small-scale models of a new social order that themselves subtly reference actual communitarian experiments. But it is Dred's swamp community, where self-emancipated people live in an open collective, that stands as the premier intentional community in the novel, one that generates others. In the figure of Dred, Stowe thus connects militant with social revolution. Cedric Robinson's classic text, *Black Marxism: The Making of the Black Radical Tradition*, treats the maroon colonies of the New World as the inauguration of Black Radicalism and an alternative to European socialism, where New World Africans separately developed an independent analysis of capitalism and established nonwestern formulations of communitarianism, entirely their own. The narrative of *Dred* makes repeated visits to the maroon community, remarking on the labor and domestic arrangements there and gradually revealing the extent of the Black underground network that it sustains and is sustained by. Dred is a literal heir to Vesey, but the blasted tree at whose roots he is buried signals a broader network of inheritance and resistance in which individual death is not a limit to revolution and fathers give way to movements. In the image of Dred's burial place, Stowe seems to pay homage to Toussaint Loverture, who claimed his death would be a blow to "only the trunk of the tree of liberty; it will spring up again from the roots, for they are many and they are deep." All characters must first pass through Dred's swamp before dispersing and reorganizing into new combinations at the North. Resistance is not an individuated affair incubated in the nuclear family, nor is revolution Oedipalized as patricide and the replacement of one father for another. As with Fuller's *Woman*, in *Dred*, each heroic entry is only another turn of the wheel of revolution in a long-term collective endeavor.

Rather than either Black or white characters resuming "the kind of relationship disrupted or foreclosed by the economics of slavery," such as male wage earning, marriage, and restitution of a heteronormative family, a generic expectation imposed on the fugitive slave narrative and adopted by Stowe for her fugitives in *Uncle Tom's Cabin*, the northern communities of Milly and Tiff, even the Claytons, are cross-class and cross-racial collectives.[46] One group "assumes the character of a family," a slave-holding family, in the collective exodus from the South, but the very act of passing indicates how transitive familial organization has become as characters break with the patriarchal property relations of slavery.[47] As Tess Chakkalakal has remarked, marriage certificates and wedding ceremonies are largely absent. Even coupling is conspicuously missing. Tiff and Milly, like Fuller's avuncular kin, each "rove" outside the traditional family, extending love and caretaking to children without homes and parents, and Clayton triangulates his companionate bliss with both his sister and Livy Ray, with a wink to Lucy Stone's public refusal of marriage. Sons must extract themselves from the Father's law, performing the radical abolitionist injunction to "come out" from institutions corrupted by slavery, which Stowe overlaps with the family: Edward Clayton from the authoritarianism his own father's court upholds and Harry Gordon from the blood laws that leave him unable to assume his father's house or protect his sisters, Black or white, from its heritable curse. Instead of usurping their father's place, they find themselves attached to collectives – a utopian community explicitly based on Elgin, the abolitionist agrarian settlement for fugitive slaves in Canada – as well as to more intimate but egalitarian bonds with women. The final clusterings in *Dred*'s conclusion differ markedly from the novelistic restitution of separate, generational, blood families at the end of *Uncle Tom's Cabin*. Rather than restore characters to families, Stowe suggestively remakes collectivities, shifting away from the heteropatriarchal white family as the essential economic unit and sketching out potential lines of gender, race, and economic reorganization.

Yet there is a speculative, provisional, "what if?" quality to these quick final chapters as they telescope into the future. The characters are settled, in nonslave territory and into new forms of relation, but we are not yet to close the book, for these are not the novel's final words. Stowe concludes her book cathecting the messier, uncertain, temporally disjunctive form of assemblage with that of the novel at her narrative's exit. We are asked to imagine an asterisk at the end of these characters' story lines when Stowe appends three documentary appendixes, the nearly complete *Confessions of Nat Turner*, a section on court decisions upholding the absolute authority of the master including the brutal Souther case, and two chapters from *A Key* documenting official Church support for slavery. The three documents qualify the settled resolution into interracial, antiracist communities. Assemblage keeps the movement of the text going, opening it back up, and revives the agitation, working on the reader.

Scholars have made much of the structure of feeling fomented by the novel, locating its most radical work there. Justine S. Murison points to the text's embrace, as a form of power, of the "enthusiasm," fanaticism, and insanity of which abolitionists were frequently accused.[48] Don James McLaughlin further reads the "dread" of the text as Stowe's appropriation and redirection of the politics of fear and phobia that galvanized proslavery.[49] The dread of the text, however, is something not just wielded or personified by her eponymous main character; it is also experienced by him and his ensemble cast. Dread is the lurking mood of the novel as the novel interrogates each facet of the slave system, and the complacencies (Clayton), naivete (Nina), idealism (Harry), or faith (Milly) of all but the titular character, who has always known such dark revelation, are gradually exposed and extinguished. Dread as affect is the anticipatory admission of the necessity of violent revolution in the face of absolutism. But as such it also encompasses much more than personal fear of revolt or war. It marks the slow peeling away of illusion, hope, and faith and the gradual exposure of an absolute system beyond the control of any one hero or villain or any single battle. No novel plot can stage its vanquishing. The ending acknowledges this reality – this dread is not to be resolved by the catharsis of battle; the anticipated contest is still anticipated because racial slavery is still entirely intact.

For a similar appendixing that restructures the feeling of a politically progressive resolution, we might turn to Black filmmaker Spike Lee's appending of footage from the Charlottesville 2017 Unite the Right rally to his 2018 film *BlacKkKlansman*, about the successful cross-racial coalitional infiltration of the KKK in the 1970s, led by Ron Stallworth. To adapt the phrasing of Christina Sharpe, the somber endnotes of these texts "annotate" the progressive politics of the narratives they append, striking a tonal shift and creating a factual drag on their happy endings.[50] The potentiality of interracial coalitional change – signified by the police force that took down the Klan at the direction of their new Black officer happily mugging for Lee's camera, or Stowe's snapshots of interracial communities of fugitives living in newly meaningful and prosperous relation to each other – is tenuous. The anti-Black climate, to borrow from Sharpe again, requires vigilance; it does not pass and remove the need for resistance, the storms roll around again, as David Duke and the Klan resurface in Lee's appended footage and as the judges and clerics of Stowe's appendix at the time of her writing still enact the anti-Black logics of church and state and foster vigilantism as the enforcement arm. Lee's editing brings into focus the incredulity and fear of one white female protestor chanting "Black lives matter!" as she hears the anti-Semitic chants of the young white supremacist "torch bearers" on the University of Virginia Lawn and the anguish of a young Black man protesting, "This is my town!" in the seconds after a car killed Heather Heyer when it plowed into counter protesters as they were chanting "Whose streets? Our streets!". Fear, incredulity, anguish – bracing for the return, the ceding of progress, and the effort required to move forward anyway: the end "notes" of these texts strike a key of dread. Rather than taking up the prophecy of Turner's *Confession*, prefiguring God's judgment in a definite teleology of end times, epic battles cycle around again in these appendixes, signaling less dramatically to rounds of struggle that do not end. Dread, as the structure of feeling induced by the turn of the wheel of revolution and the turn of the page or reel to these endnotes, emerges as the antithesis of complacency: faith in the present or future of progress is dangerous, these texts warn. Even while the characters are settled, the issues of slavery and white supremacism are not and the forces of resistance and oppression will continue to battle.

Reframing for an American Age of Fourier Dimock's assessment that the reach and extent of Fuller's *Woman* well into the ranks of the "planetary dead" honors and "embraces the unfinished task of the dead," we might argue that Fuller's and Stowe's creative assembly and temporal extensions of revolutionary lines and their trials, failures, and remaking teach us about the daunting scale social movements must assume, one that matches the scale of the systems they seek to change. In every age, it seems, Woman must be built out again against incursions and diminishments, and dialogue restored where it is silenced. The revolutionary speech and action of Turner, Garner, and Dred is necessarily incomplete, but the recurrence of such resistance, signaled in Stowe's return to Turner at the narrative's exit, is as certain as the system of racial slavery, or its legacy, that calls it out. So arranged as to prod, reposition, and involve, the passions of the Age of Fourier course through *Woman in the Nineteenth Century* and *Dred*, pulling the reader into their sweep. To maintain the momentum, the texts unravel the temporality of their own composition, opening back up at the end, moving us to take up the burden of their further composition. Embracing the unfinished tasks of these works, while ongoing, is not always a project of going forward. We must sometimes go back to the boards, even back to the important books we have not (yet) written to find out where we are going. Resigned only to the necessity of going on, social movements must abide in the long durée of the climate they seek to change.

Notes

1 F. O. Matthiessen, *American Renaissance: Art and Expression in the Age of Emerson and Whitman* (New York: Oxford University Press, 1968 [1941]), viii.

2 Charles Fourier, *The Theory of the Four Movements*, ed. Gareth Stedman Jones and Ian Patterson (New York: Cambridge University Press, 1996), 42, 5.

3 Gareth Stedman Jones, introduction to Fourier, *The Theory of the Four Movements*, xix.

4 Fourier, *Four Movements*, 4.

5 Roland Barthes, *Sade, Fourier, Loyola*, trans. Richard Miller (Baltimore, MD: Johns Hopkins University Press, 1976), 96.

6 Ibid., 82.

7 Margaret Fuller, *Woman in the Nineteenth Century*, in *The Essential Margaret Fuller*, ed. Jeffrey Steele (New Brunswick, NJ: Rutgers University Press, 1992), 315, 314.

8 Larry J. Reynolds, *European Revolutions and the American Literary Renaissance* (New Haven, CT: Yale University Press, 1988).

9 Manisha Sinha, *The Slave's Cause: A History of Abolition* (New Haven, CT: Yale University Press, 2016), 3, 1. Adam Tuchinsky similarly argues that the socialist critiques of labor and land use in the 1840s carried through to abolitionist platforms: *Horace Greeley's "New York Tribune": Civil War Era Socialism and the Crisis of Free Labor* (Ithaca, NY: Cornell University Press, 2009).

10 Sinha, *The Slave's Cause*, 3. For excellent discussion of Stowe's involvement with radical abolition and with Black radical abolitionists, see Robert Levine, *Martin Delaney, Frederick Douglass, and the Politics of Representative Identity* (Chapel Hill: University of North Carolina Press, 1997), and Martha Schoolman, *Abolitionist Geographies* (Minneapolis: University of Minnesota Press, 2014).

11 Levine, *Martin Delaney, Frederick Douglass*, 148.

12 See Charles Capper, *Margaret Fuller: An American Romantic Life, vol. 1: The Private Years* (New York: Oxford University Press, 1994), 296. For Fuller's dialogic relationship with Ralph Waldo Emerson, see Christina Zwarg, *Feminist Conversations: Fuller, Emerson, and the Play of Reading* (Ithaca, NY: Cornell University Press, 1995). Fuller's dialogism and networks are at the center of much recent work, especially the collections *Margaret Fuller and Her Circles*, ed. Brigitte Bailey, Katheryn P. Viens, and Conrad Edict Wright (Durham: University of New Hamphire Press, 2013), and *Toward a Female Genealogy of Transcendentalism*, ed. Jana L. Argersinger and Phyllis Cole (Athens: University of Georgia Press, 2014).

13 Fuller, *Woman*, 256–57, 260, 277, 340. Some of the most striking moments in Stowe's *A Key* involve the gathering and interpretive reading of fugitive slave signs and auction advertisements. Harriet Beecher Stowe, *A Key to Uncle Tom's Cabin; Presenting the Original Facts and Documents upon Which the Story Is Founded. Together with Corroborative Statements Verifying the Truth of the Work* [1853] reprint (Port Washington, NY: Kennikat Press 1968), 129–47, 175–84.

14 Margaret Fuller, *New York Tribune* dispatch, January 6, 1850, in Steele, ed., *Essential Margaret Fuller*, 434.

15 Ibid., 434.

16 Fuller, *Woman*, 266–67.

17 Ibid., 269.

18 Ibid., 343. See also Dorri Beam, *Style, Gender, and Fantasy in Nineteenth-Century American Women's Writing* (Cambridge: Cambridge University Press, 2010) for Fuller's theory of gender.

19 Ibid., 272.
20 Ibid.
21 Ibid., 269.
22 Ibid., 343.
23 Ibid.
24 Ibid., 314.
25 Ibid., 298.
26 Ibid., 298–99.
27 Ibid., 301.
28 Ibid., 298.
29 Wai Chee Dimock, *Through Other Continents: American Literature across Deep Time* (Princeton, NJ: Princeton University Press, 2006), 57.
30 Fuller, *Woman*, 267.
31 Dimock, *Through Other Continents*, 58.
32 Fuller, *Woman*, Appendix E, 364; F, 365; G, 365.
33 Ibid., Appendix G, 377.
34 Lara Langer Cohen, "Notes from the State of Saint Domingue: The Practice of Citation in *Clotel*," in *Early African American Print Culture*, ed. Lara Langer Cohen and Jordan Alexander Stein (Philadelphia: University of Pennsylvania Press, 2013), 164. See also Eric Gardner, *Black Print Unbound: The Christina Recorder, African American Literature, and Print Culture* (New York: Oxford University Press, 2015), and Derrick R. Spires, *The Practice of Citizenship: Black Politics and Print Culture in the Early United States* (Philadelphia: University of Pennsylvania Press, 2019).
35 Susan Gillman, "Networking *Uncle Tom's Cabin*; or, Hyper Stowe in Early African American Print Culture," in Cohen and Stein, eds., *Early African American Print Culture*, 231–49.
36 Levine, *Representative Identity*.
37 Cindy Weinstein, "*Uncle Tom's Cabin* and the South," in *The Cambridge Companion to Harriet Beecher Stowe*, ed. Cindy Weinstein (Cambridge: Cambridge University Press, 2004), 39–57; Susan Ryan, *The Grammar of Good Intentions: Race and the Antebellum Culture of Benevolence* (Ithaca, NY: Cornell University Press, 2004).
38 Harriet Beecher Stowe, *A Key to Uncle Tom's Cabin: Presenting the Original Facts and Documents upon Which the Story Is Founded* [1853] (New York: Dover Reprint, 2015), 15.
39 Harriet Beecher Stowe, *Uncle Tom's Cabin* [1852] (New York: Modern Library, 1996), 13.
40 See Edward E. Baptist, *The Half Has Never Been Told: Slavery and the Making of American Capitalism* (New York: Basic Books, 2014). See also Eric Williams, *Capitalism and Slavery* (Chapel Hill: University of North Carolina Press, [1944] 1994), and Cedric Robinson, *Black Marxism: The Making of the Black Radical Tradition* (Chapel Hill: University of North Carolina Press, [1983] 2000).
41 Stowe, *A Key*, 152, 139.

42 Spires, *The Practice of Citizenship*, 220.

43 Eric J. Sundquist, *To Wake the Nations: Race in the Making of American Literature* (New York: Belknap Press, 1994).

44 See Spires for an extensive discussion of how Garner figures in Harper's revision of "The Slave Mother.". See also Mark Reinhardt, *Who Speaks for Margaret Garner?* (Minneapolis: University of Minnesota Press, 2010).

45 Manu Samriti Chander and Patricia A. Matthew, "Abolitionist Interruptions: Romanticism, Slavery, and Genre," *European Romantic Review* 29.4 (2018): 431–34, 431.

46 Houston A. Baker, Jr., *Blues, Ideology, and Afro-American Literature* (Chicago: University of Chicago Press, 1984), 48. For a critique of this masculinist prerogative, see Deborah E. McDowell, "In the First Place: Making Frederick Douglass & the African-American Narrative Tradition," in *Critical Essays on Frederick Douglass*, ed. William Andrews (Boston: G. K. Hall, 1991).

47 Harriet Beecher Stowe, *Dred: A Tale of the Great Dismal Swamp*, ed. Robert Levine (Chapel Hill: University of North Carolina Press, 2000), 539. For thoroughgoing readings of family, property, and collectivity in *Dred*, see Holly Jackson, *American Blood: The Ends of the Family in American Literature 1850–1900* (New York: Oxford University Press, 2014); Jeffory A. Clymer, *Family Money: Property, Race, and Money in the Nineteenth Century* (New York: Oxford University Press, 2014); and Maria Karafilis, "Spaces of Democracy in Harriet Beecher Stowe's *Dred*," *Arizona Quarterly: A Journal of American Literature, Culture, and Theory* 55.3 (1999).

48 Justine S. Murison, *The Politics of Anxiety in Nineteenth-Century American Literature* (Cambridge: Cambridge University Press, 2011).

49 Don James McLaughlin, "Dread: The Phobic Imagination in Antislavery Literature," *J19: The Journal of Nineteenth-Century Americanists* 7.1 (Spring 2019): 21–48.

50 Christina Sharpe, *In the Wake: On Blackness and Being* (Durham, NC: Duke University Press, 2016); see chapter 4 on Black annotation and redaction. I adapt these "modes of making sensible" to these texts' central concerns with movements for social change and racial justice, through the editorial arts of selection, emphasis, organization, and supplement.

CHAPTER 22

Hawthorne/Winthrop

Christopher Castiglia

Perhaps no commonplace is truer than: you can't choose whom you love. The adage suggests the waywardness of attachments, particularly emotional, erotic, and romantic ones. We are drawn to people we know are wrong for us. We have fondness – even obsessions – for things that do not seem, rationally, to warrant our devotion. Heartsickness is endemic. Still, the heart wants what it wants, often in defiance of common sense, good advice, well-being, or laws and conventions.

Over the course of the twentieth century those attachments were often subjected to regulation, criminality, injunctions to secrecy, and shame. Freud contended that certain erotic attachments – of children to parents, of siblings to each other, to people of the same gender, to fetishes and other objects of obsessive attention – are neuroses to be "cured." Sexologists such as Havelock Ellis in England and Richard von Krafft-Ebing in Germany initiated the scientific study of human sexuality. Their effort to liberalize attitudes toward sexual variety produced taxonomies that turned erotic attachments into fixed sexual identities that more conservative scientific authorities designated as incorrectly or incompletely developed, biologically deformed, or perverse. By the late nineteenth century, most forms of emotional, sexual, and erotic attachment became things to be treated as problems to be cured, straightened out, explained away. And when those therapeutic approaches did not work, new laws made certain sexual acts, identities, and representations illegal, subject to fines and imprisonment.

Yet, as scholars of sexuality have shown, there was a period before all that, when attachments proliferated that later generations condemned as strange, unnatural, perverse, or obsessive, some not even recognizable to us today as "sexual."[1] Although these attachments could attract shame and punishment, they escaped the fates that awaited them half a century later. In the first half of the nineteenth century, American literature depicted a range of strange, unregulated, intense attachments – to people of the same sex, to material objects, to animals and nature – that, at the time, did not always seem to require punishment. In what follows I call those attachments wayward, strange, intense, and, most often, queer, even though those labels may say more about our restricted notions than they do about the early nineteenth century. I focus primarily on two very different authors – Nathaniel Hawthorne (1804–1864) and Theodore Winthrop (1828–1861) – whose novels show a wide range of intense, perverse, or unruly attachments. I contrast these authors to highlight the emergence of forms of shame, punishment, and discipline that became dominant in the next century. Alongside these responses, this literature also demonstrates the coming-into-being of a concept of subculture, of wayward attachments not only as individual but as collective phenomena.[2] The differences between these authors show, in other words, the beginning of the conflicting agencies – one regulatory, institutional, and punishing, the other informal, contingent, and pleasurable – that grew stronger in opposition to each other, coming to a head in New York in 1969, when police harassment of a bar called the Stonewall Inn met resistance from patrons who occupied a queer demimonde, an event widely cited as signaling the rise of the modern gay rights movement.

Nathaniel Hawthorne was no stranger to obsessive, unruly, queer attachments. In *The Scarlet Letter* (1850), the intense and lawless attachments between the single Puritan woman Hester Prynne and her minister lover Arthur Dimmesdale and between the young Hester and her older, obsessively vengeful husband Roger Chillingworth; the sadomasochistic relationship between Chillingworth and Dimmesdale; and the relationship between the community and the scarlet A Hester wears on her breast as a shameful reminder of her adultery are obsessive, rebellious, uncontrollable. One might use similar adjectives to describe the relationships among three American artists living in Rome in Hawthorne's late romance *The Marble Faun* (1860), and between each artist and the beautiful, young, Italian nobleman Donatello, who bears an uncanny resemblance to an ancient sculpture of a faun, a mythological creature between man and animal associated with unbridled sexuality. The intense friendship between the two women, the infatuation of the two women and their male companion with the animal-man Donatello, and one artist's fanatical devotion to the art of the Old Masters all supply the messy, absorbing, unmanageable attachments that characterize Hawthorne's fiction.

Sometimes attractions to things and places are as disconcerting, at least to modern readers, as those to people. Take, for instance, Hawthorne's 1851 *The House of the Seven Gables*, a tour de force virtual compendium of queer attachments. The story centers on the Pyncheon family, whose "curse" arises from and becomes an unshakable obsession. We might even say obsession *is* the Pyncheons' curse. In the seventeenth century, an ancestor of the present-day Pyncheons became obsessed with obtaining the land on which the House of the Seven Gables is built, to the point of having its rightful owner, Matthew Maule, hanged as a witch. On the scaffold Maule cursed Pyncheon, resulting, it would seem, in the latter's death and the loss of a deed granting the Pyncheon family ownership of a large tract of land in Maine. That deed then becomes a family obsession through the generations, especially for the unscrupulous present-day Judge Pyncheon, who, believing he is about to inherit the family wealth, has his cousin Clifford wrongly convicted and imprisoned for murder. Clifford's sister, Hepzibah, mourns for him obsessively, while the family's ancestral home grows as decrepit as Hepzibah herself. When Clifford is ultimately released, he seems mad, soothed only by certain aesthetic objects to which he has an inordinate attachment. In the end, the deed, now worthless, is discovered behind another Pyncheon fetish, a portrait of the ancestor who began the chain of calamitous attachments. *The House of the Seven Gables* thus comprises a host of odd, unhealthy, intense, obsessive attachments, including a near-incestuous devotion of a sister for her brother; a family's fetishistic attachment to a house, a deed, and a portrait; an aesthetic fascination bordering on insanity; and an unshakable attachment to a curse.

Nevertheless, *The House of the Seven Gables* ends pretty well for the Pyncheons, who move into the mansion that had been the home of the corrupt judge, united in what promises to be a satisfactory, if not exactly blissful, future. The novel is brought to its seemingly happy ending by a resolution many have found contrived, the romantic union of the cheerful young Phoebe Pyncheon and the reformer and daguerreotypist Holgrave, a Maul descendent. Heterosexual union resolves the long-lived curse, then, and frees the Pyncheons from their gloomy fate. At what price, though? Hawthorne's conclusion forecloses the other, in many ways more interesting, attachments the rest of the novel chronicles, aligning heterosexual romance with health and happiness, a future-oriented attachment. Queerness becomes a thing of the past, associated with insanity, ill-health, and joylessness, leaving the family not in the home they love but in the Judge's domicile. Thus *The House of the Seven Gables* anticipates the control the late nineteenth century saw exercised on strange or unruly attachments by psychiatry, medicine, and the law. The novel is also typical of the ways women in particular are forced to bear the weight of normative heterosexuality, since it is by and large the queer attachments of

Hawthorne's characters – Hepzibah's attachment to Clifford, Hester's to Dimmesdale, Zenobia's to Hollingsworth, and so on – that are punished in the romances.[3]

Queer attachments meet an even worse fate in Hawthorne's third romance, *The Blithedale Romance* (1852), also a story of obsessions and misplaced attachments. Its four main characters – the gruff prison reformer Hollingsworth; the abused young girl Priscilla; her haughty, feminist sister Zenobia; and the effete, at times comical, narrator, Coverdale – inhabit a utopian farm community called Blithedale. Priscilla maintains an obsessive devotion to Zenobia, who treats her with contempt. Zenobia, for her part, carries an inextinguishable flame for Hollingsworth, whose interest in her extends only as far as her substantial fortune, which, he sees, might fund his plan for prison reform. Otherwise, he rejects her not only because of his obsession with that reform but also because of his passionate attachment to Coverdale. Along the way the novel features a host of fetishes: the veil that covers a mysterious woman who can be placed in a trance from which she divulges the secrets of paying customers; the gold teeth of Westervelt, an ominous character with a secret past; the purses made by Priscilla; and the exotic flowers Zenobia wears in her hair. Each of these objects is shrouded with danger and foreboding, as ill chosen as the characters' passions for other people, all of which end in tragedy. Zenobia, scorned, drowns herself. Priscilla gives her life to the unfeeling Hollingsworth, who is destroyed by his single-minded adherence to prison reform.

But that obsession is not the only thing that destroys Hollingsworth. He also has a queer attachment. Despite his iron-willed sternness, Hollingsworth is capable of startling tenderness toward Coverdale. In those moments, "his dark, shaggy face looked really beautiful with its expression of thoughtful benevolence."[4] When Coverdale becomes ill, Hollingsworth will allow no one else to serve as Coverdale's nurse. Despite Coverdale's claim that men "really have no tenderness," the novel describes how "something of the woman moulded into the great stalwart frame of Hollingsworth, nor was he ashamed of it, as men often are of what is best in them" (39). At the worst stage in the illness, Coverdale reports, "I besought Hollingsworth to let nobody else enter the room, but continually to make me sensible of his own presence by a grasp of the hand, a word, a prayer, if he thought good to utter it" (39).

There is no future for this tender attachment, however, at least not for Coverdale, who can imagine their intimacy only in death. He regrets "that I did not die then, when I had tolerably made up my mind to, for Hollingsworth would have gone with me to the hither verge of life, and have sent his friendly and hopeful accents far over on the other side" (39). Perhaps for this reason, when Hollingsworth's passion reaches a fever pitch, Coverdale throws water on the flame. Hollingsworth begs Coverdale to join him in his prison reform, telling him that "'there is not the man in this whole world whom I can love as I could you. Do not forsake me!'" (124). But Coverdale rebuffs him, confessing, "Had I but touched his extended hand, Hollingsworth's magnetism would perhaps have penetrated me," but, he claims, "I stood aloof" (124). When Hollingsworth asks one last time if Coverdale will be his "friend of friends forever" (125), Coverdale's refusal is devastating. Of himself, the narrator states, "The heart-pang was not merely figurative, but an absolute torture of the breast." The impact on the reformer is worse. The rebuff strikes him "like a bullet. A ghastly paleness – always so terrific on a swarthy face – overspread his features. There was a convulsive movement of his throat, as if he were forcing down some words that struggled and fought for utterance." The despondent Hollingsworth can only say "Well!" and walk away, heartbroken, like most of Hawthorne's queer lovers such as Hester, Hepzibah, or Miriam in *The Marble Faun*, who seem self-destructively incapable of letting their attachments go (126).

Unlike those lovers, Coverdale seems to walk away unscathed. This seems related to the fact that he professes no queer attachments of his own, unless we count the novel's closing lines, in which out of the blue he announces he has loved Priscilla all along, a passion the novel has given no evidence of. As with *The House of the Seven Gables*, this imposition of a conventional ending has the effect of suddenly, even violently foreclosing other, odder attachments. By the time Coverdale proclaims his love for Priscilla, the girl is unavailable, and his declaration risks little in terms of his having to follow through with an actual heterosexual union. While safe in that regard, however, Coverdale remains alone, the condition of Hawthorne's other queer characters – Hester Prynne, Hepzibah Pyncheon, Zenobia – who, isolated in their nonnormative attachments, are doomed to silence, despair, disappointment, and even death.[5]

To say that Hawthorne's novels enjoy a canonical status denied to those of Theodore Winthrop is an understatement. A descendant of several eminent New England families dating back to the Puritan governor John Winthrop, Theodore Winthrop is perhaps best known to historians today not as a novelist but as the first Union officer killed in a Civil War land battle. Yet Winthrop wrote three novels, *Edwin Brothertoft*, *Cecil Dreeme*, and *John Brent*, and a travel narrative of his adventures in the Pacific Northwest, *The Canoe and the Saddle*, all published posthumously, as was a volume containing his poems and a brief biography of the author, *The Life and Poems of Theodore Winthrop*. Winthrop's fiction has remained virtually unknown until recently, and even now only *Cecil Dreeme* has been republished. Yet for those interested in the literary history of sexuality, Winthrop's work is essential reading.

Winthrop's best-known novel, *Cecil Dreeme* (1862), begins with its narrator, Robert Byng, newly returned from Europe, occupying a friend's bachelor pad – affectionately named the Rubbish Palace – which is crammed with incongruous artworks and relics organized by their owner's quirky taste. Already we are in a world of obsessive preoccupation with objects made "magic, phantasmagorical" by that attachment.[6] Like fetishes, these objects are imbued with life by their beholder: the things in the Rubbish Palace, Byng says, "seemed to retain their former semi-animation, to desire to be the properties of an actual drama, to long to sympathize with joy and sorrow, as they had dumbly sympathized long ago" (52). Exerting a "dreamy influence" over Byng, these seductive objects awaken what he calls a "certain romantic feeing of expectation" (39).

That expectation is heightened by another "dreamy influence" when Byng learns of a mysterious artist named Cecil Dreeme. Byng's obsessive attachment begins before it even has an object, as he imagines himself the object of a mystical seduction. "The melodious vagueness of the name," he asserts, "greatly attracted me" (57), and instantly Byng begins "to long to be acquainted with this gentleman" (58). The two begin a friendship "more precious than the love of women" (235). Byng reports of Dreeme, "there was in this strange young genius a passionate ardor, always latent, only waiting to flame forth, when his heart was touched" (212). At the same time that he imagines the effect of his passion on the aptly named Dreeme, Byng registers Dreeme's power over him: "How strangely his personality affects me!" (213). Dreeme's strange influence lifts Byng from a life "monstrously dull, pale, and prosaic" (203), and he proclaims to Dreeme, "'I often feel, now, as I stir about among men, collecting my budget of daily facts, that I only get them for the pleasure of hearing your remarks when I unpack in the evening'" (208). In his life apart from Dreeme, Byng continues, "'I train my mental muscle with other people. You give me lessons in the gymnastics of finer forces. My worldly nature shrivels, the immortal Me expands under your artistic touch'" (208). That touch turns physical when, walking one evening, Dreeme "dropped his cloak and took my arm" in his first "slight token of intimacy." In that instant the narrator learns the truth of what another friend has told him, namely, when one is eager to love, friendship "'soon ripens to frenzy'" (89).

In addition to the queer interest of Byng's friendship with Dreeme, an even queerer attachment in the novel is that between the narrator and Densdeth, a villain with a "dark, handsome face" (62) and "a delicate lisp" (74). Capable of "'perfect sensitiveness and perfect enjoyment'" (63), Densdeth finds his pleasure particularly in toying with the susceptible Byng, who states, "'When his eyes were upon me, I felt something stir in my heart'" (65). Byng wonders, with a combination of panic and titillation, "Will he master my will?" The answer is: yes, with a particular emphasis on "master." Densdeth exercises "an irresistible attraction" (180), and, unlike Byng's friendship with Dreeme, this seems a queerly sadomasochistic relationship. Densdeth exerts "attraction by repulsion" (178), for, as Byng acknowledges, "Pain is the elder brother of Pleasure" (192). Awakening such a painful pleasure, Densdeth posed "an unwholesome test of my self-control" (66), Byng reports. For his part, Densdeth finds Byng "'worth buying, worth perverting'" (64).

Cecil Dreeme would seem to end like Hawthorne's romances, with an eleventh-hour resolution of queer attachments into normative relationships (or the suggestion of them). But Winthrop does not bring queer attachments to an unhappy conclusion, although he comes close. When Cecil turns out to be the disguised heiress Clara Denman, Byng's dream threatens to becomes a nightmare. Considering his friendships with men "more precious than the love of women" (235), Byng is dismayed by the turn of events. Although Clara assures him, "'We shall not be friends the less'" (337), Byng has his doubts, claiming of his friendship with Cecil: "This was love, – unforced, self-created, undoubting, complete. And now that the friend proved a woman, a great gulf opened between us. Thinking thus, I let fall Cecil's hand, and drew apart a little" (347–48). Yet perhaps his preferred attachment is not quite severed: even after Clara's revelation, Byng continues to use the masculine pronoun and his friend's pseudonym, "for so I must call him" (338). Byng's attachment to Densdeth meets a more conclusive end, as the latter dies a violent death cradled in Byng's arms. Densdeth lives on, however, in Byng's melancholic absorption of the villain's sadistic power. Now Byng reveals his own "devilish passions" "slumbering lightly, and ready to stir whenever [they] knew a comrade was near" (330). Despite Densdeth's death and Cecil's eventual return to Clara, social conventions in *Cecil Dreeme* remain haunted by queer attachments in the form of persistent memory and desire.

Those attachments prove even more enduring in Winthrop's *John Brent* (1862), a novel composed of strange obsessions, homoerotic object choices, and unshakable attachments. The novel begins with its narrator, Richard Wade, in a state of ennui. He has been working in a California mine but finds the work unrewarding, both emotionally and financially. When his sister on the East Coast unexpectedly dies, Wade sets out to care for her orphaned children. This start might seem to promise what Wade later calls "the tame, limited, submissive civilization that hangs about lattices and trellises and pets its chirping pleasures, keeping life as near the cradle as it may be."[7] Yet the family plot quickly disappears and the orphaned children are never mentioned again. Instead, Wade begins a chain of queer attachments, the first of which exceeds human society altogether.

In order to travel east, Wade must attain a horse. Watching a group of horses, Wade's attention is drawn to one in particular, and apparently the horse shares the instantaneous attractions, as it begins nuzzling Wade. "A horse knows a friend by instinct," Wade reports. "So does a man. But a man, vain creature! Is willing to repel instinct and trust intellect, and so suffers from the attempt to revise his first impressions, which, if he is healthy, are infallible" (15). Throwing off the constraints associated with human "intellect," Wade accepts his attraction to the horse whose name, Don Fulano, also connotes forms of otherness associated by upper-class New Englanders with ethnicity and nationality, enhancing the appeal of this "dark" horse. Wade and Don Fulano find themselves "growing fast friends," as Wade, operating through what he calls "the law of love" (26), makes a previously untamable beast into a loving companion. The two enjoy "as close a brotherhood as can be between man and beast" (34). Noting of the horse, "'To look at such a fellow is a romance'" (50), Wade confesses, "'If I had ever seen a woman to compare with that horse, after her kind, I should not be here'" (50). Later, describing how he was drawn to the horse "by a gentle seduction," Wade says of Don Fulano, "'His coquetries are as beautiful as a woman's'" (287). Smitten, Wade declares, "I loved that horse as I have loved nothing else yet, except the other personage with whom and for whom he acted in this history" (34).

That "other personage" is John Brent, a friend Wade has not seen since their childhoods. On his first view of Brent as an adult, before he recognizes him as his long-lost friend, Wade exclaims, "'The Adonis of the copper-skinned!'" and professes his wish to be a "squaw, to be made love to by him" (38). Wade idealizes Brent, stating, "Nothing could damp his enthusiasm. Nothing could drench his ardor. No drowning his energy.

He never growled, never sulked, never snapped, never flinched" (55). When Wade first knew him, Brent had been "a delicate, beautiful, dreamy boy" (41), and now, encountering him in full manhood, Wade professes, "I learned to love the man John Brent, as I had loved the boy; but as mature man loves man. I have known no more perfect union than that one friendship. Nothing so tender in any of my transitory loves for women.. . . Such a friendship justifies life" (57–58).

Brent seems to inspire such queer attachments wherever he goes. When he is shot and dangerously wounded, for instance, Brent is carried to Fort Laramie, where he finds instant admirers in Commander Ruby and Doctor Pathie, who declares of his patient, "'I love the boy. I keep my oldish heart pretty well locked against strangers; but there is a warm cell in it, and in that cell he has, sleeping and waking, made himself a home.'" Ruby makes clear the erotic and romantic implications of this love for Brent and another equally handsome patient: "'Ah, Doctor,' said Ruby, 'you and I, for want of women to love, have to content ourselves with poetic rovers like Brent. He and Biddulph were balls, operas, champagne on tap, new novels, flirtations, and cigars to me last winter'" (267). Winthrop proliferates male admirers for Brent throughout the novel, imagining a world in which such passions flourish in the open. What is worth noting is that these relationships are not discrete nor do they lead to antagonism between rivals. Rather, the relationships between men in *John Brent* are cumulative, as men pass in and out of each other's lives, singly and in pairs, forming attachments that are passionate but not permanent, intimate but unexpected, and always recognizable to other men who share the capacity to form queer attachments.

At one point Wade comes close to making the nature of this network explicit. Brent and Wade meet an elderly British man, Hugh Clitheroe, who has been brought to the United States by a Mormon recruiter who has deceitfully promised to restore Clitheroe to his former standing after he is ruined by his excessive generosity. As is their wont, Wade and Brent form an immediate attachment to Clitheroe, as he does with them. The encounter prompts Wade to disclose, "there is a small but ancient fraternity in the world, known as the Order of Gentlemen" (101), comprising those who know each other unerringly wherever they meet" (102). Wade claims, "No disguise delays this recognition. No strangeness of place and circumstances prevents it. The men meet. The magnetism passes between them. All is said without words. Gentlemen know gentlemen by what we name instinct." Bypassing the conscious choice that might invite censure, "instinct," the term Wade also uses to describe his attachment to Don

Fulano, is a force that the body can no more resist than it can breathing, a natural phenomenon – "magnetism" – that Wade calls "the spirit's touch" (103). Although attachment is instinctual, however, it becomes social through acts of interpretation: understanding that "[e]very look, tone, gesture of a man is a symbol of his complete nature," "gentlemen" communicate "in feeling and demeanor" (103) rather than in ways that would make them recognizable to those outside the "order." That partial legibility allows "gentlemen" "'to be complete and not conventional,'" while retaining what Winthrop in *Cecil Dreeme* calls "public privacy" (41). The Order of Gentlemen seems to anticipate what the twentieth century developed as sexual subculture, bringing those who experience queer attachments together in structures of support, sympathy, and strength, protected from those who would neither understand nor approve.

Wade's "Order," like later sexual subcultures, offers solace and strength to those who have suffered. The men who attract Wade have all known physical, emotional, and spiritual pain. When he first encounters the character Brion Biddulph, for example, Wade states, "I love him for his strong sorrow" (294). Hugh Cliterhoe's anguish is apparent from his frail, broken body. When Wade first sees Don Fulano, the horse has been whipped in an attempt to break his spirit. And John Brent's painful youth "went near to crush all the innocence, faith, hope, and religion out of my friend's life" (43). "Steady disappointment, by and by, informs a man that he is in the wrong place" (9), Wade observes, and Brent's suffering drove him "out of the common paths, to make him a seer instead of a doer" (43). These characters, knowing suffering, recognize and sympathize with it in others, as is the case with the "midget" engineer, George, to whom Wade is drawn, claiming that his "dwarfishness makes him sympathetic," adding, "instead of souring, it softens him to the feeble'" (316). The ability to turn suffering into compassion is, for Wade, "an innovation, a revolution" (313).

Even though he might have found a site of commonality with Mormon polygamy, a queerness that at the time he wrote *John Brent* was the target of social censure and legal suppression, Winthrop contrasts the Order of Gentlemen with the Mormon settlement, for which Wade and Brent have nothing but contempt.[8] The men seem particularly troubled by Mormonism's inversion of the subtle and undisclosed codes of gentlemen. Same-sex attachment becomes spiritualized heteronormativity, subcultural connection becomes institutional authority, the subtle and contingent signs that make gentlemen visible to each other become codified ritual, human effort becomes divine miracle, and vision through suffering becomes vision as prophylactic against suffering, all bringing about the "mean, miserable, ludicrous invention of Mormonism" (177). Of the charismatic Mormon orator Suzzum, Wade writes, "Coarse joys were the only joys for such a body; coarse emotions, the pleasures of force and domination, the only emotions crude enough for such a soul" (92). The subtle subcultural codes of gentlemen are, by contrast, anything but rhetorical, operating through attraction, not force; subtlety, not coarseness; and voluntary membership rather than coerced obedience, and, of course, queer attachment rather than dogmatic and normative heterosexuality.

Yet that very heterosexuality threatens to separate the two friends. Although Wade did "'not expect to develop a taste for Mormon ladies'" (51), Brent falls in love with Hugh Clitheroe's daughter, Ellen. All evidence to the contrary, Brent proclaims, "'I have yearned to be a lover for years'" (172). The incredulous Wade, who has perhaps believed Brent came into the wilderness yearning for *him*, exclaims, "'You are not cruising the plains for a lady-love!'" When Brent insists that is exactly why he has gone adventuring with Wade, Wade tries to persuade Brent not to abandon him, reminding him, "Our close friendship passed into completed brotherhood. Doubts and scruples vanished. We gave ourselves to our knight-errantry" (186). The appeals seem at first to succeed – Brent's "face lighted up with the beauty of his boyhood" (186) – but that light fades, prompting Wade to betray his rival, and in so doing his friend. When kidnappers come for Ellen at night, Wade, although he hears her screams, pretends not to have recognized her voice. Brent, rightly dubious, decides to take off after Ellen without the untrustworthy Wade.

This would appear to be the heart-breaking conclusion queer attachments so often meet in Hawthorne's romances. When Wade states of Brent, "I saw that the sudden doom of love had befallen my friend," and that "love here was next to despair" (134), it is plausible to read Wade's projection of his own despair now that (heterosexual) love has proven *his* doom. But the novel does not end there. Instead, Wade has yet another adventure. He meets George Short, apparently another "gentleman," who shows Wade his design for improving the steam engine. Before he can have it produced, however, he needs a model, which he believes only one man, the British "midget" George, can make to his satisfaction, so Wade sets off for London. When he finds George in his workshop, he also discovers Ellen's drawing of Don Fulano on the wall. George, it turns out, has been harboring the escaped Hugh Clitheroe and his daughter. As Wade rushes off to tell the good news to Brent, whom he has "accidently" encountered in London, the novel concludes, not with the happy reunion of Ellen and Brent, but with the promise of another adventure for Wade and his friend. "'Come!'" Wade exclaims to his friend, "and as we hurried away, there was again the same light in his eye, – the same life and ardor in his whole being, as when in that wild Love-Chase on the Plains, we galloped side by side" (359). Wade ends up neither desolate nor isolated. The Order has sustained him between the loss and return of his attachment to Brent, and the open-ended setting out at the novel's conclusion suggests that queer attachments can persist, without necessary permanence or continuity. Contingent yet sustaining, queer attachments, like the subculture they make and that maintains them, are the promise of an as yet unwritten future.

This comparison of the novels of Nathaniel Hawthorne and Theodore Winthrop registers important developments in the history of both sexuality and literary taste. These novels make clear that, although sexual taxonomies were not yet fixed in place by the mid-nineteenth century, there was already a great deal of anxiety about distinctions between proper and improper attachments, gender identities, sexual object choices, and obsessions. Although, as historians of sexuality point out, sexual "identities" (terms like homo- and heterosexual) did not come into being until later in the nineteenth century, these rubrics sought to name and regulate certain kinds of queer attachment that were thriving by mid-century, despite the ways they were constricted by social censure, ostracism, shame, gossip, and physical and emotional abuse. These dynamics produced anxieties that animate the plots of Hawthorne's and Winthrop's romances.

The history of sexuality involves more than the story of discipline and punishment, however, and more than just the "invention" of homosexuality as an identity written on individual bodies. It also involves a genealogy of subculture, of collective formations of collective identifications and the codes and practices that made them into cultural forms. That history is discernible in the fiction of Theodore Winthrop, who allowed his novels to end without shameful disavowals of queer attachments or the imposition of tidy – if tellingly implausible – conventional endings. Characters like Richard Wade avoid sad endings because the secrecy into which queer attachments were banished also made possible forms of subculture visible, like Wade's gentlemen, through gesture, feeling, taste, and unspoken communication. At the same time, we can see in the Order of Gentlemen the exclusions, often systematic and violent, that constitute this subculture's borders.[9] In *John Brent*, Ham, a fugitive from slavery, is helped by Wade and Brent, but not credited as a "gentleman." Fort Laramie, where the friends meet Ruby and Pathie, was the largest US military post in the war against the Sioux. And the one woman who plays a key role in the novel – Ellen – is repeatedly subjected to dangers from which only men can rescue her. Subculture is not ideal, although for many, including, as other nineteenth-century fiction shows, those excluded from Wade's particular Order, other subcultural formations of different kinds enabled survival and sustenance. For good and bad, the emergence of subcultures is as important to the history of sexuality as is the institutionalizing of individualized sexual identities, and Winthrop's fiction provides important insights into that development.

Given that importance, we might ask why Hawthorne's fiction became canonical while Winthrop's by and large remain in obscurity.[10] Jane Tompkins, analyzing Hawthorne's enshrinement in the American literary canon, argues that "works that have attained the status of classic, and are therefore believed to embody universal values, are in fact embodying only the interests of whatever parties or factions are responsible for maintaining them in their preeminent position." Tompkins continues, "[T]he literary works that now make up the canon do so because the groups that have an investment in them are culturally the most influential."[11] Given that in the period Hawthorne wrote his romances the privileges granted to those occupying the identity "heterosexual" increased in proportion to the subordination, even denigration, of other attachments, it is plausible that the influential group invested in making Hawthorne's works "classic" was invested in the rise of normative heterosexuality as a central feature of cultural authority. Hawthorne's canonization reflects *how* normative heterosexuality became a "preeminent position," while retaining traces of the disciplining of strange, unwieldy, transgressive, same-sex, and queer attachments, a punitive and shaming regulation on which "canonical heterosexuality" depends. As a result of the equation of normative heterosexuality and canonicity, Winthrop's more permissive, even celebratory novels, not surprisingly, appeared – like those who would want to read them – undisciplined, even licentious and therefore "minor." Comparing the literary reputations of Hawthorne and Winthrop, then, we might ponder a disturbing question: Is the only *serious* affect in the American canon shame?

Even if we grant that Winthrop's exclusion from the canon is due to the baggy, episodic, histrionic, implausible nature of his novels, we can analyze how what are considered literary "flaws" might be signs of efforts to create an aesthetic suitable to queer attachments. Lauren Berlant contends that "desires for intimacy that bypass the couple form and the life narratives it generates have no alternative plots, let alone few laws and stable spaces of culture in which to clarify and to cultivate them." Asking, "What happens to the energy of attachment when it has no designated place? To the glances, gestures, encounters, collaborations, or fantasies that have no canon?" Berlant answers, "As with minor literatures, minor intimacies have been forced to develop aesthetics of the extreme ... by way of small and grand gestures."[12] Winthrop's novels comprise just such an "aesthetics of the extreme," with their excessive accumulation of plots, over-the-top romantic language, and repeated implausibilities. It is worth noting that *John Brent* not only appears to be "minor literature" because of its fore-grounding of the "energy of attachment" involved in "minor" attachments, but also because it generated, in its depiction of the subcultural "order of gentlemen," something like what Berlant calls "stable spaces of culture in which to clarify and to cultivate" minor intimacies. Its "badness," in other words, signals *John Brent*'s efforts to create an "alternative plot" for queer attachments and spaces in which those plots can be lived.

What we can see by comparing the literary reputations of Nathaniel Hawthorne and Theodore Winthrop, then, is the relationship between aesthetic values, heteronormative privilege, and the denigration of the aesthetic gestures that, while they may make for "bad" literature, also enable the plots and styles of queer attachment. The connection between literary and social values is demonstrated by Hawthorne's own son, Julian, when, reviewing *Cecil Dreeme*, he called the novel "morbid and unwhole-some," its characters "artificial and unnatural."[13] The younger Hawthorne's conjoining of aesthetic terms like "artificial," often used to dismiss "minor" literature, with words like "morbid," "unwholesome," and "unnatural," used to disparage queer attachments, suggests the relationship between the two forms of negative judgment. Hawthorne found *John Brent* to be aesthetically superior to *Cecil Dreeme*, comparing the former to his father's *Blithedale Romance*. Whether Julian intended to compliment the former's aesthetic value in bringing Winthrop's fiction together with his father's or to acknowledge, perhaps subconsciously, the "morbid" and "unwholesome" flirtations with queer attachment in the latter, we can only guess. Today, however, we can see not the sharp distinction in quality or attitude that Julian Hawthorne was prompted to discern and announce, but rather the queer attachments between the two authors, the rich social history they together reveal, and the pleasures – and anxieties – our attachments to their novels can awaken.

Notes

1 On the "earliness" of sexuality in the literature of nineteenth-century America, see Peter Coviello, *Tomorrow's Parties: Sex and the Untimely in Nineteenth-Century America* (New York: NYU Press, 2013); Christopher Looby, intro-duction to *Cecil Dreeme*, ed. Christopher Looby (Philadelphia: University of Pennsylvania Press, 2018); Heather Love, *Feeling Backward: Loss and the Politics of Queer History* (Cambridge, MA: Harvard University Press, 2009).

2 Unlike countercultures or counterpublics, which represent purposeful rejections of mainstream ideologies, subcultures often emerge from those who are vulnerable and marginalized; they exist primarily to protect their members, provide spaces where they can meet and interact, and enable their members to create and enjoy cultural forms of self-expression. Subcultures may also be countercultural but are not necessarily or entirely so. Subcultures may contain groups within groups, specific practices or self-identification within larger subcultures (transvestism within the gay male subculture, for example, or butch/femme communities within a larger lesbian subculture). Subcultures can serve a regulatory function (who can and cannot be considered a member of a subculture, what practices and identification will and will not be tolerated), and often reproduce the same prejudices of mainstream society. While subcultures serve an important function for the marginalized, they are, as Winthrop's novels show, rarely if ever ideal. For histories of late nineteenth- and early twentieth-century sexual subcultures, see Lillian Faderman, *Odd Girls and Twilight Lovers* (New York: Columbia University Press, 2012); Elizabeth Lapovsky Kennedy and Madeline D. Davis, *Boots of Leather, Slippers of Gold* (New York: Routledge, 2014); George Chauncey, *Gay New York: Gender, Urban Culture, and the Making of the Gay Male World, 1899–1940* (New York: Basic Books, 1995); Allan Berube, *Coming Out under Fire: The History of Gay Men and Women in World War II* (New York: Free Press, 2000). On how sexual subcultures became a political movement, see John D'Emilio, *Sexual Politics, Sexual Communities*, 2nd edi. (Chicago: University of Chicago Press, 1998).

3 For feminist analyses of Hawthorne, see Jane Tompkins, *Sensational Designs: The Cultural Works of American Fiction, 1790–1860* (New York: Oxford University Press, 1986); Jamie Barlowe, *The Scarlet Mob of Scribblers: Rereading Hester Prynne* (Carbondale: Southern Illinois University Press, 2000); Michael Broek, "Hawthorne, Madonna, and Lady Gaga: *The Marble Faun*'s Transgressive Miriam," *Journal of American Studies* 46, no. 3 (2012): 625–40; Maria O'Malley, "Taking the Domestic View in Hawthorne's Fiction," *The New England Quarterly* 88, no. 4 (2015): 657–80; Susan Van Zanten Gallagher, "A Domestic Reading of *The House of the Seven Gables*," *Studies in the Novel* 21, no. 1 (1989): 1–13; and Dana Medoro, "This Rag of Scarlet Cloth: Nathaniel Hawthorne's Abortion," *Studies in the Novel* 49, no. 1 (2017): 24–48.

4 Nathaniel Hawthorne, *The Blithedale Romance* (New York: Norton, 1978), 28. All other citations to this novel will be in the text.

5 On queerness in *The Blithedale Romance*, see Coviello, *Tomorrow's Parties*; David Greven, *The Fragility of Manhood: Hawthorne, Freud, and the Politics of Gender* (Columbus: Ohio State University Press, 2012); Lauren Berlant, "Fantasies of Utopia in *The Blithedale Romance*," *American Literary History* 1, no. 1 (1989): 30–62; Jordan Alexander Stein, "*The Blithedale Romance*'s Queer Style," *ESQ: A Journal of the American Renaissance* 55, no. 3 (2009): 211–236; and Benjamin Grossberg, "'The Tender Passion Was Very Rife

among Us': Coverdale's Queer Utopia and *The Blithedale Romance*," *Studies in American Fiction* 28, no. 1 (2000): 3–25; on queerness in *The Scarlet Letter*, see Brant Torres, "Gold Rush: Alchemy and the Queer Potentialities of *The Scarlet Letter*," *Studies in American Fiction* 41, no. 2 (2014): 149–174; on queerness in *The House of the Seven Gables*, see Christopher Castiglia, *Interior States: Institutional Consciousness and the Inner Life of Democracy in the Antebellum United States* (Durham, NC: Duke University Press, 2008), chapter 7.

6 Theodore Winthrop, *Cecil Dreeme* (Boston: Ticknor and Fields, 1862), 38. All other citations to *Cecil Dreeme* will be in the text.

7 Theodore Winthrop, *John Brent* (Boston: Ticknor and Fields, 1862), 56. All other citations to *John Brent* will be in the text.

8 See Peter Coviello, "Plural: Mormon Polygamy and the Biopolitics of Secularism," *History of the Present* 7, no. 2 (2017): 219–241, which considers how the consolidation of liberal secularism required the suppression of non-normative forms of sexuality, in this case, Mormon polygamy.

9 For an analysis of *Cecil Dreeme* that considers its engagement with racial politics, see Travis Foster, "The Queer Young American Comes of Age," *Common-Place: The Journal of Early American Life* 17, no. 2 (2017): http://common-place.org/book/the-queer-young-american-comes-of-age/.

10 For a compelling critical account of the causes of and "cultural work" done by Hawthorne's canonical reputation, see Tompkins, *Sensational Designs*, chapter 1: "Masterpiece Theater."

11 Ibid., 618.

12 Berlant, "Fantasies of Utopia in *The Blithedale Romance*," 5.

13 Looby, "Introduction," xv.

CHAPTER 23

Melville/Whitman

Kelly Ross

In the spring of 1855, as Walt Whitman was finalizing the first edition of *Leaves of Grass*, Herman Melville's latest novel, *Israel Potter: His Fifty Years of Exile*, went on sale in the United States and England (following its serialization in *Putnam's Monthly Magazine* from July 1854 to March 1855). Whereas *Leaves of Grass* would eventually be recognized as a watershed moment in literary history, *Israel Potter* left little mark on the literary landscape and remains one of his less-studied novels today. Yet these two books may share more in common than critics have previously recognized. An adaptation of an 1824 first-person narrative about a Revolutionary War soldier, Melville's "comically loopy work" (in Robert S. Levine's words) critiques the patriotic mythos of the American Revolution through the pathetic figure of Israel Potter, a common soldier.[1] As many readers have noted, Potter's frequent changes of clothes signal that his identity is performative and fluid, not stable. Early in the narrative, after volunteering for the US Navy and almost immediately being captured by a British warship, Potter exchanges his English sailor's costume, which he has been wearing as a prisoner-of-war on a British prison hulk at Spithead, for a ditch digger's rags. A few pages later he meets a knight who hires him as a gardener and offers to "give [him] coat and breeches for [his] rags," since, the knight remarks, "as you tell me you have exchanged clothes before now, you can do it again."[2] These rapid changes of clothes and the roles they signify, from sailor to prisoner to beggar to gardener, initiate a succession of such exchanges that recurs through the rest of the novel. In Gale Temple's analysis, Potter "becomes an abstract cipher, waiting for yet another ideal or icon to fill him with some form of intelligible, habitable identity . . . a 'self' . . . that will belong in significant ways to the collectivity that is the nation."[3]

What is Potter's journey, then, but a tragic inversion of Whitman's poetic method in *Leaves of Grass*, his democratic incorporation of "one and all"?

And these one and all tend inward to me, and I tend outward to them,
And such as it is to be of these more or less I am.. . .
A farmer, mechanic, or artist . . . a gentleman, sailor, lover or quaker,
A prisoner, fancy-man, rowdy, lawyer, physician or priest.[4]

While Potter's successive disguises index his desperate attempts to find a place to belong, the speaker of *Leaves of Grass* celebrates his ability to become other people, from farmers to sailors, from prisoners to gentlemen. The speaker's description of this ability varies throughout the first poem of *Leaves*, however, as he sometimes claims to speak for others, sometimes to "be of these" others, and sometimes to disguise himself as others, such that their experiences are merely "one of [his] changes of garments," as the speaker himself describes it when he discusses the "agonies" of "the hounded slave" and the "wounded person" (65). Philip Fisher has argued that Whitman claims "to speak for these voices, and finally, to impersonate them . . . Where Whitman sees their suffering he interposes himself at once to say, 'I am the man, I suffer'd, I was there.' This resonant, brave statement of Whitman's is, when looked at more closely, one of the most morally dubious acts of appropriation ever described or, in fact, boasted of."[5] This tension between being and seeming, thematized through figures of disguise in both Melville's *Israel Potter* and Whitman's *Leaves of Grass*, reflects the thorny questions about who belonged to the body politic that roiled the United States as it fought to expand its territory from the 1820s through the 1850s.

Both Melville and Whitman, in their 1855 books, were grappling with the problems of US American identity and empire after the upwelling of patriotic nationalism following the US "victory" in the War of 1812 and what Levine calls the "coercive fetishizing of the American Revolution."[6] Examining these issues in the 1855 works of these two great writers reveals their shared concern with the legacy of the American Revolution, which is perhaps not surprising given that Whitman and Melville were almost exact contemporaries. Both authors were born in New York in 1819: Whitman on May 31 in West Hills (on Long Island) and Melville on August 1 in Manhattan. New York, particularly Manhattan and Brooklyn, would remain significant to both authors throughout their careers. Furthermore, both Whitman and Melville had ancestors who fought in the American Revolution and whose tales were passed down as family lore. Whitman's maternal grandmother, Naomi Van Velsor, told him stories of her father, Captain John Williams, who had fought under John Paul Jones. Melville's paternal grandfather, Major Thomas Melvill, took part in the Boston Tea Party, and his maternal grandfather, General Peter Gansevoort, led the defense of New York's Fort Stanwix against the British.

Though Melville and Whitman are rarely read in conversation, there has been a recent surge of ground-breaking work on both authors' volumes of Civil War poems: Melville's *Battle-Pieces and Aspects of the War* (1866) and Whitman's *Drum-Taps* (1865).[7] As Cody Marrs teaches us, Melville and Whitman are "transbellum authors" par excellence, whose careers extend from the antebellum period across the Civil War to the postbellum period and who repeatedly engage with the Civil War long after its official conclusion in 1865.[8] Extending Marrs's emphasis on transbellum literature backward in time to the Revolutionary War as well as to the numerous wars the United States was engaged in during the first four decades of Melville's and Whitman's lives allows us to understand these authors as interrogating patriotic nationalism and the failures of the American Revolution's ideals. As Matthew Dennis notes, the "post–War of 1812 inclination [was] to emphasize triumph and self-possession, despite the actual record" of military ineptitude, "set[ting] the country on a particular course – encouraging a self-righteous, hubristic, and militarist expansionism"[9] achieved through violent conquest. Detailing the "number of wars waged for and against empire, slavery, expansion, and sovereignty before . . . the war between the states," Jesse Alemán reminds us that "the antebellum era was one of the most bellicose periods of the nineteenth century."[10] Indeed, even to use the term "antebellum," he and Shelley Streeby argue, "begs the question: before which war?" given that the decades following the War of 1812 included the three waves of "so-called Seminole Wars" (1814–1819, 1835–1842, and 1855–1858); the 1832 Black Hawk War and other "armed conflicts waged against Native America"; the 1830s battles of the Alamo, Goliad, and San Jacinto; and the US-Mexico War (1846–1848).[11] Moreover, the Kansas–Nebraska Act, passed in 1854, which gave residents of new territories the right to decide whether to allow slavery, led to a wave of violent conflicts between proslavery and antislavery settlers in Kansas. In the midst of this bellicose period, both Melville and Whitman looked back to the American Revolution to discern the roots of this never-ending warfare, seemingly the primary characteristic of the young country. Attending fully to Melville's and Whitman's position in the midst of this violent period of territorial expansion, rather than reading their writing as prefiguring the Civil War, allows us to reconsider their early careers and, particularly, their responses to the legacy of the US Revolution and to US continental empire building.

Melville's and Whitman's 1855 volumes are most clearly linked through their depictions of an infamous Revolutionary War naval battle between

US Captain John Paul Jones's *Bonhomme Richard* and British Captain Richard Pearson's *Serapis*. Early reviewers of *Israel Potter* singled out Melville's depiction of the battle, though they were divided on its merit. While one reviewer asserted the chapter "is a masterpiece of writing," another complained, "from this praise we would exclude the account of the battle between the *Bon Homme Richard* and the *Serapis*. A battle so sanguinary and brutal in its whole character cannot form an attractive episode in a work of high art; and it is to be regretted that Mr. Melville should have dwelt so minutely upon its details."[12] Whitman also treated this battle at length in the 1855 *Leaves of Grass*, in the poem that he would eventually title "Song of Myself." Both Melville and Whitman used Jones's letter to Benjamin Franklin describing the battle as a source text for their accounts. Moreover, some critics have argued that Whitman read Melville's account of the battle in *Israel Potter* and "appropriated some of his account."[13]

Though the battle is famous for Jones's tenacious refusal to strike his colors – "'I have not yet begun to fight,' howled sinking Paul" (Melville 145), both Whitman and Melville undercut the mythos of the Revolution by dwelling on the battle's chaos and carnage. There is no distinction between the two sides, as the British and American ships are so close "the yards entangled" (Whitman 68), or, as Melville states, "that bewildering intertanglement of all the yard and anchors of the two ships . . . confounded them for the time in one chaos of devastation" (136). The fighting leaves the so-called victorious "vessel riddled and slowly sinking . . . / Formless stacks of bodies and bodies by themselves . . . dabs of flesh upon the masts and spars" (Whitman 69). While both authors portray the grisly realities of battle, they diverge in their depictions of John Paul Jones.

After recounting the extensive deaths on both sides of the fight, Melville venerates not the ostensible victor, Jones, but the conquered Captain Pearson for his humanity: "it seemed as if, in this fight, neither party could be victor. Mutual obliteration from the face of the waters seemed the only natural sequel.... It is, therefore, honor to him as a man, and not reproach to him as an officer, that, to stay such carnage, Captain Pearson, of the Serapis, with his own hands hauled down his colors" (Melville 147). Unlike Pearson, Jones is, according to Melville's narrator, "intrepid, reckless, predatory, with boundless ambition, civilized in externals but a savage at heart" (136). Melville's emphasis on predation and ambition here has led many critics to view Jones as a figure of the United States' "brutal policies of expansionism, its 1846–48 war with Mexico, and its sustained support for slavery."[14] Whitman's speaker, on the other hand, approves Jones's ability to remain "compose[d]" and "serene" (68 and 69) amid the chaos. The contrasting portraits of Jones as Melville's reckless predator and Whitman's noble stoic reflect a larger pattern in their evocations of Revolutionary memory. Both authors berate the United States for its failure to live up to its founding ideals, but while Melville warns readers of the inevitable decline that follows imperial ambitions, Whitman justifies expansionism as manifestation of those ideals.

Every time Whitman refers to the American Revolution in the 1855 *Leaves of Grass*, he juxtaposes it with a passage that alludes to the racial conflicts underwriting US expansionism, demonstrating that he is testing Jacksonian era warfare against the democratic ideals mythologized in stories of the Revolutionary War. This juxtaposition begins in the prose preface to *Leaves*, when Whitman lists "the haughty defiance of '76" as one of the "real things and past and present events" that "enter" the American "bard" (Whitman 7–8). For many, this reference signals Whitman's belief in "the triumph and promise of New World democracy."[15] In the same paragraph, however, Whitman also stipulates that the American bard "incarnates [his country's] geography," and goes on to envision this geography: "The blue breadth over the inland sea of Virginia and Maryland and the sea off Massachusetts and Maine and over Manhattan bay and over Champlain and Erie and over Ontario and Huron and Michigan and Superior, and over the Texan and Mexican and Floridian and Cuban seas and over the seas off California and Oregon" (Whitman 7). Kirsten Silva Gruesz points out that the last phrase "neatly catalogs the march of Manifest Destiny through the 1840s and 1850s." Moving from "the Texan and Mexican and Floridian seas" to "the seas off California and Oregon," Gruesz argues, the speaker moves "from the Caribbean theater to the northern Mexican one [and] describes a not-yet-existent passage from one to the other that was seen as vitally necessary to the success of the expansionist project."[16] Moreover, this geographical vision erases the indigenous populations of the Eastern Seaboard and the Great Lakes region, which were displaced by previous generations of settler colonialists.

As in the prose preface, Whitman links Revolutionary memory to contemporary racial conflict to justify US expansionism in the poems, though his strategy changes depending on the ethnicity of the nonwhite group: he villainizes Mexicans, sentimentalizes Native Americans, and erases African Americans. In the first poem of *Leaves*, the depiction of Jones's battle against the *Serapis*, which I discussed above, follows immediately after passages about two battles in the Texas Revolution, which led to the US annexation of Texas and the US -Mexico War. Along with the subsequent section on the Revolutionary War naval battle, these three historically specific events intrude suddenly and strangely into Whitman's rapturous catalogs of occupations, animals, places, and persons. First, in a two-line section, the Whitmanian speaker rejects the possibility of narrating "the fall of Alamo . . . not one escaped to tell the fall of Alamo, / The hundred and fifty are dumb yet at Alamo" (Whitman 66). In contrast to the tragic tone of this unnarratable story, the next section villainizes General Santa Anna and the Mexican soldiers at the battle of Goliad as cold-blooded assassins. Announcing, "Hear now the tale of a jetblack sunrise, / Hear of the murder in cold blood of four hundred and twelve young men," the speaker praises the Texans as "the glory of the race of rangers, /. . . Large, turbulent, brave, handsome, generous, proud and affectionate, /. . . None obeyed the command to kneel" (Whitman 66–67). Reading this exaggerated valorization of the Texans alongside Whitman's editorials for the *Brooklyn Eagle* from 1846–1848 (the years of the US–Mexico War), Donald Pease argues that "[i]n describing the militia who were executed at Goliad as sacred martyrs whose blood called out for vengeance, Whitman evoked the memory of Goliad to reestablish a norm of U.S. hemispheric dominance that recognized no other sovereignty."[17] The doomed Rangers' defiance in the face of "the command to kneel" links them to the "defiance of '76" that Whitman celebrated in the preface, thereby justifying US expansionism in the Southwest as a fitting outgrowth of Revolutionary ideals.

The references to daily cycles of time that frame the Goliad and the *Serapis* battles underscore this contrast between craven murder and laudable combat. In the Goliad battle, the unnatural "jetblack sunrise," a phrase Whitman repeats at the beginning and end of the section, sets the tone for a contest that Whitman describes as a cowardly "massacre" of courageous Texans (Whitman 66 and 67). As Mexican historians have noted, this is an inaccurate view of the battle, but Whitman's framing uses this memory of a specific moment in US history to advocate for US expansionism across the Southwest.[18] If the Mexican "massacre" is a perversion that blackens the sunrise, then it must be righted by US retaliation. On the other hand, the Romantic image of the "light of the moon and stars" that opens the *Serapis* battle section and the "beams of the moon" that comes toward the section's end idealizes the battle as an honorable clash between equals. Whitman begins his account by honoring the English "foe" as "no skulk in his ship . . . / His was the English pluck, and there is no tougher or truer, and never was, and never will be" (Whitman 68). The final stanza of the section, however, exceeds this frame and underscores the grisly reality of war for both sides. Just after the second "moon" image, Whitman details the aftermath of the battle, depicting Jones "giving orders through a countenance white as a sheet" (Whitman 69). Two corpses – a cabin boy and an "old salt" – stand in for the mass casualties (Whitman 69). Though the account of the battle contained within the two "moon" images memorializes Revolutionary heroism, the final stanza strongly echoes Melville's account in *Israel Potter*, facing up to the enormous cost of battle. Whereas Whitman ennobles the British enemy in the Revolutionary War battle, he vilifies the Mexican enemy in the Goliad battle, naturalizing the justification for annexing their land.

Whitman takes a different approach when he juxtaposes Revolutionary memory with the displacement of Native Americans: here he sentimentalizes Native "disappearance." In the poem that Whitman would later call "The Sleepers," he pairs two scenes of leave-taking and remembrance: the first, George Washington's farewell to his officers at Fraunces Tavern; the second, the "go[ing] away" of a "red squaw" (113) who had spent an afternoon with Whitman's mother when she was a young woman. Not only does the Native American woman section immediately follow the Washington section, but Whitman accentuates the connection between the two sections by incorporating diction associated with Native Americans ("braves" and "chief") into the Washington scenes. Eliding the victories that led to the Treaty of Paris in 1783, Whitman focuses on images of loss and dispersal, beginning the Washington section with the "defeat at Brooklyn" (112) in 1776 and ending with Washington "bid [ding] goodbye to the army" on December 4, 1783. Whitman's portrait of Washington "stand[ing] on the entrenched hills," unable to "repress the weeping drops" as he watches the "slaughter of the southern braves" (112), likens him to the stock sentimental figure of the Native American chief stoically weeping as his warriors are tragically defeated by settler colonialists – Mononotto in Catherine Maria Sedgwick's *Hope Leslie*, for example. Whitman reinforces this sentimental imagery in the next stanza, when "the chief [Washington] encircles [his officers'] necks with his arm and kisses them on the cheek" (112). The dispersal of the army in this section works to frame the disappearance of the Native American woman in the next stanza as a "vanishing Indian," thus sentimentalizing the colonial and US imperial displacement of indigenous populations.

Brian W. Dippie has identified the myth of the "vanishing Indian" as a way for white US Americans to assuage their guilt over the genocidal policies of Indian Removal.[19] According to this myth, which was widely circulated in antebellum print culture, Native Americans were a doomed race, destined to disappear in the face of superior Euro-American culture, and thus they could provide the grounds for a sentimental leave-taking as they vanished into the sunset. The Native American woman in "The Sleepers" appears at Whitman's mother's "old homestead" seeking work "rushbottoming chairs" (112) – the same occupation Israel Potter turns to in his extreme poverty and desperation after he is exiled in England at the close of the American Revolution. Whitman's mother reveres the woman's "step," "voice," and "beauty," and though "She had no work to give her . . . she gave her remembrance and fondness" (113), as Washington gave his officers. Absent from this anecdote is the agency of settler colonists such as Whitman's ancestors, who by the time of Whitman's mother's girlhood in the 1810s had displaced Long Island's indigenous people and disrupted their traditional ways of life, forcing them to turn to subsistence economic activities such as rushbottoming chairs. In the "middle of the afternoon," the woman "went away" (113). Like Washington, who first weeps as he looks upon his troops being defeated and then loves them as he says goodbye, Whitman's mother performs the appropriate sentimental response to the woman: "The more she looked upon her she loved her" (112). By linking honorable defeat at the Battle of Brooklyn and Washington's bittersweet farewell to the Continental Army with the disappearance of one noble Native American woman, who "never came nor was heard of there again" (113), Whitman esteems the memory of Native Americans, dignified despite their fall, even as he sentimentalizes the Indian Wars and Indian Removal as the inevitable vanishing of a doomed race.[20]

Finally, the poem that Whitman would eventually call "A Boston Ballad (1854)" evokes the memory of the American Revolution in its description of a march of "federal foot and dragoon" through Boston. The poem's speaker declares that he "rose this morning early" in hopes of seeing the "stars and stripes" and hearing the "fifes . . . play Yankee Doodle" (135). The patriotic symbols of flag and unofficial national anthem are diminished by the ragged, ghostly appearance of the men who come to watch the parade, however. The procession has called forth

> the dead out of the earth,
> The old graveyards of the hills have hurried to see; . . .
> Cocked hats of mothy mould and crutches made of mist,
> Arms in slings and old men leaning on young men's shoulders. (135)

There are no current, living patriots to watch this procession, the speaker implies, because the United States has betrayed the ideals of these long-dead soldiers. Instead, the contemporary young men and women have been distracted by consumerism: "here gape your smart grandsons . . . their wives gaze at them from the windows / See how well-dressed" (136). The speaker suggests that these docile grandchildren have reinstated monarchical rule in the United States, so Boston's mayor may as well exhume George III's skeleton, send it to the United States, and reconstitute it in Boston, "set[ting] up the regal ribs and glu[ing] those that will not stay" (137). This bizarre and vivid image seems disproportionate to the situation if all the grandchildren have done is watch a processional in nice clothing. The sense of the poem is difficult to parse in the 1855 edition, since it lacks the later title that clues readers in to the occasion for this march, which is in fact the rendition of a fugitive enslaved man, Anthony Burns, to Virginia under the mandate of the 1850 Fugitive Slave Act. As Ivy Wilson argues, "the specificity of chattel slavery is vacated from the precincts of the poem in order to constitute it as an archetypal lamentation and a ballad for America ... Whitman's maneuver in the poem is characteristic of a nation that had formulated an intricate labyrinth of denying the presence of African Americans."[21] Burns, the fugitive enslaved man, is absent from the poem, and the speaker's complaint hinges not on a specific condemnation of slaveholders but on the more generalized compliance of Bostonians that has enabled a reintroduction of the tyrannical rule that the American Revolutionaries fought against. Britain, not the South, is the enemy in this poem, just as it was when northern and southern colonies united to throw off King George's rule in 1776. Whitman thereby deflects any criticism from the expansionist policies underwriting the westward spread of slavery.

Whitman pairs all of his evocations of American Revolutionary memory in *Leaves* with references to the United States' contemporary struggles with nonwhite peoples – Mexicans, Native Americans, African Americans – and uses the references to the founding war to justify or elide US violence in the service of continental expansion. To emphasize these interludes of historical specificity in *Leaves* is to read against the grain, since most of the book consists of exuberantly transhistorical claims such as "The past and present wilt ... I have filled them and emptied them, / And proceed to fill my next fold of the future" (87) or "Is today nothing? Is the beginningless past nothing? / If the future is nothing they are just as surely nothing" (100). Yet dwelling on Whitman's deployment of Revolutionary War memory encourages us to consider who can be contained in Whitman's democratic multitudes and who must be evacuated from the national space. According to Ed Folsom, Whitman believed that "the end of slavery would come ... when the slave owner and the slave could both be represented by the same voice, could both hear themselves present in the

'I' and the 'you' of the democratic poet … It was a kind of spiritual and ontological abolition, a desperate attempt to speak with a unifying instead of a divisive voice."[22] Yet as Fisher points out, "With only the rarest exceptions, no one speaks in Whitman's poetry other than the poet himself. No one tells his or her own story." This tension between the speaker's voice as unifying or as solipsistic, Fisher goes on to explain, is at both "the heart of [Whitman's] strength in opening up a remarkably nuanced, transpersonal self and the heart of his evasiveness, weakness, egotistical appropriation, his occupation and evacuation of others."[23] Whereas Whitman obliquely justifies US expansionism through Revolutionary remembrance, Melville cautions readers that in its imperial ambitions, the United States is in danger of becoming the very tyrannical power that the US revolution renounced.

Although *Israel Potter* is, as Levine has argued, "much more than a cynical and despairing demythologizing of the American Revolution," the novel's final chapter certainly drives this ironic treatment of the Revolutionary mythos home.[24] Finally returned to his native land after fifty-one years of exile in England, Israel's ship docks in Boston right in the midst of a Fourth of July parade. Israel is nearly run over by "a patriotic triumphal car in the procession, flying a broidered banner, inscribed with gilt letters: – 'BUNKER-HILL 1775. GLORY TO THE HEROES THAT FOUGHT!'" (190). Making his escape, Israel retreats to the soldiers' graveyard on Copp's Hill, where he had once fought the British during the Siege of Boston, and surveys the commemorative activities from above: "Sitting down here on a mound in the graveyard, he looked off across Charles River towards the battle-ground, whose incipient monu-ment, at that period, was hard to see" (190). Much criticism of the novel has focused on its ironic treatment of commemoration culture centered around the ground-breaking for the Bunker Hill monument that Potter watches from the hillside graveyard, which reifies democracy "as a monu-mental structure" but erases the individual, common man who actually fought in the battle.[25] I want to attend more particularly to the ways in which Melville's sardonic staging of a commemorative processional, with a ghostly figure of an actual Revolutionary War soldier watching from the hills, resonates with Whitman's "Boston Ballad," with its occlusion of the fugitive enslaved man who occasioned it.

Earlier in the novel, Melville describes Israel's multiple escapes from the British soldiers who imprison him as a "Yankee prisoner of war" (31) or as a British deserter (24). For several chapters, Israel is on the run, hunted by British soldiers, who are "like bloodhounds" (35): Israel is "[h]arassed day and night, hunted from food and sleep, driven from hole to hole like a fox in the woods" (32). As Carolyn Karcher, Anne Baker, and Robert K. Wallace have noted, Melville's language portrays Israel as a fugitive enslaved man, an analogy that would have resonated with readers in 1855 following infamous cases such as that of Anthony Burns.[26] Previous scholarship on the novel has not examined the way in which the British nobility shelter and aid Israel during his long period as a runaway, however. As a fugitive, Israel is aided by "the secret good offices of a few individuals, who, perhaps, were not unfriendly to the American side of the question, though they durst not avow it" (31); "the houses where he harbored were many times searched; but thanks to the fidelity of a few earnest well-wishers, and to his own unsleeping vigilance ... the hunted fox still continued to elude apprehension" (35). This "underground railroad" enables him to get to the safe houses (or, rather, estates) of first Sir John Millet and later King George III, who both treat Israel with kindness and generosity. The king promises Israel, "So long as ye remain here at Kew, I shall see that you are safe" (34). Millet hires Israel as a gardener, but also clothes him, feeds him plentifully, and gives him leave to recover from his exhaustion and starvation. Moreover, Millet assures Israel, "I perceive that you are ... an escaped prisoner of war.... I pledge you my honor I will never betray you" (29). Millet's country has declared Israel an enemy who should be remanded to state custody and imprisoned, but Millet is sympathetic to Israel's plight and disobeys his duty as a subject of the king. Not only does Melville repeatedly underscore the analogy between Israel and fugitive enslaved people in the United States in the 1850s, but he also likens the British nobility to practical abolitionists in the United States, who put themselves at personal risk by disobeying the 1850 Fugitive Slave Act in order to harbor runaways.

The structure of Melville's complex analogy between US abolitionists and British nobility reminds readers that the United States was once a colonial possession of the British empire, though it now occupies the role of imperial power, working to extend its reach across the North American continent. As Edgar Dryden argues, Melville draws on this strategy throughout *Israel Potter*, establishing a "parallelism between New England and Old England" that undermines the claim to "America's absolute novelty."[27] By betraying the ideals of liberty and democracy that it fought for in the Revolution, the United States, Melville suggests, is on the path to becoming yet another tyrannical empire. Melville's other texts from 1854 and 1855, "The Encantadas" and *Benito Cereno*, offer similar warnings about the dangers of US expansionism in the Southern

Hemisphere. Rodrigo Lazo demonstrates that "The Encantadas," published in *Putnam's*, "suggests the folly of imperial attempts to control faraway places."[28] In *Benito Cereno*, as Greg Grandin has detailed, Melville links US imperial ambitions to the rotting remains of the Spanish empire, symbolized by the decaying former grandeur of the slave ship *San Dominick*. The numerous nineteenth-century wars to acquire territory beyond the borders of the United States and extend the empire of slavery westward, as well as the legislative compromises that coerced northerners into abetting the southern slave power, all supported this imperial aim.

Whereas Whitman justified US westward expansion, Melville critiqued the ideology of US expansionism by placing it in the context of the cycle of decline that afflicted empires. The United States' overreach would lead to its fall, Melville posited. Nevertheless, for both Melville and Whitman, the anxiety about US imperialism centered on its betrayal of Revolutionary ideals, rather than on concern for the actual nonwhite populations who were being killed, displaced, and enslaved to further those imperial goals. Israel Potter is a laboring-class white man who is "subject to enslavement" (174) in England, not an African American enslaved man. Lamenting the erasure of the Revolution's "anonymous privates" (2), Melville brings the common white man's story back into the American narrative. Similarly, as Folsom and Kenneth Price state, Whitman "frame[d] issues in accordance with working-class interests – and for him this usually meant *white* working-class interests" (12). Even in such trenchant critiques of the United States' failure to fulfill its democratic ideals as Whitman's and Melville's, their imagination of the US body-politic still could not envision nonwhite citizens as full participants.

This ability to imagine a racially diverse citizenry might strike some as too tall an order for authors in the 1850s, before slavery was even abolished in the United States; it might, that is, seem an unreasonably presentist demand. Bringing together Melville's and Whitman's multifaceted, at times oppositional, engagements with Revolutionary memory in 1855, however, demonstrates these authors' acumen about the complexities of historiography and the way in which each generation creates its past. Both Melville and, to some degree, Whitman exemplify Jeffrey Insko's theory of "Romantic presentism." In contrast to teleological views of history as a steady, gradual march of progress, Romantic presentism "imagin[es] history as an always-unfinished activity happening *now* and remaking – as opposed to trying to know – *then*"; it recognizes that "the shape of our present ... motivates (or 'conditions') our particular historical interests in the first place."[29] Melville's historiography in *Israel Potter*, Insko argues, "paradoxically, is devoted less to the past than to the present ... [It] attempts to render not what we know about history, but to capture the experience of living and acting in it."[30] Whitman, too, anchors the opening of "Song of Myself" firmly in the "now":

> I do not talk of the beginning or the end.
> There was never any more inception than there is now,
> Nor any more youth or age than there is now;
> And will never be any more perfection than there is now,
> Nor any more heaven or hell than there is now. (28)

Though Insko, concentrating on the radical possibilities of immediatist abolition, celebrates the liberatory potential of Romantic presentism, Whitman's example attests that being immersed in the present moment does not preclude embracing militarist expansionism.

In the spirit of Melville's *Israel Potter*, which works against the monumentalization of history, my argument has examined the concerns with US imperialism and identity that energize Melville's and Whitman's 1855 books and remain unsettling today. To Americanist literary scholars trained to think of the antebellum era as a prelude to the transformative event of the US Civil War, however, Melville's and Whitman's interest in Revolutionary memory has been less pertinent than their prophesies of and reflections on the Civil War. The antebellum/postbellum periodization of the nineteenth century has often led us to privilege accounts of US identity that concentrate on strife and reconciliation between white northerners and white southerners. Emphasizing the imperative need to reunify a divided nation, these accounts obviate any dispute about the United States' right to occupy that territory in the first place. Attending to the tension between Revolutionary memory and the many nineteenth-century wars of expansion, on the other hand, creates space to investigate the history of US imperialism. By shifting our focus to Melville's and Whitman's accounting of the United States' Revolutionary past, we are able to perceive the ways that nonwhite populations were erased or villainized in order to keep the Revolutionary ideals alive.

Notes

1 Robert S. Levine, "Introduction," in Herman Melville, *Israel Potter: His Fifty Years of Exile* (New York: Penguin Books, 2008), vii.
2 Melville, *Israel Potter*, 29. All subsequent references will be cited parenthetically.

3 Gale Temple, "Fluid Identity in *Israel Potter* and *The Confidence-Man*," in *A Companion to Herman Melville*, ed. Wyn Kelley (Malden, MA: Blackwell, 2006), 455–456.

4 Walt Whitman, *Complete Poetry and Collected Prose* (New York: Literary Classics of the United States, 1982), 42–43. All subsequent references will be cited parenthetically.

5 Philip Fisher, *Still the New World: American Literature in a Culture of Creative Destruction* (Cambridge, MA: Harvard University Press, 1999), 81.

6 Robert S. Levine, "The Revolutionary Aesthetics of *Israel Potter*," in *Melville and Aesthetics*, ed. Geoffrey Sanborn and Samuel Otter (New York: Palgrave Macmillan, 2011), 159.

7 See the special issues published by *Leviathan*, "Melville the Civil War Poet," edited by Christopher Sten and Tyler Hoffman (17.3 [October 2015]), and *The Mickle Street Review*, "Whitman, Melville & the Civil War" (21 [2016], also edited by Tyler Hoffman). These essays form the core of a forthcoming book, *"This Mighty Convulsion": Whitman and Melville Write the Civil War*, ed. Christopher Sten and Tyler Hoffman (Iowa City: University of Iowa Press, 2019). Other scholars who have brought Whitman's and Melville's Civil War poems into conversation include Lawrence Buell, "American Civil War Poetry and the Meaning of Literary Commodification: Whitman, Melville, and Others," in *Reciprocal Influences: Literary Production, Distribution, and Consumption in America*, ed. Steven Fink and Susan S. Williams (Columbus: Ohio State University Press, 1999), 123–138; Peter Coviello, "Battle Music: Melville and the Forms of War," in *Melville and Aesthetics*, ed. Samuel Otter and Geoffrey Sanborn (New York: Palgrave Macmillan, 2011), 193–212; Cody Marrs, *Nineteenth-Century American Literature and the Long Civil War* (Cambridge: Cambridge University Press, 2015); and Eliza Richards, *Battle Lines: Poetry and Mass Media in the U.S. Civil War* (Philadelphia: University of Pennsylvania Press, 2019).

8 Marrs, *Nineteenth-Century American Literature and the Long Civil War*, 3.

9 Matthew Dennis, "Reflections on a Bicentennial: The War of 1812 in American Public Memory," *Early American Studies* 12.2 (Spring 2014): 277, 300.

10 Jesse Alemán, "The Age of US Latinidad," in *Timelines of American Literature*, ed. Cody Marrs and Christopher Hager (Baltimore: Johns Hopkins University Press, 2019), 161 and 160.

11 Alemán, "The Age of US Latinidad," 160; and Jesse Alemán and Shelley Streeby, *Empire and the Literature of Sensation: An Anthology of Nineteenth-Century Popular Fiction* (New Brunswick, NJ: Rutgers University Press, 2007), xiv. To this list Alemán and Streeby add the "filibustering schemes" of Narciso López, William Walker, and others in Cuba and Latin America – schemes that the US government supported, even if it did not officially sanction them.

12 H. W. Hetherington, *Melville's Reviewers: British and American, 1846–1891* (Chapel Hill: University of North Carolina Press, 1961), 243; and "Israel

Potter: His Fifty Years of Exile," *The Life and Works of Herman Melville*, July 25, 2000, www.melville.org/hmisrael.htm.

13 Jack Russell, "Israel Potter and 'Song of Myself,'" *American Literature* 40.1 (1968): 76. See also John Hay, "Broken Hearths: Melville's Israel Potter and the Bunker Hill Monument," *The New England Quarterly* 89.2 (June 2016): 212, and Joseph Flibbert, *Melville and the Art of Burlesque* (Amsterdam: Rodopi, 1974), 138–139.

14 Levine, "Introduction," xxvi. Jeff Insko has recently offered a counter-reading of Jones as a figure of queerness who helps us "imagine alternative forms of existence." Insko, "John Paul Jones: Queer and Wild," *Leviathan* 20.3 (2018): 31.

15 David Haven Blake, "The American Revolution," in *Walt Whitman: An Encyclopedia*, ed. J. R. LeMaster and Donald D. Kummings (New York: Garland Publishing, 1998), 18.

16 Kirsten Silva Gruesz, *Ambassadors of Culture: The Transamerican Origins of Latino Writing* (Princeton, NJ: Princeton University Press, 2002), 133.

17 Donald Pease, "The Mexican-American War and Whitman's 'Song of Myself': A Foundational Borderline Fantasy," in *Immigrant Rights in the Shadows of Citizenship*, ed. Rachel Ida Buff (New York: New York University Press, 2008), 387.

18 See Fernando Alegria, *Walt Whitman en Hispano America* (Mexico City: Ediciones Studium, 1954); and Mauricio Gonzalez Garza, *Walt Whitman: Racista, Imperialista, Antimexicano* (Mexico City: Malaga Collection, 1971). Pease explains that "the Texas Rangers' acts of looting … violated the sovereignty of the Mexican state" and provoked the events at Goliad ("The Mexican-American War and Whitman's 'Song of Myself,'" 387).

19 Brian W. Dippie, *The Vanishing American: White Attitudes and U.S. Indian Policy* (Lawrence: University Press of Kansas, 1991).

20 This strategy also characterizes Whitman's earlier writings on Native Americans, such as the 1840 poem "The Inca's Daughter," in which an indigenous Inca woman poisons herself rather than submit to Spanish conquistadores: "Now, paleface see! the Indian girl / Can teach thee how to bravely die."

21 Ivy G. Wilson, *Black and Tan Fantasy: Walt Whitman, African Americans, and Sounding the Nation* (New York: Oxford University Press, 2011), 84–85.

22 Ed Folsom, "Erasing Race: The Lost Black Presence in Whitman's Manuscripts," in *Whitman Noir: Black America and the Good Gray Poet*, ed. Ivy G. Wilson (Iowa City: University of Iowa Press, 2014), 8.

23 Fisher, *Still the New World*, 74 and 63.

24 Levine, "Introduction," vii.

25 Russ Castronovo, *Fathering the Nation: American Genealogies of Slavery and Freedom* (Berkeley: University of California Press, 1995), 146. See also Joshua Tendler, "A Monument upon a Hill: Antebellum Commemoration Culture, the Here-and-Now, and Democratic Citizenship in Melville's *Israel Potter*,"

Studies in American Fiction 42.1 (2015): 29–50; and Hay, "Broken Hearths: Melville's *Israel Potter* and the Bunker Hill Monument."

26 Carolyn L. Karcher, *Shadow over the Promised Land: Slavery, Race, and Violence in Melville's America* (Baton Rouge: Louisiana State University Press, 1980); Anne Baker, "What to Israel Potter Is the Fourth of July?: Melville, Douglass, and the Agency of Words," *Leviathan* 10.2 (2008): 9–22; Robert K. Wallace, *Douglass and Melville: Anchored Together in Neighborly Style* (New Bedford, MA: Spinner Publications, 2005). Baker specifically compares Melville's and Frederick Douglass's treatment of "the Fourth of July . . . as a day ideally suited to pointing out the nation's failure to live up to its promise of liberty for all" (9).

27 Edgar A. Dryden, *Monumental Melville: The Formation of a Literary Career* (Stanford, CA: Stanford University Press, 2004), 43.

28 Rodrigo Lazo, "The Ends of Enchantment: Douglass, Melville, and U.S. Expansionism in the Americas," in *Frederick Douglass & Herman Melville: Essays in Relation*, ed. Robert S. Levine and Samuel Otter (Chapel Hill: University of North Carolina Press, 2008), 213.

29 Jeffrey Insko, *History, Abolition, and the Ever-Present Now in Antebellum American Writing* (Oxford: Oxford University Press, 2018), 5–6, 18. In the words of Pragmatist philosopher George Herbert Mead, "In a reversal of our ordinary understanding of cause and effect, it's the occurrence in the present that causes our reconstruction of events in such a way as to account for that occurrence. This process repeats endlessly: just as the present is ever changing, so too is the past because each new event requires another reconstruction, a new account of the past" (qtd. in Insko, *History, Abolition, and the Ever-Present Now*, 18).

30 Ibid., 155.

CHAPTER 24

Harper/Stewart

Nazera Sadiq Wright

Frances E. W. Harper and Maria W. Stewart are two early African American women writers whose fictional representations of the moral and formal education of black girls taught readers to pursue fulfillment of spiritual goals, participate in public service, and access the public sphere.[1] Their works function as prescriptive texts that offer black readers a new path for their futures. Their writings were also templates for how parents and community members in the nineteenth century should nurture young black girls, particularly those who have suffered losses and have unusual natures that do not seem to fit in with the rest of the community. Harper wrote from her own experiences of loss, of harsh treatment from relatives, of feeling compelled to explore her identity as a poet when others felt she should be working to support herself, and of finding useful work in service to her people. Most likely drawn from her own youthful girlhood, Harper wrote a serialized novel in 1888–1889 titled *Trial and Triumph* about a black girl's struggle as she learns to integrate a deep interior life with an unusual intellect in the service of meaningful work. In her work as a public lecturer and through her fictional representations, Harper offered to readers the possibility of independent work for single young black women. Harper likely drew on her experiences before and after the Civil War, first as an unmarried abolitionist lecturer in the North and later as a widowed emissary to the freed people of the South. Written from her own life, Harper's poems, speeches, and novels offered optimism that reached her community and opened their hearts. Like other black women writers who published short stories, novels, and slave narratives in the nineteenth century, such as Maria W. Stewart, Harriet Wilson, and Harriet Jacobs, Frances E. W. Harper drew on her life experiences to create works that spoke to the black community, specifically the working-class black community and especially young black women. Her works showed audiences a way ahead. She instructed parents and community members how to interact with and raise young black girls who had rich interior lives and passionate emotions. Her message about such girls was that they could become valuable resources to the community if they were carefully and properly nurtured.

While Frances Watkins lost her parents early in life and was raised by extended family members, she was of an earlier generation than the character she creates in *Trial and Triumph* (1888–1889), a novel she serialized in the *Christian Recorder* in the same years. *Trial and Triumph* tells the story of a black girl named Annette Harcourt who comes of age in an urban city in the North in the post–Civil War years. Harper used the novel as a way to deliver to the wider black community the messages featured in her lectures after the Civil War. A remarkable feature of the novel is the absence of institutions and organizations that lobbied for the rights of northern and southern black people in these decades. This novel was written with the goal of promoting change at the pre-institutional level – within the homes of black families.

Although Maria W. Stewart is primarily known as a lecturer, a journalist, an abolitionist and a women's rights activist, a recently recovered six-page short story she wrote, "The First Stage of Life" (1861), illuminates her contribution to children's print culture through her portrayal of an orphaned black girl named Letitia whose representation and journey serve to define community networks as vital for black women's survival against the impact of laws passed before the Civil War. In 1861, the *Repository of Religion and Literature* serialized Stewart's short story "The First Stage of Life" in the April, July, and October issues.[2] The *Repository*, which was published from 1858 to 1863, was a black magazine administered by black men and designed for black readers.[3] Each issue of the magazine, which was published quarterly, included around twenty-two pages of poems, parables, and essays. The magazine attracted black households with rising amounts of disposable income and leisure time. Today, the *Repository* is available on microfilm only at the Indiana State Library; one extant issue is housed in Harvard University's Houghton Library.[4]

Letitia's growth from abjection to awareness with the help of a worthy and nurturing black community allegorizes the personal effects of an increasingly hostile white culture on the everyday lives of African American women in the antebellum period. Stewart presents Letitia as a lonely black girl without the care of a nurturing mother figure, illustrating the hardships many African American families experienced when mothers who were free or enslaved laborers could not always be available to their children. Stewart also approximates in the story the experiences of African

American women on the lecture circuit, including her own as an orator
and activist in the 1830s and who navigated the public lecture circuit and
faced hostile receptions. Stewart's 1833 "Farewell Address to the People of
Boston," delivered in the African Masonic Hall to an audience of black and
white, male and female listeners was perhaps responsible for the abrupt
termination of her career as a public lecturer. Although speaking in this
predominately black male space was considered a "politically delicate"
matter, Stewart declared that she was given the spiritual authority that
she found lacking in black men to assume the task of racial uplift. Stewart
states, "Methinks I heard a spiritual interrogation – 'Who shall go forward
and take off the reproach that is cast upon the people of color? Shall it be a
woman?'" Because her narrative stance was considered aggressive, and
likely because she was a black woman speaking at the podium, Stewart
received hostile reactions to this speech and was driven out of Boston.

The addition of "The First Stage of Life" into Stewart's corpus broadens
her literary identity from orator and activist to fiction writer. Although
Letitia suffers throughout Stewart's story, community members help her to
cultivate certain habits that teach independence and discipline, and she
emerges triumphant. The abuse and loneliness Letitia experiences in "The
First Stage of Life" are similar to early nineteenth-century texts that feature
black girls as main protagonists, such as the anonymously authored *The
Tawny Girl* (1823), "Theresa – A Haytien Tale" (1828; signed by "S"),
Harriet Wilson's *Our Nig or, Sketches from the Life of a Free Black* (1859),
Harriet Jacobs's *Incidents in the Life of a Slave Girl* (1861), Julia
C. Collins's *The Curse of Caste; or, The Slave Bride* (1865), and Harper's
Trial and Triumph.

Stewart's character Letitia was orphaned after her mother dies and lives
with an uncaring relative, an aunt who neither nurtures nor teaches her.
She must decide on her own that she wants to be "a good girl," and
initiates this transformation through learning the Bible and doing her
chores. Like Letitia, who eventually finds comfort in the home of community members, Frances Harper's character, Annette, gains nurturance
and support from Mr. Thomas, a teacher, and Mrs. Lassette, a community
member. While Letitia's training culminates in the ultimate goal of spiritual salvation, Annette's tutelage encourages her to participate in public
service. Thus, while education and moral uplift in the antebellum period
end with the fulfillment of spiritual goals in the writing of African
American women, in the post-Reconstruction period, the moral and
formal education of black girls led to independence, mobility, and access
to the public sphere.

Harper and Stewart join nineteenth-century African American writers and activists who incorporated representations of black girls in their literary works to address their political and social agendas. These agendas included national issues of concern to the black community, such as safety and survival during the decades when the Fugitive Slave Act was in effect, activism in pursuit of full citizenship rights and the abolition of slavery, support for finding work in the post–Civil War industrialized North, and strategies for educating the next generation. The black girls they wrote about carried stories of warning and hope, concern and optimism, struggles and success. At an early age, these black girls often exhibited adult behaviors, such as self-reliance, resourcefulness, and resistance. Evaluating early African American literature through the lens of black girlhood encourages readers to consider literary and aesthetic values that resist traditional canonization. These characters work as powerful rhetorical strategies that uncover the significance of autobiographical influence, black community uplift, and political and social agendas. Through their representations of black girls, Frances Harper and Maria Stewart guide us to a new valuation of literature in the nineteenth century, one that contributes to the importance of black girls to the literary canon.

Frances E. W. Harper and Black Girl Intimacies

Frances E. W. Harper was born in Baltimore in 1825. Her mother died when she was three years old, and her father remained absent from biographical details about this part of her life. Both parents were born free, but as her friend, antislavery activist William Still observed, the family was still "subjected of course to the oppressive influence which bond and free alike endured under slave laws."[5] Although numerous recent works focus on the role of her uncle, William Watkins, in Harper's upbringing, Still and Elizabeth Lindsay Davis write that she lived with an aunt after the death of her mother, likely until 1839, when she began service in the home of a local minister at the age of thirteen. Thus, by living with an aunt, Harper's experiences with her aunt would impact her later fiction. William Still suggests that the relationship with the aunt who took her in may not have been a happy one. He wrote that "she fell into the hands of an aunt" and that during her girlhood Harper "had many trials to endure which she would fain forget."[6] Hallie Quinn Brown wrote that "her childhood days were desolate."[7] The feeling that she was an outsider was compounded by the status of her race in a slave-owning republic. She later said, "Not that we have not a right to breathe the air as freely as anybody else in Baltimore, but we are treated worse than aliens among a people whose language we speak, whose religion we profess and whose blood flows and mingles in our veins. Homeless in the land of our birth and worse off than strangers in the home of our nativity."[8]

The one family asset of an orphaned free black girl living in a slave state was the fact that an uncle, William Watkins, operated a school for black children. William had high standards and offered a strong curriculum that included the Bible, classical literature, music, and philosophy in addition to the three Rs.[9] While practicing his trade as a shoemaker, he had taught himself languages and medicine, and sometime in the 1820s he opened the Watkins Academy for Negro Youth. He trained his students in elocution, preparing them to be leaders of their race. He taught his students to regard their voices as instruments and was "so signally precise that every example in etymology syntax and prosody had to be given as correctly as a sound upon a keyboard."[10] He was also a local leader in the African Methodist Episcopal church and was a frequent contributor to abolitionist newspapers.[11] From her uncle, Harper received training in public speaking, a devotion to the abolitionist cause, and a lifelong commitment to the Christian faith. However, his methods in the classroom were harsh. A former student who later graduated from Princeton and became a highly respected minister recalled that Watkins used a strap to make "profound orthoepical, orthographical, geographical and mathematical impressions" and that he was "strict from the first letter in the alphabet down to the last paragraph in the highest reader."[12] No matter how young the student was, they would learn – or face the strap. Thus, both at home and at school, it is likely that young Frances Watkins contended with a complex mixture of gratitude for being cared for and educated and resentment about the harsh treatment. The fact that she did not attempt to reunite with either the aunt who raised her or the uncle who educated her after she was put out to work speaks volumes about her feelings about these relatives.

Harper needed to work beginning at the age of thirteen. She was responsible for sewing and caring for the children of a Baltimore bookseller in her new situation, likely in the home of the Armstrong family, half of the prominent bookselling and publishing firm of Armstrong & Berry.[13] Yet she did not abandon her studies. Various sources have referred to this time as an "apprenticeship" with the bookseller for whom she worked, but William Still, who doubtless got his information from Harper herself, makes clear that she was hired to do domestic work. By that time, she knew that she wanted to be a poet, and within a year her literary efforts had impressed the wife in whose household she worked, who encouraged her.

We learn from Still that "through the kindness of her employer, her greed for books was satisfied so far as was possible from occasional half-hours of leisure." She spent her free time reading and studying, "rarely trifling away time as most girls are wont to do in similar circumstances."[14] Armstrong & Berry published classics such as William Whiston's translation of *The Works of Flavius Josephus* and sold advice literature such Margaret Coxe's *The Young Lady's Companion*, texts such as *Elements of Rhetoric and Literary Criticism* by J. R. Boyd ("designed for common schools and academies"),[15] and fiction by women such as *Sowing and Reaping; or, What Will Become of It* and *Sorrowing, Yet Rejoicing, or A Narrative of Recent Successive Bereavements in a Minister's Family* by Mary Howitt, who was advertised as the author of another book, *Strive and Thrive*.[16] Young Frances had access to the most recent publications in genres that enabled her to continue her education and learn what women were writing. This doubtless encouraged her to continue her own efforts, and probably within two years of being put out to work (Still says "scarcely had she reached her majority," likely meaning age sixteen),[17] she was publishing poems in the black press. Around 1845, while she was likely still doing domestic work in the home of the Armstrongs, she published her first volume of poetry, *Forest Leaves*.[18]

Harper spent the early years of her womanhood as a teacher and an abolitionist lecturer. She also contributed financial resources to the Underground Railroad. She was a strong supporter of John Brown and sent money to his widow after he was executed. She published several volumes of poetry before the Civil War and published poetry in the abolitionist press. Harper published *Forest Leaves* around 1845, at the age of twenty, but no copy has survived. Nine years later, in 1854, she published *Poems on Miscellaneous Subjects* (Boston: J. B. Yerrinton & Son), a book of antislavery poems. *Poems on Miscellaneous Subjects* sold 12,000 volumes in four years, making her the most well-known black poet since Phillis Wheatley. She also published in numerous antislavery newspapers, including *The Liberator* and *The North Star*, Frederick Douglass's paper.[19]

In 1853, her home state of Maryland had passed a law that made it legal to capture black people who entered the state and sell them as slaves. Harper had responded to this law with her voice and her pen. Thus, one year later, her book of antislavery poems was published and she delivered her first antislavery speech, "Education and the Elevation of the Colored Race," in New Bedford, Massachusetts. The success of this lecture led to a career as a public lecturer. The Maine Anti-Slavery Society hired her as a traveling lecturer for two years, and until the Civil War she lectured up and down the East Coast and as far west as Ohio. Frances married in 1860, at the age of thirty-five. Her husband, Fenton Harper, was a widower with three children who owned a dairy farm near Columbus. She bore one child, a daughter named Mary. When her husband died four years later, she was left with four children to raise and no income. In fact, her husband was in debt when he died, and three months after his death most of his property was seized. She wrote that the administrator "swept the very milk-crocks and wash tubs from my hands."[20] The experience made the injustice of property laws very real to her. She was keenly aware that if she had died instead of her husband, no property would have been seized to repay the family's debts. Harper resumed her career as a lecturer, traveling throughout the South to speak to both black and mixed audiences on the themes of temperance and education for the black community, among others. In 1871, she settled in Philadelphia.[21]

The press described the impact of Harper's public speaking in similar ways in the 1850s, when she worked to persuade white northerners to take up the abolitionist cause, and the 1870s, when she spoke to black and mixed audiences about how to move forward after the war. When she lectured in Philadelphia in 1856, the *Provincial Freeman* wrote that "the lady like ease and modesty of her deportment and the poetic beauty and pathos of her speaking alike delight and surprise her hearers." A year later, when she spoke to a white audience in Norristown, Pennsylvania, a white newspaper reported that she "melt[ed] her audience into sympathy and tears for the poor slave."[22] She often spoke extemporaneously, without notes and responding to cues from her location and audience. A clipping from a paper that Harper characterized as "one of the leading advocates of rebeldom" reported that it was clear that her speech was not "cut and dried ... for she was as fluent and as felicitous in her allusions to circumstances immediately around her as she was when she rose to a more exalted pitch of laudation of the 'Union,' or of execration of the old slavery system. Her voice was remarkable – as sweet as any woman's voice we ever heard, and so clear and distinct as to pass every syllable to the most distant ear in the house."[23] On that occasion, her "quaint humor" frequently brought her entire audience of 500 to laughter. Harper knew what it felt like to hold an audience in the palm of her hand and move them with her words, and she used that experience to describe a key moment in the life of her character Annette Harcourt in *Trial and Triumph*, the last of three novels serialized in the black newspaper the *Christian Recorder*.

Harper's decision to publish three novels in serial form in the *Christian Recorder* gave a broad and growing African American reading community access to her work. Serialization helped democratize literature by putting new work into the hands and homes of every economic and social class on a regular basis.[24] Many black writers in the nineteenth century published their first longer fictional pieces in serialized newspapers. Harper's *Minnie's Sacrifice, Sowing and Reaping,* and *Trial and Triumph* were serialized in *The Christian Recorder.* The *Colored American* serialized three of Pauline Hopkins's novels: *Hagar's Daughter: A Story of Southern Caste Prejudice* (1901–1902), *Winona: A Tale of Negro Life in the South and Southwest* (1902), and *Of One Blood; or, The Hidden Self* (1902–1903). Katherine Davis Chapman Tillman's *Beryl Weston's Ambition: The Story of an Afro-American Girl's Life* (1893) and *Clancy Street* (1898–1899) appeared in the *A. M. E. Church Review.* Frederick Douglass published his novella *The Heroic Slave* in *The North Star* in 1853.

The *Christian Recorder* was a logical choice for Harper. The African Methodist Episcopal Church, which published the journal, was her religious home at the time and was one of the leading venues where black writers could publish fictional anecdotes and serialized novels. In addition, as Eric Gardner argues, the *Recorder* may be viewed as a "public meeting place" that increased "multiple literacies" within the black community by teaching such subjects as "genre and geography, politics and poetic form, religion and rhetoric." It served as a site for discussing "real-world concerns and struggles and embody[ing] the black community's debates on gender roles, household structures, a massive war [and] questions of freedom and faith." Subscribers to the paper had access to information about diverse issues and to many African American voices that were otherwise absent from the dominant print culture. The *Recorder* functioned as a congregation of sorts for readers who were working to build community after the war. The average subscriber to *The Christian Recorder* was a married black man in his forties living in the Northeast with significant ties to the church and his family.[25]

The *Recorder's* status as a family paper made it an attractive site for black writers seeking to publish fiction with black girl figures whose actions reinforced the concepts of racial reconciliation and duty to family values. Stories about girlhood helped advance the church's mission by presenting images of well-functioning families with well-run households. Importantly, during the war, other stories about black childhood functioned as "textual interactions" between black soldiers, their families, and the church. These "soldier-subscribers," as Eric Gardner calls them, would have read the *Recorder's* girlhood stories and imagined their households functioning efficiently in their absence.

Serial publications introduced a literary form that helped black women gain access to the public sphere. Weekly installments meant that readers came to every issue primed and eager to engage with the material. As black readership grew, the black press became a viable option for novelists seeking to serialize their fiction in the nineteenth century. The growth of literary societies and increased access to printing technologies led to the development of a substantial reading community in the North.[26] In the late 1880s, the message of hope and a brighter future in Harper's novel *Trial and Triumph* would have been greatly encouraging to this population. And in laying out the social landscape of the black community in a northern urban center, it would have provided them with valuable information they needed as they planned their futures. As Michelle Campbell Toohey notes, Harper's serialized novels "addressed the complex social and political concerns of the postwar black community with the intimacy required for building community from the inside."[27]

In 1888, when she began serializing *Trial and Triumph*, Harper had been the national head of the "Negroes department" of the Woman's Christian Temperance Union for five years; she held the position until 1890. In 1887, she participated in the annual convention of the American Woman Suffrage Association. She was a voice for the rights of black women in both of these white-dominated national organizations.[28] Harper wrote a story that focused on the needs and desires of a determined and ambitious black girl. The novel tells the story of Annette Harcourt, a poor, dark-skinned black girl who becomes orphaned after her mother abandons her to run off with an intemperate man and eventually dies. Forced to live with an uncaring grandmother, Annette is encouraged by members of her community to pursue an education, become a teacher, and travel south rather than marry so as to devote her life to racial uplift. Harper's dark-skinned character represents black women's and girls' increasingly active and *visible* roles in political life, and her story warned readers of the often-unspoken compromises imposed on the personal lives of black women who break from feminine conventions and choose a life of work and political activism.

Youthful Girlhood in Maria W. Stewart's "The First Stage of Life" (1861)

Maria W. Stewart experienced a youthful girlhood that was similar to Harper's. Of her girlhood, Stewart writes: "I was born in Hartford, Connecticut, in 1803; was left an orphan at five years of age; was bound out in a clergyman's family; had the seeds of piety and virtue early sown in my mind; but was deprived of the advantages of education, though my soul thirsted for knowledge. Left them at 15 years of age; attended Sabbath Schools until I was 20; in 1826, was married to James W. Stewart; was left a widow in 1829."[29] The determination that Stewart exhibits to educate herself and move forward at such an early age is reflected by her protagonist, Letitia, in her short story, "The First Stage of Life." The story begins with a northern black mother's early death. The loneliness and isolation that Letitia experiences as a result conveys the hardships Stewart endured in her own childhood.

Stewart's description of Letitia's lonely wandering as a child likely mirrors the racial isolation that she herself encountered in her work as a widowed writer and public speaker on the American lecture circuit in the 1830s. In her September 21, 1833, "Farewell Address," presented in Boston, Stewart revealed the hostile reactions her public speaking provoked.[30] She draws on the powerful voices of biblical women to insist on her rightful position as a public speaker. Stewart questions her audience: "What if I am a woman; is not the God of ancient times the God of these modern days? Did he not raise up Deborah to be a mother and a judge in Israel? Did not Queen Esther save the lives of the Jews? And Mary Magdalene first declare the resurrection of Christ from the dead?"[31] Stewart encourages men in the audience to consider these ancient examples as they look upon her as a public speaker: "If such women as are here described have once existed, be no longer astonished, then, my brethren and friends, that God at this eventful period should raise up your own females to strive by their example, both in public and private, to assist those who are endeavoring to stop the strong current of prejudice that flows so profusely against us at present."[32] Stewart expresses that the high stakes of her activism result in her suffering: "Well was I aware that if I contended boldly for his cause I must suffer. Yet I chose rather to suffer affliction with his people than to enjoy the pleasures of sin for a season."[33] The suffering Stewart encountered on the public lecturing circuit became the material that led to her depiction of the suffering of Letitia in "The First Stage of Life."

"The First Stage of Life" tells the story of a six-year-old black girl named Letitia, who is orphaned after her mother dies and sent by her father to live with an uncaring aunt. Lacking nurturing parents and proper instruction, Letitia must discover the world on her own terms and make sense of her loneliness and unguided impressions. Community members eventually take in Letitia, raise her, and contribute to her survival. With the first

installment of "The First Stage of Life" published in April 1861, the same
month and year as the beginning of the Civil War, Stewart allegorizes this
tumultuous historical moment through the rebellious actions of a willful
and determined black girl figure.

Stewart seems to be describing the uneducated black child who per-
ceives vividly through her senses. We first meet Letitia when she is six years
old. Instead of the innocence and youthful curiosity, Letitia's girlhood
reveals she is unaware and fearful of the world: "The first time Letitia ever
noticed the blue sky, and the light of day, she was sent with another little
girl to get a pail of water, she climbed upon a ledge of rocks, she fell, and
then one of the rocks fell upon one of her limbs, she was wounded, she saw
the blood flow. How she got home, or when she recovered, she knows not,
she only knows that it was." The outdoors causes confusion and terror.
Stewart writes: "The first time Letitia was ever out in the sable orb of
night, that she recollects her attention attracted by the light of the lamps.
All was dark above, she saw no moon nor stars, she knew not what they
were, and passing by a shop she saw a monstrous large boot, she was filled
with fear, she thought it was God's boot, and walked away very softly. This
was the first idea Letitia ever had of God."[34] Letitia experiences physical
violence when she becomes orphaned after her mother dies and she is sent
to live with her uncaring Aunt Sally. Similar to Harper's upbringing,
Stewart represents how extended family often had to care for black girls
when biological parents were unable to perform this duty. Stewart exposes
the tensions that may have manifested in this extended familial relationship: "The first time Letitia remembers of having her face and hands
washed, was by her aunt Sally, but not without the threat of rubbing all
the skin off from her arms, if she did not behave herself."[35] Threats of a
brutal bath gave Letitia an early impression of uneasy and painful relations
between children and extended family members.

After a period of lonely wandering, Letitia reached a low point in her
girlhood and divine intervention led her to seek out members of the
community for assistance: "But God knew who Letitia was, and directed
her infant steps to an old man called Uncle Pete, and he told her to call on
a certain lady and gentleman, and tell them, that her aunt had gone off and
left her in the street, and that she had no father or mother." The unnamed
"lady and gentleman" from the community stepped in to become Letitia's
guardians and aid in her instruction because she "was almost a ruined
child, she was so bad." The couple "took the little stranger under their
charge; and when her Aunt Sally came after her, they would not let her go."

Under the tutelage of community members, Letitia "entered upon a new career. She was taught about God, to read, to pray, and was catechized. However, unable to retain her lessons and remain inside, Letitia found reprieve outdoors and was "always outdoors, robbing bird's nests, rambling in the woods, picking chestnuts and walnuts, and, in the winter, sliding on the ice." Her ramblings suggest that she lived outside the conventional rules of domesticity. Her disobedient disposition prevailed, as she "never liked to work very hard, and when she had to work harder than she felt disposed, she would cry, and make such a fuss, that they would send her to bed, or somewhere else, to get rid of her noise."[36] Letitia's surrogate parents proved unsuccessful in managing her unruly, immoral temperament. Letitia's roaming and living without a "settled home" reinforced her lack of awareness of social conventions, and her physical movements outdoors transgressed the restrictive mores of decorum and domesticity.

Although Letitia is still six years old when the story concludes, she has evolved from a youthful girlhood rooted in rebelliousness to a more mature stage in which she became "prematurely knowing" and aware of changes she needed to make in her behavior in order to thrive. Early African American writers often introduce black girl characters at the age of six, which is a period that I call "youthful" girlhood. The age of fifteen or sixteen, what Harriet Jacobs in *Incidents in the Life of a Slave Girl* calls "prematurely knowing" girlhood, identifies a common stage of transition when black girls were forced to become aware of adult concerns or sexual knowledge.[37] These age markers convey that black girls did not have much time to be youthful before they arrived at the age when they needed to make mature decisions and take on adult roles. Black girls needed to find strategies to protect themselves and find a future at an early age. Letitia's growth is recognized not in her age or sexual knowledge but in her level of consciousness. Because her unruliness contributed to her loneliness, Letitia developed a "religious desire to be a good girl." Her decision to change "from being one of the most abject and despised, [to] ... one of the most caressed and admired among her associates" suggests that Stewart sought to represent in Letitia's decision the exercise of individual will, in this case the desire to acquire religious instruction and live a moral life. Letitia channeled her naughtiness into a willful intention to know God and become good. Eric Gardner rightly argues that while Letitia decided to become good, the narrator "never tells *how* – never suggests any human agency much less the saving and symbiotic work of the itinerant minister and a group of settlers."[38] However, what is implicit about Letitia's decision is that she has matured. This growth was measured by her newfound awareness and acceptance of God, which led to her transformation: "The last time I heard from her she was like a tree planted in the house of my God, towering like some of the tall cedars of Lebanon, considering all things as loss compared to the excellency of Jesus Christ."[39] Letitia's feelings of loneliness and loss became the *necessary* emotional turmoil that led to her decision to become "good." By quelling her unruliness and deciding to become "good," Letitia managed herself: she read the Bible, returned from the outdoors, and lived in an actual home. Letitia's growth in awareness through religious conversion and her desire to become "good" conveys that she understood that living a religious life and abiding by conventional understandings of goodness would ensure her future. Stewart presented Letitia as fully aware of her unknowingness and portrays her time of wandering as a necessary stage in the journey to become aware, decisive, and knowing. In this process, Stewart emphasized the healing power of the community in forging relationships and nurturing black youth.

"The First Stage of Life" was published during an era in which there was a growing presence of black girl figures featured in mainstream children's print culture. Didactic story lines showed youthful readers how to be sympathetic to the needs of those who were living in poverty and introduced readers to the concept of a social conscience. The characters in these texts demonstrated altruism and steadfastness during adversity, and their morality was marked by an unselfish concern for the welfare of others, regardless of race or class. The moral rhetoric and small size of the *Repository* made the magazine inviting to youthful readers and their parents. In contrast to the large pages of *Freedom's Journal* and the *Colored American*, which were almost two feet in vertical length, the *Repository* was compact and portable like a book and small enough to fit in one's pocket.[40] Elizabeth McHenry argues that the *Repository*'s portability was intended to "expand the literary habits of black readers to include more attention to individual, solitary reading" and that this was "representative of notable changes taking place in the black community on the eve of the Civil War."[41] For black people, carrying a magazine that looked like a book contributed to the formation of bourgeois character that could be performed visibly on the street. The size and portability of the *Repository* allowed its editors to label the magazine an "intimate companion of all classes . . . capable of providing the individual reader with opportunities to engage in a communal model of literary activity even when away from the company of peers at the literary society meeting or in the lecture hall."[42] While the appeal of earlier newspapers such as *Freedom's Journal* and the *Colored American* was due to their nationalist mission as a newspaper for the people, the *Repository* focused on the morality and behavioral practices of the individual. Scholarly attention has turned toward this resource only recently. The *Repository* is archived in only three libraries – at Harvard, Yale, and Indiana State – and it has not been digitized.

Stewart was a pioneer in creating literature for and about black children. She strongly supported the development of African American children's print culture and indicted white authors and publishers for excluding black children from their publications.

> I have taken a survey of the American people in my own mind, and I see them thriving in arts, and sciences, and in polite literature. Their highest aim is to excel in political, moral and religious improvement. They early consecrate their children to God, and their youth indeed are blushing on artless innocence.... But how very few are there among them that bestow one thought upon the benighted sons and daughters of Africa, who have enriched the soils of America with their tears and blood; few to promote their cause, none to encourage their talents.[43]

"The First Stage of Life" was published in "The Children's Room" column of the *Repository*, a literary space devoted to black children and their parents. In the issues in which Stewart's story was serialized, this column published religious selections for children such as the poems "All Fulness in Christ" and "Prayer for a Heathen."[44] Essays on parenting included "Sleeping without the Light," which explores "the treatment by mother of [a] little boy's dread of sleeping in the dark," and "Bad Example," in which a boy reminds his father who is on the way to the distillery with fruit to make alcohol "that it would be a bad example for a member of the church to take peaches to a distillery."[45] Bishop Payne's essay on education, "The Duty of Children to Get Knowledge," asks readers, "Can children think? Can they learn to speak? Can they learn to read and write? Well, then, God made children to know." Payne tells young black readers how to be responsible for their own education: "How shall a child get knowledge? By thinking, thinking, thinking. By studying, studying, studying. By finding out the meaning of words; by comparing one word with another; and one thing to another, so as to find out their difference and their natures."[46] These selections reveal how invested the *Repository* editors were in ensuring that black children and their parents had access to a diverse range of children's texts.

The poems and parables printed in "The Children's Room" column were designed for African American children, parents, and community members who were engaged with public institutions such as schoolrooms and churches.[47] The conduct that the column promoted contributed to what historian Erica Ball calls "middle-class self-fashioning," a set of behaviors and values that was "deemed crucial to the personal transformations required to become independent, virtuous, ideal men and women."[48] Through the articles, poems, and stories published in "The Children's Room" column, *Repository* editors described respectability, literary taste, and middle-class values to young black readers. "The Children's Room" functioned as a literary space where African American writers could publish essays and create poems to be read and shared with parents and their children.

The selections published in "The Children's Room" encouraged black parents to teach their children ideals of honesty and perseverance that might protect them from the impact of hostile laws during the pre–Civil War era, such as the Fugitive Slave Act of 1850, which gave whites the right to repossess fugitives even if they escaped to a free state. The act resulted in an increase of illegal capture and enslavement of black people, including men and women who were already free or self-emancipated. Black activists and writers countered acts of illegal seizure through stories that taught morals and didactic lessons designed to protect black families against increasing threats of violence. To combat this institutional terror, black families were advised to secure the strength and stability of their homes. Articles in sections devoted to children in the black press routinely centered the emotional and physical health of black children, particularly their girls, by instructing parents to prepare their daughters through care for the body, intemperance, and feminine conventions through conversations between mothers and daughters.[49] "Keep your Temper," published in July 1858, uses rhetoric that instructs black girls to maintain their equanimity even in frustrating and difficult circumstances. When a girl named Emma misplaces her sewing implements and cries, "I can never keep anything!" and stamps about "with vexation," Emma's mother replies with a simple instruction: "keep your temper; if you will only do that, perhaps, you will find it easy to keep other things." The mother counsels Emma to control her passion: "You got into a passion – a bad way of spending time, and you have accused somebody, and very unjustly, too, of taking away your things and losing them. Keep your temper, my dear; when you have mislaid any article[,] keep your temper and search for it."[50]

Articles also urged black girls to learn as much as they could. In "Young Ladies, Read!," the anonymous author denounces idle behavior in young women as detrimental to the good of the black community:

> They lounge or sleep their time in the morning. They never take hold of the drudgery, the repulsive toil, which each son and daughter of Adam should perform in the world. They know nothing of domestic duties, they have no habits of industry, no taste for the useful, no skill in any really useful art. They are in the streets, not in the performance of their duty, or for the acquisition of health, but to see and be seen.[51]

The author encourages parents to make sure their girls master domestic skills: "What a mistake is then made by our young girls and their parents when domestic education is unattended to! Our daughters should be taught practically to wash and iron, to arrange the table, to do every thing that pertains to the order and comfort of the household."[52] These articles intended to "hold[] the larger community together" through their moral instructions. The absence of fathers in these articles on conduct and behavior suggests that, at this point, the instruction of children was seen as wholly the concern of mothers. In "Conversations between a Mother and her Children," published in July 1858, a mother tells her son and daughter why they should not waste bread by telling a story about a male slave in Georgia who was very thankful to receive a loaf of bread because he was starving. The conversation ends with the mother saying to her son: "Rejoice, my boy, that you are sorry for your fault; always remember, love, that *to acknowledge a fault* is the first step to improvement." Through invoking slavery in the antebellum South, the author instructs black children on moral behavior and warns them to be thrifty or fall victim to a life of labor and suffering.[53]

Despite the attention the *Repository* gave to articles devoted to proper parenting in "The Children's Room" column, Stewart's story emphasizes communal networks and suggests that the protection of a nuclear family was perhaps unattainable for many black girls in the antebellum period. Stewart's story reshaped the dominant narrative about the impoverished girl who eventually dies through a representation of a black girl who survives hardships and whose personal experiences illustrate strategic steps toward hopeful beginnings instead of an inevitable tragic ending. Stewart identifies an alternative support structure for black women and girls in the antebellum era when she reveals how her black girl protagonist gains awareness, education, and spiritual enlightenment outside the protection of a nuclear family or a nurturing mother.

Harper's serialized novel about an educated and accomplished black girl and Stewart's serialized story about a black girl's coming-of-age broadens scholars' understanding of the contributions African American women have made to nineteenth-century print culture. Their early emphasis on black girlhood invites further study on the methodologies, frameworks, and emerging trends that continue to shape the canon of early African American literature and print culture.[54] Two other narratives by black women writers, Harriet Wilson's *Our Nig* and Harriet Jacobs's *Incidents in the Life of a Slave Girl*, demonstrate black girls' growth from unruly children to educated and moral women. These works recognize the courses of action black women needed to pursue in order to ensure their survival. In these narratives, education occurs in both formal and informal ways. Representations of black girls in these narratives offered a new set of principles to assist both free and enslaved black women in acquiring independence. Mapping black girlhood in early African American literature contributes to our understanding of black female experiences and brings attention to the lives of black girls in the nineteenth century. These are fictionalized versions of the realities that many black women faced as girls. The stories focus on hope and survival, willfulness and resourcefulness. Although the black girls come from families torn apart by hardship, they develop their own strategies to remain triumphant, move forward, and survive. Frances Harper and Maria Stewart are central, significant writers who use representations of black girls to advocate a literary valuation of black girlhood in print networks that were central to African American communities in the nineteenth century.

Notes

1 For an extended discussion on these two authors, see Nazera Sadiq Wright, *Black Girlhood in the Nineteenth Century* (Urbana: University of Illinois Press, 2016).

2 Literary historian Eric Gardner recently discovered two examples of Maria Stewart's writing from the 1860s. The first discovery is a transcription of a lecture on parenting and Christian education. The second is the story "The First Stage of Life." See Eric Gardner, "Introduction: Two Texts on Children and Christian Education," *PMLA* 123, no. 1 (2008): 156–165.

3 The *Repository* was based in Indianapolis. In 1861, the year Stewart's short story was published, its chief editor was John Mifflin Brown.

4 For context about the *Repository*, see Eric Gardner, *Unexpected Places: Relocating Nineteenth-Century African American Literature* (Jackson: University of Mississippi Press, 2010), 56–91; Elizabeth McHenry,

Forgotten Readers: Recovering the Lost History of African American Reading Societies (Durham, NC: Duke University Press, 2005), 132–133, 137; Quentin Story McAndrew, "Location, Location, Location: Remapping African American Print Culture in the Nineteenth-Century United States," *Criticism* 53, no. 2 (2011): 335; and Frances Smith Foster, "Frances Ellen Watkins Harper (1825–1911)," in *Kindred Hands: Letters on Writing by British and American Women Authors, 1865–1935,* ed. Jennifer Cognard-Black and Elizabeth MacLeod Walls (Ames: University of Iowa Press, 2006), 43.

5 William Still, "Frances Ellen Watkins Harper," in Still, *The Underground Rail Road: A Record of Facts, Authentic Narratives, Letters, &c., Narrating the Hardships, Hair-Breadth Escapes and Death Struggles of the Slaves in Their Efforts for Freedom* (Philadelphia: Porter and Coates, 1872), 755. See also Elizabeth Lindsay Davis, "Frances Ellen Watkins Harper," in Davis, *Lifting as They Climb* (Washington, DC: National Association of Colored Women, 1933), 231.

6 Still, "Frances Ellen Watkins Harper," 755–756.

7 "Frances Ellen Watkins Harper," in Hallie Quinn Brown, *Homespun Heroines and Other Women of Distinction* (Xenia, OH: Aldine Publishing, 1926), 97.

8 Ibid., 98.

9 Shirley Wilson Logan, *We Are Coming: The Persuasive Discourse of Nineteenth-Century Black Women* (Carbondale: Southern Illinois University Press, 1999), 48.

10 These are the words of one of Watkins's students; see ibid.

11 Louis Filler, "Harper, Frances Ellen Watkins," in *Notable American Women, 1607–1950, vol. 2: G–O,* ed. Edward T. James, Janet Wilson James, and Paul S. Boyer (Cambridge, MA: Harvard University Press, 1971), 135–139; Cassandra Jackson, "Harper, Frances Ellen Watkins," in *African American Lives,* ed. Henry Louis Gates and Evelyn Brooks Higginbotham (Oxford: Oxford University Press, 2004), 374–375.

12 Johnson quoted (without full citation) in Frances Smith Foster, "Introduction," in *A Brighter Coming Day: A Frances Ellen Watkins Harper Reader,* ed. Frances Smith Foster (New York: Feminist Press, 2000), 7. Johnson's later career is briefly mentioned in James A. Wind, *American Congregations, vol. 1: Portraits of Twelve Religious Communities* (Chicago: University of Chicago Press, 1994), 244, 283.

13 Louis Filler's biography of Harper for *Notable American Women* said that she "went to live in the household of a Baltimore bookseller named Armstrong" in order to earn her living. Armstrong & Berry is the only bookseller I have been able to locate in Baltimore city directories of this period associated with the surname Armstrong. Filler, "Harper, Frances Ellen Watkins," 137.

14 Still, "Frances Ellen Watkins Harper," 756.

15 Armstrong & Berry advertisement in *American Republican and Baltimore Daily Clipper,* November 14, 1844, 2.

16 Armstrong & Berry advertisement in *The Pilot and Transcript* (Baltimore), January 21, 1841, 3.

17 Ibid.

18 Filler, "Harper, Frances Ellen Watkins," 136. Apparently, no copies of this volume have survived.

19 Ibid., 137–138.

20 Frances Watkins Harper, "We Are All Bound Up Together," in *Proceedings of the Eleventh Woman's Rights Convention, New York, May 1866*, reprinted in *A Brighter Coming Day: A Frances Ellen Watkins Harper Reader*, ed. Frances Smith Foster (New York: Feminist Press at the City University of New York, 1990), 217–219, quoted in Alison M. Parker, "Frances Watkins Harper and the Search for Women's Interracial Alliances," in *Susan B. Anthony and the Struggle for Equal Rights*, ed. Christine L. Ridarsky and Mary M. Huth (Rochester: University of Rochester Press, 2012), 148.

21 Filler, "Harper, Frances Ellen Watkins," 137–138.

22 Both quoted in Davis, "Frances Ellen Watkins Harper," 232.

23 Ibid., 231–232.

24 For more information on serialization, see Robert Patten, "Serial Literature," in *Oxford Reader's Companion to Dickens*, ed. Paul Schlicke (Oxford: Oxford University Press, 1999), 514–519.

25 Eric Gardner, "Remembered (Black) Readers: Subscribers to the *Christian Recorder*, 1864–1865," *American Literary History* 23, no. 2 (2011): 234, 251, 246.

26 Elizabeth McHenry, *Forgotten Readers: Recovering the Lost History of African American Literary Societies* (Durham, NC: Duke University Press, 2002), 4–5. According to US census data, the percentage of the black population that was literate increased from 30 percent in 1880 to 70 percent in 1910. The low literacy rate in 1880 is explained by the fact that the population included former slaves who had been excluded from education. For Harper's involvement with *The Christian Recorder*, see Frances Smith Foster, "Gender, Genre and Vulgar Secularism: The Case of Frances Ellen Watkins Harper and the AME Press," in *Recovered Writers/Recovered Texts*, ed. Dolan Hubbard (Knoxville: University of Tennessee Press, 1997).

27 Michelle Campbell Toohey, "'A Deeper Purpose' in the Serialized Novels of Frances Ellen Watkins Harper," in *"The Only Efficient Instrument": American Women Writers and the Periodical, 1837–1916*, ed. Aleta Feinsod Cane and Susan Alves (Iowa City: University of Iowa Press, 2001), 203.

28 Filler, "Harper, Frances Ellen Watkins," 137–138.

29 Maria W. Stewart, *Productions of Mrs. Maria W. Stewart: Presented to the First African Baptist Church and Society of the City of Boston* (Boston: Friends of Freedom and Virtue, 1845), 3–4.

30 See "Mrs. Stewart's Farewell Address to Her Friends in Boston," *The Liberator*, September 28, 1833, reprinted in *Maria W. Stewart: America's First Black Woman Political Writer: Essays and Speeches*, ed. Marilyn Richardson (Bloomington: Indiana University Press, 1987), 65–74. For a description of Stewart's difficult life circumstances at the time she wrote this story, see "Sufferings during the War," first published in 1879 in *Meditations*

from the Pen of Mrs. Maria W. Stewart: (Widow of the Late James W. Stewart) Now Matron of the Freedman's Hospital, and Presented in 1832 to the First African Baptist Church and Society of Boston, Mass., reprinted in Richardson, *Maria W. Stewart*, 98–10.

31 Maria S. Stewart, *Meditations from the Pen of Mrs. Maria W. Stewart (Widow of the Late James W. Stewart) Now Matron of the Freedman's Hospital, and Presented in 1832 to the First African Baptist Church and Society of Boston, Mass.* (Enterprise Publishing Company, 1879), 76.

32 Ibid., 77.

33 Ibid., 82.

34 Maria W. Stewart, "The First Stage of Life," *Repository of Religion and Literature of Science and Art* 1 (January 1861), reprinted in *PMLA* 123, no. 1 (2008): 162–163.

35 Ibid., 162.

36 Ibid.

37 Harriet Jacobs, *Incidents in the Life of a Slave Girl*, 1861; repr. (New York: Dover Publications, 2001), 27.

38 Eric Gardner, *Unexpected Places: Relocating Nineteenth-Century African American Literature* (Jackson: University of Mississippi Press, 2011), 87.

39 Stewart, "The First Stage of Life," 165.

40 See Jacqueline Bacon, *Freedom's Journal: The First African American Newspaper* (New York: Lexington Books, 2007), 37.

41 McHenry, *Forgotten Readers*, 138–139.

42 Ibid.

43 Maria W. Stewart, "Prayer," in *Productions of Mrs. Maria W. Stewart: Presented to the First African Baptist Church & Society of the City of Boston* (Boston: Friends of Freedom and Virtue, 1835), 12.

44 Bishop Payne, "The Duty of Children to Get Knowledge," *Repository of Religion and Literature*, October 1861, 185–186.

45 "Bad Example," *Repository of Religion and Literature*, April 1861, 86; "Sleeping without the Light," *Repository of Religion and Literature*, July 1861, 141.

46 Payne, "The Duty of Children to Get Knowledge," 185–186.

47 Gardner, "Introduction," 157.

48 Erica Ball, *To Live an Antislavery Life: Personal Politics and the Antebellum Middle Class* (Athens: University of Georgia Press, 2012), 2–3.

49 See "A Daughter's Request" (July 1859), "Dialogue between a Mother and Her Children" (October 1859), "Politeness" (January 1861), "The Dress" (January 1861), and "Letters to Little Children" (July 1861).

50 "Keep Your Temper," *Repository of Religion and Literature*, July 1858, 95.

51 "Young Ladies, Read!," *Repository of Religion and Literature*, January 1860, 34. Reprinted from the *Hartford Daily Courant*.

52 Ibid.

53 "Conversations between a Mother and Her Children," *Repository of Religion and Literature*, July 1858.

54 This essay contributes to scholarship on African American print culture. See
   Wright, *Black Girlhood in the Nineteenth Century*; Lara Cohen and Jordan
   Alexander Stein, eds., *Early African American Print Culture* (Philadelphia:
   University of Pennsylvania Press, 2012); Joycelyn Moody and Howard
   Rambsy, eds., Special Issue on "African American Print Cultures," *MELUS:
   Society for the Study of Multi-Ethnic Literature of the United States* 40.3 (2015);
   Eric Gardner's *Black Print Culture Unbound* (Oxford: Oxford University
   Press, 2015); and Brigitte Fielder and Jonathan Sencheyne, eds., *Against a
   Sharp White Background: Infrastructures of African American Print* (Madison:
   University of Wisconsin Press, 2019).

Index

Printed by Printforce, United Kingdom